THE HISTORY OF
HIGHER EDUCATION

THE HISTORY OF HIGHER EDUCATION

Major Themes in Education

Edited by
Roy Lowe

Volume V
Elite formation, system building and
the rise of the student estate

Routledge
Taylor & Francis Group

LONDON AND NEW YORK

First published 2009
by Routledge
2 Park Square, Milton Park, Abingdon, Oxon, OX14 4RN, UK

Simultaneously published in the USA and Canada
by Routledge
270 Madison Avenue, New York, NY 10016

Routledge is an imprint of the Taylor & Francis Group, an informa business

Typeset in 10/12pt Times NR MT by Graphicraft Limited, Hong Kong
Printed and bound in Great Britain by
MPG Books Ltd., Bodmin, Cornwall

British Library Cataloguing in Publication Data
A catalogue record for this book is available from the British Library

Library of Congress Cataloging-in-Publication Data
The history of higher education : major themes in education / edited by Roy Lowe.
p. cm.
Includes bibliographical references and index.
ISBN 978-0-415-37854-3 (set) – ISBN 978-0-415-38469-8 (vol. 1, hardback) –
ISBN 978-0-415-38470-4 (vol. 2, hardback) – ISBN 978-0-415-38471-1
(vol. 3, hardback) – ISBN 978-0-415-38472-8 (vol. 4, hardback) –
ISBN 978-0-415-38473-5 (vol. 5, hardback)   1. Education, Higher–History.
I. Lowe, Roy.
LA173.H584 2008
378.09–dc22
2008008884

ISBN10: 0-415-37854-0 (Set)
ISBN10: 0-415-38473-7 (Volume V)

ISBN13: 978-0-415-37854-3 (Set)
ISBN13: 978-0-415-38473-5 (Volume V)

Publisher's Note

References within each chapter are as they appear in the original
complete work.

CONTENTS

CONTENTS

ACKNOWLEDGEMENTS

The publishers would like to thank the following for permission to reprint their material:

Taylor & Francis for permission to reprint Martin Trow, 'Elite and Popular Functions in American Higher Education', from *Higher Education: Demand and Response*, W. R. Niblett (ed.). Copyright © 1969 Tavistock Publications.

Simon and Schuster for permission to reprint Allan Bloom, 'The Student and the University', in Allan Bloom, *The Closing of the American Mind*, Simon and Schuster, New York, 1987, pp. 336–382.

Martin Wiener, excerpt from M. J. Wiener, *English Culture and the Decline of the Industrial Spirit, 1850–1980*, Penguin Books, Harmondsworth, 1981, pp. 16–24, 174–177.

R. D. Anderson, 'Universities and Elites in Modern Britain', *History of Universities*, vol. X 1991, Oxford University Press, pp. 225–250.

Elizabeth J. Morse, 'English Civic Universities and the Myth of Decline', *History of Universities*, vol. XI, 1992, Oxford University Press, pp. 177–204.

Klett-Cotta for permission to reprint Roy Lowe, 'English Elite Education in the Late Nineteenth and Early Twentieth Centuries', in W. Conze and J. Kocka (eds), *Bildungsbürgertum im 19. Jahrhundert*, Teil I, Klett-Cotta, Stuttgart, 1985, pp. 147–162.

Klett-Cotta for permission to reprint Roy Lowe, 'The Expansion of Higher Education in England', in K. H. Jarausch (ed.), *The Transformation of Higher Learning, 1860–1930*, Klett-Cotta, Stuttgart, 1981, pp. 37–56.

Klett-Cotta and Sheldon Rothblatt for permission to reprint Sheldon Rothblatt, 'The Diversification of Higher Education in England', in K. H. Jarausch (ed.), *The Transformation of Higher Learning, 1860–1930*, Klett-Cotta, Stuttgart, 1981, pp. 131–148.

Oxford University Press for permission to reprint Antonio García y García, 'The Medieval Students of the University of Salamanca', *History of Universities*, vol. X, 1991, Oxford University Press, Oxford, pp. 93–105.

Oxford University Press and Princeton University Press for permission to reprint Robert L. Church, 'Economists as Experts: The Rise of an Academic Profession in the United States, 1870–1920', in L. Stone (ed.), *The University in Society*, vol. II: *Europe, Scotland and the United States from the Sixteenth to the Nineteenth Century*, Princeton University Press and Oxford University Press, 1975, pp. 571–609.

Cambridge University Press and Sheldon Rothblatt for permission to reprint Sheldon Rothblatt, 'Donnishness', in Sheldon Rothblatt, *The Revolution of the Dons: Cambridge and Society in Victorian England*, Cambridge University Press, London, 1968, pp. 181–208.

Sheldon Rothblatt for permission to reprint Sheldon Rothblatt, 'The Academic Role', in S. Rothblatt, *Tradition and Change in English Liberal Education*, Faber and Faber, London, 1976, pp. 174–194.

Princeton University Press for permission to reprint Arthur Engel, 'Emerging Concepts of the Academic Profession at Oxford 1800–1854', in L. Stone (ed.), *The University in Society*, vol. I: *Oxford and Cambridge from the 14th to the Early 19th Century*, Princeton University Press, 1974, pp. 305–351.

Oxford University Press for permission to reprint A. H. Halsey, 'Women and Men', in A. H. Halsey, *Decline of Donnish Dominion: The British Academic Professions in the Twentieth Century*, Clarendon Press, Oxford, 1995, pp. 216–234.

Taylor & Francis for permission to reprint Carol Dyhouse, 'Patterns of Provision: Access and Accommodation', from *No Distinction of Sex? Women in British Universities, 1870–1939*, C. Dyhouse, Copyright © 1995 Taylor & Francis.

Harvard Education Publishing Group for permission to reprint Linda Eisenmann, 'Reconsidering a Classic: Assessing the History of Women's Higher Education a Dozen Years after Barbara Solomon', *Harvard Educational Review*, vol. 67, no. 4, Winter 1997, pp. 689–717.

Disclaimer

INTRODUCTION

Higher education has long been recognised, in various parts of the world, as playing an important role in elite formation. Through the development of recognised hierarchies and differentiated practices in differing institutions, professional elites are shaped, power systems are reinforced and societies gain a political and social stability which underpins both the polity and social intercourse. The establishment of systems of higher education, as well as questions around the recruitment of students from particular social cadres, are in themselves key elements in this process. This final volume brings together contributions whose central concern is for one or other aspect of this process. It reflects some of the more significant work that has been done on the ways in which higher education in general, and the universities in particular, play a part in elite formation and, in so doing, become vital agencies in the determination of what those societies aspire to and how they hold together.

It is appropriate therefore that the collection begins with an essay by Martin Trow, one of the most perceptive commentators of the last half century, writing about the tension which existed (and which still persists) in North American higher education between its elite and popular functions. Although this essay, reproduced here as Chapter 98, reflected precisely the concerns and tensions confronting all those involved in shaping higher education during the late 1960s, it raised questions which were of long-term significance.

Twenty years later, Allan Bloom, in a book that was to reopen a major debate on the role of the universities in a modern society, reflected on the ways in which the academy might fulfil its obligation to civilise its students in an increasingly barbarous world. Whilst his eye-catching subtitle promised to demonstrate the ways in which American higher education had failed democracy and impoverished the souls of its students, he nonetheless held out some hopes for a society in which the universities might still 'philosophise' those passing through them. The passage selected as Chapter 99 is that which encapsulates the core of this argument.

England is the country that has generated most debate on the role of higher education in the generation and preservation of elites. This may be because of the unique nature of the British elite or because of a particular pattern to educational developments in the United Kingdom; perhaps both.

1

A number of essays have been chosen to illustrate the important controversies that this interest has kindled. First, in Chapter 100, Harold Perkin outlines the ways in which a system developed between 1860 and 1930 in England, and offers a sympathetic view of the extent to which the universities were open to new trends and to entrants from unfamiliar backgrounds. For him the universities were one key to understanding the adaptation and modernisation of British society at this time. The account by Halsey and Trow of the evolution of British universities during the nineteenth and twentieth centuries (Chapter 101) argues that the radical changes taking place necessarily threw them into the arms of government, thus making the state an increasingly powerful arbiter of their role in elite formation.

In complete contrast, in Chapter 102 Martin Wiener argues that the role of the universities and the public schools, functioning almost as a synchronised system, was to retard modernisation and to impede the kind of social transformations that were becoming overdue in an industrialised society. A contribution from the work of R. D. Anderson informs this debate. In Chapter 103 he offers a masterly overview of the debate on the universities and elite formation in Britain, drawing widely on the recent literature, and goes on to detail the changing patterns of recruitment to the universities, showing the ways in which they became increasingly the arbiters of recruitment to the professional classes at the very time that they were restricting expansion and resisting what some have since called 'massification'. In these ways, Anderson argues, the universities were central to any determination of the precise form taken by the late twentieth-century middle classes.

In a thoughtful riposte to Anderson, Elizabeth J. Morse, in Chapter 104, contends that the distinctions between the ancient universities in England and the Redbricks cannot be overlooked in any analysis of the transformations taking place. Her work carries an implicit criticism of earlier work which had been over-focused on Oxbridge. In similar vein, Roy Lowe argues in two essays, first, that the expansion of higher education in England was marked by an increasing stratification of the system (Chapter 105), and second, that the dramatic increases in the number of full-time students during the late nineteenth and early twentieth centuries were only made possible by the emergence of technological and vocational routes as 'safety valves' which ensured continuing stratification of the middle classes as a whole (Chapter 106). Finally, in a typically provocative essay, Sheldon Rothblatt (Chapter 107) argues that it was the preparedness of the universities in Britain to engage with the state during the late nineteenth century that ensured that they developed on a European rather than an American model, with private enterprise being marginal to their functioning for most of the twentieth century.

Meanwhile, in France, Fritz Ringer argues in Chapter 108, it was the particular characteristics of the universities and of secondary education, which were inextricably related one to another, which determined the nature of the emergent middle class and, in particular, recruitment to it. Ringer has been one of the most pre-eminent commentators on the systematisation of higher education in Europe during the late nineteenth and early twentieth centuries. This extract is a typical example of his tightly argued and exhaustively researched work.

There follow three essays relating to what Eric Ashby called, in a memorable phrase, 'the rise of the student estate'. First, Brian Simon in Chapter 109, one of his early public pronouncements, reflecting his involvement in the National Union of Students during the late 1930s, offers a student's view of the universities. This reflects both the growing self-consciousness of the student body and a preparedness (which marked his work throughout a lengthy career) to relate educational change to wider political causes, in this case the threat of Fascism. Eric Ashby himself became one of the leading commentators on developments in higher education. In 1970 he reflected on the recent upsurge in student political activism with an account of the rise of the student movement (Chapter 110), and this contribution captures the mood and spirit of much thinking at this time within academia around the question of what were the proper bounds of student political activity. Finally, a carefully researched essay by Antonio García y García (Chapter 111) reminds us that there has been extensive work done by scholars on other European societies and on earlier periods which brings into focus issues around both the social origins of the student body and the question of the extent to which universities were local rather than national or pan-European institutions.

There has also been significant work done on the rise of the academic profession. Four essays have been selected to illustrate some of the key themes of this research. First, in Chapter 112, Robert L. Church throws a spotlight on the way in which the emergence of the university career in the United States was linked inextricably to a growing concept of the academic as a lobbyist and advisor of government and policy-makers. Second, in Chapter 113, Sheldon Rothblatt, who has arguably done more than any other scholar to explain and illuminate the origins of the academic career in England, reflects on 'Donnishness' in an extract from his masterly work on the 'revolution of the dons' in nineteenth-century Oxbridge. In an extract from his subsequent work *Tradition and Change in English Liberal Education* (Chapter 114), Rothblatt shows how changing concepts of the academic role during the nineteenth century shaped the whole nature and concept of a university education. Rothblatt's work has been complemented by that of Arthur Engel, whose research on developments at Oxford during the first half of the nineteenth century showed the linkages between the staffing of the university, the enduring strength of the collegiate system and the ideal of a liberal education. As Engel shows in Chapter 115, whilst developments at Oxford owed much to foreign systems, particularly the German, what emerged was something that was unique to Oxford.

Three essays on the participation of women in higher education remind us that gender has been, in recent years especially, an increasingly significant focus for researchers. Although numerous contributions earlier in the collection have had something to say about issues of gender, these three have it at the heart of their enquiry. In Chapter 116 A. H. Halsey chronicles the increasing participation of women in British universities, illustrating the ways in which the gendering of roles within academia reflected trends across the economy more generally. The same theme was tackled by Carol Dyhouse in her ground-breaking book on women in British universities between 1870 and 1939. Her focus on the extent and nature of separatism shows how complex and ambiguous was the entry of females to universities in Britain (Chapter 117). Turning to the American scene, in Chapter 118 Linda Eisenmann's reassessment of Barbara Solomon's classic text on women in American higher education provides a valuable historiography of the development of this field of study in North America.

ELITE AND POPULAR FUNCTIONS IN AMERICAN HIGHER EDUCATION

Martin Trow

Source: W. R. Niblett (ed.) *Higher Education: Demand and Response*, London: Tavistock, 1969, pp. 181–201.

I

If we consider American higher education today with any degree of detachment, we are struck by a paradox. On one hand, the system seems to be in serious trouble and perhaps even in crisis. Almost every major university, and many others as well, has been the scene of student demonstrations, disturbances, and even insurrections. Events at Columbia and Berkeley and San Francisco State become national news; on many other campuses (Northwestern and Boston University, Fordham and New York University, San Jose and Howard), militant blacks and whites and dissident faculty confront their university's authorities with bold demands, threats, strikes, and sit-ins. On the other hand, if looked at from another perspective, and especially from a European perspective, American higher education is successful and thriving, and indeed provides the model for educational reformers in almost every European country. Seen in this way, it surely is a success. American research and scholarship make contributions to every field of learning, and dominate many. In applied science and technology we are the envy of the world: as Servan-Schreiber[1] has observed, the Americans have worked out 'a close association between business, universities, and the government which has never been perfected nor successful in any European country'. Our universities are deeply involved in the life of the society, and contribute much to the efforts to solve its problems, from social medicine to the problems of the inner city. And finally, this sprawling system of some 2,500 colleges and universities enrols about 40 per cent of the age grade, over

50 per cent of all high school graduates, and those proportions are steadily rising. In some large states like California, where some 80 per cent of high school graduates go on to some form of higher educcaion, our system of mass higher education begins to be very nearly universal. Whatever one's assessment of those figures and their implications, they must be counted a considerable achievement.

But I do not believe there is much gain in celebrating the triumphs of American higher education just at the moment, especially when scarcely a day goes by without another report of a confrontation and a disruption on a campus. There is perhaps more profit in considering its difficulties. I believe these, of which student unrest is only the most visible, can be better understood in the light of the continuing tension between the popular and the elite functions of American colleges and universities.

American colleges and universities, almost from their beginnings, have performed two different sets of functions. I have called these respectively, 'elite' and 'popular' functions, but perhaps more accurately the distinction is between those for which the university sets its own aims, and those which the university takes on in response to external needs and demands. The line between these is not hard and fast; ultimately, it can be argued, all university activities are in some sense responsive to societal interests. But the distinction is a useful one, perhaps most clearly to Europeans, whose universities until recently have largely confined themselves to their traditional and autonomous functions and have resisted accepting tasks set for them by other parts of the society or the population at large.

At the heart of the traditional university is its commitment to the transmission of the high culture, the possession of which has been thought to make men truly civilized. This was really the only function that Cardinal Newman, and more recently Robert Hutchins, have thought appropriate to the university. Closely related to this, and certainly central to our conception of liberal education, is the shaping of mind and character: the cultivation of aesthetic sensibilities, broader human sympathies, and a capacity for critical and independent judgement. The second autonomous function of the American university is the creation of new knowledge through 'pure' scholarship and basic scientific research. Another elite function, of greater importance for European universities than in this country, though it is by no means absent from our own most prestigious private universities, is the selection, formation, and certification of a social elite: the learned professions, the higher civil service, the politicians, and (though less in Britain than on the Continent), the commercial and industrial leadership, as well as the teachers in the preparatory secondary schools where the children of that elite are educated and prepared for their accession to elite status. These functions involve values and standards which are institutionalized in the universities and elite private colleges, and are maintained by them autonomously and even in resistance to popular demands and sentiments.

6

The popular functions fall into two general categories. First, there is a commitment on the part of the system as a whole to provide places somewhere for as many students as can be encouraged to continue their education beyond high school. For a very long time, it has been believed in this country that talented youth of humble origins should go to college. But the extension of these expectations to all young men and women, as something between a right and an obligation, dates no further back than the Second World War. In part this notion is a reflection of the erosion of the legitimacy of class cultures, and of the growing feeling in every industrial society, but most markedly in the United States, that it is right and proper for all men to claim possession of the high culture of their own societies. In school and through the mass media, ordinary people are encouraged to send their children to college to share in the high culture, both for its own sake and for its instrumental value in gaining entrance to the old and the emerging elite occupations. Higher education is assuming an increasingly important role in placing people in the occupational structure, and thus in determining their adult class positions and life chances. Social mobility across generations now commonly takes the form of providing one's children with more education than their parents had, and the achievement of near universal secondary education in America by the Second World War provided the platform for the development of mass higher education since then. The tremendous growth of occupations demanding some form of higher education both reflects and further stimulates the increase in college and university enrolments. All this shows itself in yet another way, as a marked rise in the educational standard of living of the whole population. Throughout the class structure, already fully accomplished in the upper-middle but increasingly so in the lower-middle and working classes, higher education comes to be seen as appropriate not just for people of wealth or extraordinary talent or ambition, but as possible and desirable for youngsters of quite ordinary talent and ambition.

In the past the relative accessibility of higher education brought large numbers of students to American colleges who had little interest in learning for its own sake, but who had powerful vocational orientations, and wanted the degree and sometimes the skills which would help them better their position. We are now seeing large numbers from more affluent homes who similarly enter college without much interest in learning, but who also are less interested in vocational preparation – who either have little ambition for a middle-class career, or else take it completely for granted, or, as in many cases, both. Such students pose a special problem – they are rather bored, querulous people, resentful at having to be in college, and quite vulnerable to the various quasi-hippy and radical doctrines floating around. For example, it is fashionable among some to deprecate ambition and hard work, and to resent a curriculum which, they charge, threatens to build them into the business world, fit them for jobs, careers, and so forth in a

7

sick society, and whose counter-ideology to the notion of achievement is 'Look, man, you're just putting us on the treadmill and driving us, and your lives are just running around doing things, why don't we smell the flowers a little more . . .' I can't pursue this subject here, except to say that the ancillary functions of higher education for a mass student body – of entertainment and custodial care – are now beginning to take on rather different forms as the character and characteristics of this mass intake changes.

Changes in the occupational structure and educational values are the driving force behind the explosion of enrolments and the emergence of mass higher education in America. But that development has been facilitated by the absence of a national standard or a national system of higher education. The radical decentralization of decision-making in American higher education, together with the extreme heterogeneity in the quality and character of the institutions that it comprises, make the net effect of their decisions highly responsive to social and economic forces. A given college may choose not to grow, but there are ten others that will. And while competition for places in the most desired colleges becomes ever more intense, it is still true that there is a college somewhere in America for everybody. The commitment to a conception of public service is strong enough in American higher education, both public and private, so that the number of places is basically set by the consumer's demand in the market for education, rather than by production agreements among educational producers, as in most other advanced societies. The effective demand for higher education in the American population is a function of how much people want to attend college (or send their children there) and how expensive a college education is. Educational aspirations are rising, while the growth in numbers of municipal, state, and junior colleges, in part in response to the rise in educational aspirations, contributes to their further rise by bringing inexpensive, non-residential colleges nearer to many who could not afford high tuition fees or the costs of college residence.

If one popular function is the provision of mass higher education to nearly everybody who applies for it, the second is the provision of useful knowledge and service to nearly every group and institution that wants it. The service orientation of American higher education is too well known to need discussion. But the demand on the universities for such service is increasing all the time. This in part reflects the growth of the knowledge-base created by the scientific explosion of the past few decades. Not only is much of this new knowledge of potential applied value to industry, agriculture, the military, the health professions, etc., but also new areas of national life are coming to be seen as users of knowledge created in the university. We may know more about how to increase corn production than how to educate black children in our urban slums, but it is likely that the universities will shortly be as deeply involved in efforts to solve our urban problems as ever they were in agriculture.

II

How has American higher education been able to fulfil both its elite and its popular functions? Put differently, what have been the institutional mechanisms through which the colleges and universities have been able, on one hand, to contribute to both the transmission and creation of knowledge, and, on the other, to serve the variety of other demands the society has made on them?

The chief such mechanism has been the division of labour between and within institutions. A very large number of American colleges are essentially single-function institutions, either elite or popular. Swarthmore College or Haverford or Reed are essentially preparatory colleges for graduate and professional schools. Their faculties for the most part are men who have taken the Ph.D. in distinguished universities, but who prefer a career in a teaching college rather than in a big university. In addition there are the elite private universities – the Ivy League universities, or Rice, or Cal. Tech., or Stanford, for example – which are highly selective in admissions, and which subordinate service to research and the transmission of the high culture.

By contrast, a very large number of American colleges are essentially service institutions. The roughly two hundred teachers' colleges, the many small, weak, denominational colleges, the less ambitious engineering schools, the over seven hundred junior colleges: these are serving primarily vocational ends, preparing youngsters from relatively modest backgrounds for technical, semi-professional, and other white-collar jobs.

There is another group of institutions, most notably the big state universities, which carry on elite and popular functions within the same institution. On the one hand, these institutions, along with the state colleges and junior colleges, have taken the brunt of the enormous expansion of enrolments in recent decades. They are the centres for community service of every kind, they train the teachers, the social workers, the probation officers, the market researchers, and the myriad other new and semi-professions required by this service-oriented post-industrial society. On the other hand, they are also centres of scholarship and basic research, and contribute to the advancement of knowledge in every academic subject. Moreover, they offer, in their undergraduate colleges of letters and science, the full range of academic subjects, many of which centre on the transmission of the high culture, and are concerned less with public service than with the cultivation of sensibility and independence of judgement, a sense of the past, of the uniqueness of the individual, of the varied forms of human experience and expression – in brief, all the desired outcomes of liberal education.

Within the university the popular and elite functions are insulated from one another in various ways – ways that serve to protect the highly vulnerable elite functions of liberal education and basic research and scholarship from the direct impact of the larger society whose demands for vocational training, certification, service, and the like are reflected and met in the popular

9

functions of the university. These insulations take various forms of a division of labour within the university. There is a division of labour between departments, as for example between a Department of English or Classics, and a Department of Education. There is a division of labour in relatively unselective universities between the undergraduate and graduate schools, the former given over largely to mass higher education in the service of social mobility and occupational placement, entertainment, and custodial care, while the graduate departments in the same institutions are often able to maintain a climate in which scholarship and scientific research can be carried out to the highest standards. There is a familiar division of labour between graduate departments and professional schools. Among the faculty there is a division of labour, within many departments, between scientists and consultants, scholars and journalists, teachers and entertainers. More dangerously, there is a division of labour between regular faculty and a variety of fringe or marginal teachers – teaching assistants, visitors, and lecturers – who in some schools carry a disproportionate load of the mass teaching. Within the administration there is a division of labour between the dean of faculty and graduate dean, and the dean of students. And among the students there is a marked separation between the 'collegiate' and 'vocational' sub-cultures on one hand, and academically or intellectually oriented sub-cultures on the other.

Now, despite the strains which have developed around these divisions of function between and within American colleges and universities, they have worked surprisingly well, especially in the eyes of observers in European universities who have opposed the encroachment of popular functions on the universities as incompatible with their traditional functions to further knowledge, transmit the high culture, and shape the character of the elite strata. American higher education, as a system, has been able to do those things, and *also* give a post-secondary education, often within the very same institution, to millions of students, while serving every institution of society, every agency of government.

But I believe that these mechanisms of insulation and protection are currently breaking down under the impact of a new wave of pressures to expand the popular functions of American higher education. And I should like to discuss a few of the ways in which the enormous expansion of American higher education, in both its number and its range of activities, is creating very great strains on these insulating mechanisms, and thus threatening the traditional functions of the university. Let me sketch a few of these, and then return to them in rather more detail.

First, the expansion of the university is involving it more directly in controversial issues, and is thus increasing the number and range of significant publics in the larger society, including the political parties, which are attentive to what goes on in the university. This in turn is causing severe problems for boards of trustees and regents, and for the overall governance of the universities and the protection of their autonomy. These problems are reflected back on campus in the growing politicization of both the faculty and the student body (a trend that also has other sources). The intrusion of politics on to the campus has many consequences, among them the threat to the procedures by which these institutions govern themselves. At the same time, the growth of enrolment brings to the campus large numbers of students who do not accept the institution's authority to define the form and content of higher education: some of these are middle-class whites, while an increasing number are militant blacks. The characteristic forms of protest by radical whites and militant blacks are in important respects quite different, but both are at variance with the university's traditional functions.

III

Let me turn first to the changing role of Boards of Trustees or Regents. The role of trustees in American higher education is a peculiar one. They are, by law, the ultimate authority over these corporate bodies: they own the physical resources of the institution, they select its chief administrative officers, they possess the formal authority which is exercised by delegation by the administrative officers and faculty alike. And yet two parallel tendencies have been at work to reduce the actual importance of the trustees in recent decades: on the one hand, more and more power has drained away from the trustees with the growth of major alternative sources of funds for academic programmes over which the trustees have in fact had little or no control; and, on the other, the increasing assertion, on the part of administrators and faculty, that powers that have over time been delegated to them are theirs by right. The growth of the contract grant system has enormously increased the power of the faculty in relation to administration as well as to trustees; and the tight competitive market for academic men, together with institutional ambitions for prestige in the academic league standings, have ensured that trustees rarely exercise control over the funds granted to research professors. Trustees have been relatively ineffective in controlling capital expansion, one remaining bastion of their power, when funds for new buildings come essentially to support new research programmes for which professors and administrators have jointly applied. Moreover, administrators are increasingly turning to outside funds, especially to foundations, to support new academic programmes – to set up experimental colleges, or to bring more minority group students on campus. And again, trustees are really not consulted about these. External sources of funds mark a major diminution of the trustees' power to shape the character or guide the direction of 'their' institution.

In addition, the broad encompassing concept of 'academic freedom' has meant that both administrators and faculty members come to feel that the

11

powers they exercise over instruction, admissions, appointments, the internal allocation of resources, and even, increasingly, the physical design of the campus, all are theirs by right. Some of the forces that have led to the extension and deepening of the concept of academic freedom have had to do with the enormous influence of the most distinguished American universities as models for all the others. Characteristically, it is in the most distinguished universities that the academic community had the widest autonomy, the broadest control over its own conditions of life and work. And many lesser institutions have come to see faculty power and institutional autonomy as a mark of institutional distinction, and to be pursued as part of the strategy of institutional mobility to which so much of the energy and thought of academic men is devoted.[2]

Boards of trustees traditionally have looked in two directions: inwardly to the government and direction of their universities; outwardly, to the groups and interests which provide the support, and make claims for services, on the university. On the one hand, as I have suggested, boards have been losing power over their own institutions: many things are done, and funded, so to speak, behind their backs. At the same time (and this applies more to public than to private universities) their constituencies, and their relation to their constituencies, have been changing. Boards have traditionally dealt with very specific 'relevant publics': legislative committees, wealthy donors, alumni organizations. In the leading universities, their job has been to get support from these publics while resisting inappropriate interference. And in this task boards of public universities have not been so different from those of private universities: in most of their relationships they have been dealing with people very much like themselves, known quantities, in many cases graduates of the same state university, men of similar sentiments and values and prejudices. And these relationships could be, for the most part, cosy and private. The University of California until recently could imagine itself to be a private university operating largely on public funds, in a relationship to public authorities not wholly unlike that of the British universities.

Today, the constituencies, the relevant publics, of state universities are much wider, more heterogeneous, and less familiar. In part, the growth of relevant publics has accompanied the simultaneous expansion of the universities, and of their functions. When I arrived at Berkeley eleven years ago, the University of California consisted of two major campuses, three small undergraduate colleges, and a medical school, with a total enrolment of about 40,000, operating on a state budget of a little over one hundred million dollars. Today the university consists of 9 campuses with over 100,000 students and a state budget of over three hundred million dollars, with nearly as much again from outside sources. The student body and faculty are not only bigger, but more heterogeneous, reflecting a variety of interests, many of which touch directly on very sensitive and controversial public issues. The School of Agriculture still does research on more fruitful crops and more effective pest control, but other students and faculty are active in support of the movement to organize migratory farm workers; the School of Education still produces schoolteachers and administrators, but also provides expert advice to school boards embarked on programmes of total integration, while others testify in defence of black militants and invite Black Panthers to give lectures on campus; administrative officers still define and defend academic criteria for admissions, while other administrative officers press for the admission of larger numbers of minority-group students outside the ordinary admissions criteria. And the university is just embarking on a major commitment to the solution of urban problems which inevitably will involve it in the most intense and passionate political controversies.

As a result of the expansion of the university, both in numbers and in the range of activities, more and more people in California have come to take an interest in it, and have come to feel that they have views on the university which ought to be heard. In some uncertain sense, the constituency of the university has become the population of the state. But it is out of just this uncertainty about the nature and composition of the university's 'relevant publics' that the regents' anxieties arise. As the constituency of the trustees has grown, it has become less distinct: it is unclear just who the relevant publics are to which the regents should attend. Moreover, with the disruption of the old 'cosy' relations of the regents to specific limited publics, the regents can no longer know their constituents' minds by consulting with them, or by reading their own. And as the regents lose touch with their constituents, so also they come to be less well known and trusted by their new constituents: they become not people one can phone or one has talked to, but merely a remote part of the apparatus of government – the powerful people who need to be pressured. And some unrepresentative part of the anonymous public begins to write letters complaining about the university, and the regents, for want of a genuine relation to these new publics, begin to read them, and become anxious and worried. For one important difference between specific and differentiated publics and a mass undifferentiated public is that the former reflect specific interests which can be met, or compromised with, or educated, or resisted. A mass public, by contrast, does not have interests so much as fears and angers – what it communicates to the trustees is 'Why can't you clear up that mess at the university – all those demonstrating students and unpatriotic faculty?'

These two tendencies – the trustees' sense of a loss of control over their university, and the emergence of a mass public of uncertain size and composition and temper with whom the trustees have no clear representative or communicating relationship – can undermine a board of trustees' conceptions of who they are and what their role is, and generate in them anger and anxiety. This year the Regents of the University of California have reacted to an event at Berkeley with what appears to have been panic and rage. The event was the creation of an experimental course to which Eldridge

Cleaver, a leader of the militant Black Panthers, was invited to give a series of ten (unpaid) lectures. The course had been proposed by some students, gained the participation of four faculty members, and then was reviewed, revised, and approved by the regular faculty committee which had been charged with instituting such experimental courses. It was to have had an enrolment of about 200 out of a total undergraduate enrolment of some 15,000 and a total student enrolment of some 28,000 at Berkeley. One can have varying views about the academic value or wisdom of the course (which can be said about a great many of the thousands of courses offered each year at Berkeley) without seeing it as a serious danger to the university or to the students who would be attending it. Under pressure from the Governor, and from what it took to be 'public opinion', the Regents intervened directly in the instructional programme and passed a series of resolutions prohibiting the course as designed from being offered for credit, and censuring the faculty members who had sponsored it and the faculty committee which had approved it. At the same meeting they also quite gratuitously condemned a production of a play that they had not seen which had been put on by the Drama Department at Berkeley during the summer, and directed that future productions should 'conform to accepted standards of good taste . . .' These directives, besides being violations of the regents' own standing orders, were clearly violations of academic freedom even narrowly conceived. More to the point, they had all the marks of a panic response–impulsive, disproportionate to the occasion, and deeply and unnecessarily provocative of the *internal* constituencies, the students, faculty, and administration, which essentially constitute the institution the board is nominally governing, and which strongly opposed the regential action. The situation was of course exploited by militant groups of students, and their effort to create another Columbia disaster at Berkeley was narrowly averted. But the action created a serious crisis of authority within the university – what might be called a constitutional crisis, centring on who actually controls the curriculum and appointments of staff, which is not yet resolved. If it is not resolved, or if it leads to bitter struggles between the faculty and the regents, or between the university and the state government, which involve punitive actions against the budget or individual campuses, then Berkeley's (and the whole university's) capacity to sustain a climate of intellectual excellence will be gravely threatened: its ability to perform all its functions, but most especially its elite functions as an international centre of learning, will be seriously weakened.

California is in many ways a populist democracy: the Governor and legislature discuss and revise the university's annual operating budget in an atmosphere increasingly directly political and responsive to popular sentiments and indignation; and the whole electorate votes directly on proposed bond issues that are required for capital expansion. The Board of Regents, a majority of whom are appointed to sixteen-year terms, was conceived precisely as a buffer between the university and popular or political pressures, to protect the necessary freedom of the university to explore issues and engage in educational innovations that might not have popular support at any given moment. But, as we are seeing, the board appears unable to perform that function; instead of defending the university to its external publics, it begins to function as a conduit of popular sentiment and pressure on the university. And this, as I have suggested, places the elite functions of the university in grave jeopardy.

But the problems I have been discussing are not confined to public state universities in populist societies. The emergence of a mass undifferentiated and angry public indeed poses a special threat to universities. But the more general pattern in which university expansion creates new and easily neglected bodies of constituents can be illustrated in the events at Columbia University in the recent past. As Walter Metzger has noted, the physical expansion of Columbia, situated right at the edge of Harlem, made of that community a highly relevant and attentive public. Over many years Columbia has been expanding its operations into areas and buildings from which minority-group people have 'necessarily' been evicted. But its board of trustees, and unfortunately also its administration, simply had not begun to see that Harlem was at least as relevant to Columbia's fate as were its alumni, and wealthy donors, and great foundations. And it was the representatives of the black community, within the university as students, who precipitated the crisis that then was exploited by white militants, and greatly exacerbated by undisciplined police action.

The transformation of the constituencies of a university from a relatively small known set of relevant publics to a large undifferentiated mass public may be the inevitable consequence of the expansion of a state university system governed by a single board, and thus perceived as a single entity. Decentralization has been argued in universities on educational grounds – as providing diversity, variety, and an educational context of human scale which allow stronger and closer relationships to develop between teachers and students. I would argue decentralization also on political grounds: that enormous universities and university systems which constantly extend their influence must engender mass audiences. One way to reduce the impact of mass publics on the university is to decrease the size of the authoritative (i.e. autonomous) units within it. A university cannot experiment, which implies the certainty of making errors and the near certainty of offending somebody, if it has to satisfy the lowest common denominator of popular sentiment on every issue. What brings many issues to public attention is that they are decided, or at least approved, at a very high level, and thus are seen to have widespread consequences. Many of the popular functions of the universities in the past – mass education and public service – have indeed been popular in the other sense of the word, and have gained the support of the general public. But, as I have suggested, it seems inescapable that the university will

15

in the future be involved much more frequently in highly controversial issues and actions for which mass support cannot always be gained. Such activities may have a better chance of not becoming the focus for a major crisis (as the Cleaver course did) if decisions about it are not taken at the state-wide level in ways that require politicians and other politically ambitious people to take public stands. Reducing the size of the authoritative units (perhaps even smaller than a single campus) may also help to bring the representatives of the larger society closer to the educational process. And there is very clearly a need to educate them to the nature and requirements of the institutions whose governments they head.

IV

I want now to turn to the question of student activism, which is certainly the most visible form our current troubles take. First, this phenomenon has served as a kind of ink-blot to the world: all kinds of people impute to it meanings which support their own diagnoses of what is wrong with the university. We hear from the unlikeliest sources statements that begin, 'the students are trying to tell us . . .' and end with the interpreter's own notions of what ought to be changed.

My own view is that student activism on American campuses has to he seen as the outcome of a number of different developments and forces which have the appearance of a unity only when we do not look beyond the demonstrations themselves. First, the protests do not arise out of widespread discontent with the curriculum and forms of instruction in American universities. I myself believe there is considerable need for reform of the curriculum and organization of teaching, especially at the undergraduate level. But there is evidence in surveys that the bulk of American undergraduates are not seriously discontented with the education they are receiving, indeed, are far less so than many academic men feel they should be. In my own view, discontent with the forms and content of American higher education is centred in the teaching staff and, to a very large degree, in the humanities and social science departments of the big universities. The radical student uprisings themselves are political acts with educational consequences, rather than educational actions with political overtones. They centre on political issues in the larger society, most importantly the Viet Nam war and the racial revolution, and on the university chiefly by way of increasing the amount and changing the character of its involvement in social issues and conflict. At the heart of confrontations are small but passionate and sometimes well-organized groups of political students – some nihilists, some anarchists, some highly ideological neo-Marxists and Maoists. These groups have discovered how fragile universities are, how easily disrupted; they have also learned how to politicize and mobilize much larger numbers by exploiting clumsy or brutal responses by the institutions they attack. The analysis of these movements is not possible here. But it should be noted that their success in causing major disruptions on a campus is affected not only by their own numbers and will, but also by the amount of hostility present in the faculty towards the administration; the administration's own freedom to deal with internal problems without interference from repressive external forces; the adequacy of the administration's assessment of the situation, that is, its intelligence in the several meanings of that word; and the discipline of the local police force. In addition, it is crucially important whether the administration is able to prevent the exploitation of black protest by the radical white movement. As a rule of thumb, where administrators have been able to prevent that coalition, have the support of their faculty, and work with a disciplined police force, the white radical confrontations are not likely to escalate.

But we have to distinguish sharply between the militant blacks and the radical white political activists. Their rhetoric is often equally abusive, their tactics similarly disruptive, and at times it appears that they are in close alliance against the institution and its policies and procedures. But I believe that they are fundamentally different, in that the genuinely radical white activists want to bring down the society and its institutions, while the blacks for the most part want a larger role and more power within them. The different consequences of this for their respective tactics and behaviour are very great: the white radicals are really not interested in negotiation and reform. Their ends, and not just their means, are disruption, the discrediting of authority, and the politicization and radicalization of as many students as possible through the cycle of confrontation, disruption, police repression, mass indignation, and subsequent radicalization of heretofore moderate or liberal students and faculty. By contrast, militant blacks on American campuses typically demand specific changes in institutional policy or practice, centring upon the recruitment and admission of more black students without constraint by what they see as inherently 'racist' academic standards, the recruitment of more black faculty and administrators, the provision of a programme of black studies, under the control of the blacks themselves, more economic aid for blacks, administered by them, and living and dining arrangements also reflecting their new emphasis on separation and autonomy. These are real, as opposed to rhetorical demands, and are in most cases negotiable. The negotiations may be tough, the demands expensive, in varying ways, the accompanying rhetoric and action frightening, but finally the blacks have the one interest without which genuine negotiations for a redistribution of power and rewards in an institution are not possible – that is, an interest in the survival of the institutions on which the demands are being made. This is an interest that the most radical activists, the self-styled revolutionaries, do not have. For them Berkeley or Columbia are merely part of the hated 'power structure', and convenient places to demonstrate its iniquities and gain recruits. The blacks, for the most part, know this, and

17

are not enthusiastic for the alliances which the white radicals urge on them, and for which the whites are prepared to make any concessions, adopt any posture, support any demand. But in general, black militants have run their own show, not only out of a passion for autonomy and self-direction, but also out of an awareness that, however the white radicals join them in their diatribes against the white racist establishment, their goals and interests are really quite fundamentally different and even opposed. So at Columbia the blacks expelled the whites from Hamilton Hall, and thereafter the two movements were really quite separate, with different means as well as ends, running parallel in the same campus at the same time. On the Berkeley campus this Fall the blacks were not prepared to take violent action over the Cleaver case, especially after the campus administration, which has in a variety of ways demonstrated its basic sympathy with black students and their demands, had made provision to permit the course to be given, with Cleaver lecturing. The blacks were not prepared to take to the streets and seize buildings over the issue of course credit; the white radicals had to exploit the issue without the help of the blacks, and their seizure on successive nights of two campus buildings were ended by police arrests. The arrests were made without bloodshed or brutality – the discipline of police on campus is of course a crucial factor in the success or failure of a 'confrontation' – and the Columbia disaster was not reenacted at Berkeley this Fall.

In general, as I have suggested, militant blacks on campuses have resisted the alliance with white militants and have done their own thing in their own way. One apparent exception to this is the current crisis at San Francisco State. In my own opinion, the alliance there has been forged more by the failures of the local administration and the interventions of the Governor and state administration than by any natural coincidence of interest between blacks and white radicals. Moreover, even there the alliance is uneasy and, I believe, temporary.

But while it is possible to negotiate with blacks on the basis of specific demands, in a way it is not with the radical white groups, it is not yet clear what effects the continuing and growing black student movement will have on our universities, and especially on our public universities. American higher education has been extraordinarily hospitable to new demands from the community and the public at large, and many are now trying to respond to the demands of the black community in the same spirit, spurred, in varying degrees, by a bad conscience, a sense of the genuine importance of educating larger numbers of black students, and a lively apprehension of what may happen if they don't. And there is good reason to believe that the universities, and especially the big state universities, will try to take on this new function as they have so many others. If we look at the black demands themselves, the demand to modify or set aside ordinary admissions standards in order to admit more black applicants is, in my view, reasonable, since the criteria are not very good predictors of academic performance anyway, and probably even poorer for black students. More serious is the legitimacy of applying different criteria on racial grounds; that is likely to be challenged from outside as well as causing grave misgivings within the university. There would be fewer objections if the special admissions were made on the basis of inadequate early schooling or poverty than if they were made on the basis of race. Some observers are concerned that separatist colleges or departments of black studies may apply different academic standards to the work of their own students than do other departments. But, there again, the variability among departments in the big universities is already very great, and not especially troublesome. More serious is the question of whether racial or political passions will interfere with the free play of critical inquiry in these new programmes. But they are simply too young yet for any such judgements to be made. Quite separate is the issue of how black students will press future demands on universities. If they turn regularly to coercive demonstrations, which seem to be so effective in the early stages of the movement, the damage to the university from the demonstrations or from repressive backlash will be very great. Here one can only hope that militant blacks will soon find themselves having as strong an interest in the preservation of a climate that permits serious teaching and learning on campus as does anyone else. But it would be foolish to ignore the possibility that the universities may be the scene of a great deal of militant action by the black students, with potentially very serious effects on the intellectual life of the university itself.

This leads me to the impact of external pressures and student activism on the internal government and climate of universities. There are a number of forces which tend to limit the extent and intensity of disputes within the university, which tend to mute them and press towards compromise and accommodation between differing points of view. One of these is the broad acceptance of the legitimacy of the multiple functions of a university. The practical effect of this conception of the university is to remove from dispute the sharpest and fundamentally irreconcilable issues; disputes then can take the form of arguments about relative emphasis to be given to different views or the relative support allocated to different programmes. And even those disputes are further diluted in situations in which there is secular growth and expansion throughout the university, and where disputes then become merely questions of 'priority' and time.

Disputes are also softened by a general agreement to conduct them within the regular academic and administrative machinery – the system of committees and meetings through which major universities govern themselves. Disputes are still further softened by the institutional (and often also the geographical) insulation of conflicting views. For example, the humanistic scholars are typically centred in a university's college of letters and science, or its equivalent; the service orientations in the professional schools, or in the graduate departments. Historians and engineers may have very different

19

conceptions of the primary functions of the university, but they very rarely have occasion to confront one another in argument.

Conflict between different conceptions of the university is also minimized by making the department, rather than the college or the university, the unit of effective educational decision. The departments, or most of them, are more homogeneous than the faculty as a whole, and they have their own strong mechanisms for compromise and accommodation, not least of which is to minimize the number and importance of issues involving collective decision, allowing what might be called the privatization of intellectual life, a withdrawal to one's own classroom and research. On the graduate level, the university *is*, for all practical purposes, the aggregation of departments and professional schools, their satellite research centres and institutes, and the supporting infrastructure of libraries, labs, buildings, and mostly routine administrative help (though in a university, routines are not all that routine, and may require a considerable level of skill and talent). The departments effectively govern their own appointment and promotion of staff (subject to certain review procedures by extra-departmental committees), admit their own graduate students, and organize their instruction. On the undergraduate level (I am speaking here of the central liberal arts college), there is, of course, the necessity to organize some structure of education that is not confined to a single department. The form this takes at many institutions is a set of distribution requirements – so many units required in fields outside one's major, so many in a major field, the remainder electives. This system, whatever its educational justification, has the very substantial virtue of reducing the amount of academic decision-making that is necessary. This reduces the occasions for conflict involving educational values and philosophies, thus letting men get on with their own work. What we see at work there is a spirit of *laissez-faire*, within broad administrative constraints set by limitations of space, time, staff, and other resources, that mirrors the broader philosophy of the multiversity as a whole.

This pattern may be seen as an institutional response to the problem of combining higher education offered to very large numbers of students of the most diverse character with the highest standards of scholarly and scientific work. But the events of the past few years have revealed basic weaknesses in the system which are in a sense the defects of its virtues. One of these is the lack of a central, widely shared sense of the nature of the institution, and a weakness in its capacity to gain the loyalties and devotion of its participants. This means that the institution operates on a relatively thin margin of error. Closely related to this is its tendency to generate among both students and faculty somewhat diffuse resentments, feelings of frustration and alienation from an institution which provides services and facilities but seems singularly remote from the concerns of individuals, responsive only to pressures and problems that are organized and communicated through the regular channels, and not always even to those. It is this kind of institution marked by weak faculty loyalties, vague resentments, and complex administrative arrangements, which is likely to prove to be highly vulnerable to political attack from without and within.

These attacks have other consequences than the disruptive demonstrations and sit-ins that are most widely publicized. The attacks, whether from a governor or a radical student group, work to politicize a campus, to polarize a faculty, and to force its members to make choices in an atmosphere of passion and partisanship. The differences that crystallize around the issue I have been describing differ from the ordinary issues of academic politics: for one thing, they involve the students more directly; for another, they are more stable, more closely linked to deep-rooted values and conceptions of the nature of the institution. Moreover, at Berkeley, and I suspect elsewhere, they are being institutionalized in the form of faculty parties, which will persist as permanent elements in the governmental process, further contributing to the polarization of the faculty out of which they arise. Perhaps most importantly, these tendencies threaten to disrupt the informal processes of consultation, negotiation, and compromise among and between senior faculty and administrators by which universities are ordinarily governed. And they threaten to break through all the devices for softening conflict that I was describing. In their place are put forward two powerful democratic models from the government of institutions. One is the model of representative democracy, complete with a party system and judicial review. The other is the model of direct democracy in the self-governing small community. Both have been advocated for the university, as well as a combination of the two involving the formalization of the governmental process in addition to the provision of a high degree of participatory democracy. Such a system would require a relatively high and continuous level of faculty involvement in the issues and instruments of university government, as well as a basic decision regarding the extent of citizenship – that is, the role of the students in the decision-making machinery. And indeed, both these issues have been raised in a recent student–faculty report on university governance at Berkeley which calls for a high level of participation by both faculty and students in units of government at every level, from the campus as a whole down to the individual department. Now many arguments can be made against such a proposal – its cumbersomeness, the impermanence of the students (they do not have to live very long with the consequences of their decisions on a campus), their incompetence to decide certain matters, and so forth. But in my own view, more important than any of these is the absolute level of political activity and involvement required of teachers and students under these arrangements. The cosy and rather informal method by which faculty members and administrators govern a campus may have many failings, most clearly visible to those who are not part of such a government. Its chief virtue is that it has allowed students and teachers to get on with their work of teaching and learning. Students and faculty who want radically to

21

transform the universities are at least consistent in wanting to change the form of governance, for some, as at Berkeley, by making the process of government itself a central part and focus of a university education. But liberal education, scholarship, and research are not inherently political activities, even when they take politics as their subject. And they are threatened by a highly politicized environment, both by its partisanship and demand for loyalties and commitments, and also by its distractions, its encroachments on one's time and energies. The reactions of academic men who are not much interested in university governance is usually to withdraw their attention, and let others govern. But this only works if those others, who *are* interested in politics, share the faculty's basic values, and are concerned to create and protect an environment in which the older functions of teaching and research can go on without distraction or intimidation. That is an unlikely outcome of any arrangement that makes its own government a central activity of the university, ensures that all disputes pass through its formal machinery, and brings students and faculty with a passion for politics to the centre of the governing process. But that is the direction of much student and faculty sentiment at the moment, and of reforms on many campuses.

One outcome of the heightened political atmosphere on our campuses may be that we will be seeing some academic men leaving the colleges and universities for research centres and institutes where they are more protected from popular pressures and their echoes in campus politics. If the numbers and quality of those who leave are significant, that would be a very grave threat to the quality and character of the universities as we know and cherish them.

V

My theme has been very broad. The growth of numbers, functions, and political pressures within universities takes many forms, and I have touched on only a few of those which I believe are an especially serious threat to the university's core functions of liberal education, scholarship, and basic research. I have not spoken of the crisis in undergraduate education arising out of the complete collapse of any generally shared conception of what students ought to learn; nor of the role of teaching assistants in the big state universities, who carry a great part of the undergraduate teaching on the cheap, and begin to see themselves as exploited employees and organize in trade unions. Nor have I had time to discuss the changing character of our undergraduates, of the boredom of some and the apparently unquenchable anger of others. Merely to point to these issues is to affirm that I do not judge the state of our universities by the conventional measures of success that I mentioned in my opening remarks. But let me close by saying that I am an admirer of American higher education, which, as a system and in its representative institutions, has managed both to fulfil its commitments to liberal education and the advancement of knowledge, and also to serve a nation and a people in all the ways that it has. The problem now, as it has been for a hundred years, is whether those functions can be performed in the same institution. The problem is acutely one for the great public universities. If the core functions of the state universities are threatened and then crippled by the great flood of popular pressures and demands being made on them, then those functions, at their highest levels of performance, will be confined to the great private universities, or forced outside the university altogether. And if that happens, something very precious – the presence within institutions of popular democracy of the highest standards of intellectual life – will have been lost in America.

Notes

1 J-J. Servan-Schreiber, *Le Défi américain*, Paris, 1967.
2 It could perhaps be argued that the power of the faculties in the most distinguished universities flow precisely from their academic distinction, through the familiar academic transmutation of prestige into power. The faculties of weaker institutions see the relation, but endeavour to turn the causal connection on its head: they mean to gain the power and transmute it into prestige, for their institutions directly and themselves indirectly.

99

THE STUDENT AND THE UNIVERSITY

Allan Bloom

Source: A. Bloom, *The Closing of the American Mind: How Higher Education Has Failed Democracy and Impoverished the Souls of Today's Students*, New York: Simon and Schuster, 1987, pp. 336–82.

Liberal education

What image does a first-rank college or university present today to a teen-ager leaving home for the first time, off to the adventure of a liberal education? He has four years of freedom to discover himself—a space between the intellectual wasteland he has left behind and the inevitable dreary professional training that awaits him after the baccalaureate. In this short time he must learn that there is a great world beyond the little one he knows, experience the exhilaration of it and digest enough of it to sustain himself in the intellectual deserts he is destined to traverse. He must do this, that is, if he is to have any hope of a higher life. These are the charmed years when he can, if he so chooses, become anything he wishes and when he has the opportunity to survey his alternatives, not merely those current in his time or provided by careers, but those available to him as a human being. The importance of these years for an American cannot be overestimated. They are civilization's only chance to get to him.

In looking at him we are forced to reflect on what he should learn if he is to be called educated; we must speculate on what the human potential to be fulfilled is. In the specialties we can avoid such speculation, and the avoidance of them is one of specialization's charms. But here it is a simple duty. What are we to teach this person? The answer may not be evident, but to attempt to answer the question is already to philosophize and to begin to educate. Such a concern in itself poses the question of the unity of man and the unity of the sciences. It is childishness to say, as some do, that everyone must be allowed to develop freely, that it is authoritarian to impose a point of view on the student. In that case, why have a university? If the response

24

is "to provide an atmosphere for learning," we come back to our original questions at the second remove. Which atmosphere? Choices and reflection on the reasons for those choices are unavoidable. The university has to stand for something. The practical effects of unwillingness to think positively about the contents of a liberal education are, on the one hand, to ensure that all the vulgarities of the world outside the university will flourish within it, and, on the other, to impose a much harsher and more illiberal necessity on the student—the one given by the imperial and imperious demands of the specialized disciplines unfiltered by unifying thought.

The university now offers no distinctive visage to the young person. He finds a democracy of the disciplines—which are there either because they are autochthonous or because they wandered in recently to perform some job that was demanded of the university. This democracy is really an anarchy, because there are no recognized rules for citizenship and no legitimate titles to rule. In short there is no vision, nor is there a set of competing visions, of what an educated human being is. The question has disappeared, for to pose it would be a threat to the peace. There is no organization of the sciences, no tree of knowledge. Out of chaos emerges dispiritedness, because it is impossible to make a reasonable choice. Better to give up on liberal education and get on with a specialty in which there is at least a prescribed curriculum and a prospective career. On the way the student can pick up in elective courses a little of whatever is thought to make one cultured. The student gets no intimation that great mysteries might be revealed to him, that new and higher motives of action might be discovered within him, that a different and more human way of life can be harmoniously constructed by what he is going to learn.

Simply, the university is not distinctive. Equality for us seems to culminate in the unwillingness and incapacity to make claims of superiority, particularly in the domains in which such claims have always been made—art, religion and philosophy. When Weber found that he could not choose between certain high opposites—reason vs. revelation, Buddha vs. Jesus—he did not conclude that all things are equally good, that the distinction between high and low disappears. As a matter of fact he intended to revitalize the consideration of these great alternatives in showing the gravity and danger involved in choosing among them; they were to be heightened in contrast to the trivial considerations of modern life that threatened to overgrow and render indistinguishable the profound problems the confrontation with which makes the bow of the soul taut. The serious intellectual life was for him the battleground of the great decisions, all of which are spiritual or "value" choices. One can no longer present this or that particular view of the educated or civilized man as authoritative; therefore one must say that education consists in knowing, really knowing, the small number of such views in their integrity. This distinction between profound and superficial—which takes the place of good and bad, true and false—provided a focus for

serious study, but it hardly held out against the naturally relaxed democratic tendency to say, "Oh, what's the use?" The first university disruptions
at Berkeley were explicitly directed against the multiversity smorgasbord
and, I must confess, momentarily and partially engaged my sympathies. It
may have even been the case that there was some small element of longing
for an education in the motivation of those students. But nothing was
done to guide or inform their energy, and the result was merely to add
multilife-styles to multidisciplines, the diversity of perversity to the diversity
of specialization. What we see so often happening in general happened here
too; the insistent demand for greater community ended in greater isolation.
Old agreements, old habits, old traditions were not so easily replaced.

Thus, when a student arrives at the university, he finds a bewildering
variety of departments and a bewildering variety of courses. And there is no
official guidance, no university-wide agreement, about what he *should* study.
Nor does he usually find readily available examples, either among students
or professors, of a unified use of the university's resources. It is easiest
simply to make a career choice and go about getting prepared for that
career. The programs designed for those having made such a choice render
their students immune to charms that might lead them out of the conven-
tionally respectable. The sirens sing *sotto voce* these days, and the young
already have enough wax in their ears to pass them by without danger.
These specialties can provide enough courses to take up most of their time
for four years in preparation for the inevitable graduate study. With the
few remaining courses they can do what they please, taking a bit of this
and a bit of that. No public career these days—not doctor nor lawyer nor
politician nor journalist nor businessman nor entertainer—has much to do
with humane learning. An education, other than purely professional or
technical, can even seem to be an impediment. That is why a countervailing
atmosphere in the university would be necessary for the students to gain a
taste for intellectual pleasures and learn that they are viable.

The real problem is those students who come hoping to find out what
career they want to have, or are simply looking for an adventure with
themselves. There are plenty of things for them to do—courses and disciplines enough to spend many a lifetime on. Each department or great division
of the university makes a pitch for itself, and each offers a course of study
that will make the student an initiate. But how to choose among them? How
do they relate to one another? The fact is they do not address one another.
They are competing and contradictory, without being aware of it. The problem of the whole is urgently indicated by the very existence of the specialties,
but it is never systematically posed. The net effect of the student's encounter
with the college catalogue is bewilderment and very often demoralization.
It is just a matter of chance whether he finds one or two professors who
can give him an insight into one of the great visions of education that have
been the distinguishing part of every civilized nation. Most professors are

specialists, concerned only with their own fields, interested in the advancement of those fields in their own terms, or in their own personal advancement in a world where all the rewards are on the side of professional distinction. They have been entirely emancipated from the old structure of the university, which at least helped to indicate that they are incomplete, only parts of an unexamined and undiscovered whole. So the student must navigate among a collection of carnival barkers, each trying to lure him into a particular sideshow. This undecided student is an embarrassment to most universities, because he seems to be saying, "I am a whole human being. Help me to form myself in my wholeness and let me develop my real potential," and he is the one to whom they have nothing to say.

Cornell was, as in so many other things, in advance of its time on this issue. The six-year Ph.D. program, richly supported by the Ford Foundation, was directed specifically to high school students who had already made "a firm career choice" and was intended to rush them through to the start of those careers. A sop was given to desolate humanists in the form of money to fund seminars that these young careerists could take on their way through the College of Arts and Sciences. For the rest, the educators could devote their energies to arranging and packaging the program without having to provide it with any substance. That kept them busy enough to avoid thinking about the nothingness of their endeavor. This has been the preferred mode of not looking the Beast in the Jungle in the face— structure, not content. The Cornell plan for dealing with the problem of liberal education was to suppress the students' longing for liberal education by encouraging their professionalism and their avarice, providing money and all the prestige the university had available to make careerism the centerpiece of the university.

The Cornell plan dared not state the radical truth, a well-kept secret: the colleges do not have enough to teach their students, not enough to justify keeping them four years, probably not even three years. If the focus is careers, there is hardly one specialty, outside the hardest of the hard natural sciences, which requires more than two years of preparatory training prior to graduate studies. The rest is just wasted time, or a period of ripening until the students are old enough for graduate studies. For many graduate careers, even less is really necessary. It is amazing how many undergraduates are poking around for courses to take, without any plan or question to ask, just filling up their college years. In fact, with rare exceptions, the courses are parts of specialties and not designed for general cultivation, or to investigate questions important for human beings as such. The so-called knowledge explosion and increasing specialization have not filled up the college years but emptied them. Those years are impediments; one wants to get beyond them. And in general the persons one finds in the professions need not have gone to college, if one is to judge by their tastes, their fund of learning or their interests. They might as well have spent their college years in the Peace

Corps or the like. These great universities—which can split the atom, find cures for the most terrible diseases, conduct surveys of whole populations and produce massive dictionaries of lost languages—cannot generate a modest program of general education for undergraduate students. This is a parable for our times.

There are attempts to fill the vacuum painlessly with various kinds of fancy packaging of what is already there—study abroad options, individualized majors, etc. Then there are Black Studies and Women's or Gender Studies, along with Learn Another Culture. Peace Studies are on their way to a similar prevalence. All this is designed to show that the university is with it and has something in addition to its traditional specialties. The latest item is computer literacy, the full cheapness of which is evident only to those who think a bit about what literacy might mean. It would make some sense to promote literacy literacy, inasmuch as most high school graduates nowadays have difficulty reading and writing. And some institutions are quietly undertaking this worthwhile task. But they do not trumpet the fact, because this is merely a high school function that our current sad state of educational affairs has thrust upon them, about which they are not inclined to boast.

Now that the distractions of the sixties are over, and undergraduate education has become more important again (because the graduate departments, aside from the professional schools, are in trouble due to the shortage of academic jobs), university officials have had somehow to deal with the undeniable fact that the students who enter are uncivilized, and that the universities have some responsibility for civilizing them. If one were to give a base interpretation of the schools' motives, one could allege that their concern stems from shame and self-interest. It is becoming all too evident that liberal education—which is what the small band of prestigious institutions are supposed to provide, in contrast to the big state schools, which are thought simply to prepare specialists to meet the practical demands of a complex society—has no content, that a certain kind of fraud is being perpetrated. For a time the great moral consciousness alleged to have been fostered in students by the great universities, especially their vocation as gladiators who fight war and racism, seemed to fulfill the demands of the collective university conscience. They were doing something other than offering preliminary training for doctors and lawyers. Concern and compassion were thought to be the indefinable X that pervaded all the parts of the Arts and Sciences campus. But when that evanescent mist dissipated during the seventies, and the faculties found themselves face to face with ill-educated young people with no intellectual tastes—unaware that there even are such things, obsessed with getting on with their careers before having looked at life—and the universities offered no counterpoise, no alternative goals, a reaction set in.

Liberal education—since it has for so long been ill-defined, has none of the crisp clarity or institutionalized prestige of the professions, but nevertheless perseveres and has money and respectability connected with it—has always been a battleground for those who are somewhat eccentric in relation to the specialties. It is in something like the condition of churches as opposed to, say, hospitals. Nobody is quite certain of what the religious institutions are supposed to do anymore, but they do have some kind of role either responding to a real human need or as the vestige of what was once a need, and they invite the exploitation of quacks, adventurers, cranks and fanatics. But they also solicit the warmest and most valiant efforts of persons of peculiar gravity and depth. In liberal education, too, the worst and the best fight it out, fakers vs. authentics, sophists vs. philosophers, for the favor of public opinion and for control over the study of man in our times. The most conspicuous participants in the struggle are administrators who are formally responsible for presenting some kind of public image of the education their colleges offer, persons with a political agenda or vulgarizers of what the specialties know, and real teachers of the humane disciplines who actually see their relation to the whole and urgently wish to preserve the awareness of it in their students' consciousness.

So, just as in the sixties universities were devoted to removing require-ments, in the eighties they are busy with attempts to put them back in, a much more difficult task. The word of the day is "core." It is generally agreed that "we went a bit far in the sixties," and that a little fine-tuning has now become clearly necessary.

There are two typical responses to the problem. The easiest and most administratively satisfying solution is to make use of what is already there in the autonomous departments and simply force the students to cover the fields, i.e., take one or more courses in each of the general divisions of the university: natural science, social science and the humanities. The reigning ideology here is *breadth*, as was *openness* in the age of laxity. The courses are almost always the already existing introductory courses, which are of least interest to the major professors and merely assume the worth and reality of that which is to be studied. It is general education, in the sense in which a jack-of-all-trades is a generalist. He knows a bit of everything and is inferior to the specialist in each area. Students may wish to sample a variety of fields, and it may be good to encourage them to look around and see if there is something that attracts them in one of which they have no experience. But this is not a liberal education and does not satisfy any longing they have for one. It just teaches that there is no high-level generalism, and that what they are doing is preliminary to the real stuff and part of the childhood they are leaving behind. Thus they desire to get it over with and get on with what their professors do seriously. Without recognition of important questions of common concern, there cannot be serious liberal education, and attempts to establish it will be but failed gestures.

It is a more or less precise awareness of the inadequacy of this approach to core curricula that motivates the second approach, which consists of what one might call composite courses. These are constructions developed especially for general-education purposes and usually require collaboration of professors drawn from several departments. These courses have titles like "Man in Nature," "War and Moral Responsibility," "The Arts and Creativity," "Culture and the Individual." Everything, of course, depends upon who plans them and who teaches them. They have the clear advantage of requiring some reflection on the general needs of students and force specialized professors to broaden their perspectives, at least for a moment. The dangers are trendiness, mere popularization and lack of substantive rigor. In general, the natural scientists do not collaborate in such endeavors, and hence these courses tend to be unbalanced. In short, they do not point beyond themselves and do not provide the student with independent means to pursue permanent questions independently, as, for example, the study of Aristotle or Kant as wholes once did. They tend to be bits of this and that. Liberal education should give the student the sense that learning must and can be both synoptic and precise. For this, a very small, detailed problem can be the best way, if it is framed so as to open out on the whole. Unless the course has the specific intention to lead to the permanent questions, to make the student aware of them and give him some competence in the important works that treat of them, it tends to be a pleasant diversion and a dead end—because it has nothing to do with any program of further study he can imagine. If such programs engage the best energies of the best people in the university, they can be beneficial and provide some of the missing intellectual excitement for both professors and students. But they rarely do, and they are too cut off from the top, from what the various faculties see as their real business. Where the power is determines the life of the whole body. And the intellectual problems unresolved at the top cannot be resolved administratively below. The problem is the lack of any unity of the sciences and the loss of the will or the means even to discuss the issue. The illness above is the cause of the illness below, to which all the good-willed efforts of honest liberal educationists can at best be palliatives.

Of course, the only serious solution is the one that is almost universally rejected: the good old Great Books approach, in which a liberal education means reading certain generally recognized classic texts, just reading them, letting them dictate what the questions are and the method of approaching them—not forcing them into categories we make up, not treating them as historical products, but trying to read them as their authors wished them to be read. I am perfectly well aware of, and actually agree with, the objections to the Great Books cult. It is amateurish; it encourages an autodidact's self-assurance without competence; one cannot read all of the Great Books carefully; if one only reads Great Books, one can never know what a great, as opposed to an ordinary, book is; there is no way of determining who is to decide what a Great Book or what the canon is; books are made the ends and not the means; the whole movement has a certain coarse evangelistic tone that is the opposite of good taste; it engenders a spurious intimacy with greatness; and so forth. But one thing is certain: wherever the Great Books make up a central part of the curriculum, the students are excited and satisfied, feel they are doing something that is independent and fulfilling, getting something from the university they cannot get elsewhere. The very fact of this special experience, which leads nowhere beyond itself, provides them with a new alternative and a respect for study itself. The advantage they get is an awareness of the classic—particularly important for our innocents; an acquaintance with what big questions were when there were still big questions; models, at the very least, of how to go about answering them; and, perhaps most important of all, a fund of shared experiences and thoughts on which to ground their friendships with one another. Programs based upon judicious use of great texts provide the royal road to students' hearts. Their gratitude at learning of Achilles or the categorical imperative is boundless. Alexandre Koyré, the late historian of science, told me that his appreciation for America was great when—in the first course he taught at the University of Chicago, in 1940 at the beginning of his exile—a student spoke in his paper of Mr. Aristotle, unaware that he was not a contemporary. Koyré said that only an American could have the naive profundity to take Aristotle as living thought, unthinkable for most scholars. A good program of liberal education feeds the student's love of truth and passion to live a good life. It is the easiest thing in the world to devise courses of study, adapted to the particular conditions of each university, which thrill those who take them. The difficulty is in getting them accepted by the faculty.

None of the three great parts of the contemporary university is enthusiastic about the Great Books approach to education. The natural scientists are benevolent toward other fields and toward liberal education, if it does not steal away their students and does not take too much time from their preparatory studies. But they themselves are interested primarily in the solution of the questions now important in their disciplines and are not particularly concerned with discussions of their foundations, inasmuch as they are so evidently successful. They are indifferent to Newton's conception of time or his disputes with Leibniz about calculus; Aristotle's teleology is an absurdity beneath consideration. Scientific progress, they believe, no longer depends on the kind of comprehensive reflection given to the nature of science by men like Bacon, Descartes, Hume, Kant and Marx. This is merely historical study, and for a long time now, even the greatest scientists have given up thinking about Galileo and Newton. Progress is undoubted. The difficulties about the truth of science raised by positivism, and those about the goodness of science raised by Rousseau and Nietzsche, have not really penetrated to the center of scientific consciousness. Hence, no Great Books, but incremental progress, is the theme for them.

Social scientists are in general hostile, because the classic texts tend to deal with the human things the social sciences deal with, and they are very proud of having freed themselves from the shackles of such earlier thought to become truly scientific. And, unlike the natural scientists, they are insecure enough about their achievement to feel threatened by the works of earlier thinkers, perhaps a bit afraid that students will be seduced and fall back into the bad old ways. Moreover, with the possible exception of Weber and Freud, there are no social science books that can be said to be classic. This may be interpreted favorably to the social sciences by comparing them to the natural sciences, which can be said to be a living organism developing by the addition of little cells, a veritable body of knowledge proving itself to be such by the very fact of this almost unconscious growth, with thousands of parts oblivious to the whole, nevertheless contributing to it. This is in opposition to a work of imagination or of philosophy, where a single creator makes and surveys an artificial whole, But whether one interprets the absence of the classic in the social sciences in ways flattering or unflattering to them, the fact causes social scientists discomfort. I remember the professor who taught the introductory graduate courses in social science methodology, a famous historian, responding scornfully and angrily to a question I naively put to him about Thucydides with "Thucydides was a fool!"

More difficult to explain is the tepid reaction of humanists to Great Books education, inasmuch as these books now belong almost exclusively to what are called the humanities. One would think that high esteem for the classic would reinforce the spiritual power of the humanities, at a time when their temporal power is at its lowest. And it is true that the most active proponents of liberal education and the study of classic texts are indeed usually humanists. But there is division among them. Some humanities disciplines are just crusty specialties that, although they depend on the status of classic books for their existence, are not really interested in them in their natural state—much philology, for example, is concerned with the languages but not what is said in them—and will and can do nothing to support their own infrastructure. Some humanities disciplines are eager to join the real sciences and transcend their roots in the now overcome mythic past. Some humanists make the legitimate complaints about lack of competence in the teaching and learning of Great Books, although their criticism is frequently undermined by the fact that they are only defending recent scholarly interpretation of the classics rather than a vital, authentic understanding. In their reaction there is a strong element of specialist's jealousy and narrowness. Finally, a large part of the story is just the general debilitation of the humanities, which is both symptom and cause of our present condition.

To repeat, the crisis of liberal education is a reflection of a crisis at the peaks of learning, an incoherence and incompatibility among the first principles with which we interpret the word, an intellectual crisis of the greatest magnitude, which constitutes the crisis of our civilization. But perhaps it would be true to say that the crisis consists not so much in this incoherence but in our incapacity to discuss or even recognize it. Liberal education flourished when it prepared the way for the discussion of a unified view of nature and man's place in it, which the best minds debated on the highest level. It decayed when what lay beyond it were only specialties, the premises of which do not lead to any such vision. The highest is the partial intellect; there is no synopsis.

The decomposition of the university

This became all too clear in the aftermath of the guns at Cornell, and I had a chance to learn something about the articulation of the university as it decomposed. In general, no discipline—only individuals—reacted very well to the assault on academic freedom and integrity. But various disciplines reacted in characteristic ways. The professional schools—engineering, home economics, industrial-labor relations and agriculture—simply went home and closed the shutters. (Some professors in the law school did indeed express indignation, and a group of them finally spoke out publicly for the dismissal of the president.) These faculties were supposed, in general, to be conservative, but they just did not want trouble and did not feel it was their fight. The complaints of the black students were not about them; and whatever changes in thought were to take place, they would be untouched. In spite of the common complaints about the great variety of disciplines unbalancing the university and causing it to lose its focus, everyone knows that the arts and sciences faculty is where the action is, that the other schools are ancillary to it, that it is the center of learning and prestige. This much of the old order has been preserved. The challenge at Cornell was issued to the College of Arts and Sciences, as was the case everywhere throughout the sixties. The problem thus had to be faced by the natural sciences, the social sciences and the humanities. They were asked to change their content and their standards, to eliminate elitism, racism and sexism as "perceived" by students. But the community of scholars proved to be no community. There was no solidarity in defense of the pursuit of truth.

The natural scientists were above the battle, an island unto themselves, and did not feel threatened. I believe that only one natural scientist at Cornell spoke out against the presence of guns or the bullying of professors. The university's most famous professor, a Nobel prizewinning physicist, became a leading spokesman in defense of the president without once consulting those professors whose lives had been threatened or posing the question of what was at stake. He deplored the violence but took no action or uttered any word indicating where a line should be drawn. As far as I know, none of the natural scientists was in cahoots with the thugs, as were some social scientists and humanists. It was the absolute independence of their work from the rest of the university's activity, and their trust that theirs is the important work, that made them indifferent. They did not share a common good with the rest of us. Walking to the meeting where the faculty capitulated to the students—a truly disgraceful event, a microcosm of cowardly acquiescence to the establishment of tyranny—in the company of a friend who had had to suffer the humiliation of leaving his home and hiding out with his family after receiving explicit threats, I heard a professor of biology loudly asking, perhaps for our benefit, "Do these social scientists really believe there is any danger?" My friend looked at me sadly and said, "With colleagues like that, you don't need enemies."

Because the student movements were so untheoretical, the natural sciences were not a target, as they had once been in high-grade fascism and communism. There were no Lenins thundering against positivism, relativity or genetics, no Goebbels alert to the falseness of Jewish science. There had been the beginnings of an offensive against the scientists' collaboration with the military-industrial complex, as well as their role in producing the technology that abets capitalism and pollutes the environment. But none of this went to the heart of the serious scientists' research. They were able to avoid the fury by distancing themselves from certain unpopular applications of their knowledge, by insulting the government which supported them, and by declaring themselves for peace and social justice. Here too the great Cornell physicist has, predictably, distinguished himself by making a habit of apologizing for physics' hand in producing thermonuclear weapons. But these scientists were not asked to change one thing in their studies, their classes or their laboratories. So they opted out.

This behavior was not merely selfishness and self-protectiveness, every man for himself, although there was a good deal of that, accompanied with the usual distasteful moralizing rhetoric. The atmosphere of crisis caused a not entirely conscious reassessment of natural science's relation to the university. Crises in the intellectual world as well as in the political one tend to bring to the surface tensions and changes in interest that it is easier not to face as long as things are calm. To break old alliances and form new ones is always a painful business, as, for example, when liberals broke with Stalinists at the beginning of the Cold War. The scientists found themselves confronted with the fact that they had no real connection with the rest of the university, and that to cast their lot with it was costly. One cannot imagine that biologists would have been so callous if chemistry had somehow become a target for cultural revolution, and young Red Guards monitored its teachings and terrorized its practitioners. Chemists are biologists' blood relations, and their knowledge is absolutely indispensable for the progress of biology. But it is not now conceivable that a physicist qua physicist could learn anything important, or anything at all, from a professor of comparative literature or of sociology. The natural scientist's connection with the rest of humane learning is not familial but abstract, a little like our connection with humanity as a whole. There may be a formulaic invocation of rights applicable to all, but nothing that moves with the burning immediacy of shared convictions and interests. "I can live without you" is the silent thought that steals into one's mind when such relations become painful.

The reality of separateness has existed since Kant, the last philosopher who was a significant natural scientist, and Goethe, the last great literary figure who could believe that his contributions to science might be greater than his contributions to literature. And, it should be remembered, it was not that they were philosopher and poet who happened to dabble in science, but that their writings were mirrors of nature and that their science was guided and informed by meditation on being, freedom and beauty. They represented the last gasp of the old unity of the questions before natural science became the Switzerland of learning, safely neutral to the battles taking place on the darkling plain. Henry Adams—whose life bridged the last epoch when gentlemen, such as Jefferson, thought science both attainable and useful for them, and the one where scientists speak an incomprehensible language that teaches nothing about life but is necessary to life as information—takes note of this change in his quirky way. When he was young he had studied natural science and had given it up; when as an old man he looked again in that direction, he found that he was in a new world. The old university traditions and ideals had concealed the fact that the ancient bonds had decayed and the marriage was washed up. The great scientists of the nineteenth century and twentieth century were in general cultivated men who had some experience of, and real admiration for, the other parts of learning. The increasing specialization of the natural sciences and the natural scientists gradually caused the protective fog to lift. Since the sixties the scientists have had less and less to say to, and to do with, their colleagues in the social sciences and humanities. The university has lost whatever polis-like character it had and has become like the ship on which the passengers are just accidental fellow travelers soon to disembark and go their separate ways. The relations between natural science, social science and humanities are purely administrative and have no substantial intellectual content. They only meet on the level of the first two years of undergraduate education, and there the natural scientists are largely concerned with protecting their interest in the young who will be coming their way.

A perfect illustration of this situation appeared a few years ago in a *New York Times* account of the visit of a professor of music to Rockefeller University. The life scientists working there brought bag lunches to the musicologist's lecture. The project was inspired by C. P. Snow's silly conceits about "the two cultures," the rift between which he proposed to heal by getting humanists to learn the second law of thermodynamics and physicists to read Shakespeare. This enterprise would, of course, be something other than an exercise in spiritual uplift only if the physicist learned something important for his physics from Shakespeare, and if the humanist similarly profited from the second law of thermodynamics. In fact, nothing of the sort ensues. For the scientist the humanities are recreation (often deeply respected by him, for he sees that more is needed than what he offers, but is puzzled about where to find it), and for the humanist the natural sciences are at best indifferent, at worst alien and hostile.

The *Times* quoted Joshua Lederberg, the president of Rockefeller University, from which philosophy had recently been banished, as saying after the lecture that C. P. Snow was on the right track but "counted wrong"—there are not two but many cultures, one example of which is that of the Beatles. This represents the ultimate trivialization of a trivial idea that was just a rest station on a downward slope. Lederberg saw in the humanities not the human knowledge that complements the study of nature but merely another expression of what was going on in the world. In the end, it is all more or less sophisticated show business. With a kind of wink at his audience Lederberg lets us know that in this sea of democratic relativism natural science stands out like Gibraltar. All the rest is a matter of taste.

This disposition affected the natural scientists' behavior at Cornell and everywhere else. In the attempt to use the admission of students and appointment of faculty as means for this or that social goal, which has lowered university standards and obscured the university's purpose, they cooperated with the new agenda, in their own way. They adopted the rhetoric of anti-elitism, antisexism and antiracism, and quietly resisted doing anything about the issues in their own domain. They passed the buck to the social scientists and the humanists, who proved more accommodating and could be more easily bullied. Natural scientists too are Americans, in general favorably disposed to the mood of the times. But they are also pretty sure of what they are doing. They cannot deceive themselves that they are teaching science when they are not. They have powerful operational measures of competence. And inwardly they believe, at least in my experience, that the only real knowledge is scientific knowledge. In the dilemma that faced them—mathematicians wanted, for example, to see more blacks and women hired but could not find nearly enough competent ones—they in effect said that the humanists and social scientists should hire them. Believing that there are no real standards outside of the natural sciences, they assumed that adjustments could easily be made. With the profoundest irresponsibility, scientists went along with various aspects of affirmative action, assuming, for example, that any minority students admitted without proper qualifications would be taken care of by other departments if they did not do well in science. The scientists did not anticipate large-scale failure of such students, with the really terrible consequences that would entail. They took it for granted that these students would succeed somewhere else in the university. And they were right. The humanities and social sciences were debauched and grade inflation took off, while the natural sciences remain largely the preserve of white males. Thus the true elitists of the university have been able to stay on the good side of the forces of history without having to suffer any of the consequences.

To find hysterical supporters of the revolution one had, not surprisingly, to go to the humanities. Passion and commitment, as opposed to coolness, reason and objectivity, found their home there. The drama included a proclamation from a group of humanities teachers threatening to take over a building if the university did not capitulate forthwith. A student told me that one of his humanities professors, himself a Jew, had said to him that Jews deserved to be put in concentration camps because of what they had done to blacks. Finally these men and women were in action instead of idling away their time in libraries and classrooms. But they worked to their own undoing, for it is the humanities that have suffered most as a result of the sixties. The lack of student interest, the near disappearance of language study, the vanishing of jobs for Ph.D.s, the lack of public sympathy, came from the overturning of the old order, where their place was assured. They have gotten what they deserved, but we have unfortunately all lost.

The reasons for this behavior on the part of many humanists are obvious and constitute the theme of this book. Cornell was in the forefront of certain trends in the humanities as well as in politics. It had for several years been a laundering operation for radical Left French ideas in comparative literature. From Sartre, through Goldmann, to Foucault and Derrida, each successive wave washed over the Cornell shores. These ideas were intended to give new life to old books. A technique of reading, a framework for interpretation—Marx, Freud, structuralism, and on and on—could incorporate these tired old books and make them a part of revolutionary consciousness. At last there was an active, progressive role for the humanists, who had been only antiquarians, eunuchs guarding a harem of aging and now unattractive courtesans. Moreover, the almost universal historicism prevailing in the humanities prepared the soul for devotion to the emergent. Added to this was the expectation that in such changes culture would take primacy over science. The intellectual antiuniversity ideology of which I have spoken found its expression in these conditions, as the university could be thought to be the stage of history. Lucien Goldmann told me a few months before his death that he was privileged to have lived to see his nine-year-old son throw a rock through a store window in the Paris of '68. His studies of Racine and Pascal culminated in this. *Humanitas redivivas!* Students took to the action but not to the books. They could work on the future without the assistance of the past or its teachers. The avant-garde's fond expectation that the revolution would introduce an age of creativity, that art rather than antiquarianism would flower, that imagination would finally have its innings against reason, did not find immediate fulfillment.

The professors of humanities are in an impossible situation and do not believe in themselves or what they do. Like it or not, they are essentially involved with interpreting and transmitting old books, preserving what we call tradition, in a democratic order where tradition is not privileged. They are partisans of the leisured and beautiful in a place where evident utility is the only passport. Their realm is the always and the contemplative, in a setting that demands only the here and now and the active. The justice in which they believe is egalitarian, and they are the agents of the rare, the refined and the superior. By definition they are out of it, and their democratic inclinations and guilt push them to be with it. After all, what do Shakespeare and Milton have to do with solving our problems? Particularly when one looks into them and finds that they are the repositories of the elitist, sexist, nationalist prejudice we are trying to overcome.

Not only did the thing in itself require a conviction and dedication not often really present in the professors, the clientele was disappearing. The students just were not persuaded that what was being offered them was important. The loneliness and sense of worthlessness were crushing, so these humanists jumped on the fastest, most streamlined express to the future. This meant, of course, that all the tendencies hostile to the humanities were radicalized, and the humanities, without reservations, were pitched off the train. Natural and social science found their seats by demonstrating a usefulness of one kind or another. This the humanities were unable to do.

The apolitical character of the humanities, the habitual deformation or suppression of the political content in the classic literature, which should be part of a political education, left a void in the soul that could be filled with any politics, particularly the most vulgar, extreme and current. The humanities, unlike the natural sciences, had nothing to lose, or so it was thought, and, unlike the social sciences, they had no knowledge of the intractableness of the political matter. Humanists ran like lemmings into the sea, thinking they would refresh and revitalize themselves in it. They drowned.

This left the social sciences as the battleground, both the point of attack and the only place where any kind of stand was made. They were the newest part of the university, the part that could least boast of great past achievement or contribution to the store of human wisdom, the part the very legitimacy of which was questionable and where genius had participated most modestly. But the social sciences were principally concerned with the human things, were supposed to be in possession of the facts about social life and had a certain scientific conscience and integrity about reporting them. The social sciences were of interest to everyone who had a program, who might care about prosperity, peace or war, equality, racial or sexual discrimination. This interest could be to get the facts—or to make the facts fit their agenda and influence the public.

The temptations to alter the facts in these disciplines are enormous. Reward, punishment, money, praise, blame, sense of guilt and desire to do good, all swirl around them, dizzying their practitioners. Everyone wants the story told by social science to fit their wishes and their needs. Hobbes said that if the fact that two and two makes four were to become a matter of political relevance, there would be a faction to deny it. Social science has had more than its share of ideologues and charlatans. But it has also produced scholars of great probity whose works have made it harder for dishonest policy to triumph.

Thus it was in social science that the radicals first struck. A group of black activists disrupted the class of an economics teacher, then proceeded to the chairman's office and held him and his secretary (who suffered from heart disease) hostage for thirteen hours. The charge, of course, was that the teacher was racist in using a Western standard for judgment of the efficiency of African economic performance. The students were praised for calling the problem to the attention of the authorities, the chairman refused to proffer charges against them, and the teacher disappeared miraculously from campus, never to be seen again.

This kind of problem-solving was typical, but some professors in the social sciences did not like it. Historians were being asked to rewrite the history of the world, and of the United States in particular, to show that nations were always conspiratorial systems of domination and exploitation. Psychologists were being pestered to prove the psychological damage done by inequality and the existence of nuclear weapons, and to show that American statesmen were paranoid about the Soviet Union. Political scientists were urged to interpret the North Vietnamese as nationalists and to remove the stigma of totalitarianism from the Soviet Union. Every conceivable radical view concerning domestic or foreign policy demanded support from the social sciences. In particular, the crimes of elitism, sexism and racism were to be exorcised from social science, which was to be used as a tool to fight them and a fourth cardinal sin, anticommunism. Nobody of course would dare to admit to any of these sins, and serious discussion of the underlying issue, equality itself, had long been banished from the scene. As in the Middle Ages, when everyone except for a few intrepid and foolish souls professed Christianity and the only discussion concerned what constituted orthodoxy, the major student activity in social science was to identify heretics. These were scholars who seriously studied sexual differentiation or who raised questions about the educational value of busing or who considered the possibility of limited nuclear war. It became almost impossible to question the radical orthodoxy without risking vilification, classroom disruption, loss of the confidence and respect necessary for teaching, and the hostility of colleagues. Racist and sexist were, and are, very ugly labels—the equivalents of atheist or communist in other days with other prevailing prejudices— which can be pinned on persons promiscuously and which, once attached, are almost impossible to cast off. Nothing could be said with impunity. Such an atmosphere made detached, dispassionate study impossible.

This suited many social scientists, but a new, tougher strain emerged out of the struggle. Some saw that their objectivity was threatened, and without respect and protection for scholarly inquiry any one of them might be put at risk. The pressure revived an old liberalism and awareness of the importance of academic freedom. Pride and self-respect, unwillingness to give way before menace and insult, asserted themselves. These social scientists knew that all parties in a democracy are jeopardized when passion can sweep the facts before it. Most of all, an instinctive disgust at loudspeakers blaring propaganda was roused in them. Such social scientists were not necessarily all of the same personal political persuasion. Their fellow feeling consisted in mutual respect for the motives of colleagues with whom they did not always agree but from whose disagreement they might profit, and in attachment to the institutions that protected their research. At Cornell one found social scientists of left, right and center—on the admittedly narrow spectrum that prevails in the American university—joining together to protest the outrage against academic freedom and against their colleagues that took place there and continues in more or less subtle forms everywhere. It is not an accident that the challenge to the university was mounted in its most political part, and that there it was best understood. The political perspective is the one in which the moral unity of learning naturally comes into focus and the goodness of science is tested.

I unfortunately cannot assert that this crisis has caused social science to broaden its concerns or has induced the other disciplines to reflect on their own situations. But it was inspiring to be momentarily with a band of scholars who were really willing to make a sacrifice for their love of truth and their studies, to discover that the pieties could be more than pieties, to sense community founded on conviction. The other disciplines have, in general, not put their professed attachment to free inquiry to the test. Their immunity is a large part of the story behind the fractured structure of our universities.

The disciplines

How are they today, the big three that rule the academic roost and determine what is knowledge? Natural science is doing just fine. Living alone, but happily, running along like a well-wound clock, successful and useful as ever. There have been great things lately, physicists with their black holes and biologists with their genetic code. Its objects and methods are agreed upon. It offers exciting lives to persons of very high intelligence and provides immeasurable benefits to mankind at large. Our way of life is utterly dependent on the natural scientists, and they have more than fulfilled their every promise. Only at the margins are there questions that might threaten their theoretical equanimity—doubts about whether America produces synoptic scientific geniuses, doubts about the use of the results of science, such as nuclear weapons, doubts that lead to biology's need for "ethicists" in its experiments and its applications when, as scientists, they know that there are no such knowers as ethicists. In general, however, all is well.

But where natural science ends, trouble begins. It ends at man, the one being outside of its purview, or to be exact, it ends at that part or aspect of man that is not body, whatever that may be. Scientists as scientists can be grasped only under that aspect, as is the case with politicians, artists and prophets. All that is human, all that is of concern to us, lies outside of natural science. That should be a problem for natural science, but it is not. It is certainly a problem for us that we do not know what this thing is, that we cannot even agree on a name for this irreducible bit of man that is not body. Somehow this fugitive thing or aspect is the cause of science and society and culture and politics and economics and poetry and music. We know what these latter are. But can we really, if we do not know their cause, know what its status is, whether it even exists?

The difficulty is reflected in the fact that for the study of this one theme, man, or this *je ne sais quoi* pertaining to man, and his activities and products, there are two great divisions of the university—humanities and social science—while for bodies there is only natural science. This would all be very well if the division of labor were founded on an agreement about the subject matter and reflected a natural articulation within it, as do the divisions between physics, chemistry and biology, leading to mutual respect and cooperation. It could be believed and is sometimes actually said, mostly in commencement speeches, that social science treats man's social life, and humanities his creative life—the great works of art, etc. And, although there is something to this kind of distinction, it really will not do. This fact comes to light in a variety of ways. While both social science and humanities are more or less willingly awed by natural science, they have a mutual contempt for one another, the former looking down on the latter as unscientific, the latter regarding the former as philistine. They do not cooperate. And most important, they occupy much of the same ground. Many of the classic books now part of the humanities talk about the same things as do social scientists but use different methods and draw different conclusions; and each of the social sciences in one way or another attempts to explain the activities of the various kinds of artists in ways that are contrary to the way they are treated in the humanities. The difference comes down to the fact that social science really wants to be predictive, meaning that man is predictable, while the humanities say that he is not. The divisions between the two camps resemble truce lines rather than scientific distinctions. They disguise old and unresolved struggles about the being of man.

The social sciences and the humanities represent the two responses to the crisis caused by the definitive ejection of man—or of the residue of man extracted from, or superfluous to, body—from nature, and hence from the purview of natural science or natural philosophy, toward the end of the eighteenth century. One route led toward valiant efforts to assimilate man to the new natural sciences, to make the science of man the next rung in the ladder down from biology. The other took over the territory newly opened up by Kant, that of freedom as opposed to nature, separate but equal, not requiring the aping of the methods of natural science, taking spirituality at least as seriously as body. Neither challenged the champion, natural science, newly emancipated from philosophy: social science tried humbly to find a place at court, humanities proudly to set up shop next door. The result has been two continuous and ill-assorted strands of thought about man, one tending to treat him essentially as another of the brutes, without spirituality, soul, self, consciousness, or what have you; the other acting as though he is not an animal or does not have a body. There is no junction of these two roads. One must choose between them, and they end up in very different places, e.g., Walden II, known as Brave New World by the other side, and The Blessed Isles (a favorite retreat of Zarathustra), known as The Kingdom of Darkness by its opponents.

Neither of these solutions has fully succeeded. Social science receives no recognition from natural science.[1] It is an imitation, not a part. And the humanities shop has turned out to be selling diverse and ill-assorted antiques, decaying and ever dustier, while business gets worse and worse. Social science has proved more robust, more in harmony with the world dominated by natural science, and, while losing its inspiration and evangelical fervor, has proved useful to different aspects of modern life, as the mere mention of economics and psychology indicates. Humanities languish, but this proves only that they do not suit the modern world. It may very well be the indication of what is wrong with modernity. Moreover the language that in an unscholarly way influences life so powerfully today emerged from investigations undertaken in the realm of freedom. Social science comes more out of the school founded by Locke; humanities out of that founded by Rousseau. But social science, while looking to natural science, has actually received a large part of its impulse in recent times from the nether world. One need only think of Weber, although Marx and Freud are similar cases. It cannot be avowed, but *man*, to be grasped, needs something the natural sciences cannot provide. Man is the problem, and we live with various stratagems for not facing it. The strange relations between the three divisions of knowledge in the present university tell us all about it.

To look at social science first, it might seem that it at least has a general outline of its field and a possible systematic ordering of its parts, proceeding from psychology to economics to sociology to political science. Unfortunately there is nothing to this appearance. In the first place, it leaves out anthropology, although I suppose that if I were desperate to make a case I could find a way of squeezing it in; and it also leaves out history, about which there is dispute as to whether it belongs to social science or humanities. More important, these various social sciences do not see themselves in any such order of interdependence. Largely they work independently, and if they, to use that hopeless expression, "interface" at all, they frequently turn out to be two-faced. Within most of the specialties, about half of the practitioners usually do not believe the other half even belong among them, and something of the same situation prevails throughout the discipline as a whole. Economics has its own simple built-in psychology, and that provided by the science of psychology is either really part of biology, which does not help much, or flatly contradicts the primacy of the motives alleged by economics. Similarly, economics tends to undermine the normal interpretation of political events that political science would make. It is possible to have an economics-guided or -controlled political science, but it is not necessary; and it is equally possible to have a psychology-guided political science, which would not be the same as the former. It is as though there were a dispute among the various natural sciences about which is primary. Actually each of the social sciences can, and does, make a claim to be the beginning point in relation to which the others can be understood—economics arguing for the economy or the market, psychology for the individual psyche, sociology for society, anthropology for culture, and political science for the political order (although this latter is the least assertive about its claim). The issue is what is the social science atom, and each specialty can argue that the others are properly parts of the whole that it represents. Moreover each can accuse the other of representing an abstraction, or a construct, or a figment of the imagination. Is there ever a pure market, one not part of a society or a culture that forms it? What is a culture or society? Are they ever more than aspects of some kind of political order? Here political science is in the strongest position, because the reality of states or nations is undeniable, although they can in turn be considered superficial or compound phenomena. The social sciences actually represent a series of different perspectives on the human world we see around us, a series that is not harmonious, because there is not even agreement as to what belongs to that world, let alone as to what kinds of causes would account for its phenomena.

A further source of dispute within social science concerns what is meant by science. All agree that it must be reasonable, have some standards of verification and be based on systematic research. Moreover, there is a more or less explicit agreement that the kinds of causes admitted within natural science should somehow apply within social science. This means no teleology and no "spiritual" causes. Pursuit of salvation would, for example, need to be reduced to another kind of cause, like repressed sexuality, whereas pursuit of money would not. Search for material causes and reduction of higher or more complex phenomena to lower or simpler ones are generally accepted procedures. But to what extent the example of the most successful of the modern natural sciences, mathematical physics, can or should be followed within social science is a matter of endless discussion and quarreling. Prediction is the hallmark of modern natural science, and practically every social scientist would like to be able to make reliable predictions, although practically none have. Prediction appears to have been made possible in natural science by reducing phenomena in such a way as to be amenable to expression in mathematical formulas, and most social scientists want the same thing to happen in their discipline. The issue is whether various efforts in that direction cause distortion of the social phenomena, or lead to the neglect of some that are not easily mathematized and the preference for others that are; or whether they encourage the construction of mathematical models that are figments of the imagination and have nothing to do with the real world. A kind of continuous guerrilla war goes on between those who are primarily enthusiasts of science and those who are primarily attached to their particular subject matter.

Economics, held to be the most successful of the social sciences, is the most mathematized—both in the sense that its objects can be counted and that it can construct mathematical models for at least hypothetically predictive purposes. But some political scientists, for example, say that the Economic Man may be very nice for playing games with but that he is an abstraction who does not exist, while Hitler and Stalin are real and not to be played with. Economic analysis, they say, not only does not help us to understand such political actors but makes it more difficult to bring them within the purview of social science by systematically excluding or deforming their specific motives. Economists, seeking mathematical convenience, turn us away from the consideration of the most important social phenomena, assert the objectors (including the small, vociferous band of Marxist economists who are rigorously excluded from the core of the discipline, the only social science in which this has happened). So it goes between the various disciplines and within several of them where the adherents of the different approaches have no common universe of discourse.

Publicity aside, what students actually see today when they first encounter social science are two robust, self-sufficient, self-confident social sciences, economics and cultural anthropology, extremes forming the antipodes, having almost nothing to do with each other—while political science and sociology, quite heterogenous, not to say chaotic in their contents, are strung tensely between the two poles.[2] It should not be surprising that these two disciplines are more explicit than are the other social sciences about their founders: Locke and Adam Smith, on the one hand, and Rousseau on the other. For these sciences have as their clear presuppositions one or the other of the two states of nature. Locke argued that man's conquest of nature by his work is the only rational response to his original situation. Locke emancipated greed and showed the illusory character of the countervailing motives. Life, liberty and the pursuit of property are the fundamental natural rights, and the social contract is made to protect these rights. These principles agreed upon, economics comes into being as *the* science of man's proper activity, and the free market as the natural and rational order (a natural order unlike other recognized natural orders in that it requires establishment by men, and they, as economists are constantly telling us, almost always get it wrong). Economists have in general stuck to this, are in general old liberals of one kind or another and supporters of liberal democracy, as the place where the market exists. Rousseau argued that nature is good and man far away from it. So the quest for those faraway origins becomes imperative, and anthropology is by that very fact founded, Lévi-Strauss is unambiguous about this. Civilization, practically identical to the free market and its results, threatens happiness and dissolves community. From this follows immediately admiration for tight old cultures that channel and sublimate the economic motive and do not permit the emergence of the free market. What economists believe to be things of the irrational past—known only as underdeveloped societies[3]—become the proper study of man, a diagnosis of our ills and a call to the future. Anthropologists have tended to be very open to many aspects of the Continental reflection, from culture on down, to which economists were completely closed (Nietzsche's influence was already evident more than fifty years ago in Ruth Benedict's distinction between Apollonian and Dionysian cultures); they have tended to the Left (because the extreme Right, equally viable in their system, had no roots here) and to be susceptible to infatuations with experiments tending to correct or replace liberal democracy. Economists teach that the market is the fundamental social phenomenon, and its culmination is money. Anthropologists teach that culture is the fundamental social phenomenon, and its culmination is the sacred.[4] Such is the confrontation—man the producer of consumption goods vs. man the producer of culture, the maximizing animal vs. the reverent one—between old philosophic teachings present here but not addressed. The disciplines simply inhabit different worlds. They can be of marginal use to one another, but not in a spirit of community. There are few economists who also think of themselves as anthropologists, and vice versa, although there are, for example, many political scientists and sociologists who cross one another's borders, as well as those of economics and anthropology. The economists are the ones most ready to jump the social science ship and go it on their own, and think themselves closer than the others to having achieved a real science. They also have substantial influence on public policy. The anthropologists have no such influence beyond the academic world but have the charms of depth and comprehensiveness, as well as the possession of the latest ideas.

A few words about political science and its peculiarities might help to clarify the problems of social science as a whole. To begin with, it is, along with economics, the only purely academic discipline that, like medicine, engages a fundamental passion and the study of which could be understood as undertaken in order to ensure its satisfaction. Political science involves the love of justice, the love of glory and the love of ruling. But unlike medicine and economics, which are quite frank about their relations to health and wealth, and even trumpet them, political science turns modestly away from such avowals and would even like to break off these unseemly relations. This has something to do with the fact that she is a very old lady indeed, who would prefer not to show her age. Political science goes all the way back to Greek antiquity and has the dubious parentage of Socrates, Plato and Aristotle, all with bad reputations in the land of modern science. The other social sciences are of modern origin and part of the modern project, while political science persists, trying to modernize and get with it but unable entirely to control old instincts. Aristotle said that political science is the architectonic science, a ruling science, concerned with the comprehensive good or the best regime. But real science does not talk about good and bad, so that had to be abandoned. However, both medicine and economics really do talk about good and bad, so the abandonment of the old political goods had the effect only of leaving the moral field to health and wealth in the absence of the common good and justice. This accords with Locke's intention, which was not at all "value-free," but was to substitute lower but more solid, more easily attained goods for those that had been classically proposed. Political science's transformation into a modern social science did not further social science but did further the political intentions of modernity's founders. It has tried to reduce the specifically political motives into subpolitical ones, like those proposed in economics. Honor is not a real motive; gain is.

Of course Locke himself was still much more a political scientist than an economist, for the market (the peaceful competition for the acquisition of goods) requires the prior existence of the social contract (the agreement to abide by contracts and the establishment of a judge to arbitrate and enforce contracts) without which men are in a state of war. The market presupposes the existence of law and the absence of war. War was the condition of man prior to the existence of civil society, and the return to it is always possible. The force and fraud required to end war have nothing to do with the market and are illegitimate within it. The rational behavior of men at peace, in which economics specializes, is not the same as the rational behavior of men at war, as was so tellingly pointed out by Machiavelli. Political science is more comprehensive than economics because it studies both peace and war and their relations. The market cannot be the sole concern of the polity, for the market depends on the polity, and the establishment and preservation of the polity continuously requires reasonings and deeds which are "uneconomic" or "inefficient." Political action must have primacy over economic action, no matter what the effect on the market. This is why economists have had so little reliable to say about foreign policy, for nations are in the primitive state of war with each other that individuals were in prior to the social contract—that is, they have no commonly recognized judge to whom they can turn to settle their disputes. The policy advice of some economists during the Vietnam war attempted to set up a kind of market between the United States and North Vietnam, with the United States making the cost of South Vietnam prohibitive to North Vietnam; but the North Vietnamese refused to play. Political science, as opposed to economics, must always contemplate war with its altogether different risks, horrors, thrills, and gravity. Churchill formulated the difference between a political perspective and a market perspective in commenting on Coolidge's refusal to forgive the British war debts in the twenties. Coolidge said, "They hired the money, didn't they?" To which Churchill responded, "This is true, but not exhaustive." Political science must be exhaustive and this makes it a sticky subject for those who want to reform it so as to accord with the abstract projects of science. Consciously or unconsciously, economics deals only with the bourgeois, the man motivated by fear of violent death. The warlike man is not within its ken. Political science remains the only social science discipline which looks war in the face.

Political science has always been the least attractive and the least impressive of the social sciences, spanning as it does old and new views of man and the human sciences. It has a polyglot character. Part of it has joined joyfully in the effort to dismantle the political order seen as a comprehensive order and to understand it as a result of subpolitical causes. Economics, psychology and sociology as well as all kinds of methodological diagnosticians have been welcome guests. But there are irrepressible, putatively unscientific parts of political science. The practitioners of these parts of the discipline are unable to overcome their unexplained and unexplainable political instincts—their awareness that politics is the authoritative arena of effective good and evil. They therefore engage in policy studies whose end, whether it is stated or not, is action. Defense of freedom, avoidance of war, the furthering of equality—various aspects of justice in action—are hot subjects of study. The good regime has to be the theme of such political scientists, if only undercover, and they are informed by the question "What is to be done?" And, in a real peripety, it turns out that the area of political science where mathematics has had the greatest success is elections, the most exciting and decisive part of democratic life, where public opinion turns into government and policy. The most scientific element of political science is one that makes its practitioners friends and allies of real politicians, enlightening them and learning from them. Science here parallels the greatest political thrills and has no need of changing the perceived nature of its object to study it scientifically.

So political science resembles a rather haphazard bazaar with shops kept by a mixed population. This has something to do with its hybrid nature and its dual origins in antiquity and modernity. The reality with which it deals lends itself less to abstractions and makes more urgent demands than do any of the other social science disciplines, while the tension between objectivity and partisanship in it is much more extreme. Everything in modern natural and social science militates against the assertion that politics is qualitatively different from other kinds of human association, but its practice repeatedly affirms the contrary. Its heterogeneity is perhaps debilitating, and one finds here choice theorists of the economic-models school, old-fashioned behavioralists, Marxists (who are never at home in economics), historians and policy researchers. Most unusual of all, political science is the only discipline in the university (with the possible exception of the philosophy department) that has a philosophic branch. This has long been an embarrassment to it, and political philosophy was scheduled for termination in the forties and fifties. "We want to be a real social science," cried the terminators with an exasperated stamp of the foot. But a combination of serious and fervent scholarship on the part of a few thinkers and the muscle of the rebellious students in the sixties gave political philosophy a reprieve that now looks permanent. It became, for the best and the worst of reasons, the bastion of the reaction against value-free social science and the new social science as a whole. It has, where its presence is at all serious, proved to be continuously the most attractive subject in the field for both graduate and undergraduate students. And as the new scientific persuasion has lost much of its élan and the field has fragmented in various directions dictated at least partly by fidelity to the political phenomena, many of those who were once fierce enemies of political philosophy have become its allies. Political philosophy is far from ruling, but it provides at least a reminiscence of those old questions about good and evil and the resources for examining the hidden presuppositions of modern political science and political life. Aristotle's *Politics* is still alive there, as well as Locke's *Treatise on Civil Government* and Rousseau's *Discourse on the Origins of Inequality*. Aristotle asserts that man is by nature a political animal, which means that he has an impulse toward civil society. Reading Aristotle helps to lay bare the hidden premise underlying modern social science, that man is by nature a solitary being, and could provide the basis for making a debate of it again.[5]

Obviously, then, the glory days of social science from the point of view of liberal education are over. Gone is the time when Marx, Freud and Weber, philosophers and interpreters of the world, were just precursors of what was to be America's intellectual coming of age, when youngsters could join the charms of science and self-knowledge, when there was the expectation of a universal theory of man that would unite the university and contribute to progress, harnessing Europe's intellectual depth and heritage with our vitality. Natural science was to culminate in human science; Darwin and Einstein would tell social science as much as they had told natural science. And modern literature—Dostoyevski, Joyce, Proust, Kafka—expressed our mood and provided the insights that social science would systematize and prove. Psychoanalysis provided the link between private experience and public intellectual endeavor. So unified was the experience that personal desire was intimately connected with intuition of the comprehensive order of things, a simulacrum of the old understanding of philosophy as a way of life. On a much less sophisticated level but expressing something of the same ethos, Margaret Mead had a new science that took one to exotic places, brought back new understandings of society and also proved the legitimacy of one's repressed sexual desires. To young people, the sociologists and psychologists who trod the university's grounds could look like heroes of the life of the mind. They were initiated into the mysteries and might help us to become initiates too. Old-style philosophy had been overcome, but names like Hegel, Schopenhauer and Kierkegaard were thought to offer some of the experience required for our adventure.

Such an atmosphere as surrounded social science in the forties was obviously of ambiguous value for both students and professors. But something akin to it is necessary if American students are to be attracted to the idea of liberal education and the awareness that the university will cause them to discover new faculties in themselves and reveal another level of existence that had been hidden from them. American students, it must be remembered, if they have learned anything at all in high school, have learned natural science as a technique, not as a way of life or a means of discovering life. If anything other than routine specialized learning is to touch them, they must be given a shock treatment—even if it is only to make them think about their commitment to natural science and its meaning, inasmuch as their earlier training has been more of an indoctrination, more of a conformism, than the discovery of a vocation. The social science inebriation of the forties was not, I believe, the genuine article, but it reproduced something of the intellectual excitement surrounding theoretical new beginnings. It proved fertile for many students and scholars, generated its own ancillary bohemia and affected the substance of people's lives. It was not just a profession.

The hopes for a unity of social science have faded, and it cannot present a common front. It is a series of discrete disciplines and subdisciplines. Most are modest, and although there is a lot of nonsense, there are also a fair number of really useful parts practiced by highly competent specialists. The expectations are radically lowered. Economics is a specialty that has universal pretensions to explain and encompass everything, but they are not quite believed, and its popularity does not rest on them. Political science does not even try to make good its ancestral claim to comprehensiveness and only covertly and partially makes its special and rightful appeal to the political passion. Anthropology is the only social science discipline still exercising the charm of possible wholeness, with its idea of culture, which appears more really complete than does the economists' idea of the market. Both the superpolitical cultural part and the subpolitical economic part claim to be the whole, while neither sociology nor political science, apart from certain individuals, really seems to make any claims over the whole social science enterprise. There is no social science as an architectonic science. It is parts without a whole.

Similarly, with the possible exceptions of computer science as a model for man, and sociobiology, the expectation of substantive unity between natural science and social science has faded, leaving social science a consumer only of natural science method. Gone is the cosmic intention of placing man in the universe. In the direction of the humanities, it is again only anthropology that has maintained a certain opening, particularly to the merchandise being hawked in comparative literature, but also to serious studies, e.g., Greek religion. No other social scientists expect to get much from nineteenth- and twentieth-century art and literature, which fascinated many significant social scientists a generation ago, and there are fewer and fewer social scientists who have much familiarity with that sort of thing in a personal way. The social sciences have become an island in the university floating alongside the other two islands, full of significant information and hiding treasures of great questions that could be mined but are not. Notably, the social science intellectual in the German or French mold, looked upon as a kind of sage or wise man who could tell all about life, has all but disappeared.

The students are aware of this and do not turn to the social sciences in general for the experience of conversion. Particular things or particular professors may be of interest to them for one reason or another, but for any who might happen to be looking for the meaning of life, or who might be able to learn that that is what they should look for, social science is not now the place to go. Anthropology, to repeat myself, is something of an exception. The secret of social science's great early success with intelligent young Americans was that it was the only place in the university that seemed, however indirectly, to seek the answer to the Socratic question of how one should live. Even when it was most vigorously teaching that values cannot be the subject matter of knowledge, that very teaching taught about life, as shown by such once exciting contrivances as Weber's distinction between the ethics of intention and the ethics of responsibility. This was not textbook learning, but the real stuff of life. Nothing like this is to be found there today.

Moreover, a great disaster has occurred. It is the establishment during the last decade or so of the MBA as the moral equivalent of the MD or the law degree, meaning a way of insuring a lucrative living by the mere fact of a diploma that is not a mark of scholarly achievement. It is a general rule that the students who have any chance of getting a liberal education are those who do not have a fixed career goal, or at least those for whom the university is not merely a training ground for a profession. Those who do have such a goal go through the university with blinders on, studying what the chosen discipline imposes on them while occasionally diverting themselves with an elective course that attracts them. True liberal education requires that the student's whole life be radically changed by it, that what he learns may affect his action, his tastes, his choices, that no previous attachment be immune to examination and hence re-evaluation. Liberal education puts everything at risk and requires students who are able to risk everything.[6] Otherwise it can only touch what is uncommitted in the already essentially committed. The effect of the MBA is to corral a horde of students who want to get into business school and to put the blinders on them, to legislate an illiberal, officially approved undergraduate program for them at the outset, like premeds who usually disappear into their required courses and are never heard from again. Both the goal and the way of getting to it are fixed so that nothing can distract them. (Prelaw students are more visible in a variety of liberal courses because law schools are less fixed in their prerequisites; they are only seeking bright students.) Premed, prelaw and prebusiness students are distinctively tourists in the liberal arts. Getting into those elite professional schools is an obsessive concern that tethers their minds.

The specific effect of the MBA has been an explosion of enrollments in economics, the prebusiness major. In serious universities something like 20 percent of the undergraduates are now economics majors. Economics overwhelms the rest of the social sciences and skews the students' perception of them—their purpose and their relative weight with regard to the knowledge of human things. A premed who takes much biology does not, by contrast, lose sight of the status of physics, for the latter's influence on biology is clear, its position agreed upon, and it is respected by the biologists. None of this is so for the prebusiness economics major, who not only does not take an interest in sociology, anthropology or political science but is also persuaded that what he is learning can handle all that belongs to those studies. Moreover, he is not motivated by love of the science of economics but by love of what it is concerned with—money. Economists' concern with wealth, an undeniably real and solid thing, gives them a certain impressive intellectual solidity not provided by, say, culture. One can be sure that they are not talking about nothing. But wealth, as opposed to the science of wealth, is not the noblest of motivations, and there is nothing else quite like this perfect coincidence between science and cupidity elsewhere in the university. The only parallel would be if there were a science of sexology, with earnest and truly scholarly professors, which would ensure its students lavish sexual satisfactions.

The third island of the university is the almost submerged old Atlantis, the humanities. In it there is no semblance of order, no serious account of what should and should not belong, or of what its disciplines are trying to accomplish or how. It is somehow the repair of man or of humanity, the place to go to find ourselves now that everyone else has given up. But where to look in this heap or jumble? It is difficult enough for those who already know what to look for to get any satisfaction here. For students it requires a powerful instinct and a lot of luck. The analogies tumble uncontrollably from my pen. The humanities are like the great old Paris Flea Market where, amidst masses of junk, people with a good eye found castaway treasures that made them rich. Or they are like a refugee camp where all the geniuses driven out of their jobs and countries by unfriendly regimes are idling, either unemployed or performing menial tasks. The other two divisions of the university have no use for the past, are forward-looking and not inclined toward ancestor worship.

The problem of the humanities, and therefore of the unity of knowledge, is perhaps best represented by the fact that if Galileo, Kepler and Newton exist anywhere in the university now it is in the humanities, as part of one kind of history or another—history of science, history of ideas, history of culture. In order to have a place, they have to be understood as something other than what they were—great contemplators of the whole of nature who understood themselves to be of interest only to the extent that they told the truth about it. If they were wrong or have been completely surpassed, then they themselves would say that they are of no interest. To put them in the humanities is the equivalent of naming a street after them or setting up a statue in a corner of a park. They are effectively dead. Plato, Bacon, Machiavelli and Montesquieu are in the same condition, except for that little enclave in political science. The humanities are the repository for *all* of the classics now—but much of the classic literature claimed to be about the order of the whole of nature and man's place in it, to legislate for that whole and to tell the truth about it. If such claims are denied, these writers and their books cannot be read seriously, and their neglect elsewhere is justified. They have been saved only on the condition of being mummified. The humanities' willingness to receive them has taken them off the backs of the natural and social sciences, where they constituted a challenge that no longer has to be met. On the portal of the humanities is written in many ways and many tongues, "There is no truth—at least here."

The humanities are the specialty that now exclusively possesses the books that are not specialized, that insist upon asking the questions about the whole that are excluded from the rest of the university, which is dominated by real specialties, as resistant to self-examination as they were in Socrates' day and now rid of the gadfly. The humanities have not had the vigor to fight it out with triumphant natural science, and want to act as though it were just a specialty. But, as I have said over and over again, however much the humane disciplines would like to forget about their essential conflict with natural science as now practiced and understood, they are gradually undermined by it. Whether it is old philosophic texts that raise now inadmissible questions, or old works of literature that presuppose the being of the noble and the beautiful, materialism, determinism, reductionism, homogenization—however one describes modern natural science—deny their importance and their very possibility. Natural science asserts that it is metaphysically neutral, and hence has no need for philosophy, and that imagination is not a faculty that in any way intuits the real—hence art has nothing to do with truth. The kinds of questions children ask: Is there a God? Is there freedom? Is there punishment for evil deeds? Is there certain knowledge? What is a good society? were once also the questions addressed by science and philosophy. But now the grownups are too busy at work, and the children are left in a day-care center called the humanities, in which the discussions have no echo in the adult world. Moreover, students whose

nature draws them to such questions and to the books that appear to investigate them are very quickly rebuffed by the fact that their humanities teachers
do not want or are unable to use the books to respond to their needs.

This problem of the old books is not new. In Swift's *Battle of the Books*
one finds Bentley, the premier Greek scholar of the eighteenth century, on
the side of the moderns. He accepted the superiority of modern thought
to Greek thought. So why study Greek books? This question remains
unanswered in classics departments. There are all sorts of dodges, ranging
from pure philological analysis to using these books to show the relation
between thought and economic conditions. But practically no one even tries to
read them as they were once read—for the sake of finding out whether they
are true. Aristotle's *Ethics* teaches us not what a good man is but what the
Greeks thought about morality. But who really cares very much about that?
Not any normal person who wants to lead a serious life.

All the things I have said about books in our time help to characterize the
situation of the humanities, which are the really exposed part of the university. They have been buffeted more severely by historicism and relativism
than the other parts. They suffer most from democratic society's lack of
respect for tradition and its emphasis on utility. To the extent that the
humanities are supposed to treat of creativity, professors' lack of creativity
becomes a handicap. The humanities are embarrassed by the political content of many of the literary works belonging to them. They have had to alter
their contents for the sake of openness to other cultures. And when the old
university habits were changed, they found themselves least able to answer
the question "Why?," least able to force students to meet standards, or to
attract them with any clear account of what they would learn. One need
only glance at the situation of the natural sciences in all these respects to
see the gravity of the problem faced by the humanities. Natural science is
sovereignly indifferent to the fact that there were and are other kinds of
explanations of natural phenomena in other ages or cultures. The relation
between Einstein and Buddha is purely for educational TV, in programs put
together by humanists. Whatever its practitioners may say, they are sure its
explanations are true, or truth. They do not have to give reasons "why,"
because the answer seems all too evident.

The natural sciences are able to assert that they are pursuing the important truth, and the humanities are not able to make any such assertion. That
is always the critical point. Without this, no study can remain alive. Vague
insistence that without the humanities we will no longer be civilized rings
very hollow when no one can say what "civilized" means, when there are
said to be many civilizations that are all equal. The claim of "the classic"
loses all legitimacy when the classic cannot be believed to tell the truth. The
truth question is most pressing and acutely embarrassing for those who deal
with the philosophic texts, but also creates problems for those treating purely
literary works. There is an enormous difference between saying, as teachers

once did, "You must learn to see the world as Homer or Shakespeare did," and saying, as teachers now do, "Homer and Shakespeare had some of the same concerns you do and can enrich your vision of the world." In the former approach students are challenged to discover new experiences and reassess old; in the latter, they are free to use the books in any way they please.

I am distinguishing two related but different problems here. The contents of the classic books have become particularly difficult to defend in modern times, and the professors who now teach them do not care to defend them, are not interested in their truth. One can most clearly see the latter in the case of the Bible. To include it in the humanities is already a blasphemy, a denial of its own claims. There it is almost inevitably treated in one of two ways: It is subjected to modern "scientific" analysis, called the Higher Criticism, where it is dismantled, to show how "sacred" books are put together, and that they are not what they claim to be. It is useful as a mosaic in which one finds the footprints of many dead civilizations. Or else the Bible is used in courses in comparative religion as one expression of the need for the "sacred" and as a contribution to the very modern, very scientific study of the structure of "myths." (Here one can join up with the anthropologists and really be alive.) A teacher who treated the Bible naively, taking it at its word, or Word, would be accused of scientific incompetence and lack of sophistication. Moreover, he might rock the boat and start the religious wars all over again, as well as a quarrel within the university between reason and revelation, which would upset comfortable arrangements and wind up by being humiliating to the humanities. Here one sees the traces of the Enlightenment's political project, which wanted precisely to render the Bible, and other old books, undangerous. This project is one of the underlying causes of the impotence of the humanities. The best that can be done, it appears, is to teach "The Bible as Literature," as opposed to "as Revelation," which it claims to be. In this way it can be read somewhat independently of deforming scholarly apparatus, as we read, for example, *Pride and Prejudice*. Thus the few professors who feel that there is something wrong with the other approaches tend to their consciences.

Professors of the humanities have long been desperate to make their subjects accord with modernity instead of a challenge to it. One sees this in a puerile form in the footnotes to Paul Shorey's edition of Plato's *Republic*, on which I cut my teeth, where he is eager to show that Plato had already divined this or that discovery made by some American professor of psychology in 1911, while he remains studiously silent about Plato's embarrassing disagreements with current views. Much study in the humanities is just a more or less sophisticated version of the same thing. I do not deny that at least some professors love the works they study and teach. But there is a furious effort to make them up-to-date, largely by treating them as the matter formed by some contemporary theory—cultural, historical, economic or psychological. The effort to read books as their writers intended them to be read has been made into a crime, ever since "the intentional fallacy" was instituted. There are endless debates about methods—among Freudian criticism, Marxist criticism, New Criticism, Structuralism and Deconstructionism, and many others, all of which have in common the premise that what Plato or Dante had to say about reality is unimportant. These schools of criticism make the writers plants in a garden planned by a modern scholar, while their own garden-planning vocation is denied them. The writers ought to plant, or even bury, the scholar. Nietzsche said that after the ministrations of modern scholarship the *Symposium* is so far away that it can no longer seduce us; its immediate charm has utterly vanished. When it comes down to it, the humanities scholar is not motivated by inner necessity, by any urgency, certainly not one dictated by old books. The scholar who chooses to study Sophocles could just as well have chosen Euripides. And why a poet, and not a philosopher or a historian; or why, after all, a Greek, and not a Turk?

There are a few humanities departments in universities that have been able to escape respectably into the sciences, such as archeology and some aspects of the languages and linguistics. They have almost entirely broken off relations with the contents of books. Fine art and music are, of course, in large measure independent of the meanings of books, although the way of treating them does, at least to some extent, depend on the prevailing views about what art is and what is important in it. There is in humanities a great deal of purely scholarly work that is neutral, useful and intended to be used by those who have something to say, such as the making of dictionaries and the establishment of texts.

The list of departments is dominated by the long catalogue of the various departments of language and literature, usually one for each of the Western languages, and conglomerates for the others. Except for English, they all are responsible for teaching foreign languages. The teachers have had to learn a difficult language well and must teach it to a population of students who do not really want to learn languages very much. Now, in addition to the language, there are books written in that language, and the learning of the language entails reading those books. Hence, having learned the language in effect qualifies the teacher to teach the contents of the books, particularly since the books do not now belong anywhere else. However, the teachers' real knowledge of and affinity with those books is not ensured by their mastery of the language. The books are the important thing, but the language tail tends to wag the literature dog. These departments are the primary guardians of the classic literature and protect their dominion over their works ferociously. University convention submerges nature. It issues licenses, and hunting without one is forbidden. Moreover, because of these conventions the professors also listen to one another more attentively than to outsiders, and are listened to more attentively than others by outsiders, as doctors are more impressive to laymen in matters of health than are other laymen. A cozy self-satisfaction of specialists easily results (until there are rude jolts from the outside, such as occurred during the sixties). Professors of Greek forget or are unaware that Thomas Aquinas, who did not know Greek, was a better interpreter of Aristotle than any of them have proved to be, not only because he was smarter but because he took Aristotle more seriously.

This arrangement of the language and literature departments entails other structural difficulties. Do Greek poetry, history and philosophy belong together, or again, is not the secondary fact of the Greek language determining the articulation of the substance? And is it not possible that the proper connections go beyond Greece altogether, constituting such pairs as Plato and Farabi or Aristotle and Hobbes? Willy-nilly these departments are forced to adopt historical premises. Greek philosophers are of a piece and, more likely, the whole of Greek culture or civilization is a tightly woven tapestry of which the Greek scholar, not the philosopher or the poet, is the master. From the outset this arrangement answers the crucial questions about the relation between the mind and history before they are raised, and does so in a way contrary to the way Plato or Aristotle would answer them.

Most interesting of all, lost amidst this collection of disciplines, modestly sits philosophy. It has been dethroned by political and theoretical democracy, bereft of the passion or the capacity to rule. Its story defines in itself our whole problem. Philosophy once proudly proclaimed that it was the best way of life, and it dared to survey the whole, to seek the first causes of all things, and not only dictated its rules to the special sciences but constituted and ordered them. The classic philosophic books are philosophy in action, doing precisely these things. But this was all impossible, *hybris*, say their impoverished heirs. Real science did not need them, and the rest is ideology or myth. Now they are just books on a shelf. Democracy took away philosophy's privileges, and philosophy could not decide whether to fade away or to take a job. Philosophy was architectonic, had the plans for the whole building, and the carpenters, masons and plumbers were its subordinates and had no meaning without its plan. Philosophy founded the university, but it could no longer do so. We live off its legacy. When people speak vaguely about generalists vs. specialists, they must mean by the generalist the philosopher, for he is the only kind of knower who embraces, or once embraced, all the specialties, possessing a subject matter, necessary to the specialties, which was real—being or the good—and not just a collection of the matters of the specialties. Philosophy is no longer a way of life, and it is no longer a sovereign science. Its situation in our universities has something to do with the desperate condition of philosophy in the world today, and something to do with its peculiar history as a discipline in America. With respect to the former, although reason is gravely threatened, Nietzsche and Heidegger were genuine philosophers and able to face up to and face down both natural science and historicism, the two great contemporary opponents of philosophy. Philosophy is still possible. And on the Continent even now, school-children are taught philosophy, and it seems to be something real. An American high school student knows only the word "philosophy," and it does not appear to be any more serious a life choice than yoga. In America, anyhow, everybody has a philosophy. Philosophy was not ever a very powerful presence in universities, although there were important exceptions. We began with a public philosophy that sufficed for us, and we thought that it was common sense. In America, Tocqueville said, everyone is a Cartesian although no one has read Descartes. We were almost entirely importers of philosophy, with the exception of Pragmatism. One need not have read a line of philosophy to be considered educated in this country. It is easily equated with hot air, much more so than any of the other humane disciplines. So it always had an uphill fight. Students who did seek it could, however, find some refreshment at its source.

But it has succumbed and probably could disappear without being much noticed. It has a scientific component, logic, which is attached to the sciences and could easily be detached from philosophy. This is serious, practiced by competent specialists, and responds to none of the permanent philosophic questions. History of philosophy, the compendium of dead philosophies that was always most lively for the students, has been neglected, and students find it better treated in a variety of other disciplines. Positivism and ordinary language analysis have long dominated, although they are on the decline and evidently being replaced by nothing. These are simply methods of a sort, and they repel students who come with the humanizing questions. Professors of these schools simply would not and could not talk about anything important, and they themselves do not represent a philosophic life for the students. In some places existentialism and phenomenology have gained a foothold, and they are much more attractive to students than positivism or ordinary language analysis. Catholic universities have always kept some contact with medieval philosophy, and hence, Aristotle. But, in sum, the philosophy landscape is largely bleak. That is why so much of the philosophic instinct in America used to lead toward the new social sciences and is now veering off toward certain branches of literature and literary criticism. As it stands, philosophy is just another humanities subject, rather contentless, without a thought of trying to take command in the crisis of the university. Actually it contains less of the exhilarating presence of the tradition in philosophy than do the other humanities disciplines, and one finds its professors least active of the humanists in attempts to revitalize liberal education. Although there was a certain modesty about ordinary language analysis—"We just help to give you clarity about what you are already doing"—there was also smugness: "We know what was wrong with the whole tradition, and we don't need it anymore." Therefore the tradition disappeared from philosophy's confines.

All the language catalogued in Part Two was produced by philosophy and was in Europe known to have been produced by philosophy, so that it paved a road to philosophy. In America its antecedents remain unknown. We took over the results without having had any of the intellectual experiences leading to them. But the ignorance of the origins and the fact that American philosophy departments do not lay claim to them—are in fact just as ignorant of them as is the general public—means that the philosophic content of our language and lives does not direct us to philosophy. This is a real difference between the Continent and us. Here the philosophic language is nothing but jargon.

The evident weakness of the division of literature on the basis of the language in which it was written led, a half-century ago, to the sensible project of trying to reunite it. Thus comparative literature was founded. But as is the case with all such undertakings in our times, there was considerable perplexity about what the new discipline was trying to do, and it tended to generate systems of comparison that dominated the literary works, tributes to the ingenuity of their founders rather than openings through which the works could reveal themselves freed from arbitrary constraints. Comparative literature has now fallen largely into the hands of a group of professors who are influenced by the post-Sartrean generation of Parisian Heideggerians, in particular Derrida, Foucault and Barthes. The school is called Deconstructionism, and it is the last, predictable, stage in the suppression of reason and the denial of the possibility of truth in the name of philosophy. The interpreter's creative activity is more important than the text; there is no text, only interpretation. Thus the one thing most necessary for us, the knowledge of what these texts have to tell us, is turned over to the subjective, creative selves of these interpreters, who say that there is both no text and no reality to which the texts refer. A cheapened interpretation of Nietzsche liberates us from the objective imperatives of the texts that might have liberated us from our increasingly low and narrow horizon. Everything has tended to soften the demands made on us by the tradition; this simply dissolves it.

This fad will pass, as it has already in Paris. But it appeals to our worst instincts and shows where our temptations lie. It is the literary complement to the "life-styles" science I discussed in Part Two. Fancy German philosophic talk fascinates us and takes the place of the really serious things. This will not be the last attempt of its kind coming from the dispossessed humanities in their search for an imaginary empire, one that flatters popular democratic tastes.

Conclusion

These are the shadows cast by the peaks of the university over the entering undergraduate. Together they represent what the university has to say about man and his education, and they do not project a coherent image. The differences and the indifferences are too great. It is difficult to imagine that there is either the wherewithal or the energy within the university to constitute or reconstitute the idea of an educated human being and establish a liberal education again.

However, the contemplation of this scene is in itself a proper philosophic activity. The university's evident lack of wholeness in an enterprise that clearly demands it cannot help troubling some of its members. The questions are all there. They only need to be addressed continuously and seriously for liberal learning to exist; for it does not consist so much in answers as in the permanent dialogue. It is in such perplexed professors that at least the idea might persevere and help to guide some of the needy young persons at our doorstep. The matter is still present in the university; it is the form that has vanished. One cannot and should not hope for a general reform. The hope is that the embers do not die out.

Men may live more truly and fully in reading Plato and Shakespeare than at any other time, because then they are participating in essential being and are forgetting their accidental lives. The fact that this kind of humanity exists or existed, and that we can somehow still touch it with the tips of our outstretched fingers, makes our imperfect humanity, which we can no longer bear, tolerable. The books in their objective beauty are still there, and we must help protect and cultivate the delicate tendrils reaching out toward them through the unfriendly soil of students' souls. Human nature, it seems, remains the same in our very altered circumstances because we still face the same problems, if in different guises, and have the distinctively human need to solve them, even though our awareness and forces have become enfeebled.

After a reading of the *Symposium* a serious student came with deep melancholy and said it was impossible to imagine that magic Athenian atmosphere reproduced, in which friendly men, educated, lively, on a footing of equality, civilized but natural, came together and told wonderful stories about the meaning of their longing. But such experiences are always accessible. Actually, this playful discussion took place in the midst of a terrible war that Athens was destined to lose, and Aristophanes and Socrates at least could foresee that this meant the decline of Greek civilization. But they were not given to culture despair, and in these terrible political circumstances, their abandon to the joy of nature proved the viability of what is best in man, independent of accidents, of circumstance. We feel ourselves too dependent on history and culture. This student did not have Socrates, but he had Plato's book about him, which might even be better; he had brains, friends and a country happily free enough to let them gather and speak as they will. What is essential about that dialogue, or any of the Platonic dialogues, is reproducible in almost all times and places. He and his friends can think together. It requires much thought to learn that this thinking might be what it is all for. That's where we are beginning to fail. But it is right under our noses, improbable but always present.

Throughout this book I have referred to Plato's *Republic*, which is for me *the* book on education, because it really explains to me what I experience as a man and a teacher, and I have almost always used it to point out what we should not hope for, as a teaching of moderation and resignation. But all its impossibilities act as a filter to leave the residue of the highest and non-illusory possibility. The real community of man, in the midst of all the self-contradictory simulacra of community, is the community of those who seek the truth, of the potential knowers, that is, in principle, of all men to the extent they desire to know. But in fact this includes only a few, the true friends, as Plato was to Aristotle at the very moment they were disagreeing about the nature of the good. Their common concern for the good linked them; their disagreement about it proved they needed one another to understand it. They were absolutely one soul as they looked at the problem. This, according to Plato, is the only real friendship, the only real common good. It is here that the contact people so desperately seek is to be found. The other kinds of relatedness are only imperfect reflections of this one trying to be self-subsisting, gaining their only justification from their ultimate relation to this one. This is the meaning of the riddle of the improbable philosopher-kings. They have a true community that is exemplary for all other communities.

This is a radical teaching but perhaps one appropriate to our own radical time, in which proximate attachments have become so questionable and we know of no others. This age is not utterly insalubrious for philosophy. Our problems are so great and their sources so deep that to understand them we need philosophy more than ever, if we do not despair of it, and it faces the challenges on which it flourishes. I still believe that universities, rightly understood, are where community and friendship can exist in our times. Our thought and our politics have become inextricably bound up with the universities, and they have served us well, human things being what they are. But for all that, and even though they deserve our strenuous efforts, one should never forget that Socrates was not a professor, that he was put to death, and that the love of wisdom survived, partly because of his *individual* example. This is what really counts, and we must remember it in order to know how to defend the university.

This is the American moment in world history, the one for which we shall forever be judged. Just as in politics the responsibility for the fate of freedom in the world has devolved upon our regime, so the fate of philosophy in the world has devolved upon our universities, and the two are related as they have never been before. The gravity of our given task is great, and it is very much in doubt how the future will judge our stewardship.

Notes

1 Natural science simply does not care. There is no hostility (unless it is attacked) to anything that is going on elsewhere. It is really self-sufficient, or almost so. If some other discipline proved itself, satisfied natural science's standards of rigor and proof, it would be automatically admitted. Natural science does not boast, is not snobbish. It is genuine. As Swift pointed out, its only habitual and apparently necessary sortie from its own proper domain is into politics. This is where it itself, if only in confused fashion, recognizes that it is a part of a larger project, and that it is dependent on that project, which is not a product of its methods. Lowly, despised politics points toward the need for philosophy, as Socrates originally said, in such a way that even scientists have to admit it. Natural scientists have no respect for political science as a science, but they have a passionate concern for politics. This is a beginning point for rethinking everything. Is the danger of nuclear war or the imprisonment of Sakharov just an accident?

2 Psychology is mysteriously disappearing from the social sciences. Its unheard-of success in the real world may have tempted it to give up the theoretical life. As the psychotherapist has taken his place alongside the family doctor, perhaps his education now belongs to something more akin to the medical school than to the sciences, and the research relevant for him is more directed to treatment of specific problems of patients than to the founding of a theory of the psyche. The Freudian theories have been incorporated into some aspects of sociology, political science and anthropology, and it appears that the self alone had nothing more to tell the social sciences. This leaves open the question of what the solid ground is on which therapy stands, and where its newer ideas come from. Serious academic psychology is left with the segment that has to all intents and purposes fused with physiology.

3 Undeveloped, bad; developing, better; developed, good—for man and for the science of economics.

4 I am tempted to say that psychology teaches that sex is the primary phenomenon. It is closer to economics when understood as stimulus-response, closer to anthropology when understood as a hang-up. If one wants something more from psychology, one meets a road sign saying "To the Humanities."

5 History, sharing Greek origins with political science, also has elements of the ancients-moderns identity crisis, in addition to the other problems of the strictly modern social sciences. As already mentioned, both participants and observers are unsure whether it is a social science or one of the humanities. Its matter is resistant to the techniques of the behavioral sciences, since it is particular, and therefore not easily generalizable, deals with the past, and is therefore beyond controlled experiments; but it does not want to be merely literature. I believe that none of the other social sciences includes history as part of the social science schema, with the exception of that part of political science which is concerned with political practice as opposed to social science, e.g., some aspects of American politics and of international relations. History until the nineteenth century meant primarily political history; and it, unlike political science, was not refounded in early modernity. Its traditional role was enhanced during the new foundings because it told what happened, as opposed to old political science, which told what ought to have happened. Therefore history was understood to be closer to the truth of things. History had to wait until the nineteenth century for its modernization by historicism, which argued, as it were, that being, certainly man's being, is essentially historical. Historicism appears to have been a great boon for history, a radical step upward in status. But the appearance is somewhat deceptive. Historicism is a philosophical, not a historical, teaching, one not discovered by history. Rather

than the prestige of philosophy adhering to history, the reverse occurred. All humanities disciplines are now historical—not philosophy, but history of philosophy, not art, but history of art, not science, but history of science, not literature, but history of literature. Thus history is all of these, but also none of them, because they are discrete disciplines in the humanities. History became the empty, universal category encompassing all the humanities, except insofar as it remained its modest, narrow political self. But because it does not have an anchor in political passion as does political science, it could float easily away from that dock under the influence of the prevailing winds, as politics was depreciated by so many other things, especially historicism. So, history, a wonderful, useful study, full of most learned individuals, is as a whole a medley of methods and goals, six disciplines in search of a self-definition.

6 It is to be noted that many students who come to the university intending to go into natural science change their intention while in college. It never, or almost never, happens that a student who was not interested in natural science before college discovers it there. This is an interesting reflection on the character of our high school education in general and science education in particular.

100

THE PATTERN OF
SOCIAL TRANSFORMATION
IN ENGLAND

Harold Perkin

Source: K. H. Jarausch (ed.) *The Transformation of Higher Learning, 1860–1930*, Stuttgart: Klett-Cotta, 1981, pp. 207–18.

Between 1850 and 1930 there took place in England a revolution in higher education. It was a revolution in the meaning, purpose, size and personnel, both staff and students, of the English universities, and it was arguably more profound than any change since the 13th century foundation of Oxford and Cambridge or before the transition towards mass higher education of the 1960s. In round terms it was nothing less than the transformation of the university from a marginal institution, an optional finishing school for young gentlemen and prospective clergymen, into the central power house of modern industrial society.

The measure of this revolution can be taken by asking what difference it would have made to English society in 1850 and again in 1930 if the universities had suddenly disappeared. In 1850—almost none. The 850-strong Oxbridge intake, mostly sons of landowners and clergy, could easily, like most of their class, have found alternative ways of passing the time and, if they wished, of qualifying for the Church or other liberal professions in foreign travel, military college, articled clerkships or the theological seminaries. Neither ordination for the Church, which took 38% of Cambridge graduates between 1800 and 1849, nor the professions of law, medicine, public administration and teaching, which took 21%, required a university degree, nor was a degree sufficient training for law or medicine. Hardly any Oxford or Cambridge man, even of the handful (6% at Cambridge) who came from business families, went into business.[1] The only occupation which might have suffered, and that a largely unpaid one, was politics—and most peers and M.P.s did not have a degree.

The 375 or so full-time internal students at London University in 1861 and the 50 at Durham were scarcely more relevant to the needs of the new industrial society of mid-Victorian England, apart perhaps from the majority who studied medicine and the few scientists and engineers; and most doctors and engineers were still trained on the job by a form of apprenticeship.[2]

The broadening of social recruitment

In the English as distinct from the Scottish universities, where in Glasgow as many as a third of the students in the 1830s were working-class, there was scarcely a single workman's son.[3] At Oxford in 1835 there was one and in 1860 no "plebeian," a term which embraced everyone below "gentleman" and the clergy,[4] and there is no reason to think that there were more poor students at Cambridge, London or Durham, where the fees ensured that only the middle and upper class could afford them. Even the middle class were mostly absent from Oxford and Cambridge. Nearly two-thirds (63%) of Cambridge students between 1800 and 1849 came from landed and clergy families, 21% from the liberal professions, and only 6% from business and banking.[5] All the Oxford students in 1835 and 1860 were sons of land-owners, clergy and "gentlemen," though the 21 percent to 32 percent of the latter must have included some professional and business men.[6] In no university in Britain were women of any class admitted. In total the English universities admitted less than 0.3% of what is now called the student age group, and if the Scottish universities admitted a larger share of a smaller population, most of these were between 15 and 18 years old and were not university students in the modern sense at all.[7]

As for the academic staff, they were chiefly drawn, as Arthur Engel has shown for Oxford, from the "gentlemanly" classes. Between 1813 and 1830, 45% of his sample were sons of clergymen, 28% of squires, armigers and "gentlemen," 15% of business and professional men, and only 5% from the "non-gentlemanly" classes. As late as the years 1881 to 1900 over 80% still came from the gentlemanly classes.[8] More to the point, most of the dons at Oxford and Cambridge were "poor relations," young men of good parentage but little inherited wealth, who became temporary celibate fellows while they waited their turn for a college living in the Church which they needed because their families lacked the patronage or wealth to provide one. Only 15% remained in the university for life, either because they gained a professorship or headship of a college which allowed them to marry or because a Church living never came their way. The professors at London and Durham, almost all recruited from Oxford and Cambridge, only differed from most dons in that they had gained a life appointment with freedom to marry similar to the Oxbridge professors and heads of houses. Only these few career academics would have permanently missed the universities of 1850.

Nor could the English universities claim to be vital to intellectual culture or scientific research. Not one of the intellectual giants of the early 19th century (Bentham, Coleridge, Malthus, Ricardo, Davy, Faraday or Darwin) was a university don, and the few academic scientists like Wheatstone, Daniell and Lyell were only to be found at the new University of London. The Royal Commission of 1852 on Oxford feared that "the clergy and gentry who are educated at the university" would in their ignorance of physical science be left behind by their social inferiors, to the serious injury of both science and other branches of knowledge.[9]

Lest it should be thought that Scotland was more advanced—as it certainly had been in the 18th century with the European leadership of Adam Fergusson, Dugald Stewart, Adam Smith, John Millar and the Scottish historical school of philosophy—one Scottish historian has talked of "the intellectual paralysis of intellectual life associated with Victorian Scotland." If that is exaggerated, the undergraduate faculties of Scottish universities were really secondary schools for 12- to 17-year-olds—"miserable filthy little urchins" as *Blackwood's Edinburgh Magazine* called those of Glasgow in 1823.[10] Their output, chiefly of kirk ministers and village dominies, was no more relevant to modern industrial society than that of Oxbridge.

In sum, the universities of Britain in 1850 could have been abolished with no great loss to the British economy and society. They were, indeed, less important than in the early 17th century, when on the eve of the Civil War they had educated 1.1% of the age group, over three times the percentage of 1850.[11]

By contrast, what if the universities had disappeared in 1930? That would have inflicted an immense loss on society and industry. By that date there were, including the five Scottish ones, 22 universities and university colleges in receipt of Treasury grants (24 if we include the unfunded colleges at Hull and Leicester) and 58 institutions if we count the separately funded colleges and schools of London and the University of Wales. They catered to about 50,000 students, representing 1.7% of the age group, or at least six times the percentage of 1850.[12] More important, it was a more critical percentage, a true elite which would supply most of the top positions in the Cabinet, the civil service, the medical and legal professions, and made a substantial contribution to the owners and managers of banking and big business.

As for the social origins of the students, the universities now catered, if unequally, to the whole social range. Nearly a quarter (23%)—more than a quarter of the men (27%)—were children of manual workers, a larger percentage than in any other West European country.[13] Although the child of a professional or managerial father had over 30 times the chance of getting to university of that of an unskilled worker, what has more often been overlooked is that only about one-third of upper class off-spring got there, which meant that two-thirds were beaten in the climb up the educational ladder by children from below.[14] Women, too, now found a place there, with

23% of the student body, though fewer of them (13%) came from the working class.[15] (To complete the picture we should add the large non-university sector of higher education, mainly teacher training and technical colleges, which contained another one percent of the age group and far more women and working-class students.)

The university teachers, too, had changed out of all recognition. No longer mainly clergymen waiting for permanent employment, they had become secular professional academics with a recognizably structured lifetime career. There is little information on their social background until after the Second World War. Of those in a 1968 sample who had entered university service before 1945 most, 83.2%, came from the professional and managerial classes and only 5.3% from the working class; but what is perhaps more significant is that the largest group, 42.5%, came from lesser managerial and professional families and, if we add the non-manual workers, half (49.6%) came from the lower middle class, and more than half (54.9%) from below the top social class.[16] Allowing in the latter for professional and salaried fathers with very little capital, there can be little doubt that the vast majority of academics were middle-class men (only about 10% were women, as now) with little family wealth and wholly dependent on their university salaries. As the best examinees of their peer group, they reflected belatedly the changed composition of the student body, but with a bias towards the scholarship boy from the grammar and direct grant schools, from which came no less than 72.3 percent. Although the largest single group, 43.4%, were graduates of Oxbridge, where nearly half came from the public boarding schools, only 22.3% of the university teachers were boarding-school products—a much smaller percentage than in most elites in Britain at that time.[17] University teaching had become a meritocratic profession mainly for the bright but poorer sons of the middle class.

The rising importance of higher learning

Meanwhile the whole meaning and purpose of the university as an institution had changed. Apart from educating a large fraction of the elite in most occupations and acting as a narrow but effective channel of social mobility especially from the lower middle ranges of society, the university had come to play a much more central role in the economy and indeed in matters of life and death. Michael Sanderson has chronicled the increasing involvement of the universities from the late 19th century onwards in industry, beginning with shipbuilding, chemicals and electrical engineering and continuing with man-made fibers and plastics, pharmaceuticals, dyestuffs and electronics, a development to which we shall return.[18] Beyond that, university science had begun to explore the keys to life in cellular biology, bacteriology, virology, genetics, and to death as well as life in atomic research. One has only to recall a few of the names—Rutherford in nuclear physics,

Fleming in antibiotics, Blackett in operational research—to realize how blindingly relevant the universities had become to the survival of man on this planet.

On a humbler level, the universities had begun to take over from apprenticeship and the professional institutions the advanced education of most of the higher professions. As the Vice-Chancellor of London University put it, belatedly in 1946, "The truth is that all the professions are pressing us, as universities, to take on the greater part, if not the whole, of the requisite professional or technical training for their own professional subjects." He went on to mention accountancy, veterinary medicine, estate management, youth leadership and journalism[19]—marginal professions compared with those which had already been absorbed. The U.G.C. annual listings from 1925–26 of "branches of study in which advanced students were engaged" chronicle this trend: 7 kinds of engineering, 10 of agricultural science, at least 12 industrial technologies from aeronautics and brewing to oil and textiles, 28 specialisms in medicine, and a new and burgeoning range of economic and social sciences.[20] We must not exaggerate the extent to which the universities were the progenitors of a more qualified, professional society, but academics were already on the way to becoming the key profession, the profession which provides both the expertise and the experts for most of the other professions.[21] If the universities had disappeared in 1930, they would have left a gaping hole in the social and industrial fabric—and Hitler would have won the Second World War.

It would be interesting to trace the stages by which this extraordinary change between 1850 and 1930 in the meaning, purpose, size and personnel of universities came about. The story would begin with the seething discontent of the new industrial classes at the exclusiveness and complacency of Oxford and Cambridge, which had come to monopolize for the Anglican clergy and gentry a national resource originally founded for poor scholars. It would follow the movement for reform both outside Oxbridge, in the effort to found alternative institutions for middle-class sons in London and the great industrial cities, and inside, with the help of parliamentary pressure coming to the aid of clerical dons seeking a lifelong career compatible with marriage and an opportunity to study and teach more relevant subjects like history, modern languages, the physical sciences and economics. It would bring in their increasing involvement in industry, with massive donations from industrialists on one side and on the other the penetration of academic inventors and consultants into the process of technological advance. It would show the increasing financial support of the state from the first minute grant of £15,000 to university colleges in 1889, through the establishment of the Department of Scientific and Industrial Research in 1917 and of the U.G.C. in 1919, to the shouldering by the 1930s of about one-third of university expenditure and the consequent "remote control" of academic remuneration. Above all, it would trace the construction of an educational ladder, from the higher grade elementary schools of the 1880s and the state-supported secondary schools of 1902 through the grammar school scholarship of 1907 to the state and L.E.A. university studentships from 1920 onwards.[22]

This story has, however, been more than adequately chronicled by Armytage, Sanderson, Sheldon Rothblatt, Arthur Engel and others.[23] In the space available it is more important to ask why this revolution took place at all, and why in so short a time, in what was by any standards the most aristocratic, conservative and class-ridden of modern industrial societies. It is not enough to point, with A. H. Halsey, to "the remarkable absorptive capacity, the judicious and un-Marxist Fabianism of the upper classes."[24] The upper classes were not Fabian except perhaps in the original Roman sense of knowing when to retreat to still stronger positions, and attitudes are not causes but effects which themselves need explanation. Just as the most important reason for the first Industrial Revolution can be found not in the progressive attitudes of English landlords but in the material self-interest underlying those attitudes—they stood to gain in increased rent from the enclosures, mines, canals, railways and new towns[25]—so their part in the early stages of the university revolution can best be explained by self-interest, including their interest in political survival and the art of compromise to avoid something worse.

But first we must rid ourselves of the unhistorical and intellectualist fallacy that the universities before the great transformation were as important to the ruling classes as they have since become to intellectuals. It is salutary to be reminded how contemptuous the old landed class could be of academic pursuits. As a student one of my friends, now a senior Oxford don, was found reading by his fox-hunting aunt, a female squire. "What!" she said, "Are you still reading a book? Most unhealthy! Why don't you get out and ride a horse?" There were aristocratic politicians in 1850 who were scholars, like the Earl of Derby who preferred translating Homer to being Prime Minister, or Peel and Gladstone who both took double firsts at Oxford. But the great majority thought brain work only marginally superior to manual work and, when necessary to their well-being, preferably done by other people for the pitiful wages it was worth. Education was mainly valued for the group unity and social superiority it brought, including the ability to understand the Latin tags in parliamentary speeches, but this was more a product of the great public schools than of the ancient universities, which were "optional extras." As for the modern universities, they were objects of charity for the lower orders, much like the village church schools on a larger scale, important for political support and social control, but on no account to be attended by one's own children.

The defence of the privileges of Oxford and Cambridge was really the defence of the Church of England monopoly, which by 1851, when it was discovered that only a minority of the population attended the established

Church,[26] had become indefensible. Even Gladstone, M. P. for the University and a high Anglican and loyal alumnus, was not prepared to defend it and introduced the bill to reform Oxford himself." It was, like the 1832 Reform Act or the Repeal of the Corn Laws, a concession which gave nothing vital away. The dissenters would be pleased and, as long as Latin and Greek were prerequisites for admission, the sons of the clergy and gentry and those professions which chose to be "civilized" in the public schools would still have the edge over all competitors. Moreover, once Oxford and Cambridge were reformed it became possible to justify new forms of privilege, such as their near-monopoly of the competitive examinations for the civil service from 1870. Reform was a retreat to a stronger position.

In the same way the new civic universities could be tolerated and even encouraged with royal charters and, eventually, government funds because they infringed upon no aristocratic interest, they drew middle-class political support, and they were, in their view, only a higher form of that "technical instruction" which the government already supported via the science and Art Department from the 1850s and the "whiskey money" after 1889.[28] It was also in the national interest and in the interests of increased urban rents if the country was prosperous in the face of international competition. It would be a mistake, however, to attach too much importance to the fear of foreign competition engendered by the international exhibitions of 1851, 1867, and 1878.[29] This may have been a factor in state support for evening classes and technical colleges but at the university level it assumes at too early a stage a strong and direct connection with industrial employment which was simply not there. Only seven percent of Cambridge graduates in 1850–99 went into business, including banking, and though the figures for London or the civic and Scottish universities are patchy, the percentages there around the turn of the century were not much greater.[30] The great majority of graduates both from Oxbridge and from the provincial universities down to the First World War went into the professions, including the clergy (dissenting as well as Anglican), public administration, law, medicine and teaching. Even the scientists and engineers tended to prefer public employment, teaching or private professional practice to industry.[31] Industrialism was certainly the main driving force behind higher education, as it was behind the expansion of the professions, but it was industrialism in the broadest sense of the growth of a new urban class society demanding more and better professional and administrative services, not in the narrower sense of the employment needs of industry itself. These could still best be met, it was generally agreed, by training on the job supplemented by mainly part-time technical instruction below the university level. With a few significant exceptions in particular science and engineering departments where the seeds of the future were being sown,[32] the new and reformed universities down to the early years of the 20th century were chiefly schools preparatory to the literate and liberal professions and instruments for turning the sons of the other classes, whether landowners, business men or the few, notably in Wales and Scotland, from the working class, into professional men.

The causes of the social transformation

We are thus left with a paradox. If the reforms and new foundations of the Victorian age had only succeeded in changing the universities from finishing schools for young gentlemen and prospective clergymen into preparatory schools for the professions, how then did they manage to become by 1930 so vital to modern industry and society? Mainly because of changes *outside* the universities which transformed the structure of demand for their products, both for knowledge and for graduates. These changes, which began in the late 19th century and came to full fruition in the interwar period, can be summed up as follows:

1   the rise of big business and with it of a plutocratic class by an amalgamation of the new millionaires with the old great landowners;
2   the relative decline of the landed gentry (the rural squires) and of the clergy whose incomes were heavily dependent on falling agricultural prices;
3   the emergence of new science-based industries closely linked to university research and graduate employment;
4   the growth of state administration and its more direct involvement in the economy and social life;
5   the narrowing, by taxation and educational policies as well as by big business and big government, of the channels of social recruitment and their concentration in the system of education and qualification.

The rise of big business between the 1880s and the 1920s is well-known in its economic aspects, but its social effects have been little studied. The number of joint-stock companies rose from 11,000 in 1888 to about 65,000 in 1914,[33] but more to the point was the rise of giant enterprises like Lever Brothers, Courtaulds, J. and P. Coats and Brunner-Mond, predecessor of I. C. I. The social effects of this development, coupled with those of the so-called "Great Depression" of 1874–96 on agricultural prices and rents, were profound. The wealth and status of the majority of the landed class were undermined, but the richer landlords, like the great London dukes with urban property, mines and other resources were joined in a new plutocratic, London-based class by great capitalists, many of them self-made millionaires like Lord Leverhulme, Lord Northcliffe, Cecil Rhodes and Sir Thomas Lipton.[34] The aristocracy rushed to diversify their holdings and incomes, on the one side to join the boards of joint-stock companies—one-quarter of the peerage became company directors by 1896—and on the other side to join the "flight from the land" which, after the 1909 "People's Budget" with its supertax and threatened land taxes, began the biggest transfer of land since the Conquest.[35] The plutocrats were few, however, and for most of the upper class a leisured life on the land was no longer an automatic right. Their children would have to fend for themselves and compete, admittedly with competitive advantages, with others for the top jobs in society.

The decline in agricultural rents and prices, to which the clergy's incomes were tied, removed overnight the attraction of the main alternative career for younger sons and for the sons of the clergy themselves. At the same time the secular professionalization of college fellowships removed another reason for ordination.[36] The proportion of Cambridge graduates going into the Church plummeted from 38% between 1850 and 1899 to six percent in the 1930s. The two largest classes which still between 1850 and 1899 supplied 50% of Cambridge graduates clearly had to find other jobs to do, often without higher education, and their numbers fell to nine percent by the 1930s. Their places were taken partly by children of the professional class, who increased from 26% to 30% of a much larger student body, but much more by those of the business class, who increased from 15 percent to 46 percent.

Still more striking was the change in social destinations. The share of those going into the Church and landowning as a career shrank from 45 percent to six percent (0% in land) and they were replaced partly by an increase in professional employment from 39% to 49%, still more by an increase of those going into business from seven percent to 31 percent.[37] Sanderson's figures show larger percentages of Cambridge graduates going into industry and business between the Wars, rising to 52% in 1929 and averaging 40% for the whole period.[38] Oxford, allowing for its larger weighting of arts degrees, had a similarly dramatic increase in business careers, from seven percent between 1906 and 1910 to 31% in 1938, and averaging 24% in the 1920s and 1930s.[39] Curiously enough, apart from Birmingham, Liverpool and Newcastle, which averaged 32%, 52% and 64% in the early 1920s, most provincial universities had smaller proportions going into business than Oxford and particularly Cambridge.[40] This underlines the fact that the upper and upper middle classes who still dominated Oxbridge were much quicker to seize the new opportunities in business, and were more welcome as recruits with "the right social background" than provincial graduates. Such indeed was the aim of the Appointments Boards set up in Oxford and Cambridge in the 1890s with the help of business men like Sir Douglas Fox, Lord Rothschild and Nathaniel Cohen with the express purpose of recruiting graduates for big business.[41] Even an Oxbridge arts graduate, it was assumed, was a better prospect for management than a provincial scientist or engineer, and it is noticeable that the graduates from other universities were nearly all scientists and engineers, mainly recruited for research and production and only rarely for management training.

Graduate scientists and engineers, however, were certainly needed for the new science-based industries of the 20th century. Many of these, such as steam turbines, electrical engineering, electronics and broadcasting, dye-stuffs, pharmaceuticals, manmade fibers and petrochemicals, were based on fundamental research done mainly in 19th century universities, often with active collaboration between industrialists and professors like Sir Henry Roscoe, Lord Kelvin, MacQuorn Rankine and J. J. Thomson. Such science professors acted not only as consultants but as recruiting agents between their students and business, and their departments became the seedbeds of whole new industries.[42] By the inter-war period the universities had become vital to the development and survival of the most advanced and rapidly growing sectors of British industry.

The growth of big government which began in the late 19th century also provided opportunities for graduate employment and academic consultancy. The number of civil servants which had scarcely kept pace with population for most of the 19th century leapt from 50,859 in 1881 to 116,413 in 1901, to 317,721 in 1922 (during the post-War decline) and to 350,293 in 1936.[43] The increase was due to the growth in government responsibility for an ever-widening range of services, including education, public health, factory inspection, industrial arbitration and conciliation, as well as the rising scale of military operations, and above all to the incipient rise of the welfare state, which took central government offices for the first time (except for the Customs and Excise) into every provincial town and placed new burdens on the local authorities as well. By no means all the new civil servants and local government officials were graduates but those in the higher echelons were, and the highest grade of the civil service was almost exclusively recruited from Oxford and Cambridge.[44] At lower levels, such as factory inspection and social work, other graduates could find a foothold. The London School of Economics, for example, set up the first course in welfare work.[45] The universities, and especially Cambridge and London began increasingly to furnish the government with consultants on social and economic problems like J. M. Keynes, R. H. Tawney and W. H. Beveridge, though it did not always accept their advice.[46] Here again the universities found themselves at the heart of one of the most far-reaching developments of modern society, the expanding corporate state.

The combined effect of all these four developments was to converge on the fifth, the channelling of recruitment to most of the elites in society through education and the qualification systems, at the apex of which now stood the universities. Given the closing of other avenues, into leisured landownership or the Church, even the children of the upper class were forced to seek higher education if they wished to be certain to reach the top. With the rise of big business and the operation of super-tax and death duties it became more difficult (though not impossible) for middle-class and the few working-class entrepreneurs to build up a business and make a fortune,[47] and so hopes of social mobility were channelled towards education. The educational ladder itself diverted middle and working-class talent away from traditional forms of social climbing, and many a potential self-made man became a professor or a civil servant instead. The ladder brought talent from below into competition with the children of the higher classes. By a quirk of the English system it was easier for a really bright but poor child to go to Oxford or Cambridge than to a provincial university since, after the reforms of the 1870s, there were far more open scholarships there to be won. Although the scholars were few, they had by definition to be good at competitive examinations, and they tended to get better degrees and a larger share of university fellowships and civil service places, which accounts for the rapid shift in those professions towards recruitment from the lower middle ranges of society.[48] Thus the competition was immediately felt by the sons of the higher classes, who had to strive harder in the educational competition or shift their attention to careers where social background and "character" gave them an advantage, in business and the socially superior and more expensive professions such as law and medicine.

The net result of this convergence of recruitment upon the educational route was what may be called a "threshold effect." With dramatic suddenness, between the first and third decades of the 20th century the percentage of the age group enrolled in universities doubled, from 0.8 percent to 1.5 percent. Higher education became fashionable, almost a necessity, even for the rich who wished to reach the top of the great functional elites and even for those who came from the business class and/or hoped to get into management. They avoided the provincial universities, but both Oxbridge and the rest became more vital to the middle classes, both for those who followed the now traditional routes into the professions and the more adventurous who were willing to take their chances in business. For bright boys and (fewer) girls from the working class all their hopes of social mobility came to center on the grammar school and university, preferably Oxbridge. For all classes the university became the normal route to high status and income. This was an aspect of the rise of professionalism as the guiding principle of modern society.

Thus the revolution in British higher education, though from one point of view occupying the whole period between 1850 and 1930 and by no means complete even then, from another passed its critical turning point almost overnight, between, say, 1900 and 1920. The war, though not itself the cause, accelerated the transition, by extending the role of the state, challenging the automatic leadership of the traditional ruling class, bringing forward new leaders from the ranks, and shaking up old assumptions about what men—and women—from different social backgrounds could do and not do. But the causes lay much deeper, in the profound shifts in income, social structure and expectations about the distribution of life chances which began in the late 19th century. At the risk of massive oversimplification of complex developments, the revolution may be summed up in a sentence. Before, 1900, despite many undercurrents of change, the universities are still in the world of leisured gentlemen and the gentlemanly professions; after 1920, despite many hangovers from the past, they are in the bustling, strenuous world of business and the competitive professions, where serious preparation for high status and incomes is channelled increasingly through higher education. By the 1920s the university is no longer a finishing school for young gentlemen; it is the central power house of modern industry and society.

Notes

1 Lawrence Stone, "The Size and Composition of the Oxford Student Body, 1580–1910" in L. Stone, ed., *The University in Society* (2 vols., Princeton, 1974), 1:91–2, tables 1 A and 1 B (for both Oxford and Cambridge admissions); Fritz K. Ringer, *Education and Society in Modern Europe* (Bloomington, 1979), 236 (for social origins and subsequent careers of Cambridge students, abstracted from Hester Jenkins and D. Caradog Jones, "Social Class of Cambridge Alumni of the 18th and 19th centuries," *British Journal of Sociology*, 1 [1950] and a 1938 survey by the Cambridge University Appointments Board).

2 Figures from R. A Lowe, Table 1, in his contribution to this volume; for the preponderance of medical students at London University and other civic colleges see W. H. G. Armytage, *Civic Universities* (London, 1955), 170–75.

3 Michael Sanderson, *The Universities and British Industry, 1850–1970* (London, 1972), 148.

4 Stone, 93.

5 Ringer, 236.

6 Stone, *loc. cit.*; Ringer, 239.

7 Sanderson, 149; Harold Perkin, *Key Profession: The History of the Association of University Teachers* (London, 1969), 6.

8 Arthur J. Engel, "From Clergyman to Don: The Rise of the Academic Profession in 19th-century Oxford" (Diss., Princeton University, 1975) Appendix 2.

9 *Report of the Royal Commission on the University of Oxford* (1852), 79–80.

10 "Vindiciae Gallicae," *Blackwood's Edinburgh Magazine*, 13 (1823), 94: the undergraduate Faculty of Arts was "a school where boys from twelve years of age to sixteen or seventeen" were instructed in elementary Classics, Mathematics, Logic, Ethics, etc., and were not to be compared with those of Eton, Westminster, Winchester, or Harrow (English grammar boarding schools) .

11 Stone, 103.

12 University Grants Committee, *Report for the Period 1929–30 to 1934–35* (London, H. M. S. O., 1936), 11; Robbins Committee, *Report on Higher Education* (London, H. M. S. O., 1963), 16.

13 The figures are for those of university admission age (18) in 1928–47 and are taken from Jean Floud "The Educational Experience of the Adult Population of England and Wales as at July 1949" in D. V. Glass, ed., *Social Mobility in Britain* (London, 1954), cited by A. H. Halsey, *Trends in British Society Since 1900* (London, 1972), 189, 219.

14 Figures from Jean Floud, cited by Ringer, 243.

15 Halsey, 217 and 219.

16 Perkin, 262.

17 Perkin, 259, 260.

18 Sanderson, *passim*.

19 *Home Universities Conference, 1946: Report of Proceedings* (Association of Commonwealth Universities, London, 1946).

20 University Grants Committee, *Returns from Universities and University Colleges* ... (annually from 1925–26 onwards) (London, H. M. S. O., 1926).

21 Cf. Perkin, *Key Profession*, Chap. 1.

22 Cf. A. H. Halsey, A. F. Heath and J. M. Ridge, *Origins and Destinations: Family, Class and Education in Modern Britain* (Oxford, 1980), 25: the proportion of scholarships or "free places" in grammar schools rose from a required 25% under the 1907 regulations to an actual 45% in 1931 (drawn mainly from the less affluent middle class and the upper working class). See also R. H. Tawney, *Secondary Education for All* (London, 1922), 20: "The number both of pupils and school places in 1922 is ... all too small. But, inadequate as they are, they represent something like an educational revolution compared with the almost complete absence of public provision which existed prior to 1902" (quoted *ibid.*). A more detailed account may be found in G. A. N. Lowndes, *The Silent Social Revolution* (2nd ed., Oxford, 1969).

23 Armytage, *op. cit.*, Sanderson, *op. cit.*, Sheldon Rothblatt, *The Revolution of the Dons: Cambridge and Society in Victorian England* (London, 1968), Engel, *op. cit.*

24 A. H. Halsey, "British Universities and Intellectual Life" in A. H. Halsey, J. T. Floud and C. A. Anderson, eds., *Education, Economy and Society* (London, 1961), 506.

25 Cf. Harold Perkin, *The Origins of Modern English Society, 1780–1880* (London, 1969), esp. chap. 3.

26 *Census of England and Wales, 1851: Religious Worship* (London, H. M. S. O., 1854).

27 John Morley, *Life of Gladstone* (London, 1908), 1:369–79.

28 O. M. V. Argles, *From South Kensington to Robbins: An Account of English Technical and Scientific Education since 1851* (London, 1964), chap. 2.

29 Cf. Argles; Armytage, 219–22.

30 Ringer, 236; Sanderson, 100–101, 111–14, 173–79.

31 Sanderson, *loc. cit.*

32 Sanderson, esp. 83–93, 107–11, 160–65.

33 Sir John H. Clapham, *An Economic History of Modern Britain* (Cambridge, 1926), 3:202, 222.

34 Cf. F. M. L. Thompson, *English Landed Society in the 19th Century* (London, 1963), chap. 11; and Harold Perkin, "Land Reform and Class Conflict in Victorian Britain" in John Butt and P. F. Clarke, *The Victorians and Social Protest* (Newton Abbot, 1973).

35 Thompson, 306–07, 321–26.

36 Cf. Engel, 467.

37 Ringer, 236.

38 Sanderson, 279.

39 Sanderson, 279.

40 Sanderson, 279.

41 Sanderson, 55–58.

42 Sanderson, 100–101, 111–14, 173–79.

43 H. Finer, *The British Civil Service* (London, 1937), 24.

44 Cf. R. K. Kelsall, *Higher Civil Servants in Britain from 1870 to the Present Day* (London, 1955).

45 Lord Beveridge, *The London School of Economics and its Problems, 1919–37* (London, 1960), 86.

46 Keynes was an economic adviser to the British delegation to the Versailles Treaty conference, 1919; Tawney the leading member of the Hadow Committee on secondary education, 1926; and Beveridge's contributions range from assistance to Churchill over labor exchanges, 1909, to his famous report on *Social Insurance and Allied Services*, 1942.
47 For the changing social origins of large company chairmen and millionaires, see H. J. Perkin, *Elites in British Society since 1880* (unpublished report to S. S. R. C., 1976, deposited in British Library Lending Division).
48 Perkin, above, and "The Recruitment of Elites in British Society since 1880", *Journal of Social History*, Winter 1978.

101

THE EVOLUTION OF THE BRITISH UNIVERSITIES

A. H. Halsey and M. A. Trow

Source: A. H. Halsey and M. A. Trow, *The British Academics*, London: Faber and Faber, 1971, pp. 38–64.

Introduction

Our task now is to examine and explain the British case in the light of the history of British society. But we may briefly anticipate the outstanding characteristics of the present system of universities in Britain so as to order the comparative and historical sketch of their development which follows. First, this group of institutions is relatively small and slow in its rate of expansion: measured in terms of the number of graduates per 10,000 population in 1958 it was smaller than the U.S.A., the U.S.S.R., Canada or Japan.[1]

Second, the British universities have a strong centrifugal tendency evident in the comparable standard of their degrees which has been maintained hitherto by a voluntary system of external examining involving the interchange of staff between universities for examining purposes, by the role played by London in the development of provincial colleges and by the more diffuse influence of Oxford and Cambridge.

Third, there is concerted control over standards and numbers of entrants, partly through a national system of undergraduate and graduate scholarships, partly through a customarily agreed ratio of about one teacher to eight taught, partly through a linked system of secondary-school examining boards and, in recent years, through centralised inter-university machinery for undergraduate applications.

Fourth, there is an evolving standardisation of financial and administrative procedures which derives from the dependence of the universities on state finance. While this dependency is not unique to Britain, the method of organising the amount and distribution of resources through the University Grants Committee has been a distinctive feature of the British system and we shall examine it in detail in Chapter 4.

Finally, there is, as we shall try to show in Part II, an 'English Idea of the University' which gives a common stamp to universities in this country despite differences of age, size and location. In other words, there are norms in British universities which mark them as reflecting a more or less unified conception of university education.

British universities in the nineteenth century

The social and cultural unity of England and the political incorporation of Scotland and Wales into Great Britain are centuries old. They pre-date the Industrial Revolution and had already generated aristocratic and religious traditions which have acted as a powerful brake against movement towards the incorporation of the university into the service of the technological society. Modernisation began early in England, but the university response to it has been most strongly contained within an educational hierarchy corresponding to the structure of power and prestige of the wider society. The needs of the aristocracy, the gentry and the clergy (who were closely linked to them) were already provided for in Oxford and Cambridge, whose dominance over British university life was attained by the defeat of the migration to Stamford in 1334.[2] In the fourteenth century Oxford and Cambridge, backed by royal power, established themselves as national institutions with a monopoly over higher learning. The monopoly was challenged frequently but unsuccessfully until the rise of the universities in the industrial provincial cities of the nineteenth century, and even then monopoly only gave way to pre-eminence. The technical changes which precipitated the Industrial Revolution of the late eighteenth and early nineteenth centuries were linked to entrepreneurship rather than to the formal development of scientific research and the training of scientists and technologists in the manner of those countries, like Germany and France, whose industrialisation came later.[3] In Britain, the challenge of industrialism and of religious non-conformity was met partly by reform and expansion of the ancient foundations, partly by assimilation of the sons of successful businessmen through the colleges and the public schools which supplied them, and partly by the movement of Oxford and Cambridge dons to teach in the newly created universities.

As a result, two university traditions emerged: Oxford and Cambridge were national universities connected with the national élites of politics, administration, business and the liberal professions offering a general education designed to mould character and prepare their students for a gentlemanly style of life: the rest were provincial, all of them, including London, addressed to the needs of the professional and industrial middle classes, taking most of their students from their own region[4] and offering them a more utilitarian training for middle-class careers in undergraduate courses typically concentrated on a single subject.[5]

Until the middle of the nineteenth century these two traditions existed side by side with little contact. But the assimilating processes of the latter half of that century resulted in the twentieth century in a two-tier structure with Oxford and Cambridge at the apex. In summary, then, what we have to analyse in Britain is the slow and faltering development of an élitist system of higher education during the course of the century which preceded the Robbins Report.

In 1850 there were four universities in England – Oxford, Cambridge, London and Durham. There were also four universities in Scotland but none in Wales. Owen's college in Manchester was about to be founded, representing the rising aspirations of the provincial industrial bourgeoisie, which were to gain expression in 'Redbrick' civic universities at the end of the century. The University of London had been formed fourteen years earlier by a combination of University College and King's College but was itself only an examining body and was not to become a full teaching university for another half-century. Durham, like Owen's college and other provincial university centres, was scarcely viable in the 1850's, turning out only a handful of graduates. It was in any case an Anglican foundation concerned mainly with preparing young men for the ministry. The English scene was dominated by Oxford and Cambridge, ancient, rich and secure, but together admitting less than eight hundred students each year and providing an education for the upper classes and those intending to be ordained in the Anglican Church. Their traditions and curricula inhibited either concern with the technological requirements of industry or training for the new scientific professions, and in this respect they were less responsive to the new needs of the middle classes than they had been at earlier times. Compared with Germany, the major source of inspiration to those bent on university reform, England and Wales had roughly one-tenth as many university students per head of population.

The absence of competition indicated by Ben-David might have been reversed if there had been independent religious, regional or ethnic groups with the material resources and cultural tradition necessary to challenge the English aristocratic hierarchy. Scotland provided the only example of such conditions and the situation there was indeed very different. No religious tests were imposed on would-be entrants. There was already a long-standing tradition of broadly based secondary education, and of encouragement for clever boys to go to the university from the agricultural areas; the university year accommodated itself to the cycle of agriculture. 'While Oxford and Cambridge slept, insulated by Anglicanism from influences from abroad, the Scottish universities maintained a constant traffic of ideas especially with the universities of Holland . . . In philosophy, science and medicine, they provided an austere but healthy diet; moreover they precipitated the reform of higher education in England, for it was the immoderate animadversions of Sir William Hamilton in the *Edinburgh Review* which helped to stimulate Oxford and Cambridge to adapt themselves to the Victorian age.'[6]

Religion and the universities

The triumph of secular learning is now so complete that the English educational world of the 1850's seems almost inexplicably remote.[7] Religious thought was then still inextricably mixed with attempts to define the educational aims of a society recognised as changing; and Church interests were deeply entrenched in both schools and universities.

Here is John Sparrow's description of Oxford in the late 1840's. It was 'an entirely Anglican and largely clerical society: it contained no dissenters, no Roman Catholics and, among the Dons, a minority of laymen. Every undergraduate had to sign a declaration that he had read the XXXIX Articles and to subscribe to them in order to qualify for a degree. Most Fellowships required their holders to take Holy Orders, and for many undergraduates the degree was simply a step on the road to Ordination; it has been calculated that of rather over twenty-five thousand men who matriculated at Oxford in the first half of the century, about one thousand four hundred were called to the Bar and over ten thousand were Ordained; Oxford in other words, was turning out about two hundred Clergymen a year.'[8]

It is true that, in a Victorian context, Mark Pattison thought of Oxford as having undergone revolutionary change in its climate and preoccupations between 1840 and 1850: and there were indeed reformist stirrings against the Anglican establishment inside as well as outside the Colleges. Yet in Pattison's nearest neighbour college, Exeter, one of the tutors, William Sewell, had publicly burned Froude's *The Nemesis of Faith* only the year before. It is true too that Tractarianism was receding from the centre of debate at that time and that academic minds were turning to the challenge of the flourishing new scientific scholarship led by a distinguished professoriate in the German universities. Nevertheless, insofar as the country's need for new men in science, literature and the learned professions had been recognised at all, the new class had been identified by Coleridge as 'the Clerisy'.[9]

Moreover it was in the 1850's that Cardinal Newman began to write the letters and discourses which he eventually published as *The Idea of a University* – a book which, for all its emancipated catholicism, embodied a conception of the essential place of religion in university institutions and a denial of the place of scientific research which would make nonsense of the actual development in British universities in this century. Newman's ideal was a fusion and preservation of classical and Christian knowledge. 'In the nineteenth century, in a country which looks out upon a new world, and anticipates a coming age, we have been engaged in opening the schools dedicated to the studies of polite literature and liberal science, or what are called the arts, as a first step towards the establishment on catholic ground of a Catholic university. And while we thus recur to Greece and Athens with pleasure and affection, and recognise in that famous land the source and the school of intellectual culture, it would be strange indeed if we forgot to look further south also, and there to bow before a more glorious luminary, and a more sacred oracle of truth, and the source of another sort of knowledge, high and supernatural, which is seated in Palestine. Jerusalem is the fountainhead of religious knowledge, as Athens is of secular.'[10]

But those who were to shape the future of higher education were already beginning to turn their eyes further north: and those who saw the vital reform as that of altering the character of Oxford and Cambridge colleges found themselves in direct conflict with Church interests. The Commissions set up in 1850 instantly roused theologians and ecclesiastics to resist the intrusion of Parliament into the affairs of the ancient universities. The Bishop of Exeter described the Commissions as having 'absolutely no parallel since the fatal attempt of King James II to subject them [Oxford and Cambridge] to his unhallowed control'.[11]

Parliamentary interest was in opening Oxford and Cambridge to dissenters – a debt owed by Russell to his supporters in the growing non-conformist middle class. But, backed by a small professorial group,[12] the attack was generalised into a campaign against the extensive decay of scholarship which was held to have afflicted Oxford and Cambridge over the past century and a half, and against the inadequacy of arrangements for the training of professional people. The Commissioners pointed, for example, to the complete absence of a school of medicine in Oxford and its unsatisfactory connection with the profession of law.[13] They even charged Oxford with having 'no efficient means for teaching candidates for Holy Orders in those studies which belong particularly to their profession', and they complained of the rarity of learned theologians in the university.

In both the ancient foundations the struggle to establish higher standards of learning and teaching developed into a conflict over traditional forms of collegiate life and the relation of the colleges to the university. For learning the model was the German universities with their powerful professoriate. For teaching the problem was to get rid of closed fellowships which were linked to the distribution of Church employment and preferment. As Frederick Temple of Balliol put it to the Commissioners in discussing restrictions on election to fellowship, 'men who are naturally well fitted to be country clergymen are bribed, because they are born in some parish in Rutland, to remain in Oxford as Fellows, until they are not only unfit for that, but for everything else. The interests of learning are entrusted to those who have neither talents nor inclination for the subject. Fellowships are looked upon and used as mere stepping stones to a living. A large number of Fellows live away from the place and thus, in reality, convert the emoluments to a purpose quite alien from that for which they were intended.' Temple later became Archbishop of Canterbury, but his opinions were emphatically not those of the dominant Church party in Oxford. Dr. Pusey, who was their leader, was strenuously opposed to the introduction of a lay professoriate, seeing it as a threat to the traditional morals and religious life of the university. Armytage[14] quotes Henry Mansel to illustrate the prevailing animosity to secular and professorial development, and in particular to the supporters of the professorial interest who collaborated with the Royal Commissioners.

> *Professors we,*
> *From over the sea*
> *From the land where Professors in plenty be;*
> *And we thrive and flourish, as well we may,*
> *In the land that produced one Kant, with a K,*
> *And many Cants with a C.*

College fellows were celibate. Their fellowships were tenable for life but were forfeited on marriage or the taking up of a College living. The idea of university teaching, as a profession, secular and full-time as we now know it, had no place in Oxford or Cambridge in 1850. Only about a third of the fellows actually lived there. Tutors had yet to realise their interests in securing well-paid and permanent careers in their colleges, freed from Church connections. They sought control of colleges and of the university in order to create the conditions of appointment, teaching and examining which would make such careers possible. Meanwhile, as John Sparrow puts it, 'being a tutor was not well enough paid to be looked upon as a vocation or profession, or even a regular post; a tutorship was simply a perquisite, a job with which a junior fellow would occupy a year or two while he was waiting for a college living. When a tutorship became vacant, the head of the college would offer the post to the fellows in residence in order of seniority, without regard to their abilities, easily passing over those who were not in orders.'[15] All in all Oxford and Cambridge had changed little since the seventeenth century in their system of fellowships and selection of undergraduates until the 1850 Commissions and the reforming legislation of 1854 and 1856.

Outside Oxford and Cambridge the most important innovation in the first half of the nineteenth century was the secular foundation in London of University College. When a Bill of Incorporation was introduced by Brougham in the House of Commons in 1825, the established Church opposed the grant of a charter to what W. M. Praed satirically termed 'the radical infidel college'. When this failed Church interests turned instead to establishing a rival institution with the same function but under Anglican control. This led to the foundation of King's College. But the orthodox and the godless institutions had enough in common to combine and were given a charter as the University of London in 1836. This was the first non-sectarian university to be established in England with the power to grant degrees in Arts, Law and Medicine. But the battle over Church influence in London did not end there. Thus, Thomas Arnold resigned from the University senate in 1839 in protest against its refusal to make examination in scripture compulsory for undergraduates. Nevertheless, especially as an examining body and a centre for the affiliation of provincial institutions, the new University in London was an essential step in breaking the Anglican grip on university studies.

The other university in England at this time was at Durham.[16] It was concerned mostly with the training of the Anglican clergy, but also set out from the beginning to offer professional training of other kinds, including engineering. Durham university remained an unimportant and ailing institution in its early years, and by the end of the 1850's it had declined to the point of granting only a handful of degrees each year. It was rescued by parliamentary action in the 1860's, when new degrees in science and theology were established, along with new professorships in chemistry, geology and mining.

Social stratification and the universities

In nineteenth-century Britain, as elsewhere, access to the universities was almost wholly denied to the working classes. For the mass of the population there was no viable avenue from the primary and secondary schools to the colleges. Before 1870 even primary education was by no means universal. The existence of primary schools was dependent on local church and voluntary provision, which had an uncertain relation to the rapid movement of population out of agriculture into the industrial centres of the North and West. In 1841 nearly half the women and a third of the men who were married in England and Wales signed the register with a mark and the percentages were still 27 and 20 in 1870, when the Forster Act provided for a national system of state primary schools. It was not until 1880 that compulsory attendance was introduced, and then only up to the age of ten, the age being raised to eleven in 1893 and to fourteen in 1918.

The link to universities through secondary education was also almost non-existent for the working classes throughout the nineteenth century. A national system of secondary schools only began to develop in the twentieth century after the 1902 Education Act. There were, of course, endowed and proprietary secondary schools including grammar schools of mediaeval origin, but even by the end of the century they contained no more than 100,000 children. And the public schools, though they grew rapidly during the nineteenth century in response to the needs of the upper and middle classes to prepare their sons for careers which increasingly demanded professional qualifications, were schools from which the mass of the public were excluded. In the main and throughout the century, elementary education was for 'workmen and servants', concerned not with the promotion of talented individuals but with inculcation among the masses of discipline, piety, and respect for private property and the existing social order.[17] There were some exceptions, some narrow channels through local grammar schools which carried poor boys into the universities. Nevertheless, their social isolation continued and they remained insulated from the kind of populist sentiment which contributed heavily to the expansion of the American universities in the second half of the nineteenth century.

The economy and the universities

The Great Exhibition of 1851 declared Britain's lead among the industrial countries. Yet, as we have seen, the universities were still more closely tied to the Church than to business. As D. S. Cardwell, referring to the 1840's, points out, 'professional studies, even at that late date, had no place in the university. Law was studied at the Inns of Court, Medicine at the London Hospitals and for the clergy, no special training was thought necessary. The Victorian engineer and his predecessors were trained in the old craft apprenticeship system . . . the universities were concerned with the liberal education of men of a privileged class who would later adopt suitable professions or else follow a life of leisure. The educational ideal was the Christian gentleman; if he was a scholar, then so much the better; if not, then he would benefit from the corporate life in the university.'[18]

Why was this so? Why was it that, in sharp contrast to Germany, Britain failed to develop university institutions for the training of scientists and technologists and the development of applied scientific research ? Again the answer lies partly in the social isolation of the ancient English universities. Dons were not at all concerned to reduce the social distance between themselves and the Victorian business classes, while businessmen regarded colleges with the greatest suspicion.

According to one estimate, only about 7 per cent of all Cambridge undergraduates entered business, to include banking, in the period 1800–99, or less than half the percentage of students coming from business backgrounds. . . . Leaders of commerce and industry returned the resentment. Not only were they reluctant to employ arts graduates, they saw little use for science and engineering graduates as well. For at least sixty years prominent intellectuals, parliamentary spokesmen, heads of scientific associations and institutions, government committees and royal commissions had urged the schools and the universities to produce scientists and technologists to staff industry and increase the importance of British manufacturing. University colleges, which grew into universities, and colleges of technology had been founded to help produce men of science and technology. Government had been used to establish adequate science teaching in schools. Voices demanding the union of science and industry had become more strident and occasionally hysterical with the rise of industrial Germany and America, but industrialists had not responded. The overwhelming majority of trained science and engineering graduates from all universities, chemists as well as physicists, were employed in teaching rather than in industry. Manufacturers continued to favour industrial chemists or engineers who had received their training essentially in the works itself. The attitude that college life ruins a man for a business career was still prevalent.[19]

Nor did it die with the nineteenth century.

There was support for, even idealisation of, the professional man among dons, but the word 'professional' had ethical and status as well as occupational connotations. 'The professional man, it was argued by those who distrusted and feared the ethical implications of the acquisitive aspects of industrialism, thought more of duty than of profit. The gratitude of his client rather than the market defined his reward, and technically he was not paid but granted an honorarium. He earned his reputation by discretion, tact and expert knowledge rather than by advertising and financial success. He was a learned man, and his education was broad and comprehensive. Unlike the businessman, who operated within an impersonal market situation, the professional man was involved with his clients at a personal, intimate level. Ideally he did not have to compete with others of the same profession, at least not to the same extent as the businessman. The professional society, with its principles of restricted entry, embodied in the professional examination and the *numerus clausus*, insulated him from the severer pressures of supply and demand. There was, therefore, a certain self-restraint in his manner, a gentlemanly quality which distinguished him from the brash and aggressive industrialists of the Midlands and the North.'[20]

Nor was there anything resembling the German demand from industrial employers for trained scientists and engineers or any appreciation of the contribution they could make to industrial efficiency. Most British employers did not think it worth while to make the necessary investment in training and research. On the contrary, as Landes has argued, 'they were convinced the whole thing was a fraud, that effective technical education was impossible, scientific instruction unnecessary. Their own careers were the best proof of that: most manufacturers had either begun with a minimum of formal education and come up through the ranks or had followed the traditional liberal curriculum in secondary and sometimes higher schools. Moreover, this lesson of personal experience was confirmed by the history of British industry. Here was a nation that had built its economic strength on practical tinkerers – on a barber like Arkwright, a clergyman like Cartwright, an instrument maker like Watt, a professional "amateur inventor" like Bessemer, and thousands of nameless mechanics who suggested and effected the kind of small improvements to machines and furnaces and tools that add up eventually to an Industrial Revolution.'[21] Britain thus paid the price of its historical precosity as an industrialising nation.

'In sum, job and promotion opportunities for graduates in science and technology were few and unattractive. The most remunerative field . . . was chemistry, and even there the best positions were often reserved for men trained abroad; undoubtedly the mediocre quality of many British graduates served to reinforce the scepticism of management.'[22]

Hitherto, science in England had not been a profession. It was in the hands of amateurs who could pursue their interests only on the basis of private means. In 1851 Charles Babbage could list only a small number of official scientific posts, including 'a few professorships; the Royal Astronomers; the Master of Mechanics to the Queen; the Conductor of the Nautical Almanac; the Director of the Museum of Economic Geology and of the Geological Survey; Officers of the same; Officers of the Natural History Museum'.[23]

Cardwell summarises the situation as follows:

> The mid-century was that time during which the beginning of the social organisation of science can first be seen. Primarily it took the form of the organisation of studies by the reform of the older universities in the matter of the inclusion of the progressive sciences in the examination syllabuses; by the foundation of the Government School of Science and the Owen's College; by the introduction of London Science degrees, and by the beginning of State aid to scientific education through the agency of the Science and Art Department. Perhaps the central fact of these reforms was the institution of examinations, for these . . . are associated with the 'expert', with discipline and, ultimately, with professionalism.[24]

We have noted the general lack of opportunity for children to go to universities and this of course also affected potential scientists.

> The major defect in the structure was the chaotic state of education; both primary and secondary. The public schools and the old endowed grammar schools were hardly touched by science. Only occasionally would a headmaster include science in his syllabus. Generally it occupied no place in the school; at Eton, in the early sixties there were twenty-four classical masters, eight mathematics masters and three to teach all other subjects. This meant that youths went up to the universities unprepared for science and even if inclined that way would be discouraged by the simple fact that there was little prospect of being able to make a living as a scientist; certainly not at the 'old school' at any rate.[25]

Social and educational stratification kept amateur science apart from industrial processes in nineteenth-century Britain. 'There was practically no exchange of ideas between the scientists and the designers of industrial processes. The very stratification of English society helped to keep science isolated from its applications: it was admitted that the study of science for its useful applications might be appropriate to the labouring classes, but managers were not attracted to the study of science except as an agreeable occupation for their leisure.'[26] This social division has deeply affected the relation between the universities and industry down to the present day, despite the rise of the Redbrick universities in the industrial provinces, the government pressures generated by twentieth-century wars and the almost continuous alarms raised in Parliament and Press from the earlier years of the nineteenth century, with their theme that scientific and technological 'manpower' was the key to British survival in a modern internationally competitive industrial world.

This relation between university pure science and industrial technology, or rather the absence of it, is well illustrated in the history of the aniline dye industry. The first of the aniline dyes was discovered in 1856 by W. H. Perkin while working in the Royal College of Chemistry. Together with his father and brother he set up a manufacture of the new dye at Greenford Green, being aware of its commercial potentialities. The Perkin family soon made a fortune and retired. This new discovery was of immense potential importance to British industry in that it could be manufactured from coal and thus relieved the necessity to import dye-stuffs. The facts were recognised but it was the German chemical industry and not the British which took advantage of the possibilities of industrial exploitation, establishing dye factories at Höchst, Ludwigshafen, Elbefeld, Berlin and elsewhere. 'Although the actual discovery was made by an Englishman, many German scientists had worked and were working in that and collateral fields; . . . the Prussian government, having decided that the facilities for advanced chemistry were inadequate at the universities of Bonn and Berlin, resolved to erect new laboratories. These attracted wide attention all over Europe and with reason for, at a time when Owen's College was still installed in Cobden's old house, these laboratories were built on a palatial scale.'[27]

The Royal Commission on Technical Education of 1881–84 showed that the German organic chemical industry had taken a strong lead over Britain. The applied science laboratory was not yet a feature of British industry whereas in Germany and Switzerland close links had been established between chemists in the universities and technical Hochschulen and research development laboratories in industrial firms. 'In the evidence given to the Commission, W. H. Perkin showed that Germany, in 1879, produced some £2-million worth of coal-tar colours and Britain some £450,000. There were seventeen colour works in Germany and five in this country. Thus the industry which it was anticipated in 1862 would render Britain independent of foreign dye-stuffs, an industry which originated in England and depended for raw material on England's greatest asset – coal – had been lost to Germany in less than thirty years from the date of original discovery.' By the end of the century the German aniline dye industries were supreme and the German universities were responsible for two-thirds of the world's annual output of original chemical research. Germany had four thousand trained chemists in industry and this 'had all begun in 1862 with the founding of the aniline dye industry' behind which was 'the educational system of the country, and not least, the original Giessen laboratory of 1825 and the vision of von Humboldt'.[28] Meanwhile in Britain the industrial research laboratories remained in their infancy.

The rise of the provincial universities

Nevertheless, the later years of the nineteenth century saw the beginnings of what may now be seen as a fundamental change in the relation of the university to the economy in Britain. Though modified at every point by the older Oxford and Cambridge ideals of a liberal education for gentlemen, this has gradually and belatedly widened the conception of admissible professions and vocations, and has come to some sort of terms with the applied sciences and business studies. At bottom, these changes, in Britain as elsewhere, represent the establishment of science as an institution, incorporated into the universities as an integral part of their life as teaching and research bodies, and into industry as a widening range of new professions concerned with the practical development of fundamental research in the sciences and its application to industrial processes.

The story is mainly a provincial one – provincial aspirations, provincial pressures and provincial responses. By the end of the century, after fifty years of fitful and transient attempts, there were universities firmly established in the provincial cities.

Among the forces which led to this situation were the Mechanics Institutes. These had their origins in Glasgow in the eighteenth century and came to London in 1805 with George Birkbeck, the founder of the London Mechanics Institution whose name was subsequently given to one of the colleges of the University of London. The movement spread throughout the country during the first half of the century until in 1853, for example, there were no less than 100 branches of a union of Institutes in Yorkshire alone, with twenty thousand members. However, although the Institutes had begun as places for the further education of young artisans and ambitious young workers, they gradually fell into the hands of middle and lower-middle-class students, putting decreasing emphasis on technological instruction and more on 'liberal education'.

It was in the 1850's that a suggestion was made for a new national industrial university with the Mechanics Institutes as constituent colleges. It failed, but the underlying aim of providing for technological education did not exhaust itself and the needs of the provinces were becoming increasingly recognised. Thus, for example in the 1860's, Matthew Arnold was arguing that 'we must plant faculties in the eight or ten principal seats of population, and let the students follow lectures there from their own homes with whatever arrangements for their living they and their parents choose. It would be everything for the great seats of population to be thus made intellectual centres as well as mere places of business; for the want of this at present, Liverpool and Leeds are mere overgrown provincial towns, while Strasbourg and Lyons are European cities.'[29] And the reform movements in Oxford and Cambridge also led to attempts at colonisation of the provinces through the University Extension movement which has continued to the present day.

Nottingham and Sheffield both exemplified the influence of the Oxford and Cambridge Extension movements. Nottingham was the first town to run an extension course. It was organised in a re-built Mechanics Institute and held under the direction of Henry Sidgwick of the University of Cambridge. Out of this extension movement and with the support of trade unionists, private donors and the civic authorities (who levied a $1^1/_2$d rate on the town for the purpose) a University College was founded in 1881. This, like Exeter, Southampton, Leicester and Hull, was a college which prepared students for the examinations of the University of London until it received an independent charter after the Second World War.

But the main thrust came from the industrial cities themselves. In 1869 Leeds proposed to establish a college of science in Yorkshire, which was built by 1874. The Newcastle College of Physical Science dates from 1871. Josiah Mason College opened in Birmingham in 1880. A College of Science for the West of England was founded at the same time in Bristol and the University College of Liverpool began in 1882, according to Armytage 'in a disused lunatic asylum in the midst of a slum district'. In Manchester, Owen's College, which still had only 116 students in 1867, became the first constituent college of the new Victoria University in 1880 with the backing of its energetic professor of chemistry H. E. Roscoe and the powerful support of Mark Pattison of Oxford and Lyon Playfair. Liverpool joined in 1884 and Leeds (the Yorkshire College of Science) in 1887, both bringing with them a local medical school.

The character of the provincial universities thus derives from the convergence of two nineteenth-century movements. One was local – a desire to bring the perceived benefits of metropolitan liberal culture to civic life, and this was supported by the University Extension movements of the ancient English universities. The other was a national movement which aimed to bring higher technological education into the service of industry. It was inspired by fear of industrial competition from the Continent, appreciation of the industrial benefits gained by Germany, France and Switzerland from their polytechnics and admiration of the American land grant colleges.

The slow and tentative assimilation of an older aristocratic and gentle-manly conception of education with the newer and more practical orientations representing a response to industrial needs was therefore reflected in a fusion of contrary educational philosophies which gave technological study a place in university life. 'The leaders of educational thought in Britain were under the spell of Newman's lectures, Pattison's essays and Jowett's teaching. It is not surprising, therefore, that they opposed the segregation of technological education into separate institutions. The manager-technologist must receive not only a vocational training: he must enjoy also the benefits of a liberal education; or at least he must rub shoulders with students who are studying the humanities.'[30] On the other hand, there was also opposition in the same circles to the idea that the lower middle classes needed the cultural benefits of higher education and so, contrarily, 'the most powerful argument for the new university colleges was one based on their utilitarian value'.[31]

Thus technology established itself in the civic colleges in Scotland and in London and finally spread to the older English universities to become an integral part of the university curriculum. At the same time, however, tech-nological and applied studies never gained the prestige accorded to them in either the separate technological institutions of Germany or France, or such American institutions as the Massachusetts Institute of Technology or 'Cal. Tech.'. Once established, the provincial universities tended everywhere to shift the scope and balance of their stud/es to resemble as closely as possible the norms set by Oxford and Cambridge. But they lacked the wealth,[32] the independence of cultural tradition, the social status and the political connec-tions to offer a serious challenge to the entrenched position of the ancient foundations.

British universities in the twentieth century

We 'have tried to show that the British universities developed slowly in the nineteenth century and entered the twentieth century as a restricted and élitist group of institutions. In England Oxford and Cambridge stood at the centre, the University of London had emerged as a federation of hetero-geneous colleges in the capital, and university charters were being granted to colleges in the major provincial cities. Scotland, meanwhile, had four well-established universities. The system as a whole mustered only 20,000 students out of a population of forty million.

In the twentieth century there has been more substantial growth from this tiny base. The number of students has risen from twenty-five thousand before the first war to twice as many between the wars and nearly eight times as many at the present time, so that in 1966–67 there were nearly one hundred and ninety thousand university students on full-time or 'sandwich' courses.[33]

The two wars stimulated this growth; partly because they created climates of opinion favourable to reform in general and to educational reform in particular and thus increased the effective demand for university places, and partly because they dramatised the utility of university research for military and industrial efficiency. Also underlying these accelerating forces of war there has been the steady pressure from beneath, made possible by the increase in the number of grammar schools which followed the creation of a national system of secondary schooling in 1902.[34] At the same time the demand for graduates has strengthened slowly as the managerial and professional occupations have expanded in government, in industry and in the educational system itself.[35] The universities, moreover, not only supply a larger market for graduate teachers; during the course of the century they have also increased their ratio of staff to students as they have become centres of every kind of research in the sciences and the arts.

Although the growth of the universities has been continuous throughout the century, and although the two wars accelerated the trends, it is clear that social and economic developments since the second war have surpassed all previous pressures towards expansion and will continue to do so. The change in opinion about the scale of provision of university and other forms of higher education since the mid-1950's is quite unprecedented.[36] At that time only a very small minority of radical expansionists were ready to contemplate 10 per cent of the age group in universities. By the time the Robbins Committee reported, middle-class opinion, including academic opinion, as we show in Chapter 11, had already shifted to accept the idea of educating some 20 per cent of the age group to this level by 1980. Behind this shift lie fundamental changes of political and social outlook: aspirations to this higher standard of education are now taken for granted in the middle classes and are penetrating into working-class families, especially those in which the parents have themselves had some experience of education beyond the minimal school-leaving age. And the old fear of industrial decline, with its invidious international comparisons and its acceptance of the theory that skill and training make the largest marginal contributions to the productivity of the economy, have resulted in political support for the ever-growing higher education budget.

Moreover, the older class conceptions of education have been eroded rapidly in the post-war years. Statistics of inequality of educational opportunity have become popular knowledge and have turned access to the universities into an almost commonplace criterion of distributive justice. This motif has been strengthened by the economic aim of eliminating waste of potential talent in the work force and particularly by the insistent attack on the assumption of a restricted 'pool of ability' which has come to be seen as a rationalisation for preserving class privileges. In this process the ideological defence of an élite system of universities has been seriously undermined and policy for the development of higher education has come to be seen more in terms of economic feasibility.

The course of expansion has had three phases. The first began around the turn of the century with the foundation of the civic universities and continued after the First World War until the depression years of the 1930's. The second, which was more rapid, occurred after the Second World War. Unlike its predecessor, it did not fade out but instead has formed the basis for the third phase in the 1960's and 1970's. At the beginning of the first period Oxford and Cambridge were numerically, as well as academically and socially, preponderant. By the end of it, just before the second war, they had been surpassed in numbers of students and staff by the major Redbrick universities and overtaken by London. Within the first decade of the century Birmingham, Bristol, Leeds,[37] Manchester[38] and Sheffield[39] all gained charters as independent universities; together with Durham and its Newcastle constituent, they began to lead the expansion of the British university system and they have continued to do so ever since.

The second period of growth after the second war included the granting of independent charters to the former provincial university colleges at Nottingham, Southampton, Hull, Exeter and Leicester.[40] The last-named became independent in 1957 bringing the total number of British universities to twenty-one. Meantime the establishment of the University College of North Staffordshire at Keele[41] without tutelage from London was the precursor of a much publicised movement at the end of the 1950's to found new universities with independence *ab initio*. The first of these, Sussex,[42] admitted its first students in 1961. Subsequently East Anglia, York, Essex,[43] Kent, Warwick and Lancaster have received charters and four new Scottish universities have been formed, one at Strathclyde (out of the Royal College of Science at Glasgow), one at Stirling, Heriot Watt in Edinburgh and one at Dundee. No doubt these new foundations will contribute greatly to the third phase of expansion. But in the second phase they counted for little. The bulk of the expansion between 1947 and 1964 was borne by the established universities in the industrial provincial cities, by London, by Wales and by the ancient universities in England and Scotland.

Numerically a more important addition has been the translation of nine English colleges of advanced technology to university status.[44] Their incorporation into the university system during the three or four years after the Robbins Report has produced a group which is larger than either the new English universities, the ancient English colleges or the University of Wales. Moreover, with their heavy concentration on engineering and the applied sciences and their keenness to develop the sandwich type of course, they have in some respects a greater claim to newness than the new universities. Academically the new universities have distinguished themselves from the older foundations in their attempts to move away from the dominant single-subject honours degree to wider and more flexible curricula and this has had its organisational counterpart in a blurring of the lines and reduction of the autonomy of disciplinary departments. But the new technological universities embody a no less radical departure in the stress which they put on co-operation with local industry and particularly the development of teaching arrangements interposed and in partnership with industrial experience.

With the establishment of engineering studies in Cambridge and London and the rise of the provincial universities at the end of the nineteenth century technological studies found their way into the British university system. But their scope was limited by the persistence of the older established ideas of liberal education, and technological education continued for the most part in sub-university institutions. In the twentieth century the struggle on behalf of technology has continued and a new chapter in the story opened with the Robbins proposals for expanding this sector of university life. The new group of technological universities also represents a radical departure from tradition in that the institutions concerned are specialised from the outset.[45]

The CATs were designated in 1957 (except for Bristol in 1960, and Brunel in 1962) and were taken from the control of the local education authorities, who had nurtured them from their nineteenth-century origins, to be given independent status under the direct control of the Ministry of Education in 1962. Robbins' recommendation that they be upgraded to university status was accepted (though not the linked proposal for the creation of five Special Institutions for Scientific and Technological Education and Research) and all except Chelsea, which has been absorbed into the University of London, now have an independent charter. Only two of them have retained the technological label in their titles–Loughborough University of Technology and Bath University of Technology. The Bradford Institute of Technology has become the University of Bradford, Northampton College of Advanced Technology has become the City University, Battersea College of Technology has become the University of Surrey and has moved to Guildford, Brunel College has moved ten miles away from Acton to a larger site near Uxbridge as Brunel University.[46]

The State and the universities

The expansion of the universities in the twentieth century in Britain and the beginning, since the publication of the Robbins Report in 1963, of their incorporation into a emerging system of higher education, has involved massive government patronage of education of the kind which began much earlier in other countries. Higher education in Britain in the nineteenth century was largely a matter of private enterprise, though lacking the competitive character which resulted in the rapid expansion of the American system from the middle of that century. In the twentieth century the state has provided almost all of the resources for expansion.

Thus the role of the state has been transformed. For the Victorians the task was to re-examine and to widen narrow liberal definitions of state responsibility ('interference'). Now it is to manage purposeful social change, to administer development and to reconcile competing interest groups. Then the universities were small, private and inconsequential for the mass of the population, exercising the freedom of irrelevance. Now they are a crucial foundation of the economy, conceived since Robbins as integral to a higher education system which supplies scientific man-power and technological innovation for economic growth and widening opportunities to a rising proportion of the population. They are thus also of crucial political import-ance and are in any case pressed into responsibility, or at least responsiveness, to the state as the manager of economic growth, and the dispenser of indi-vidual opportunity for participation.

Increasing state control over higher education is the common theme of current discussion and, in his standard work on the modern history of the relation between the universities and government, Berdahl summarises the general tendency in Britain. 'From having almost no contact with the instruction of its citizens before the nineteenth century, the state has now reached a position in which it is necessarily interested in every facet of education from the primary school to the university.'[47] No doubt this is an over-simplification. For example, in explaining 'the low level of thought and life' characteristic of both Oxford and Cambridge in the seventeenth and eighteenth centuries G. M. Trevelyan attributes the major responsibility to the 'control and outside interference exercised by King and Parliament'.[48] But, until at least the middle of the nineteenth century, positive state inter-ference with the pre-industrial English universities was concerned with regulating their life and practices in the interests of Anglican religious orthodoxy. Freedom to develop non-conformist and industrial university institutions was negatively hampered, on the other hand, by a failure of state support which contrasts markedly with German and French experi-ence. It was reluctant and niggardly in relation to industrial needs and, as we have seen, was confined largely to emancipating the don and his univer-sity from constricting clerical influences. However, it has become clear in the present century in Britain that the incorporation of the sciences and the adaptation of higher learning to an industrial, democratic and secular age involves much more than a dismissal of clerics. Whether necessary or not, the form of secondary education, the creation of industrial and military research organisations, the provision of student scholarships, academic salaries, and university buildings and research facilities have in fact trans-formed the scale and character of state intervention.

It would of course be highly misleading to suppose that the magnitude of this transformation was foreseen at the beginning of the century. What actually happened was that means were sought of channelling funds to the universities which paid every possible respect to the interests of both academic freedom and the tax-payer's pocket. The principle was that of the 'buffer or shock absorber': the mechanism, established in 1919, was the University Grants Committee.

The terms of reference of the U.G.C. as laid down in a Treasury minute in 1919 were 'to enquire into the financial needs of university education in the United Kingdom and to advise the government as to the application of any grants that may be made by Parliament to meet them'. In 1952 the following words were added, 'to collect, examine and make available information related to university education throughout the United Kingdom and to assist, in consultation with the universities and other bodies concerned, the preparation and execution of such plans for the development of the universities as may from time to time be required in order to ensure that they are fully adequate to national needs'.

This reformulation of U.G.C. functions raises at every point fundamental issues about the idea of a university, the meaning of phrases like 'academic freedom', 'national needs' and 'plans for development' which will form part of our discussion of the characteristics of British universities in the next chapter. Here we shall confine ourselves to the formal relations between the universities and the state.

A recent publication of the University Grants Committee contains a succinct description of the principle of these relations:

'There is no doubt that in the early days, when relationships between the Government and the universities were being tentatively and gradually established, the "buffer" concept was advantageous to both sides. It relieved the Government of assuming direct responsibility for the universities, and it safeguarded the universities from political interference. More positively, it was an earnest of the Government's willingness to provide money for the universities "without strings", and it enabled the universities to enjoy public funds without the fear that the gift might turn out to be a Greek one.'[49]

The key to the working of the principle is again accurately described in the Committee's passage on its relation to the Government:

'From 1919 until 1963 the University Grants Committee was the direct concern of the Treasury. Its staff consisted of Treasury Civil Servants. It was always clear, and totally accepted, that once they "came to the University Grants Committee" these Civil Servants were the servants of the Committee and not of the Treasury. But they knew the Treasury, its habits, its ways of thinking; and they knew personally the individual Treasury officials with whom they were dealing on the Committee's behalf.

'Not only was this fact a source of immense strength to the Committee, through its officials and their day-to-day dealings with their Treasury colleagues. More, the authority of the Treasury was behind the Committee in its dealings both with the Government and with, for example, the Public Accounts Committee. The Treasury was deeply committed to the "buffer" principle, and guarded most jealously the Committee's independent status. A succession of highly paid Treasury officials, among whom the most determined was Sir Edward (now Lord) Bridges, defended with all their acumen and experience the autonomy of the universities, and of the Committee, against every attack from whatever quarter.'[50]

What in short is being described here is an historical continuity, within the framework of a recently completed parliamentary democracy of *de facto* control of élitist institutions by likeminded members of the élite. It has worked through fifty years of Conservative and Labour governments because, as the Committee put it, 'it has been rooted and grounded in one indispensable element, reciprocal confidence between the bodies concerned'.[51] The observer might specify the tribute more closely to the extraordinary stability of the British system of élite recruitment to positions of political, industrial or bureaucratic power.

The growth of state power expresses itself dramatically in Table 1 which shows the income of universities from 1920 to 1968 distributed by their source.

Since the creation of the U.G.C. the total income of the universities on the grant list has risen from just over £3 million in 1920–21 to over £216 million in 1968: and these figures do not include non-recurrent grants by parliament for new building and equipment which in 1966–67 amounted to a further £77.4 million[52] bringing total expenditure in that year to something near £270 million. There are two essential features of the statistics. First, the rate of growth in the 1960's, associated of course with the Robbins enquiry and the redefinition of higher education which has increased the number of universities from twenty-four to forty-four in the last ten years, dwarfs all previous experience. Second, an increasing proportion of this now vast income is provided by the state. Direct parliamentary grants alone account for 82.7 per cent. The local authorities contribute 0.2 per cent and in any case take out through rate charges more than they put in.[53] Oxford and Cambridge 'are still regarded as a source of revenue by local authorities'[54] and the nineteenth-century foundations now have a 'favourable balance of trade': for example the University of Birmingham in 1963–64 received £56,150 in contributions from the neighbouring cities and paid out £198,578 in rates.[55] Thus the expansion of university studies, especially in the natural and applied sciences (to which more recently must be added a tremendous growth of the social sciences[56]), has almost completely eroded the financial basis of autonomy, converting the universities to this extent into state dependencies and thus placing the burden of maintaining academic freedom on the beliefs and sentiments of those who wield power in the modern system of government and administration. The question therefore becomes: who are the power wielders and, more specifically, who exercises what kind of power in, over and through the University Grants Committee? We shall return to this question in Chapter 4.

Table 1 Sources of university income, 1920–68.

Year	Total income of universities £	Sources as percentage of total income					
		Parliamentary grants	Grants from L.A.'s	Fees	Endowments	Donations and subscriptions	Other sources (a)
1920–21	3,020,499	33.6	9.3	33.0	11.2	2.7	3.3
1923–24	3,587,366	35.5	12.0	33.6	11.6	2.5	4.8
1928–29	5,174,510	35.9	10.1	27.8	13.9	2.4	6.9
1933–34	5,593,320	35.1	9.2	32.8	13.7	2.4	6.8
1938–39	6,712,067	35.8	9.0	29.8	15.4	2.6	7.4
1946–47	13,043,541	52.7	5.6	23.2	9.3	2.2	7.0
1949–50	22,009,735	63.9	4.6	17.7	5.7	1.7	6.4
1953–54	31,112,024	70.5	3.6	12.0	4.3	1.6	8.0
1955–56	36,894,000	72.7	3.1	10.8	3.8	0.9	8.7
1961–62	74,113,000	76.5	2.1	9.0	2.7	0.9	8.9
1964–65	124,161,715	79.9	1.4	8.1	1.9	0.6	8.1
1967–68	216,204,321	72.9[b]	0.9	7.4		1.7	17.1[b]

(a) includes payment for research contracts from 1955–6.
(b) The amount of parliamentary grant shows an apparent drop in 1967–8 because for that year only grants from the Exchequer are distinguished in the statistics. Grants and payments for research from other government departments are included in 'other sources'. Previously all parliamentary grants had been grouped together.

Source: U.G.C. Returns and information.

Notes

1 See Joseph Ben-David, 'The Growth of the Professions and the Class System', in R. Bendix and S. M. Lipset (eds.), *Class, Status and Power*, 2nd ed., The Free Press, 1966.

2 H. Rashdall, *The Universities of Europe in the Middle Ages*, Oxford, The Clarendon Press, 1936, Vol. 3, pp. 89–90.

3 'If the universities, through the persons of Grocyn, Colet and Erasmus and through Cranmer, Latimer and Ridley, had played a part in the Renaissance and the Reformation, they had little to do with the Scientific and still less with the Industrial Revolution. Trinity College, Cambridge, had offered house-room to Newton, though even he, it is said, had worked out his main discoveries before he returned as a fellow. Glasgow University had lent working space to James Watt to save him from the restrictive regulations of the City Corporation. Apart from him, almost the only inventor connected with a university was the Rev. Edmund Cartwright, sometime fellow of Magdalen College, Oxford, and inventor of the power loom, a wool-combing machine, a precursor of the bicycle and even a form of internal combustion engine; but he resigned his fellowship to marry an heiress long before he turned his mind to mechanical invention.' H. J. Perkin, *Key Profession: The History of the Association of University Teachers*, Routledge and Kegan Paul, 1969, p. 4.

4 The percentage of students drawn from within thirty miles in 1908–9 were, at Bristol 87 per cent, Leeds 78 per cent, Liverpool 75 per cent, Manchester 73 per cent, University College London, 66 per cent.

5 These degree courses were, of course, directed especially towards the newer technological and professional occupations created by industrialism, such as chemistry, electrical engineering, state grammar school teaching and the scientific civil service.

6 Eric Ashby, *Universities: British, Indian, African*, Weidenfeld and Nicolson, 1966, p. 7. Ashby also points out that all was not well with the Scottish universities, especially in their government and their adherence to out-dated curricula (see pp. 23–4).

7 A book like Sir Walter Moberly's *The Crisis in the University*, SCM Press, though published as recently as 1949, would almost never be mentioned as relevant to the 'crisis' as defined in contemporary discussion, precisely because of its preoccupation with the religious tradition of the universities.

8 John Sparrow, *Mark Pattison and the Idea of the University*, Cambridge University Press, 1967, pp. 82–3.

9 W. H. G. Armytage, *Civic Universities*, Ernest Benn, 1955, p. 167.

10 John Henry Newman, *The Idea of a University*, Doubleday, 1959, p. 259.

11 Quoted by Armytage, *op. cit.*, p. 147.

12 There were about twenty-five professors in Oxford in 1850.

13 'It is true that before 1850 Cambridge had effectively lost contact with lawyers and doctors whose professional education took place elsewhere.' Sheldon Rothblatt, *The Revolution of the Dons: Cambridge and Society in Victorian England*, Faber and Faber, 1968, p. 249.

14 W. H. G. Armytage, *op. cit.*, p. 202.

15 John Sparrow, *op. cit.*, pp. 66–7.

16 There had been a college set up at Durham in 1656 by Cromwell, but it never obtained university powers, mainly because of Oxford and Cambridge opposition, and was swept away during the Restoration. Not until nearly two centuries later was the university founded, and then not without considerable Church

opposition. The Bishop of Exeter, one of the wealthy oligarchs in the Chapter of Durham, held the view that 'to establish a university from the Chapter incomes was unwise, for it would only increase discontent in the country and add to the excess of educated people for whom there were already too few positions' (Armytage, p. 175). The Chapter did in the end co-operate by enfranchising their South Shields estates for £80,000 which enabled them to give the university £3,000 a year. A charter was granted empowering the new university to award degrees in 1837.

17 Cf. D. V. Glass, 'Education and Social Change in Modern England', in M. Ginsberg (ed.), *Law and Opinion in England in the 20th Century*, Stephens, 1959.

18 D. S. Cardwell, *The Organisation of Science in England*, Heinemann, 1951, p. 45.

19 Sheldon Rothblatt, *op. cit.*, p. 268.

20 *Ibid.*, pp. 91–2.

21 David S. Landes, *The Unbound Prometheus: technological change and industrial development in Western Europe from 1750 to the present*, Cambridge University Press, 1969, p. 345.

22 *Ibid.*, p. 346.

23 Charles Babbage, *The Exposition of 1851*, quoted by Cardwell, *op. cit.*, pp. 60–1.

24 D. S. Cardwell, *op. cit.*, pp. 80–1.

25 *Ibid.*, p. 81.

26 Sir Eric Ashby, *Technology and the Academics*, London, Macmillan, 1958, Chapter 3.

27 D. S. Cardwell, *op. cit.*, p. 80.

28 *Ibid.*, p. 136.

29 M. Arnold, *Schools and Universities on the Continent*, London, 1868, p. 276 (quoted by Armytage, *op. cit.*, p. 220).

30 Eric Ashby, 'On Universities and the Scientific Revolution', in A. H. Halsey *et al.* (eds.), *Education, Economy and Society*, The Free Press, 1961, p. 220.

31 *Ibid.* 'The utilitarian argument', he adds, 'was less persuasive in Wales. In Aberystwyth and Bangor it was the idea of a university as a place for liberal education which aroused public support.' See B. E. Evans, *The University of Wales: A Historical Sketch*, Cardiff, 1953.

32 Their private endowments were modest and by the end of the First World War were negligible by comparison with governmental grants. The income from endowments in 1919–20 was, at Birmingham University £7,500, Bristol University £8,000, Leeds University £7,100, Manchester University £30,500. U.G.C. Returns, 1919–20, Cmd. 1263, H.M.S.O.

33 The latest official estimates, based on projections of recent numbers of qualified school leavers, anticipate four hundred and sixty thousand university students by 1981. *Student Numbers in Higher Education in England and Wales*, Education Planning Paper No. 2, H.M.S.O., 1970.

34 The percentage of seventeen-year-olds in full-time education doubled from 2 per cent to 4 per cent between 1902 and 1938 and rose further to 15 per cent by 1962.

35 The professional class grew from a little over 4 per cent in 1911 to a little under 8 per cent in 1959. See G. Routh, *Occupation and Pay in Great Britain, 1906–60*, Cambridge University Press, 1965.

36 For a graphic description of the changing climate of opinion see Noel Annan, 'Higher Education', in B. Crick (ed.), *Essays on Reform 1967: A Centenary Tribute*, Oxford University Press, 1967.

37 A. H. Shimmin, *The University of Leeds*, Cambridge University Press, 1954.

38 H. B. Charlton, *Portrait of a University 1851–1951*, Manchester University Press, 1951.

39 A. D. Chapman, *The Story of a Modern University: A History of the University of Sheffield*, Oxford University Press, 1955.

40 J. Simmonds, *New University*, Leicester University Press, 1958.

41 W. B. Gillie, *A New University: A. D. Lindsay and the Keele Experiment*, Chatto and Windus, 1960.

42 Sir John Fulton, *Experiment in Higher Education*, Tavistock Pamphlet No. 8, 1964; and David Daiches (ed.), *The Idea of a New University: An Experiment in Sussex*, André Deutsch, 1964.

43 A. E. Sloman, *A University in the Making*, British Broadcasting Corporation, 1964.

44 These are Aston, Bath, Bradford, Brunel, Chelsea, City, Loughborough, Salford and Surrey.

45 For a discussion of the technological universities see R. A. Buchanan, 'The Technological Universities', *Universities Quarterly*, December 1966. Mr. Buchanan discusses ten ex-CATs by excluding Scotland and Northern Ireland but including the Welsh College of Advanced Technology at Cardiff which has its origin in a science and arts school dating from 1866. It became a CAT in 1957.

46 A discussion of the staff of the ex-CATs by Oliver Fulton is included in Appendix A below.

47 R. O. Berdahl, *British Universities and the State*, Cambridge University Press, 1959, p. 105.

48 G. M. Trevelyan, *British History in the Nineteenth Century*, Longmans, 1923.

49 U.G.C., *University Development 1962–67*, Cmnd. 3820, H.M.S.O., 1968, para. 554.

50 *Ibid.*, paras. 576–7.

51 *Ibid.*, para. 555.

52 The total capital expenditure on buildings and equipment from public and private sources has risen from less than £30 millions in the 1952–7 quinquennium to £99 millions in 1957–62 and to –295 millions in 1962–7.

53 See the figures compiled by the Estimates Committee in their Fifth Report for 1964–5, H.C.P. 283, H.M.S.O., 1965. As Lord Bowden has remarked, this report 'was a most important and illuminating document which has . . . been forgotten much too soon'.

54 *Ibid.*, p. xxxvi.

55 *Ibid.*, Appendix G, p. 275.

56 Between the end of the last but one quinquennium (1961–2) and the end of the last (1966–7) undergraduates in faculties of social studies increased by 181.2 per cent and postgraduates by 149 per cent. Comparable increases for the total student body were 62.3 per cent and 65.1 per cent. The numbers were:

		1961–2	*1966–7*
Undergraduates	Social Studies	10,554	29,675
	Total	93,781	152,230
Graduates	Social Studies	1,907	4,749
	Total	19,362	31,973

Source: U.G.C., *op. cit.*, Table 5, p. 19.

Excerpt from
ENGLISH CULTURE AND THE DECLINE OF THE INDUSTRIAL SPIRIT, 1850–1980

Martin J. Wiener

Source: M. J. Wiener, *English Culture and the Decline of the Industrial Spirit, 1850–1980*, Harmondsworth: Penguin, 1981, pp. 16–24.

The shaping of a gentleman

Ironically, the educational system that Arnold's father did so much to shape played a leading role in fixing this separation, and the attitude and values that went with it, upon English society. The public school was of particular importance, for this "peculiar institution" unique to England had become by the end of Victoria's reign the shared formative experience of most members of the English elite. For all their vaunted independence, the public schools, through new institutions like Headmasters' Conference, converged on a common model. Despite the absence of state direction, they came to constitute a system,[1] one that separated the next generation of the upper class from the bases of Britain's world position – technology and business.

The decade of the eighteen-sixties had seemed to be destined to be a time of sweeping reform in secondary education. A spreading awareness of the need to modernize the unsupervised hodgepodge of existing schools led to the creation of two royal commissions. The Clarendon [Public Schools] Commission, appointed in 1861, was to examine the nine most prestigious endowed schools, and the Taunton [Schools Inquiry] Commission, created three years later, was to look at all the other endowed schools. Their reports did indeed lead to acts of Parliament, but the thrust for fundamental reform was deflected. The main effect of the prolonged attention was to establish the nine ancient public schools, more or less as they were, as *the* model of secondary education for all who aspired to rise in English society. After examining in detail the faults of the public schools, the Clarendon Commission turned to their greater merit:

> These schools have been the chief nurseries of our statesmen; in them, and in schools modelled after them, men of all the various classes that make up English society, destined for every profession and career, have been brought up on a footing of social equality, and have contracted the most enduring friendships, and some of the ruling habits of their lives; and they have had perhaps the largest share in moulding the character of an English Gentleman.[2]

There was change – new schools appeared, new subjects were introduced, improvements in physical facilities and innovations in school procedures were made – but only the minimum necessary to preserve and extend the social dominance of the public school pattern. This aim was attained: In the later nineteenth century the sons of the middle classes flocked in increasing numbers into schools modeling themselves upon the "Clarendon nine." What was usually desired was expressed in a fictional parent's enthusiasm for the reinvigorated Shrewsbury: "Just the very place: new buildings, old traditions. What could possibly be better?"[3]

The most obvious example of the public schools' detachment from the modern world was the virtual absence of science of any sort from their curricula. In the teaching of science the public schools lagged far behind schools of lesser social standing. It was first taught in private and Dissenting academies in the eighteenth century, and by Victoria's accession it was a normal part of the curriculum in most such schools, and in many grammar schools.[4] Yet it did not penetrate the schools of the upper class for some years thereafter, and then only over determined obstruction.

At Rugby, the pioneer of public school science instruction, the first science teachers were barely tolerated. J. M. Wilson, an astronomer, was allowed after 1859 to offer four hours a week of "natural philosophy" as long as it did not interfere with the fourteen hours he put in on algebra, geometry, and trigonometry. For this science instruction no room could be found on the premises at Rugby, and "the experiments were performed out of sight, in the cloakroom of the Town Hall a hundred yards away down the road from the school, with the apparatus locked up in two cases so that the townspeople could use the space for other purposes at night."[5] This was the situation the Public Schools Commission found at the most scientifically minded of the leading schools! Even after the commission urged the development of science instruction, the pace of change was slow. Graham Wallas (1858–1932), at Shrewsbury between 1871 and 1877, later recalled that "we had no laboratory of any kind, and I never heard in my time of any Shrewsbury boy receiving a science lesson."[6]

This neglect of science rested on an educational ideology. Its positive face was exaltation of the Greek and Roman classics as the basis of any liberal education. Its negative side was a fear of science as antireligious, which sharply waned as the century drew on, and an association of science with vulgar industry, artisans, and commercial utility, which did not diminish so readily. Headmasters, more or less equating the classics (together with Christianity, of course) with civilization and ideal mental training, were eloquent in defense of a purely classical curriculum, and they were backed up by most educated persons of note. No less a figure than Gladstone added his views: "What I feel is, that the relation of pure science, natural science, modern languages, modern history and the rest to the old classical training, ought to be founded on a principle . . . I deny their right to a parallel or equal position; their true position is ancillary, and as ancillary it ought to be limited and restrained without scruples."[7]

Most significant for the future, science was linked in the public mind with industry, and this damaged its respectability in upper-class eyes. Industry meant an uncomfortable closeness to working with one's hands, not to mention an all-too-direct earning of money. The question of science teaching was enmeshed in the class system: Despite the tradition of Hooke, Boyle, and their contemporaries of the great days of the Royal Society, it was not until the twentieth century that experimental science was fully accepted again in England as a fit occupation for a gentleman. The fact that the classics were a mark of social class worked to prevent the application of parental pressure for "modern" instruction. As the Taunton Commission concluded in 1868:

> They [the great majority of professional men and poor gentry] would, no doubt, in most instances be glad to secure something more than classics and mathematics. But they value these highly for their own sake, and perhaps even more for the value at present assigned to them in English society. They have nothing to look to but education to keep their sons on a high social level. And they would not wish to have what might be more readily converted into money, if in any degree it tended to let their children sink in the social scale.[8]

Although argument raged in the reviews over the nation's need for education in science, when it came down to the crucial question of one's own sons, the modernists rarely pushed principle to the point of practice. Isambard Kingdom Brunel (1806–59), the greatest engineer of his generation, sent two sons to Harrow, where they were hardly likely to follow their father's profession; T. H. Huxley (1825–95) sent a son to University College School; Lyon Playfair (1818–98), another leading critic of outdated public school curricula, sent one to Cheltenham; and so on.[9] When science teaching finally arrived in the public schools, it came late, marked by a social stigma and a bias against those aspects that bordered on engineering.

Similarly, the public schools resisted calls for particular training to prepare boys for the expanding professions. Vocational preparation – for law,
medicine, or any newer profession – carried the stigma of utility. Edward
Thring (1821–87), of Uppingham, a highly successful headmaster, found
it "absolutely impossible to direct the studies of a great school to this
end [professional education] beyond a certain degree, without destroying
the object of a great school, which is, mental and bodily training in the best
way, apart from immediate gain."[10] Thring was stating a platitude against
which it was extremely difficult for gentlemen to take a stand. One exception was Dean Farrar (1831–1903), who observed that a scientific education
would be useful.

> And no sooner [Farrar wrote] have I uttered the word "useful" than
> I imagine the hideous noise which will environ me, and amid the
> hubbub I faintly distinguish the words, vulgar, utilitarian, mechanical
> . . . Well, before this storm of customary and traditional clamour
> I bow my head, and when it is over, I meekly repeat that it would
> be *more useful* – more rich in practical advantages, more directly
> available for health, for happiness, for success in the great battle of
> life. I for one am tired of this "worship of inutility." One would
> really think it was a crime to aim at the material happiness of the
> human race.[11]

Thring's view remained pedagogical gospel. The weight of prejudice was
heavily against the compatibility of liberal education (increasingly *the* mark
of a gentleman) and utility. Yet if the public school produced exceedingly
few scientists, and even fewer engineers, they did send forth increasing
recruits to the growing ranks of professional men. As landed society entered
its decline, and public schools expanded and increased in number, they
became the nursery of professionals. Their disparagement of specialized and
practical studies reinforced the traditional content of the professional ideal
– the imitation of the leisured landed gentleman – at the expense of the
modern role of the professional as expert.

If the technical skills necessary for professionalism were discouraged
at public school, the world of business was openly disparaged. Pre-Victorian
public schools had been little more than finishing schools for sons of the
landed gentry, with an admixture of farmers' sons and a few town boys.
Aristocratic values were unchallenged, and trade despised. Arnoldian
reforms retained – even deepened – the low valuation of commerce. In *Tom
Brown's Schooldays*, that testament of gratitude to Dr. Arnold, Thomas
Hughes spoke scornfully of England's previous "twenty years of buying
cheap and selling dear." When Tom Brown, son of an idealized country
squire, wishes upon leaving Rugby to "be at work in the world, and not
dawdling away three years at Oxford," he is set straight by a master. Nothing

was a greater vice to Arnold or Hughes than "dawdling," but there was work and there was work:

> You talk of "working to get your living" and "doing some real good in the world" in the same breath. Now, you may be getting a very good living in a profession, and yet doing no good at all in the world, but quite the contrary, at the same time. Keep the latter before you as your only object, and you will be right, whether you make a living or not; but if you dwell on the other, you'll very likely drop into mere money-making.[12]

Despite Thomas Hughes's assertion of the sovereignty of individual character "apart from clothes, rank, fortune, and all externals whatsoever,"[13] no children of businessmen were in evidence at Tom Brown's Rugby, and none of the characters so much as contemplated a commercial career. In a later and very popular novel about Harrow, Horace Vachell's *The Hill* (1905), a businessman's child arrives at school, but under a cloud of suspicion. Though rising by ability to captain of the cricket team, he remains an outsider, and ends by being expelled for dishonesty. "One is sometimes reminded," another boy typically comments, "that he is the son of a Liverpool merchant, born in or about the docks,"[14] Given this stigma, it is hardly surprising that one of the most successful means of resisting the introduction of modern subjects was to associate them with the world of business. When the Taunton Commission was told by the inspector of schools for London that "I have been assured by several men of business that few things would please them better than a successful attack upon classical studies," a potent weapon was handed to the opponents of curricular change.[15]

The public schools gradually relaxed their entrance barriers. Boys from commercial and industrial families, however, were admitted only if they disavowed their backgrounds and their class. However many businessmen's sons entered, few future businessmen emerged from these schools, and those who did were "civilized"; that is, detached from the single-minded pursuit of production and profit.[16] "Somehow or other," the zealous founder of public schools, Nathaniel Woodard (1811–91), had written the bishop of Manchester in 1871, "we must get possession of the Middle Classes . . . and how can we so well do this as through Public Schools?"[17] Although Woodard's ambitious scheme for a vast network of boarding schools to embrace the entire middle class did not go far, the success of the public schools on a more modest and indirect scale gave a new lease on life to traditional social values. Their very physical environment held the urban industrial world at arm's length, and evoked the life of the old landed gentry. Disproportionately, whether new or ancient, they were distant from cities and industrial regions. Southern England had a very high proportion of the most prestigious public schools.[18] New schools were placed, whenever possible, deep in the countryside. Older schools sited in the cities moved out, like Charterhouse to the Surrey Hills. Every public school acquired, or sought to acquire, an estate to ensure its undisturbed rural character.[19] In this endeavor they were ironically assisted by the economic difficulties of the landed aristocracy; particularly after the First World War many large country houses were taken over by old and new public schools.[20]

The ethos of the schools, in keeping with their surroundings, exalted the careers colored by the aristocratic ideals of honor and public leadership – the military, politics, the civil service, and the higher professions. Public school boys made excellent administrators of a far-flung empire, but the training so admirably suited for that task ill fitted them for economic leadership.[21] The public schools nurtured the future elite's political, not economic, abilities, and a desire to maintain stability and order far outweighed the desire to maximize individual or national wealth.

During the second half of the nineteenth century the public schools took a central place in the life of the English upper classes. More than this, although less than one in twenty Englishmen ever passed through them, they became an archetypal national institution. "When we are criticizing its products," noted a typical defender in 1929, "whether by way of praise or blame, it is really to a great extent the English character that we are criticizing."[22] The public schools, observed Roy Lewis and Angus Maude (not unsympathetically) as late as 1949, enjoyed an "invisible empire" among the middle classes, who avidly read the new genre of public school literature.[23] Those who could afford it, sent their sons; those who could not, sought a grammar school as close as possible to the public school model. This latter quest was made easier after 1902, as a state system of secondary education was developed by public school men committed to public school ideals. Soon after it was established in 1899, the secondary school section of the Board of Education came under the control of the Headmasters' Conference.[24] Public school standards became the standards of the section and its officials. The chief official, Sir Robert Morant (1863–1920), who wrote and administered the Education Act of 1902 (for a prime minister with two public school headmasters in his family), "believed," a critic complained in Parliament many years later, "that the best form of education was that which had been given to him at Winchester," and consequently sought to replicate that education as far as practicable throughout the upper reaches of the state system.[25] Supported by nearly all the civil servants involved, this effort succeeded, and the new secondary schools developed a curriculum, an outlook, and forms of organization in line with the ideals of the education of the gentry. This molding of state education, affecting every inhabitant of Britain in one way or another, was a legacy equal in importance to the continued direct education in public schools of the bulk of the country's elite.[26] Through one or the other route, the late-Victorian public school outlook continued to shape British attitudes and values in the twentieth century.

The later-Victorian ancient universities present much the same picture as the public schools. Socially of less significance (most public school boys did not go on to university), they too witnessed a "conservative revolution" beginning in mid-century that revivified them and increased their contribution to the life of the nation, while preserving the essentials of traditional gentry culture. In the eighteen-fifties and sixties, "modern" subjects were scarcely in evidence in the Oxbridge curriculum. Sixteen years after two royal commissions had urged reform, T. H. Huxley could relate to a parliamentary committee the following experience at an Oxford dinner party: "I asked whether it would be a fair thing to say that any one might have taken the highest honours at the university, and yet might never have heard that the earth went round the sun? and all the gentlemen present ["very distinguished university men"] with one consent said 'Yes.'"[27] As with the public schools, very few undergraduates came from business backgrounds. Oxford and Cambridge, even more than the public schools, were precincts reserved for the sons of gentry, clergy, and the more distinguished professions.[28] Both curricula and admissions were widened during the rest of the century, but, as in the public schools, within the context of a reinvigorated ideal of liberal education and the role of the don that perpetuated many attitudes of the past. The "new model" don was reminiscent of the new public school master, a "moral gentleman" who sought to form the character of students; the new ideal of giving moral and spiritual leadership to a materialist society through liberal education was consonant with the ideals of the great headmasters: The ethos of later-Victorian Oxbridge, a fusion of aristocratic and professional values, stood self-consciously in opposition to the spirit of Victorian business and industry: It exalted a dual ideal of cultivation and service against philistine profit seeking.[29] Businessmen were objects of scorn and moral reproval, and industry was noted chiefly as a despoiler of country beauty. Whenever the subject of business arose at Oxford between Tom Brown and his friend Hardy, it was denounced: Hardy despised Carthage as a trading nation and feared that England was going the same way.[30] Well into the twentieth century, undergraduates were regularly discouraged from pursuing commercial careers, and alarms were sounded against the infection of these rarified precincts by vulgar influences from without. The defeat of proposals to abolish compulsory Greek at both universities in 1904 and 1905 revealed, among other things, a continuing determination to suppress the wishes of vulgar commercial elements. So deeply rooted was the disdain for the values represented by commerce and industry that, as Sheldon Rothblatt concluded, "numerous dons and non-resident M.A.'s decided the worth of an academic subject by its usefulness to commerce and industry. In their view almost no subject which could be turned to the benefit of business deserved university recognition."[31]

Like the public schools, later-Victorian Oxford and Cambridge provided a common formative experience for much of the British elite, and at the same time came to represent a *national* way of life. Like the public schools, they became the model for other institutions of education. The civic universities represented an exception to this rule, for they set out to provide a more modern and practical education. They had their successes, but never threw off the lower status that went with their task. Even they frequently imitated Oxbridge practice. Indeed, the post-1960 "Plateglass" universities, the first to seriously challenge the social supremacy of Oxbridge, were closer in many ways to the ancient than to the Victorian foundations. Despite their self-conscious modernity, largely expressed in a great emphasis on the social sciences, they by and large shared Oxbridge's lack of interest in technology and business. The "Plateglass" universities, significantly, were located away from large centers of population, in the cathedral town-country estate setting that had become typical of elite schools. In these cases, physical form followed social and psychological function – the embodiment of an ideal of "civilization" bound up with preindustrial, preurban models – forming an amalgam of an idealized medieval church and a similarly idealized eighteenth-century aristocracy.

Oxbridge institutionalized Victorian resistance to the new industrial world. As Rothblatt reflected, "the disdain of *homo oeconomicus* in Cambridge [and Oxford] was altogether too complete."[32] Oxbridge trained a political leadership with a minimum of interest in or knowledge of the industrial world. Recruits to the higher civil service, for many years predominantly graduates of these two universities, were, Oliver Macdonagh concluded, "almost without exception lacking in scientific, mechanical, technological or commercial training or experience."[33] If Oxbridge insulated the sons of older elites against contact with industry, it also gradually drew sons of industrial and commercial families away from the occupations of their fathers, contributing to a "hemorrhage" of business talent.[34]

The educated young men who did go into business took their antibusiness values with them. As businessmen sought to act like educated gentlemen, and as educated gentlemen (or would-be gentlemen) entered business, economic behavior altered. The dedication to work, the drive for profit, and the readiness to strike out on new paths in its pursuit waned.[35]

Thus, revivified public schools and ancient universities furnished the reformed and cohesive English elite with a way of life and an outlook that gave little attention or status to industrial pursuits. This development set England apart from its emerging rivals, for in neither the United States nor Germany did the educational system encourage a comparable retreat from business and industry.[36] In education, as in the composition and character of its elite, later-Victorian England marked out its own path, foreshadowing its twentieth-century achievements and difficulties.

Notes

1 For a detailed substantiation of this claim, see J. R. de S. Honey, *Tom Brown's Universe: The Development of the Victorian Public School* (London, 1977), ch. 4.

2 *Parl. Papers 1864 20, Report of H. M. Commissioners appointed to inquire into the Revenues and management of certain Colleges and Schools and the Studies pursued and instruction given therein* [hereafter called *Public Schools Commission*] *1*, 56. As the novelist and translator Rex Warner, himself a schoolmaster, observed in a brief popular account, the Clarendon report "is evidence of the complete acceptance of the public school system as the best possible means of education for those who were to be leaders of the country in peace or war." (Rex Warner, *English Public Schools* [London, 1945], 30).

3 Quoted in T. W. Bamford, *The Rise of the Public Schools* (London, 1967), 15.

4 See J. H. Plumb, "The New World of Childhood in the Eighteenth Century," *Past and Present*, no. 67 (May, 1975), 64–95, and Bamford, *Rise of the Public Schools*, 87, 97.

5 Bamford, *Rise of the Public Schools*, 88.

6 Quoted in Martin J. Wiener, *Between Two Worlds: The Political Thought of Graham Wallas* (Oxford, 1971), 6.

7 *Public Schools Commission 2*, 42. J. R. de S. Honey concluded (*Tom Brown's Universe*, 128), "The position of the classics, public schools and in English education in general, was if anything more powerful at the end of the nineteenth century then it had been at the beginning."

8 *Parl. Papers 1868 28, Report of the Schools Inquiry Commission 1*, 17–18.

9 See Bamford, *Rise of the Public Schools*, 105.

10 *Education and School* (1864), quoted in W. J. Reader, *Professional Men* (New York, 1966), 108.

11 F. W. Farrar, "Public School Education," *Fortnightly Review 3* (new series) (March, 1868), 239–40.

12 Thomas Hughes, *Tom Brown's School Days* [1857] (New York, 1968), 46, 276–7. The dean of Lincoln, addressing Wellington College on its fiftieth anniversary, typically described the school as a place where the young might "learn to put honour before gain, duty before pleasure, the public good before private advantage" (*Wellington College Year Book*, 1909, quoted in David Ward, "The Public Schools and Industry in Britain After 1870," *Journal of Contemporary History 2*, no. 3 [July, 1967], 49).

13 Hughes, *Tom Brown*, 54.

14 Quoted in Ward, "Public Schools and Industry," 38.

15 *Schools Inquiry Commission 1*, 18. See E. C. Mack, *Public Schools and British Opinion, 1780–1860* (New York, 1938), 391.

16 See, for example, Rupert Wilkinson and T. J. H. Bishop, *Winchester and the Public School Elite* (London, 1967), passim.

17 Sir John Otter, *Nathaniel Woodard: A Memoir of His Life* (London, 1925), 240. Woodard, a High Church clergyman, was the son of a country gentleman of modest means. See Honey's account of Woodard's and others' efforts to provide public schools for a wider section of the middle classes (*Tom Brown's Universe*, ch. 2).

18 See Honey, ibid., 286.

19 See Bamford, *Rise of the Public Schools*, 16. When cities threatened to encroach, as at Eton and Harrow, expensive defensive measures were taken: Both schools, in effect, sealed off their buildings with a green belt. Harrow's land purchases between 1885 and 1898 were described at the time as a necessary preservative of the invaluable "beauty and dignity" of the school's "rural" setting, upon which "the romantic affection which gathers round an ancient public school" would soon erode (C. Colbeck, quoted in E. W. Henson and G. T. Warner, *Harrow School* [London, 1898], 155).

20 See W. H. G. Armytage, *Four Hundred Years of English Education* (London, 1970), 232.

21 Foreign imitations of the public schools, developing in different societies, moved in different directions. Wilkinson and Bishop, for example, found that comparing their subject, Winchester, with the most fashionable boarding schools in the eastern United States brought out all the more clearly "how often the public schoolboy's outlook on careers resisted the pull of private money-making": "Although the founders of Groton and St. Paul's tried sincerely to emulate the public school way, it has been estimated that the major American boarding schools have sent less than one percent of their boys into government since 1900" – a vastly lower proportion than that at Winchester (Wilkinson and Bishop, *Winchester and the Public School Elite*, 72).

22 Bernard Darwin, *The English Public School* (London, 1929), 28.

23 Roy Lewis and Angus Maude, *The English Middle Classes* (London, 1949), 22, 232.

24 See Brian Simon, "Introduction," in *The Victorian Public School*, ed. Brian Simon and Ian Bradley (London, 1975), 16–17.

25 Chuter Ede, in Parliament, 4 February 1943; quoted in Bamford, *Rise of the Public Schools*, 260.

26 One effect was, in Bamford's view, to delay "lower-class (elementary school) aspirations . . . for a generation and more. With those aspirations went any hope of a massive development of technical and scientific education that the scientists and industrialists had been urging for half a century" (*Rise of the Public Schools*, 261).

27 *Parl. Papers 1868 15, Report of the Select Committee on Scientific Instruction*, 402. In that very year a proposal that the Cambridge colleges should contribute to the establishment of a temporary professorship of experimental physics and a laboratory (that eventually became, with outside money, the Cavendish Laboratory) was foundering before fierce opposition. "A Prussian is a Prussian," said Dr. Phelps, the master of Sidney Sussex, "and an Englishman is an Englishman, and God forbid it should be otherwise" (quoted in Armytage, *Four Hundred Years*, 167).

28 See Michael Sanderson, *The Universities and British Industry, 1850–1970* (London, 1972), 48–50; and Sheldon Rothblatt, *Revolution of the Dons* (London, 1968), 86–7.

29 Philip Elliot (*The Sociology of the Professions* [London, 1972], 52) has summarized this development in Britain: "The ideology of liberal education, public service and gentlemanly professionalism was elaborated in opposition to the growth of industrialism and commercialism. This is one reason why it drew so heavily on the older tradition of gentlemanly leisure and the established professions. It incorporated such values as personal service, a dislike of competition, advertising and profit, a belief in the principle of payment in order to work rather than working for pay and in the superiority of the motive of service."

30 Thomas Hughes, *Tom Brown at Oxford* [1861] (London, 1869), 100–1, 305, 395. See Rothblatt, *Revolution of the Dons*, 244–6, 256–7, 267–73; Sanderson, *The Universities and British Industry*, 51–2.
31 *Revolution of the Dons*, 256–7.
32 Ibid., 273.
33 Oliver Macdonagh, *Early Victorian Government* (London, 1977), 212. Macdonagh noted an "irony" about the creation of the new civil service: "that the radical ideals of open competition and selection of the fittest by examination contests should have been interlinked with the reactionary ideal of education as an experience and an exercise rather than the acquisition of particular skills or knowledge, or being graded according to intellectual attainment." Newman's *Idea of a University*, published almost contemporaneously with the Northcote-Trevelyan report, proved as influential as the latter in shaping the character of the new governing class. The result of the battle launched by Trevelyan and the other education and administrative reformers was, à la 1832, "to enlarge and rebuild, not to destroy or even weaken the exclusive elite" (Macdonagh, *Early Victorian Government*, 212–13).
34 See the statistics on recruitment and later occupations of Oxford and Cambridge undergraduates in Sanderson, *The Universities and British Industry*, 37, 53–4, and Rothblatt, *Revolution of the Dons*, 272–3.
35 See Chapter 7.
36 See David Landes, *The Unbound Prometheus* (Cambridge, 1969), 343–8, and Peter Mathias, *The First Industrial Nation* (London, 1969), 423–4.

UNIVERSITIES AND ELITES
IN MODERN BRITAIN

R. D. Anderson

Source: *History of Universities* X (1991): 225–50.

This paper discusses the relation of British universities to élites and élite formation in the light of some recent general theories about university development, notably those in the collective volume on *The Transformation of Higher Learning, 1860–1930* (1983) edited by Konrad Jarausch, and in Harold Perkin's *The Rise of Professional Society: England since 1880* (1989). From these books, and from other contributors to the debate like Fritz Ringer and Harmut Kaelble, four main points seem to emerge. One is that the years from the 1860s to the1930s form a distinctive period, the middle phase of a transition, in Jarausch's words, 'from traditional elite higher learning to modern mass higher education'. Jarausch sees a 'seismic shift' within this period, as 'a small, homogeneous, elite and pre-professional university turned into a large, diversified, middle-class and professional system of higher learning'.[1] There was a substantial rise in enrolments, but (and this is the second point) the key to expansion remained middle-class demands. Working-class students were few, and some authors have claimed that in this period those poorer students whom tradition had formerly admitted were squeezed out as competition for middle-class positions intensified. Thus Kaelble sees this as the era of 'competitive opportunities', coming between those of 'charitable' and 'welfare' opportunities, with the last phase not starting before 1914. Jarausch too considers that 'only after World War One did conscious attempts to create equality of educational opportunity begin to have an impact on enrollments'. For England, Perkin would put the process a little earlier, seeing the period 1900–1920 as the 'critical turning point' both for the entry of talent from below, and for the process by which 'the university became the normal route to high status and income'.[2]

It is Perkin who discusses most fully the third point, the link between university expansion and the phenomenon of professionalization. In *The*

Origins of Modern English Society 1780–1880 (1969), Perkin examined the triumph of the 'entrepreneurial' over the aristocratic ideal, part of the struggle being to wrest control of education from the hands of the old élite; this was expressed in the two great middle-class university campaigns, for the foundation of the University of London, and for the reform of the ancient universities of Oxford and Cambridge. In this struggle the professional class, especially the intellectuals within it, figured as allies of the entrepreneurs. In Perkin's new book the professionals come to the front of the stage, and since 1880 their ideal of 'trained expertise and selection by merit' has had an ever-increasing grip on status and influence. Part of this story was the third wave of middle-class action, the creation of the provincial or 'civic' universities, with their distinctively scientific and vocational mission. As universities progressively took over the training of the professions, and formal qualifications replaced earlier systems of personal patronage or apprenticeship, universities became key social institutions. By 1930, Perkin argued in his contribution to the Jarausch volume, a 'revolution' had taken place in British higher education, transforming the university from a marginal institution, a 'finishing school for young gentlemen', into 'the central power house of modern industry and society'.[3]

The fourth point is one of the themes of Fritz Ringer's *Education and Society in Modern Europe* (1979): that this period of development (the 'high industrial' phase in his terminology) saw a marked incongruence between the actual needs of industrial society and the aristocratic or pre-industrial values which schools and universities transmitted to the bourgeoisie through the classics and the ideal of liberal education; the gentlemanly ideal gave the professions or public service higher prestige than business, and diverted talent away from the latter.[4] This phenomenon is a well documented one in France, Germany and other countries. Comment on it in Britain also has a long history, going back at least to Matthew Arnold, and both the ancient universities and the boarding 'public schools' which fed into them (for in Britain more than most countries, higher and secondary education cannot be discussed apart) have been praised or blamed, according to taste, for their efficacy in absorbing the new middle classes and their wealth. Recently this argument has been given a new twist by the 'Wiener thesis': Martin Wiener argued in 1981 that the British élite had adopted a set of anti-industrial, anti-urban values which were responsible for the 'decline of the industrial spirit' and the failures of the British economy in the twentieth century. By 1900, wrote Wiener, the 'nation possessed a remarkably homogeneous and cohesive élite, sharing to a high degree a common education and a common outlook and set of values . . . [which] marked a crucial rebuff for the social revolution begun by industrialization'.[5] Many scholarly commentators have been sceptical of Wiener's theory, but it has enjoyed great vogue in political, business, and journalistic circles in Britain. So have the views of Correlli Barnett, who argued in *The Collapse of British Power* (1972) and *The Audit of War* (1986) that the pursuit of an ethos of public service by Britain's governing élite led it first to cultivate imperial illusions instead of accepting the realities of power, and after 1945 to devote Britain's limited resources to the welfare state instead of industrial reconstruction.[6] For both Wiener and Barnett, the public schools were the chief villains of the piece; but the businessmen and neo-liberal politicians who have repeated their indictment of liberal education have directed it almost exclusively against the universities.

The aim here is not to argue that these theories are wrong, but rather to test and refine them. This essay addresses three main points. First, it argues that the chronology of development needs some subdivision, and that significant movement towards wider access and equality of opportunity can be seen well before 1914. Second, it suggests that until a quite recent period the link between universities and élite formation was selective: the university-educated professions were not necessarily those which enjoyed the highest prestige, while for many of the most powerful élites university education remained marginal. The two parts of Perkin's revolution should therefore be separated: democratization of the universities (of a limited kind) can be observed before 1914, but was chiefly associated with the rise of low-status professions like schoolteaching; while university education has become near-mandatory for the general range of middle-class careers only since the Second World War, and the process is not yet complete.

Thirdly, we shall seek to look at British higher education from the periphery rather than the centre, and to stress the element of national and cultural identity in 'élite formation'. It is a weakness of the Jarausch book that its essays—including the useful statistical material compiled by Roy Lowe—only cover England. Thus in a discussion of the social origins of students the 'British' figures for 1870, 1890, and 1910 are in fact those for Oxford which, not surprisingly, show few students from the lower social strata.[7] This parochially English approach is a particular weakness in comparative work, where it can lead to serious distortion, but it is common enough among historians, as is over-concentration on Oxford and Cambridge and the public schools. Michael Sanderson has pointed out, for example, that Wiener's thesis only seems plausible because it ignores the civic universities, which were 'the largest part of the university sector' and 'a prime expression of the industrial spirit, closely linked with industry, drawing their life-blood finance from it, and pumping back research and students to it'—as indeed Sanderson showed in his pioneering book of 1972 on universities and industry.[8] Again, in a recent article on 'The modern university and national values, 1850–1930', Reba N. Soffer swiftly narrows the subject down to the formation of the national élite in Oxford and Cambridge, and specifically to the role of history teaching.[9] But there were 'national values' of other kinds within the British Isles.

The relation between universities and nationalism, their role in the formation of national élites and the promotion or maintenance of distinctive national cultures, is a familiar theme in many parts of Europe. This kind of perspective has rarely been applied to Britain. Yet modern Britain is a multi-national state. Education, at both school and university level, has been central to definitions of national identity, and has been an early subject of the administrative devolution which has been combined, in the complex British political system, with unitary parliamentary representation. Ireland, the greatest problem and the greatest failure of the multi-national state, provides the most obvious example.

Only the briefest summary can be given here of the complex Irish university question. Originally there was only one university in Ireland—Trinity College Dublin, which, though open to students of all denominations since 1793, remained strongly Anglican in spirit. In 1849 the state founded three strictly non-denominational Queen's Colleges, which were intended to provide a university education acceptable to Catholics, and so bind the Catholic élite closer to British rule. These colleges were condemned by the Vatican and the Irish hierarchy, and only the college in Protestant Belfast flourished. This condemnation was followed in 1854 by the creation of a non-governmental Catholic University, which became after varying fortunes University College Dublin. These developments had religious motives, but undoubtedly contributed to the rise of national feeling among the Catholic middle class, and to the creation of a professional and intellectual élite alienated from British values. By the end of the century one cultural aspect of this was Gaelic revivalism. After many controversies, in which the significance of the colleges for the sense of identity and the professional ambitions of the different Irish communities became very clear, the settlement of 1908 combined University College Dublin with the Queen's Colleges at Cork and Galway in the National University of Ireland, while Queen's College Belfast became an entirely separate university. The National University met the longstanding demand of Catholics for a university which reflected their interpretation of Ireland's cultural traditions, and a few years later it duly made a knowledge of the Irish language compulsory for matriculation. As T. H. Moody points out, although the 1908 Act was opposed at the time by Ulster Unionists, and although Queen's University Belfast was to remain faithful to a tolerant and non-sectarian tradition, 'the university settlement of 1908 . . . was in a profoundly significant sense the prelude to the partition of Ireland in 1921'.[10]

After that date, universities in southern Ireland pass outside our scope. But it is anachronistic to treat nineteenth-century Ireland as if it were not part of the British state. The religious implications of the Irish university question made it a centre of controversy in Westminster politics, especially in the 1870s, and both the Queen's University of 1850 (a federal university granting degrees for the Queen's Colleges) and its successor the Royal University of Ireland of 1879 (a purely examining university like the University of London) were taken as models in British university debates. For neither

Irish nor Scottish universities existed in isolation: the influence of Scotland on the foundation of University College London and the English provincial colleges is well known, the state subsidies given in Ireland and Scotland were often cited enviously by proponents of university development in England and Wales, and academic staff circulated freely between the four countries. Students, too, competed for the same national positions, especially through competitive examinations like those for the Indian and administrative civil services, which gave a powerful impetus to the standardization of curricula. In medicine, schoolteaching, the clergy, and many other occupations, the outlying parts of the British Isles produced a quantity of trained brain-power which could not be absorbed locally, and which was exported both to England and to the British Empire.

In Wales, the university question was closely connected with the national revival of the late nineteenth century, and the university movement rested on a powerful 'democratic' myth. The University of Wales of 1893, incorporating the colleges founded at Aberystwyth in 1872 and at Bangor and Cardiff in the 1880s, was claimed to express a national reverence for learning which could be traced back to the days of the Celtic church, and was identified with the Nonconformist, rural, Welsh-speaking, 'peasant' side of Welsh life; it was a university of the people, which turned out schoolteachers and educationists, pastors and poets, rather than lawyers, doctors or businessmen.[11] This was a somewhat misleading image, for much of industrial Wales was also Nonconformist and Welsh-speaking. When the appeal for a Welsh university was first launched in the 1860s, it was the 'elevation' of the middle class and the need to form a native technical élite which were stressed:

> The material wealth and commercial importance of the Principality are every day increasing. Our mines and manufactures, our railways and shipping interests, are rapidly expanding. The demand for educated talent, for scientific acquirements, for engineering skill—in a word, for all the results of a liberal training—is becoming more and more imperative . . . The direction of our large and lucrative undertakings, the chief posts in the country which require superior skill and attainments, are monopolized by strangers.

But with university training, 'the enterprising Welshman, now almost always thrown into the rear, would soon be found successfully competing with the Englishman and the Scotchman for posts of lucrative employment'.[12] In practice, no doubt, the colleges did help to create a functional élite of the type hoped for, as well as a national political and cultural leadership which was well in evidence by 1914. And although Welsh was valued as an academic subject, teaching and social life were conducted in English, for one aim was to prepare Welsh graduates for posts in the wider British sphere.

Scotland had its own 'democratic' myth, well established by the end of the eighteenth century, which stressed the 'popular' character of the universities and the way in which the national élite was drawn from all social classes and parts of the country. Scots prided themselves on the distinctiveness of their universities, which were seen as a point of superiority over England, but because they were already in existence, and no battles for new foundations had to be fought, there was no university question to become the focus of nationalism. Scottish universities were funded relatively generously by the state, and their teaching was effectively remodelled to allow Scots to seize the prizes in British life.[13] This was probably one reason why the Scottish middle classes remained profoundly unionist in modern times. If the Irish universities were one of the irritants which led to the failure of the union of 1801, the Scottish ones maintained a balance of independence and integration which contributed to the success of that of 1707.

The Scots, like the Welsh, were attached to their cultural identity without seeking political separation from the United Kingdom. But unlike the Welsh, they had no major grievances over religion (the Scottish religious situation, though internally divisive, being free from English intervention) or language (Gaelic being marginal geographically, and long seen as a hindrance to social progress rather than an inheritance to be cherished). It would be wrong, however, to suggest that there was no debate about national identity. Scotland's cultural distinctiveness from England had long rested on its religion, but as secularization weakened the force of this, some Scottish intellectuals sought substitutes, whether in philosophy, history or literature. This debate is the subject of G. E. Davie's influential but controversial books *The Democratic Intellect* (1961) and *The Crisis of the Democratic Intellect* (1986). Elite formation is one of Davie's specific themes, for he argues that the Scottish tradition of philosophical education once created, and could create again if it were revived, a national leadership of an organically democratic kind. However, these ideas have not prevailed in official university culture, where assimilation to 'British' norms has generally been preferred.

It would be interesting to explore questions of cultural identity within England itself. Has the role of religion as a divisive force been underestimated? Did the London colleges have an identifiable urban or metropolitan character?[14] Did the civic universities represent a distinctive 'bourgeois', provincial, or entrepreneurial culture, as asserted by many of their historians,[15] or were the new universities captured by the values of the old and assimilated to a national pattern?[16] Here, however, we shall confine discussion to some quantifiable criteria which illustrate the significance of differences within Britain.

The first of these is the rate of expansion. According to Lowe's figures, students in English universities and university colleges rose from 3,385 in 1861 to 26,414 in 1911, and then to 37,255 in 1931.[17] In the nineteenth

Table 1 Scotland: male university students per 1000 population.

	Total	Ratio
1800	*c.* 2850	1.8
1825	*c.* 4250	1.8
1861	3399	1.1
1881	6604	1.6
1911	5924	1.2
1931	7674	1.6
1951	11149	2.2

Sources: For 1800: R. L. Emerson, 'Scottish Universities in the Eighteenth Century, 1690–1800', *Studies on Voltaire and the Eighteenth Century*, 167 (1977), 473. For 1825: R. D. Anderson, *Education and Opportunity in Victorian Scotland: Schools and Universities* (Oxford 1983), 346–7. For 1861–1951: R. D. Anderson, 'Education and Society in Modern Scotland: a Comparative Perspective', *History of Education Quarterly*, 25 (1985), 467.

century, there was a latent demand for university education which the new colleges, locally accessible and cheaper than Oxford and Cambridge, were able to tap. But in 1861, England still had fewer students than Scotland (3,399), with ten times the population. Scottish totals rose to 7,770 in 1911 and 11,072 in 1931.[18] However, these increases were accompanied by general demographic growth, and also covered the period when women were admitted; since women students were generally of the same social class as men, this did not involve any downward social penetration. If women students are left out of account, and university enrolments are related to total population, there was still a large 'real' increase in England. But in Scotland, as Table 1 shows, there seems to have been no fundamental change in the balance between the universities and society between 1800 and the Second World War. Here Jarausch's 'seismic shift' registered low on the Richter scale. Moreover, if the key to the 'modern' university is its relationship with the professions and its service of middle class needs, the Scottish universities became modern well before the 1860s. The combination of general education with vocational training for church, law and medicine was established in the late eighteenth century, and W. M. Mathew's work on Glasgow shows that students from the landed aristocracy declined from thirty-two per cent in the 1740s to seven per cent in the 1830s; by then half the students came from 'industry and commerce' (including many from the working as well as the middle class), and seventy per cent of them were absorbed by the three learned professions.[19]

The proportion of student places to population continued to vary nationally, as is shown in Table 2, which gives the situation in 1910–11. England lagged behind the less industrialized parts of Britain, and this tendency is confirmed by the ratio for 'Northern England', which compares student numbers at Liverpool, Manchester, Leeds and Sheffield with the population

Table 2 U.K.: full-time university students per 1000 population, 1910–11.

	Total	Ratio
England	19617	0.58
Northern England	3246	0.34
Wales	1375	0.68
Scotland	6736	1.4
Ireland	*c.* 3000	0.69

Sources: For England, Wales, and Scotland: *University Grants Committee. Report for the Period 1929–30 to 1934–35* (London 1936), 52–3. For Ireland, estimate based on: *The National University Handbook, 1908–1932* (Dublin 1932), 69, 127; T. W. Moody and J. C. Beckett, *Queen's, Belfast 1845–1949: the History of a University* (2 vols London 1959), ii, 663; R. B. McDowell and D. A. Webb, *Trinity College Dublin, 1592–1952: an Academic History* (Cambridge 1982), 500; Annual Reports of Queen's Colleges, for 1908–9, in PP 1909, XX.

of Lancashire, Cheshire and Yorkshire. These counties had a population of 9.6 million, larger than many European countries, and together formed one of the greatest concentrations of wealth and industry in the world. In their four university colleges there were 3246 students, only about two-thirds of whom were taking a full course leading to graduation. Were these really the power-houses of an industrial society?

The figures in Table 2 correspond to age-cohort participation ratios of around one per cent, rising to perhaps two per cent in Scotland.[20] This was considerably less than the 'middle-class' share of the population, and in this sense universities were highly élitist. But this did not mean that their student body was drawn exclusively from the higher social strata. The social origins of Scottish students are well documented, and Table 3 gives data for Glasgow and Aberdeen in 1910. Here thirty to forty per cent of the students came from below the 'bourgeois' level, their parents being members of the

Table 3 Scotland: parental occupations of students, 1910 (%).

	Glasgow		Aberdeen	
	Male	Female	Male	Female
Professional	26	27	20	24
Businessmen	25	27	13	14
Farmers	3	7	13	20
Intermediate*	20	19	16	12
Manual workers	24	18	14	15
Not known	3	1	26	15
N =	229	88	152	93

*small business, shopkeepers, white collar
Source: Anderson, *Education and Opportunity*, 310–15.

Table 4 Wales: parental occupations of students, 1910 (%).

	Aberystwyth	*Bangor*	*Cardiff*
Professional	24	18	24
Businessmen	7	3	9
Farmers	14	18	6
Intermediate	31	17	30
Manual workers	24	44	32
N =	393	222	388

Source: PP 1913, XVIII, *Royal Commission on the Civil Service. Appendix to Third Report* [Cd. 6740], 309–10.

'intermediate' group, including shopkeepers and clerks, or engaged in manual labour. Comparison with data from other periods shows a significant democratization since the 1860s, but little further change in the 1920s and 1930s.[21] The composition of the manual-worker group also changed: in the nineteenth century, these parents were predominantly traditional artisans, but by 1910, especially at Glasgow, they included skilled factory and engineering workers. At no period did unskilled workers or labourers make much of a showing. But perhaps twenty per cent of Scottish university students could properly be described as 'working class'.

Table 4 shows that in Wales the proportions were even higher. Aberystwyth and Bangor were small towns, with an important slate-quarrying industry at Bangor, while Cardiff was the commercial centre of the South Wales coalfield, and over a third of the Welsh manual-worker fathers listed in this 1910 source were miners or quarrymen. Much depends on definitions, but Jarausch's conclusion that down to 1930 it was only in post-revolutionary Russia that more than ten per cent of the students were 'recruited from the bottom half of the population' surely needs modification.[22]

The evidence suggests that the Welsh and Scottish 'democratic myths' had some substance, and that members of the British élite recruited there may have had broader social origins than their English colleagues. In practical terms, access to universities was regulated by four factors: the structure of the school system, and its ability to prepare students to university entrance standard; the cost of a university education; the financial aid available to individuals; and the occupational advantages which a university training brought—or, to put it another way, the degree to which entrance to an occupation was still possible at the age of twenty-one or twenty-two. The precocity of the Scottish universities was helped by favourable conditions in all these respects. They were accessible without formal entrance requirements, and fed by a network of rural parish schools, while in the towns the middle classes had access to cheap and efficient day schools; fees were kept low by state endowment; bursaries to support poorer students were quite widely available, and often awarded by open competition; and the careers for which university training was thought desirable included school-teaching as well as the traditional professions. From about 1890, however, England began to move in the same direction.

Although the middle class had access to effective day schools which could compete with the public schools well before 1902, it was not until the Education Act of that year that public organization and subsidy of secondary schools began, followed in 1907, as part of a conscious policy of educational opportunity, by the provision of free places for scholars from elementary schools. Outside England, however, systematic state aid began earlier. In Ireland, an Act of 1878 distributed subsidies on the basis of examination results, allowing secondary schools of all denominations a share. In Wales, the 'intermediate' schools created in 1889 were notable for putting an academic education within easy reach of students in small country towns, and remarkably high levels of access to secondary schooling underlay the success of the Welsh university colleges.[23] In Scotland, state grants to secondary schools began in 1892, and meant that there was no loss of democratic access when a university entrance examination was introduced, the age of entry rose, and university preparation was abandoned by the smaller schools. All these developments in secondary education, incidentally, greatly increased the demand for graduate teachers.

The state subsidy which universities had always received in Scotland, and which supported the Queen's Colleges in Ireland, allowed fees to be kept low. In Scotland a university education cost as little as £10–12 in arts and science (fees for medicine were always higher everywhere), and after 1901 fees ceased to be a real barrier, as the Carnegie endowment paid them for all Scottish-born students who applied. In Wales, fees were kept near the Scottish level, and state subsidy began in 1882. Annual state grants for English university colleges began in 1889, and by 1910 less than a third of university income in England and Wales was derived from fees.[24] They were thus well below the market rate, and the cost of an arts degree in English provincial universities was usually about £15–20 a year, though University and King's Colleges in London were considerably more expensive. Moderate fees put university education within reach of the reasonably prosperous middle class. Lodgings, or a place in one of the still uncommon student residences, were likely to cost £40–50 per annum. But the total cost was still well below the £200 or so needed to cover fees, college residence and the necessary lifestyle at Oxford or Cambridge, or indeed the £80–100 and upwards charged by public schools.

Even so, university education would normally be beyond the reach of the lower middle or working classes. Few of the new colleges were well enough endowed to offer scholarships. It was local authorities (county and borough councils) which came to fill this gap in England and Wales. Under Acts of 1889 and 1890, they were able to aid 'technical' education, a term which was interpreted broadly. Large industrial towns saw the development of higher technical schools, which usually had some work of degree standard and developed links with the local university, sometimes being formally affiliated or incorporated with it. Many councils also gave significant amounts for the general support of their local universities. For individuals, there were university scholarships in technical or scientific subjects, and after 1902, when the English local authorities took over schools of all levels from the former school boards, they were able to develop integrated scholarship systems leading from the elementary school via the council grammar school to the university. In 1910, the royal commission on the civil service, which carried out a systematic inquiry into educational opportunities, found that 366 boys and 143 girls left state secondary schools in England and Wales with university scholarships, 134 and twenty-seven respectively going to Oxford or Cambridge; 253 of the boys and seventy of the girls had started their careers in elementary schools. In England, local authorities maintained 1327 university scholarships, equivalent to about seven per cent of the total number of students.[25] This might not seem a high proportion, and of course these students were a tiny handful compared with the mass of working-class children in elementary schools. Yet several of the witnesses to this commission, including those from Scotland and Wales, claimed that the ladder of educational opportunity was already almost complete; their conception was the limited one of the time, under which only the exceptionally 'bright' children of the working class were expected to progress beyond elementary schooling.

The final significant development was the establishment from 1890 of 'day training colleges' for elementary teachers within the universities. The demand for elementary teachers with basic qualifications had previously been met by non-university colleges, recruited from elementary schools via the 'pupil-teacher' system. This had itself provided a significant channel of social mobility, especially for women, and in Scotland male students at the colleges were allowed to attend university classes as early as 1873. Now the state was prepared to subsidize this training within universities, and although at first the day training students might not stay long enough to graduate, a new range of experiences and potential opportunities was opened to them. New social strata were being tapped, and fears were expressed that the presence of the day training students would frighten away those from more affluent families.[26]

Generalization about the social role of the English provincial universities is hampered by the absence of systematic information about their students' backgrounds. The sources usually describe them as essentially middle-class, but this does not take us far. It is also clear that, though most students were drawn from the immediate locality, the development of specialities not offered elsewhere could make a wider appeal to students of high social status. This was especially true of the applied sciences: when Ludwig Wittgenstein

Table 5 English provinces: parental occupations of students (%).

Mason College, Birmingham, 1893		University College, Nottingham, 1911	General	Day TC
Professional	37	Professional	29	5
Businessmen	17	Businessmen	27	6
Intermediate	34	Farmers	4	5
Manual workers	13	Intermediate	19	41
N =	270	Manual workers	5	32
		Not known	16	11
		N =	75	63

Sources: For Birmingham: M. Sanderson, *The Universities and British Industry, 1850–1970* (London, 1972), 98–9. For Nottingham: PP 1913, XL, *Royal Commission on University Education in London. Appendix to Final Report* [Cd. 6718], 173.

wished to continue his studies in engineering, it was to Manchester that he came from Berlin in 1908.[27] It was said that the public-school men at the provincial universities were especially likely to study vocational subjects like engineering, medicine or architecture—and in the 1890s twenty-six per cent of the students at the Victoria University (Manchester, Liverpool and Leeds) came from public schools.[28] Arts and pure science were left to the less privileged students and the prospective teachers; in several civic universities, the day training students formed a third or a half of the arts and science faculties. This was indeed a swing away from technology or applied science, but one which could hardly have less to do with the adoption of 'aristocratic' or gentlemanly values.

Some fragmentary data for the years after 1890 are in Table 5. The figures for Birmingham come from Sanderson, and show limited working-class participation: many of the 'intermediate' group here were small businessmen. For Nottingham, however, the figures are interesting because they distinguish the day training students from the rest, and clearly show their modest origins—the miner's son D. H. Lawrence was among these students in the 1900s. This source also reveals that while nearly a third of the general students had fathers earning over £300 a year (a comfortable middle-class income), this was the case for only one of the day training students. Nottingham was exceptional because the city council was the direct sponsor of the college, and was able to make it

the coping stone of an educational edifice based on the broadest and most democratic principles. Nine-tenths of the regular students of the College, we were informed, commence their education in the public elementary schools; from these they pass to the large and well-organised municipal or high schools, and thence with the aid of scholarships to the College.

So reported the Treasury inspectors in 1907. Their predecessors in 1902 had found that 'the majority of the students belong to the artisan and lower middle classes, and many of them are very poor', and that 'though the students are drawn from all classes, the opportunities specially afforded to young working men of ability and promise are thus very considerable, and from this point of view we think that the College exhibits the nearest approach, of all the Colleges which we visited, to a People's University.' It was true that 'there are many grades between the extreme types of a People's University . . . and the ideal towards which the largest and best endowed of the Colleges are striving, of carrying Oxford and Cambridge into populous centres'.[29] But there were other universities like Liverpool, Sheffield or Leeds where the local authorities took a similar benevolent interest, and Leeds told the civil service commission that 'there is in Yorkshire a complete system of scholarships by which the children of poor parents are assisted to pass from the elementary schools to the Universities and to secure in after life positions suitable to their capacities'. It was 'well known' at Leeds that many 'of its most distinguished alumni have been the sons and daughters of working men, assisted by scholarships from the elementary stage upwards'.[30]

It is unnecessary to discuss Oxford and Cambridge at length. Stone on Oxford, and Jenkins and Jones on Cambridge, have established their social exclusiveness and their close links with the public schools.[31] The establishment of day training colleges, the attempt to reduce living expenses by founding cheaper colleges and introducing 'non-collegiate' students, and the ability of state secondary schools to compete for college scholarships must have had some democratizing effects before 1914. But these universities retained a special 'national' role in several ways: their recruitment, like that of the public schools, was not localized; they were the universities normally chosen by the landed aristocracy and the wealthiest of the middle class; they had a connection with the highest reaches of national power in law and politics; and academically or socially ambitious students came to them from the Scottish or provincial universities.

Studies of the educational background of specific élite groups usually show the predominance of Oxford and Cambridge over other universities. One such study, of over 3000 élite members between 1880 and 1970, lies behind Perkin's recent work. Whereas in *The Transformation of Higher Learning* Perkin placed the 'revolution' in higher education before 1930, elsewhere he has acknowledged that the tight connexion between universities and professionalization is more recent, and that many powerful élites previously did without higher education. Nevertheless, Perkin provides convincing evidence that the nineteenth-century emphasis on educational qualifications did shift influence from the traditional élite to the middle classes.[32] W. D. Rubinstein, using the same data as Perkin, has pushed this argument further, arguing that attendance at a public school or an ancient university should not be seen as evidence of privileged status, and that British élites were recruited from comparatively wide social backgrounds. It is certainly true that the public schools and universities helped the sons of clergymen, army officers, colonial civil servants and other relatively modest members of the middle class to improve their social status through education. But one may question Rubinstein's description of these families as the 'lower middle classes', and although he uses the term 'meritocracy', it was only middle-class merit which could benefit, for public schools (and the preparatory schools which became an essential preliminary) remained expensive.[33]

If Oxford and Cambridge did draw on a wider middle class, graduation often led to positions of useful obscurity rather than power. In Compton Mackenzie's novel *Sinister Street* (1913), the hero Michael Fane spends four years at Oxford, with no particular occupation in mind, for he has a private fortune in prospect. He meets an old school-fellow:

'I'm just down from Oxford,' Michael informed him.
'Pretty good spree up there, eh?'
'Oh, yes, rather,' said Michael.
'Well, I had the chance to go,' said Drake. 'But it wasn't good enough. It's against you in the City, you know. Waste of time really, except of course for a parson or a schoolmaster.'[34]

Oxford and Cambridge had a glamorous role as finishing schools for a life of leisure, and gave a serious intellectual preparation to those whose wealth and family background were likely in any case to secure them an influential position in business or a profession. But their strictly meritocratic function was more humdrum, and training parsons and schoolmasters was not so different from what less famous universities were doing. This is illustrated by Table 6, which shows the career destinations of students from Aberdeen and Bangor. Aberdeen had an important medical school, but otherwise it is the predominance of teaching as a university outlet, especially for women, which is most striking. The detailed data also show that teaching and the church were classic 'transitional' professions: the ones most likely to be chosen by students with modest social backgrounds, with low continuity from one generation to the next.[35]

Few students from Aberdeen or Bangor went into business. The background of business élites has attracted a good deal of recent historical work, which has generally shown both that businessmen had less higher education than other élite figures, and that British businessmen had less than their continental or American counterparts.[36] In a preliminary analysis of business leaders between 1860 and 1980 included in the *Dictionary of Business Biography*, David Jeremy found that twenty-nine per cent went to a university, though the proportion rose in the twentieth century.[37] A similar analysis of the *Dictionary of Scottish Business Biography, 1860–1960* shows that eighty-three (twenty-two per cent) of the 381 men included attended a university or

Table 6 Occupations of former students, Aberdeen and Bangor (%) Occupations of graduates of Aberdeen, 1901–25, and of students at Bangor *c.* 1884–1904.

	Aberdeen Men	Aberdeen Women	Bangor
Education	27	68	59
Church	9	0	16
Medicine	42	11	3
Civil service	5	1	0
Law	3	0	1
Business	4	2	1
Engineering			3
Science	3	1	1
Agriculture	3	0	14
Miscellaneous	3	2	2
None, married, died	2	16	
N =	2912	1627	1303

Sources: For Aberdeen: T. Watt, *Roll of the Graduates of the University of Aberdeen, 1901–1925* (Aberdeen 1935), 943. For Bangor: J. G. Williams, *The University College of North Wales: Foundations, 1884–1927* (Cardiff 1985), 214.

higher technical school. None went to Oxford, only ten to Cambridge. The commonest pattern was study at a Scottish university, sometimes in science or engineering, more often in the general arts course, though many stayed for only a year or two and did not graduate. Higher technical training was most likely to be found among men in mining, steel or shipbuilding, and was acquired at the Royal School of Mines in London, at English provincial universities chosen for their specialization in applied science, or at the college which is today Strathclyde University. On the whole, the choice of higher education was a pragmatic one, and revealed little movement away from business values.

The same was true of secondary education, where Scottish habits differed from English. The founders of businesses often had a rudimentary education, but later generations were sent to the best local day schools, including some which had a technical bias like Allan Glen's in Glasgow. Only twenty-three (six per cent) went to English public schools. If they were not destined for higher education, the sons of business families usually left school at fifteen or sixteen to enter the family business or to take up an apprenticeship. This habit of early school leaving persisted even after several generations of wealth.[38] Thus if Scottish industry failed to adapt to the challenges of the twentieth century—and some of the men in this dictionary presided over spectacular entrepreneurial disasters—it would seem to be due less to the absorption of anti-industrial values through education, than to rejection of theoretical training, and outdated adherence to the mystique of learning on the job. G. W. Roderick, in a study of Welsh industrialists, comes to rather similar conclusions.[39]

It is also striking that all the Scottish business leaders who went to a university, with one exception, were of the second or later generations, and owed their positions to inheritance, not to managerial careers based on trained expertise. The exception, Donald Matheson, general manager of the Caledonian Railway between 1910 and 1922, was trained as an engineer at Watt College, Edinburgh and Owens College, Manchester.[40] As a gardener's son, he was also the only one of these 381 men whose career resembled that of the classic 'lad of parts' rising through education: the men of humble origin among the business élite usually left school at the earliest opportunity and reached the top through qualities of character and practical experience. This probably changed later with the decline of family control—the *Dictionary* is confined to those whose business careers were completed by 1960—but Paul Robertson has concluded from his study of Scottish universities and industry that 'on balance, except for Glasgow and Edinburgh engineering graduates, businessmen appear to have had almost no interest in the products of Scottish university education before 1914.'[41] There were few salaried posts in industry, and in commerce, which absorbed the bulk of the boys who left secondary schools, educationists were still trying to persuade employers to accept entrants at seventeen rather than the traditional fourteen or fifteen. For these very important careers, which certainly led to positions of wealth and power, universities were decidedly marginal institutions.

This leads to our first conclusion: that the categories of 'graduates' and 'élites' overlapped, but did not coincide. On the one hand, university graduates ranged from cabinet ministers to village schoolteachers; on the other, it was quite normal—not only for businessmen—to reach élite positions without attending a university. Universities were important for the endorsement of élite status based on birth or wealth, but their role in élite *formation* was limited. Medicine was virtually the only profession which concentrated its training in degree-granting institutions. Other 'graduate' professions (sometimes with professional training elsewhere) included the higher civil service, the Scottish clergy, the Anglican clergy in England and Ireland, barristers in England and Ireland and advocates in Scotland, university and secondary teachers, and professional scientists. The main new professions to develop university training before 1914 were engineering and architecture, but still only in conjunction with the traditional apprenticeship system. Other professions or semi-professionalized occupations used either apprenticeship, or specialized colleges which might or might not have university affiliations. Trainee solicitors, bankers or accountants might attend university lectures without graduating; but for commerce and most family-run enterprises university education was the exception. For the army and navy—professions of high prestige which attracted the aristocracy—it was both unnecessary, and difficult to combine with the usual modes of entry.

What mattered more was schooling. The choice of secondary school accurately reflected social status, and above a certain level to send sons to a public school (or a day school of equivalent status in Scotland) was *de rigueur*. After that, whether a son was sent to a university would depend on the planned career. If business was aimed at, he would normally not be. This tends to invalidate the argument that universities diverted talent away from entrepreneurial careers: for every businessman's son who went to Oxford and became a civil servant, there may well have been a civil servant's son who did not go to Oxford and became a businessman. A Scottish aristocratic example to illustrate this is that of the second and third marquesses of Aberdeen, brothers born in 1879 and 1883. Both went to Harrow, but while the eldest son was then sent to St Andrews and Oxford, and duly inherited the title, his brother was apprenticed to an Aberdeen shipyard, and went on to an English industrial career, ending as chairman of a Sheffield steel firm, and serving as president of the Federation of British Industries. He inherited the marquessate at the age of 81; his own son was at Harrow and Oxford, then apprenticed as a land agent in preparation for managing the family estate. It was Harrow School which was the common educational element for this family.[42]

The same perspective may be applied to the education of women. The admission of women is surely the most significant single development in European universities before 1914, yet the élites/professionalization approach has little to say about it; the question is almost ignored in the Jarausch book. The prominence of women from the leisured upper middle classes in the early years of the women's education movement makes it difficult to explain in terms of career demands, and the main occupation for which universities did prepare women, teaching, was neither fully professionalized nor of high status. Apart from medicine, the main professions were closed to women until after the First World War, and this put a limit on the expansion of student numbers.[43]

It perhaps makes sense to think of a 'middle-class leaving age' for full-time education. In the mid-nineteenth century (when working-class children left school at ten or eleven) this was commonly fifteen or earlier, and only the small élite who used the old public schools stayed till eighteen. By 1914, it was the accepted pattern that middle-class children of both sexes were kept at school until between sixteen and eighteen. But after that, university education was an option, in which three broad patterns may be discerned. First, there were the leisured or wealthy classes, who were likely to choose Oxford or Cambridge for social reasons, with a career decision postponed until later. Second, there was the broad mass of the professional and business middle class, especially in the provinces. Only a minority of their sons was likely to be sent to a university, and the expense had to be justified by a clear intention to enter a profession, or to acquire specialized scientific or engineering skills. This class was more likely to give its daughters a higher education than the wealthy upper class, and cases can certainly be found where a daughter went to university, to become a teacher, while her brothers went straight into business. Thirdly, there were the lower middle and working classes, small numbers of whose children reached a university through luck or talent, and whose choice of occupation thereafter was limited by lack of resources or family influence.

Although most of the evidence in this paper comes from before 1914, there was no fundamental change after the First World War. The extension of secondary education continued to work itself out, more scholarships were available from local authorities and after 1920 also from the state, and the value of a university education was more widely appreciated. Enrolments rose after 1918, and remained on a new plateau. Access ratios increased —though only to 1.7 per cent of the age-group in 1938.[44] By the 1930s numbers were stagnant, and there were few symptoms of an imminent breakthrough to a new era. That only came after the Second World War, due partly to spontaneous and unanticipated demand, and partly to the series of educational reforms which ran from the Education Act of 1944 via the Robbins report of 1963 to the introduction of comprehensive secondary education.

It is as part of this process, and only since the 1950s, that the 'middle-class leaving age' has been raised to twenty-one or twenty-two. As university training has become necessary for a much wider range of careers, including those in business, competition for posts has forced the middle classes to use the universities far more than before; one outcome is that a large expansion of enrolments has taken place without a fundamental shift in the social composition of the student body. Motivation towards university attendance continues to vary by class, and to some extent by gender, and Britain remains a country where higher education is thought of as something for the privileged or the especially able rather than as a standard aspiration. It is also a country where, according to recent surveys, only a minority of business managers have any sort of higher education, a situation illustrated in David Lodge's latest academic novel *Nice Work* (1988), and relevant too to Perkin's interpretation of recent British politics as a conflict between the public-service professionals with university training and the corporate professionals committed to entrepreneurial values.[45]

A further post-1945 development was the system of mandatory state grants, which made it no more expensive to attend a distant university than a local one. Combined with the centralized system of selection required by the new competition for places, this produced for the first time something like a homogeneous university system recruited on a national basis. The distinctiveness of Scottish, Welsh and civic universities, subject to powerful assimilative influences ever since the late nineteenth century, and undermined by a more general decline of regional cultures and societies in the face of broad economic forces, seemed destined to wane into insignificance.

In the 1950s and 1960s, when new universities were being founded, the Oxford and Cambridge-derived model of the residential, character-forming university, once vigorously challenged by rival ideals, had acquired an extraordinary ascendancy. Whether this model inhibited a genuine transition from élite to mass higher education in Britain, and whether the ideal of liberal education associated with it led to a new incongruence between the curriculum and the wide range of occupations for which universities now prepared, are among the many questions which there is no space to pursue here.

References

1. K. H. Jarausch, 'Higher Education and Social Change: some Comparative Perspectives', in *The Transformation of Higher Learning, 1860–1930: Expansion, Diversification, Social Opening, and Professionalization in England, Germany, Russia, and the United States* (Chicago 1983), 10, 36.
2. H. Kaelble, 'Educational Opportunities and Government Policies in Europe in the Period of Industrialization', in P. Flora and A. J. Heidenheimer (eds), *The Development of Welfare States in Europe and America* (New Brunswick 1981), 239–68; Jarausch in *Transformation*, 17; H. Perkin, 'The Pattern of Social Transformation in England', ibid., 218.
3. H. Perkin, *The Rise of Professional Society: England since 1880* (London 1989), xiii; Perkin in Jarausch, *Transformation*, 218.
4. F. Ringer, *Education and Society in Modern Europe* (Bloomington 1979), 6–12.
5. M. Wiener, *English Culture and the Decline of the Industrial Spirit, 1850–1980* (Cambridge 1981), 11–12. Cf. J. Raven, 'British History and the Enterprise Culture', *Past and Present*, 123 (1989), 178–204.
6. C. Barnett, *The Collapse of British Power* (London 1972), 19–43; C. Barnett, *The Audit of War: the Illusion and Reality of Britain as a Great Nation* (London 1986), 201–33.
7. Jarausch, *Transformation*, 24.
8. M. Sanderson, 'The English Civic Universities and the "Industrial Spirit", 1870–1914', *Historical Research*, 61 (1988), 103; M. Sanderson, *The Universities and British Industry, 1850–1970* (London 1972).
9. R. N. Soffer, 'The Modern University and National Values, 1850–1930', *Historical Research*, 60 (1987), 166–87.
10. T. W. Moody, 'The Irish University Question of the Nineteenth Century', *History*, 43 (1958), 109. For a fuller account, see T. W. Moody and J. C. Beckett, *Queen's, Belfast 1845–1949: the History of a University* (2 vols London 1959).
11. W. C. Davies and W. L. Jones, *The University of Wales and its Constituent Colleges* (London 1905), xi–xiii, 160, 197–8.
12. Ibid., 74, 82. For the Welsh university question generally, see K. O. Morgan, *Rebirth of a Nation: Wales 1880–1980* (Oxford 1981), 106–11.
13. R. D. Anderson, *Education and Opportunity in Victorian Scotland: Schools and Universities* (Oxford 1983).
14. S. Rothblatt, 'London: a Metropolitan University?', in T. Bender (ed.), *The University and the City, from Medieval Origins to the Present* (New York 1988), 119–49.

15. E.g. Sanderson, cited above, and D. R. Jones, *The Origins of Civic Universities: Manchester, Leeds & Liverpool* (London 1988).
16. E.g. Barnett, *Audit of War*, 222–3. A more nuanced view is that of R. Lowe, 'The Expansion of Higher Education in England', in Jarausch, *Transformation*, 53–4, and 'Structural Change in English Higher Education, 1870–1920', in D. K. Müller and others (eds), *The Rise of the Modern Educational System: Structural Change and Social Reproduction, 1870–1920* (Cambridge 1987), 163–78.
17. Jarausch, *Transformation*, 13. Most new foundations in Britain started as 'university colleges', unable to award their own degrees; but for convenience the generic term 'universities' has been used in this article.
18. R. D. Anderson, 'Education and Society in Modern Scotland: a Comparative Perspective', *History of Education Quarterly*, 25 (1985), 467.
19. W. M. Mathew, 'The Origins and Occupations of Glasgow Students, 1740–1839', *Past and Present*, 33 (1966), 78, 85.
20. Ringer, *Education and Society*, 229; Jarausch, *Transformation*, 16, 52.
21. Anderson, *Education and Opportunity*, 148–53; R. D. Anderson, *The Student Community at Aberdeen, 1860–1939* (Aberdeen 1988), 138–41; I. J. McDonald, 'Untapped Reservoirs of Talent? Social Class and Opportunities in Scottish Higher Education, 1910–1960', *Scottish Educational Studies*, 1 (1967), 52–8; A. Collier, 'Social Origins of a Sample of Entrants to Glasgow University', *Sociological Review*, 30 (1938), 161–85, 262–77.
22. Jarausch, *Transformation*, 36.
23. G. E. Jones, *Controls and Conflicts in Welsh Secondary Education, 1889–1944* (Cardiff 1982), 45, 80, 82–3.
24. In 1912–13, fees were 28% of income in institutions receiving Treasury grants: *Board of Education. Reports for the Year 1912–13 from those Universities and University Colleges in Great Britain which are in Receipt of Grant from the Board of Education* (2 vols London 1914), i, pp. xiv–xv.
25. Parliamentary Papers (hereafter PP) 1914, XVI, *Royal Commission on the Civil Service. First Appendix to Fourth Report* [Cd. 7339], 47, 55, 86.
26. PP 1902, LXXX, Parliamentary Return of 2 July 1902 incorporating inspectors' reports, 15.
27. B. McGuinness, *Wittgenstein, a Life: Young Ludwig, 1889–1921* (paperback ed. London 1990), 61.
28. PP 1897, LXX, Parliamentary Return of 17 June 1897 incorporating inspectors' reports, 7, 31; PP 1902, LXXX, Parliamentary Return of 2 July 1902, 31, 64, 74; T. Kelly, *For Advancement of Learning: the University of Liverpool, 1881–1981* (Liverpool 1981), 92, 136. For the percentage of public-school students, see PP 1895, XLIX, *Royal Commission on Secondary Education. Vol. IX. Appendix. Statistical Tables* [C. 7862–VIII], 426–7.
29. PP 1907, LXIV, Parliamentary Return of 23 July 1907 incorporating inspectors' reports, 93; PP 1902, LXXX, Parliamentary Return of 2 July 1902, 16, 94, 96.
30. PP 1913, XVIII, *Royal Commission on the Civil Service. Appendix to Third Report* [Cd. 6740], 315–16.
31. L. Stone, 'The Size and Composition of the Oxford Student Body, 1580–1910', in L. Stone (ed.), *The University in Society. Volume I. Oxford and Cambridge from the 14th to the Early 19th Century* (Princeton 1975), 66–7, 93, 103; H. Jenkins and D. C. Jones, 'Social Class of Cambridge University Alumni of the

18th and 19th Centuries', *British Journal of Sociology*, 1 (1950), 93–116. For Cambridge, see also S. Rothblatt, *The Revolution of the Dons: Cambridge and Society in Victorian England* (London 1968), 280–1.

32. H. Perkin, 'The Recruitment of Elites in British Society since 1800', *Journal of Social History*, 12 (1978–9), 222–34, and *The Structured Crowd: Essays in English Social History* (Brighton 1981), 151–67. Cf. *Rise of Professional Society*, 87–91.

33. W. D. Rubinstein, 'Education and the Social Origins of British Elites, 1880–1970', *Past and Present*, 112 (1986), 163–207.

34. C. Mackenzie, *Sinister Street* (new ed., London 1949), 652.

35. R. K. Kelsall, 'Self-Recruitment in Four Professions', in D. V. Glass (ed.), *Social mobility in Britain* (London 1954), 308–20; for the Aberdeen case, see also Anderson, *Student Community*, 11, 139–40.

36. H. Kaelble, 'Long-Term Changes in the Recruitment of the Business Elite: Germany compared to the U.S., Great Britain, and France since the Industrial Revolution', *Journal of Social History*, 13 (1979–80), 404–23; F. K. Ringer, 'The Education of Elites in Modern Europe', *History of Education Quarterly*, 18 (1978), 159–72.

37. D. J. Jeremy, 'Anatomy of the British Business Elite, 1860–1980', *Business History*, 26 (1984), 12.

38. A. Slaven and S. Checkland (eds), *Dictionary of Scottish Business Biography, 1860–1960* (2 vols Aberdeen 1986–90). Cf. editors' conclusion, ii, 430.

39. G. W. Roderick, 'South Wales Industrialists and the Theory of Gentrification, 1770–1914', *Transactions of the Honourable Society of Cymmrodorion*, 1987, 65–83.

40. Slaven and Checkland, *Dictionary*, ii, 302–4.

41. P. Robertson, 'Scottish Universities and Scottish Industry, 1860–1914', *Scottish Economic and Social History*, 4 (1984), 49.

42. A. Gordon, *A Guide to Haddo House* (Edinburgh 1981), 18–19.

43. Cf. J. Howarth and M. Curthoys, 'The political economy of women's higher education in late 19th and early 20th-century Britain', *Historical Research*, 60 (1987), 208–31.

44. Ringer, *Education and Society*, 229.

45. Perkin, *Rise of Professional Society*, 505, 517–19.

104

ENGLISH CIVIC UNIVERSITIES AND THE MYTH OF DECLINE

Elizabeth J. Morse

Source: *History of Universities* XI (1992): 177–204.

I

In his article, 'Universities and Elites in Modern Britain',[1] R. D. Anderson argues persuasively in favour of new perspectives on the recent history of higher education in the British Isles. He warns against a too-trusting acceptance of the role of universities in the formation of professional elites and advocates an end to the assumption that all university development of any note took place along what has become known as the London-Oxford-Cambridge axis. In this piece, I shall argue that these perceptions are both a cause and a symptom of certain inequalities in the English system of higher education.

Significantly, the concept of a triangular locus of power, centred on the South of England and encompassing the two ancient universities originated with the sociologist Edward Shils in the 1950s, and it has been widely adapted since then to describe apparent cultural trends in England, especially those relating to the development of higher education.[2] Anderson argues that the too-ready adoption of this model leads to a 'parochially English approach' which distorts much recent historical writing, either by encouraging historians to ascribe their discoveries about the ancient universities to the system of higher education as a whole, or by assuming that those trends in university history that were atypical of Oxford and Cambridge were, therefore, aberrant. Although Anderson notes the existence of powerful forces for assimilation at work on the peripheral universities from the time of their inception, he is more inclined to stress the separate national identity of the non-English periphery, the universities of Scotland, Ireland and Wales.

The aim of this article is to expand on Anderson's critique of English university historiography (leaving to others the discussion of other British universities) and to suggest reasons why the majority of English universities have been neglected by historians in the past. To achieve this, reasons must first be found for the civics' failure, although they were more numerous and accessible to a far greater number of students than the ancient universities of Oxford and Cambridge, to compete with the Oxbridge-based idea of a university in the public mind. Although historians delight in obscure discoveries and recondite themes, in the case of university history it appears that scholarly attention has accurately mirrored public apathy in the recent past.

The practice of twentieth-century English social history has been skewed by this neglect, especially in the area of the 'decline of Britain' debate. The theory that the elitist English universities promoted anti-business values and catered not at all to the children of businessmen was propounded by the historian Martin Wiener in 1981, at a time when the political climate in Britain made the universities exceptionally vulnerable to charges of elitism, extravagance, and social uselessness.[3] Wiener provided ample anecdotal evidence to support this contention with respect to Oxford and Cambridge, but was able to avoid the powerful contradictory example of the civic universities only by ignoring them.[4] For instance, Wiener overlooked evidence that the majority of the civic universities not only catered to the children of merchants and businessmen, as well as to those of the artisanal and lower middle class, but aimed to send their graduates back into industry, when industry could be persuaded to accept university-trained engineers, scientists and managers.[5] It is arguable that Wiener's thesis that university education gentrified its recipients out of industrial careers found widespread acceptance partly because of the void in the historiography that allowed the common reader to assume that the two ancient universities were indeed typical of the English university system as a whole.

Five years ago, virtually nothing had been published on the history of civic or provincial universities, except for commemorative histories of individual institutions, written on the occasion of a centennial or other milestone in the institution's history. The limitations of this medium were such that none was able to offer a balanced view of the civic university in its social or historical setting. Apart from one very general history of the civic universities, the only work to discuss them in historical context was Michael Sanderson's definitive history of the universities' relationship with industry, which was, and remains the most perceptive study of the civic universities' role in the higher education system.[6] Since 1986, there have been reassuring indications that the vacuum is slowly being filled: doctoral research (especially in the United States, a geographic perspective of some importance,) publications and ongoing non-commemorative research by scholars at the civic universities promise a shift in perspective away from an exclusive concentration on the ancient universities.[7] This body of work evinces an interest in the civics on the part of historians of universities, and may be evidence of stirrings of public consciousness of the importance of provincial and non-elite forms of higher education. The challenge for the historian is to argue the case for the civic universities' uniqueness and to refrain from analysing them solely as separate but unequal colleagues of the ancient universities.[8] Having done this, some arguments can be advanced as to why the civic universities have suffered these 'invidious comparisons' for so long and why they themselves were unable or unwilling to find for themselves a more positive self-image.[9]

Such has been the subordinate role of the civic universities that no agreed-upon name for them has evolved. Although the terms 'civic,' 'provincial' and 'redbrick' have been used interchangeably in the past, I have preferred the term 'civic universities' as it was the name those institutions chose for themselves and because it is the only one of the three that carries no pejorative connotation. Although even this term is imperfect (it is questionable whether the universities of Durham or London can properly be called 'civic,' for example) it has the advantage of being both contemporary and neutral.

At the turn of the twentieth century, there were five English universities —Oxford, Cambridge, London, Durham and the Victoria University, the last a loose federation composed of the university colleges of Manchester, Liverpool and Leeds. By the end of the year 1900, they were joined by the fire-new University of Birmingham, the first 'unitary' civic university, which both taught and examined for its own degrees. By 1945, the English civic universities and the University of London numbered nine in all (including the three component colleges of the old Victoria university, now the Universities of Manchester, Liverpool and Leeds,) together with six university colleges that taught for the University of London degree examinations. Together they educated over three times as many students as the ancient universities.[10] Although most still recruited more students locally than nationally, by 1947 many recruited as many as half their students from outside their immediate area. This figure suggests that the civics drew at least a portion of their students by reputation, rather than sheer convenience, although no true national market would be possible before the 1950s, when a national system of grants offered the poor student a real alternative to living at home and attending the local university.[11]

Civic universities, then, were numerous and catered to a far higher proportion of the country's undergraduates than did the ancient universities, but how influential were they? Despite a profusion of evidence that the work of individual departments had reached international calibre, less can be said about the overall quality of civic university education, especially in the areas of social life and customs. This is the case in part because the ancient universities and their graduates have hitherto exercised indisputed control of standards for excellence in universities. Oxbridge has set the standard for the ideal forms of tuition, of student life, for the relationship of arts to sciences and the proper balance in which they should be held, and finally, for the 'idea of a university' itself. This last is of critical importance for understanding the apparent decline of the civic universities in the 1930s and

1940s, and the utter neglect of their unique attributes in the formation of a plan for university expansion in the 1950s and beyond.

At the birth of the civic universities, towards the end of the nineteenth century, two ideas of a university competed for dominance in England. The civic university idea was of comparatively recent currency, although there had been calls for regional universities as early as the seventeenth century, and Oliver Cromwell had briefly lent his support to a university for the north of England. It differed from the elite idea of a university in its openness to teaching new or vocational subjects, its cheapness, which implied mass instruction rather than the labour-intensive tutorial, together with non-residence, which also cut the costs of a university education. Nineteenth-century accretions to the idea decreed that it should be non-sectarian and that it should offer some instruction to women. It was by nature urban and geared towards the needs of the residents of the great industrial towns.

This idea of a university found supporters in two of the key figures in the civic university movement. Richard Haldane and Joseph Chamberlain. Both were liberal imperialist in their politics and may have derived their interest in improved education for the governing classes from their political views. Chamberlain was concerned with both municipal reform and the improvement of regional education and presided, as Member of Parliament for Birmingham, over the transformation of Mason College into the first wholly autonomous civic university in 1900. Haldane, whose bias was in favour of national strategies for education, was less concerned with the development of a specific region and more interested in the provision of higher technical education in the German manner. First as barrister, then as Privy Councillor, and finally as a member of Sir Henry Campbell-Bannerman's cabinet, Haldane promoted regional and technical higher education on the German model in the English civic universities whose charter campaigns he supported from his position in government, as well as in the Welsh and Irish universities.[12] City councillors supported this idea of a university (though never unanimously), partly out of civic pride, from a desire to improve local industry through technical training, and partly from a sincere regard for the benefits of higher education, even in its non-vocational forms. Central government never had a plan for the expansion of higher education in this period, preferring cautious sponsorship of local initiative at small cost to the state.

Foremost among local motivations was a desire for the prestige a university conferred on its community.[13] Michael Sanderson has described the romantic impulse behind university-building and presented the civics' much-maligned Victorian exteriors as a hymn to civic pride:

> ... a kind of secular religiosity, the architectural expression of family and civic pride, the ideals of learning or the belief in material

progress through science. . . . to observe these exterior forms of the old colleges is to appreciate that they could not have been conceived by their founders totally as the product of Victorian rational economic calculation.[14]

But did the public—parents, would-be students, city councillors accept the civic universities in this spirit? It appears that, after the initial enthusiasm of the 'foundation period,' they did not. Although the universities were welcomed by local parents, eager to find a cheap non-sectarian alternative to the ancient universities, they did not attract lasting public loyalty. Reasons for this failure, which brought the civic universities into low repute and sometimes desperate financial straits in the mid-twentieth century, include their distaste for and inept conduct of publicity, their essentially regional loyalties which prevented them from developing a national clientèle, their inability to create for themselves an image that would appeal to the paying public, but most of all the existence of an older, stronger and more captivating 'idea of a university' based firmly and immutably upon the ancient foundations at Cambridge and Oxford. Perhaps it is the aura of broken romance that clings to the civic universities, the sense that they belong to a state of mind now fallen from fashion, once both innovative and utterly of their time, that makes them such a fascinating but often melancholy subject for historical inquiry.

The traditional idea of a university, based on observation and experience of the ancient universities' collegiate organisation, their face-to-face relationships between tutors and undergraduates, and their atmosphere of privilege, has been thoroughly discussed so frequently that it is not necessary to discuss it in more detail here. In their 1971 study of the British academic profession, A. H. Halsey and Martin Trow anatomised that idea and, through their analysis of contemporary attitudes, demonstrated its continuing power. There were, they argued, six defining characteristics that constituted the English idea of a university: antiquity, cosmopolitanism (that is, national, rather than local student recruitment), selectivity, 'education' rather than 'training' (emphasizing liberal, rather than vocational studies), domesticity (students residing in college), and intimacy (a high ratio of staff to students.)[15]

It would be inadequate to say that seven hundred years without competition had been sufficient to root this 'Oxbridge' idea firmly in the English mind, for it is only since the nineteenth century that universities have impinged much on the public consciousness. Furthermore, there existed four Scottish universities of great antiquity, offering a form of instruction and of corporate life much closer to that of the civic than to that of the ancient universities. In the late nineteenth and early twentieth century, widespread anxiety about England's ability to compete as a world power led English observers to study the higher education systems of industrial competitors, especially Germany and the United States, and to make recommendations for better provision for advanced technical training.[16] The civic universities were clearly in a position to provide such training on the highest level, so there was no practical reason why their strength in science and engineering should not dovetail nicely with the newly-perceived national needs. They did so in practice, but never in theory, for the idea of higher education in applied science found no resonances in the public mind.

Could not a wealthy and powerful nation support two ideas of a university? The civic universities did not seek to replace the ancient institutions, nor even, in the early years, to achieve the same level of prestige.[17] Rather, they viewed their role as supplementary, to supply cheaply and efficiently the demand for unadorned technical, scientific and liberal education on a regional level.[18] Yet the story of the civic universities, for all their triumphs, is a sad one, for they never escaped the ancient idea of a university. Instead, they were ineluctably drawn into habits of emulation and undue deference, falling victim to a barrage of criticism in the 1930s and 1940s, which pointed to their failure to attain an ideal to which they had never aspired and for which they were fundamentally unsuited.

Before discussing the period of apparent decline, it will be useful to look in some detail at the kind of image a newly-established civic university was trying to achieve, at the ways in which pressure to emulate the ancient universities was exerted, the resistance and eventual yielding of the civic universities to this pressure, and the ways in which the resultant mixture of ancient and modern was received by the public. An episode in the early history of the University of Bristol illustrates all of these themes.

II

The University of Bristol, founded in 1909, was the last of the civic universities to receive its charter before the First World War. It had its roots in the university extension movement of the 1870s, by which members of the ancient universities sought to bring university education to provincial cities. Bristol's early patrons included the Master of Balliol College, Oxford, Benjamin Jowett. The university itself consisted of an uneasy alliance between two rival institutions, one of which was the old university college which had evolved from the informal extension classes. It emphasized liberal and medical studies and enjoyed the support of local Liberals. The second was the Merchant Venturers' Technical College, the recent creation of the powerful Society of Merchant Venturers, supported by local Tories and devoted to the study of practical subjects, especially engineering, then rarely seen as a university subject. The amalgamation of the two colleges produced a sometimes uneasy union. Although the number of students more than doubled between 1900 and 1913, the University was one of the smaller civic universities, with 375 students in the latter year.[19] Unlike the northern universities, Bristol owed the bulk of its endowment to one family, the Wills (manufacturers of Woodbine cigarettes) who relieved it of the necessity of attracting a broad spectrum of local financial support. Its history set it apart from the older, northern universities, for it incorporated two opposing political and educational views, providing a focus for community divisions to a degree unknown by the other civic universities.

This lack of a solid base of local support may have been the cause of apparent public apathy towards the University in its early years and may help to explain the young institution's uncommon ability to get itself into trouble with its public. Civic universities did not, in general, attract a great deal of public attention, but, when the public did become aware of their affairs, it displayed a number of assumptions about the nature and dignity of universities, together with an implicit hierarchical ranking of these institutions. Existing cases of civic universities' catching the public eye, therefore, are extremely suggestive of popular ideas of what a university should be. The Bristol degree scandal offers an unparalleled case study of such an incident.

In 1912, only three years after receiving its university charter, the University of Bristol became the centre of a national scandal. It started simply enough, with the installation of Lord Haldane, the civic universities' principal spokesman in government, as university Chancellor. On such ceremonial occasions it is usual for universities to award a handful of honorary degrees to men and women of academic distinction, and civic universities had adopted this custom, bestowing degrees sparingly and with care. On this occasion, however, the University of Bristol awarded seventy honorary degrees to a wide variety of individuals, many of whom appeared to be distinguished primarily by the material support they had given to the new university.

Whose idea was this magnificent, foolhardy gesture? In his memoirs, the Bristol physicist Arthur Tyndall blamed the Vice-Chancellor, Sir Isambard Owen for the excessive number of honours.[20] It was not the first time Owen's love of pageantry had led to tasteless excess; on one memorable occasion he overrode the recommendations of the committee appointed to choose a design for university gowns, replacing its chaste selection with a garish combination of red and salmon pink, intended to evoke the colours of the Avon Gorge after rain.[21] On the other hand, the inflated degrees list may have been the work of a committee, of whose members none was willing to offend friends of the university by deleting names and which abdicated responsibility by passing the list intact to Owen.

Although it is impossible to say for certain why such an inflated number of degrees was thought necessary, the list of names offers some clues to possible motives, suggesting that a well-defined agenda lay behind its composition. Many of the honours were conferred on persons of undoubted merit: the DLitt to the popular poet Henry Newbolt and the English scholar

Sir Arthur Quiller-Couch, for instance, and the LLD to a number of university vice-chancellors, to the Lord Bishop of Bristol and, *in absentia*, to the Prime Minister. It is true that a number of local city councillors, aldermen and local notables were honoured, but so were the heads of local secondary schools, together with twenty-one past and present members of the university teaching staff. The composition of the list suggests no miscalculation, but rather a plan to establish the university's place among other universities and as the centre of the educational establishment in the West of England. It may also be suggested that the university's aim was to create a past for itself, to tighten its links with other educational institutions through a web of mutual obligation, to heighten its own status through the instant creation of a distinguished academic staff, and to enrich its own history by honouring the luminaries of its past. If this was the case, the attempt failed and instead exposed the proud young institution to ridicule.[22]

Two strands of opinion within the university itself first opened up the scandal to the public scrutiny. The students were the first to protest, (before the event there had been murmurs of dissent from Convocation, the representative body of former graduates, but no vocal objections.) The first public protest was a scathing editorial in the medical students' journal:

> No university in the world, of any repute, would permit such an action for a moment, and we must conclude that our authorities here wish to vie with the tenth-rate American institutions, only they have not even the privilege of paying a few pounds for their honours![23]

Students and recent graduates of the new university would have had good cause to be concerned for the reputation of their *alma mater*, for the public's acceptance of and respect for the institution determined the value of their degrees on the employment market.

Second, the honorary degrees provided the locus for a bitter dispute between the university administration and staff, the latter accusing the former of arrogance, authoritarianism and bad government. Preferring to hang together, most members of staff kept their protests muted, but one professor, Maurice Gerothwohl, published his protest in the national press and, subsequently, was hanged separately. After the sacking of Gerothwohl, questions were asked in the House of Commons and the Privy Council contemplated an investigation. The University of Oxford representative on the University Court, the constitutional body responsible for upholding Bristol's public image, called for the intervention of the Visitor, as provided in the university's charter, but the Court defeated the motion, preferring to settle its affairs internally and privately.[24]

This public display of discord, with its implications of unplumbed depths of impropriety in university administration, probably did more than the original degree scandal itself to provoke a storm of critical comment by press and public. Indeed, even at the height of the scandal, most critics of the degrees were careful to avoid singling out any individual degree-holder as unworthy of that honour. Two local newspapers, the *Western Daily Press* and the *Bristol Guardian* voiced dissatisfaction with the granting of the MA to persons of no academic distinction but approved of rewarding the university's friends. They proposed a degree of Civic Merit, which would express gratitude without debasing the degree currency.[25]

As the university derived a portion of its income from the Bristol City Council, it could be threatened with financial consequences if its reputation sank low enough to bring shame to the city. There does not seem to have been a serious threat of financial sanctions, thanks to the support of the Lord Mayor in the council, but the affair raised questions, both in the City Council and in the press about the true extent and nature of the university's local service function. Critics asked whether the ordinary Bristolian was getting value for money from a university that educated a tiny minority of the population. Why, it was asked, did foreign faces appear among the students, and was it the city's place to subsidize them?[26] In this manner, the degree scandal called into question all of the civic university's functions, raised questions about its utility and internal affairs that had no bearing on the original controversy, and demonstrated the weakness of the tie that linked the university with its parent town.

Despite the new institution's undoubted practicality, the controversy arose because the idea of a civic university had not replaced the dominant ancient idea in the public mind. A local university might be asked to respond to local needs, cater to local students, and at the same time to conform to standards of excellence and selectivity (in the honours it conferred, if not in its admissions) set by the ancient universities. At the time of the degree scandal, *The Times* published an article entitled 'New Universities and Old Truths'. Although appreciative of the new institutions' local orientation and function, it contained a warning to them to stay within the established hierarchy:

> While they have refused to hamper themselves with the fetters of medieval tradition, it is nevertheless to the example of Oxford and Cambridge that the younger universities turn for lessons in the art of building the fabric of a liberal education.[27]

The affair ended in anti-climax. The Privy Council declined to conduct an inquiry. A generous gift from a local benefactor enabled the university to embark on an ambitious building programme, which had the effect of shoring up both public confidence and the university's self-esteem.[28] Shortly thereafter, the outbreak of the first world war deflected public attention from university matters. The lesson had been truly learned, however, and the University of Bristol was careful not to offend against conformity again. Public opinion had left no doubt that, while the new university might experiment with brightly-coloured gowns if it chose to do so, in matters of more importance, it would be held to an exacting standard, upheld by the ancient universities and endorsed by the general public.

In his essay on Victorian institutions' attempt to establish legitimacy by the 'invention of tradition,' David Cannadine has pointed to a trend common to all new institutions of the period. To gain legitimacy, '. . . venerable and decayed ceremonials were revived, and new institutions were clothed with all the anachronistic allure of archaic but invented spectacle.' The civic universities were part of this trend, '. . . with their deliberately anachronistic styles of architecture, their aristocratic chancellors, their antique gowns and lavish degree ceremonies. . . .'[29] The evidence of the Bristol degree scandal suggests at modification of this argument. Civic universities conformed to the strict letter of the ancient idea of a university under compulsion, and the threat of public censure quickly brought an end to their attempt to free themselves in any important way from traditional customs. The failure of the new idea of a university was foreshadowed by these early events.

III

At the end of the first world war, the civic universities found themselves in serious financial trouble, partly as a result of the loss of student fees during the war and partly as a consequence of high levels of postwar inflation. In 1921, the government grant to universities was cut from £1,500,000 to £1,200,000, a temporary economy that reflected no dissatisfaction with the universities' performance but which was felt as a blow, coming as it did on top of the financial privations of wartime. In desperation, the universities launched public appeals for funds to offset their losses, an exercise in self-help warmly applauded by the new University Grants Committee.[30] In an unprecedented attempt to commercialize its product, Bristol University placed itself in the hands of a professional publicist, who produced a remarkable pamphlet designed to spur public giving by a combined appeal to the public's aesthetic and patriotic impulses.

The most striking feature of this pamphlet is its military tone and style, reminiscent of wartime recruitment propaganda, a similarity that cannot have escaped its readers. From its title, 'The First Line of National Defence,' the reader moves to its frontispiece, an illustration featuring a busy construction site. In the foreground of this picture stands a stern-visaged young man, arms crossed, chin raised, staring purposefully out from the page. This picture is captioned: 'In the mental training, guidance and development of our youth lies the wealth of the Empire.' Facing page one is a map of the West of England, drawn in a style familiar from wartime news reports, with Bristol at the centre and, radiating out from it the trade routes to Europe, the Americas and the Empire. The war, in which the public's alliance was sought was not of conquest, then, but of trade.[31]

The text is equally forceful: 'The destiny of the Empire rests upon the action of every citizen of Great Britain to-day . . . first of all upon the action of virile youth. Brains are our First Line of National Defence.'[32] The universities were characterised as 'power stations of mind,' whose function was to train: 'the forces of character and intellect, originality and knowledge, thought and judgement, vision and action, wisdom and enterprise.'[33] The list of qualities suggests a cunning blend of the traditional academic desiderata: force of intellect, knowledge, thought and wisdom, with those of the practical man: force of character, originality, judgement, action and enterprise. The university, it is implied, will produce neither cloistered academics nor philistine men of action, but a new breed combining the best features of both.

Next, an appeal is made to the competitive spirit, first nationally, in reference to the superior funding of higher education in the United States, then locally, in reference to the rise of the port of Liverpool to a position of dominance over the older port of Bristol in the nineteenth century, and to its new ability to outstrip Bristol in the quality of its higher education. The reader, whipped to a frenzy of patriotism and local pride, is quickly reassured as to the type of institution that seeks his help. In a section entitled 'The Modern Ideal University,' the idea of a civic university, situated in the heart of a great city, oriented toward the practical and the modern, is enunciated, together with a reassurance that the modern university can combine modernity with a respectful sense of the past.[34] There follows an attempt to invest the university with the city's antiquity, praising the distinction of its buildings, 'which for spaciousness, convenience and architectural merit are held to surpass anything else of the kind in England outside Oxford and Cambridge.'[35] The pamphlet then turns to Bristol's halls of residence, advocating residential life, for the formation of 'character and culture,' and for providing the vital elements of conversation and friendship integral to the intimate atmosphere of the elite university.[36] In this fashion, the pamphlet's authors attributed the ideas of antiquity and domesticity to the new universities in an effort to bestow legitimacy on institutions which were, by their own account, neither antique, nor elite, nor offering education at the expense of training.

The appeal itself was couched in the frankest possible terms: 'There are none who do not benefit, and no sum is so small that it will not be welcome.'[37] In addition, county councils were reminded that they benefited from the university, both in its capacity as an educational institution and through the work of its agricultural research station. Detailed instructions were given on how to write one's cheque or devise a bequest to the university.

It is not known how the public reacted to these uncharacteristically bold merchandizing techniques, nor how many actually saw the pamphlet.

Financially, the appeal was not a success. Arthur Tyndall recalled that the university staff recoiled in horror from the crude commercialization of the appeal, the publicist's 'vulgar propaganda methods, suitable for advertising a new face cream but not a University.'[38] When the university's principal donors, the Wills family, gave £100,000 to cover post-war building expenses incurred by the building programme they had funded, to everyone's horror the advertising agency claimed a cut of the donation. The Wills brothers (regular donors to the university who would not have regarded their donation to their own project as a response to the appeal) were affronted, and the University had quickly and quietly to buy off the advertising firm, abandoning the appeal in the process.[39]

This incident, small in itself, illustrates a dilemma common to all civic universities—how to advertise when advertisement is by definition an ungentlemanly thing to do. The ironic side of the incident is that the pamphlet was in fact a fair reflection of the university's real needs. Its appeal to civic pride and competition, its use of the prewar national efficiency rhetoric were all in the best traditions of civic university fund-raising and what Americans would call boosterism. It was not, however, the pamphlet's contents that were held to be at fault, but rather the university's recourse to advertising techniques, and, for a major educational institution, reticence in this matter spelt hard times ahead as the century unfolded. Without advertising, the university would be limited in its ability to disseminate information about its services and its needs, but with advertising it would lay itself open to charges of vulgarity. In the case of the Bristol appeal, it was the university itself, rather than the public, that recoiled from the reality of fundraising tactics. Better to trust to luck and to the eventual restoration of the full government grant, it seemed to say, than to soil one's hands by extending them, palm upward, to the public. The transatlantic observer cannot help but notice the contrast with the American universities, with their shameless self-advertisement, willingness to court public favor, and their significantly higher levels of funding.

IV

It has been suggested that the study of the new English universities, their ideals, aims and attempts to find a place among established institutions, can often be undertaken profitably by outsiders, and this has been equally true of the American universities.[40] This section will examine some English views of American higher education in the pre-1940 period, revealing on the part of the observers a very much more relaxed attitude toward the diversity and occasional follies of these institutions. In part, the observers expected mediocrity. As the evidence of the University of Bristol's honorary degree scandal indicates, the presumed low quality of the American university was a readily-available image with which to beat those English counterparts which displayed excessive entrepreneurial spirit at the expense of quality. There were, however, English observers whose study of American institutions was sufficiently objective to allow them to make balanced and perceptive comments which provide the modern historian with valuable points of comparison.

In his study of late nineteenth-century American political and social institutions, *The American Commonwealth*, James Bryce devoted a chapter to the country's universities. In common with other English observers, Bryce noted that the majority of universities were not, in fact, doing university-level work, both because of their students' inadequate preparation at secondary school level and the universities' lack of adequate teaching staff.[41] He was, however, struck by the variety of the American institutions, by the infinite capacity of any given college to grow and to attain status, and by the popular appeal of even the humblest. Contrast his tolerant, even laudatory attitude towards the weak young American institutions with the expectations of excellence for the new English universities discussed above:

> They light up in many a country town what is at first only a farthing rushlight, but which, when the town swells to a city, or when endowments flow in, or when some able teacher is placed in charge, becomes a lamp of growing flame, which may finally throw its rays over the whole State in which it stands.[42]

Bryce concluded that the multiplication of small universities caused no danger to educational standards but rather that excellence was promoted by the very number of colleges and universities in the country, which multiplied the chances that one would eventually produce a scholar of distinction.

In a frontier society, unfettered by long traditions and existing models, new universities very similar in spirit and conception to the English civic universities were able to expand and flourish, with no constraints upon their growth or their potential to achieve excellence. The absence of a well-established 'idea of a university' in American society allowed for a rich growth of institutions of all types and standards, from powerful state universities to tiny denominational colleges, to which a form of natural selection applied. Colleges and universities either throve or failed according to the fortunes of their host community, their ability to attract students and staff, and the entrepreneurial abilities of those who governed them.

The ability of American universities to be all things to all men was certainly not viewed by contemporaries as an entirely desirable trait, and attracted criticism at home and abroad. In the 1930s, the American academic Abraham Flexner excoriated both the American and the English civic universities for their ready acceptance of 'non-university' subjects designed to bring them profit but little academic recognition. Writing on English vice-chancellors, Flexner noted that: 'The English scorn—and very properly—the "advertiser" and "money-raiser" who have latterly emerged in America.'[43] He did not address the problem of how to attract funding without some sort of appeal to the public and adopted an entirely anti-vocational stance towards the university curriculum, deploring the existence of even such well-respected departments as Automobile Engineering at Bristol and Brewing at Birmingham.[44] At the same time, Flexner displayed some ambivalence toward the ancient idea of a university, to which he was powerfully attracted:

> In all countries, history, traditions, vested interests hamper recon-struction. Obstacles are not always bad: a rich and beautiful past may interfere with reconstruction, while at the same time offering considerable compensation.[45]

Ultimately, it seemed, Flexner would have the civic universities resign themselves to their dependence on the ancient university ideal.

Despite its freedom from a monolithic, all-controlling and detailed 'idea of a university,' America did have very definite ideas about what a univer-sity should be. Overarching assumptions about the function of a university linked institutions of widely-differing quality into something like a coher-ent whole. In the 1920s, Edward Fiddes (historian and Registrar of the University of Manchester) returned from a visit to America and reported his impressions in a lecture. In common with all English observers, he noted the high percentage of American youth in higher education, but, like Bryce, was quick to point out the elementary nature of much of that instruction.[46] As Bryce had done, he commented on the universities' wide appeal to all social strata and on the wealth of many of these institutions. Unlike Flexner, he was not dismayed by the universities' forays into non-academic or voca-tional teaching, because he perceived that their unifying principle, that which made them universities in American eyes, was not the dissemination of an agreed-upon body of knowledge but rather the transformation of immi-grants and aliens into Americans. As long as the university performed this function, what did it matter if liberal and vocational education jostled within its portals, or if the latter sometimes appeared to dominate the curriculum? Fiddes quoted an unnamed American critic as having said:

> It [the university] is the educational power station of the land, occupying itself to a most burdensome extent with even minor forms of the education that leads to prosperous and understanding American citizenship.[47]

It may be remembered that the University of Bristol was forced for very shame to withdraw its pamphlet characterizing British universities as 'power stations of mind.' To the average American reader, however, neither the metaphor, nor the universities' mixed agenda would have seemed incongruous.

V

To the English observer and critic at home, however, the issue of what a civic university was, or ought to be, too often became enmired in comparisons between the ancient and the modern, and it was the rare inside observer who could overcome the influence of the ancient idea of a university and give a clear picture of the civic university as it was, or as its founders intended it to be.

Between the two world wars, the civic universities adopted a new course, attempting to conform, insofar as they could, to what they felt to be the essentials of the traditional idea of a university. Lack of funds inhibited them from going the whole way; I know of no civic university that seriously considered adopting the tutorial system, for instance, or offering its staff residential rooms in college. Other areas, such as antiquity, were obviously intractable, although there were rather pathetic attempts to link the universities with anything ancient in their surroundings. The area most amenable to change proved to be that of student residence, and new building projects were put in hand in the inter-war period. Bristol, for instance, expressed the intention of becoming fully residential, although this was never realized.[48] Even at the time, it must have been obvious that full residence was a quixotic dream for these underfunded institutions. Bristol, with less than one third of its students living in halls in 1928, would have had an even better chance of achieving this ambition than the big northern universities whose proportion of students living in halls was closer to one fifth.[49] Shortly after the first world war, Bristol's Vice-Chancellor referred to the halls of residence as 'residential college[s] on the lines of similar Colleges at Oxford and Cambridge', so it is clear that university administrators viewed residence as an area in which they could and should emulate the ancient universities.[50] Whether the proposed changes were insufficient, or whether critics perceived the fatal loss of focus implicit in such slavish copying, the promise of improved provision of residence was not enough to stem the tide of criticism, both from outside and from within, that was to swamp the civic universities in the inter-war years. By the 1930s, it was obvious that the roots of the dissatisfaction lay much deeper than wrangles over student residence, for instance, would seem to imply.

In this period, economic depression and high unemployment, together with fears for the future of liberal democracy combined to create widespread dissatisfaction with the guardians of liberal culture, including the universities. Eric Ashby has traced the increasing influence of the National Union of Students in this period to the twin issues of university reform and the growth of a student political consciousness.[51] More detailed study of this period suggests that, while students at the ancient universities became involved with politics, particularly on the Left, those at the civic universities were more profoundly affected by the scarcity of jobs, especially in the teaching profession.[52] Many of these were scholarship students, whose families had made sacrifices to allow them to continue their education, on the understanding that a professional qualification would lead to improved employment prospects. Although they felt the political currents of their day, they had too much invested in a university education to accept with equanimity the risk, however slim compared with that of other workers, of unemployment.[53]

There were other, perfectly genuine causes for complaint about the quality of the universities' service to the state; Michael Sanderson has called their lack of provision for the bright working-class child '. . . not only . . . socially unjust but also economically bizarre.'[54] Paradoxically, this very real shortcoming seems to have attracted very little contemporary attention. Instead, universities in general and civic universities in particular were made to bear the blame for what were essentially social, economic and ultimately cultural limitations of their society. The civics' real loss of prestige occured when they began to be viewed as Victorian fossils, remnants of that proud provincial culture that had flourished in the nineteenth century and then declined to pitifully low levels in the twentieth.

A multiplicity of explanations exist for the decline of provincial culture. In his history of the English provinces, Donald Read cites, among other causes, 'centralisation *upon* London as the centre of government and standardisation *from* London as the arbiter of standards.'[55] Specific causes included the rise of pressure group politics, the growth of the professions and of professional organisations, decline in provincial interest in politics, the decline of the provincial great towns, including the phenomenon of 'moving out,' in which leading families deserted the centre of town for the suburbs and the consequent disappearance of networks of important local families. There were causes linked to technical innovations, such as improved communication and faster travel, the rise of a national press, followed by the influence of radio and television. Finally, Read blames the effects of standardisation in education, including the failure of the civic universities to make a local impact.[56] The last factor is hardly just. The civic universities were caught in a trap from which they could not escape: they were, like it or not, linked into a national system by their common indebtedness to the University Grants Committee, by participation in such organizations as the National Union of Students and the Association of University Teachers, by the national and international professional activities of their staff, and later by the national recruitment of students; at the same time they still paid lip service to an ideal of local service that had lost all power to command and only served to degrade them in the public eye. Among their other national affiliations, the civic universities were forced to accept allegiance to the elite idea of a university, following the collapse of more suitable and congenial local roles.

During the second world war, much serious critical thought was given to the post-war university, and it was commonly accepted that the universities, in particular the civics, had sunk to unacceptably low depths during the previous two decades. Paradoxically, even those who wrote with appreciation of the civic universities' unique role were forced into total negation of the idea of a civic university because they would have them conform to the impossible ideals of intimacy and domesticity. At the same time, critics frequently advocated a return to local service as the civic universities' best chance of rediscovering a role.

In 1949, Sir Walter Moberly, the Oxford-educated Vice-Chancellor of the University of Manchester, published a Christian tract advocating the rebirth of the university as a counter-poise to the evils of technocracy, totalitarianism, and secularism. He praised the alchemical transforming power of universities, but lamented that this effect was limited to Oxford and Cambridge, calling the nonresidential civics, 'a bargain-counter, at which certain specific articles . . . are purveyed.'[57] In his judgement, the civic university student was in great need of transformation:

> The 'Redbrick' universities at least cater predominantly for a clientèle which is 'suburban,' without roots and without standards; and they have too much taken their colour from their environment.[58]

Although he suggested that they might be able to join in a spiritual reformation, Moberly utterly denied the civics' ability to effect transformation solely through the influence of place. The ancient universities were expected to wield this transfiguring power over their undergraduates and there were many who claimed to have experienced it. The civic universities had never aspired to such powers, now it was clear that these were necessary for survival but, for them, tantalizingly unattainable.

Moberly did not advocate simple-minded emulation of the ancient universities, regarding such copying as snobbish and unproductive. Rather, their proper role should be to play Martha to the ancient universities' Mary, and to this end they should, 'cultivate a somewhat greater austerity' than Oxford or Cambridge.[59] Even in the post-war world, their function was to serve the needs of the local community, not to aspire to a national role. Moberly realized that there was a price to be paid for this severe dedication to local service:

> Instead of spacious and stately buildings, green lawns, and the glamour of a historic tradition splendidly embodied, you have buildings frequently dingy and cramped and sometimes sordid, set in an environment of smoke and slums.[60]

It was scarcely an inviting prospect, and not one to promote competition with the ancient universities for the most promising students. It could only work if the civics confined their aspirations to the second rank.

Surprisingly, in view of his description of their domestic life, Moberly concluded that the civic universities had not succumbed to a sense of inferiority, suggesting that they might yet become flagships of local education and culture by forging tighter links with their parent towns.[61] It was a hopeless prescription for institutions which, for almost half a century, had been part of an increasingly rigid, hierarchical university system, and whose localities had little use left for them.

The most famous, most devastating and, paradoxically, the most constructive criticism of the university system as a whole appeared during the war, misleadingly entitled *Red Brick University*. Its author, the Oxford-educated Edgar Allison Peers, professor of Modern Languages at the University of Liverpool, considered the work subversive enough to prefer the anonymity of the pseudonym Bruce Truscot, a cover which was only broken at his death.[62] His programme for university reform was sweeping and brutal in its treatment of the upper- or middle-class student idler and of the idle don. Although he made cutting remarks about the ancient universities' population of 'pass men,' tutorials empty of content and lectures delivered year by year from yellowing notes, it was towards the civic universities that he directed his most detailed recommendations. The civics' career as local service institutions must end, he wrote, if they were to take their place as potentially equal members of a university system. He proposed a vastly-increased government grant with a threefold purpose: to bring most students into halls of residence, to offer more open entrance scholarships (promoting national, rather than local student recruitment) and the development of specialised subjects within the universities.[63] In other words, the civic universities would adopt two features of the traditional idea of a university, residence and cosmopolitanism, while the ancient universities joined with them in a hitherto unimagined pastime, competition.

Bruce Truscot is better-known for painting the life of the civic university in its blackest hues. His imaginary industrial city 'Drab-town' with its dreary university buildings of red brick (a medium ineluctably associated in the public mind with asylums and board schools) left a far deeper impression on his numerous readers than his constructive program for reform. Even after history had left him behind (Truscot opposed any major increase in numbers, either of universities or of students) English readers continued to savour the Truscot duality for which their culture had prepared them: Oxbridge elegance *versus* Redbrick drabness.[64] Although Truscot offered a more realistic assessment of the university problem than did Moberly, the latter recognised a reality that Truscot was prepared to ignore: the civics could never be the equals of the ancient universities because to be an English university was to be Oxbridge. The 1960s saw the working out of this dilemma.

VI

At the time of the university expansion of the 1950s and 1960s, the civic idea of a university was more deeply discredited than at any time in its history. Planners of new universities bypassed them, even though the civics themselves were undergoing a period of expansion. The new universities were deliberately sited in cathedral towns, despite the lobbying of industrial towns for universities of their own. Their settings were pastoral, and, if they were ill-served by the fashionable architects of the day, they could often count on one ancient building to sustain the desired effect. Norwich offered the new University of East Anglia a site with an eighteenth-century house whose 'warm stucco walls and . . . miniature Tom tower . . . have already a fittingly collegiate flavour.'[65] Creative course planning did away with the perceived narrowness of the single-subject degree, while the group tutorial and semi-collegiate system created instant intimacy and domesticity. The simultaneous creation of a separate tier of technological universities, with limited arts sides, such as Aston and Salford which grew out of former Colleges of Advanced Technology (CATs), ensured that the new universities' commitment to liberal education, not training, remained untarnished. Of course there were exceptions and anomalies. Warwick University, for instance, combined a cathedral town setting with an industrial one, and suffered the odium of its staff and students when its connections with industry grew too intimate. Despite such variations in the model, it is clear that the new institutions answered to the traditional idea of a university, ascribing little if any spiritual ancestry to the civic universities.

This study has attempted to demonstrate why civic universities have received less than their share of attention from historians and why interest in them has been revived mainly by scholars outside Britain. The trends discussed above give some clues as to why this has been the case and to why it is beginning to change. The nature of the historical profession itself suggests some further answers. The generation of historians described by David Cannadine in his article, 'British History: Past, Present—and Future?,' who came up to university in this period of expansion preferred, as historians do, to study historical trends with implications for the future.[66] If they knew nothing else about universities, they knew their Truscot and they had learned from him that the civics were worthy but dull. Historians prefer continuities: Oxbridge begat the new universities, Redbrick begat nothing. Nothing except the Commonwealth universities, where the federal principle was to find its fullest expression, the ex-CATs, and the first round of polytechnics to attain university status. No inconsiderable legacy, thinks the outsider.

If historians have now decided to remedy this situation, as the recent body of historical writing suggests, and to put the civic universities back in their place as pioneers of popular, meritocratic university education in England, some caution must be exercised. Little will be accomplished if we imagine them as dingy, utilitarian utopias, in which leisure, aesthetics, friendship and the transforming power of place have been discarded as expensive, elitist frills, unnecessary beautification of the grim face of learning. To do this is to cast our lot with the elitists, to imagine that the civic universities contributed nothing to the pleasures of the mind and spirit. No one who has set foot inside a civic university could imagine such a thing, and that is where we should begin.

References

1. R. D. Anderson, 'Universities and Elites in Modern Britain', *History of Universities* x (1991).
2. Edward Shils. 'British Intellectuals in the Mid-Twentieth Century,' in *The Intellectuals and the Powers and Other Essays.* (Chicago and London, 1972), 135–153.
3. Martin J. Wiener. *English Culture and the Decline of the Industrial Spirit, 1850–1980* (Cambridge, 1981), 22–24.
4. Michael Sanderson. 'The English Civic Universities and the "Industrial Spirit", 1870–1914.' *Historical Research* 61 (1988), 90–104.
5. Michael Sanderson. *The Universities and British Industry 1850–1970* (London, 1972), 95–101.
6. Ibid. See also, W. H. G. Armytage. *Civic Universities: Aspects of a British Tradition* (London, 1955).
7. See for instance, Julie Sims Gibert. 'Women at the English Civic Universities: 1880–1920,' (Unpublished doctoral dissertation, University of North Carolina, Chapel Hill, 1988); Elizabeth Jean Morse. 'The Changing Idea of a University: The Universities of Bristol and Manchester, 1900–1940,' (Unpublished doctoral dissertation, University of California, Berkeley, 1990). I would like to thank Sarah Barnes of Northwestern University for sharing her research for a dissertation on the comparative histories of Northwestern and the University of Manchester. For recent published works on the civic universities, see David R. Jones, *The Origins of Civic Universities: Manchester, Leeds and Liverpool* (London, 1988), and Peter R. H. Slee, *Learning and a Liberal Education: The Study of Modern History in the Universities of Oxford, Cambridge and Manchester 1800–1914* (Manchester, 1986). Jones's book is based on his Yale University doctoral dissertation. For articles relating to the civic universities by established scholars of English culture, see Thomas William Heyck, 'The Idea of a University in Britain, 1870–1970.' *History of European Ideas* 8 (1987), 205–219, and Sheldon Rothblatt, 'Historical and Comparative Remarks on the Federal Principle in Higher Education.' *History of Education* 16 (1987), 151–180. A recent grant to the University of Birmingham extends the promise of a major scholarly history of that institution in the near future: see 'Research in Progress', below.
8. Writers inside the civic universities have had the utmost difficulty in doing this. In his study of the post-war university novel, Ian Carter coins the term 'not-Oxbridge' to describe the attitude of both Oxbridge writers to the periphery and the attitude of civic university writers towards their own institutions. Ian Carter, *Ancient Cultures of Conceit: British University Fiction in the Post-War Years* (London, 1990).

9. For further thoughts on this subject, see A. H. Halsey. 'Invidious Comparisons: Oxford and the British Universities 1914–1970,' in B. H. Harrison (ed.), *The History of the University of Oxford*, vol. 8 (forthcoming). I am grateful to Professor Halsey for letting me read his draft version of this piece.

10. University Grants Committee. *Returns from Universities and University Colleges in Receipt of Treasury Grant, Academic Year 1947–48* (London, 1949), 5.

11. Ibid. 9.

12. Eric Ashby and Mary Anderson, *Portrait of Haldane at Work on Education* (London, 1974).

13. For a fuller discussion of the varied motivations of civic university founders see Morse. *op. cit.*, 1–2.

14. Sanderson, *The Universities and British Industry*, 81.

15. A. H. Halsey and M. A. Trow, *The British Academics* (London, 1971), 67–83.

16. See C. R. Searle, *The Quest for National Efficiency* (Oxford, 1971), 75–76.

17. For the opposing point of view, see Roy Lowe. 'Structural Change in English Higher Education, 1870–1920,' in Detlef K. Müller *et al. The Rise of the Modern Educational System: Structural Change and Social Reproduction 1870–1920* (Cambridge, 1987), 164. I do agree with Lowe's companion point, that the civic universities were eager to strengthen their arts side and to avoid the stigma of providing only technical training. For further evidence of the civics' desire to become a new kind of university, see below.

18. Morse, *op.cit.*, ch.2.

19. For student numbers, see Sanderson. *The Universities and British Industry*, 96. Note that this figure excludes students in the Faculty of Medicine.

20. A. M. Tyndall, 'Sixty Years of Academic Life in Bristol,' from a slidetalk to the Forum of the S.C.R., Bristol University, March 10, 1958, p.18. University of Bristol Archives (UBA), DM219 Box 2.

21. Don Carleton, *A University for Bristol* (Bristol, 1984), 28.

22. For a complete list of the honorary degrees, see *The Nonesuch* ii (Dec. 1912), 23–4.

23. *Stethoscope* 15 (Aug. 1912), 23.

24. Carleton, 29; *Bristol Times and Mirror* 11 April, 1913, 5 in UBA DM 526; Public Record Office PC 8/760, Folder 111190, June 1913. Handwritten notes on the cover and inner cover.

25. *Western Daily Press* 10 Sept., 1912. *Bristol Guardian* 14 Sept. 1912. UBA DM 526.

26. *Bristol Guardian* 23 Nov., 1912, and *Bristol Times and Mirror* 12 Mar., 1913. UBA DM 526.

27. *The Times* 18 Oct. 1912. UBA DM 526.

28. Tyndall, 'Sixty Years', 19–20.

29. David Cannadine, 'The Context, Performance and Meaning of Ritual: The British Monarchy and the "Invention of Tradition", c. 1820–1977,' in Eric Hobsbawm and Terence Ranger (eds) *The Invention of Tradition* (Cambridge, 1983), 138.

30. Carleton, 37, and University Grants Committee, *Report of the University Grants Committee, 3rd February 1921.* (London, 1921), 4.

31. *The First Line of National Defence* (London, nd[1921]).

32. Ibid., 1.

33. Ibid., 2.

34. Ibid., 6.
35. Ibid., 7.
36. Ibid., 12.
37. Ibid., 16–17.
38. MS note by A. M. Tyndall dated December 1949, thought to relate to the pamphlet (DM 363:23). It is ironic that Tyndall of all people should react so violently to the publicist's tactics, as he himself enjoyed a reputation as one of the most entrepreneurial academics of his generation. His reaction in this case suggests that he had a shrewd idea of the public's likely reaction to the use of advertising techniques by an institution of higher learning. For a further discussion of Tyndall's methods for promoting physics at Bristol, see S. T. Keith, 'Scientists as Entrepreneurs: Arthur Tyndall and the Rise of Bristol Physics.' *Annals of Science* 41(1984), 335–357.
39. Tyndall, MS note.
40. For an excellent example of the comparative perspective, see Martin Trow, 'The Robbins Trap: British Attitudes and the Limits of Expansion' (University of California, Berkeley. Center for Studies in Higher Education, Occasional Paper no. 63, June 1988).
41. James Bryce, *The American Commonwealth* (2nd edn, 2 vols London and New York, 1889), ii. 545–546.
42. Ibid., 568.
43. Abraham Flexner, *Universities: American, English, German* (New York, 1930), 250.
44. Ibid., 255–256.
45. Ibid., 35.
46. Edward Fiddes, *American Universities. A lecture delivered at the University of Manchester on 16th November, 1925* (Manchester, 1926), 11–14.
47. Ibid., 32.
48. A. M. Tyndall, 'The University of Bristol' (typescript n.d.), UBA DM 363:81.
49. University Grants Committee. *Report including Returns from Universities and University Colleges in Receipt of Treasury Grant, Academic Year 1928–29* (London, 1930), 57. The comparative figures for Bristol are from Manchester and Birmingham.
50. 'Draft Memorandum for issue to L.E.A.'s etc in the West of England. Sub-Committee on Closer Relationship between the University and Western Counties', Mar. 1919, p. 2, UBA DM883. For further discussion of the use of residence to emulate the ancient universities, see Morse, ch. 3.
51. Eric Ashby and Mary Anderson, *The Rise of the Student Estate in Britain* (London, 1970), 69–70.
52. For a fuller discussion of these themes, see Morse, ch. 7. For the point that the ancient universities and London were the locations of the bulk of student political activity in the 1930s, see Brian Simon, 'The Student Movement in England and Wales During the 1930s', *History of Education* 16(1987), 189–203, 191.
53. For a survey of the extent of graduate unemployment, see *The New University*. n.s. (Dec. 1934), 11. On the comparatively privileged position of the university graduate in the job market, see Armytage, 269.
54. Sanderson, *The Universities and British Industry*, 278.

55. Donald Read, *The English Provinces c. 1760–1960: A Study in Influence* (London, 1964), 207.
56. Ibid. ch. 5.
57. Walter Moberly, *The Crisis in the University* (London, 1949), 24.
58. Ibid. 25.
59. Ibid., 305.
60. Ibid., 243.
61. Ibid., 246–248.
62. For an account of the revelation of Truscot's true identity, see Peter Searby's review of Thomas Kelly, *For Advancement Learning. The University of Liverpool 1881–1981* in *History of Universities* iv (1984), 218–20.
63. Bruce Truscot, *Red Brick University* (Harmondsworth, 1951), 54–61.
64. For his views on expansion, see Truscot, 266–73.
65. *The Times Educational Supplement* 6 Feb. 1959, 218.
66. David Cannadine, 'British History: Past, Present – and Future?' *Past and Present* no. 116 (Aug. 1987), 169–91.

ENGLISH ELITE EDUCATION IN THE LATE NINETEENTH AND EARLY TWENTIETH CENTURIES

Roy Lowe

Source: W. Conze and J. Kocka (eds) *Bildungsbürgertum im 19. Jahrhundert*, Teil I, Stuttgart: Klett-Cotta, 1985, pp. 147–62.

Despite keen scholarly interest in the topic of nineteenth and twentieth century English elites, and access to them — an interest which has generated a considerable literature — there remain widely contrasting views on elite exclusivity, on the extent to which governmental, professional and industrial elites were accessible to those of humble origin and on the role of education in sustaining these elites. What may be loosely termed the "traditional" interpretation is that which emphasizes the extent to which positions of power and privilege in England were the preserve of relatively small groups at the onset of industrialisation and have remained so despite the traumatic and apparently democratising social changes of the nineteenth and twentieth centuries. John Scott, for example, has emphasized the growing power of elite educational institutions — the public schools and the ancient universities as "self-recruiting and self-perpetuating institutions composed of men recruited from the establishment"[1]. Similar judgements have been made by Stanworth and Giddens[2] writing on industrial management and by P. A. Welby in his study of the Anglican clergy[3]. Implicit in such analyses is a view of the educational system which emphasises its power in limiting access to these elites through its selective function. One recent study by Boyd has drawn attention to the continuing strong links between the public schools and Oxbridge and has argued that the growth of higher education may even have heightened social stratification by leading to the establishment of a "super league" of prestigious institutions and to lines of demarcation within higher education which may have worked to exclude the alumni of some colleges and universities from elite posts. He concluded that *despite the tempests of post-war change, the public schools and ancient universities have maintained a secure connection with the occupational hierarchy*[4]. Fritz Ringer has, in a powerful introductory chapter to his study of European education reflected on the possibilities of an "educational segmentation that tends to legitimize and to perpetuate social distances"[5]. In the event, his analysis of educational change in England drew attention as much to its rapid extension and evolution at the turn of the twentieth century as to its assumption of a "tracking" function through segmentation. But there remains much in his analysis which would sympathise with these rather gloomy accounts of social change.

The alternative view has been canvassed by Harold Perkin and W. D. Rubinstein. Perkin's claim that the evidence "argues for the university as a vehicle of social mobility rather than an obstacle to it"[6] is based on the argument that the growing power of Oxbridge to command the professions gave opportunities for small but significant numbers of relatively poor middle class scholars to aspire to positions of power. For him, the most recent one hundred years have witnessed "a significant increase in social mobility" marked by increasing recruitment from the middle ranges of society to elite positions. More recently, Perkin has extended this argument to claim that this represented *nothing less than the transformation of the university from a marginal institution an optional finishing school for young gentlemen and prospective clergymen, into the central power house of modern industrial society*[7].

W. D. Rubinstein, who was for some years Perkin's co-researcher, has augmented this view in a recent conference paper, claiming that studies which consider merely the schooling and university of alumni who subsequently aspired to elite positions disguise as much as they reveal by assuming a homogeneity among those who frequented the public schools which did not in reality exist. Rubinstein's work on the wealth and social position of the parents of public school boys suggests that their backgrounds were extremely varied. He argues from this that these elite educational institutions may therefore have played a critical part in sponsoring social mobility. For Rubinstein, the emergent middle classes provided the powerhouse of the social transformation of the early twentieth century. These middle classes, "disproportionately resident in London and the South East" thus gave a new twist to the North v. South contrast and were a catalyst to *the drift of population and wealth in this century to the south . . . a process which increasingly appears irreversible*[8]. The involvement of schooling in this process must be noted: most of the major public schools are in the south of England.

Against this background, this paper will focus upon two key developments in the process of transformation which occured at the turn of the twentieth century. First, the establishment of close links between the professions and the universities will be considered for evidence of the "standardisation" of access to elite positions. Secondly, as ancillary to this process, the opening up of scholarship routes to higher education will be examined. In combination these two phenomena may throw light on the extent to which higher education became an effective agency of social mobility during this period.

Between 1870 and 1920 the major professions moved within the ambit of the universities, which thus became the key to social and career advancement as never before. Medical education was fairly typical of this process. The standardisation of medical qualifications was approached in 1858 through legislation which introduced the registration of medical practitioners and the abolition of regional licences. Within a few years medical education was taking place increasingly within the universities[9]: by 1878 either the universities, or medical schools associated with them, were entirely responsible for medical education. This trend was formalised when those new university colleges with medical schools (Birmingham, Bristol, Liverpool and Owens) were recognized by the grant of charter at the start of the twentieth century[10]. In this process Oxford and Cambridge were able to fall back upon the defence of providing a liberal education for intending practitioners before they received their professional training elsewhere, a pattern which continued at least until the 1922 Royal Commission, which reported that *at Oxford, practically all the students have taken honours in the Physiology School. They receive their practical training elsewhere, mainly in the London hospitals*[11]. Similarly at the sister university: *London is its centre of clinical studies, and Cambridge has concentrated on giving a primary training in the fundamental sciences of medicine*[12].

The legal profession has been described at that which "showed the least interest in formal education throughout the nineteenth century"[13], probably reflecting the prestige in which the profession was held. The Law Society had been founded as recently as 1825 and in 1836 began the establishment of professional examinations which were to be used throughout the century to counter the threat of encroachments upon professional autonomy by the universities. As Arthur Engel has shown, the Law Society was still, in 1908, trying to resist the power of two provincial Universities to establish law degrees which would exempt entrants to the profession from part of their five years of articled pupilage[14].

The universities, for their part, struggled to set their house in order in the matter of legal education. A School of Jurisprudence was established at Oxford in 1850, and in the following year the mediaeval disputation was finally, removed from the qualifying examinations for the Bachelor of Civil Law Degree. As with other professions, the universities committed themselves increasingly to the inculcation of "general principles and a liberal culture" prior to entering an Inn of Court[15]. The relevance of Oxbridge to the legal profession was established in the later-nineteenth century by a succession of eminent jurists who accepted chairs, most notably Kenelm

Digby, Sir William Anson, James Bryce, A. V. Dicey and Sir Frederick Pollock. Thus, while alternative routes to a legal education remained open into the twentieth century, increasing numbers of entrants chose to follow the university route, at first via Oxbridge and later through the Law Schools established in some of the Redbrick Colleges early in the twentieth century. A glance at the admissions register of Lincoln's Inn shows clearly that by the late-nineteenth century the universities had effectively established themselves as the starting point to a legal career. In 1880 of the 78 men admitted to Lincoln's Inn, 32 had been at Oxford previously and 27 at Cambridge, 5 had degrees from the University of London, 9 came from Scotland or overseas (most of these were graduates) and only 5 had no recorded experience of higher education[16]. The Gray's Inn Register shows a smaller proportion passing through university before admission during the 1880s, but also offers clear evidence of the growing acceptability of a degree — or at least some time spent at university — before beginning a legal career[17].

The pattern of entry to the civil service underwent radical changes between 1853 and 1890, and these, too, resulted in a strengthening of the position of the ancient universities. The Trevelyan-Northcote Commission (1853–1854) had as its main object the abolition of patronage and its substitution by competitive entry to the civil service. The outcome was an examination system which, since the examinations were of a literary type, dearly favoured the university man. Ironically, the succession of modifications to the entry schemes inspired by the 1860 Select Committee, the Playfair Commission (1874–5) and the Ridley Commission (1886–90) served only to strengthen this trend. Thus, from 1890, access to the new "First Division" of civil service grades was through examinations modelled closely on the honours papers of Oxford and Cambridge. In 1895 the lower age limit for administrative class posts was raised from 18 to 22, thus effectively closing entry to all but the most affluent of those who had not attended university[18]. In 1913 Sir Richard Lodge pointed out to the McDonnell Commission that an Oxford man who had taken Classical Moderations and later Greats could win enough marks in the civil service entry papers with no extension of his education[19]. A representative of Leeds University told the same Commission that "among the class of parents from whom our students are drawn, the possibility of entering the Civil Service is at present very little known"[20]. The prestige of a civil service career was confirmed by the fact that, in response to these reforms, the proportion of Oxbridge entrants actually rose between 1916 and 1939 from 80% to 90%. Thus, between 1909 and 1914, over a quarter of the successful candidates in the open competitions for entry to junior administrative posts were alumni of the "Clarendon" schools (the nine major public schools). Hardly surprisingly, by 1929, 28% of the posts at the level of assistant secretary or above were occupied by old boys of these same nine schools. Similarly, between 1909 and 1914, whereas 80% of the open competition entrants to the civil service had attended

Oxford or Cambridge, only 2% had attended no university at all. In this case, too, "professionalisation" involved the tightening of a clearly defined career route which favoured the ancient universities[21].

The traditionally restricted access to a military career was preserved until the mid-nineteenth century by the purchase system. The high cost of army commissions made them available to only a select few. In 1846 Lord Grey commented scathingly of this system: *There is not even a pretence of making it depend upon their showing themselves to be fit*[22]. Predictably, the levelling tendencies of the mid-century saw "buying in" come under increasing attack. Examinations were introduced in 1849, although their influence was largely resisted until the final abolition of purchase in 1871. This, together with other reforms in military education instigated by Edward Cardwell, signalled what has been called "the first step towards the establishment of a professional army"[23]. These involved among other things the regularisation of the age of entry to the military colleges, so that children were now excluded. Thus the minimum age of admission to Sandhurst was raised in 1858 to 16, and, as the century progressed, the age of entry was more commonly 18 or even 20. Yet these changes did not involve the establishment of a university education as the route to the army. H. A. Vachell, who entered Sandhurst from Cambridge in 1882, and Haig who followed him from Oxford two years later, were very much the exception among army recruits down to 1914, most of whom had been at public school and had then used a crammer (as did Winston Churchill for his third successful attempt in 1893) to get themselves up to scratch for the army examinations. In this process, a few schools sustained a stranglehold. Hugh Thomas has shown that *in an average year between 1878 and 1899, out of 330 Sandhurst cadets, 17 came from Eton, 22 from Bedford Grammar School, 17 from Harrow, 18 from Clifton, 23 from Wellington, 10 from Winchester, 11 from Cheltenham and 12 from the United Services School, Westward Ho*[24]. These recruits were drawn almost exclusively from landed or upper middle-class backgrounds and two thirds of them used crammers to qualify. Brian Bond has commented: *The British Army in the second half of the nineteenth century reduced the influence of wealth and social position and substituted objective educational tests for entry and a regularised system for professional advancement. At the same time it succeeded... in excluding all but a handful of officers from the lower-middle and working classes*[25]. It is perhaps significant that this profession, which remained aloof from the universities throughout the nineteenth century, was the most successful in sustaining a very limited access to its ranks.

One further aspect of this pattern of late nineteenth-century professionalisation was the growing tendency for industry and business to seek employees from the universities. This stemmed partly from "second phase" industrialisation in the second half of the century which saw the appearance of new industries which required a highly skilled workforce equipped with technical skills. The appearance of the new "civic colleges" was in large part a response to this demand. These Redbrick colleges both taught the sons of artisans, tradespeople and businessmen and provided a core of skilled graduates who were equipped for industrial posts. Although changing terms of trade meant that demand was not consistent, at Newcastle and Manchester approximately half of the graduates were entering industry by the late-nineteenth and early twentieth century, with peaks of demand from industry during the 1890s and again immediately before the first World War[26]. There is no evidence that these two universities were untypical, and the slight fall in the percentages of graduates entering industry in the first decade of the twentieth century may reflect not only the minor economic depression of the period, but also the growth of secondary schooling which involved a growing demand for schoolteachers, thus drawing away some graduates who might otherwise have sought careers in industry. At London University, the picture was similar. One professor of chemistry estimated in 1910 that 60% of his graduates entered industry, 25% teaching, while 15% were girls who married and were lost to the labour market[27]. This final comment hints at another important social function which was performed for the Edwardian and Georgian middle-classes by the universities, that of providing a marriage market.

More surprisingly, this period saw major initiatives from Oxford and Cambridge to meet the demands of industry, not only through the establishment of new departments, but also by setting up Appointments Boards (Oxford, 1892: Cambridge, 1901) whose primary function was to locate graduates in industrial posts. Their success was startling: between 1906 and 1913 the percentage of Oxford graduates entering industry rose from seven to twenty. At Cambridge, some colleges had already developed a reputation for their links with business: it has been estimated that 15% of the graduates of Jesus College were already entering industry by the end of the century. Under the influence of the new Appointments Board the university provided growing numbers of entrants to business and industrial careers during the Edwardian period, so that, by 1914 "of the order of two to three hundred a year" were finding their way from Cambridge into these posts[28].

But these developments within the ancient universities were pregnant with significance for both the universities and industry. At both universities more students came from families with business backgrounds than left to enter business. Further, many of these entrants to industry had graduated in Faculties with no obvious links with industrial skills. Thus a tradition of the highest echelons of industry being colonised by men with a liberal education was confirmed in the early twentieth century, while Oxford and Cambridge were able to continue to prepare the sons of many businessmen for the major "nonindustrial" professions. So, the rapprochement of industry and the universities may not have involved as great an enhancement of social mobility as is immediately suggested.

Teaching was another emergent profession during this period. At the mid-point of the nineteenth century the universities, open only to communicant members of the Anglican Church, offered limited career opportunities. School teaching too, had few attractions; beyond the great public schools, the majority of secondary schools were in a run down condition and many had ceased teaching entirely. Both the universities and the schools were revivified by later nineteenth century developments.

Within Oxbridge two developments opened up teaching as a career route. The first was a redefinition of the role of a university don: the second, the introduction of teaching in new subject areas. Sheldon Rothblatt has shown how the rise of the public schools in the nineteenth century resulted in the appearance at the ancient universities of increasing numbers of undergraduates with high expectations of the scholarship and teaching ability of their tutors. Before the 1880s the enforcement of celibacy upon Oxbridge tutors had forced many scholars into the public schools. The further relaxation, between 1850 and the 1870s, of the requirement of religious conformity for college fellowships, widened competition. The "close action of the teacher on the pupil"[29] which Mark Pattison advocated to the Royal Commission on Oxford University, and whose absence had done much to damage the image of university teaching, offered self-respect to these new dons and opened the gates to the recognition of tutoring as a worthy career. Rothblatt has elegantly summarized the revolution which this involved: *A new group of dons emerged in Cambridge in the twenty years preceding the statutory reforms of 1882. They were distinguished by their professional interest in scholarship, by their intention to make university teaching a career and by their desire to revive the unique feature of a collegiate university, the close relation between fellows and students*[30]. It was the emergence of this group, and the dominance of this ethic, which led to the virtual disappearance of private tutoring at the two ancient universities during the closing years of the century. *The new dons sought a place for themselves in Victorian society... They elected to remain in the colleges. They translated the example of the schools into Cambridge and found that in forming the character of students, by which they meant restoring the influence of the teacher they regained their self-respect*[31]. In this process, it might be added, they also helped to establish an academic career among the major professions.

The second key to this process was the introduction of new subjects. It was as much to establish the propriety of a liberal education as a preparation for professional life as to respond to sweeping technological change that new schools and Faculties were established. At Oxford, the two existing schools of Mathematics and Greats were supplemented after 1852 by History, Law, Theology, English, Modern Languages, Natural Science, Medicine, Forestry and, in 1921, Modern Greats. At Cambridge, the foundation of the Natural Sciences Tripos during the mid-nineteenth century led to the establishment of chairs in various subjects, while the expansion at the turn of the century saw Economics, Law, Medicine, Agriculture and Architecture all receive formal recognition.

These changes resulted in less than 10% of Oxford dons moving on to a church career by the end of the nineteenth century, compared with 53% who took that step during the first half of the century. Although the social background of Oxford dons remained predominantly "gentlemanly", as Arthur Engel has shown, by the turn of the century the majority went on to make their career within the university[32].

This professionalisation was increased by the appearance of the "Red-brick" provincial colleges, most of which were chartered as fully fledged universities in the early years of the twentieth century. Although the justi-fication presented for the foundation of most of the colleges was the enhancement of local industries and trades, in reality the acquisition of university status was usually followed by a scramble for prestige, which meant the promotion of the liberal arts and the appointment of staff with experience at the older universities — Cambridge, with its greater commit-ment to science, was rather more successful than Oxford in this process of "colonisation" of the Redbrick universities. These Oxbridge alumni, although in a minority at the provincial universities formed a significant proportion of the graduates appointed and were particularly successful in winning the most influential posts. In 1894, of 13 professors at Liverpool, only four were not from the two ancient universities[33]. This was not untypical. Some influential Oxbridge men, such as Henry Sidgwick and his friend James Bryce, clearly saw the leadership of these provincial colleges as the proper concern of Oxbridge. In their correspondence at the turn of the century, these two men discussed likely candidates for the principalship of both Birmingham University and the Owens College at Manchester[34]. If the Red-brick universities sought at the start of the twentieth century to imitate the teaching and collegiate style of Oxford and Cambridge, this process of "colonisation" was at least a partial cause.

Schoolteaching had long offered rich rewards for its most successful practitioners. The headship of Harrow carried a salary of £10,000 as early as the 1860s, although this was exceptional, and in marked contrast with the army of assistant masters who were described by the headmasters' con-ference as "villainously paid" in 1876. The key to the growing self-respect of schoolteaching at the end of the nineteenth century lay in its emer-gence from the shadow of two other professions, those of don and cleric, for which teaching was traditionally seen as a preparation. The grip of the church upon school teaching weakened dramatically towards the end of the century. In 1870 over a half of the masters at ten great public schools were ordained, by 1906 only one master in eight at the same schools was a clergyman[35]. Despite the continuing widespread belief that it was preaching ability which provided the key to a school headship, and that the highest offices in the church were the preserve of those who had enjoyed successful tenure of a public school headship (of eight Archbishops of Canterbury during the 100 years from 1860, six were ex-public school heads, four of these with links with Rugby school), in fact the schools increasingly provided their own career rewards, particularly with the expansion of secondary schooling following on the reforms of the 1870's and 80's.

A further key to this development was the relaxation during the 1880s of the practice of enforcing celibacy upon Oxbridge dons. As college after college modified its rules for fellowships, aspiring scholars were no longer forced to make their way into the schools. The "modernisation" of school curricula through the introduction of scientific studies and modern languages led to the appearance of schoolmasters who had not been through the grind of 'Greats' and may thus have been less inclined to defer to both an exclusively Classical curriculum and to these rather idiosyncratic career outlets.

There were several tokens at the turn of the century of this increasing assurance and autonomy of the teaching profession. There was a growing trend to pension heads, thus ending the need to seek ordination to eke out retirement. The Association of Assistant Masters, founded in the 1890s and incorporated in 1902, fought a series of successful battles over salary, security of tenure, superannuation and the establishment of professional standards in schools. Although these issues were contested largely by activists from within the grammar schools, the benefits were felt within the public schools. Thus, for example, the Endowed Schools (Masters) Act of 1908 finally outlawed the practice by which a new headmaster sacked existing staff and brought in his own men. This growing self respect was marked by increasing public recognition of schoolmastering. H. A. James, a prominent member of the H. M. C. who left the headship of Rugby school for the Presidency of St. John's College, Oxford, in 1909, was awarded a Companionship of Honour, and became one of the first members of the H. M. C. to receive such an award[36]. By the end of the century over a thousand secondary schools had been reformed by the Charity Commissioners. Between 1861 and 1931 the number of children receiving secondary education in the United Kingdom rose from an estimated 37,000 to 433,000. On concomitant was the emergence of schoolteaching as a career.

This process seems to have been linked to a hardening of the stratification of schools which had been advocated by the Taunton Commissioners in 1867 and which was still thought appropriate at the end of the century. First, second and third grade secondary schools were distinguished not only by the differing social groups for which they catered and differing curricula, but also by differing staffing patterns. Thus, the Bryce Commission reported that in the great public schools — the first grade secondary schools — "practically all" of the staff were university men. By contrast, *in the second grade the proportion of university men is much smaller ... The principal is generally a graduate and in most cases he has under him one or two men who*

*are also graduates, but the whole staff seldom consists of university men
exclusively.* This was even more marked in the third grade schools, where,
Bryce found, *there are among 'the graduate' teachers few members of the
older universities, the staff being largely from the London University and
the university colleges*[37]. This graduation and separatism was reflected in the
salaries of these schools. While the average salary in the ten great Public
schools was £242, in a sample of 190 other endowed secondary schools it
was only £105. The contrasts were equally great in girls' secondary schools.
A mistress in one of the eleven best schools could anticipate a salary of the
order of £147, but the average for second and third grade schools were only
£112 and £84[38].

There is some evidence to suggest therefore that, at the very moment
that the Bryce Commissioners were emphasizing the dangers of each class
of school becoming the preserve of a particular social group, English schooling was developing a self-perpetuating characteristic by which particular
schools tended to lead to particular routes through higher education.
Significantly, the Bryce report warned that *a parent who has reason to think
that his children, if sent to a certain school, will run the risk of acquiring habits
of speech or behaviour which might be disadvantageous to them afterwards,
is entitled to decline such a risk*[39]. Thus, while the first grade school continued to aim towards a classical education at one or other of the ancient
universities — or towards the army for its less able candidates — the very
best second grade schools had different aspirations. Leeds Central School
was thought to be a model: *The classical education aimed at was limited to
such requirements as would be needed for the Victorian or London matriculation, and the degree it prepared for was the B. Sc. rather than the B. A.
What was true of the Leeds School was true of many other schools of the
same type*[40].

During the first years of the twentieth century, the swift expansion of
the new "Redbrick" universities and of the municipal secondary schools
worked towards the reinforcement of these distinctions. One inspector of
secondary schools reported in 1907 to the Board of Education: *I have
recently had occasion to bring to the notice of the Bristol L. E. A. [Local
Education Authority] a defect in their educational organisation which had
hitherto escaped notice and which I have some reason to believe exists in other
large towns. It may be briefly described as a breakdown in the 'educational
ladder' at the top.*

*The old grammar schools of every grade; with all their faults, flattered
themselves that they never let the really brilliant boy escape notice, and that
every nerve was strained to bring his work to a university scholarship standard.
The number of distinguished men who were educated at some of our humbler
grammar schools is a confirmation of this claim . . . I suppose it is generally
recognized that our new municipal secondary schools are and must remain
second grade schools that the normal leaving age will be 16 or 17 and that the*

staff will continue, for some time at any rate, to consist of elementary teachers who have obtained a London B. A. or B. Sc. in the interests of their professional work, i. e. by men and women who have ceased to be students at the age of 19 or 20, instead of, as in the first grade schools, by teachers who have had a regular university course, and have only taken up their profession at the age of about 23. It may therefore be assumed that these schools cannot, as a rule, attempt anything like a university scholarship standard of work. The result of this is that our secondary schools must be definitely graded, as indeed they are in practice[41].

Only one profession stood out during this period as the exception to the general trend. Whereas changes in recruitment to most of the major professions — and to some emergent ones — saw an increase in the significance and power of the universities, for the clergy the opposite was the case. Whereas, in the early nineteenth century, holy orders was seen by some as "the most attractive of all professions"[42], the increasing secularisation of society and the new earnestness demanded of the clergy in the wake of the Oxford Movement worked to make it less so. Although the numbers of Anglican clergymen rose steadily during the nineteenth century (15,000 in 1831 rising to 23,000 in 1911)[43] fewer of them were drawn from Oxbridge. Thus, between 1840 and 1860 there was an absolute decline in the number of graduates taking holy orders and a rapid increase in the numbers of non-graduates, and the number of Oxford men coming forward in that year was only half of the numbers ordained in 1840 with similar backgrounds[44]. The figures for Cambridge were comparable. In 1841 270 men took orders: in 1862 — 178. The removal of the requirement of ordination for many Oxbridge fellowships in the years following 1871 served only to accelerate this trend. The reasons for these changes were complex. There was a decline in the value of many livings: pluralism and non-residence among the Anglican clergy was effectively stamped out at mid-century, and the growing numbers of assistant curates (mostly from non university backgrounds) served to diminish the status of the profession too. Equally, the growing availability of other career outlets to graduates doubtless tarnished the attractiveness of the church. These changes were partly a response to the growth of Nonconformist sects, whose clergy performed similar functions but were not in the main university men: this too may have been a factor. This suggestion that the clergy were the exception to the general trend of professionalisation may help explain the spectacular clerical careers achieved by a few men of humble origin, which have been used by Rubinstein to argue for strong democratising tendencies within higher education. In brief, it may have become slightly easier for a man of relatively humble origins to aspire to an archbishopric after some of the potential opposition had been drawn away into other emergent professions.

This consideration brings us to a second major question. Who exactly were the recipients of these career advantages which the universities and schools were increasingly able to bestow? The key to a "democratisation" of the educational system was seen at the time by many as the provision and resuscitation of scholarships. The 1922 Royal Commission on Oxford and Cambridge proffered a benign view of the significance of these scholarships: *The number of poor men in residence at both universities increased materially during the last half of the nineteenth century. This increase has been very rapid in recent years owing to the improvement of local schools with the assistance of grants from Local Education Authorities, and to the consequent success of those schools in competing for open Scholarships*[45]. This Report went on to argue that by 1914 "a considerable proportion" of scholars and exhibitioners came from poor homes or at least homes where "means were at any rate moderate".

Fritz Ringer has argued that in England examinations were vital to the opening up of higher education and the professions: *England combined low enrollments per age group with a comparatively "democratic" distribution of access chances... This configuration is especially likely to engender social mobility through education... This has apparently been done to some extent in England, perhaps by way of the eleven-plus and other examinations*[46].

This rosy picture of democratisation is not borne out by a closer look at the evidence. Three contemporary reports confirm the view that, while the early years of the twentieth century did see an enhanced opportunity for lower class pupils to rise through the educational system, the dice remained heavily loaded in favour of pupils from more privileged backgrounds. The whole question of scholarships for higher education was reported on in 1916 by the Board of Education. This document confirmed that the current cost of a year at Oxbridge was £140, while scholarships were pegged at £80[47]. Consequently, a poor scholar would need to win both a school scholarship and a college scholarship to be in a position to sustain himself through an undergraduate course. It becomes clear from this report too, that the new civic universities were the more natural route for holders of L. E. A. awards. In 1911–12, for example, of the £57,000 awarded by local authorities, £5,000 sent students to Oxford, £15,000 to Cambridge, while the rest (37,000) was disbursed among students studying at the eight other English universities, which were in any case much cheaper, not least because the bulk of their students were not in residence[48]. The 400 scholarships offered by these civic universities varied from £40 to £20 annually — a stark contrast with the level of awards offered by the ancient universities. So, this report suggests that the scholarship system did in practice reinforce the hierarchical characteristics of English higher education. One passage in the report is very telling: *If the Local Education Authorities took a completely independent line in their methods of award they would cut off their pupils from the advantages offered by Oxford and Cambridge, and effect a thorough severance between the Public Schools and the old universities on one hand and the new universities and grant earning schools on the other. Such a severance is not to be desired*[49].

This gloomy picture was confirmed by Ellis's report on *The Poor Student and the University*, which appeared in 1924. Ellis showed that, during the second half of the nineteenth century, scholarships were effectively confined to the great public schools and to a few boys from endowed grammar schools. *Through this narrow gate the poor child may infrequently have reached the university*[50]. The commissions of the 1850s, Ellis argued, worsened the situation by emphasizing free competition in those very attainments which were best acquired in the public schools. Only London, an examining university with no residential requirement, offered any real chance to significant numbers of students from humble origins. Ellis went on to hint at the way in which the sudden development of both municipal secondary schools and civic universities may have led to the establishment of a "tracking" system: *These new universities coming to their full status during the very years when secondary education was being organized, cannot fail to have a particularly close relation to the secondary schools. The comparatively low range of fees, and the economical standard of living which is becoming a tradition within them, have made them relatively more accessible to the children of poor parents. The industrial and technological bias of some of the faculties has commended them to the sympathetic notice both of the working-class population and of such schools as have developed an interest in science and its applications. The fact that they are largely aided from municipal funds has meant that to some extent the university and the school have come under the same control*[51]. This was largely confirmed by the classic study of access to English universities by Glass and Gray which showed that, even as late as 1913–14, the 432 scholarships offered by the Oxbridge colleges were very unevenly shared. Of them, 374 (86%) went to public school pupils, 27 (6%) to endowed grammar pupils, 29 (7%) to pupils from municipal secondary schools and 2 (0.5%) to alumni of private schools[52]. Set against the numbers in these various sectors of secondary education the figures make even more stark reading: for the public schools, with a total population of 43,000 pupils, these figures represented 8.5 scholarships per 1,000 boys. Within the grammar and municipal schools the smaller number of scholarships was shared among a larger population (82,000), so that the number of scholarships in this sector per 1,000 boys was only 0.68. Each pupil in the endowed and municipal sector had, in 1913, one twelfth of the chance afforded his contemporary in a public school of gaining entry to Oxbridge[53]. Further, this research showed that this disparity was widened even further by the fact that the fifteen most expensive public schools won almost half of all the college scholarships awarded to these schools[54]. It becomes clear that, while devices were established to offer poor students a chance of aspiring to the ancient universities at the turn of the century (free places in secondary schools: L. E. A. scholarships), such students entered the race at a grave disadvantage.

It becomes possible, then, to attempt a few provisional judgements upon the traumatic changes which took place in both secondary and higher education between 1870 and 1920. Swiftly expanding professions offered attractive rewards and turned increasingly to the universities for their labour force. Competitive entry to these professions involved a quest for men with the breadth of vision to discharge executive responsibilities. Hardly surprisingly, the best available contemporary model — that of a humane education — was seized upon and its prestige reinforced. Consequently, the expansion of both higher and secondary education saw no immediate threat to the status of a Classical education, merely its supplementation through a broadened curriculum. Elite schools and colleges met these new demands with an expansion which admitted growing numbers of "first generation" entrants without seriously threatening the grip exercised by those social groups which were already privileged. As a further consequence it was possible to relegate the vital discussion on the most appropriate technical education to those second grade institutions whose producers would provide experts for the new industries of the period. Thus, the most contentious curricular debates were held within the endowed schools, the new municipal schools and the civic colleges. The extent to which a "tracking" function developed between these schools and the Redbrick colleges is suggested by the striking similarity between developments in the two sectors. At precisely the same moment that Robert Morant imposed a broad, humane curriculum upon all secondary schools (1904), the newly chartered Civic universities were retreating from their full-blooded commitment to applied science and settling for expansion in Arts and pure science. For these colleges, too, were involved in a scramble for status which necessitated adherence to the tried model of a humane education[55].

Competition between existing and new municipal secondary schools and between institutions of higher education resulted, then, in some similarity of curricula, and this similarity, which enabled some limited social mobility, served to obscure the divisive nature of this emergent system. For overlaying curricular similarities were disparities in status and in the aspirations of students which both fanned and were fed by the closer links between the universities and the major professions. One key to an understanding of these status disparities is the contrast in lifestyles between elite and lower status institutions. This contrast was all-pervasive and was critical: what marked the public school man and the Oxbridge scholar was a certain disinterestedness, a leisured lifestyle, a growing commitment to athleticism in the closing years of the nineteenth century and, of course, scholarship. This style had its trappings — not only of dress, but also of speech. The precise details of this lifestyle and of its historical timing may be open to debate: John Honey is currently engaged upon as yet unpublished research on the significance of accent among English elites. But what is beyond doubt is the extent to which this ethos was communicated to new and less prestigious colleges and schools, both through conscious imitation on the part of staff who introduced team games and house systems and through an unconscious imitation among the student body[56]. The host of early twentieth century novels and pamphlets which popularised the public-school ethic are also worthy of serious study. One further aspect of these contrasts concerns environment. The author has recently studied the extent to which differing revivalist architectural styles were sought at the turn of the century for colleges with differing purposes — revivalist Gothic for Oxbridge, brick and terra cotta for the new hothouses of science[57]. What is truly under consideration here is the process by which in England an emergent middle-class identified itself through the kind of conditioning which it gave its young people as they prepared for entry to elite professions. At the end of the day the marks of an educated man, at least a smattering of Classics and conformity to a particular lifestyle and set of values, were as significant as the possession of formal qualifications. A limited broadening of recruitment to the most prestigious educational institutions enabled them to prepare a rising generation for key positions in society by introducing them to this lifestyle. Inadvertently, a scholarship system which it was hoped might broaden entry to this elite became a mechanism which reinforced its exclusivity by enabling a minority of new recruits to experience this conditioning process. Through this complex network of processes the English universities were able to participate in the reinforcement of the major professions during the late nineteenth century: it is a process which deserves much further study.

Notes

1 J. Scott, *The Upper classes: property and priviliege in Britain*, London 1982, 107.
2 P. Stanworth and A. Giddens, *Elites and Power in British Society*, Cambridge, 1974.
3 P. A. Welby, "Ecclesiastical appointments, 1942–61", Prism, VI, 5, 1962.
4 D. Boyd, *Elites and their education*, NFER, 1973, 143.
5 F. K. Ringer, *Education and Society in Modern Europe*, Bloomington, 1979, 30.
6 H. Perkin, "The recruitment of elites in British society since 1800", Journal of Social History, 12, 1979, 229.
7 See K. H. Jarausch (ed.), *The transformation of higher learning, 1860–1930*, Stuttgart, 1983, 207. This collection contains several other relevant articles.
8 W. D. Rubinstein, "Education and the social origins of British elites, 1880–1970", unpublished paper given to the 1983 Conference of the Anglo-American Historical Society, See also Rubinstein's *Wealth and the Wealthy in the Modern World*, London, 1980.
9 R. M. Walker, *Medical education in Britain*, London, 1965, 23.
10 C. Newman, *The evolution of medical education in the nineteenth century*, London, 1957, 292.
11 Royal Commission on Oxford and Cambridge Universities, *Report*, London, 1922, 32.

12 *Ibid.*, 37.
13 A. Engel, "The English universities and professional education", in K. H. Jarausch, *op. cit.*, 297.
14 *Ibid.*, 303.
15 A. Harding, *A Social history of English Law*, London, 1966, 348.
16 *Lincoln's Inn Admissions Register, 1420–1893*, London, 1896.
17 *Register of Admissions to Gray's Inn*, London, 1899.
18 See R. K. Kelsall, *Higher Civil Servants in Britain from 1870 to the present Day*, London, 1955 and E. N. Gladden, *Civil Services of the U. K. 1855–1970*, London, 1967.
19 *MacDonnell Commission*, Appendix to third report, 227.
20 *Ibid.*, 265.
21 See Kelsall, *op. cit.*, chapter 6.
22 H. Thomas, *The Story of Sandhurst*, London, 1961, 104.
23 *Ibid.*, 105.
24 *Ibid.*, 151.
25 B. Bond, *The Victorian army and the staff college, 1854–1914*, London, 1972, 30.
26 M. Sanderson, *The universities and British industry, 1850–1970*, London, 1972, 101.
27 *Ibid.*, 112.
28 *Ibid.*, 52–54.
29 S. Rothblatt, *The Revolution of the Dons*, Cambridge, 1968, 194.
30 *Ibid.*, 227.
31 *Ibid.*, 246.
32 A. Engel, *From Clergyman to Don*, Oxford, 1983, 286.
33 This point has been developed by the autor in D. K. Müller, F. Ringer and B. Simon, *The Rise of the Modern Educational System: structural change and social reproduction* (forthcoming).
34 Bodleian Library M. S. Bryce, 15.
35 *J. Honey, Tom Brown's Universe*, London, 1977, 308.
36 There is a detailed account of these developments in chapter 5 of John Honey's book (above).
37 *Bryce Report*, 1895, Vol. 1, 238–9.
38 *Ibid.*, 209.
39 *Ibid.*, 74.
40 *Ibid.*, 142.
41 Public Record Office Ed. 12/139.
42 A. D. Gilbert, *Religion and Society in Industrial England*, London, 1976, 133.
43 *Ibid.*, 28.
44 W. O. Chadwick, *The Victorian Church*, London, 1966, Vol. 1, 522.
45 *Oxford and Cambridge Report*, 1922, 132.
46 Ringer, *op. cit.*, 247.
47 Board of Education, Interim Report of the consultative committee on scholarships for higher education, London, 1916, 30.
48 *Ibid.*, 33.
49 *Ibid.*, 31.
50 G. S. M. Ellis, *The poor student and the university*, London, 1942, 2. See also L. D. Witheley, *The poor student and the university*, London, 1933.
51 Ellis, *op. cit.*, 6.
52 D. V. Glass, and J. L. Gray, "Opportunity and the older universities", in L. Hogben, *Political arithmetic*, London, 1938, 428–433.
53 *Ibid.*, 438.

54 *Ibid.*, 450.
55 This argument is developed more fully in my contribution to Muller, Ringer and Simon.
56 See, for example J. A. Mangan, *Athleticism in the Victorian and Edwardian Public School*, Cambridge, 1981 and D. Newsome, *Godliness and Good Learning*, London, 1961.
57 R. A. Lowe, "Building the Ivory Tower: the social functions of late nineteenth century collegiate architecture", *Studies in Higher Education*, 7,2, 1982. See also M. Seaborne, "The architecture of the Victorian Public School", in B. Simon and I. Bradley (eds.), *The Victorian Public School, Dublin*, 1975.

106

THE EXPANSION OF HIGHER
EDUCATION IN ENGLAND

Roy Lowe

Source: K. H. Jarausch (ed.) *The Transformation of Higher Learning, 1860–1930*, Stuttgart: Klett-Cotta, 1981, pp. 37–56.

The late nineteenth and early twentieth centuries saw a phenomenal and unprecedented growth in the provision of higher education in England. At the commencement of the period, in mid-century, there were but four small university institutions and a number of provincial colleges of varying prestige and clientele. For the vast bulk of the population education beyond elementary school had to be sought through Mechanic's Institutes or Adult Schools. Within eighty years this situation had been completely transformed through a process of growth and systematization. By 1930 the different elements in what could be discerned as a system stood in a clear relationship one to another, and identified themselves with particular social groups. Similarities with higher education in other major industrial societies were now more manifest: admission qualifications and ages were, by 1930, largely standardized; specialist faculties, each linking with professional occupations, had been established, and, more importantly, a definite hierarchy of educational institutions was discernible. How did this process occur in England between 1860 and 1930?

The determinants of expansion

During these years higher education in England responded to a series of changes in the economic and commercial structure which impinged on all major industrial societies. The onset of what Fritz Ringer has called the "high industrial" phase of development involved the deployment of a far more highly skilled labor force than had previously been required as well as the swift expansion of ancillary professional services such as banking and accountancy. The first phase of British industrialization, centered largely on innovation and growth in the textile industries, was giving way to, and had helped to initiate, a second based to a greater degree on the development of coal and iron resources and the building of railways. In the seventy years after 1860 whole new industries emerged (machine tool, chemical, and electrical), with Britain becoming increasingly an industrial exporter, involved in heavy investment abroad. This growth in scale of both industrial and urban systems meant not only the rise of manufacturing regions but also more sophisticated transportation networks. Fueled by late-nineteenth century imperialism and by sharpened rivalry between nations, these changes both depended upon and, in turn, stimulated the transformation of higher education.

Two consequences were immediately apparent. On the one hand there was a sustained and growing demand for vocational training. The number of workers in engineering, the machine tool industry and shipbuilding doubled between 1851 and 1881. Despite some employers' concern that technical education might lead to the dissemination of trade secrets, these new industries necessarily increased the demand for skilled and semi-skilled workers. The second outcome was a growing sensitivity to foreign developments. This intensified competition involved a new interest in how industrial rivals trained their work force. In 1881 the Samuelson Commission was ordered to "inquire into the instruction of the industrial classes in certain foreign countries in technical and other subjects and into the influence of such instruction on manufacturing and other industries at home and abroad."

Ironically, English contemporaries did not always perceive the need for change. Often the attention of those involved in the debate on higher education concentrated upon the need to preserve significant elements of the existing system in the face of sweeping changes. The rhetoric of the day emphasized the maintenance of traditional styles as much as the necessity to adapt to new circumstances. The way in which contemporary needs were perceived was to prove critical in shaping this emerging system.

Some developments appeared irresistible. This was certainly true of one of the most significant elements in the process of growth, the enhanced demand from below. The Schools Enquiry Commissioners estimated the number in receipt of grammar school education in 1861 as nearly 37,000. By 1931 there were a total of 433,517 children in recognized secondary schools. This growth was swiftest after 1902, when the newly formed Local Education Authorities assumed responsibility for secondary education. They participated in the virtual creation of a system of girls' secondary education. The implications for higher education were immediately perceived. As early as 1870, John Percival, headmaster of Clifton College, used the annual gathering of the National Association for the Promotion of Social Science to urge the Universities to recognize

> a whole class of schools which have sprung up in obedience to a
> national want. . . . Who can fail to lament the want of real living

connection between our old universities and the great commercial and industrial centers? A great step will have been taken in this direction if the universities so reform themselves as to remain closely connected with the middle class schools, even those of modern aims and tendencies.[1]

Those involved in the debate on secondary education, which was itself rapidly expanding, demanded university reform in these terms.

As the industrial towns grew, and municipal politics became linked with civic pride, a more general critique of the isolation of the universities appeared. It was realized that local colleges, dispersed throughout the industrial north, could provide a cultural focus. Joseph Chamberlain emphasized this point in his frequently quoted 1898 pronouncement:

> To place a university in the middle of a great industrial and manufacturing population is to do something to leaven the whole mass with higher aims and higher intellectual ambitions than would otherwise be possible to people engaged entirely in trading and commercial pursuits.[2]

Equally, as Arthur Smithells, the Professor of Chemistry at the newly chartered Leeds University, spelled out, the time was ripe for the universities to replace their monastic ideal by a closer identity with these growing towns:

> English education and English life have suffered to an almost incalculable extent by the isolation of our ancient universities. The want of geographical contact between the greatest seats of learning and the busy hives of industry ... have been attended by mutual disadvantages, and ... have placed in actual opposition two spheres of human activity that, in a well-regulated world, should be coincident.[3]

This was supplemented by the observation that, since the century had witnessed a shift of population to the northern towns, new foundations were needed to obviate the expense of living away from home.[4]

Although industrial development, a revitalized secondary school system and urbanization may be readily identified as three major factors influencing the development of higher education, there was never any identifiable consensus on the kinds of growth which would best meet the national need. However, in the ferment of ideas which were canvassed, some dominant arguments did recur.

Within Oxbridge, despite the reforms of the 1850s and 1870s, which had set fair to modernize those institutions, there was little readiness for sweeping change. The unpreparedness for innovation was well summarized by Edwin Guest, Master of Gonville and Caius, who, in 1870, proffered one of the more congenial responses to the relentless prodding of the Devonshire Commissioners:

> Where there are so many conflicting interests to reconcile, it is obvious that prudence is necessary. . . . Precipitate action might do more harm than good. It would be, indeed, a sad thing if, in becoming "Physicists", we were to put into jeopardy the character of our University as the great mathematical school of Europe.[5]

That character involved adherence to the ideal of a liberal rather than a vocationally-oriented curriculum, and to a collegiate system fulfilling a strong pastoral role. For many dons, abandonment of these aims was too great a price to pay for the modernization of the two major universities.

But if Oxford and Cambridge were slow to initiate internal reform, one increasingly acceptable growth outlet, which reaffirmed the national function of the universities, was the nascent extension movement. This development, initiated by James Stuart in the early 1870s at Cambridge, with Oxford following just a few years later, arose from what one contemporary called "a widespread opinion in favor of a diversification of their revenues for the promotion of higher education in the great centers of population."[6] Increasingly, this movement, as it hardened into the Tutorial Classwork of the early Twentieth Century, was viewed by critics as an attempt to mould a refractory and dangerous proletariat in the image of "the reasonable university man."[7] For its enthusiasts, men like Mansbridge and Tawney, this was seen in the years before the First World War as a device which might offer a broad "highway" to a democratized system of higher education, rather than the selective ladder established in the wake of the 1902 Education Act. It succeeded in bringing thousands into contact with university work, and in disseminating the ideal of a liberal education among the nation at large. It is no coincidence that those of the new university colleges which grew from local extension centers—notably Nottingham and Reading—subscribed more readily at the outset to a curriculum balanced between Arts and Sciences, and did not set about an immediate radical reconsideration of the ideal of a university.

At London, too, the introduction of external degrees in 1858 and the recognition of women students in 1878 provided the framework by which the university sponsored growth in other leading towns, although both concessions were made in response to the internal problems of the London colleges rather than with an eye to growth at the national level. Similarly, at Durham, close ties with the established church retarded innovation, a fact which elicited the scorn of Lyon Playfair in 1868:

Though it does teach engineering just now, and does pay a nominal attention to science, it was so difficult, a few years ago, to get them to comprehend science in any enlarged aspect that I have not much hope of Durham. That university had a splendid opportunity of becoming a people's university for the great manufacturing counties in the north of England; but, being governed chiefly by clerical authorities, who naturally looked chiefly to the traditions of Oxford and Cambridge, the university has not taken root in the affections and sympathies of the population around it.[8]

For the subsequent structure of higher education in England this failure of the existing universities to commit themselves wholeheartedly to expansion was critical. The outcome was a whole series of new institutions aiming at a different clientele, and standing below Oxbridge and the London colleges in prestige. Further, the pre-existing universities compounded this contrast by ensuring that in those activities which did impinge upon the wider public—university extension and examining—the pattern was largely of evening teaching. Thus the precedent of a growth in "compensatory" higher educational agencies, soaking up demand which could not be met within the existing systems, was laid down at the beginning of the period under review.

In the major industrial cities the need for growth in higher education was readily perceived and forcefully articulated. The civic colleges represented a direct attack upon the concept of a university as a monastic institution offering a humane education in the liberal arts. Ironically, it was an Oxford scholar, J. R. Seeley, who most cogently spelled out the nature of the development foreseen, when, in 1887, he joined the debate on a Midland university:

It is desirable greatly to increase the number and to disperse over the country teachers of the particular type which is produced at the universities . . . who have their knowledge at first hand, speak with authority each in his department, and speak to men. . . . England, which till lately has had but two universities, will have a dozen.[9]

For Seeley, these new institutions should not be collegiate, on the Oxford model, nor must they dissipate themselves in examining. In sum their brief was to be the democratization of the knowledge of the age:

Modern civilization needs a vast quantity of science: the demand for trustworthy knowledge, scientific, sanitary, technical, economical, political, historical, moral and religious, rises with urgency from these great towns. Why should it not be met by universities founded everywhere?[10]

The debate on the founding of a Midland university, in which Seeley was joined by the professoriate of Mason College, Birmingham, elucidated most of the major strands of the argument on the kind of growth that was foreseen. In 1892, B. C. A. Windle, the Professor of Anatomy, emphasized the extent to which local needs should be met:

> Every new university should be not merely the expression of a local desire for the best form of education, but should also be informed by the spirit and influenced by the peculiar nature of the pursuits of the district in which it is located . . . we should not hesitate to strike out on new lines.[11]

E. A. Sonnenschein, the Professor of Classics, attempted to resuscitate the collegiate ideal with a proposal for a federated university with sister colleges at Nottingham, Bristol and Birmingham. His reasoning followed that which had led to the establishment of a federated Victoria University in the major northern cities a decade earlier.[12]

The real impetus to a full-blown attack on the existing university ideal stemmed from the exploration of foreign precedents. Seeley had suggested in 1887 that Heidelberg and Edinburgh both proffered valuable models of successful non-collegiate institutions. The Birmingham syndics dispatched in 1898 a three-man delegation to study Canadian and American practice. It was under their influence that W. J. Ashley was recruited from Toronto to lead the infant Faculty of Commerce at Birmingham. He immediately became the apologist for radical departures:

> Birmingham does not dream of rivalling the two older universities in the studies particularly associated with them, like Classics, Maths., Philosophy and History. It will give its energies, and turn its resources, towards those fields in which they do little, and in which the loss of the amenities of college life is counterbalanced by the advantages derived from a position in the midst of a great industrial population . . . accordingly our curriculum will be very elastic.[13]

Contentiously, Ashley went on to claim technical studies as the prerogative of the universities, citing Leipzig as the welcome exception among German universities in which commercial education was pursued at the highest level.

Similar arguments were adduced for the other civic colleges. At Leeds, local industrialists demanded a professoriate who would be "a general source of scientific enlightenment to the county."[14] Significantly, the Yorkshire College began work with no teaching in the Arts. It was only introduced under the influence of Cambridge Extension lecturers, and the first Professors in the Humanities were paid on a lower scale than their scientific brethren. At Liverpool, Ramsay Muir repeatedly emphasized that his college would offer the best vocational training: "A university is the only possible vitalising force for technical education which aims at developing capacity for a particular profession."[15] The protagonists of the new university colleges predicted a swift growth in the provision of technical and scientific places, although this was rarely, if ever, quantified.

There were significant addenda to the case for growth. One was the argument that more places must be made available for young women. Typical was Arthur Smithells, Professor of Chemistry at Leeds, who, inaugurating a course on Home Science at Kings College, London, in 1908, pleaded the feminist cause:

> We shall find plenty of young women of talent who have the inclination and the opportunity to devote a few years to this kind of higher education and who will return from it ready to enter with redoubled interest and usefulness into the realm of home life.[16]

A further reason, advanced initially in 1907 by Ramsay Muir, was that the university needed to be enlarged and democratised to ensure a supply of entrants to teaching. He pointed out that "this movement had enormously reduced the cost of university education, and brought it visibly within the reach of thousands to whom it had been unattainable. Hence has come a remarkable increase in the 'natural supply' of teachers, adequately trained at their own expense."[17] To further this process, he argued, the inadequate courses currently offered in the university day training departments should be replaced by one-year professional training following on a three-year undergraduate course. Four years later this scheme was formally adopted.

Meanwhile, the case for an expansion of vocational and technical training outside the universities was also being made. By 1870 the proselytising of Lyon Playfair and his associates had led to a Select Committee and a scheme for a National Technical University. Working through the Science and Art Department, and, after 1887 the National Association for the Promotion of Technical Education, this lobby argued consistently for governmental backing for new initiatives. The outcome was not only the first steps (from 1889) to fund the new university colleges, but also the appearance of separate institutions, financed in part by the Science and Art Department and in part from local rates, devoted to technical education. The City and Guilds College, 1881, and the Regent Street Polytechnic, acquired by Quintin Hogg in the same year, were crucial precedents, establishing the model of technical institutes outside and below the university sector. In response to the accusation that he had neglected cultural studies, Hogg replied: "I did not include the subjects you mentioned for fear of attracting a class of young men of a higher education status than those for whom the institute was intended."[18] Against this background, the rift between the university and non-university sectors hardened, so that by 1910 the Commission on University Education in London was able to report: "Universities are institutions for making officers; the polytechnics were intended to be institutions to make the rank and file the most capable rank and file in the world."[19]

Throughout this period the evening school movement gained force. In a strong plea for technical education in evening schools in 1905 C. H. Creasey emphasized that "one of the most pressing educational needs of the next few years, is to adapt instruction to the capacity of a larger number of earnest students."[20] Similarly, in the *University Review* four years later, W. J. Bees, a schools' inspector, argued for a vast increase in technical education if British industry was to match that of Germany, where a quarter of the work force had received a technical training:

> Higher education for the great mass of people in industrial districts must be evening education . . . a steady flow of evening students should pass from the advanced technical institutions to the university. This will enable the university to fulfill its function as the head of the evening school scheme in great industrial and commercial districts.[21]

In these terms the locally financed Technical Colleges and Evening Schools, which together constituted the fastest growing sector of English higher education, were condemned to inferior status.

The pattern of growth

How did these new demands relate to the pattern of actual developments between 1860 and 1930? Any statistical treatment is open to the charge that figures presented at the time were often not accurately researched or contained their own internal inconsistencies. But with the introduction of annual returns from university colleges in 1893 and the centralization of records through the Board of Education after 1899, these problems decreased during the later part of the period under review.[22]

Throughout these figures census years have been used to provide a sample which is readily comparable with overall population trends. However this technique runs the risk of distortion through the particular circumstances of individual years: for example, 1921 saw the zenith of the brief post-war economic expansion and an abnormally high demand for educational facilities from newly demobilized troops. Nonetheless, over the long run these decennial returns are a sufficiently reliable guide to the overall growth of the English system.

Broadly, the pattern which emerges confirms that pre-existing university institutions were slow to respond to changed circumstances. Consequently much work developed in relatively new institutional forms unhampered by a traditional role and readier to adjust to the demands of expansion. Because of contemporary ambiguity over precisely what constituted higher education, it was necessary to review the whole post-school provision, including work which was often of low status, but which catered to those social groups unable to aspire to a university education for historical reasons. In a country with clearly defined class boundaries, where the existing universities remained the preserve of the privileged, the shift towards a schooled society, far more of whose members aspired to higher education, took place through new "compensatory" institutions which, for reasons associated with class exclusivity, were not immediately granted recognition as institutions of higher learning. This eclectic approach is further justified, because, as part of the gradual professionalization of society, the artisans and skilled workers who looked to the adult movement or to technical classes for their own education, were themselves, in turn, to father the first-generation university entrants of the mid-twentieth century.

Even for the pre-existing universities of Cambridge, Oxford, London and Durham (Table 1) it is impossible to be entirely confident of student numbers, although these figures, researched independently, are sufficiently close to those put forward by Stone for Oxbridge to indicate that both are fairly near the mark.[23] They suggest an eight-fold growth in this sector during the whole period, with the greatest expansion occurring in the newer institutions. Thus, the figures lend credence to the view that Oxbridge was far from wholehearted in accommodating to change.

Within the new provincial university colleges (Table 2) growth was even more startling. In each case returns are shown for the original foundation from which the later university developed. Where estimates have been made, they are based on individual college histories and the best available secondary sources. Although, even by 1931, none of these universities could compare in size with Oxford, Cambridge or London, in total they constituted a new sector of higher education, with a maximum student capacity, towards the end of the period, nearly thirty times as great as that at the outset.

Table 1 Full Time Students in Pre-Existing Universities.

	CAMBRIDGE	OXFORD	LONDON	DURHAM	TOTAL
1861	1,200*	1,200*	375*	50*	2,825
1871	1,750	1,940	300	70*	4,060
1881	2,400*	2,310	700	300*	5,610
1891	2,700*	2,400*	1,100*	350*	6,550
1901	3,080	2,800	900*	250*	7,030
1911	3,970	3,400	4,120	900*	12,390
1921	5,900	4,440	6,950	1,200*	18,490
1931	5,600	4,572	10,281	1,446	21,899

*Approximation based on returns of graduates for one year only.

Table 2 New University Foundations.

				Total Numbers of Enrolled Student				
	1861	*1871*	*1881*	*1891*	*1901*	*1911*	*1921*	*1931*
Birmingham			200	650*	749	1,017	1,923	1,630
Bristol			350*	450*	542	834	1,045	954
Exeter				100*	200*	300*	450	650
Hull								100
Leeds			463	973	958	1,168	2,334	1,884
Leicester							9	100*
Liverpool				1,290*	974	1,401	2,665	2,220
Manchester	500*	1,000	1,100	1,300*	1,194	1,660	2,397	2,477
Newcastle	60	200	350	1,900*	1,612	1,435	1,628	1,411
Nottingham			1,600	1,600	1,914	1,906	1,075	1,551
Reading					500*	1,083	563	641
Sheffield			400	500	1,266	2,500	1,072	965
Southampton		270	500*	700*	900*	738	940	772
TOTAL	560	1,470	4,963	9,463	10,809	14,042	16,101	15,355

*Estimate

Perhaps the most significant change concealed by these global figures is the decline of part-time teaching in these institutions (Table 3). At their outset several of these colleges proliferated evening and day-release courses, most aimed at young workers in local industries. When this function was taken on by technical colleges, and as industry increasingly demanded training through full-time courses, the pattern changed, with only those colleges which had derived originally from a strong local university extension tradition, such as Nottingham, resisting the trend until at least the First World War. The figures suggest, too, that the contraction of part-time work coincided not with the granting of full university status but with the First World War, after which no institution resumed its earlier character completely. Even Leeds, which retained large numbers of part-time students into the 1920s, eroded their part in the university by a rapid expansion of full-time capacity.

It is also interesting to consider the extent to which this growth enhanced the opportunities for women to pursue academic training (Table 4). It becomes clear that the provincial colleges were, from their inception, at least accessible to women, and, so far as one can generalize, there seems to have been little change in the ratio of men to women, despite the swift growth in overall numbers. Women remained outnumbered by three or four to one at most institutions. The two exceptions were Birmingham and Bristol, where expansion involved vastly increased numbers of male entrants while the female portion remained static in size, representing a decreasing proportion of the student body.

Table 3 Ratio of Full-Time to Part-Time Students in Provincial University Colleges.

		1893	1901	1911	1921	1931
Birmingham	FT	409	435	868	1,809	1,446
	PT	291	314	149	114	184
Bristol	FT	412	334	467	1,008	905
	PT	293	208	357	37	49
Leeds	FT	400	746	660	1,610	1,510
	PT	501	212	503	724	374
Liverpool	FT	517	683	919	2,314	1,747
	PT	776	291	482	351	473
Manchester	FT	987	1,048	1,374	2,006	2,107
	PT	320	146	286	391	373
Newcastle	FT	482	502	652	1,212	1,058
	PT	1,478	1,110	783	416	353
Nottingham	FT	431	446	242	776	644
	PT	1,329	1,696	1,664	299	907
Sheffield	FT	158	361	354	947	749
	PT	103	905	2,164	125	216
Reading	FT			335	549	626
	PT			748	14	15
Southampton	FT			204	343	474
	PT			534	597	298

Table 4 Ratios of Female Students in Provincial University Colleges.

	1893		1901		1911		1921		1931	
	M	F	M	F	M	F	M	F	M	F
Birmingham	365	335	368	381			1,354	455	985	461
Bristol	387	318	345	197			681	327	572	333
Leeds	354	46	428	139			1,288	322	1,131	379
Liverpool	447	120	559	124			1,766	548	1,203	544
Manchester	—	—	—	—	no return presented		1,425	581	1,476	631
Newcastle	1,545	415	1,364	248			980	232	783	275
Nottingham	—	—	—	—			650	126	447	197
Reading	—	—	—	—			214	335	250	376
Sheffield	194	67	1,118	87			751	196	568	181
Southampton	—	—					198	145	305	169

Another significant development in these colleges was the growing concentration upon teaching to degree level (Table 5). The first returns from the colleges show only a small minority of students proceeding to degrees. At Mason College, Birmingham in 1893, only 14 of 700 students received London external degrees. This was not untypical. In the same year 13 graduated from Bristol, 13 from Leeds, 123 from Manchester, and 17 from

Table 5 The Growth of Work at Degree Level.

	1910–11 FULL TIME STUDENTS			1920–21 FULL TIME STUDENTS								1930–31 FULL TIME STUDENTS								
				Research		P.G.		Degree		Diploma		Research		Others		Degree		Diploma	
	Degree	Diploma	P.G.	M	W	M	W	M	W	M	W	M	W	M	W	M	W	M	W
Birmingham	565	242	19	42	22	1	16	1,073	244	238	173	57	17	0	0	73	265	155	179
Bristol	232	226	9	11	0	9	23	360	216	301	88	34	10	0	0	411	260	127	63
Leeds	409	108	18	11	6	6	10	817	287	454	19	57	16	0	0	832	242	242	121
Liverpool	679	199	37	22	0	8	28	1,198	473	538	47	36	3	0	0	844	391	323	150
Manchester	936	295	117	46	21	16	35	1,125	490	238	35	57	14	4	1	1,019	503	396	113
Newcastle	458	165	2	7	1	26	8	741	184	86	2	17	2	0	0	610	194	156	79
Nottingham	133	102	6	8	1	8	3	252	43	382	79	13	0	0	0	184	72	250	125
Reading	115	125	11	4	1	0	1	109	129	101	124	8	11	0	1	147	171	195	193
Sheffield	215	76	7	13	0	12	23	469	168	257	5	30	3	1	0	416	139	121	39
Southampton	99	103	2	3	1	1	6	98	67	96	71	2	0	0	0	146	78	157	91

Nottingham. From 1911 onwards, when more systematic records are available, a majority of students were on degree courses. This concomitant of recognition as a university was part of the process by which the provincial colleges established their position in the status hierarchy. Degree courses gave access either to professional posts or to managerial positions within industry. Thus, as the period progressed, the university colleges neglected increasingly the skilled artisans whom, it had been foreseen, they might train.

But below these aspirant university colleges there was a plethora of institutions offering technical education of one sort or another. A useful index of the development of this sector is furnished by the annual returns of recognized classes and students, first to the Science and Art Department, and subsequently to the Board of Education (Table 6). The tradition of part-time study in these institutions was never seriously threatened. By 1931 only 8,000 students, from a cohort of over a million, were studying full-time in technical colleges. These were, in the main, products of elementary schools financed by either L.E.A. or industrial scholarships. The Clerk Report of 1931, which examined these colleges indicated no desire, from industrialists or educationalists, to see the English tradition of part-time technical education modified.[24] The needs of British industry were to be met by the elementary schools, with a leaving age raised to 15, or by technical secondary schools, newly sanctioned by fashionable psychological theory. Thus, technical education remained low in prestige and failed to establish clear routes to managerial positions throughout the period under review. Its growth was phenomenal, but was accomplished through the extension of part-time facilities.

The third major area to be considered in any overview of higher education is that of teacher training. It provided one of the most significant pioneer routes for social mobility, with the vast majority of entrants coming from working-class or lower-middle class origins and gaining job-security in the difficult conditions of the early twentieth century. This was, too, an area in which women preponderated, suggesting that teacher training may well have been a common outlet for able girls who could not aspire to a university education (Table 7).

The vagaries of the English system render a precise comparison with other societies, in which categories of students may be clearly delineated, difficult. In England, for example, medical education became the concern of the universities by the mid-19th century, and, for most of the period, university statistics subsume the vast majority of medical students. Legislation in 1858, which standardized admission to the Medical Register, soon led to all training taking place either in the universities or in medical schools which came under their auspices.[25] Legal training, too, became linked more usually with a university education in the late 19th century, although some census reports give returns of law students outside the universities. In 1881, for example, there were 1,600 such students, but, unfortunately, similar

Table 6 Students in Receipt of Technical Education in Recognized Classes.

	Schools	Classes	Pupils under Instruction
1861	38		1,330
1871	908		38,015
1881	1360	4839	61,177
1891	2164	8568	148,408
1901			
In day science classes			66,384
In evening science classes			98,673
In day art classes			52,533
In evening art classes			67,854
		TOTAL	285,444
1911			
In day technical institutes			3,024
In day technical classes elsewhere			11,329
In evening and similar schools			708,259
In schools of art			41,292
In art classes elsewhere			3,217
		TOTAL	767,121
1921			
In technical schools			5,434
In day technical-classes			15,976
In Schools of Art			48,109
In art classes			3,611
In part-time technical instruction			866,567
In part-time technical courses			781,619
In day continuation courses			55,261
		TOTAL	1,776,568
(The returns for 1921 are for England and Wales.)			
1931			
In technical colleges			8,030
In day technical classes			27,819
In art schools			58,700
In day continuation schools			20,656
In evening institutions			905,786
		TOTAL	1,020,991

statistics are not available for the whole period under review. It would be reasonable to assume that the figures given here omit a significant number of trainees for professional posts who cannot be readily quantified. They also overlook the host of students in the adult education movement, Mechanics Institutes, Athenaeums and the like. Since many of these had a substantial social membership, any accurate assessment of their educational functions is difficult. There is a risk, too, that the figures presented here involve some double counting, since some training colleges were recognized

Table 7 Students Training to Teach.

		No. of colleges	M	F	Total
1861					
	Church of England	15	905	844	1,749
	British	1			121
	Wesleyan	1			114
	Roman Catholic	3			145
	TOTAL				2,129
1871					
	Church of England	22	835	781	1,616
	British	3	140	203	343
	Wesleyan	2	125	105	230
	Congregational	1	22	25	47
	Home and Colonial	1	0	140	140
	Roman Catholic	2	63	88	151
	TOTALS	31	1,185	1,342	2,527
1881					
	Church of England	25	904	1,199	2,203
	British	3	130	200	330
	Wesleyan	2	117	109	226
	Congregational	1	23	32	55
	Roman Catholic	3	42	146	188
	TOTALS	34	1,216	1,686	3,002
1891					
	Church of England	26	916	1,198	2,114
	British	4	137	255	392
	Wesleyan	2	119	109	228
	Roman Catholic	3	44	186	230
	Undenominational	2	33	129	162
	TOTALS	37	1,249	1,877	3,126
1901					
	In training colleges	64	2,192	3,610	5,802
	Being taught part-time in pupil teacher centers	38	506	643	1,149
	TOTAL				6,951
1911					
	Training for elementary teaching		3,870	7,295	11,165
	Training for secondary teaching		37	145	182
	Training for domestic science teaching			910	910
	TOTAL				12,257
1921	Pupil teachers in centers		597	2,745	3,342
	Pupil teachers not in centers		159	1,710	1,869
	Student teachers		5,741	10,930	16,671
	TOTAL				21,882
1931					
	Pupil teachers in centers		150	198	348
	Rural pupil teachers		120	565	685
	Student teachers		6,757	12,727	19,484
	TOTAL				20,517

Table 8 Total Numbers in Receipt of Post-School Education in England.

Year	Oxbridge, Durham and London	Provincial Universities	Total No. of Students in Universities and University Colleges	Technical Education	Teacher Training	Total (Nearest 100)
1861	2,825	560	3,385	1,330	2,129	6,800
1871	4,090	1,470	5,560	38,015	2,527	46,100
1881	5,610	4,950	10,560	61,177	3,002	74,700
1891	6,550	9,463	16,013	148,408	3,126	167,500
1901	7,030	10,809	17,839	285,444	6,951	310,200
1911	12,390	14,042	26,414	767,121	12,257	805,800
1921	18,490	16,101	34,591	1,400,000*	21,882	1,456,400*
1931	21,900	15,355	37,255	1,020,991	20,924	1,079,200

*Estimate

as Science and Art centers with students listed in the official returns of Technical Colleges.

Despite these reservations, it is possible to attempt a rough index of the numbers in receipt of some kind of post-school education in England during the period under review (Table 8). It shows that the ten-fold growth in the numbers attending university and teacher training college was far outweighed by the growth of part-time technical education. Thus, while the right-hand column suggests that a dramatic transformation came over English society, with some kind of post-school education becoming a real possibility for many young people, it must be remembered that most of this took place in the low-prestige, part-time "compensatory" institutions whose development allowed the universities to remain above the hurly-burly of this change.

Setting these figures alongside the overall population trends for England and Wales, makes it possible to depict the student body as a percentage of the total population and of the 20–24 age group (Table 9). Thus, these years saw an increase of nearly six times in the likelihood of any individual receiving a university education, and of eighty times in access to some kind of post-school educational experience.

Finally, the statistics of growth decade by decade show the universities responding to slightly different stimuli than those influencing the technical sector (Table 10). For the universities the 1870s and 1880s were the two major growth periods, while in the technical sector the 1860s and 1880s were clearly the more significant periods. In both sectors the first decade of the century saw an upturn in growth which was not subsequently matched.

In brief, these statistics give credence to the hypothesis that in England a diverse and highly-stratified system of higher education developed partly as a consequence of the unreadiness of existing universities to respond fully to social change. In this process, the role of the emergent university colleges was crucial. In the event, their aspiration to break from the "technocratic" model and to conform with that of the Oxbridge college drove a wedge between "humane" and applied studies which was to prove immensely significant for English society in the twentieth century. It is that process which will be examined in conclusion.

The dynamics of growth

It is clear that all these developing institutions wished to appear academically respectable. This was nowhere more true than in the provincial university colleges, where a recession from the "technological" ideal, and from part-time teaching, excluded many who turned instead to the technical colleges. Within the newly-chartered universities in the early twentieth century, much energy was devoted to the resuscitation of the liberal arts. It is significant that the Yorkshire College at Leeds was at first excluded from the federated Victoria University on the grounds that its curriculum was insufficiently

Table 9 Students as a Percentage of Population (All Figures in Thousands).

			University Students		All Students	
			as % of	as % of	as % of	as % of
	Total	20–24	total	20–24	total	20–24
Year	Population	Population	population	age group	population	age group
1861	20,066	1,829	0.016	0.185	0.035	0.383
1871	22,712	2,004	0.024	0.277	0.203	2.296
1881	25,974	2,328	0.040	0.453	0.289	3.222
1891	29,003	2,646	0.055	0.605	0.579	6.350
1901	32,528	3,120	0.054	0.572	0.953	9.936
1911	36,070	3,175	0.073	0.832	2.235	25.386
1921	37,887	3,151	0.091	1.098	3.843	46.208
1931	39,952	3,494	0.093	1.066	2.701	30.882

Table 10 Percentage Growth per Decade in Student Numbers.

Year	University Students	All Students
1861–71	164	657
1871–81	190	163
1881–91	152	224
1891–1901	111	184
1901–11	148	260
1911–21	131	180
1921–31	108	74

balanced, failing to offer a liberal education. No sooner was the new University of Birmingham legitimized by the grant of a charter in 1900 than its first Vice-Chancellor, Oliver Lodge, was lamenting "the unfortunate impression abroad that Birmingham either does not possess or does not encourage a Faculty of Arts. This impression has an obvious historical origin."[26] Under his energetic guidance, the arts faculty had trebled in size within twelve years. By 1905 Lodge was already claiming that a general B.A. at Birmingham could offer "a general education in the knowledge of the time."[27] This shift towards arts and pure science rather than applied science was not universally welcomed. In 1911 a local ratepayers' association angrily petitioned the Privy Council:

So far as the Birmingham University as such is concerned, it is of no use whatever to the industrial classes; as far as we can see all that has been done by the merging of Masons Science College into the University has been to divert the funds intended for ... the industrial classes to the use of the wealthy classes, and now the middle and working classes are being asked to contribute towards the education of the wealthy and well-to-do.[28]

This process seems to have been sustained into the inter-war years and paralleled elsewhere. In 1918, Sir Charles Grant Robertson, the Dean of Arts, lamented the general impression that Birmingham University was no more than a glorified school of applied science.[29] Under his direction the policy of vigorous expansion in arts was maintained. Similarly at Leeds, both Michael Sadler and J. B. Baillie, who succeeded him as Vice-Chancellor, attempted to resurrect the collegiate ideal, pressing the scheme of a "community housed in a pleasant landscape around an artistic set of buildings."[30]

This reversion from the applied sciences reflects the strength of the university model with which the late-nineteenth century pioneers had tried to break. It also probably indicates the class exclusivity of higher education, as dons in the new provincial colleges began to fear they were ministering, through applied science, to social groups for whom the university was not the proper preserve. It must not be forgotten, too, that, during this period, the provincial colleges were largely staffed by the products of Oxbridge. At all events, whatever the reasons, there seems to have been some retrenchment along traditional lines in the Redbrick Universities in the years after 1900.

Within the technical colleges there were also growing reservations concerning the extent to which the universities had usurped major responsibility for vocational instruction. In 1909, George Beilby told the Association of Technical Institutions that the time was ripe for its members to reclaim prime responsibility for technical training:

Some of the universities have given us a noble lead in our earlier development, but I am bold enough to think we have outgrown that lead. . . . I discriminate sharply between the function of the technical college, the training of large numbers of competent craftsmen or professional men, and the development of a smaller class of scientific pioneers.[31]

Another element in the dynamic of change was the increasing involvement of the state in planning the function of these higher educational agencies. As Armytage has pointed out:

The civic universities in their struggling years, and the university colleges all along, owed the very existence of their arts faculties and in many cases their pure science faculties to the presence of a large body of intending teachers whose attendance at degree courses was almost guaranteed by the state.[32]

191

By the early twentieth century the pattern of growth in all areas was effectively controlled and directed by governmental agencies. This development had been prefigured by the Samuelson Report, which called for state funding of scientific enterprise, and by the Devonshire Commissioners who, in 1875 had gone so far as to recommend that under a Ministry of Science the state should assume general responsibility for the direction of scientific instruction at every level.[33] But it was the growth in numbers, accompanied by the development of significant industrial and scientific research at the universities, in brief the move of higher education to a more significant position within the economy, which impelled the anxious governmental supervision of all new departures and expansion. From 1889 a Treasury Committee, prefiguring the U.G.C., disbursed grants to the new colleges. In response to Fabian demands the annual commitment grew to £ 54,000 by 1904. A separate Development Commission, concerned to ensure the supply of food for a growing population, became an important agency sponsoring agricultural education and research. By at once depriving British industry of vital German products the 1914 war provided a further twist. The D.S.I.R. (1915) and the formalization of the U.G.C. (1919) were direct consequences of the radically changed situation resulting from this crisis.

This governmental involvement was frequently cloaked in a "laissez-faire" philosophy which disguised the degree to which central management went on. In July, 1910, for example, Lloyd George fobbed off an anxious deputation from Southampton, where local aspirations for a university were currently under threat, with a demand for greater local initiative. He compared Southampton unfavorably with Bangor,

> with only 15,000 in a North Wales town, where there are no great industries, no great liners running to South America, no Cunarders. . . . I am sure you will agree with me you can do more. I, as long as I am here . . . want to know what the localities are prepared to do. When you come into contact with Chancellors of the Exchequer and ask us to do this or that for the locality, we are all alike in one respect: we help those who help themselves.[34]

Perhaps a truer index of the close involvement of the government at this period is provided by the exhaustive report supplied by G. T. Beilby, who was in 1914 commissioned to inspect, for the Board of Education, all departments of Applied Chemistry.[35] Indeed, many academics at this time feared the stultifying influence of governmental planning. In 1911, Oliver Lodge pleaded with the Board of Education for greater autonomy in planning courses:

> The increased Government grant raised . . . many important questions as to the autonomy of universities in the management of their

own affairs. Universities . . . should not become appendages of State Departments of the Civil Service. . . . The only reasonable way was to trust the institutions and the experts called together to manage them.[36]

It is possible, then, to discern two major elements in the dynamics of growth. First, traditional elite views of the function and style of a university clearly influenced the pattern of growth of the new university colleges. Secondly, enhanced size and economic significance attracted greater financial support from the state, and with it a growing determination to oversee the structure of this developing system. With hindsight, the claim that the role of the U.G.C. was advisory rather than supervisory until at least 1950 seems to lack validity.

Perhaps paramount in determining the pattern of expansion was the strong sense of hierarchy within English higher education, which was briefly threatened by the kaleidoscopic nature of these changes but which, in the event, remained as strong in the 1920s as seventy years earlier. In 1882 William Siemens had argued to the Samuelson Commissioners the distinctiveness and preferability of the university to the polytechnic.[37] In 1902, Ashley was keen to emphasize that his infant Faculty of Commerce at Birmingham had as its primary object

> the education, not of the rank and file, but of the officers of the industrial and commercial army: of those who as principals, directors, managers . . . will ultimately guide the business activity of the Empire.[38]

In the *University Review* three years later, W. McDougall claimed that Oxbridge life was "on a different and altogether higher plane"[39] than that enjoyed in other institutions. Similarly, in 1932, Ernest Barker was not alone when he warned that "it is a great mistake to blur the distinction between university and technical college."[40] The grounds on which the case was made may have shifted in response to a changed situation, but the central point remained, that English society was best served by a clearly designated and hierarchical system of higher education, with democratization taking place through new compensatory institutions rather than the complete restructuring of the old. If we are to seek a single most potent factor in explaining the peculiar structure of higher education which emerged in England between 1860 and 1930, it is probably to be found in a national preoccupation with social hierarchies.

Notes

1 *Transactions of the National Association for the Promotion of Social Science*, 1870, 311–6.
2 W. H. G. Armytage, *Civic Universities* (London, 1955), 243.
3 *University Review*, 21, No. 4 (January, 1907), 146.
4 M. Sanderson, *The Universities and British Industry, 1850–1970* (London, 1972), 3.
5 Evidence given on 30 June, 1870; see *Scientific Instruction*, H.M.S.O. (London, 1870), 3: 217–8.
6 *University Extension Journal*, 3 (October 1898), 27.
7 S. Rowbotham, "The call to University Extension teaching", *University of Birmingham Historical Journal*, 12, No. 1 (1969), 71.
8 *Scientific Instruction*, 1 (1868), 59.
9 J. R. Seeley, *A Midland University* (Birmingham, 1887), 13–14.
10 Seeley, 13–14.
11 E. W. Vincent and P. Hinton, *The University of Birmingham* (Birmingham, 1947), 6.
12 Vincent and Hinton, 6.
13 W. J. Ashley, "The Universities and Commercial Education", *North American Review*, 15 (January 1903), 17.
14 A. N. Shimmin, *The University of Leeds* (Cambridge, 1954), 10.
15 Shimmin, 25.
16 *University Review*, 40 (1909), 246.
17 *University Review*, 22 (1907), 349.
18 S. F. Cotgrove, *Technical Education and Social Change* (London, 1958), 63.
19 Cotgrove, 64.
20 C. H. Creasey, *Technical Education in Evening Schools* (London, 1905), 5.
21 *University Review*, 43 (1909), 498.
22 The statistics presented are drawn from a variety of sources, most notably:
Annual Reports of the Committee of Council on Education,
Science and Art Department Annual Reports,
Board of Education: *Annual Reports,*
Statistics of Public Education,
Lists of Schools,
Reports from University Colleges (Annual, 1893–1920),
Returns from Universities and University Colleges, in receipt of grant (Annual, 1920–31),
Cambridge Historical Register,
Oxford Historical Register,
Royal Commissions on Oxford and Cambridge (1874, 1922),
University Yearbook,
Census Reports, 1861–1931,
M. Greenwood, "University Education", *Journal of the Royal Statistical Society*, 48 (1935), 241.
Where these sources failed to provide information, resort was made to works on individual colleges, cf. H. Silver and S. J. Teague, *The History of British Universities, 1800–1969: A Bibliography* (London, 1971).
23 L. Stone (ed.), *The University in Society* (Oxford, 1975), 1: 91–2.
24 Clerk Report, *Education for the Engineering Industry*, H.M.S.O. (London, 1931).
25 R. M. Walker, *Medical Education in Britain* (London, 1965).
26 Vincent and Hinton, *op. cit.*
27 *University Review*, 2 (1905), 31.

28 Public Record Office, Education 119/1.
29 Vincent and Hinton, 106–7.
30 Shimmin, 38.
31 *University Review*, 45 (1909), 643–6.
32 Armytage, 256.
33 Devonshire Committee, *Scientific Instruction, Eighth Report* (London, 1875), 27.
34 P.R.O. Ed. 119/67.
35 P.R.O. Ed. 119/27.
36 P.R.O. Ed. 119/1.
37 Evidence given in March, 1882; see *Technical Instruction*, 3 (London, 1883).
38 W. J. Ashley, *The Faculty of Commerce in the University of Birmingham; its Purpose and Programme* (Birmingham, 1902).
39 *University Review*, 7 (1905), 147.
40 Armytage, 267.

107

THE DIVERSIFICATION OF HIGHER EDUCATION IN ENGLAND*

Sheldon Rothblatt

Source: K. H. Jarausch (ed.) *The Transformation of Higher Education, 1860–1930*, Stuttgart: Klett-Cotta, 1981, pp. 131–48.

A little more than a century ago the higher education of England began the transformation that in time produced the pre-eminence in national life ascribed to it by Harold Perkin in this volume. New universities, colleges, technology schools, and government-funded research organizations were established. Whole new areas of knowledge, scarcely known in 1860 or known only in embryonic form, were introduced, first gradually and then, about 1880 or 1900, much more rapidly. Disciplines and sub-disciplines acquired the autonomy they now enjoy as professional careers, although not overnight, not at the same pace and not with the same degree of recognition in each case.

By 1930, there were in the United Kingdom two ancient English universities, a quartet of Scottish ones, universities and university colleges in Ireland north and south, a Welsh federated university, a large group of Victorian universities and colleges in London and the provinces, and a new group of twentieth century redbricks modelled on their civic predecessors. There were also non-university technical and arts colleges. In architecture and ethos, in student body, national reputation and financial support, in the style of self-government and in relation to their surrounding communities, these foundations differed greatly one from the other; but they were converging on a single type of institution, that of the present-day research and teaching university, emphasizing original scholarship and science and committed to professional training, with a small but growing postgraduate sector and a faculty chosen largely for its competence in the several fields of study and teaching. Some three-quarters of a century earlier their social and educational differences had been much sharper. In origin they were diverse, had grown up in response to different audiences, and for many decades did not always share the same higher education mission.

It is customary to associate the transformations in the world of higher learning with changes in the central direction of English history occurring in the late nineteenth century. The period after 1870 was one of imperial expansion, sharp international trading rivalry, the application of science to manufacturing, and the development of the large industrial corporation. In these changing circumstances there was room for a new university mission. New industries, especially in chemicals, metals, or synthetic textiles simply could not function without applied science or high-level technological innovation, and they did not have traditions of basic research behind them to make the necessary technical changes unaided. Furthermore, better-trained managers were required in the large, publicly-owned firms. If such people did not themselves require training in research, they certainly had to understand the technical processes vital to industry. The imperial experience also encouraged a new perspective on the uses of higher education. Overseas expansion stimulated specific kinds of scientific work, for example, in tropical medicine or in civil and mechanical engineering, especially in connection with the construction of mines, ports, railroads and factories. The growth of government was yet another reason for an enlarged university role. The expansion of government through the establishment of a civil service recruited by competitive examinations led to the development of courses of university study as preparation for them. The increasing intervention by government into the economy and society also encouraged the growth of new professions, as in the social services or teaching.

It is equally true that the connection between higher education and other institutions was most often tenuous and unpredictable. The work of building a higher education system involved large numbers of scholars, scientists, civil servants, policy makers, pressure groups, community organizations, publicists, philanthropists and industrialists, as well as professional men and women not themselves in academic life. Given the strongly individualist character of Victorian society, their efforts were not and could not have been fully coordinated. From a dirigist point of view, the transformation of higher learning in England was largely uncoordinated and haphazard, full of what in historical retrospect appear to be digressions, misplaced emphases, lost chances, false starts and conflicts. To be sure, even historical irregularity has a logic, insofar as occurrences in time cannot be wholly random but must bear some relation to the overall culture of a society. This, at least, was the joyful conclusion of the mid-Victorian positivist, Thomas Henry Buckle, who claimed to have taken the idea from the poet and philosopher Goethe. But if institutional linkages existed, they were neither mechanical nor precise, and it is well to remember the somewhat anfractious route by which the university of the nineteenth century arrived in the twentieth.

In the essay that follows I take the fact of diversification as given, and I concentrate instead on the principal causes behind the remarkable intellectual and academic transformation in higher education. "Causes" must be understood as efficient or proximate rather than final, as reasons, explanations or categories rather than prime movers. To bring these out I have adopted a mode of discussion that moves between normative and historical explanation, that asserts what may be typical in a particular transformation but also recalls what actually happened. For purposes of comparison, as well as taxonomy, a normative approach is clear and useful, but it can never be wholly satisfying. It is static while history is dynamic, a process where events assume a character specific to time and place. It is my hope, therefore, that the two approaches will complement one another.

Academic professionalism

Changes in the structure and purpose of higher education bear a closer causal relationship to the development of an urban society than to industrialism *per se,* even though the latter has an obvious effect on the former. City life mediates economic change and redistributes its effects, generating a high and continuing demand for the most varied social and personal services. The spectacular growth of an urban consumer culture in the nineteenth century provided higher education with an opportunity to supply England with large numbers of specialists who increasingly called themselves "professional men," and behind them were the academicians, the members of the "key profession," the one that trained the others.[1]

Curiously, or perhaps understandably given the magnitude of the task, there are no standard histories of academic professionalism in England, although there are studies of the metamorphosis of the Oxbridge clerical don into the career university teacher. As late as 1911 census returns put university faculty into the blanket category of "teachers."[2]

Much work remains before useful detailed conclusions can be compiled concerning the relationship between the kind of bonding we call professionalization and the diversification of university and technical instruction. Certainly what needs to be solidly appreciated is that professionalization is an aggressive process. It has a self-propelled internal quality, or to invert a Victorian aphorism more used now than then: men may not make history exactly as they please, but they do try to make it. The characteristics of academic professionalism may be identified as measurable or certifiable competence, peer approval, full-time devotion to a career, and freedom from personal subservience or independence but through association.

The service function that lies at the heart of any professional self-perception requires a high degree of control over the market. The lead time necessary to establish teaching programs, train students and faculty, plan and carry out research or any of the other familiar academic tasks necessitates insulation from short-term economic fluctuations. Independence is particularly sought by academics because, not being self-employed, they are and have been vulnerable to changes in the economy and society. Their role model has not been the independent practitioner—the lawyer or physician, for example, who enters into a personal or fiduciary relationship with his client—but the public employee, the state administrator or army officer or Church of England clergyman. But the desire for independence has remained a constant.[3] Hence from the middle of the nineteenth century onwards the move towards academic professionalism has been characterized by special efforts to keep curriculum, recruitment, career, academic disciplines and the definition of service fully in academic hands. Since at no time are professors fully protected from shifts in supply and demand, the phrase "ivory tower" has to be understood as symbolic rather than actual.

The idea of the academic as a professional man was compounded of two traditions, that of the Scottish university teacher and the Oxbridge don. The former had the greatest influence on the faculty organization of the newer universities, with the exception of Durham, which borrowed heavily from Oxbridge. Oxford and Cambridge in general contributed the idea of academic self-government, which itself was a borrowing from certain practices of a land-owning oligarchy long accustomed to sinecures, appanages, patronage, and a relatively free hand in English government and society. From the aristocracy, as well as from the two senior universities, came yet another influence, known to the Victorians as the "clerisy" ideal, a neologism of the Romantic poet Samuel Taylor Coleridge, and to present-day scholars as the "aristocratic model of professional growth."[4] This consisted of a gentlemanly style of living, a preference for public rather than private employment with the concurrent claim to be acting in the general good, and a group rather than an individualist ethic of behavior. The clerisy ideal was not wholly aristocratic, however, for it also included nineteenth century beliefs in merit, career, hard work and useful employment, as well as the necessity of competition as proof of good character, although in practice attention-getting had to be played down in the interests of group harmony. It should be apparent that such a guide or model for professional behavior has the latent function of reinforcing a sense of academic independence and of softening the suggestion of self-interest and ambition.

To the question posed in Konrad Jarausch's introduction, at what point in its history is an academic activity considered to be a profession, I return the tentative theoretical answer that this occurs when a branch of learning is considered to be the basis of a career, when that career becomes a virtual end in itself, and when its practitioners believe they have fundamental control over the survival, growth and perpetuation of their occupation. Thus the professor of botany at Cambridge in the 1850s was not a professional scientist because he thought of himself primarily as a parish priest. In the same period Sir Henry Maine, one of the pioneers of cultural anthropology, explained that as he could not earn a living as a professor, he practiced law as well.[5] None of this, however, is to be confused with the notion that academic professionalism depends upon absolute agreement on the methods of a particular field, for under situations of an expanding knowledge base such agreement is not likely to occur.

If professionalism was the ultimate thrust of academicians in mid-Victorian England when the "take-off" began, then it must also be acknowledged that the conditions for academic independence were not achieved in the nineteenth century. Arguably they have been more closely approximated in the twentieth century. In Victorian England there was considerable intervention into the affairs of Oxford, Cambridge and the Scottish Universities by Parliament and the Privy Council. Newer foundations were inadequately financed and matriculation levels too uneven to provide for either stability or predictable expansion. Furthermore, the civic universities, Durham, London and even the new collegiate foundations of Oxford and Cambridge were in varying degree subject to the authority of lay councils. Only the medical faculties of universities enjoyed comparative independence by virtue of their earlier recognition as part of a liberal profession. Beginning about 1900 academic senates began to take a stronger part in institutional decision making, and from then on in the provincial universities diversification was essentially a matter over which faculty had a larger degree of control.[6]

Finally, it must be understood that the phasing in of new subjects, new methods of research, new staffing patterns, library and museum development and innovation in general occurred at differential rates of change according to location, funding, sense of mission and institutional organization. Each segment of the academic profession followed a chronological development peculiar to itself, so that at any point in the last half of the nineteenth century the historian encounters status uncertainties, internal disagreements over curricula, widely divergent views on career and service, different measurements of competence, and a mixture of role model and reference groups within each branch of learning. A checkered history is more typical of academic professionalism than normative discussions can possibly suggest.[7]

Medicine jumped out first in the nineteenth century and led the way towards academic professionalism and consequently diversification. This was not surprising. The condition of cities called for a major epidemiological effort, and the consumer demands of a society with increased per capita income and concern for the quality of everyday life certainly favored the growth of a medical profession. Furthermore, physicians, if not surgeons or apothecaries, enjoyed a certain historic prestige which could be capitalized upon when needed. Medicine became the umbrella under which new scientific subjects entered the university, e.g., physiology, bacteriology, medical physics and organic chemistry. For centuries, in fact, medicine held an honorable place in the pantheon of university disciplines (if less honorable in the eighteenth century).[8] Physicians, surgeons and apothecaries often led the way in finding support for science. They were the prime movers, for example, behind the scheme to establish a Royal College of Chemistry in 1845.[9] They were the principal founders of medical schools in the provinces, and several of these, such as Sheffield and Birmingham, became the nuclei of civic universities. Physicians like George Birkbeck had a strong hand in the establishment of what became known as University College, London, and the metropolitan evening college that today bears his name. It is a well-known fact that the success of the medical school at U.C. enabled it to survive a difficult childhood. One of the reasons that University College with its nonconformist, utilitarian and radical backing, and King's College, an Anglican foundation, were able to bury their differences and associate together as the University of London in 1836 was probably the common interest in medicine. By 1851 nearly 60 medical colleges, mostly free standing but some part of hospitals, were affiliated with the London University, which at that date was an examining rather than a teaching institution, the burden of instruction falling upon the constituent colleges and schools.

Some form of profession building had been going on in England since the eighteenth century, but from 1870 to 1880 onwards the movement towards academic professionalism accelerated. Furthermore, it now took a turn towards a wholly new objective, mission or purpose. This can be illustrated by the work of the famous commissions of inquiry appointed by the Crown and by Parliament to inquire into the teaching, studies, revenues and discipline of Oxford and Cambridge. The two that reported in the 1850s were concerned with the improvement of tutorial or collegiate instruction, but the ones that came after concentrated on improving the university or professorial part of instruction, and this began to include a formal research mission. The first set of commissioners thought in terms of a teaching institution, keeping before them the traditional "idea" of a university as a place for the dissemination of knowledge, not its advancement, and for the moral superintendence of young and immature students rather than for the imparting of skills and competencies. Even in the middle decades of the nineteenth century German science and scholarship were considered means of improving teaching, not a set of methods for pursuing basic knowledge. While the teacher might be allowed to undertake systematic inquiry in a particular field, it was not held to be an essential requirement for teaching. Because research, stressing critical inquiry, was thought to have a subversive dimension, it was far better to imitate than innovate. By contrast, the later commissions talked about encouraging research, improving technology and professional competence, and building up new specialties and disciplines. The problem was no longer one of making available to new social groups the knowledge that well-educated people already possessed, but of engaging higher education in the task of national advance and prosperity.

Demand for higher education

Few topics in the history of the growth and diversification of higher education are so poorly understood as the function of demand. It is still glibly assumed that shifts in social stratification, or profound changes in the economy or evidence of a growing working-class consciousness provide undeniable proof of the existence of strong demand for increased access to institutions of higher education or of a new audience for new subjects. Such was simply not the historical case. The evidence for demand from below is almost always contradictory, confusing and ambiguous, whether for basic literacy or numeracy or higher education.[10] There is a tendency in the history of education generally to assume demand when the supply side may be the crucial variable.[11] For instance, it is all too often asserted that the educational leaders of England thwarted the demands of parents for increased access to all levels of education for their children.

Without denying that social snobbery was a feature of Victorian culture, it must nevertheless be noted that the demand for higher education throughout the nineteenth century and well into the twentieth was spotty, to say the least, and being unreliable presented newer institutions with major headaches. Since their start-up costs were high, requiring an initial large capital outlay for construction and land, money for staff was in short supply, and little in the way of funding was available for the diversification of curriculum. The civic universities and London and to a certain extent Durham were established on the liberal political premise that once in operation these institutions would be successfully responsive to market forces. Their founders hoped that sufficient fee-paying students would be attracted to make a full program of studies possible. But short run disappointments were rather the rule. Many of the newer colleges led a perilous existence for the first decade or two, skating on thin financial ice which forced them into a variety of cost-cutting and money-raising expedients. When the numbers of full-time students at Owens College, Manchester, fell so low in the 1860s and 1870s that adequate staff could not be retained, evening classes and special courses for schoolmasters were introduced in order to attract students and increase fee income.[12]

In retrospect it is easy enough to criticize this decision which inevitably pushed the new foundations towards remedial and compensatory education[13] and compromised their standing in the eyes of older and more prestigious universities, but a reliance on market factors can have this historical effect. The reasons for low enrollments at redbrick are not hard to discern. They were the result of two factors: families where the support of a full-time student was a luxury whose benefits could not be perceived and an inadequate supply of properly prepared young persons. Being hamstrung, the new universities could do little to remedy the situation except wait for the slow and cumulative effects of the Balfour Education Act of 1902. In the meantime they quickly outdistanced their logistical support. Drawing their faculty from the pre-Victorian universities with long traditions of learning and scholarship, facing new social situations with high expectations, the faculty of the civic universities became frustrated and disappointed. And as the process of profession-building continued, with new disciplines and interests developing and the research mission being everywhere adopted, the income problem was exacerbated.

At best the effect of demand on diversification is difficult to measure. It appears to have had the most impact in precisely those areas where professionalization was most prominent, for in general professions feed themselves. Certainly there was a continuous overall demand for medicine or medical biology, but individual medical schools fared badly, and their success was not necessarily built on numbers. The famous Cambridge medical school, re-established in the 1870s, attracted few students, being staffed for research.[14] At Cambridge there was a demand for classics and mathematics, and at Oxford for Literae Humaniores, but most of the new academic specialties hardly attracted career-minded undergraduates.[15] Some of the most famous Oxford professors, pioneers in the several fields of learning, lectured to empty halls right up to the First World War.[16] This was the anomalous but direct result of the historical fact that the great knowledge revolution of the nineteenth century took place when post-graduate education was in its infancy. The striking structural peculiarity of higher education at the turn of the century was the widening gap between teaching and research, which was only slowly reduced by the introduction of the research degree and the arrival of the older, often foreign-educated student in search of specialized training.

Demand for higher education in general must always be carefully distinguished from demand that produces innovation and diversification. As indicated, instances of the former can be found, but very few examples of the latter. Even so, supply more often led demand in the period up to the First World War and even beyond. Academic career-building had more to do with the transformation of higher learning than student or parental pressures, which, where its effects can be discerned, were generally conservative. Parents preferred familiar and time-tested programs of study to the new directions in knowledge so conspicuous a feature of the world of higher learning before the war. This was as true of the demand for women's education as for men's; for while there is no doubt that a significant number of young women were available for higher education, well-prepared and achievement-minded, they were primarily interested in the subjects of the traditional syllabus. Given the uphill fight against much male opposition to women in higher education and the opening up of careers in elementary, and later secondary education, there is every reason to suspect this would have been the case.

The demand for university services generally other than teaching—for consulting or laboratory research, for example—was no more pronounced in England than the demand for teaching. Despite the anti-business bias implicit in the aristocratic model of professionalism, there does appear to have been a considerable amount of industrial research undertaken by professors in the provincial universities in their early years and by the London professoriate in the period 1900 to 1914. It is entirely possible there was more owing to secret research, as in the steel industry,[17] but it appears safe to speculate that as much of this work was solicited by career-minded academics as was sponsored by profit-hungry industrialists. The failure to develop on-going research contacts between industry and some of the universities was more likely the fault of the former than the latter. In this respect the English and French situations seem comparable.[18]

The impact of donors

Before 1850 universities and colleges had benefited greatly from charitable gifts and endowments for scholarships, professorships, fellowships, lectureships, for buildings, libraries and museums. Over the centuries these had come from many public and private sources, from wealthy merchants or their wives, from bishops, aristocrats and members of the royal family and from government and academics themselves. Motives ranged from religious reasons, honor and noblesse oblige to raison d'etat. This pattern of philanthropy carried on through the nineteenth and into the twentieth centuries, and for some of the same reasons, with the addition of a sense of civic pride, the feeling that great cities must possess universities as once it was believed they must possess cathedrals. Perhaps the most significant instances of gift-giving are the endowments and capital funds that successful businessmen, professional men and civic benefactors used to establish so many of the provincial universities and local medical colleges and technical institutes. Yet the historian who has most concerned himself with Victorian charity is dissatisfied with its overall record. He points out how much gift-giving was by academics of the old boy network, especially those in the ancient foundations, and how little, relatively speaking, came from the sources of new money.[19]

One of the several difficulties in assessing the historical record of gift-giving is the very different requirements of historical periods widely separate in time. If by one measure philanthropy in the sixteenth and seventeenth centuries was more successful than later, it was largely because higher education had not yet developed the voracious appetite it has demonstrated in the past century. The growth of research as a central feature of higher education altered the historic pattern of gift-giving. Very large sums were now needed for the expansion of museums, the creation of science laboratories, the building up of research libraries in all fields, as well as for the construction of classrooms, offices and lecture halls. It was necessary to increase the size of teaching staffs when the student population started to grow but even more so when academic specialism took off. Considerable amounts were particularly required for the establishment of the new university colleges, which shortly grew to university status, and after construction costs were met, there was a need to endow chairs and pay faculty. Even wealthy Oxbridge required substantial assistance. With some exceptions, the financial strength of Oxford and Cambridge lay in the "private" part of the university—in the colleges. The "public" or university part was weakly provided for. The last nineteenth century statutory commission had attempted to correct the imbalance by forcing the colleges to contribute some of their income to a University Chest, or by allowing the university a portion of college tuition to subsidize new subjects, or by consolidating small fellowships and assigning them to university purposes. When this plan was first envisioned college income was booming. A number of colleges had made a killing in the sale of land for the construction of railroads. But after 1870 college income declined as a result of the agricultural depression, very definitely threatening expansion and diversification. Consequently, both old and new institutions were in need of additional support.

Late Victorian dons have filled the pages of university history with complaints that their institutions were left impoverished, but in fact considerable support was forthcoming from the manufacturing community, if not in equal amounts to each institution, or for every subject now the object of academic professionalism. Some famous industrialists came forward with substantial sums for laboratories, chairs and buildings, as did those grand old benefactors, the London livery companies, but not on a scale comparable to American philanthropy. The contributions of municipal corporations, local professional associations, mechanics institutes, great commercial houses and industrial firms in creating technical colleges and university colleges has often been told. Most of the money given was for science and technology, for this was where new money was most needed and where individual professors were most active in soliciting support; but insofar as research was becoming important, there was no instant or automatic response to the financial requests of professors and heads, no immediate perception by all sectors of the business community that the support of university-based science and technology was essential to national economic strength. Nevertheless the metals and engineering industries of the north developed strong working relations with Sheffield, Birmingham and the Imperial College. Ship engineering and naval architecture were features of Glasgow, Newcastle and Liverpool universities. Brewing linked up with Birmingham.[20] These connections greatly benefited the civic universities in their earliest years, and they even contributed directly to the growth of specialism, since the spinoff from applied technology could and did stimulate work in basic science. Proximity to local industry or a strong and identifiable sense of civic pride on the part of the community seemed to be a requirement for good working relations between universities and industry, because the London professoriate, which aided other industries like steel and textiles, aircraft and radio-communications, did not succeed in attracting substantial pre-war financial support from Thameside manufacturing.[21]

The success of fund-raising varied according to time and place. There was, for example, no satisfactory response to the appeals of Oxford and Cambridge for help—at least collecting fell far short of announced goals, despite a really heavily-orchestrated campaign by specially-designed fund-raising associations representing a large number of fields. The campaign, in fact, had an adverse effect upon university morale and produced a split in the faculty, a fear on the part of some dons that big science would dominate the ancient universities and compromise the college system.[22]

Here, before the First World War, was a sign of the internal fracturing of the university under the pressure of the competition for funds, an indication of the primacy of the discipline over any university-wide loyalty. The Oxbridge appeal was unsuccessful partly because of the collapse of the "natural" constituency of the two universities, the old university-clerical world, and the failure as yet to acquire a new one. Many dons still harbored an anti-business scruple, and the feeling was reciprocated, but others very busily pursued the Edwardian millionaires, oblivious of the historic taboo.

Academic interest groups

That supply is more important than demand in allowing diversification to take place receives confirmation from the actions of Victorian and Edwardian dons in securing an adequate support base for innovation and growth within higher education. English academics were not shy when it came to expressing their desires for patronage or their need for money, and from the middle of the century onwards the solicitation of funds for higher education projects was active and steady. Quite possibly the Parliamentary Committee of the British Association for the Advancement of Science was the first organized scientific pressure group on the historical scene. Reacting to the interest in applied science that followed the Crystal Palace Exhibition of 1851, it sought support for pure or basic science.[23] In the decades that followed famous names like Roscoe and Playfair, Thomas Huxley and Mark Pattison, and of a later generation, Haldane and Lockyer, kept the pressure up as very accomplished and energetic publicists. They formed professional associations, interest and lobby groups, arranged for newspaper coverage, made public speeches, contacted prominent benefactors, politicians and members of the civil service, and by so doing kept the requirements of modern universities foremost in the public consciousness. Many of them had spent some period of their early life in Germany, and they constantly referred to the German universities as the model universities, publicly comparing the support received there or in America with that in England. They were loudest on behalf of newer subjects, and because of this, as well as because of the rather strident tone of their campaigns, they irritated more reticent and less needy dons who believed that university autonomy would be adversely affected by new ties of dependency should the great publicists succeed.

Generational factors

There was a decided generational element in the diversification of higher education, but more work must be done before deciding how significant its overall contribution was. I would suggest that it was most important at the beginning of the development of a sub-discipline or at a moment of expansion, but as Joseph Ben-David and Awraham Zloczower have argued in connection with German disciplinary growth, the generational element must be combined with the structural peculiarities of an academic system in order to be significant. For structural reasons age-specific behavior is part of the history of teaching and reform at Oxford and Cambridge. The fellowships system there skewed appointments so that before the 1880s' abolition of celibacy and holy orders as requirements for tenure, fellows were either very young or very old. Younger dons were always involved in the Oxbridge reform movements of the nineteenth century because they had the most to gain in challenging what often amounted to a gerontocracy. Towards mid-century they very definitely spearheaded the attack on the "old college system," pressed for State intervention, insisted on the necessity for full-time academic careers and helped produce a revolution in teaching. Foreign and domestic observers were struck by the decidedly youthful tone of Oxford and Cambridge after the reform period. Romantics and aesthetes were enchanted by the beauty, insouciance and grace of the Oxbridge undergraduate in a setting of parks, gardens and ancient buildings; but others, who believed universities existed for the advancement of learning, were depressed by the immaturity, public school ethos and lack of intellectual seriousness in collegiate life.

The rather sudden expansion of the professoriate in the critical reform decade after 1876, partly in response to increasing matriculations and State pressure but also equally a function of professionalization, provided new career opportunities for young scholars and scientists who had been preparing themselves for precisely such a change. At Oxford the university teaching staff increased from 40 to 63, over half of whom received appointments after 1880. At Cambridge there was an even more spectacular infusion of new blood, since 61 out of 73 university appointments had been made since 1870.[24] The same effect occurred throughout the constituent colleges, providing Oxbridge with one of its most characteristic staffing peculiarities, a checkerboard of indolent old sinecurists and eager young hotshots. Certain disciplines were clearly being carried on by younger men, and this may have been true elsewhere in England during the early period of expansion. Before the institution of the research degree, long periods of academic apprenticeship were not required, and young men could be called to leadership positions early in their careers. One Principal of Firth College, Sheffield, was only 24. Sir George Humphrey was 22 when he became surgeon to Addenbrooke's in Cambridge. The study of European scientists circa 1900 by Heilbron, Forman and Weart shows that English physicists were much younger than their German counterparts,[25] and although they are reluctant to speculate on this fact, it is conceivable that this was one of a number of factors that account for the success of certain branches of physics in the period before the war. Such opportunities as existed in academic life before 1914 were not duplicated again until the great expansion of the 1960s, which likewise opened up opportunities for a younger generation of scholars and scientists.[26]

Organizational or structural characteristics of institutions

While research and specialism go together, directly affecting the process of faculty recruitment, the actual structure or constitution of an educational institution also plays a part in determining where and when innovation can enter the curriculum. However, as we shall see, no firm historical conclusions regarding the institutional forms most conducive to innovation are possible. What appears to be an organizational advantage may only be temporary, and what seems to be a structural barrier to change may turn out to be a boon. The internal organization of a university, school or college is no more independent than any other variable.[27] Nor is the age of an institution an indication of whether its faculty will readily take to fresh ideas or remain tradition-bound. It has been said of the University of Hull, which was founded in the late 1920s, that it was not innovative despite its youth, that on the contrary, it was born "middle-aged"[28] (like Falstaff, presumably, at three o'clock in the afternoon with something of a large belly).

Nevertheless, it is possible to suggest that from their inception the civic universities possessed a short-term structural advantage over Oxbridge in moving towards the research conception of a university. The organization of professors and lecturers into faculties—Arts, Sciences, Medicine, Technology, Commerce—put authority for courses of study, scholarships, prizes, appointments, degrees, diplomas, and certifications directly into the hands of faculty committees, whereas at Oxford and Cambridge right up to the war and beyond, responsibility for these was a confused matter of decision-making shared between university boards of studies, the "old schools," colleges and large bodies of alumni constitutionally empowered to vote on matters of curricula. In part the "country vote" was seen as an advantage in the earlier years of the nineteenth century when maintenance of the aristocratic and clerical ascendancy in the university was more important than innovation and discovery, but it was a decided liability three quarters of a century later when academic professionalism was attempting to reshape the intellectual character of the universities. Slowly, through a number of constitutional and structural changes that occurred in the years before the war, the university parts of Oxford and Cambridge came to dominate the colleges and to create what is now sometimes referred to as a federal system. The non-researcher, the "good college man," has been an endangered species since the Edwardian period.[29]

Another reason why the civic universities in their earliest years were able to do important work in applied research was necessity. Professorial remuneration varied greatly within redbrick, but it was usually less than what was deemed to be the necessary income of a professional gentleman. While endowments provided some income support, remuneration was also affected by matriculations, with laboratory and lecture fees providing a crucial portion of salary. Since enrollments were unreliable in the early years, professors went outside the universities into consulting and applied research, much as the old unreformed Oxbridge professoriate cast about for a living in the church or law and government, or the collegiate fellows went into private teaching. A further reason for the substantial interest in applied research at the civic universities was the generally low level of student preparation. The mathematics professors at Leeds simply refused to do remedial teaching.[30] As teaching institutions the redbrick reputation suffered in comparison with Oxbridge, but as centers of technology, their success record in applied research was substantial.

From the standpoint of profession-building, however, the situation that existed at Leeds, Sheffield, Liverpool and Nottingham was far from satisfactory. Consulting as a steady means of income supplement was not reliable, as the work depended upon the needs or desires of the consulter, as did any externally-sponsored research. Under these conditions certain kinds of intellectual problems could not be pursued; and some forms of basic science suffered. Ironically, what soon freed the redbrick professoriate was the development of research laboratories within industry itself—laboratories which no longer required the services of an outside consultant or researcher but which could still absorb graduates trained by him.[31]

The situation was different with respect to arts subjects. While the demand for instruction began to increase with direct and indirect government subsidies for the training of teachers, there were few opportunities for outside work. In addition, relations between teachers and potential benefactors or employers were sometimes strained. The establishment of arts faculties in redbrick universities owed much to Oxbridge—sponsored extension lectures and a system of local examinations. Arts lecturers and professors were often recruited from Oxford and Cambridge. Touched with the clerisy brush, believing in the civilizing purposes of liberal education, they were occasionally at odds with a community of practical-minded philanthropists and potential donors. Nathan Bodington, the Principal of Leeds, who was trained in classics at Oxford, was one of those Victorian academic leaders who did not get on with local business precisely because of his different outlook on the purposes of university education.[32]

At Oxford and Cambridge, the collegiate organization of teaching and the absence of a newer-type senate organization with overall responsibility for curriculum and instruction forced innovation along different lines. One of the reasons why the diversification of intellectual and academic life at Oxford and Cambridge is so difficult to follow is that there were so many different possible entry points into the system. Who would have predicted, for example, that the teaching of Scandinavian languages at Oxford was introduced by the Oxford University Press, which suddenly found itself with money that could, in the hands of an interested party, be diverted for the purpose,[33] or that the famous Cambridge medical school led by the physiologist Michael Foster would be partly the result of the reform movement within Trinity College, which brought him to Cambridge with a college appointment? If the collegiate structure of Oxbridge was a handicap in some ways, it was beneficial in others, and many instances of college sponsorship of new work could be cited. A college might be more interested in teaching traditional subjects than in providing for new ones, but once interested in new work and new subjects, it was easier for a single college to introduce them than open the matter to university-wide debate. Science had been coming into the universities this way ever since individual dons installed their personal, primitive laboratories in out-of-the-way college rooms at the beginning of the nineteenth century.[34]

The Cavendish Laboratory is probably the most famous example of how diversity could occur at Oxbridge. A handsome endowment from Lord Devonshire, an aristocrat-industrialist, established a well-equipped Cambridge laboratory that stood outside both the collegiate structure and the faculty organization. The Cavendish did not have to prepare students for examinations, and it was in a position to attract and train young researchers entirely out of its own resources. The lines of inquiry of the Cavendish were established by its great directors, Maxwell, Rayleigh, J. J. Thomson and Rutherford, and because of this independence the laboratory was able to take advantage of the introduction of research degrees into Cambridge in 1895 to sponsor research dissertations which could then be used by colleges—if they chose—as a basis for appointments to fellowships. The Cavendish developed a special ethos, as symbolized by its famous afternoon teas, and became the model for scientific work, expressing in perfect measure all of the requirements of academic professionalism. Some of the success of the Cavendish was repeated at Manchester, which also had a well-endowed physical laboratory; but elsewhere, because of less generous support, professors associated with laboratories had to spend a greater amount of time teaching the more elementary aspects of their subject.[35]

The action of government and the effect of war

While its role varied, the State was involved in higher education from the start. In subtle and indirect ways at first, and in direct ways later, the State can be considered one of the most decisive influences in the diversification of higher education in England. This is a somewhat unorthodox position. It is more common to contrast the English State with the German one and to point out, often deprecatingly, how uninterested it was in the problems of university education, science, technology, teacher training and academic discovery. I would like to suggest that this was not exactly the case. The historical problem has been oversimplified because of the failure, as Roy MacLeod has noticed, of historians of science (and universities) to recognize the particular features of government in the nineteenth century.[36]

It is true that in the nineteenth century the island was passing through what is commonly called a "liberal" phase. This textbook commonplace, while containing a particular kind of truth, does not tell the whole or even the most important part of the story. Talk of a minimal state in 1860 might have made good copy but poor history. Centuries of development had created a very powerful central State, and the unique history of English constitutionalism (as measured against other European countries) had allowed a fairly large and experienced group of titled and lesser aristocracy, much interpenetrated with the other strata of English society, to gain political experience at every level of government, national or local. By historical habit the landed aristocracy was interventionist. Furthermore, the English State was not what it was in Romantic thinking, an abstraction embodying national purpose, the whole to which the parts adhered and the spiritual as well as political center of national life, but a collection of ministries, boards, agencies and councils performing a variety of tasks, not always strictly coordinated, and by a complicated process of legislative and executive interaction subject to a variety of competing demands and wishes. This too was an aristocratic legacy—the product of oligarchy rather than monarchy, of a community of peers equal in status if not in power or income.[37] In these circumstances the great landlords and heads of houses could continue to exert influence at the very heart of English politics, and individual ministers, undersecretaries and other civil servants were relatively free to respond to the changing social conditions of English life as their education, networks of friends, past associations and political ambitions inclined them.

Against the Liberal doctrine of the minimal State, then, must be laid the custom of State intervention along the ancient caravan routes of aristocratic patronage. But even the Liberal State recognized the necessity of ad hoc decision-making in response to specific problems or demands. This temporary conjunction accounts for the characteristic responses of the Victorian State even as it moved forward in the second half of the nineteenth century to rational, bureaucratic government. Decision-making could occur almost

211

anywhere within the structure of government, and consequently there was indeed some provision of State aid to higher education, even to research, but it was not systematic. The various agencies of government, as yet unco-ordinated by the Treasury, made decisions independently of one another, and advice was sought where needed. Even before the enactment of the famous civil service reforms of the nineteenth century, experts and consult-ants were brought into government to advise on matters of educational policy, and even in the supposed heyday of the minimal State there was an impressive range of government assistance to the higher education sector. For example, recent writers have emphasized how much scientific research activity was sponsored by government in the first half of the nineteenth century.[38] There were tidal, ordinance and geological surveys and expedi-tions. The government supported scientific posts at the Botanical Garden at Kew, the observatory at Greenwich and the Assay Office of the Royal Mint. The Medical Department of the Privy Council contributed to various kinds of scientific projects. The Inland Revenue and Excise Department sponsored astronomical, hydrographical and munitions research, and the Commissioners of Woods and Forests encouraged geological work through the Museum of Economic Geology and the Mining Records Office. A Government School of Mines and Science Applied to the Arts was founded in 1851. Parliamentary grants were given to the various royal societies, sometimes as on-going subventions, sometimes for specific projects, so that the Royal Society, the Royal Geographic Society, the Royal Society of Edinburgh, the Scottish Meteorological Society could count on intermittent and recurrent assistance from London.

In support of teaching the government provided for the Regius pro-fessorships at Oxford and Cambridge, and, for reasons that go back to the ancient days of a separate Scottish Parliament, Whitehall assumed financial responsibility for the universities of Scotland. For the new examining University of London the government provided aid from the late 1830s onwards for the conduct of examinations, the award of prizes and honors, and for maintenance and repairs to buildings.[39]

In the later nineteenth century and twentieth century even much greater assistance went to higher education. The new universities and colleges received money (initially at their request), as did the new Welsh universities and Irish ones. The Board of Education supported the Imperial College, referred to journalistically as the new South Kensington "Charlottenburg." The Treasury increasingly supported engineering and medicine, includ-ing the medical school at Cambridge—this before the institution of recurrent state grants to Oxford and Cambridge. The National Health Insurance Act of 1911 funneled some money into medical research as well, and there-after a Medical Research Commitee of the Privy Council was formed. The Board of Agriculture gave research grants from the 1890s onwards and afterwards financial support was carried on by a Development Commission for Agriculture and Fisheries. Local authorities, too, contributed to civic universities and to London University before and after the reorganization of local government in the last decades of the nineteenth century, but the major support came from the State and its executive branches. In fact the State, in creating national systems of elementary and secondary compulsory education, did more for the teaching of science generally and indirectly for the diversification of higher education than any other single source after the turn of the century. Grants were given to all institutions possessing departments for the training of teachers. State action drove up enrollments, stabilized university income, and stimulated growth in the size of teaching and research staffs.

The First World War produced more State activity. The military technology effort led to increased aid of all kinds to the education sector. After the war, because of the running down of plants due to forced neglect, the insatiable requirements of big science and the need to find better support for junior faculty, as well as the distortion in enrollments produced by conscription and wartime manpower needs, the University Grants Committee was created to put the financing of higher education on a firm and consistent basis. In the same spirit the Department of Scientific and Industrial Research was projected in 1915.

There is no doubt that the war years were a watershed in university-State relations. Yet I would like to stress that the machinery for government intervention into the higher education system had long been in place, as well as an attitude of assistance congenial to the academician. This explains why unaffiliated intellectuals like the Benthamites, or individual Oxbridge dons, or members of the clerisy or science publicists like Playfair and Roscoe readily turned to the State for support. The Victorian intelligentsia had always been more confident of their ability to persuade government to support them than private philanthropy. They were confused about the meaning of industrialism, worried about political democracy even when they spoke in favor of it, fearful of the effects of cultural pluralism after centuries of leadership from above by the landed aristocracy and its hangers-on, the "natural leaders" of society. They worried more about the possible effects of "public opinion" than about government intervention, and as academic professionals they preferred to risk their independence with the latter than with the former. The Liberal voice of the nineteenth century may from time to time have expressed concern about the consequences of heavy state funding for higher education, but it was only one of several influential voices. And these are the reasons, if not the only reasons, why England before the First World War moved towards the European model of centrally-supported higher education rather than towards the American one of private, local and regional support, despite some of the heavily plural and decentralized features of Victorian civilization. After all, honors, recognition and prestige had always flowed downward from the Crown and government; central direction had always characterized the English State. In historical perspective the Liberal State was only an interlude.

Notes

* I wish to thank my colleagues Martin Trow and John Heilbron and the staff of the Center for Studies in Higher Education at the University of California, Berkeley, for their invaluable help in the preparation of this essay.

1 Harold Perkin, *Key Profession* (New York, 1969) and his essay in this volume.
2 Lord Ashby, "The Academic Profession," in *Minerva*, 8 (1970), 91.
3 From his study of industrial scientists and engineers today Kenneth Prandy has concluded that the self-conception of professional men and women is directly affected by a sense of autonomy. Strong feelings generate a concern for status, weak ones for class. Kenneth Prandy, *Professional Employees: A Study of Scientists and Engineers* (London, 1965), 41, 44, 175–8.
4 Magali Sarfatti Larson, *The Rise of Professionalism, a Sociological Analysis* (Berkeley, 1977), Chapter 6; Sheldon Rothblatt, *The Revolution of the Dons* (London, 1968), 86–93.
5 Ashby. See also Sheldon Rothblatt, review of *From Status to Contract: A Biography of Sir Henry Maine, 1822–1888*, by George Feaver, in *Journal of Modern History*, 43 (1971), 158–9 for the institutional source of Maine's occupational "pluralism."
6 Graeme C. Moodie and Rowland Eustace, *Power and Authority in British Universities* (Montreal, 1974), 27–38. See also Lord Ashby's remarks in A. C. Crombie, ed., *Scientific Change* (London, 1963), 727.
7 For disagreements over the use and nature of economics by academic economists see Michael Sanderson, *The Universities and British Industry, 1850–1970* (London, 1972), 189. Differences in the internal history of a particular discipline can sometimes be attributed to the work of leading personalities or to timing or to both. See Richard Southern, *The Shape and Substance of Academic History* (Oxford, 1961), 11, 14; D. J. Palmer, *The Rise of English Studies* (London, 1965), 51, 71.
8 Roy Porter, "Science and the Universities," in *British Journal for the History of Science*, 9 (1976), 321.
9 Gerrylynn K. Roberts, "The Establishment of the Royal College of Chemistry: An Investigation of the Social Context of Early Victorian Chemistry," in *Historical Studies in the Physical Sciences*, 7 (1976), 437–86.
10 Lawrence Stone, "Literacy and Education in England 1640–1900," in *Past and Present*, 42 (1969), 115–6.
11 But the mistake is not made by Thomas Walter Laqueur. See his *Religion and Respectability: Sunday Schools and Working Class Culture 1780–1850* (New Haven, 1976).
12 Palmer, 56–7.
13 See the contribution by Roy Lowe to this volume.
14 Arthur Rook, ed., *Cambridge and its Contribution to Medicine* (London, 1971), 148.
15 The more specialized parts of the Cambridge Natural Sciences Tripos, for example, did not attract students until the 1890s when it became apparent that the creation of a national system of schooling was producing careers for science teachers. See D. S. L. Caldwell, *The Organization of Science in England* (London, 1957), 186, 196.

16 Charles Edward Mallet, *A History of the University of Oxford* (London, 1968) 3: 446.
17 Michael Sanderson, "The Professor as Industrial Consultant: Oliver Arnold and the British Steel Industry, 1900–1914," *The Economic History Review*, 31 (1978), 585–600.
18 See Francois Leprieur and Pierre Papon, "Synthetic Dyestuffs: The Relation between Academic Chemistry and the Chemical Industry in Nineteenth Century France," in *Minerva*, 17 (1979), 218.
19 David Owen, *English Philanthropy 1660–1960* (Cambridge, Mass., 1964), 346 *et seq.*
20 Sanderson, *The Universities and British Industry*, 10 *et seq.*
21 Sanderson, "The University of London and Industrial Progress, 1880–1914," *Journal of Contemporary History*, 7 (1972), 243–61.
22 George Haines, *Essays on German Influence upon English Education and Science, 1850–1919* (Hamden, Ct., 1969), 143–4; Rothblatt, *Dons*, 254–6.
23 David Layton, "The Educational Work of the Parliamentary Committee of the British Association for the Advancement of Science," in *History of Education*, 5 (1976), 25–39.
24 Haines, 106.
25 Paul Forman, John L. Heilbron and Spencer Weart, "Physics *circa* 1900," in *Historical Studies in the Physical Sciences*, 5 (1975), 50–55. The median age of entry into the full professorship of physics was 32 in the United Kingdom but 37 1/2 in Germany.
26 The number of university teachers in the U. K. grew slowly if steadily from 1900 to the mid-1940s, when a sharp swing upward occurred. The graph is very steep in the 1960s and 1970s. See A. H. Halsey and Martin Trow, *The British Academics* (London, 1971), 140.
27 For a contrary view with respect to Germany, see the contribution of Peter Lundgreen to this volume.
28 Charles Carter, "On Being a Middle-Aged University," review by T. W. Bamford, *The University of Hull: The First Fifty Years* (Oxford, 1978), in *Minerva*, 17 (1979), 180–3.
29 It may even be suggested that the idea of the small American liberal arts college is also moribund, insofar as the curriculum is modeled precisely on that of the large research universities and the education of the faculty is that of the research scholar or scientist. See Rothblatt, *Tradition and Change in English Liberal Education, an Essay in History and Culture* (London, 1976).
30 A. N. Shimmin, *The University of Leeds, the First Half Century* (Cambridge, 1954), 19.
31 Sanderson, *Universities and British Industry*, 94, 119.
32 Shimmin, 13. The year was 1882.
33 Charles Firth, *Modern Languages at Oxford, 1724–1929* (Oxford, 1929), 55–7.
34 In the right academic setting with the right student even neglect plays a part in encouraging innovation. Thus it was the student subculture of collegiate Oxford that enabled the brilliant young scientist, Harry Moseley, to advance in his physics studies. See John L. Heilbron, *H. G. J. Moseley, The Life and Letters of an English Physicist, 1887–1915* (Berkeley, 1974), 37 *et seq.*
35 Romualdas Sviedrys "Physical Laboratories in Britain," in *Historical Studies in the Physical Sciences*, 7 (1976), 435.
36 R. M. MacLeod, "Science and the Treasury: Principles, Personalities and Policies, 1870–1885," in *The Patronage of Science in the Nineteenth Century*, ed., G. L. E. Turner (Leyden, 1976).

37 Hence the vulnerability of aristocratic cabinets to outside pressure groups in the early Victorian period. See D. A. Hamer, *The Politics of Electoral Pressure* (Hassocks, Sussex, 1977), 324–8.
38 MacLeod, "Resources of Science in Victorian England: The Endowment of Science Movement, 1868–1900," in *Science and Society, 1600–1900*, Peter Mathias, ed. (Cambridge, 1972), 111–66; W. H. Brock, "The Spectrum of Science Patronage," in Turner, *ibid.*
39 Eric Hutchinson, "The Origins of the University Grants Committee," in *Minerva*, 13 (1975), 583–6; Robert O. Berdahl, *British Universities and the State* (Berkeley, 1959), 20–68.

108

EDUCATION AND THE MIDDLE CLASSES IN MODERN FRANCE

Fritz Ringer

Source: W. Conze and J. Kocka (ed.) *Bildungsbürgertum im 19. Jahrhundert*, Teil I, Stuttgart: Klett-Cotta, 1985, pp. 109–46.

An adequate social history of the modern European middle classes would conceive society as a system of relatively persistent relationships among more or less dominant social groups. It would recognize that absolute changes in levels of wealth and education may fail to disturb a more enduring structure of relative inequalities, and that much limited or individual mobility may accompany the reproduction of stable relationships among groups[1]. Moreover, such a social history would be concerned not only with class differences of wealth and economic power, but also with status differentiations in Max Weber's sense, with differences in style of life and social honor. It would give serious attention, finally, to the way in which particularly the dominant social groups defined and categorized themselves in relation to each other and to less advantaged groups.

Modern European systems of secondary and higher education are best conceived as systems of interrelated institutions, curricula, and academic qualifications or credentials, that cannot be understood in isolation from each other. Educational systems have played complex and relatively autonomous roles in their societies; they have not simply been functional extensions of economic "needs", and they have not served primarily as channels of upward social mobility.

Thus during most of the nineteenth century, the leading European secondary schools and universities prepared their graduates almost exclusively for the liberal professions, the higher civil service, the church, and secondary and university teaching. There was virtually no direct relationship between advanced education and the early industrial economy, and the social distribution of educational advantages was by no means congruent with the hierarchy of wealth and economic power. From the later nineteenth century

217

to our own day, to be sure, certain forms of advanced education have been perceived and recommended as "requirements" of economic and technological progress, and the system of educational qualifications has indeed been brought into closer interaction with the occupational system of the high industrial and late industrial age. Yet while a loose and general relationship may in fact obtain between technological change and educational change, the case for economic functionalism in education has never been adequately specified, and the modern system of educational qualifications has almost certainly done as much to shape the modern occupational system as the reverse. At the same time, the evidence is increasingly against the popular notion of steadily increasing social mobility through improved educational opportunities in modern times. Even the partial incongruity between the distribution of advanced education and the hierarchy of economic advantages has survived into the late industrial era, although it has probably been attenuated by the convergence between the educational system and the occupational system that began during the high industrial period.

The present essay will briefly examine the French educational system of the nineteenth and early twentieth centuries with a view to its relevance for an adequate social history of the French middle classes. It will survey the pattern of educational institutions and qualifications, the proportions of age cohorts reaching specified levels and types of advanced education, and the social origins of students in the various sectors of the system. It will also begin to touch upon the position of academics and intellectuals in French society, and upon the issue of middle-class self-definitions and social classifications. The hope is that even summary evidence on these matters will provide important clues to the internal articulation of the French middle classes, the relationship between the status hierarchy of education and the class hierarchy of wealth and economic power, and the deeper divide between the dominant social groups and the rest of society.

The emphasis is less on social mobility that on social reproduction, on changeable but relatively persistent group relationships, and particularly on certain correspondences and interactions between the structure of the educational system and the structure of class and status relationships in the larger society. The implied hypothesis is not that all social differences can be reduced to educational differences, but roughly that the rank order of educational institutions and curricula translates a preexistent social hierarchy into the language of academic prestige, whether in the idiom of "cultivation" or of "merit". Once established and vested with a certain autonomy, the educational hierarchy acts back upon the social hierarchy, primarily to legitimate and reinforce it, but also partly to supplement and complicate it. More specifically, the educational sytsem perpetuates sociocultural traditions and confers prestige. It thus interacts primarily with the status hierarchy of life styles and social honor, rather than with the class hierarchy of wealth and economic power. During much of the nineteenth century, in fact, European educational systems transmitted status conventions and social meanings that were partly incongruent with the emerging high industrial class hierarchy. The underlying conflict between the class and status orders became particularly acute during the later nineteenth century, as educational systems came into closer interaction with certain sectors of the occupational system. Particularly affected was a range of younger professions that were at once more educated than their early industrial precursors, and arguably more relevant to commerce and industry than the older learned and liberal professions.

The method of the present essay is essentially comparative. Part of its purpose is to call attention to important structural similarities between the French and German systems of secondary and higher education. These were so remarkable, in fact, as to cast doubt on the analytical significance of ad hoc and purely national approaches in the history of eduction. On the other hand, this essay will also attempt to identify significant differences between the French and German educational systems. These were certainly smaller than the underlying similarities, but they were important nonetheless. They sustained subtle but enduring differences between the internal articulations of the middle classes in the two societies, as I would argue. Some of what follows is thus intended to show that advanced education was an integral element of bourgeois status in France, or that the French educated upper middle class was largely identical with the propertied upper middle class even during the nineteenth century, whereas the German educational system helped to define a distinctive status group of the highly educated, the *Bildungsbürgertum,* that set itself off to some degree from the economic middle classes, at least until the end of the nineteenth century.

I

The French Revolution did not end by having a "democratic" effect on French secondary and higher education[2]. It swept away the ancient universities, along with the endowments of the clerical teaching orders that had run most of the secondary schools *(collèges)* of the old regime. The educational reform projects of the Convention had few enduring consequences, and so it was Napoleon who really established the basic framework of secondary and higher education for nineteenth-century France.

Napoleon's main concern was with administrative rationalization and state control. The so-called University he created in 1806 was not an advanced institution of learning, but a hierarchically organized and centrally controlled corporation that encompassed all public secondary and higher education and its personnel. Napoleon's conception of higher education was narrowly practical. He saw a need for advanced instruction and state certification in law, medicine, and pharmacy, but the "faculties" or "schools" to which he assigned these functions were strictly professional institutions. As for the

219

faculties of letters and of sciences, heirs of the old arts faculties, they had almost no regularly enrolled students until late in the nineteenth century. Their main task was the setting and grading of the *baccalauréat*, a secondary leaving examination and certificate similar to the German *Abitur;* but they also examined and certified teachers for the state secondary schools, and they usually offered public lectures of general interest to amateur audiences. In sum, for most of the nineteenth century, France had university-level faculties, but no universities.

The other institutions of higher education favored by Napoleon were the so-called "government schools" or *grandes écoles*. Some of these dated back to the eighteenth century; others had their origins in the revolutionary period. They were clearly designed to train specialists for the various branches of the government service, including the military. The elite groups of students they accepted on the basis of highly competitive entrance examinations were educated and boarded at the expense of the state, usually for a three-year term. The two most famous *grandes écoles* of the nineteenth century were the Ecole Polytechnique (1794) and the Ecole Normale Supérieure (1795, 1808). Officially a military school, the Ecole Polytechnique prepared civil as well as military engineers for government service[3]. Among its graduates, some went on to complete their training at such older "schools of application" as the artillery and naval schools, the School of Mines, and the School of Bridges and Roads; most ended up in the military, though a good number also went into the technical branches of the high civil service, and a few transferred to private industry. The Ecole Normale, by contrast, was a purely academic institution; preparing the elite of future teachers and administrators for the state secondary schools[4].

The keystone of the Napoleonic educational system was the state *lycée,* which was patterned more on the old Jesuit *collèges* than on the so-called central schools of the revolutionary period. Established in 1802, the Napoleonic *lycées* offered an essentially classical curriculum, along with substantial training in mathematics. To put the new institutions on their feet financially, the Emperor established a cluster of state scholarships, which were also designed to aid pupils from the poorer classes, especially sons of loyal soldiers and functionaries. While these scholarships helped to lend the Napoleonic educational system an air of meritocratic opportunity, they fell short of matching the provision of free secondary education that had been funded from the endowments of the clerical teaching orders[5]. In 1808, the famous and all-important *baccalauréat* was instituted as a nationally standardized secondary leaving examination based on the curriculum of the *lycées*. It was a prerequisite for the more advanced teaching degrees in letters and sciences, and, from 1820 on, for access to the faculties of law and medicine as well.

The French *lycées* of the nineteenth century were financed directly by the central government and usually located in the larger cities. The more numerous public *collèges* were partly supported by the municipalities and typically found in the smaller towns. Their curriculum was largely that of the *lycées,* but many of them lacked the higher grades. In competition with the public secondary schools, private *collèges* attracted a substantial portion of the student population. During the early nineteenth century, a number of private secondary schools were run by laymen. Increasingly over the course of the century, however, private secondary schools were essentially Catholic schools. A few of the private *collèges* run by the Jesuits matched the most renowned Parisian *lycées* in academic standing, but there were also Catholic *collèges* that catered to a humble clientele in the countryside[6].

Though they varied, the costs of secondary schooling were probably somewhat higher in France than in Germany during the nineteenth century. In addition to substantial tuitions, roughly half of French secondary pupils paid fees to board at public or private secondary schools. Scholarship funds declined from the First Empire to the Third Republic, and did not always go to the neediest students in any case. More generally, secondary education was as rigorously separated from primary schooling in France as in Germany. Many of the youngsters who reached the secondary classes of public secondary schools at around age eleven came from elementary classes attached to public or private secondary schools. In France as in Germany, moreover, primary teachers were trained at primary normal schools, not at the secondary schools and university faculties that prepared secondary teachers *(professeurs)*.

Until the 1860s, the French secondary curriculum remained overwhelmingly classical. Small prevocational programs were attached to some municipal and private *collèges* during the early nineteenth century, but secondary schooling proper meant classical schooling. The first systematic alteration of this pattern was the curricular bifurcation of 1852, in which the four highest secondary grades were divided into a literary (classical) and a scientific (predominantly mathematical) branch. Even before this bifurcation was adopted, and again after it was dropped in 1864, students preparing to take entrance examinations for the scientific *grandes écoles* could in any case begin their study of advanced mathematics after the Third, and thus bypass much of the classical program of the highest secondary grades.

More radical than bifurcation of 1852 was the "special secondary" curriculum introduced between 1863 and 1865, which launched a whole series of structural changes in French secondary education. Influenced by the example of the German *Realschulen,* the special secondary program was meant to provide an alternative, at the lower secondary level and within the existing secondary schools, to the abstract and literary bent of the traditional curriculum. A four-year course beginning at age eleven emphasized the applied sciences, laboratory exercises and even manual training, along with French and history. More commonly found at *collèges* than at *lycées,* the special program quickly attracted substantial enrollments. Yet it did not long retain its original character. Instead, during the 1880s, it evolved in a generalist and academic direction. Its duration was extended; the practical science courses were replaced by more theoretical ones; the modern languages and French literature, taught in the traditional manner, became more important elements in the curriculum. In 1891, the "special" program officially became the "modern" stream within the French secondary system, with a duration one year short of the classical curriculum and a baccalaureate of its own[7].

The generalist shift in the special secondary program during the 1880s was aided by significant changes in French public primary education. The Ferry laws of 1881–1882 not only made public primary schooling free and compulsory for ages six through thirteen; they also accelerated the development of free public higher primary and full-time vocational education. Some of the new institutions created in this way resembled the special secondary program as originally conceived, except that they were free and "primary." The transformation of "special" into "modern" secondary education thus reduced the possibility of competition between higher primary and special secondary schooling, while laying the basis for a three-tiered hierarchy of classical secondary, modern secondary, and higher primary or full-time vocational education.

Needless to say, these structural changes were accompanied by heated public debates over the relative merits of classical and modern secondary education, and over the accreditation of the modern baccalaureate of 1891. The controversy came to a head in testimony before the parlimentary Ribot Commission, convened in 1899 to undertake a full-scale investigation of public and private secondary education. The real outcome of the commission's work was a decree of 1902, which probably owed less to the testimony collected than to the views of reform-minded education officials and to the politics of the left center in the Chamber of Deputies. In any case, the decree of 1902 established a framework for French secondary schooling that remained in place, largely unchanged, until after the Second World War. The full seven-year course of secondary studies that began with the Sixth at age eleven was divided into two cycles, four and three years in length. In the first cycle, students chose either a modern or a classical stream. In the second cycle, those coming from the first-cycle modern program continued in a course labelled (Modern) Languages-Sciences, while those coming from the classical side could opt for Latin-Greek, Latin-Sciences, or Latin-(Modern)Languages. At least in theory, the decree of 1902 recognized no difference of accreditation between the four curricular paths and the two baccalaureates that had thus been established. In practice, the strictly modern option suffered from a relative lack of prestige and from minor restrictions of access to higher education for some time to come[8].

Obviously, the French secondary baccalaureate was the decisive criterion of membership in the educated upper middle class in nineteenth-century

France. It was notorious for its difficulty and for its impact on teachers and students in the higher secondary grades. Over half the candidates might fail all or part of the required tests, and some therefore repeated the concluding grades of the secondary curriculum. From 1820 on, the baccalaureate was a prerequisite for access to the faculties of law and medicine, and thus to the *licence* in law and the doctorate in medicine, the two professional degrees typically awarded by these faculties after three to five years of additional study.

From its beginnings in 1808, the baccalaureate was also required of candidates for the three main advanced degrees offered by the faculties of letters and of sciences: the *licence,* the *agrégation,* and the state doctorate. Until late in the nineteenth century, all three were taken exclusively by future secondary and university faculty, and all three were rigidly tied to the secondary curriculum. The *licence* was just a slightly more elaborate version of the baccalaureate, required of all but the lowest ranks of secondary teachers. The more difficult *agrégation,* usually and most easily obtained after three years at the Ecole Normale, gave access to the highest positions in the state secondary system. It was awarded in the main secondary subjects, which were also the only ones represented by chairs in the nineteenth-century faculties of letters[9]. In fact, successful *lycée* teachers, usually *agrégés,* could advance from their secondary posts to positions in the faculties of letters and sciences, most easily those in the provinces, during most of the nineteenth century. The state doctorate, formally required for professorships in the faculties, was awarded on the basis of two theses, one of them in Latin; but even the non-Latin dissertation evolved only gradually from a formality before 1850 to a serious research effort by the end of the century.

Several major *grandes écoles* did not formally require the baccalaureate of those taking their entrance examinations[10]. On the other hand, these very difficult examinations themselves were largely based on the secondary curriculum. To prepare for them, students took so-called preparatory courses for two to four years beyond the highest secondary grade. Expensive and typically found only at the most renowned Parisian *lycées,* these preparatory courses constituted a formidable barrier between secondary schooling and the *grandes écoles.*

Along with the Ecole Polytechnique and the Ecole Normale, the Military School of Saint-Cyr, several naval schools, and the Colonial School figured among the notable *grandes écoles* of the nineteenth century. The Ecole Centrale des Arts et Manufactures, privately founded in 1829 and taken over by the state in 1857, was designed to train engineers, managers and entrepreneurs for French industry[11]. The Ecole Libre des Sciences Politiques remained a private school from its foundation in 1872 until after the Second World War. Its emphasis was on politics and international affairs, and it eventually acquired something close to a monopoly of access to certain departments of the higher civil service. Advanced theological education in

France has generally taken place at higher seminaries *(grands séminaires),* rather than in university faculties of theology. The famous Ecole Pratique des Hautes Etudes was founded in 1868 to permit seminarstyle ("practical") research training for small groups of advanced students in the arts and sciences. Among other purely scholarly or artistic institutions of higher education in Paris, one must count the Ecole des Chartes, which trains archivists and paleographers, the Ecole des Langues Orientales Vivantes, and the Ecole des Beaux-Arts. The ancient Collège de France is an institute of advanced study; its tenured faculty give public lectures but do not formally teach regular students.

At the side of these distinguished establishments, several clusters of younger institutions have sprung up since the late nineteenth century and especially since the First World War. Some have been oriented toward business administration; but the overwhelming majority have been specialized technical and engineering schools. Their ancestors are not so much the Ecole Polytechnique and the Ecole Centrale as the *écoles d'arts et métiers,* which did not attain university-level standing until the twentieth century[12]. The two oldest of these practically oriented schools of mechanical engineering were founded by Napoleon to train "noncommissioned officers" for French industry. The rapid development of higher primary and full-time vocational schooling from the 1880s on allowed the *écoles d'arts et métiers* to raise their standards, and they began to confer an engineering diploma in 1907. Further progress in vocational and "secondary technical" education, especially since 1945, has confirmed the now so-called *écoles nationales d'ingéniers arts et métiers,* together with many younger engineering schools, in their role of univerity-level technical institutions.

While important structural changes took place in French secondary schooling and in French higher technical education during the late nineteenth century, at least equally significant transformations altered the university faculties, especially those of letters and sciences[13]. Beginning in the 1860s, leading French academics and educational administrators began to call for reforms that would bring French higher education in the arts and sciences closer to the model of the German research university.

The reform movement achieved its first practical success with the founding of the Ecole Pratique des Hautes Etudes (1868). Then, between 1877 and 1883, the faculties of letters and sciences themselves were affected by the stepwise establishment of 350 scholarships for students working toward the teaching *licence,* and another 200 for more advanced candidates seeking the *agrégation.* For the first time, the faculties of letters and sciences thus acquired a solid core of regular students, not merely examinees and amateur auditors. They accordingly began to replace the old public lectures with "closed courses" for regular students, and with *conférences,* small-group colloquia or seminars of a type first developed at the Ecole Normale. During the 1880s, a certain degree of specialization was instituted in the preparation for the *licences* in letters and in sciences. Beyond the level of the *licence,* the so-called diploma of higher studies was introduced to attest the capacity for independent research. It eventually became a normal step on the way to the *agrégation.* In 1893, medical students were required to begin their university work with a year of basic studies in the faculties of sciences. In 1895, a further reorganization of the *licence* in sciences established a flexible system of specialized certificates, any three of which could make up the *licence.* In 1897, the university faculties were empowered to institute so-called university diplomas of their own, on the basis of whatever requirements they chose to set.

In the meantime, a series of measures taken between 1885 and 1896 transformed the French faculties into something like modern universities. In 1885, the faculties were given limited powers to manage their own funds, especially private gifts and endowments, while interfaculty councils began to link the several faculties in each town. In 1893, the financial prerogatives of these councils were broadened, and in 1896, the existing faculties were grouped together to form 16 universities in metropolitan France. While some of the new units were too small to be effective, and while none achieved the integration of their counterparts in England and Germany, one can reasonably date the creation of the modern French universities from 1896.

Even so, the real significance of the institutional changes that have been described lies in the partial loosening of the restaints that long bound especially the French faculties of letters to their teacher-training function, and thus to the major subject categories of the secondary curriculum. On the one hand, the "New Sorbonne" of the years around the turn of the century had acquired some of the autonomous character of a specialized research institution. On the other hand, a new flexibility in the system of accreditations, along with a measure of financial autonomy, enabled the stronger provincial faculties of science to seek local clients and financial support by offering applied scientific and technical courses of interest to local industries. By the beginning of the twentieth century, the French universities thus performed the full range of functions characteristic of the German universities, and perhaps some of those characteristic of the German technical institutes as well.

In France as in Germany, the period between the two World Wars brought a whole new wave of change, particularly in secondary education. On both sides of the Rhine, leading reformers were inspired by the ideal of the common school *(école unique),* which was to reduce social barriers by starting all pupils off in the same schools, and by having curricular specializations branch off from a "common trunk" as late as possible. Progress toward this goal was slower in France than in Germany during the 1920s; but then the National Socialist regime brought reform to a standstill in Germany, while change accelerated in France during the 1930s and continued almost uninterrupted into the post-World War II era.

During the 1920s, French reformers succeeded in reducing the curricular differences between elementary primary schooling and the elementary classes attached to secondary schools. In the higher secondary grades, the curricular option labelled Latin-Modern Languages was dropped, while common classes began to reduce the differences not only between the remaining secondary streams, but also between higher primary and secondary education. Then, in a stepwise sequence between 1928 and 1933, French public secondary education became free, except that students in the elementary classes of secondary schools continued to pay fees[14]. The Vichy regime temporarily reintroduced tuition for all secondary grades; but it upheld and continued a series of measures begun under the Popular Front that ultimately brought the former higher primary and full-time vocational schools into the secondary system. A further process of change in the French educational system was thus initiated that has extended nearly to our own day.

II

Table 1 describes what I call the inclusiveness of French secondary and higher education at various levels from 1840 to 1950; that is, it reports enrollments in the several layers and parts of the French educational system as percentages of the relevant age groups (access percentages, or access chances). There is no other way to assess the "size" of an educational system or of "the educated class" in any society. Absolute enrollment figures are largely meaningless, and even ratios of secondary enrollments to the population, for example, cannot be made internationally comparable, since secondary programs differ in the number of grades or years they encompasses. The calculation of access percentages of the type listed in Table 1 is admittedly somewhat problematic. Thus *total* secondary enrollments are related to the *overall* size of the appropriate number of age years in the population. The resulting percentage therefore represents declining enrollments in ascending grades as a kind of *average;* it understates enrollments in the lowest grades and correspondingly overstates enrollments in the highest grades. At the university level, total enrollments for both France and Germany are similarly related to a four-year age group, although this procedure is only roughly justified by what is known about average durations of university study in the two countries at various times. If these limitations are kept in mind, however, the indicators in Table 1 can safely be assigned an analytical significance that unrefined data would lack.

With respect to French secondary education, evidence not reproduced in the table would clearly indicate that enrollments and baccalaureate awards as of 1840–1842 were certainly no higher, and were probably somewhat lower, than they had been in 1831, in 1809, and even on the eve of the Revolution of 1789[15]. Thus, in a system that had been essentially stable for over half a century, the first notable increases in enrollments and baccalaureate awards

226

Table 1 The Inclusiveness of French Secondary and Higher Education, 1840–1950: Degrees and Enrollments as Percentages of Relevant Age Groups, with Prussian and German Comparisons*.

Enrollments and Degrees as % of Age Group in:	*1840–42*	*1854–56*	*1865–66*	*1875–76*	*1885–87*	*1910–11*	*1930–31*	*1950–51*
Secondary Enrollments	1.2	1.7	2.2	2.4	2.4	2.6	6.9	17.3
Baccalaureates	0.5	0.7	0.9	0.8	1.0	1.1	2.3	5.7
Law Degrees		0.2	0.2	0.2	0.2			
Law Students				0.2	0.2	0.7	0.8	1.5
Medical Degrees		0.1	0.1	0.1	0.2			
Medical Students				0.2	0.2	0.4	0.7	1.2
Degrees in Letts. & Scis.		(0.02)	(0.03)	(0.04)	0.1			
Students in Letts. & Scis.				(0.03)	0.3	0.5	1.3	2.4
All University Students				0.5	0.6	1.7	2.9	5.4
Prussian/German Comparisons								
Secondary Enrollments			1.7	2.5	2.6	3.2	8.8	9.1
Abiturs			0.5	0.7	0.8	1.2	3.3	4.5
Law Students			0.1	0.2	0.2	0.2	0.4	0.4
Medical Students			0.1	0.1	0.2	0.3	0.4	0.4
Students in Arts & Scis.			0.2	0.2	0.3	0.6	1.1	1.6
All University Students			0.5	0.6	0.8	1.2	2.1	2.5
Students at Tech. Inst.					0.1	0.2	0.4	0.8

Table 1 (cont'd)

* Sources: Ministère de l'Instruction Publique, Rapport au Roi par ... (Villemain) ... sur l'instruction secondaire (1843); —, Bulletin Administratif de l'Instruction Publique, 52 (April, 1854); —, Statistique de l'enseignement secondaire en 1865 (1866); —, ... en 1876 (1878); —, ... en 1887 (1889); —, Statistique de l'enseignement supérieur, 4 vols. (1868–1900); Chambre des Députés, Enquête sur l'enseignement secondaire (1889); J.-B. Piobetta, Le baccalauréat (Paris, 1937); Annuaire statistique de la France, vols. 42 (1926), 72 (1966); INSEE, Population par sexe, âge et état matrimonial de 1851 à 1962 [Etudes et Documents, 10] (Paris, 1968); Wilhelm Lexis, ed., Das Unterrichtswesen im Deutschen Reich, vol. 2 (Berlin, 1904); Statistische Mitteilungen über das höhere Unterrichtswesen im Königreich Preussen, vol. 28 (1911); Statistisches Handbuch/Jahrbuch für den Preussischen Staat, vols. 2 (1893), 11 (1913); Jahrbuch für das höhere Schulwesen im Deutschen Reich, vol. 1 (1933); Preussische Statistik, vols. 204, 236; Deutsche Hochschulstatistik, vol. 7; Statistisches Jahrbuch, vols. 9, 34, 52, 54, and vol. for 1952; Statistik der Bundesrepublik, vol. 199. For details and annotation, see Ringer, Education and Society, pp. 272–279, 291–300, 316–329, 335–341.

For France, through 1885–87, total (male) enrollments in public and private secondary schools are related to the ten-year age group 8 through 17 (both sexes); thereafter, enrollments in the Sixth and higher grades (including girls in 1930–31 and 1950–51) are related to the seven-year age group 11 through 17. This may understate secondary access slightly through 1885–87, and overstate it slightly thereafter. The corresponding data for the baccalaureate are related to age year 17. Beginning in 1875–76, enrollments in university faculties are related to the four-year age group 19 through 22. This may understate university access slightly for 1875–76, and overstate it slightly for 1930–31 and 1950–51. Insignificant numbers of theology students are included in the figures for letters and sciences; students in faculties or schools of pharmacy are not separately listed, but are included in the totals for all university students. Also included among university students are foreigners (7% in 1891, 13% in 1910–11, 22% in 1930–31, and 7% in 1950–51) and women (10% in 1910–11, 27% in 1936, and 40% in 1961). For years 1854–56, 1865–66, and 1875–76, medical doctorates, and licences awarded in law, and in letters and sciences, are related to age year 22. Adding agrégations in letters and sciences, capacités in law, and officiers de santé in medicine would not have altered the rounded figures actually tabulated.

For Prussia (secondary enrollments and Abiturs through 1910–11) and Germany (all other figures), total secondary enrollments (including girls for 1930–31 and 1950–51) are related to the nine-year age group 11 through 19 (both sexes), and corresponding figures for the Abitur are related to age year 19. University enrollments are related to the four-year age group 20 through 23, which probably understates university access slightly through 1875–76, and certainly overstates it somewhat for 1930–31 and 1950–51. (The sizes of relevant age groups for 1865–66 are estimated, not directly available.) Students in arts and sciences are those in faculties of "philosophy" or in subjects typically taught there (including pharmacy). Significant enrollments in faculties of theology (Catholic and Protestant) are not separately listed, but are included in the totals for all university students. Also included among university students are foreigners (7.5% at Prussian universities in 1900–1903, 4% at German universities in 1931, and 7.5% at German universities in 1961) and women (2.5% at German universities in 1911; 21% and 16% at all German university-level institutions, respectively, in 1931 and 1951). The German technical institutes were not considered university-level institutions until 1899.

Not covered by the table are the French grandes écoles and related institutions (e.g. écoles nationales d'arts et métiers), French private or religious institutions of higher education (grands séminaires, Institut Catholique), and various German academies (relatively low enrollments and not considered university-level institutions until the interwar period, at the earliest).

took place during the 1850s and 60s. The expansion of the 1850s was essentially confined to the private secondary schools, which benefited from the privileges granted them by the Falloux Law of 1850. The much more abrupt upswing of the 1860s occurred at the introduction of the "special" secondary program between 1863 and 1865. Thereafter, from the mid-1860s to the First World War and even into the 1920s, French secondary enrollments rose very little, in relation to the age group, although a gradually increasing proportion of the age group completed their secondary schooling and earned the baccalaureate. In fact, as more detailed breakdowns would show, what growth there was during this period took place exclusively in the "special" or "modern" secondary branch, which was simply superimposed, in effect, upon an unchanging classical mainstream.

The increase in French secondary enrollments and baccalaureates between 1910–11 and 1930–31 was due partly to further growth in the modern stream, and partly to the full accreditation of girls' secondary education during the 1920s. At the same time, a new set of structural changes began even before 1930 and accelerated during the 1930s and 40s. In this further transformation, the barriers between classical and modern secondary schooling were somewhat reduced, and even formerly higher primary and full-time vocational schools were partially integrated into the secondary system. Much of the change was nominal, not real, since visible differences of academic and social standing continued to distinguish the traditional forms of secondary education from their younger competitors. Nevertheless, a substantially increased share of the age group did earn baccalaureates of one sort or another by 1950–51, and a new set of relationships was thus established between the educational system and the white-collar hierarchy of the late industrial society.

The data on the French university faculties in Table 1 indicates a striking stability in certificates and enrollments per age group from the 1850s to the 1880s. The faculties of letters and sciences awarded very few degrees before the 1870s, remaining narrowly confined to their function of examining future secondary teachers. As a result, the numericaly dominant faculties were the professional ones, particularly those of law and medicine. In the early industrial environment, in other words, French university education consisted almost exclusively of training and certifying institutions for the legal and medical professions.

French legal and medical enrollments in fact grew substantially from the 1880s to the interwar period and through the Second World War. But the most dramatic change registered in Table 1 is the explosive expansion of the French faculties of letters and sciences from the late 1870s on. The *rate* of increase in enrollments was in fact greatest between 1876 and 1911, although growth continued at a more moderate pace to the end of the period covered in the table. What happened during the decades after 1876, obviously, amounted to a rapid and thorough transformation in the tasks performed by the non-professional faculties[16].

Looking more closely at the relationships between French secondary enrollments, baccalaureates and university access percentages, one realizes that entrants to the secondary schools must always have been roughly twice as numerous as the "average" enrollments actually tabulated. Since up to half of all candidates typically failed the baccalaureate examination, much of the "weeding out" of pupils came rather late in their secondary career. In addition, the rate of early leaving was certainly significant as well, though apparently not as high as in the German secondary system. Until late in the nineteenth century, French baccalaureate awards were a good deal more frequent, in relation to the age group, than the rate of university certificates and enrollments. Thus the baccalaureate must have been held as a terminal degree by many students who chose not to go on to the professional faculties[17].

The main purpose of Table 1, of course, is to permit comparisons between the French and the German or Prussian systems of secondary and higher education. And the most important general conclusion to be drawn from such a comparison is that the two national systems were really rather similar in structure and size. Even the rhythms of change in education were not very different east and west of the Rhine. German and Prussian data not reported in the table would demonstrate that German university enrollments declined during the later eighteenth century and reached a low point around 1801–05[18]. The recovery that followed upon the Napoleonic wars and the civil service reforms in Prussia reached a peak at 1830–1831, a year that also saw particularly high enrollments and *Abitur* awards in secondary schools. In fact, recurrent concerns about the dangers arising from an overproduction of educated men reached a crisis level in Germany during the 1830s and 40s, just as similar anxieties were expressed, with less obvious empirical grounds, in France[19]. In any case, German university enrollments per population declined sharply during the 1830s, until they reached a plateau between 1840 and 1870 that is adequately represented by the figures for 1865–66 in Table 1. German secondary enrollments and certificates per population also declined during the 1830s, but then increased gradually from 1840 on. Nevertheless, it seems reasonable to interpret the plateau in German university enrollments per population and age group between 1840 and 1870 as a kind of early industrial equilibrium, and to compare it to the relatively constant rate of French legal and medical degree awards per age group during the decades around the mid-nineteenth century.

Secondary enrollments per age group increased somewhat more vigorously in Prussia than in France from the mid-1860s to the interwar period. But in Prussia as in France, these increases during the high industrial period took place almost exclusively in the non-classical sector of the system, while enrollments in the classical *Gymnasium* stream remained essentially stable, in relation to the age group, from the 1870s to the 1920s[20]. In Germany as in France, public debates over the status of non-classical or partly classical secondary programs during the late nineteenth century were accompanied by renewed anxieties over a supposed excess of educated men and the danger of creating an "academic proletariat"[21]. In Germany as in France, finally, the interwar period witnessed the full accreditation of girls' secondary education, further substantial increases in levels of inclusiveness, and another wave of concern over a supposed overproduction of graduates during the 1930s.

One of the major differences between the French and German indicators in Table 1 is due largely to the regressive educational policies of the National Socialists in Germany between 1933 and 1945. While the French educational reforms of the 1930s were continued under the Vichy regime and into the postwar period, the National Socialists restricted access to secondary schools and universities to such a degree that the postwar resurgence had not yet reattained French levels of inclusiveness by 1950–51. As of that year, moreover, the French secondary system, unlike its German counterpart, had been enlarged in a partly nominal way by the integration of formerly higher primary and full-time vocational schools.

Secondary enrollments per age group were clearly higher in France than in Prussia around 1865, and what we know about earlier patterns in the two countries suggests that France in fact held a quantitative lead in secondary education throughout the first two-thirds of the nineteenth century. Even late in the century, the French secondary system produced more graduates, in relation to the age group, than its Prussian counterpart. The shape of the pyramid of secondary enrollments differed slightly in the two societies. Despite the high failure rate on the baccalaureate, a somewhat larger proportion of secondary students typically obtained the leaving certificate in France than in Germany during the nineteenth century. As a result, what advantage Prussia had over France in secondary schooling came after 1870, and was chiefly due to the continuous and vigorous expansion of the six-year *Realschulen* and of lower secondary education generally.

At the university level, the French system clearly produced more legally trained graduates than Germany until the 1870s, and again between 1910 and 1950. During much of the nineteenth century, this difference was undoubtedly due in part to the narrowness of the curriculum in the French faculties of letters and sciences. Roughly half of French law students sought the *licence* in law as a kind of generalist degree, without intending to enter the legal professions[22]. From the late nineteenth century on, moreover, the French law faculties offered courses, as well as a doctorate, in economic, social and political studies, so that the high enrollments per age group in the French law faculties of the early twentieth century were due in part to the expansion of the social sciences as a field of study within those faculties.

The most obvious differences between the French and German indicators in Table 1, of course, reflect the fact that the French faculties of letters and of sciences were little more than examining boards for the secondary bacca-laureate and for the teaching *licence* and *agrégation* during the entire period from the creation of Napoleonic "university" to the late 1870s. This circum-stance certainly was of decisive significance, not only for the size and character of the educated elites in nineteenth-century France, but for the history of French science and scholarship as well. The German "philosophical" facul-ties of the nineteenth century not only fulfilled their institutionally primary function of educating future secondary teachers in unique ways; they also transcended that function relatively early in the century. Parallel develop-ments in France, by contrast, did not even begin until the late 1870s. One of the consequences, obviously, was a crucial deficit in French university enrollments per age group, as compared to the corresponding indices for Germany, that remained clearly visible until sometime between 1890 and 1900.

Even so, the importance of this difference between the two systems should not be overstated. The old theory that German industrialization was crucially aided by a strong system of secondary and higher education, for example, must be radically questioned, revised, or even abandoned[23]. To sustain the theory at all, one would either have to emphasize German lower secondary schooling toward the end of the nineteenth century; or one would have to look more closely at the graduates of the German faculties of "philosophy" before about 1890. The German technical institutes were not nearly as significant, from a quantitative and comparative perspective, as has sometimes been thought. They are represented in Table 1, whereas the French *grandes écoles* and other non-university institutions of higher education were too diverse to be treated in a summary table[24]. Yet it is clear that the German technical institutes graduated a relatively small fraction of the age group before the 1890s. Both before and after that time, their output of graduates was almost certainly matched or even overmatched by the Ecole Centrale, by the *écoles d'arts et métiers,* by any of a cluster of younger technical schools created in France from the late nineteenth century on, and as of about 1900, by the French faculties of sciences as well. Moreover, even if it *were* possible to specify exactly when and where Germany had significant educational advantages over France, it would still be necessary to demonstrate that these advantages were truly relevant to actual differences in the level, pace or character of economic growth in the two countries. It seems less and less likely that such a demonstration could succeed.

We thus return to a central argument of the present essay. The develop-ment of secondary and higher education in France and Germany during most of the nineteenth century was not directly or primarily a function of economic growth. It was tied, rather, to the kind of bureaucratic rational-ization that received a new impetus, in France as in Prussia, at the beginning of the nineteenth century. It was also a consequence of state control over qualifications and access to the legal and medical professions. Since both such state control and bureaucratic rationalization proceeded in roughly parallel ways in France and Germany during our period, the systems of secondary and higher education in the two countries also developed in a generally parallel way, despite whatever differences there were in the levels and rates of industrialization in the two national economies. The main indicators in Table 1, to repeat, were remarkably similar in their orders of magnitude. During much of the nineteenth century, to be sure, the French system produced somewhat more secondary graduates per age group than its Prussian counterpart, and there were roughly twice as many legally educated Frenchmen as Germans, in relation to the age group. Prussia and Germany, on the other hand, had a slight relative advantage in the *Realschulen* of the late nineteenth century, along with a highly developed system of university education in the arts and sciences that was not fully matched in France until around the turn of the century. Nonetheless, if "the educated middle class" were defined, simply and not unreasonably, as the holders of secondary certificates, then France and Germany could be shown to have had educated middle classes of generally comparable size from the early nineteenth century on.

III

The social character of an educational system can be systematically and comparably described as more or less progressive, and more or less segmented. A progressive system is one that recruits a relatively high proportion of its students from lower middle-class and lower-class backgrounds. Progressiveness in an educational system or school should not be considered a sufficient condition for upward social mobility, since it tells us nothing about the social positions actually attained by its graduates. A segmented system is one in which different programs of study at the same age level also differ in the social origins of their students[25]. Both progressiveness and segmentation can be measured in terms of *relative access chances* or of similar indicative ratios. If 2 percent of working-class youths and 20 percent of all youths in an age group reached secondary schools, for example, then the relative access chance for the working class with respect to these schools would be 2/20 or 0.1. Similarly, if 3 percent of students actually in these schools and 30 percent of the occupational census were identified as working-class, then one could specify an *opportunity ratio* for the working class in these schools of 3/30, or 0.1 again[26]. These technicalities are worth rehearsing because of the interpretive principle they imply: *In principle,* the sort of information typically available on the social origins of students in French and German secondary schools and universities is meaningful only in relation to a norm, which can be found in the occupational census, in the corresponding data for the whole age group, or in the relevant indicators for all students in a given sector of the system. A coherent and comparable account of students' social origins and socio-occupational destinies, in turn, is one of the few ways we have to grasp the social role of the educational system, and of the educated classes, in any society.

By far the best source of information on the social character of secondary education in nineteenth-century France is a survey conducted by the French Ministry of Education in 1864 that has been extracted from the archives by Patrick Harrigan, and that is briefly summarized in *Table 2*. Within the limits of occasionally awkward categories, this valuable evidence gives us a glimpse of the French public secondary system as a whole, and of the early "special secondary" stream as well. At the time of the survey, students leaving the small special program after at most four years of study typically went into "commerce" (17 percent) or agriculture (11 percent), or into various intermediate or lower-level white-collar positions (11 and 9 percent, respectively). The vast majority of students in the secondary system as a whole, of course, were enrolled in the classical stream. Among them, about 44 percent proposed to continue their studies, or actually continued them, beyond the baccalaureate, at the university faculties and *grandes écoles,* while 23 percent became large merchants or entered "commerce" or other white-collar occupations.

Among the fathers of all secondary students, 17 percent were *propriétaires,* members of the upper and the established middle classes who owned varying but substantial amounts of land and/or securities, and who presumably liked the aristocratic connotation of being without ordinary gainful employment[27]. Since an additional 10 percent of fathers were large merchants, and 3 percent were industrialists, the older propertied and the currently active portions of the economic upper middle class jointly accounted for 30 percent of students. The liberal and educated professions, including fathers in "Education", were represented at 17 percent, or about equally with the *propriétaires* alone. Taken together, the economic and educated upper middle classes thus accounted for nearly half of all secondary students. The intermediate layers of the economic middle class were represented by a further 24 percent of the sample, while 12 percent of the fathers were farmers, 9 percent were artisans and clerks, and only 2 percent were workers.

The differences of social origin between the special secondary program and the secondary system as a whole provide a perfect example of what I call socially *vertical* segmentation. The students in the special stream were recruited from a perceptibly lower portion of the social hierarchy than those in the classical stream, or those in the system as a whole. Dividing the tabulated percentages for the special curriculum by those for all secondary education, one can calculate a whole series of indicative ratios[28]. Thus, among the parents of pupils in the special secondary stream, the liberal and educated professions were most markedly underrepresented, at ratios of 0.1 for law, and 0.2 for medicine, for "Education", and for the highly educated

Table 2 Social Origins and Educational/Occupational Choices of French Public Secondary Pupils about 1863 (Percentages by Column)*.

Univ.-Level Institutions & Occupational Groups	All Secondary Ed.		Special Sec. Only	
	IN	OUT	IN	OUT
Ecole Normale	—	1.5	—	0.5
Ecole Polytechnique	—	3.7	—	0.3
Mining (Civil Engineering)	—	1.7	—	0.1
Ecole Centrale	—	2.5	—	0.2
Arts & Métiers	—	1.9	—	6.4
Ecole Forestière	—	0.7	—	(—)
Officers/Military Schools	2.4	6.2	1.0	2.3
Law	6.4	12.3	0.6	1.6
Medicine	4.5	9.2	1.0	2.3
Other University-Level Education	—	1.7	—	1.6
Religion	0.3	2.0	} 0.8	0.7
Arts, Writers	1.0	0.8		
Subtotal	14.6	44.2	3.4	16.0
"Education"	2.3	1.7	0.4	0.2
Primary Teachers	1.7	2.7	3.0	6.2
High(er) Officials	1.6	0.1	} 2.0	0.7
Middle Officials	2.0	0.3		
Lower Military	1.3	4.6	1.2	5.7
Subtotal	8.9	9.4	6.6	12.8
"Propertied"	17.0	2.8	13.5	3.4
Industrialists	2.9	0.7	} 3.6	1.0
Engineers	0.5	0.3		
Large Merchants	9.7	2.8	7.4	2.4
Subtotal	30.1	6.6	24.5	6.8
"Industry"	1.3	3.3	} 1.2	4.2
Railroads	0.1	0.3		
"Commerce"	7.3	13.4	8.8	17.0
Shopkeepers	7.0	2.3	10.7	5.1
White Collar	7.8	6.8	5.8	10.8
Subtotal	23.5	26.1	26.5	37.1
Clerks	2.7	4.4	2.8	8.5
Farmers	12.3	7.3	21.4	11.4
Artisans	6.1	2.0	12.5	6.9
Workers	1.9	0.4	2.4	0.8
Subtotal	23.0	14.1	39.1	27.6
Abs. Total Known (100%)	12 603	26 066	1 548	1 849

* From Patrick Harrigan with Victor Negila, *Lycéens et collégiens sous le Second Empire: Etude statistique sur les fonctions sociales de l'enseignement secondaire public d'aprés l'enquête de Victor Duruy (1864–1865),* (Paris 1979), pp. 18–21, 27–30, and Tables 1, 8, 9. The IN columns report the occupations of students' fathers; the OUT columns cover the educational or occupational plans of students as of 1864, as well as the educational institutions or occupations actually reached by students who left the secondary schools (most of them with the *baccalauréat*) from the late 1850's to 1863. Harrigan used a code of 96 basic educational/occupational *categories* to record both fathers' occupations and students' goals, along with a summary code of 20 educational/occupational *groupings*. I have partly rearranged Harrigan's groupings to specify important distinctions, in so far as Harrigan's (and the source's) basic categories themselves made this possible. The grouping 'White Collar' as used in this table covers a cluster of predominantly private white-collar employees of a middling or unspecified level, while the grouping 'Clerks' represents the French *employés*.

as a group. Less pronounced underrepresentations or slight overrepresentations, with ratios between 0.8 and 1.1, characterized the middle and higher officials, the economic upper middle class, and the lower portions of the white-collar hierarchy. Notable overrepresentations can be calculated for "Commerce" (1.2), shopkeepers (1.5), farmers (1.7), primary teachers (1.8), and artisans (2.0). Obviously, the special secondary curriculum was markedly more progressive in its recruitment than the larger and more prestigious classical branch. Though quite small as of 1864, the non-classical sector of French secondary education clearly attracted a disproportionate share of students from lower middle-class families, who would probably have been prevented from entering the classical program by the practicalities and risks involved, and by a kind of social distance from the esoteric world of the traditional secondary schools.

Even so, the French secondary system of 1864 as a whole cannot be considered particularly progressive or "democratic"[29]. In the French census of 1872, the liberal professions, magistrates, and secondary and university professors jointly made up around 1 percent of the working population, while all business owners and wholesale merchants accounted for 4.4 percent, and the propertied and rentiers for another 4.8 percent[30]. No matter how one interprets and "matches" the socio-economic categories of the census with those of the student survey, one has to come up with very substantial overrepresentations for the economic upper middle class, and with even larger ones for the educated and professional elite.

To be sure, the English "public schools" of the early nineteenth century were decidedly more aristocratic than the French *lycées* and *collèges* of the 1860s[31]. But comparisons with Prussia provide a rather different perspective, and a more pertinent one. Thus among parents of about 1600 pupils in selected but roughly representative Prussian secondary schools around 1800, according to Jeismann, some 40 percent were civil servants (all ranks) or members of the educated professions (including officers); another 33 percent were clergymen and secondary teachers; 2 percent were landowners; 6 percent were merchants and manufacturers, and 19 percent were noncommissioned officers and soldiers, primary teachers, artisans and workers, farmers and day laborers[32]. What stands out about these figures is the very low share of the propertied and entrepreneurial upper middle class, which accounted for 30 percent of fathers in the French survey of 1864. The place of this group was taken in Prussia by additional representatives of the educated and noneconomic middle classes, by Protestant clergymen, and by remarkably large contingents of secondary teachers and civil servants of all ranks.

A similar comparative conclusion seems warranted by a report on the social origins and career plans of the roughly 85 thousand pupils who graduated from all Prussian secondary schools between 1875 and 1899[33]. Among these, fully three-quarters meant to enter the liberal and learned professions, including the high civil service, the church, secondary and university teaching, and the officer corps, whereas a mere 4 percent clearly intended to take positions in industry and commerce. The comparable figures in the French survey of 1864 were less than 50 percent, and more than 25 percent, respectively.

Among the fathers of Prussian secondary graduates, 22 percent were members of the educated middle class, including 6 percent who were Protestant clergymen; 8 percent were landowners and industrialists; and 21 percent were merchants, shopkeepers and innkeepers. Here the corresponding percentages in the French survey of 1864 were 17 for the educated middle class without clergymen; 30 percent for *propriétaires,* large merchants and industrialists, and 23 percent for "Industry", "Commerce", shopkeepers, and white-collar employees. On the other hand, at least 20 percent of the Prussian fathers were middle and lower-ranking civil servants and primary teachers, a figure that cannot nearly be matched by any combination of corresponding categories in the French survey. Only the shares of farmers, artisans and workers were of roughly equal size in the two samples, at some 18–20 percent in all, and even this circumstance has to be interpreted in light of the fact that all of the Prussian students canvassed were secondary graduates, whereas the French survey included early leavers and students currently enrolled. Both at the beginning and at the end of the nineteenth century, in sum, the Prussian secondary schools appear to have had markedly less connection than the French *lycées* and *collèges* with an established economic upper middle class, and indeed with the economy in general.

Interestingly enough, small portions of the Prussian graduates under discussion came from the non-classical *Oberrealschule* and the incompletely classical *Realgymnasium,* rather than from the numerically dominant classical *Gymnasium.* As in the French survey of 1864, one can therefore compare the social indicators for the "modern" curricular streams with those for the secondary system as a whole, arriving at ratios of over- and underrepresentation for various social groups. Some of what one discovers in this way can easily be described as socially *vertical* segmentation, in that groups higher on the social scale were predictably underrepresented in the *Realgymnasium* and especially in the *Oberrealschule.* At the same time, one can discern an element of what I call socially *horizontal* segmentation, in that "industrialists", for example, were actually overrepresented in the *Oberrealschule,* whereas the sons of primary teachers were underrepresented in this most "modern" of the three school types, although they would have to be ranked below the "industrialists" on a unlinear social scale[34].

What this kind of horizontal segmentation reflects is a behavioral difference between education-oriented and economy-oriented social groups at roughly comparable social "altitudes", or a horizontal articulation of society into sectors or strands that cut across the predominant pattern of vertically differentiated layers. In nineteenth-century France, the economically dominant elites also held very strong positions in secondary education, which in turn sent graduates into the leading positions in industry and commerce, not only into the liberal and learned professions. In Prussia during much of the nineteenth century, by contrast, the traditional secondary schools were more rigorously separated from the economy, both in their recruitment and in the projected careers of their graduates. By the end of the century, moreover, the less prestigious "modern" schools in Prussia attracted disproportionately large representations from an emerging industrial middle class, and not merely from the lower regions of the social scale, as in France. The difference between the two patterns should not be exaggerated; for in France as in Prussia, it was the educated upper middle class, rather than the economic elite, which was most markedly overrepresented in the classical secondary program and in the secondary system as a whole. Nevertheless, there was something like a divide between the educated and the propertied in Germany, whereas the French pattern can be *fairly* adequately described in terms of the vertical distance between the upper and the lower middle classes.

These impressions can be confirmed and further clarified by what data is available on the social origins of students at French university faculties and *grandes écoles*. Thus in the survey of 1864, secondary students who proposed to pursue university studies in law or medicine, or who had already begun such studies, came overwhelmingly from propertied as well as educated upper middle-class families. Among prospective members of the legal professions, the indicative percentages were 37 for the liberal and educated professions, including "artistic professions" and military officers; 29 percent for the *propriétaires;* 10 percent for large or wholesale merchants and industrialists; and a round 75 percent for the upper middle classes generally. Among prospective physicians, the coresponding percentages were 37 (again) for the liberal and educated professions, 22 percent for the *propriétaires,* 11 percent for large merchants and industrialists, and a round 70 percent for the upper middle classes generally[35]. Considered in relation to the census, these are very high numbers indeed.

Figures for the leading *grandes écoles* of the nineteenth century are equally drastic. At the Ecole Polytechnique, according to Shinn, the transformation of "special" into "modern" secondary education after 1880 produced a substantial shift in a progressive direction. Comparing students who entered the school between 1848 and 1879 with those who entered between 1880 and 1914, one obtains the following percentages for the fathers' professions[36]

	1848–79	1880–1914
Liberal professions and high officials	37	20
Propriétaires and entrepreneurs	52	38
Middle and lower officials	7	20
Shopkeepers and artisans	4	10
"Popular classes"	1	11

Before 1880, in other words, nearly 90 percent of students at the Ecole Polytechnique came from upper middle-class backgrounds.

For the Ecole Centrale, Weiss has summarized a more detailed account of students' social origins in the following broad categories and percentages[37].

	1830–47	1881–1917
Upper bourgeoisie	68	57
Middle bourgeoisie	16	21
Employees and lower cadres	4	14
Popular classes	10	7

It was the same general pattern, although the Ecole Centrale ranked somewhat below the Ecole Polytechnique in academic and social distinction.

In the context of this upper middle-class domination of major *grandes écoles,* the Ecole Normale stood out all the more sharply as a socially unique institution. Its division for the natural sciences was a little more progressive in its recruitment, on the whole, than the division of letters. Moreover, the school as a whole appears to have undergone a slight shift in a progressive direction during the late nineteenth century. Looking beyond these finer distinctions, however, one can arrive at the following summary of Smith's data on the fathers of students who entered the school between 1868 and 1909[38].

Liberal professions	12%
Higher officials and commissioned officers	8%
Owners of capital and businessmen	13%
Secondary and university professors and administrators	19%
Primary and vocational school teachers and administrators	9%
Middle and lower officials and white-collar employees	19%
Artisans, shopkeepers, tradesmen	6%
Lower classes	14%

The unusual elements in this distribution are not only the substantial percentages for the lower middle and lower classes, but also the very high representation of academics and teachers. Nearly 30 percent of students' fathers were professional educators.

The Ecole Normale was almost certainly the most purely "academic" institution in Europe. Throughout the nineteenth century, its graduates were in fact the elite of French secondary teachers, and of professors in the faculties of letters and sciences as well[39]. One has to remember that until late in the century, there was no sharp separation between the functions and career patterns of secondary teachers and those of their colleagues in the faculties of letters and sciences. The highest positions in the more distinguished secondary schools were as desirable and prestigious as chairs in some of the faculties, especially those in the provinces. A *lycée professeur* might jointly hold an appointment in a faculty, or he might be "promoted" to a faculty, where he would spend much of his time examining baccalaureate candidates. It was only after 1880 that holders of chairs in faculties of letters were routinely expected to engage in research, or that some of their students aspired to careers other than secondary teaching. The Ecole Normale thus long remained part of a closed system that encompassed the secondary schools as well as the faculties of letters and sciences, and whose main function was the teaching and examining of secondary students.

The German university professors of the nineteenth century were clearly set apart from the German secondary teachers. Their immense prestige was derived partly from their role as research scholars and scientists, and partly from their control of an examination system that gave access to positions of power outside as well as inside the academic world. The French *professeur,* by contrast, was essentially a secondary teacher, or a teacher of secondary teachers, even if he had attended the Ecole Normale and earned the *agrégation.*

What information we have on the social origins of French secondary teachers as a group suggests that they typically came from relatively humble circumstances. In a sample from the late nineteenth century, only 17 percent were the sons of *propriétaires* and business owners, high civil servants, officers, and members of the liberal professions[40]. Just over a third came from the families of small merchants and artisans, of middle and lower-ranking officials and white-collar employees. An additional 27 percent of the fathers were farmers, lower-ranking military and policemen, and workers; 7 percent were secondary *professeurs* themselves, and 15 percent were primary teachers. Regarded in the light of this distribution — or of the occupational census, of course, the *Normaliens* of the late nineteenth century were a social elite, and not just an academic one. Viewed in another context, however, the Ecole Normale was much more progressive and much more purely academic in the social origins of its students than any other *grande école,* or than the faculties of law and medicine[41].

All of these relationships can be charted more precisely, though at the cost of a sharp change of chronological focus. During the late 1950s, French statisticians began to report on the fathers of university students in a well-articulated set of socio-occupational categories resembling those of the French census of 1954. In the early 1960s, a government report applied the new scheme to the *grandes écoles* as well. It thus became possible to construct a systematic survey of students' social origins for all of French higher education. The interest of such a survey is not much reduced by changes in the social character of the French educational system between the late nineteenth and the mid-twentieth century. The traditional *grandes écoles* in particular remained small elite institutions, even while the university faculties took in substantially increased fractions of the age group.

Of course there have been changes in the occupational census, and in certain key social classifications as well. The ubiquitous *propriétaires* of the nineteenth century have essentially disappeared, although a residual category of "rentiers, without profession" has continued to be used, in the distributions of students' fathers, if not in the census of the "active population". On the other hand, the so-called *cadres supérieurs* and *cadres moyens* have become very significant classifications, encompassing executive and middle-level white-collar workers and experts in the public as well as the private sector. Needless to say, these new categories, like the old ones, reflect mentalities — and symbolic conflicts, and not only social realities in the white-collar hierarchy of the late industrial society[42].

Table 3 summarizes some of the most significant distributions of fathers' occupations for all sectors of French higher education around 1961–63 in the new system of classifications. At the bottom of the table, the summed percentages for the liberal and learned professions are added to those for the industrialists and executive employees to yield indicative percentages for the educated and economic upper middle classes, taken together. Since the census percentages are listed at the left of the table, the opportunity ratios for all social groups and institutions can be quickly calculated or estimated. Looking at the university faculties alone, for example, one can see at a glance that the faculty of law ranked somewhat below the faculty of medicine by the early 1960s. At the same time, a more substantial social distance separated the two professional faculties from the faculty of letters. Though not covered in the table, the faculty of sciences resembled the faculty of letters, while the percentages for French university students generally fell between those for law and those for letters[43].

Among non-university institutions of higher education, as the table indicates, the traditional *grandes écoles* stood well above the university faculties in the social origins of their students: The representation of the upper middle classes at these elite schools ranged from 62 percent at the Ecole Polytechnique to some 50–53 percent at the Ecole Normale, the Ecole Centrale, and the former Ecole Libre des Sciences Politiques, grouped here with several younger Instituts d'Etudes Politiques. The higher commercial schools followed with an upper middle-class percentage of 46, and with particularly high representations not only for industrialists and executive employees, but also for commerce and for middle-level white-collar employees. The higher commercial schools are now generally considered *grandes écoles* in a wider sense of that term, and so are such schools of engineering (ENSI) as those for electricity, aeronautics, and chemistry. The upper middle-class representation at the ENSI for chemistry in 1961 was a good deal lower than it was at the higher commercial schools; but it still exceeded 29 percent, the comparable indicator for the university faculties. Only the now so-called Ecoles Nationales d'Ingénieurs Arts et Métiers ranked somewhat below the university faculties in the social origins of their students. They should really be

Table 3 Social Origins of Students at French University-Level Institutions, 1961–63 (Percentages by Column)*.

Fathers' Occupations and (% of 1954 Census)	University Faculties, 1963				Selected Grandes Ecoles, 1961–62						
	Law	Medicine	Letters	All Facs.	Nor. male	Poly techn.	Centrale	Inst. Pol.	Commerce	ENSI Chem.	Arts & Métiers
1. Lib. professions (0.6)	11	20	7	10	7	16	7	15	8	7	3
2. High officials (0.4)	6	8	6	7	7	19	16	11	8	10	6
3. Professors (0.9)	3	4	4	4	33	8	4	3	1	3	2
1.–3. Sum (1.9)	20	32	16	20	47	43	27	29	17	20	11
4. Teachers (2.0)	3	3	6	5	14	9	5	3	2	5	5
5. Mid. officials (1.1)	7	6	7	7	5	3	6	7	6	7	6
6. Agriculture (26.8)	6	3	8	7	1	1	2	8	4	5	6
7. Industrialists (0.4)	5	4	2	3	2	5	3	8	12	5	4
8. High white coll. (1.0)	7	6	5	6	4	14	20	15	17	10	8
9. Commerce (7.7)	8	9	10	9	5	6	7	8	17	10	6
10. Mid. white coll. (2.8)	6	4	7	6	7	3	7	3	6	7	8
11. Artisans (3.9)	3	3	5	4	2	2	2	3	3	4	9
12. Low white coll. (10.9)	7	7	8	7	5	8	9	8	5	11	10
13. Workers (38.9)	5	4	11	9	3	2	2	3	5	8	19
14. Rentiers, without prof. (—)	8	7	10	8	4	1	6	3	5	5	5
15. Others (2.6)	16	3	6	7	1	3	4	2	1	3	3
16. Unknown (—)	1	10	—	2	—	—	—	—	—	—	—
1.–3., 7.–8. Sum (3.3)	32	42	23	29	53	62	50	52	46	35	23

* Sources: Ministère de l'Education Nationale, Informations statistiques, 69 (1965); Les Conditions de développement, de recrutement, de fonctionnement et de localisation des grandes écoles en France (La Documentation Française, 1964); INSEE, Recensement général de la population de mai 1954: Résultats du sondage au 1/20 ème, Population active, I: Structure professionnelle. 'Professors' includes secondary teachers (along with "literary and scientific professions" in the census); 'Teachers' are chiefly primary teachers (combined with middle-level employees in medical and social services in the census); 'High white collar' covers engineers as well as administrative cadres supérieurs in the private sector, although the engineers are not separately mentioned in the survey of students; the same is true of "technicians" in relation to cadres moyens; 'Low white collar' encompasses private commercial as well as public and private office clerks (employés); 'Workers' includes small percentages of public employees and of servants (personnel de service); 'Others' is further described in the census as encompassing artists, clergy, and the military and police. The faculties of pharmacy and of sciences are not separately treated in the table; the faculty of sciences resembled that of letters in the social origins of its students. The schools listed as grandes écoles (with the number of institutions surveyed in each case) are: Ecoles Normales Supérieures (2, including the one at Sèvres, which prepares teachers for girls' secondary schools), Ecole Polytechnique (1), Ecole Centrale des Arts et Manufactures (1), Instituts d'Etudes Politiques (5, including "Sciences-Po", the former Ecole Libre des Sciences Politiques), Ecoles Supérieures de Commerce (12), Ecoles Nationales Supérieures d'Ingénieurs (ENSI) for chemistry (14), Ecoles Nationales d'Ingénieurs Arts et Métiers (6). For details, see Ringer, Education and Society, pp. 344–348.

considered the apex of the French system of full-time vocational education, although they are now clearly university-level institutions.

The columns on the Ecole Polytechnique, the Ecole Centrale, and the Instituts d'Etudes Politiques in Table 3 typify what might be called the integrally *bourgeois* character of some of the traditional *grandes écoles*. In modern French usage, the word *bourgeoisie* does not refer loosely to the entire "middle class," or to the intermediate social strata termed *classes moyennes*. It certainly does not have the specifically economic, entrepreneurial, or "capitalist" connotation associated with the Anglo-American notion of a commercial and industrial "bourgeoisie". Instead, it describes the highest altitudes in the social hierarchy, or the "upper middle class"[44]. It also typically implies a *combination* of social advantages, a plenitude encompassing wealth and economic control, social influence and political power, along with the high status or *distinction* associated with a quasi-aristocratic, "cultured" style of life[45].

To see the *reality* behind this idea of a thrice-blessed *bourgeoisie,* one only has to look at the Ecole Polytechnique. The students of that academically and socially distinguished institution had already passed through the best secondary schools and the select and expensive preparatory courses before reaching the school. After graduating from it, they became not only elite military officers, but also high public administrators, technologists, and business leaders. Among the students' fathers, high officials and members of the liberal professions were hugely over-represented; but so were industrialists and executive employees. Thus the Ecole Polytechnique was no more progressive and just as *integrally bourgeois* in its recruitment during the early 1960s as it had been during the late nineteenth century.

The former "Sciences-Po" and other Instituts d'Etudes Politiques typically prepared their students for the highest positions in the civil service[46]. Though not quite as exclusive as the Ecole Polytechnique, they were even more balanced in their recruitment from the several subgroups *within* the upper middle class. Similarly, the Ecole Centrale drew almost as large a share of its student body from the families of high officials (*cadres supérieurs,* public sector) as from those of executive-level business employees (*cadres supérieurs,* private sector). Here again, the notion of an *integrally bourgeois* pattern of recuitment seems appropriate.

In the early 1960s as during the late nineteenth century, the Ecole Normale was a kind of "academic" antithesis to the integrally bourgeois *grandes écoles*. This remarkable institution drew 47 percent of its students, more than the Ecole Polytechnique, from the liberal and learned professions. Its total percentage for the upper middle class was 53, the second highest in the table. Yet one could hardly describe the school as a bourgeois stronghold. After all, almost one-quarter of its students came from lower middle-class backgrounds, and almost half had fathers who were university professors, secondary *professeurs,* and primary teachers. As during the late nineteenth century, the Ecole Normale thus stood out not so much for its progressive as for its overwhelmingly "academic" recruitment.

Among students at all university-level institutions in the German Federal Republic as of 1963, and among students of law, of the humanities, and of technological subjects at these institutions, the following percentages had fathers in selected socio-occupational groups[47].

	All Fields	Law only	Humanities	Technology
Medicine and other Liberal professions	14	18	10	11
High officials	9	16	9	8
Secondary and university teachers	6	5	8	4
Learned and Liberal professions	29	39	27	23
Big businessmen and executive employees	23	22	20	28
Workers	6	4	7	6

To compare these percentages with those in Table 3 is obviously to run the risk of taking differences of categorization for genuine differences of recruitment. The German figures were not reported in the terminology of the German occupational census, so that they cannot easily be converted into opportunity ratios. The two societies differed somewhat in their occupational structures in any case. On the other hand, the quantitative differences between the French and German patterns were substantial, so that a few comparative generalizations may justifiably be attempted.

As of the early 1960s, it is probably safe to conclude, the German system of university-level education as a whole was somewhat less progressive in its recruitment than the French university faculties considered alone. We know that the French faculties were a good deal more inclusive than the German system at that time. We also know of at least two occasions when increases in the inclusiveness of French secondary and higher education may have engendered minor gains in progressiveness as well. The first such change began during the 1880s, with the stepwise accreditation of "modern" secondary schooling and the explosive expansion of the faculties of letters and sciences[48]. The second transformation occurred between the late 1930s and the late 1950s, with the integration of the former higher primary and full-time vocational schools into the French secondary system. Certainly this second wave of change had no full counterpart in Germany, where educational growth was checked by the policies of the National Socialists. Thus the German educational system, almost surely the most progressive one in Europe during the early nineteenth century, had lost that rank by the 1960s.

In its internal articulation, the German system of the early 1960s was characterized by relatively mild and predictable differences between the pre-professional fields of study and the humanistic subjects. This part of the German pattern was closely paralleled in France. The French faculties of letters and of sciences once differed markedly from the faculties of law and medicine, but these differences had been much reduced by the mid-twentieth century. Much more specifically characteristic of the German system, on the other hand, was the social distinction between university studies and the subjects typically taught at the technical insitutes. Though itself no more than a muted echo of a formerly sharper division, this social distinction had no parallel in France. It should be noticed that the German economic upper middle class of the early 1960s was more strongly represented in "technology" than in law or in the humanities, whereas the learned and liberal professions were relatively underrepresented at the technical insitutes. In a way, therefore, the distinctiveness of technology as a field of study entailed something like a socially horizontal segmentation in German higher education[49].

In France around 1960, by contrast, the Ecole Polytechnique stood at the very apex of the educational hierarchy. It was a partly technical school, but it drew its students from all sectors of the upper middle class. Even such younger technical schools as the ENSI for chemistry clearly outranked the university faculties of letters and of sciences in the social origins of their students. The Ecoles Nationales d'Arts et Métiers, to be sure, were much more progressive in their recruitment than other sectors of French higher education. But even this instance of segmentation in the French system was socially vertical, not mainly horizontal. It reflected the social distance between the upper middle classes on the one hand, and the lower middle and working classes on the other, whereas the social place of the German technical institutes faintly recalled a divide between the educated and the economic sectors *within* the middle and upper middle classes.

In sum, the German data cited throws into even sharper relief the three major traits of the French educational system that have held our attention. These are the sharp and socially vertical distinction between most of the *grandes écoles* and the university faculties, particularly those of letters and of sciences, which certainly cancelled any "democratic" consequences of progressive recruitment in the faculties; the integrally bourgeois character of the Ecole Polytechnique and other traditional *grandes écoles,* which tended to absorb advanced education into the conjoined attributes of a thrice-blessed *bourgeoisie;* and the contrast between the Ecole Polytechnique and the Ecole Normale, which embodied an antithesis between the *bourgeois* and the *professeur* that took the place of a wider tension between property and education in modern France.

IV

Table 4 describes large and random samples from two leading contemporary biographical dictionaries, one French and the other German. Entries

Table 4 University-Level Education of French and German Elites, 1830–1930 (Percentages by Column and by Row)*.

a) French Elite Groups

University-Level Education: Percent by Row

Occupationl. Categories	(% by Col.)	No Uni-Level	Type Unknown	Law, Letters	Medicine, Sci.	Polytechnique	Normale	Oth. Grand Ecole	Relig, Milit.
Writers, Arts, Scholars	(23)	52	4	16	2	1	2	23	2
Academics	(16)	3	5	18	19	4	25	16	10
Clergy	(7)	14	2	4	—	—	1	2	78
Military, Landowners	(19)	17	—	—	—	25	—	—	58
High Officls.	(5)	14	18	44	1	8	—	12	3
Politicians	(7)	51	3	32	3	3	2	3	3
Lawyers	(4)	—	2	96	—	1	1	1	—
Med. & Oth. Lib. Prof.	(6)	1	2	1	89	1	—	5	1
Entrepreneurs, Techn. Prof.	(9)	25	5	5	8	28	3	25	1
Other, Unknown	(3)	61	7	13	6	—	—	6	8
All Groups	(100)	25	4	16	10	9	5	12	19

b) German Elite Groups

University-Level Education: Percent by Row

Occupationl. Categories	(% by Col.)	No Uni-Level	Type Unknown	Law Hum., Theol.	Med., Sci.	Technical Inst.	Prof. Acads.	Military Acads.
Writers, Arts, Scholars	(13)	28	5	38	9	2	19	—
Academics	(45)	3	4	40	45	4	4	—
Clergy	(4)	31	2	66	2	—	—	—

Military, Landowners	(3)	56	3	14	1	2	—	24
High Officls.	(8)	9	13	43	17	11	7	—
Politicians	(4)	28	8	60	2	1	1	—
Lawyers	(1)	—	13	88	—	—	—	—
Med. & Oth. Lib. Prof.	(3)	—	6	1	93	—	—	—
Entrepreneurs, Techn. Prof.	(15)	42	8	7	19	15	8	—
Other, Unknown	(3)	59	2	23	7	3	5	—
All Groups	(100)	18	5	35	29	6	7	1

* The table reports on random samples from the leading French and German biographical encyclopedias. In the case of the incomplete *Neue Deutsche Biographie*, vols. I–IV (Berlin, 1953–1964), all entries for males born 1800–1899 through Grasman (N: 2366) are considered. The *Dictionnaire de biographie française*, vols. I–X (Paris, 1933–61) also incomplete, treats more persons per letter more briefly than its German counterpart, so that coverage was restricted to entries at least 25 lines in length for males born 1800–1899 through Dallière (N: 2953). 'Writers, Arts, Scholars' includes all full-time writers outside the sciences, journalists, editors and publishers, along with the creative and performing arts, and a few private scholars or intellectually active "rentiers". 'Academics' includes academic secondary school teachers, librarians and archivists. 'Military, Landowners' are predominantly officers, though a few are owners, managers or lease-holders of large estates, 'High Officials' includes judges and diplomats. 'Politicians' covers full-time elected politicians, whether national or local, along with leaders of political parties and labor unions. "Medical and other Liberal Professions' are chiefly medical men. 'Entrepreneurs, Technical Professions' are owners, managers and (rarely) executive employees of large enterprises, along with somewhat smaller contingents of scientists, engineers, inventors, explorers, architects and technicians who were not *explicitly* linked with business or the academic world. 'Other' is made up chiefly of such "non-elite" occupations as farmers, shopkeepers, artisans, and lower-level civil servants. 'No University-level Education' means that no *attendance* was specified at institutions considered at university level around 1930, except that university-level education was assumed in the legal and medical professions in which it was required. 'Type Unknown' consists mostly of individuals who were said to have "finished their studies in Paris", or "studied at Heidelberg and Berlin". *In section a*, around four-fifth of cases under 'Law, Letters' are law students, just as about four-fifth of those under 'Medicine, Sciences' studied medicine or (in a few cases only) pharmacy. 'Ecole Polytechnique' includes individuals who went on from that institution to various "schools of application". The category of 'Other Grandes Ecoles' is dominated by the higher art and music schools (125 cases); but it also encompasses the Ecole des Chartes (55 cases), other high-level scholarly institutions in Paris (15 cases), "Sciences-Po" (11 cases), the Ecole Centrale (29 cases), and a cluster of less distinguished technical, professional, and higher commercial schools (43 cases). 'Religious, Military' covers the higher seminaries, theological faculties, and the Catholic Institute, together with the military schools, chiefly Saint-Cyr and the Ecole Navale. *In section b*, 'Law, Humanities, Theology' includes the social sciences as well. 'Medicine, Sciences' also includes pharmacy, dentistry, and mathematics, along with a handful of cases of university study of business. 'Technical Institutes' covers the "polytechnical" ancestors of these institutions as well. 'Professional Academies' encompasses art, music, and other professional and technical academies (mining, agriculture, forestry) other than the technical institutes. For details, see Fritz K. Ringer, "The Education of Elites in Modern Europe", in *History of Education Quarterly*, vol. 18 (1978), pp. 159–172.

considered are males born between 1800 and 1899, who are classified in terms of their occupations and their university-level educations, if any. Of course the criteria of eminence used by the editors of such encyclopedias are not really specified, and probably cannot be; the judgments made in the process of selection are partly subjective. On the other hand, such judgments are neither gratuitous choices; nor are they based on merely individual opinions. In addition to the objective circumstances in which eminence was achieved, they reflect a partly collective sense of what constitutes eminence in a given social world. Thus, from a rather special perspective, the samples that will be described do tell us something about the role of education and of the educated in that world.

At the left of both sections of the table, the occupations of the eminent biographees appear as percentages by column. One is not surprised to find that entrepreneurs and members of the technical professions were more numerous in the German than in the French sample. These men would have been active between about 1830 and 1960, a period when industrial development based on advanced technology was probably more characteristic of Germany than of France. A notable feature of the French sample was a high proportion of lawyers and of parliamentary politicians, many of whom were in fact politically active lawyers. The prominence of electoral and parliamentary politics under the Third Republic seems to account for this characteristic of the French elites. Much more surprising is the large number of military officers among eminent Frenchmen of this period. Many of them were members of landed and aristocratic families. Perhaps the visibility of colonial exploration and conquest during the late nineteenth century also contributed to this pattern. In Germany, despite the social importance of the officer corps as a whole, military men and landowners made up only 3 percent of the sample. Apparently then, there can be a difference between the visibility of eminent individuals and the recognized importance of an institution.

Particularly pertinent to the concerns of the present essay are the figures for academics and for the "unattached intelligentsia" of writers, artists and private scholars in the two samples. Among Germans who achieved eminence sometime between 1830 and 1960, no less than 45 percent, or almost half, were university professors. Writers, artists and scholars added another 13 percent, to bring the total for German intellectuals other than clergymen to 58 percent. In the French sample, the total for the two groups of secular intellectuals came to less than 40 percent, and among these, the academics were much less prominent, at 16 percent, than the unaffiliated writers, artists and scholars. Here is a double contrast that sheds light on the role of higher education and on the structure of the educated elites in the two countries. While the universities and university professors played an extraordinarily prominent role in German society, the academic community as a whole long held a relatively unimportant position in France.

At the same time, the typically most eminent French intellectual of the nineteenth century was the free-lance writer or publicist, rather than the research scholar or scientist. Indeed, as the table indicates, this French "man of letters" often had no university-level education at all, although he probably held the secondary baccalaureate. Perhaps the literary market, especially the network of intellectual journals for general audiences, was more highly developed in France than in Germany. Perhaps, too, some talents that would have been attracted to academic careers in Germany found less fully institutionalized intellectual roles in France, whether as private scholars dependent on family incomes, as politically active writers, or as more purely literary men of letters. In any case, some of the most interesting data in Table 4 reflect profound differences in the organization of intellectual life in the two societies that must have deeply affected the predominant styles of thought as well.

The last line in each of the two sections of Table 4 summarizes the role of higher education in the formation of prominent Frenchmen and Germans during our period. As might be expected, a somewhat larger proportion of the biographees terminated their formal schooling before the university level in France than in Germany. Moreover, only about one-quarter of the French elites had attended the university faculties, almost always those of law and medicine, while an exactly equal proportion had received their advanced education at the Ecole Polytechnique, at the Ecole Normale, or at a few other non-university institutions of higher education, not including purely military schools, higher seminaries and other theological centers. The relevant percentages are really quite remarkable, since the traditional *grandes écoles* enrolled only minute fractions of the student population. Almost two-thirds of eminent Germans were educated at the universities, many of them at the "philosophical" faculties. In France, by contrast, the Ecole Polytechnique alone accounted for almost as many of the biographees as the university faculties of medicine and of sciences combined. Among eminent French academics, some 41 percent were graduates of the Ecole Normale or of other non-university institutions, as against only 37 percent who had attended any of the university faculties. The contrast with the German pattern would presumably have been even sharper if the nineteenth century alone had been considered. Some 85 percent of academics in the German sample, as might be expected, had been educated at the universities.

The data on the entrepreneurs and technical professionals in Table 4 will provide a final indication of the important role played by the *grandes écoles* in French society. In the German sample, over 40 percent of entrepreneurs and technologists had no university-level education at all; this is another symptom of the divide between the educated and the economic and technical elites in nineteenth-century Germany. Just under 20 percent of the German entrepreneurs and technologists had engaged in scientific university studies, while another 23 percent came from the technical institutes and professional academies. Among eminent French entrepreneurs and technical professionals, a considerably smaller proportion (25 percent) were without university-level education, and only 8 percent had attended university faculties of sciences. Over half had been educated at the *grandes écoles,* and the Ecole Polytechnique alone accounted for 28 percent of the group! Since the Ecole Polytechnique also trained one-quarter of the French military elite and 8 percent of eminent high officials, it must have been an unusually versatile and immensely influential school. One can scarcely imagine an institution more characteristic of the relationship between elite higher education and *bourgeois* predominance in nineteenth-century France.

Notes

1 See Pierre Bourdieu, *"Cultural Reproduction and Social Reproduction",* in Jerome Karabel and A. H. Halsey, eds., *Power and Ideology in Education* (New York 1977), pp. 487–511.
2 The brief institutional history that follows is essentially a summary of Fritz K. Ringer, *Education and Society in Modern Europe* (Bloomington & London 1979); see esp. pp. 113–156 and the Bibliography. See also Antoine Prost, *Histoire de l'enseignement en France 1800–1967* (Paris 1969), and two excellent new anthologies in the field: Donald N. Baker & Patrick J. Harrigan, eds., *The Making of Frenchmen: Current Directions in the History of Education in France, 1679–1979* (Historical Reflections VII, 1980), and Robert Fox & George Weisz, *The Organization of Science and Technology in France 1808–1914* (Cambridge & New York 1980). Detlef Müller, Fritz K. Ringer & Brian Simon, eds., *The Rise of the Modern Educational System: Structural Change and Social Reproduction, 1850–1920* is forthcoming.
3 Terry Shinn, *Savoir scientifique & pouvoir social: L'Ecole Polytechnique, 1794–1914* (Paris 1980).
4 Robert J. Smith, *The Ecole Normale Supérieure and the Third Republic* (Albany 1982).
5 R. R. Palmer, *"Free Secondary Education in France before and after the Revolution",* in *History of Educational Quarterly* (1974), pp. 437–452.
6 John W. Bush, *"Education and Social Status: The Jesuit Collège in the Early Third Republic",* in *French Historical Studies,* 9 (1975), pp. 125–140.
7 C. R. Day, *"Technical and Professional Education in France: The Rise and Fall of l'enseignement secondaire spécial, 1865–1902",* in *Journal of Social History,* 6 (1972–1973), pp. 177–201; Fritz K. Ringer, *"Structural Change in French Secondary Education, 1865–1920",* in Müller, Ringer & Simon, *Rise of the Modern Educational System,* for this and what follows.
8 A regulation of 1907 still required Latin for the *licence* in letters. Classical graduates were long given advantages even in the entrance examination for the Ecole Polytechnique. See esp. Terry Shinn, *"Educational Stratification and Conflict: The French Case, 1880–1914",* in Müller, Ringer & Simon, *Rise of the Modern Educational System.*
9 The faculties of sciences were somewhat less rigorously tied to the secondary curriculum than the faculties of letters. See Victor Karady, *"Recherches sur la morphologie du corps universitaire littéraire sous la Troisième République",* in *Le mouvement social,* 69 (1976), pp. 47–79; Victor Karady, *"L'accès aux grades et*

leurs fonctions universitaires dans les facultés des sciences au 19ᵉ siècle: examen d'une mutation", in Baker & Harrigan, *Making of Frenchmen,* pp. 397–414, for this and what follows.

10 This was true of the Ecole Polytechnique and of the Ecole Centrale, for example. Between 1860 and 1880, about three-fourths of entrants to the Ecole Polytechnique had the baccalaureate, according to Shinn, *Savoir scientifique,* p. 51.

11 John H. Weiss, *The Making of Technological Man: The Social Origins of French Engineering Education* (Cambridge, Mass. 1982).

12 C. R. Day, *"The Making of Mechanical Engineers in France: The Ecoles d'Arts et Métiers, 1803–1914"*, in *French Historical Studies,* X (1978), pp. 439–460.

13 For what follows, see George Weisz, *The Emergence of Modern Universities in France, 1863–1914* (Princeton, New Jersey 1983); Victor Karady, *"Restructuring the Faculties of Letters and Sciences in Late 19th-Century France"*, in Müller, Ringer & Simon, *Rise of the Modern Educational System;* Terry Shinn, *"The French Science Faculty System, 1808–1914: Institutional Change and Research Potential in Mathematics and the Physical Sciences"*, in *Historical Studies in the Physical Sciences,* X (1979), pp. 271–332.

14 John E. Talbott, *The Politics of Educational Reform in France, 1918–1940* (Princeton 1969).

15 Ringer, *Education and Society,* pp. 131–134, and the following pages for what follows.

16 In 1912–1913, for example, French sciences faculties awarded some 1250 basic science certificates for medical students, and almost 500 university diplomas in applied science and engineering, as compared to less than 400 *licences* in sciences. See Weisz, *Emergence of Modern Universities in France,* p. 184.

17 In 1910–11 and 1930–31, university enrollments per age group appear to have been somewhat higher than the number of secondary graduates per age group. Foreign students at French universities and French candidates for university diplomas in technology, who did not need the baccalaureate, probably account for much of this anomaly.

18 Ringer, *Education and Society,* pp. 45–50.

19 Lenore O'Boyle, *"The Problem of an Excess of Educated Men in Western Europe, 1800–1850"*, in *Journal of Modern History,* 42 (1970), pp. 471–495. See also George Weisz, *"The Politics of Medical Professionalization in France 1845–1848"*, in *Journal of Social History,* 12 (1978–1979), pp. 3–30, esp. pp. 17–20.

20 Ringer, *Education and Society,* pp. 52–54, and the following pages for what follows.

21 James C. Albisetti, *"French Secondary School Reform in German Perspective"*, and Detlef Müller, *"Secondary Education in Germany in the Late 19th Century"*, in Müller, Ringer & Simon, *Rise of the Modern Educational System;* Detlef Müller, *Sozialstruktur und Schulsystem: Aspekte zur Theorie und Praxis der Schulorganisation im 19. Jahrhundert* (Göttingen 1977), pp. 274–280.

22 Weisz, *"Politics of Medical Professionalization"*, p. 28 notes that only 2052 out of 4895 law students in 1867 intended to pursue legal careers. See also Weisz, *Emergence of Modern Universities,* pp. 188–189, for what follows.

23 Ringer, *Education and Society,* pp. 149–156.

24 The following are approximate sizes of each of three classes at some notable *grandes écoles* at various times: Ecole Normale: 20–30 during the early 19th century, and 35–45 from the late 19th century on; Ecole Polytechnique: 125–175 during the early nineteenth century, and 225–275 from the late nineteenth century on; Ecole Centrale, around 100 soon after its foundation in 1829, 225–275 during the late nineteenth century, and 250–325 by the mid-20th century. The

écoles d'arts et métiers were also three-year schools, with approximate class sizes, collectively, of around 200 during the early 19th century, around 400 during the late nineteenth century, and some 600–700 by the early twentieth century. Enrollments at the Ecole Centrale and at the *écoles d'arts et métiers* together amounted to around 0.1% of the age group during the late nineteenth century. If enrollments at the *grandes écoles* and related institutions were added to university enrollments, the latter would be increased by some 10–15% from the 1880s on, and another 5–6% could be added for religious higher education as well. See Ringer, *Education and Society*, pp. 338–340.

25 Ringer, *Education and Society*, pp. 22–31; Fritz K. Ringer, *"On Segmentation in Modern European Educational Systems"*, in Müller, Ringer & Simon, *Rise of the Modern Educational System*.

26 If the percentage for the working class in the occupational census were equal to the number of working-class children in the relevant age group, incidentally, then the opportunity ratio for the working class would be mathematically identical with its relative access chance.

27 For the *propriétaires* as a peculiar social category in nineteenth-century France, see Shinn, *Savoir scientifique*, p. 66; Ringer, *Education and Society*, p. 162; Weiss, *Making of Technological Man*, p. 71, and further annotation and bibliography there.

28 I have used the term *distribution ratios* to designate these measures of segmentation in Ringer, *"On Segmentation"*. Unlike opportunity ratios, in which the denominator is taken from an occupational census, distribution ratios are mathematically identical with relative access chances with respect to the restricted population made up of all students in the secondary system as a whole.

29 Like R. Anderson before him, Harrigan has been impressed by the number of students in the survey who came from lower middle-class homes. While recognizing that the lower classes were essentially excluded, he has stressed the relatively "democratic" character of the French system; but he has not fully specified his standards of comparsion. He *has* insisted that secondary students were no less progressively recruited in France than in Germany during the nineteenth century; but he has not in fact considered the comparative data discussed here and in Ringer, *Education and Society*, pp. 160–170. See Patrick J. Harrigan, *Mobility, Elites, and Education in French Society of the Second Empire* (Waterloo, Ontario 1980), esp. pp. 14, 17–19, 26–27.

30 Statistique de la France, *Résultats généraux du dénombrement de 1872* (Nancy, 1874), and Ringer, *Education and Society*, pp. 177–178 for annotation.

31 Ringer, *Education and Society*, pp. 231–232, which draws on T. W. Bamford, *"Public Schools and Social Class, 1801–1850"*, in *British Journal of Sociology*, vol. 12 (1961), pp. 224–235.

32 K. E. Jeismann, *Das preußische Gymnasium in Staat und Gesellschaft . . . 1787–1817* (Stuttgart 1975), p. 165. The chronological gap between Jeismann's sample and the French survey is unfortunate, of course. But the intervening enrollment changes were not great in either system, and Prussian data for 1875–1899 (discussed below) confirm much of what Jeismann observed for 1800.

33 Wilhelm Ruppel, *Über die Berufswahl der Abiturienten Preussens in den Jahren 1875 bis 1899* (Fulda 1904), and Ringer, *Education and Society*, pp. 70–78, 280–284 for what follows.

34 The most pertinent ratios (relation of *Oberrealschule* graduates to all graduates in the Prussian survey) are: learned professions 0.26, primary teachers 0.33, technical professions 1.8, "industrialists" 2.2, commerce 1.3, artisans 2.1. It should be recalled that the corresponding ratios for the "special" program in the French

survey of 1864 were: *propriétaires,* large merchants, intermediate white-collar employees, and industrialists and engineers 0.8–1.1, and primary teachers 1.8.

35 Harrigan, *Lycéens et collègiens,* table 15.

36 Shinn, *Savoir scientifique,* p. 185; Ringer, *Education and Society* pp. 170–173.

37 Weiss, *Making of Technological Man,* pp. 72, 74.

38 Smith, *Ecole Normale,* p. 42. For a somewhat different grouping of Smith's data, see Ringer, *Education and Society,* pp. 175–176.

39 Victor Karady, *"L'expansion universitaire et l'évolution des inégalités devant la carrière d'enseignant au début de la IIIe République",* in *Revue française de sociologie,* vol. XIV (1973), pp. 443–470.

40 Victor Karady, *"Normaliens et autres enseignants à la Belle Epoque",* in *Revue française de sociolgie,* vol. XIII (1972), pp. 35–58. Karady's sample of Normaliens and his categories differ somewhat from Smith's. See also Gérard Vincent, *"Les professeurs du second degré au début du XXe siècle",* in *Le Mouvement social,* May 1966, pp. 47–73, and Paul Gerbod, *La Condition universitaire en France au XIXe siècle* (Paris 1965), esp. pp. 110, 581–582.

41 Unfortunately, differences and imprecisions of categorization prevent a comparison of data presently published on the Normalien elite, or on French academics generally, with the summary but important account of German university professors' social origins in Christian von Ferber, *Die Entwicklung des Lehrkörpers der deutschen Universitäten und technischen Hochschulen 1864–1954* [Helmuth Plessner, ed., *Untersuchungen zur Lage der deutschen Hochschullehrer,* vol. III] (Göttingen 1956), pp. 177–178. Someone really ought to attempt such a comparison on the basis of manuscript sources on French Normaliens and academics, and of the rich and incompletely exploited source materials accumulated by Plessner's team in the 1950s, which are still available at the Institut für Bildungsforschung in Berlin. My own strong impression is that by the late nineteenth century, at any rate, German university professors came from generally higher social origins than French Normaliens and academics generally. See also Fritz K. Ringer, *Der Niedergang der deutschen Mandarine* (Stuttgart 1982), and Fritz K. Ringer, *"The German Academic Community",* in *Internationales Archiv für Sozialgeschichte der deutschen Literatur,* vol. III (1978), pp. 108–129.

42 Luc Boltanski, *"Taxinomies sociales et luttes de classes: la mobilisation de 'la classe moyenne' et l'invention des 'cadres'",* in *Actes de la recherche en sciences sociales,* no. 29 (Sept. 1979), pp. 75–104 is a fascinating case study.

43 Ringer, *Education and Society,* pp. 191–201, 344–348 for this and following paragraphs.

44 See Natalie Rogoff, *"Social Stratification in France and in the United States",* in Reinhard Bendix and S. M. Lipset, eds., *Class, Status and Power: Social Stratification in Comparative Perspective* (New York 1966).

45 My concern here is with social realities; but they are sometimes hard to separate from social "mentalities" or classificatory propensities. I mean to return to these in another context; but my thinking about them has been much affected by Pierre Bourdieu's definition of the *habitus* as a *structure structurante.* See Bourdieu's brilliant *La distinction: Critique sociale du jugement* (Paris 1979).

46 On the relationship between the Instituts d'Etudes Politiques and the crucial Ecole Nationale d'Administration, see Ringer, *Education and Society,* pp. 125–126.

47 From Gerhard Kath, ed., *Das soziale Bild der Studentenschaft in Westdeutschland und Berlin, Sommersemester 1963* (Deutsches Studentenwerk, Berlin 1964) as annotated and discussed in Ringer, *Education and Society,* pp. 104–110, 201–205, 312–315. Less than 2 percentage points for the liberal professions pertain

to men without university education; 'big businessmen' are manufacturers, whole-sale merchants and a few others in business with university education; 'executive employees' include employed engineers and architects; 'workers' must include domestics, as in the French data in Table 3, since they are not otherwise mentioned.

48 See Ringer, *Education and Society,* pp. 90–97, 110–112 for this and what follows.

49 This train of argument has been challenged by Peter Lundgreen *"Bildung und Besitz Einheit oder Inkongruenz in der europäischen Sozialgeschichte? Kritische Auseinandersetzung mit einer These von Fritz Ringer",* in *Geschichte und Gesell-schaft,* vol. 6 (1980), pp. 262–275; but Lundgreen's argument seems to me to suffer from confusions about technicalities in the assessment of segmentation, and to offer no support for the counterthesis it seems to propose. See also Fritz K. Ringer, *"Bestimmung und Messung von Segmentierung: Eine Teilantwort an Peter Lundgreen",* in *Geschichte und Gesellschaft,* vol. 8 (1982) pp. 280–285.

109

THE STUDENTS
AND THE FUTURE[1]

Brian Simon

Source: B. Simon, *A Student's View of the Universities*, London: Longmans, Green and Co., 1943, pp. 120–42.

The student movement had begun to realize the dangers of Fascist domination during the period of the Spanish war, but the general outbreak of war in 1939, and especially the subjection of Europe by the Nazis in 1940, aroused the great majority of students to a social consciousness and a sense of responsibility which far exceeded anything that had gone before. The totality of the war was understood, implicitly at least, from the beginning, and this made it possible to integrate the immediate needs of the war situation with ideas about the ultimate future of the universities. The students' criticisms of the universities centre round the fact that the universities have a function in society and a duty to the people which, owing to the restrictions on entrance and the nature of the teaching, they do not fulfil. Their hatred of Fascism is based on the fact that its victory would mean the total destruction of science and culture, of freedom and progress. They believe, therefore, that the complete defeat of the Fascist Powers is the essential prerequisite to the establishment of a planned, stable, and progressive society.

In the attainment of this victory over Fascism, the universities clearly have an important part to play, and in order that they may efficiently fulfil their rôle, certain reforms become necessary. These reforms are, in addition, steps leading to universities which are consciously planned to make the maximum contribution to at peaceful community. Thus the two objectives, of winning the war and the peace, are envisaged as being inextricably bound together.

This single view of the situation has been specially noticeable in the sphere of student activities. There are two ways in which students may effect changes in the universities: by expressing a point of view with a united voice, and attempting by negotiations, publicity, and other means to have it accepted by the authorities; by directing day-to-day activity into such progressive channels that they themselves increase the scope and effectiveness of the universities.

In the latter sphere the ideal is a student community representative of the people and actively concerned with the social, political, and cultural issues of the time. The last few years have seen notable advances made. There has been no tendency for the students of this country to hide behind the walls of the universities and let the world pass them by. They have broken down the old traditions of academic isolation, and have largely undermined student apathy. It has been in the course of making these changes that they have formulated their proposals for reform. Therefore to assess the value of student action, we must examine both the progress made in increasing the contribution of the universities to society, and the instances where reform has been obtained on immediate issues by direct negotiation.

In working out their conception of the rôle of the universities in war-time, students have drawn on the experience of Spain, China, and, more recently, the Soviet Union. The changes in these countries during the periods of invasion have illustrated the social value of a university in war as well as in peace. In China tremendous importance has been assigned to education, and the great collective efforts made to maintain the universities under very difficult conditions are well known and enthusiastically supported in student circles in this country; the heroic treks of universities bombed out of their original sites, and the practical application of the slogan "every cave a classroom," contain the real essence of a new spirit of education. In Spain, despite the combined onslaught of Franco and the Moors, Germans and Italians, the Spanish Republican Government took special pains to provide for the children and built thousands of schools during the three years of war. Similarly university education was expanded by the creation of workers' institutions (*Instituto obrero*) for those between the ages of fifteen and forty-five, which were considered to be of sufficient value to the community to justify the payment of a monthly wage to the students.

Finally, in the U.S.S.R., while many students are inevitably at the front or working in factories and hospitals, tremendous efforts are being made to develop and increase the contribution of the universities to the struggle of the people. A speech by a member of the Soviet Academy of Science to medical students in Moscow usefully crystallizes the spirit of these three countries.

We are beginning our studies in days that will go down in history. The whole world is rising to fight for freedom, for civilization, for science. Mankind has taken up arms so that millions of young people like yourselves might be able to continue studying and acquire knowledge and culture, and so that your fathers, brothers, and sisters might be saved from the Fascist slavery which threatens them. Years will pass and you will be proud to recall that you lived in the days of the great patriotic war. With even greater pride you will recall that you took part in it, for each one of us working in the rear is helping the front.

I know, I feel, that your hearts are burning with the desire to be right in the thick of it. That is a noble desire, but you have a different task to perform. You must study—go on studying in defiance of the enemy who is endeavouring to spread confusion in our ranks with the wings of death. We must study in spite of everything. Study twice and three times as hard as in previous years.

The theme of the above speech has also been the central theme for student activity in this country during the war. Many instances will be given later of the work done by students outside the lecture-room and the laboratory, but they have constantly recognized their main task to be hard academic study. At Easter, 1943, 1000 students stated: "Our own share in the great struggle for victory consists in hard and consistent work to qualify for full service in the forces, science, medicine, education, and other spheres. In our most important field of work we must achieve the greatest possible efficiency." At the same time, the methods of study produced by high specialization in the schools, and by the competitive examination system, were condemned. Many students are concerned only with amassing a vast quantity of data in order to push ahead of their colleagues in the race for jobs, whereas the real duty of the student is to ensure that, by the pooling of ideas and knowledge, the entire student body should be as well trained as possible. On this basis, co-operative work among students, and assistance to those finding themselves in difficulties, are steadily increasing.

The faculty societies have already changed radically from the pre-war period, and are now beginning to take the form of "tutors" to the students. The most valuable methods of helping students to reach a high academic standard are, however, reached only by staff-student co-operation, and nationally, and in each of the colleges and universities, students are attempting to form closer links with the staff. Curriculum reform, the institution of tutorials and discussions in the place of lectures, and a widening of student interests have resulted.

The faculty and departmental societies have also succeeded in affecting courses by other means. During the war they have organized less academically abstruse lectures than formerly, and have devoted more time to the wider aspects of the particular subject. Inter-society meetings have helped to break down the false isolation of the various sections of human knowledge, and to relate them to each other and to human society as a whole. Such improvements in the system of study, co-operation with the staff, and discussions on social topics, have inevitably led to a broadening of university education.

257

The firm belief in the necessity for constant academic work has also been expressed in the demand for a fourth academic term during the summer vacation. The N.U.S. has stated: "In war-time a student has to train himself in the shortest possible time to take his place as a member of the forces of democracy against fascism. The primary aim of the 'Fourth Term' is to cut down the university course, to increase the amount of organized study carried ont in the short time available. The peace-time advantages of the summer vacation are part of the student's sacrifice for victory."[2] The extra term means that a normal degree course of nine terms can be completed in two years and three months, and it is estimated that by 1944 the majority of colleges and universities will be operating this or a similar shortening system. Good relations between staff and students again form the foundation for this innovation, since it creates many difficulties which can be met only if there is full co-operation between all members of the university.

The various forms of national service instituted since 1939 have provided a sounder basis for student activities along lines tending to draw the universities closer to the community as a whole. The kind of work the students wished to do was different from the old slumming parties, carried on in a spirit of condescension with an attitude of "knowing what's best for the lower classes," and the air offensive against our towns pointed the way to a real identity of interest. Students said: "We must identify ourselves with the people, learn from them, and make our contribution in a spirit of equality. We must recognize that our interests are identical with those of the whole people."[3] This spirit was soon translated into practice.

The first large-scale opportunity occurred when London and, later, the provincial cities were heavily raided. During the Christmas vacation, 1940–41, about 120 students worked in Stepney in air-raid shelters, rest centres, and hospitals. They came from all parts of the country and stayed from one to five weeks. Substitute staff were provided for a number of rest centres, educational talks, discussions on current events, and lectures on health were given in air-raid shelters, and a survey of shelter conditions in the area was made and a report produced. The students who did this work also housed and fed themselves. In Manchester, Liverpool, and the other large university towns similar jobs were done, many hundreds of students giving up all their spare time. Medical students staffed first-aid posts, engineers helped with the rescue squads, teams of men drained Anderson shelters, whilst in some towns the student unions were opened for bombed-out people, and washing and bathing facilities made available. In particular were the reports on shelter conditions very useful, since they enabled mistakes to be noted, and in certain cases definite improvements resulted.

At the same time educational and social work was carried on in towns and villages in reception areas. Surveys of local conditions were made in conjunction with local organizations, and help given to the billeting authorities. Groups of students toured areas with dramatic and variety shows. Many students are helping with army education, in particular by providing "student brains trusts." Other contacts have been made during the course of day-to-day spare-time work in hospitals and factories, since nowadays most student unions have a permanent organization to mobilize their members for the war effort. In some colleges a student workshop has been established, and small parts made under the direction of a local firm. Elsewhere machines in particular factories are constantly staffed by rotas of students. During the long vacation this work is intensified, and the summer of 1942 saw many thousands working on the land and in factories, or helping with education.

One particular aspect of this type of student activity needs special emphasis. The years prior to the war saw an increasing solidarity between students and other young people of their age, which has since developed rapidly. In several towns students initiated the formation of local youth committees, uniting all young people in the area, which, in co-operation with the official Youth Committees, have done splendid work in the educational and social spheres. Many students work in youth clubs, and special schools have been organized to train more students to undertake this work.

These developments have revitalized the main student organizations. The annual Congresses of the N.U.S., which before the war had an average attendance of 150, attracted 600 students in 1940, 1100 in 1941, and 1500 in 1942—a symptom of increased interest in social and academic affairs brought about in part by the student societies. In preparation for these Congresses study groups were held attracting people of diverse views, inter-society meetings became frequent, and local conferences were organized in many places. The student societies were seen as the main opportunity to bring right into the university all those political, social, and cultural problems which interest the present generation, and in this way to supplement the formal education. The difficulty in obtaining national speakers of note, and the magnitude of the problems to be discussed, necessitated far more collegiate activity than before. Isolation into cliques became far less noticeable, and debates and open forums were very popular. The subjects discussed at the congresses were directly related to the immediate problems in the universities, and thus each year a large number of active "missionaries" returned from Congress with a policy for student activity. In this way the congresses have become the focal point of the student year, and by this year, 1943, have reached the stage where a real concrete programme of action is produced.

There is still a considerable body of students who are not covered by the society activities; but compulsory S.T.C. training, the organization of lectures during fire-guard duty, and the wide acceptance of spare-time and vacation war work have eradicated entirely the anti-social student of prewar years. The intellectual life of the universities may to-day miss those dazzling stars which flashed across the pre-1940 period, but the general appreciation of social and cultural issues is far higher. Students have also shown a consistent spirit of international friendship, and have attempted, by participation in the work of international youth bodies, by the creation of an International Council of Students, and by contacts with Soviet and American student delegations, to enrich their studies with the experiences of the world student movement.

Thus the efforts of students to improve the universities are taking concrete forms, and are centred round the belief that the universities are important social institutions with a valuable rôle to play no matter what the general political situation. This belief was expressed from the outbreak of war by the demand that the universities and colleges should be maintained and not allowed to seep away into ineffectiveness as during the 1914–18 War. It would be ridiculous to claim that this attitude of students produced the war-time regulations, which although stringent have, with few exceptions, realized the value of higher education in the present situation. The student movement did, however, appreciate the necessity for intellectual life, research, and free discussion, and understood the urgent need for trained professional workers of all categories. The new and grave responsibilities thrown on to the universities and colleges were seen as a changed aspect of peace-time responsibilities, and the limitations which had been noted in peace were even more evident in war. War-time problems have therefore led naturally to discussion of the reform of the universities, and N.U.S. congresses and conferences have provided regular opportunities for proposals to be worked out in a communal way. The following is a summary of the policies adopted.

The student programme

The universities and colleges, no matter what the state system, form an integral part of the whole educational process; as such they can be reformed only in conjunction with the general reform of education. Furthermore, both universities and schools are closely related to the social process, and a radical alteration in society is necessary if they are to be fully effective. Democracy, which exists in England in the political field to a large extent, must be extended to give far more economic equality. The resources of the country should be utilized for the benefit of all the people, and production planned to meet the needs of the community, this involving the abolition of private profit as the mainspring of industry and the removal of monopoly from private hands. Under such conditions the schools could become the fountain-head of the democracy for which we are fighting, and indeed, if the attacks of Fascism are to be overcome completely, the democratization of the educational system is essential.

The school system

The present school system, with its injustices and inequalities, is founded on class privilege, and must be replaced by a system in which there is equality of educational opportunity for all citizens. In detail this involves:

1. Local authorities compelled to provide nursery schools for all children, with appropriately trained staff.
2. Free compulsory full-time school attendance up to the age of sixteen years, maintenance grants to be given where necessary.
3. Maximum size of classes to be thirty pupils.
4. Common system of primary education, with parallel schools of equal status at the post-primary stage, each child receiving the type of education best suited to his talents and inclination. Transfer from one type to another to be possible at any time.
5. Public schools and all privately owned schools to be brought entirely under the central scheme.
6. Free meals and free compulsory medical and dental services in all schools.
7. Abolition of dual control and its replacement by a unified administration.[4]

The impact of the school system on the universities is not confined to such considerations as these. The reform of university entrance standards requires "equality of opportunity" to be translated into practice by the provision of adequate buildings, teachers, facilities, and finances. The post-primary or secondary schools, providing compulsory education for all up to the age of sixteen, must also provide free training, with maintenance grants available, for those pupils for whom further full-time education is deemed justifiable. This extra period should be given on the basis of merit alone, and transfer to full-time education should be possible for all those carrying on in part-time day continuation schools.

The changes needed in university curricula, though facilitated by these developments, call also for complete reorganization of the teaching in primary and secondary schools. The present school examination system, and its corollary, early specialization, brings about increasing specialization in the universities, which in their turn react on the schools with a continuously stultifying effect. This vicious circle must be broken simultaneously at both stages.

The fundamental reforms outlined above, especially the abolition of all fees, will destroy any excuse for the examination system of to-day. Curricula should be altered so that all pre-university education is of a general character. All pupils should be educated in the sciences, one or more foreign languages, literature, history, music, the arts, and social subjects. General science, for instance, must not be taken to mean the lumping together of two separate courses in physics and chemistry, but should include a study of biology, geology, astronomy, and practical mechanics, integrated together as far as possible. Similarly history, geography, literature, and the elements of ethics should not be treated in isolated compartments. No specialization, on the side of science or the humanities, should be allowed. This is a very brief picture of the education envisaged as a foundation on which the universities and colleges must be built.

Entrance to universities

Entrance to the universities and colleges must be awarded on one criterion alone, that of the fitness of the student to benefit from this particular type of education. Before the war only about 0.6 per cent. of ex-elementary school pupils managed to reach the universities compared with some 20 per cent. of non-elementary school children. The state bursaries awarded during the past two years have indicated that a large proportion of the present secondary-school students are of sufficiently high standard to benefit from further education, and recent social studies have proved beyond doubt that further untapped sources of talent will be found when the transition from elementary to secondary school becomes general.

It is not sufficient, however, to draw solely upon these schools, since many people taking part-time courses may be fully fitted for the universities and colleges. Professional and industrial workers who show particular interest and aptitude for education should be enabled to enter higher educational institutes, if necessary passing first through special pre-training schools. At present there are, undoubtedly, large numbers of such people who are denied a higher education by limiting regulations and financial difficulties. The regulations are easily altered, and the provision of adequate finances will be necessary if progress is to be made. Ideally university education should be free, with maintenance grants provided for all students, and the least that must be done is to extend the number of scholarships and grants to several times their present number. The amount of money given to the student should be sufficient to enable him to live in reasonable comfort so that financial worries will not engage his attention to the detriment of his education.

The curriculum

In addition to reforms of the methods of entry, reforms in curriculum will make new functions for the universities possible. Changes in the present economic and social order, which restricts university education, must be followed by radical alterations in academic teaching. The conception fundamental to proposals for this new teaching is that education must be related to social needs. The student is primarily a citizen, both during his time at the university and later on in whatever profession he may follow. To-day a sense of social responsibility is achieved by students despite the universities rather than because of them. In certain departments, particularly in the training of teachers, whether in the universities or the training colleges, there has been a deliberate attempt to prevent political discussion and the study of economic and social problems which is only now being overcome.

In the future the courses must be so planned that from them arises not only a knowledge of the particular specialism, but also a real understanding of its place in society. Furthermore the rôle of professional workers and the intelligentsia must be made clear. They are not a separate section of the nation, free to develop in isolation whilst the rest face tremendous daily problems. Rather do they constitute a section of the community particularly concerned with these problems, which must study the experiences of the people, and contribute from their knowledge to the solution of the problems.

Throughout the period of education, therefore, knowledge must be acquired in its social context. The linkages between various subjects must be made evident by the teaching, since the social relations of any particular subject cannot be understood if it seems isolated from all other spheres of knowledge. While the main effect of this isolation is to obscure the real relations of any subject, both to human society and to the body of knowledge, it also makes teaching of the specialism itself a complex yet incomplete matter. It is only possible to integrate one field of knowledge with another when the fundamentals of both are understood. In the universities the first year should be one in which science is taught to all students, along with history, economics, and a foreign language. In the later years there must be concentration upon one side or another, but the physicist, say, should never be allowed to treat his subject as an end in itself, but should constantly visualize its application to and effects on other sciences, and how the development of other sciences affects physics itself.

These principles are best illustrated by a brief study of the proposals made for each particular faculty. In science the first step should be the removal of those false divisions between subjects which lead to narrow erudition, and the institution of a general approach to science as a whole. This general course should cover the bases of the physical sciences, and in addition the history and philosophical implications of science. Science history must be taught so that the social causes of scientific investigation are shown clearly, and current philosophical theories are given a true perspective in the light of the progress of society. Lectures and discussions should not be treated academically, but integrated with practical work and industrial applications. Laboratory training must be revised so that experiments are less of a routine nature, and give more opportunities for initiative on the part of the student. During the whole of the course the ultimate objectives of the students should be kept in view, and periods of practical training provided in the industries or professions they intend to enter. Science students should work in adult and youth organizations to help to develop the science education of the community as a whole. Finally, all students must be encouraged to take part in the activities of professional scientific organizations so that they may participate in the control which will be necessary if their work is to be properly applied.

The faculty of medicine requires similar reforms. Preclinical training in botany, zoology, chemistry, and physics is to-day far too academic and a general course in the study of life in all its forms would be far more useful. During clinical training subjects should be more closely related to each other and the syllabus revised to eliminate unnecessary detail. There must be more preparation for general practice, and emphasis on preventive medicine rather than curative. The study of social problems, philosophy, industrial and public health should be included in the curriculum, and in general far more co-operation with the faculty of social science is necessary. Finally, a critical attitude to medical propaganda should be developed, and students organized to help to combat such social evils as tuberculosis and venereal disease.

The study of the arts should widen the knowledge of the ways in which men of all nations have thought, felt, and acted on lines other than our own, and of the social, intellectual, and psychological problems which have arisen in the past. This knowledge should be used to view present-day society in its proper perspective, and to help in the solution of current problems. Subjects must be interrelated—for example, history, economics, and geography must be closely connected, and some study of history and philosophy should be incorporated in literature courses. The teaching of history cannot be separated from existing social conditions, and the syllabus must be revised on a non-national basis. Literature courses must develop the critical and creative faculties rather than the memory, and philology should be treated in an historical manner. Courses in classics should be viewed less from the point of view of translating pieces of literature and widened to cover all aspects of ancient civilizations. Corresponding adjustments are needed in the other departments. Finally, all arts students should work for a society in which true cultural values can be realized.

Social science should form a part of every course, and, especially in those departments where it is the central subject, its study must be closely related to social needs. Practical work and training, including participation in social surveys, should be integrated with academic preparation, and all students should be taught psychology and social administration. In the departments of engineering there must be far closer contact with industry and the provision of long periods of industrial training. The curriculum should include the study of industrial conditions, administration, and planning.

Although policies in more detail than these have been worked out for other subjects, one final example will suffice to indicate student opinion. Any educational programme must be sterile unless teachers are trained to

264

work the system. Intending teachers should, whether attending universities or training colleges, receive a four-year course, the first part of which gives a general education in sociology, psychology, general science, and politics. More opportunity must be given for individual research, and all students should work in educational spheres such as youth clubs, army education, or nurseries. The present binding grants, whereby students have to promise to take up teaching as a profession before entering on their training, and even in some cases have to guarantee not to marry for three years, must be replaced by adequate scholarships with no limitations attached. In the selection of teachers as great attention should be paid to personality and human attributes as to specific academic qualifications, and the conditions in the profession, both from the point of view of salary and social standing, should be more fitting to the responsible position teachers hold in society.

Methods of teaching

Recognition that the scientist, doctor, or teacher cannot assume a position of ethical neutrality in society, and must therefore concern himself with moral and political questions, alone calls for changes in university teaching methods, even if the present system did not stand condemned by its own criteria. Methods of teaching should be changed in order to develop the free capabilities and critical faculties of the students. The first step in this direction must be the provision of people specially trained for teaching in universities and colleges, and not chosen on the basis of their research experience as at present. The lecture which reproduces current text-books must be cut out of the courses, and there should be a liberal distribution of books and printed lecture notes or synopses. Library facilities could well be increased to help in this field.

Teaching should consist far more of discussion on the basis of previous reading, informational lectures being reduced to a minimum. Seminars, in which students take a full part in discussion, and tutorials should be increased, whilst individual tuition should be provided on as wide a scale as possible. Such reforms would eliminate the present rigidity in methods, and make for a more flexible system which appreciates students as responsible people who wish to make the most of their training, and is designed to assist their individual work and development. Such changes are essential if graduates are to be capable of independent judgment and able to apply their knowledge and abilities in new situations.

Examination system

The examination system, revised to fit in with these reforms, would be a test of adaptability and intelligence rather than of memory and speed of handwriting. Practical work done during the course, and any individual work completed, should be taken into account. Oral examinations and written tests should be considered with this for the final assessment.

In the formulation of curricula and syllabi, and the organization of teaching methods and examination systems, students have a contribution to make. New regulations and adjustments will constantly be required, and it is essential that the student view should be heard. Therefore staff-student committees should be instituted based on the departments and linked up, first in faculty groups and finally on a complete college basis. They should have administrative powers, not being advisory only as at present, and should have the double function of advancing university education and of developing social responsibility among the students.

Technical and training colleges

The reforms so far outlined, though applicable to any higher educational institution, have been based mainly on experiences in the universities. There has developed, however, an attitude to the technical and training colleges which is fully consistent with the programme. At present these colleges are isolated from the universities, have fewer facilities, and are regarded as giving an inferior training. In the future they must be on a par with the universities in matters of entrance, curricula, and degree standards. Co-operation between them and the universities must be intimate and continuous, and transfers of pupils from one to the other should be made possible. Higher education would thus become an entity rather than several separate categories of institutions.

Students' physical welfare

Since the universities and colleges will be responsible for young people over a period of four to seven years, it is essential that they concern themselves with all sides of the individual's development during this period, which is, for most students, a critical one. They must therefore ensure a high standard of physical health and well-being among the students. The universities have been considering this question during the past seven years, and their proposals are of great interest. Before the war many schemes were being planned which had to be cancelled in 1939, but the need for them still exists.

The colleges form compact units, in which the student works, plays, and in many cases lives, and hence they are particularly adapted to complete schemes of preventive medicine. The policy advocated by the students falls into three parts—measures to promote a higher standard of general health: a scheme for regular physical examination and immunization against certain diseases: a contributory scheme for the treatment of illness. These will be outlined very briefly in turn.

Living conditions should be subject to regular inspection and supervision by joint committees of staff and students, and diet and housing standards set up and maintained. This must be done, as the rest of the health programme, in conjunction with similar health schemes for the community as a whole. Facilities for physical training and athletics must be made freely available, and each college should have a P.T. instructor specially trained for university work. Although compulsory participation in some form of physical exercise would be undesirable, a similar effect may be achieved by education in the principles of hygiene and biology; regular lectures on health should include such topics as the importance of exercise, sleep, and recreation, and the medical officer of the university should teach the elementary facts of disease, form and function, and sex. Eventually, however, a great deal of such education should take place in the pre-university stages.

Every university should have a full-time, paid medical officer, who, with suitable assistance, will examine every student on entry, and at regular intervals afterwards; an X-ray film of the chest, in order to assist early diagnosis of tuberculosis, is essential to the examination. The object should be to detect chronic diseases, physical defects, or malnutrition, and a recognized standard record should be kept of each student. Inspection of eyesight, hearing, and dental condition should be included.

Facilities for the diagnosis and treatment of everyday illnesses should be available under a contributory scheme. Fees would be collected with tuition fees by the college authorities, and the payment would be compulsory. If the Beveridge Report were implemented, the students would be provided for as ordinary citizens: otherwise a plan along similar lines would be necessary.[5]

Students' social activity

The initiation of such a health programme would go far to ensure that the graduate left the university healthy in mind and body and would have a profound effect on the intellectual and moral life in all the universities and colleges. It must be supplemented, however, by provision for a full social life. The liberal regulations previously suggested would be of great assistance in this connection, as would the removal of financial difficulties; the reasons why 70 per cent. of students have not in the past taken part in sporting activities, and 50 per cent. have even ignored social functions, are lack of time, energy, and finances. Certain limitations, however, do not fall into these categories. Of recent years students have been prevented from holding meetings by various college and university authorities, and the proctors of Oxford and Cambridge have been particularly rigid and undemocratic in their restrictions and vetoes. If the students are to make full use of their opportunities at the universities there must be complete freedom of discussion, organization, and publicity. Unless they are able to hear and express all points of view they will not be in a position to make their own judgment on the problems that face society, and so themselves. Though many universities have no restricting rules, there have been enough cases in the past of bans on discussion, organization, and student newspapers, to illustrate the bad effects of this curtailment of liberties. Such censorship is unworthy of the universities and a direct menace to their development as institutions with a responsibility to society.

In student hostels there should be far more scope for self-government, and students must be represented on all hostel committees. Costs of residence should be drastically reduced to be within the means of all people, since hostels are undoubtedly of value in the social and intellectual life of the university community.

Other lines along which university life can develop are adequately illustrated by student activities during the war. Their common basis is that the student enjoys a privilege by attending a university which carries with it certain responsibilities. An essential condition of his university education is that he should strive continuously to improve the universities, and should participate in any movement outside them which aims at bringing about a society in which they can be fully effective. This necessity for political action has been the keynote of most student conferences in the last few years. It is of little value trying to reform the education system if the need to reform society is realised only in an academic way. Direct work among the progressive forces in society has been, and should be, a fundamental principle for all members of the universities.

International co-operation

Closely related to these considerations is the question of international co-operation. Education must itself be international in outlook so that the bigoted prejudices of the present day are avoided. A true realization of the value of one's national culture can be found only amidst an appreciation of the forward movement of humanity as a whole, and in relation to the achievements of all civilized nations. In setting such a standard, the universities will have an important part to play. Regular exchanges of students between the nations must be a feature of post-war education, and special provision should be made to cater for large numbers of foreign students in this country. International co-operation between students should be extended to cover all members of the universities, and professors and lecturers encouraged to make international tours. These and similar measures would ensure an outlook which would make the misunderstandings of to-day impossible. During the immediate period after the war the universities in such countries as Britain and America, where material destruction has been relatively slight, should cement international friendship by giving the maximum possible help to the higher educational institutes of Europe, the U.S.S.R., and China. Many have been destroyed and their equipment stolen, and immense efforts will be needed before they can reoccupy the place in world culture which it is essential they should fill.

Post-graduate and research work

Other aspects of university reform have not entirely escaped attention, though proposals are so far somewhat tentative and sketchy. Research work in the universities and colleges should be planned on a national scale, and information exchanged with research workers in other countries. In general the work should cease to be sponsored by private firms and should be published if the standards reached merited this. Post-graduate education and research should be interrelated, and special courses designed for people coming to the universities from industry. Theses in post-graduate syllabi should be far less academic and abstruse in character, and correlated more with practical experience. Extra-mural education should be extended along the lines developed since the war, *i.e.* more week-end schools on particular subjects, and co-operation with the W.E.A. and army education authorities. Work of the type carried on by the W.E.A. should be extended and nationally financed. Students should be encouraged to help in all such work, which should form an important part of adult education.

Adult education

The education of children up to the age of sixteen has already been mentioned, but there must be a national policy based on the recognition of education as being lifelong, and providing facilities in accord with this belief. Continuation schools for young people over sixteen should replace entirely the present night-school system; attendance should be compulsory, and financial assistance given so that no pecuniary loss is incurred. More youth clubs should be set up, governed democratically by the young people themselves, in which social affairs, politics, music, drama, and the arts can be approached in a practical way and creative efforts encouraged. In these clubs students should play a part, not as superior leaders, but as individuals with a contribution to make to the efficient running of the club.

Graduate employment

Finally, the economic situation prior to the war and questions about the economics of the post-war period have led to a consideration of graduate employment. In the past large numbers of graduates have been unemployed, and many more misemployed. The fundamental solution to this lies in the development of a society in which the professional and intellectual workers will be used for the benefit of the community as a whole, and where a rational and planned approach to all employment is a *sine qua non*. There has always been a great need of doctors, scientists, and teachers, and unemployment in these professions has been the result solely of an inefficient and undemocratic social system. Given a properly organized society, it will be possible, by the provision of vocational guidance and the extension and national co-ordination of the University Appointments Boards, to ensure that each graduate obtains work suitable to his personality and qualifications.

Finance

This programme of reform is clearly incomplete without mention of the financing and control of the universities and colleges. The main source of finance must be the Government, which should provide grants of such a magnitude that the various institutions are free to develop and extend their facilities, undertake experimental work, and give to their staff adequate salaries, without having to depend upon private charity. There should also be some measure of central direction, so that entrance standards, degree standards, and general functions are nationally planned. This could be achieved by a system leaving considerable autonomy to the individual universities and colleges to use methods and carry out work best suited to themselves.

Conclusion

The policy put forward by British students thus includes a mixture of long-term and immediate reforms, and covers also those aspects of social change without which no development of the universities would be possible. Whenever such topics as health or political freedom have been discussed, it has been emphasised that the health and freedom of the student depend on proper health services for the people as a whole and real freedom of Press, speech, and organization in the national community. Some students, it is true, remain apathetic or indifferent to such problems but, despite this limitation, there is a growing movement in the universities which has a vital attitude to social and cultural questions and to the part that the student or graduate can play. Political and religious differences have not caused rifts, and the most controversial subjects have been discussed with tolerance and understanding and a genuine desire to find truth. In working towards their aims students have had the active assistance of the more progressive professors, lecturers, and teachers, who, with their wider culture and experience, can be of tremendous assistance to student societies.

In the introductory chapter of this book a number of questions were posed concerning the position and activities of the universities to-day. It is true that the proposals of the students do not answer all of these questions, nor are they sufficiently detailed to provide a blue-print of the future pattern of the universities. Such a task could be carried out effectively only by the co-operative effort of many people with experience of all sides of the industrial and social system, and after the amassing of the necessary social facts and figures. Nevertheless the proposals made indicate the main lines of advance. They show at least the beginning of a rational attitude to the universities, which takes into account the social, scientific, and economic factors operating at the present time. They substitute for the present lack of conscious aim clearly defined objectives closely related to the needs of the modern era, which must be attained if the universities are consciously to develop all sides of their work in fruitful directions.

They show finally that the spirit animating British students is fundamentally opposed to Nazism. The dictators are the worst enemies of youth, who see their hopes and ideals for the future menaced by his greedy imperialism. Young people in the British universities are pledged to put their utmost into the struggle for the destruction of Fascism—the immediate task which must precede the building of the "good" society they are working to attain. It will be a society in which the hopes and aims of man and the possibilities of material and cultural advance are no longer frustrated and repressed, but where culture and science, and so the universities, will have free and full possibilities of development in accordance with the needs of the people. For the universities, and all that they stand for, can only reach full stature when there is social control over production and distribution, and the progress of society is planned in the interests of the whole people.

Under such conditions the universities will draw to themselves the best of the nation's youth, for equality of opportunity will be a reality and no longer a phrase. Apart from training them as efficiently as possible for their jobs, they will equip them with the knowledge and the social and scientific understanding necessary if they are to be acutely aware of the problems facing society, to realize the necessity for action, and to apply their talents in the service of the community. Research and teaching posts will be held by men and women with the best minds in the community, who are capable of adapting themselves to new conditions and new problems. The universities will also be intimately concerned with all industrial, economic, political, social, and cultural movements. They will use their resources to raise the standard of living in the most general sense, and so to provide the conditions for the development of human personality which is the end and aim of such activity. By their educational functions they will become centres of a vital and creative culture, shedding their light over thousands and millions of people in their locality, closely linked with daily activities and problems, and essentially, therefore, at the disposal of the people.

Such could be the future of the universities—a future they will surely attain if they ally themselves with the forces of progress all over the world to overthrow the enemies of culture and science.

Notes

1 This chapter describes the activities and ideas of the more active sections of university students during the war, and throughout the chapter the collective term "students" must be taken to refer to these sections. The main sources of information have been the reports, published by N.U.S. of the Annual Congresses of the N.U.S., 1940–43, and echoes from these reports will be found throughout this chapter, direct quotations being acknowledged in footnotes.
2 *The Fourth Term.* N.U.S.
3 *Students and the Blitz.* N.U.S.
4 A programme along these lines was officially adopted by the N.U.S. Council in February 1943.
5 See *Memorandum on Student Health Service.* British Medical Students' Association.

110

THE STUDENT MOVEMENT

Eric Ashby

Source: E. Ashby, *Masters and Scholars*, London: Oxford University Press, 1970, pp. 25–49.

I invite you to spend this lecture with me in the placid waters of history (I called it in my first lecture a historical *andante*), and I begin by reading to you extracts from a handbill posted by students on the gates of a university.

> If you wish to regain your infringed rights . . . if you wish to make the Professors redeem that pledge . . . which they have . . . refused to fulfil . . . if you would banish dogmatism and supercilious pedantry from [the University] then . . .

But I must not go on, or it will give away the origin of the handbill. It is obviously not of very recent origin, for it does not include expressions like 'repressive tyranny of the military industrial complex' or 'prostituted by the consumer society'. But some indignation and defiance are there just the same. In fact the handbill is 145 years old. It was published by the students of Marischal College, Aberdeen, when they were campaigning for the re-election of Joseph Hume as rector.

The circumstances were as follows. The rector of a Scottish university is nowadays elected by the students alone. He, and an assessor appointed by him, represent the students on the university's governing body, called the court. But he is much more than a students' Ombudsman. He is the titular head of the university. Originally he was appointed by the whole body corporate, the Masters and Scholars. But in four of the five Scottish universities this privilege of taking part in the election had been filched from the students. In Edinburgh the rectorship had become a perquisite of the Lord Provost of the city. In St. Andrews the university allowed students to vote but permitted only four candidates to stand: the four were the professors of divinity and ecclesiastical history and the principals of the two colleges; an arid choice, from the students' point of view. In Aberdeen there were two universities; in one of them (King's College) the students took no part in the election of rector. In the other (Marischal College) the students still voted but it had long been made quite clear to them that they were to elect a man whose name was proposed to them by the professors.

In 1824 the students of Marischal College, Aberdeen, asserted their rights under the charter. In defiance of the professors they elected a radical Member of Parliament, Joseph Hume, as their rector. To the alarm of the college, the rector intimated that he would take his duties seriously. And he did: on the instigation of the students he held a rectorial court for the first time since 1738, and after a public enquiry, reproved the professors for unpunctuality, a reproof which, by all accounts, they fully deserved.

This was one of several occasions in the early nineteenth century when students protested about their rights in rectorial elections. In 1858 an act was passed which entrusted to the students the sole responsibility for electing a rector. He was still titular head of the university, but since he was not put there by the Masters *and* the Scholars, he and his assessor were regarded as the representatives of the Scholars on the court. In those days the court was a small body (only six to eight members); so the representatives of the students, although they were not students themselves, constituted one-third to one-quarter of the university's governing body.

But the rectorship was not much used by the students as a channel of participation between themselves and the university. Each year, at election time, it created knots of solidarity among students supporting rival candidates. There was a rectorial address (sometimes very stormy: in 1861 Maitland, the solicitor general, delivered his rectorial address in Aberdeen with blood trickling down his face from a missile which had struck him during the uproar), but once the rectorial address was over the rector usually disappeared, the students dispersed, and any corporate opinion which had been generated among them ran into the ground for another year.

Then, in 1883, a trivial incident occurred which I regard as the source of the student movement in Britain. A young man from Edinburgh University who had been studying in Germany saw a placard on a door of one of the buildings in Strassburg (as it was then spelt) labelled '*Studenten Ausschuss*', Student Committee. He got a copy of the constitution and studied it under the shadow of Strassburg cathedral. The young man—his name was Fitzroy Bell—decided that this was the sort of organization students ought to have in Edinburgh. In January 1884 Bell called a meeting of student representatives from the various faculties and societies in the university, and a Students' Representative Council was set up. The representatives were elected by constituencies of students according to faculties, or classes. The objects of the council were to represent the interests of students, to be the official recognized channel between students and the university authorities, and to promote social life and academic unity among students. The council earned golden opinions from the start by persuading the student body to behave with dignity and decorum (a remarkable achievement for Scottish students in those days) at the tercentenary of the university which was held shortly afterwards. On the strength of the goodwill it earned in this operation the council began—and has kept up ever since—a 'firm but friendly pressure' on the university authorities. It secured improvements in the library; it organized a staff-student consultative committee to reform the clinical instruction in the faculty of medicine; it criticized the high failure rate for the M.A. degree; it proposed something similar to the free university which present-day activists regard as very up-to-date and 'with it', namely an arrangement whereby anyone, not just the appointed faculty, should be free to advertise and give courses in the university, and that students should be able to choose which courses to attend so that, in philosophy for instance, they would not need to be exposed to what the S.R.C.'s student newspaper called 'the sterilising influence of a systematic dosing of one school of thought'.

Of course the Students' Representative Council in Edinburgh did not persuade the authorities to take all its advice. But there is no doubt whatever that since 1884 there has been an effective student movement in Edinburgh University with corporate student opinion which has been taken seriously by the authorities and which has influenced the university.

Very soon after 1884 S.R.C.s were created in the other Scottish universities and in 1888 the student movement in Scotland took another historic step. Let me spend a few minutes on it because it illustrates a theme which I want to bring out in these lectures. The theme is that the most effective way for students to acquire rights is for them to shoulder responsibilities. In January 1887 it was announced in the Queen's speech at the opening of parliament that legislation would be introduced for the reform of the Scottish universities (bills had been before parliament on and off for four years, with never enough time allowed to get them through). Immediately the S.R.C. in Edinburgh set up a sub-committee to influence the contents of the bill, and by November a memorial was presented to the Scottish members of the government. The memorial sets out the reforms which students wanted—an interesting list and, although it is eighty-three years old, how very familiar: an improvement in the faculty–student ratio; less emphasis on lectures as a means of instruction; greater freedom of choice among courses for degrees; account to be taken of teaching ability in the appointment of professors. Meanwhile the bill was dropped again and revived in the following year. Student activity was not confined to Edinburgh. The S.R.C. in St. Andrews proposed joint consultations among students at all four universities; these gave birth to a second memorial which was carefully timed to reach Westminster just before the committee stage of the bill. The memorial requested amendments to the bill which would strengthen the constitutional position of student councils. Among the amendments were: (i) increased representation on the courts, which were the governing bodies (for the bill proposed to halve the voting strength of the students' representatives by increasing the size of courts without increasing the number of rector's assessors); (ii) student representation on senate committees; and (iii) an assurance of the right of access of S.R.C.s to the courts and the senates and also to the commissioners who, if the bill was passed, would have the task of revising the ordinances for all the Scottish universities.

The bill was passed and it contained much, though not all, that the students had asked for. The essential provisions, however, were there. Students' Representative Councils were recognized by parliament as integral parts of the constitution of Scottish universities—the student movement was now established in the statute book of Westminster. The act laid down, too, that the commissioners might include students among those to be consulted about the new university ordinances.

The commissioners were duly appointed and for nearly ten years they laboured at the revision of ordinances. The two memorials I spoke about just now had evidently made such a favourable impression on the commissioners that they were in a receptive mood to receive further suggestions from students. This meant that over a stretch of years students interested in university reform were able to take an active part in it. Indeed the authorities encouraged them to do so. The S.R.C.s of the four universities accepted this challenge. The Edinburgh students' council prepared another statesmanlike document, this time for the commissioners. They asked for some assured income for S.R.C.s (they suggested a shilling per head raised by an increase in the matriculation fee); they asked that the S.R.C. should have an opportunity to comment on draft ordinances before they were adopted; they asked to be consulted as to who should be appointed to the important office of rector's assessor, for the assessor was the man who really represented their interests on the court; they wanted (a surprising request) a fairly stiff entrance examination to be passed before a student was admitted to a degree course.

This document for the commission and the two memorials to the government convey a sense of responsibility and good judgement and concern for higher education. The carefully worked out and tactfully worded requests had their reward. The commissioners did submit draft ordinances to the S.R.C.s of all Scottish universities for comment. They gave the S.R.C.s a privilege not provided in the act, namely direct right of access to senates—the act provided only for access to courts. And most of the requests about academic matters which were made by the students appeared as ordinances. In brief, the students of the Scottish universities in the stretch of years between 1887 and 1900 had an indubitable influence on higher education in Scotland. They won the confidence of the university authorities: 'You as students,' said the Principal of St. Andrews University in one of his annual addresses, 'may help in moulding these alterations [the new ordinances] so as to make them beneficial.' And, by exercising their influence responsibly, they acquired for the student movement as a whole valuable and lasting rights. One further outcome of these combined operations conducted by the students' councils led them to form a consortium which still flourishes, now renamed as the Scottish Union of Students. It was the first national forum for corporate opinion among students in Britain.

This strong current of cohesion did not affect Oxford or Cambridge, because there the student's loyalty was to his college, not to the university, and colleges were small intimate societies which did not at that time feel the need for any formal machinery of student government. The first English university to form a students' council was Liverpool. This was in 1892. Its direct inspiration was from Scotland. Its birth, like that of the Edinburgh S.R.C., coincided with a state occasion, the opening of the Victoria building. But this time there were no golden opinions earned. The authorities had, very unwisely, decided to exclude students from the opening ceremony. The students organized a biting petition of protest. The authorities responded by opening the gallery to students; but their magnanimity was rewarded with what must have been regarded as the basest ingratitude, for the students who were admitted to the hall disrupted the proceedings by making unseemly noises; and, as the chancellor rose to speak, an enormous biscuit, three feet in diameter, was lowered from the ceiling until it cut off the astonished chancellor from his audience. Upon the biscuit was an inscription explaining that it was a gift to the university senate, 'which took the biscuit for its impertinence in trying to exclude the students'.

I tell you of this incident not simply to entertain you, but as an example of another way in which cohesion is achieved among students. You can imagine the indignation among the worthy citizens of Liverpool, and the affront to the majesty of the academic senate, which this sort of episode caused in 1892. This in turn united the students in self-defence, and it put upon the new student council a heavy responsibility to atone for the disgrace and to guarantee it would not be repeated.

Between the turn of the century and the outbreak of World War I, students' councils were formed in other civic universities, and the charter which established the University of Birmingham in 1900 took a further step in recognition of the student estate by providing that there 'shall be a Guild of Graduates of the University and a Guild of its Students' each having representatives on the Court of Governors. This secured for the English universities a recognition of the student movement, similar to that accorded eleven years earlier to the Scottish universities. But not quite the same; for the court in Birmingham (and in similar civic universities in England) is not a small executive governing body; it is a mammoth assembly likely to meet only once a year. Nevertheless students were able to be represented on this body by 'real' students not, as had been the tradition in Scotland, by distinguished adults elected by students. Only in one institution, the Queen's University of Belfast, was provision made for a student, the president of the S.R.C. (provided he was a graduate), to sit on the executive governing body.

Inspired by the Scottish example, the English students' councils sought some way to pool their corporate opinion by having annual congresses. These were pleasant social occasions, and they discussed several important topics but did nothing much about them. Perhaps the only useful practical outcome was an interest in self-governed residence halls (the prototypes of a modern commune)—and even this took its lead from Scotland. Regarded as attempts to concentrate and consolidate opinion among students the congresses failed. The reason was that in those days there were no issues likely to unite the interests, or to inflame the passions, of students at a national level. Students did not think of themselves as a class having rights or responsibilities.

When the storm-clouds of war lifted in 1918 and young men came back to reconstruct Europe, there seemed to be a great opportunity and a great responsibility for students to contribute to peace. The universities were filled by men who had survived a tragedy past comprehension. They were promised, and they believed it then, that it had been a war to end wars. One way to seal this promise was for the students of Europe to co-operate. To this end students from France resumed their annual meetings by organizing a student congress in Strassburg (now spelt Strasbourg) in 1919 which set up a *Confédération internationale des étudiants*. The idea was that this C.I.E. (as it came to be called) would have affiliated to it the national students' unions of European countries. But England had no national students' union; and that was how one came to be founded, in 1992, composed of representatives of the students' councils or guilds of separate universities.

It would weary you to hear details about the rising and falling fortunes of the N.U.S. in the twenty years between the wars. Ex-servicemen at the universities left and were replaced by schoolboys, for whom war was only a story told by their elder brothers and their parents. The C.I.E. did many useful things: it facilitated travel, it organized international games, it promoted friendship between individual students. But it did not help much to heal the wounds of Europe; on the contrary, it solidified into a Gallic bloc which refused to allow the Germans and Austrians back into a partnership for peace; and later on it changed and became an agent for Mussolini's fascism. On the home front the N.U.S. made useful enquiries over graduate unemployment (a great anxiety in the early 1930s), student health, and so on. But the word 'apathy' which haunts all student organizations became more and more frequent in the records of the union's meetings. Criticism grew louder, enthusiasm wilted, and the membership began to fall away. It was the students' guild at Liverpool, the oldest representative council in England, which halted this decay. The guild sent a circular to all the constituent members of the N.U.S. asking, in effect, what use did they want to make of a national student movement. This stimulated the union's leaders to get their priorities straight; and the union applied itself to a critical appraisal of universities themselves. There was much to criticize: the squalid conditions in which many students had to live and work; inadequate facilities in some of the smaller universities at a time when government grants were being cut; a suspicion that curricula needed adaptation to a new kind of world and that teaching methods could be improved. There was, too, a dry wind of disillusionment which troubled the minds of sensitive students. The future was not secure. Wars had not ended. There was an economic depression. There were students whose parents were on the dole. Appeals to take the thorny path of pacificism were made by those who now realized that it was not just the wickedness of the Kaiser which had shattered the peace of Europe. Then came Italy's invasion of Abyssinia and the farce of sanctions (a farce recently repeated with different stage props in Rhodesia); the war in Spain; the crying necessity for independence in India; the Jewish exodus: a rising tidal wave of anxieties which had a cumulative effect on the conscience of student leaders in Britain. One can sense among some of them a stirring of collective responsibility, a belief that somehow the corporate voice of students should be heard both inside universities, to improve them, and outside universities, to work for the improvement of society.

Responsibility meant engagement: criticism inside the universities and political commitment outside. The N.U.S. banned political topics from its debates; yet it is difficult to take a stand about the ills of society without some sort of political commitment. These circumstances began to give purpose and a fresh thrust of energy to the student movement, and a note of militancy was audible at the annual meetings of delegates. This was encouraged by some of the elder statesmen of the student movement. In 1939 Ramsay Muir, who as a student had founded the first students' council in England (at Liverpool), addressed the N.U.S. at its annual meeting. He was then a veteran of sixty-seven. He deplored the fact that universities made no proper provision for teaching about such topics as nationalism, the working of representative democracy, the relationship with the Third World; and he is then reported to have said: 'Why should not the student bodies demand and insist that guidance on such themes, and opportunities for discussion, should be opened to them?' Students ought to be insisting that their need for this sort of curriculum should be satisfied. Why, he asked, don't students do this? 'I think,' he said, 'one main reason is that they have not been hitherto organised as corporate bodies, with leaders of their own.'

Ramsay Muir's subversive remarks evidently took his audience by surprise, but it was just the sort of encouragement which leaders of the student movement needed. The pronouncements of the union had become sharper. 'No person with the required ability should be precluded from attendance at a University' was one policy statement issued in 1938: it is one which the union has stuck to ever since. To a Canadian audience this doubtless sounds like a jumbo-size platitude; but you must recollect that in 1938 the chance of an English boy or girl going to a university was about three in a hundred, compared with the present chance of a Canadian, which I am told is at least eighteen in a hundred. And in 1940, when the annual meeting of delegates was held under the presidency of an earnest and convinced Marxist, the congress issued a Charter of Student Rights and Responsibilities (which will be the theme of my next lecture), and it was told by its president that students 'working together for similar and constructive ends, can be a force and influence of real strength in a sick world'. The congress demanded the immediate independence of India and condemned the system of imperialism. It also affirmed its belief 'that the principles of Socialism, Federation, and Democracy, are all essential for the establishment of a new world order'. That was thirty years ago. There were a lot of resolutions about university reform, some of them admirable, and there was some shrewd criticism of the British academic scene. It is easy to say, and I think it is correct to say, that the enthusiastic solidarity of this conference did not reflect opinion among the rank and file of students in Britain. The rank and file were not interested in these wider issues and had no opinion about them; but it was the opinion of the articulate elected representatives of these students, and surely in all systems of representative democracy there is, except on specific issues in times of crisis, a similar contrast between the engagement of the representatives and the apathy of their constituents. At the congress in the following year (1941) the impetus of interest was maintained, for the attendance nearly doubled (there were 1,100 delegates) and the discussions and resolutions, though free from the Marxist jargon so evident in 1940, were still vividly concerned with really important problems: the relevance of curricula to social needs, the need to preserve civil liberties, and a reassertion of the need to bring higher education within reach of all who could benefit from it; framed (as a newspaper editorial put it) 'in no spirit of self interest but in the light of the wider interests of the community'. Here is evidence of the stirring of corporate student conscience. Student congresses continued during the war years, with attendances at over one thousand. When victory was in sight, the British people, tired but heroically hopeful, turned a second time to build a new world, and the student movement produced a blueprint for its small sector of the new world. It was the result of considered discussion among the constituent unions in different universities. Its proposals are now so familiar that I do not need to recite them. In any case the significance of the document for my present theme is not in its content; it is in its style. It was subdued, reasoned, persuasive: not a catalogue of demands from a trade union but an *aide mémoire* of suggestions for reform. This was the spirit in which the student movement in Britain emerged from the war and it is the style in which spokesmen for the movement have done business with the university authorities since; at any rate until very recently.

That was twenty-six years ago. The achievements since 1944 of the National Union of Students and their constituent unions and councils and guilds have, in my view, been a complete vindication of this policy. It is a style jeered at by the New Left as 'sherry diplomacy' and 'compromise with the system'. Well, it should be judged by its results.

For a time after 1945 it seemed as though history would be repeating itself. The British student movement survived the war better than any other student movement in Europe and its leadership from 1946 was influenced by a new generation of ex-servicemen. The leaders believed that Britain had a responsibility to restore the international amity of students. There was not only Europe to think about now but the Third World: students from Africa, India, Malaya. In 1947 the National Union of Students affiliated itself to the International Union of Students. But again political rifts soon appeared. The I.U.S. was considered to be run from behind the Iron Curtain; to belong to it was therefore to flirt with communism. British students tried to hold their own independent point of view at its meetings but eventually they had to withdraw. It is a melancholy thought that international student movements, launched with such high hopes and manned by young people with such vivid enthusiasm, have always been shipwrecked in political storms. Having extricated itself from the I.U.S., the British joined a new organization, the International Student Conference; until it was disclosed that this body was being financed by the notorious United States Central Intelligence Agency. Again they withdrew.

But these misfortunes abroad did not weaken the influence of the student movement inside Britain. There have of course been struggles for power between those who sought influence by patient negotiation with the Establishment, and those who sought not influence but confrontation. You have, I understand, had a similar experience in the Canadian student movement. There are, you see, two ways to win a game of chess. One is to outplay your opponent. The other is to bash him over the head with the chessboard. In both cases the opponent is beaten, but there is an important difference in the quality of the victory. Students' councils in the separate universities, and, at national level, the N.U.S. and its independent Scottish elder brother, the Scottish Union of Students, have—with a handful of exceptions —played the game by the rules of negotiation and have won several very important rounds.

First, the student movement had to get its facts straight. So the London office of N.U.S. set up a research unit which has produced some impressive reports. In a similar way some individual students' councils have presented their universities, and the University Grants Committee which finances British universities, with incontrovertible data about working and living conditions in universities. Then the student movement had to cut a channel of communication between itself and the authorities. In most of the universities communication is already good; and the University Grants Committee reserves an hour at each university it visits to have an off-the-record talk with a delegation of students. At national level communication was not at first so easy. The Minister of Education declined to listen to the student voice. But this changed dramatically when David Eccles became Minister. He welcomed the N.U.S. and encouraged it to lay its views before his ministry. And in 1960 the chairman of the University Grants Committee addressed a conference of delegates from the universities arranged by the union, encouraging them to express their views about the development of higher education in the quinquennium 1962–7.

Thereafter the channels of communication between the N.U.S. and the Establishment became busy with traffic. The union had by now extended its membership to include colleges outside the university system. (It may be necessary to explain to a Canadian audience that in Britain only 53 per cent of the students having full-time higher education are in universities; the rest are at colleges of education or colleges of technology, art, or commerce. These students were not eligible to belong to the N.U.S. until 1937 and their numbers have greatly increased in the last ten years.) Conditions for students in some of these non-university institutions were deplorable. Girls in some colleges of education were bound by rules which would have been appropriate to a medieval nunnery. In some colleges of further education the students had no control even over their own union. The spokesmen for students therefore had plenty of lobbying to do. They learnt the techniques of lobbying as (to go back to my analogy) a keen chess student would learn from master players in chess. Exchanges of correspondence with ministers, circulars to Members of Parliament, press conferences, and TV appearances, became each year more sophisticated. The most effective technique was the evidence given to the national committees which were reviewing higher education at that time, especially to the famous Robbins Committee. There is an astonishing resemblance between some of the forty recommendations made by the N.U.S. to this committee and the policies proposed in the committee's report. I do not, of course, imply that one caused the other; most of the ideas were in the air anyway at that time. But the corporate student view did undoubtedly influence those policies, (as I know, from my own experience on the University Grants Committee, the corporate student view influenced that committee's policies). Perhaps the crowning symbolic moment was in the spring of 1965 when the executive of the National Union of Students was invited to dine with the Prime Minister at 10 Downing Street. The public knew, then, that the government recognized a student estate in Britain. It had become a body whose corporate opinion had to be reckoned with; its membership had in 1965 reached nearly 300,000.

How did the spokesmen for the student estate use this influence? I have time to give you only two examples. In 1965 the colleges of advanced technology (C.A.T.s, as they were called) which were in the public sector of education, were being transformed into autonomous universities. In Britain that means that they had to receive royal charters and new constitutions approved by the Privy Council. The governing bodies of some of the C.A.T.s prepared draft charters without consulting their students, a mistake they might not have made if they had read the history of Scottish universities. This was discovered at Battersea Polytechnic, which was to be the new University of Surrey. The student union there got hold of a draft surreptitiously. The draft had not, in their view, made proper provision for an adequate disciplinary procedure; it had not made adequate proposals for participation; and it had not given students control of their union. Here was a clear case for intervention on behalf of the student estate. The N.U.S. issued a printed pamphlet of amendments to the draft charter which it sent to the Privy Council; it then publicized the case by a press conference, and sent a letter to the Prime Minister. By return it received a letter from the Secretary of State for Education and Science, written on the authority of the Privy Council, to say that the Privy Council was advising all sponsors of new university charters to make three provisions: (i) for an association representing the student body, (ii) for joint committees composed of student representatives and representatives of senate and council, and (iii) for a right of appeal over decisions on discipline. This was tantamount to saying that the Privy Council would not be likely to approve any new charter which did not comply with these three suggestions. Not all the amendments were agreed to; the N.U.S. did not get all it asked for, but it had scored something of a diplomatic success. But now the campaign had to be carried into the older universities which were not revising their charters and statutes. The student leaders, despite their success by the use of 'sherry diplomacy', were under pressure from the militants to use the techniques of confrontation, demand, non-violent direct action, in order to exact more concessions more quickly. Notwithstanding warnings from the president of the N.U.S., the delegates to the council passed a resolution supporting 'non-violent direct action' when university and college authorities fail to respond to student demands. In 1968 there were mild outbreaks of unrest in a dozen British universities. The vice-chancellors, sensitized by shock waves from Berkeley, Berlin, and Paris, prepared themselves to deal firmly with trouble. Here was a second opportunity for the representatives of the student estate to act as mediators and to avoid a head-on collision. To their great credit they seized this opportunity. During the summer of 1968 a joint statement was worked out and on 7 October it was issued in the names of the Committee of Vice-Chancellors and the National Union of Students. It set out, as clearly as any such diplomatic statement could be expected to do, the rights of students to take part in decision-making in universities and the limitations of these rights. It set out the essential principles for discipline in a world where the idea that a faculty member could or should act *in loco parentis* had become an abandoned myth. It hinted at the reforms which the student movement would press universities to adopt over examinations and curricula. Not, by and large, a dramatic document in content but—as for the postwar blueprint produced twenty-four years earlier—it was an historic document in style. For it stood for a partnership between senior and junior members

283

of the university, achieved not by the 'abject subjection of Quisling students to the Establishment' (this is how one militant critic described it) but by blunt talk and hard bargaining between two groups in a community with common aims: the Masters and the Scholars.

These two examples of student diplomacy are further illustrations of the theme which I proposed to you when I described the negotiations between the Scottish student representative councils and the government three-quarters of a century ago: student councils which act responsibly will acquire rights. By 'act responsibly' I do not mean 'act with deference' and I certainly do not mean 'act in a spirit of subjection'. There was a time, I know, when professors did not expect students to think for themselves. There was a famous master of Trinity College, Cambridge, in the nineteenth century who declared that the student should 'entertain a docile and confiding disposition towards his instructor'. Our aim as university teachers now is just the opposite: to provoke a disciplined critical attitude towards knowledge, and we must not be surprised if this attitude is adopted towards our universities and even towards ourselves. This, I believe, is one of the rights of students, provided it is accompanied by a corresponding responsibility.

I believe that this balance of rights and responsibilities does exist in Britain today, but it would be misleading to leave you with the impression that the student movement now occupies a secure place in the policy of British higher education. It is, rather, balanced in a delicate equilibrium. I have described, in this historical *andante*, how it has grown from the resolve of a Scottish student, sitting in the shadow of Strassburg cathedral eighty-seven years ago, into well-organized movements represented locally in each university or college by a students' council or guild, and nationally by the Scottish Union of Students and the much larger, and now much more vigorous, union representing students in the rest of Britain. It is a movement with over 400,000 members. For the most part they are inarticulate and reasonably contented, but they have shrewd and forceful and articulate representatives as their spokesmen. It is a movement which has campaigned for good conditions of work for its members and which has defended their rights of free speech and protected them against possible miscarriage of justice. But, far more important than these trade union activities, the representatives of the student movement have thought about the content and style of education they wish students to receive and have put forward useful and constructive views which have influenced policy. Among the more sincere and thoughtful students who shape corporate opinion, responsibilities to their institutions and to society loom larger than rights. But not all student leaders are sincere and thoughtful. Cohesion in the student movement is still fragile. It seems to me that the movement faces two major decisions. Will it choose to become a trade union, bargaining across the table with the administration and faculty as bosses, not sitting down with them as partners? Or will it rest its influence upon the belief that the Masters and Scholars are members of a corporation consenting to the same ends? That is the first major decision to be made. And the second: will the movement succumb to the infection which has afflicted three international student movements—the infection of alignment in politics? Last April the N.U.S. altered Clause Three of its constitution which—for nearly fifty years—has protected the union from resolutions on political issues. By allowing its representatives to become a pressure group in politics, and not simply in education, the movement could lose its influence and its liberties—just as, in the past, universities which have corporately dabbled in politics have lost their influence and liberties. Or the representatives of the student movement could alienate public confidence by magnifying their own rights, and applying sanctions to secure them, at the expense of their responsibilities. In my next lecture I shall reflect on some of these rights and responsibilities.

111

THE MEDIEVAL STUDENTS
OF THE UNIVERSITY OF
SALAMANCA*

Antonio García y García

Source: *History of Universities* X (1991): 93–105.

1. Introduction

The University of Salamanca has had a chequered history. The difficult early stage in the thirteenth and fourteenth centuries (1218/1219–1380) gave way to a period of consolidation, beginning at the end of the fourteenth century and running until the end of the Middle Ages (1381–1500). This was followed by the golden age of the University in the sixteenth century when its numbers and reputation were at a height. The University later experienced gradual but irregular decline until the first half of the twentieth century, when it again grew in importance. These vicissitudes notwithstanding, it was the foremost of the Spanish universities until the end of the ancien régime. This article only discusses the University during the late middle ages, from its foundation until the latter part of the reign of the Catholic King and Queen, Ferdinand and Isabella.

The University, established in the winter of 1218–19, found its first patron and author of its first statutes (1254) in King Alphonso X (1252–84). The protection of the Crown was also evident during the reigns of John II of Castile (1406–54) and of the Catholic King and Queen (1474–1516). Amongst Popes noted for their protection of Salamanca were Benedict XIII and Martin V. The former in 1381 as cardinal legate gave the University a set of statutes, which have not survived, but which formed the basis for others which he gave as Pope in 1411. Martin V was author of the statutes of 1422, which remained in effect until the early modern period was well advanced. The local Salamancan church contributed to the University in several ways. Besides helping to provide buildings and personnel, it endowed the University with a third of the tithes of the diocese of Salamanca, which were applied towards the payment of the teaching staff. In addition to the above, the late medieval University had other benefactors of lesser importance whose assistance is recorded in University documents.[1]

On the basis of the available documentation, I shall attempt to determine the geographical background of the students who came to Salamanca in the late middle ages and whether their extraction was from the nobility, the bourgeoisie, or the poorer classes. I shall also discuss briefly the sources of funding for university studies as well as the distribution of the students amongst the various faculties.

No general work on the University of Salamanca in the late medieval period which uses modern historical methods exists. A first attempt to provide such a study is to be found in the two chapters on this subject in the first volume of the new *Historia de la Universidad de Salamanca*.[2] The reader is referred to these two chapters for a detailed account of the historical background to the present article, as well as for information about the rather scant existing bibliography on the medieval period of the University of Salamanca.

In an attempt to organize the available information, I shall distinguish between the difficult early period of the University of Salamanca from its foundation in the winter of 1218–19 to 1380, and the period of consolidation, from 1380 to 1500. The dates are approximate.

2. The difficult early period: from the foundation to 1380

The source material for the history of the University of Salamanca in the late middle ages provides no direct information on the students of the thirteenth century nor those of the first forty years of the fourteenth; thus we are unable today to determine their total numbers, social origin, sources of financing, or any other details other than those which may be inferred from the existing information from the end of the first half of the fourteenth century, assumptions which would be unreliable. In the author's opinion, all that can be assumed retrospectively is that nearly all the scholars were clerics, for the most part canon lawyers, and to a much lesser extent students of civil law, and that secular clergy financed their studies principally by means of ecclesiastical benefices, while members of the regular clergy were provided for by the order to which they belonged.

Such official and private books as may have existed for the fourteenth century in which were recorded the names of scholars of the University of Salamanca have now been lost. This unfortunate gap can only be overcome, albeit very inadequately, using the documents contained in the *Bulario* and *Cartulario* of the University. For the period 1343–80 there are fifty-one references to students in about fifty documents, corresponding in all to thirty-five scholars. However some of these were studying in more than one faculty; hence the presence of fifty-one entries in Table I (see Appendix below). These documents provide information about the students' diocese of origin, to what category of the clergy they belonged, whether they were bachelors or students who had not yet obtained this degree, the faculty in which they studied (although this information is frequently omitted) and the benefices for which they were applying (where this is the case). It is evident that nearly all were clerics bound for the Church. Admittedly, according to contemporary canon law, applicants for ecclesiastical benefices need only to have been tonsured and were not necessarily destined for a career in the clergy. But in this case it must be stressed that students who appear for the first time in a document as clerics continue to appear as such in later *acta*, even in those sometimes written several years afterwards. In fact there are only two laymen to whom reference is made at all in these documents. One was the physician to the King of Navarre, Angel de Costefort, who graduated from Salamanca in 1362, having been financed by a donation from his King, Carlos III, amounting to 73 *libras*, 19 *sueldos* and 11 *dineros carlines*.[3] The other was not a student but a doctor of both canon and civil law called Juan Alfonso, who asked that he and his wife might choose a confessor *in articulo mortis*. Obviously, the fact that all but two of the thirty-five scholars discussed here were bound for the Church does not give much indication about the number of lay students who may have attended Salamanca contemporaneously.

It has been affirmed that in respect to thirteenth and fourteenth century Bologna,[4] most of the scholars were clerics and that amongst these the predominant group held canonries. At Salamanca the proportion of clerics was probably greater than at Bologna. Of the thirty-five members of the University discussed here, eighteen were canons, thirteen are described simply as clerics, one was a priest, and one a deacon. One thing seems clear from this documentation: those who were not canons wished to be so, and those who were often aspired to another or other subsequent canonries. Interestingly in this period, there was no monk or member of the regular clergy who asked for or received an ecclesiastical benefice, which was not the case in the following period. The only student who was a member of the regular clergy in these registers was the Navarran Franciscan Pedro de Isaba, who in 1355 received 12 *libras* from the Infante Luis of Navarre, brother of King Carlos II the Bad, to attend the 'schools of Salamanca'.[5]

To interpret correctly this information, it is necessary to point out that in most cases the sources reveal that the students were studying at the University at the moment the document was written. In some cases, however, the students seem to have studied prior to this date so that it is likely that some became canons after leaving the University. In the case of several students, the relevant document does not say that they had studied at Salamanca at all, simply that the University of Salamanca requests ecclesiastical bene-fices for them. It can only be assumed they were or had been students of Salamanca. There are also two cases in which enrolment at Salamanca was based only on the fact that those involved were important personages who had established foundations for students at Salamanca.

Finally, it must be asked what can be known about the average total attendance at Salamanca in this period 1343–80 for which there is only specific information about thirty-five students. Again, there is no direct evidence of the total number of students. But a register of 1378 does exist[6] in which the person in charge of the school of the *Decretals* states that in them 'at least 200 scholars' could be seated, which allows us legitimately to suppose that there was another hall of the same capacity for the schools of the *Decretum* (The *Decretals* of Gregory IX and the *Decretum* of Gratian were the chief texts read in the faculty of canon law.) Table I (although obviously biased towards clerics) suggests that canonists far outnumbered civilians. Supposing that the latter did not exceed one hundred, it would seem that in 1378, the number of canon- and civil-law students was about 500. Table I also suggests that the number of scholars who studied in the other faculties (theology, arts and medicine) was much lower too. In all, the scholars must have numbered about 1,000 at most. Such a relatively small total number of students *c.* 1378 allows us to suppose that the number must have been much smaller in the thirteenth century, about which, as mentioned above, we have no sources at all.

In the period 1347–80, it should be said, total attendance may have fluctuated wildly. At different times during this century Castile was subject to plague, drought, and bad harvests. To what extent these factors have affected attendance, however, cannot be ascertained.

In the documentation no mention at all is made of the social origin of the students identified. We can only presume they were mainly from the bour-geoisie, as was the general tendency of the time, and as can be observed in the following period at Salamanca for which the documentation reveals the existence of a mere handful of poor students and nobles, implying that the rest were drawn from the middle classes. Certainly there can have been few poor students at the University at the time. One way of assisting such students was through the provision of free accommodation in hostels and university colleges. These institutions appeared late at Salamanca compared with their date of introduction in the universities of France and England. In Salamanca in this period only a few of these institutions were created, such as the hostels for sixteen scholars of canon and civil law, whose establish-ment in Salamanca was undertaken in 1364 by a canon of Burgos, Alfonso Pérez.[7] Pérez was a great collector of ecclesiastical benefices, some of which even gave rise to litigation over their rightful ownership. As compensation he was required to establish the aforementioned hostel, although we do not know if it ever opened its doors.

3. Period of consolidation of the University of Salamanca, 1381–1500

The University of Salamanca grew in importance from the 1380s, principally due to the protection given by Benedict XIII, especially after his dispute with the University of Paris. In addition to the two sets of statutes he gave to the University of Salamanca mentioned above, Pope Luna also granted the University's request in 1403 that 318 of its members be given ecclesiastical benefices (Table VI). In addition, he was responsible for the organization and consolidation of the theology faculty, which had hitherto been operating in the Dominican and Franciscan convents of Salamanca, and only in the University itself on an impermanent basis. While we are uncertain of the date that the theology faculty was first established, Benedict XIII's reorganization dates from 1395–96. To achieve this, he took maximum advantage of the material and intellectual resources of the two great mendicant orders, the Franciscans and the Dominicans. He created five chairs, three in the University and two in the Dominican and Franciscan convents of St Steven and St Francis, whose standards were recognized to be high. At the same time the cathedral chapter was affiliated to the theology faculty on the same terms as the mendicant orders. These measures produced a larger influx of students wishing to study theology at Salamanca, and throughout the fifteenth century teachers emerged, not only of local but worldwide importance, such as Juan de Segovia, Juan Alfonso de Mella, Alonso de Madrigal and others.

The other faculties also improved in quality and expanded in numbers of students, but they did not attain the standard of the two law and theology faculties.

The special protection of Juan II of Castile and above all the Catholic King and Queen was also very influential in consolidating and strengthening the University after 1380.

This is the context in which to view the comments made below on the students of the University of Salamanca during this second period of consolidation which precedes the University Salamanca's golden age in the sixteenth century.

A few years after the outbreak of the papal schism the University of Salamanca sent a *rotulus* to the Avignon Pope, Clement VII, soliciting ecclesiastical benefices and, exceptionally, spiritual graces or dispensations for the University's professors and especially its students. The *rotulus* was accepted by the Pope on 29–31 October 1381. This was the first known occasion on which a Pope granted a large number of ecclesiastical benefices (to several hundred fortunate people) at the request of the University of Salamanca (see Table II). There were doubtless two reasons for this concession: Salamanca and the kingdom of Castile were already of considerable importance in the academic world and in contemporary Christian politics; in addition, the Avignon Pope needed the support of the universities, which easily could transfer their obedience from Avignon to Rome, or back again if they did not receive special treatment when this was demanded.

Scholars on the *rotulus* came from nearly every diocese of the two kingdoms of Castile and Portugal. But no student came from Navarre. This had not been the case among the groups of scholars identified from the period 1343 to 1380 which, as mentioned above, include a layman and a Franciscan from the kingdom of Navarre, if admittedly both were maintained by the royal family of the kingdom.

Apart from the diocesan clerics, a Benedictine from the Monastery of Samos (diocese of Lugo) appears in the 1381 *rotulus*, who asked to be appointed a prior in Santiago or Braga. The faculty in which he studied is not supplied.[8] Conversely, there is a cleric from the diocese of León who aspired to a benefice whose collation was in the hands of the monks of the monastery of Sahagún.[9]

Of the students on the 1381 *rotulus*, several were bachelors and of these, some were recruited as teachers. Admittedly, to obtain a bachelor's degree a period of teaching was obligatory for experience in 'reading' or 'teaching' formed part of the *curriculum studiorum*. In these cases, however, it would appear that the bachelors occupied paid teaching positions, which was, in principle, against the statutes, since such teachers were required to be licentiates or doctors. Presumably, the shortage of qualified teachers led to this lowering of the statutory requirements. On this *rotulus* benefices were also requested for eight doctors or masters: for a Franciscan doctor of theology, four doctors in canon law, one in civil law and two in music.[10] Music, at this point, did not constitute a faculty, but was rather a unique discipline taught in the *schola cantus*.[11] However, no scholar appears in the *rotulus* who claimed to be studying music. On the other hand, one of the music masters was definitely at the same time a scholar of canon law.[12] But studying in two faculties or teaching in one and studying simultaneously in another was a relatively common occurrence in Salamanca.[13]

This *rotulus* contains little indication of the social background of the scholars. Social class is only denoted in the case of noblemen, of whom eleven are mentioned, amongst others, Gonzalo Gómez de Aguiar, son of Prince Fernando, in turn son of the King of Castile, Enrique II.[14] On the other hand, another student is said to have been the son of the beadle of the University,[15] who presumably was not a nobleman, but who none the less was an influential person in the university corporation.[16]

Although there is no specific evidence to support this, it can be supposed that the remaining students were drawn from the bourgeoisie. In other *rotuli* of this kind there is specific mention of poorer students, their poverty stated as being the reason for requiring the benefice solicited. In the 1381 *rotulus*, however, no one claims poverty as an excuse.

Thirty-three students appear in a second *rotulus* of 13 October 1392. In it are listed benefices or graces sought for scholars belonging to ten dioceses all within the kingdom of Castile. In addition to the bachelors and simple students, only one doctor (of law) appears in this *rotulus*. His presence has not been recorded in Table III. One of the students held the position of university *consiliarius* that year.[17]

More interesting than the *rotulus* of 13 October 1392 for purposes of this discussion is the *rotulus* of 9 August 1393, by means of which the same Avignon Pope Clement VII granted benefices to 113 Salamancan scholars from twenty-three dioceses of the kingdom of Castile as well as to a monk from the monastery of Santo Domingo de Silos (diocese of Burgos) who studied canon law (see Table IV). Seventeen were bachelors of canon law and eight of civil law; eleven were students of civil law, one of arts, and one of theology; in the case of thirty-four their faculty is unknown.

Examination of the evidence also shows that just as most of the students were studying law, so most of the professors soliciting benefices were lawyers. Benefices were solicited for three doctors in civil law, three in canon law, one licentiate *in utroque iure* who was also a bachelor of arts, two licentiates in canon law, and one licentiate in canon law who was also a student in civil law. It seems odd that no teacher of theology appears; this is undoubtedly due to the fact that these teachers usually were members of mendicant orders, who rarely solicited ecclesiastical benefices. We do not know if the teachers in medicine of this date were laymen and hence excluded from soliciting for benefices. Indeed, we do not even know if the faculty had a significant number of students in this period, albeit far fewer than the number of students in the law faculties and the theology faculty.

A student who 'per septennium in Studio Salamantino scholas grammaticales tanquam bachalarius rexit'[18] is also mentioned, as is another who had similarly taught for seven years in the grammar schools. In this second case there is no indication of the supplicant's current teaching position or any other activity.[19]

As regards the information on social extraction, the *rotulus* lists the son of the nobleman, Arnaldo Bonal (doctor of decrees),[20] a son of a military man,[21] and the son of Antonio Sáchez, doctor of canon law and *auditor* of the King of Castile.[22]

A fourth *rotulus* exists dated 16–17 October 1403 presented to the pope by the Bishop of Niza and soliciting benefices for thirty-three members of the University of Salamanca (see Table V). It does not appear to have been granted, perhaps because Benedict XIII was about to accept another *rotulus* of 318 scholars only a few days later. In addition to the students from the twelve dioceses of the kingdom of Castile this list contains the name of a Frenchman from the diocese of Oloron, who was a student of canon law. Distributed according to faculty, this *rotulus* contains the names of two

BAs, three bachelors of canon law, and two in civil law, plus two students in arts, twenty-three in canon law, and one in civil law.

The second largest surviving *rotulus* of all is that granted by Benedict XIII on 19–23 October 1403 (see Table VI). In it appear the names of 318 scholars, plus the names of those who appear as teachers (one doctor of civil law, another of canon law, and a licentiate of civil law). Another teacher, a Toledan cleric, is also mentioned, who was responsible for the 'cathedra cantus' and was studying canon law.[23]

These 318 students were drawn from twenty-seven dioceses of the kingdom of Castile and from three French dioceses (two from Mende and one from Oloron). From the kingdom of Aragon, there were only two scholars from the diocese of Saragossa. Significantly, no Portuguese is recorded, undoubtedly because the Portuguese kingdom had refused obedience to Pope Luna. There also appear three members of the Third Order of Saint Francis and a canon regular from the collegiate church of San Isidro de León.

Amongst these scholars, two are listed as belonging to the nobility[24] and one as a military man.[25]

By faculty, in descending order of numerical importance, there were 102 whose faculty is unknown, twenty-three bachelors and ninety-eight students in canon law, ten bachelors and twenty students in civil law, fifty-seven students in arts, seven in theology, and a single BA. There was also a bachelor in *utroque iure*[26] and a bachelor in both canon law and arts.[27] One of these students was *consiliarius* of the University[28] and another its syndic.[29]

During this period three university colleges were founded: one of the five *colegios mayores* (the *Colegio de San Bartolomé*) and two of 'minor' ones (the *Colegio Viejo de Oviedo*, known vulgarly as 'Bread and Coal', and the college of the Archbishop of Toledo, Alfonso Carrillo). It must be emphasized that the terms *colegio mayor* and *colegio minor* refer to a later period. There was no difference in legal structure between the two types of college, only a difference of importance. Eventually, there were six *colegios mayores* in the Spanish university system, of which four belonged to the University of Salamanca. The *Colegio de San Bartolomé* was the only one founded in the middle ages.

These three colleges were founded for poor scholars, as is indicated by the very title of the first statutes of the *Colegio de Oviedo: Ordinatio Collegii pauperum scholarium civitatis Salmantinae*. This college was founded by Gutierre de Toledo in 1381, who drew up some preliminary statutes to enable it to open, the title of which is transcribed above. The definitive statutes date from 1386 and were amended in the seventeenth century. In the founder's *Ordinatio*, it was set out that the college was established for six poor scholars to study canon law, to be chosen from the candidates from the diocese of Oviedo. Should there be an insufficient number of these, then candidates from the dioceses of Toledo and Palencia could be elected instead.[30]

The minor Salamancan college founded in 1479 by Archbishop Alfonso Carrillo de Acuña offered twelve places for students from the Archbishopric of Toledo or from other dioceses if there was an insufficient number of candidates. The scholars were required to study either in the faculties of theology or canon law.[31]

The first statutes of the *Colegio de San Bartolomé* were drafted in 1414–16. They were adapted from the statutes of the *Colegio de San Clemente de los Españoles* established at the University of Bologna. San Bartolomé's founder was Diego de Anaya y Maldonado, then Bishop of Cuenca, hence the name also given to the college, *Colegio de Cuenca*. The founder later became Bishop of Salamanca and subsequently Archbishop of Seville. The college was intended to provide places for fifteen poor scholars drawn only from the kingdom of Castile, of which five were to study theology and ten canon law. The statutes of 1414–16 were drafted definitively in 1435, amended in 1437, then amended further on other occasions.[32]

Undoubtedly, the preference given to students of canon law in filling the places in these colleges only reinforced the numerical dominance of the faculty of canon law, which almost certainly existed from the university's inception. It is also one of the reasons why attendance in the faculty continued to increase during the sixteenth century while in other countries the number of canonists fell in relation to the numbers studying civil law or other subjects of greater interest.

4. Conclusion

The papal *rotuli* of requests or collective petitions for ecclesiastical benefices for poor students are an important source for medieval university history, despite their limitations, especially in the period of the Avignon popes, who tried to attract supporters thereby. The chief country to benefit from this rich manna was France. Castilians benefited in their hundreds from papal munificence during the Great Schism, but Frenchmen were rewarded in their thousands. In 1378 French universities presented Pope Clement VII with a total figure of 4,788 requests for benefices for students. In 1403, they sought 4,478 benefices from Pope Benedict XIII.[33] The largest *rotulus* of graces for Salamanca benefited only slightly more than 300 students; over the epoch of the Great Schism only 825 Salamancan students are known to have sought papal aid.

Obviously, the *rotuli* of requests say relatively little about the total student population at the date of their presentation. Not all students had the qualifications that permitted them to be included in the list of petitioners. Fortunately for Salamanca we have another apparently insignificant but actually quite important source from which to determine the total number of students in 1378, as we have already seen. Working from information about the capacity of the lecture hall for students of canon law following a course on the *Decretals*, we have estimated that at this date there were some 1,000 students at Salamanca. This figure, high for a Castilian or any other Iberian university in the period, was modest compared with many contemporary Italian, French, and English universities.[34] Clearly, too, the collegiate provision at Salamanca was meagre compared with the great universities of northern Europe. In both respects, moreover, the University of Salamanca at the turn of the fifteenth century was in no way comparable with its successor in the reign of Philip II. At its zenith in the late sixteenth century Salamanca enrolled 5,000, not 1,000, students per annum and boasted fifty colleges, not three.[35]

References

* Translated from Spanish by Kathy Ross Landazabal.

1. V. Beltrán de Heredia, *Bulario de la Universidad de Salamanca* vol. I (Salamanca, 1966): hereinafter cited as BUS; idem, *Cartulario de la Universidad de Salamanca* vol. I (Salamanca, 1970): hereinafter CUS.
2. Various authors, *Historia de la Universidad de Salamanca* (3 vols., Salamanca, 1989–90), i. 13–34 'Los difíciles inicios (Siglos XIII–XV)' and 35–48 'Consolidaciones del s. XV': hereinafter HUS.
3. CUS, i. 639, no. 59.
4. S. Stelling-Michaud, *L'Université de Bologna et la pénétration des droits romain et canonique en Suisse aux XIIᵉ et XIVᵉ siècles* (Geneva, 1955), pp. 130–1.
5. CUS, i. 637, no. 56.
6. CUS, i. 646–7, no. 71.
7. BUS, i. 393–4, no. 109, and BUS, i. 396–7, no. 113.
8. BUS, i. 439, no. 70. A similar case is found in BUS, i. 442, no. 147.
9. BUS, i. 451, no. 327.
10. BUS, i. 434–5, nos. 4–8.
11. BUS, i. 441 and 443, nos. 132 and 161. Cf. BUS, i. 568, no. 33.
12. BUS, i. 443, no. 161.
13. BUS, i. 442–3, nos. 148, 161, 166, etc.
14. BUS, i. 441, no. 117.
15. BUS, i. 443, no. 159.
16. See the chapters cited in HUS, note 2 above.
17. BUS, i. 491, no. 7. For this office see the chs. cited in HUS, note 2 above.
18. BUS, i. 504, no. 104.
19. BUS, i. 504, no. 98.
20. BUS, i. 501, no. 45.
21. BUS, i. 501, no. 46.
22. BUS, i. 501, no. 47.
23. BUS, i. 568, no. 33.
24. BUS, i. 567, no. 11; BUS, i. 580, no. 279.
25. BUS, i. 573, no. 121.
26. BUS, i. 567, no. 5.
27. Ibid., no. 14.

28. Ibid., no. 9.
29. Ibid., no. 10.
30. L. Sala Balust, *Constituciones, estatutos y ceremonias de los antiguos colegios seculares de la Universidad de Salamanca* vol. I (Madrid, 1962), pp. 73–7.
31. Ibid., pp. 95–104.
32. Ibid., vol. 3 (Madrid, 1964), pp. 7–194.
33. J. Verger, *Les Universités au moyen âge* (Paris, 1973), pp. 124–5.
34. See esp. T. H. Aston, 'Oxford's Medieval Alumni', *Past and Present* 74 (1977), 6–10; G. D. Duncan and T. A. R. Evans, 'The Medieval Alumni of the University of Cambridge', *Past and Present* 86 (1980), 35, 74–5.
35. L. E. Rodríguez San Pedro Bezares, *La Universidad Salmantina del Barroco. Periodo 1598–1625* 3 vols. (Salamanca, 1986).

112

ECONOMISTS AS EXPERTS

The rise of an academic profession in the United States, 1870–1920

Robert L. Church

Source: L. Stone (ed.) *The University in Society*, vol. II: *Europe, Scotland and the United States from the Sixteenth to the Nineteenth Century*, Princeton: Princeton University Press and Oxford: Oxford University Press, 1975, pp. 571–609.

I

Historians have usually described the development of the academic social sciences as a steady progress from concern with reform toward an increasingly exclusive concern with scientific method, with objectivity, and with understanding social organization for the sake of understanding and not application. In the beginning, the story goes, social science, hardly deserving of the name, was moralistic, practical, and therefore biased, but the fields rapidly advanced toward objectivity, disinterest, and scientific abstraction. Social sciences progressed from "lore" to "science," from social reform to social science.[1] A more accurate and revealing point of view, however, is one that pays particular attention to the academic social scientists' continuing desire to make their knowledge influential in the real world and that interprets the various definitions of social science as different strategies adopted at different times to enhance the social scientists' influence outside the academy.

In part the social scientists desired to influence social development in order to impose the values and interests of their social class on society. Because of very restricted access to college and professional academic training in the United States before World War I (probably less restricted than in Europe at the time but much more so than in the contemporary United States), the vast majority of academic social scientists came from the more comfortable classes. Social science attracted them in part because it appeared to offer them a chance to maintain the values of these classes against challenges from other social groups.[2]

At another level more germane to this essay, the academic social scientist desired to make a difference in order to enhance his sense of worth and identity and to justify his choice of career. Perhaps this has been a special problem in the United States where widespread anti-intellectualism and utilitarianism have forced the academic to justify—to himself at least—his decision to withdraw from the "real" world and the competition of the marketplace.[3] To argue that ideas and research do affect the real world has been a powerful antidote to the criticism that the academic was isolated, impractical, and irrelevant.

As the social science disciplines organized and professionalized, they built into each discipline's very structure the justification that careers in that field "made a difference" in the real world. They came to define contributing to the literature of political science or economics or sociology as *ipso facto* "making a difference." Socialization to the profession and its internal reward structure has reassured most workers in the vineyard of their extra-academic influence. Just how knowledge achieves that influence, they have left to their field's basic theorists and philosophers. Among those committed to exploring the basic purposes of social science, those charged with applying its findings, and those innovators interested in changing a discipline's methods or scope or focus, however, the problem of relating knowledge and action is always present and often controversial. They are always concerned with determining what social science "is for" and with defining how it affects the real world that social scientists study. When a social science discipline is relatively stable, controversy over relating thought and action is often muted—even though practitioners may disagree fundamentally on the issue. When fields are developing, as in the period under study here, or facing fundamental challenges over method and purpose as they are at present, the controversy is open and often rather heated.[4] In those years before academic social sciences achieved the stability of purpose and procedures that would ultimately shield most practitioners from the problem of defining their work's relevance to the real world, the relation of social science and social action was at the forefront of concern for a great number of academic social scientists. There is a further point. Most academics probably, and surely almost all social scientists, expected—even before such expectations were built into professionally defined roles—their work eventually to contribute to social or individual betterment. The historian of academic disciplines must determine how soon the academic thinks his work will become relevant or meaningful in the real world in order to specify how various scholars define their obligations to society. Those most concerned with seeing their ideas make a difference will expect the shortest time span between their research and its application. Throughout the period under discussion here social scientists continued to expect academic knowledge to have an immediate impact on social action.

The remainder of this essay proposes to test the explanatory power of this point of view by surveying the development of academic economics in the United States between 1870 and 1920.[5] The academic economist first sought to affect social action by teaching popular audiences or public opinion what he thought were correct principles of social and economic organization. He depended on informed public opinion to force officials to effect appropriate policy changes. By 1920 the economist had adopted the role of the expert in which he sought to affect policy by passing his findings, his advice, and his conclusions about public policy directly to public officials who would, he hoped, transform them immediately into policy. Although academic economists basically redefined the strategy they employed for influencing social action between 1870 and 1920, they did not alter their desire to make a difference in the society. The shift from a stress on moralism and reform to a stress on objectivity and science, which the standard histories of social science have identified, is best seen as a shift in strategy designed to enhance the economist's capacity to affect society. In the fifty-year period under survey the introduction of empirical observation and quantitative analysis made economics more complex, more sophisticated, more capable of comprehending and accounting for observed social phenomena, which in turn increased economics' applicability in the determination of public policy. The techniques and the rhetoric of science increased the economist's sense of worth by increasing his capacity to make a difference in the real world. What had changed in the fifty years between 1870 and 1920 was the means which academic economists adopted to affect public policy rather than any fundamental change in their attitude toward reform and their duty to encourage it. What also changed as a consequence of the economists' shift in strategy was that university teaching and "making a difference," once tightly entwined, had become separate and unconnected functions.

II

Faculty, administrators, trustees, and donors cooperated to establish social science in the American college and university after the Civil War as part of a wider effort to nurture socially responsible ideas in the nation's present and future leaders. Isolated professors of political economy or of the science of politics or, more typically, of modern history taught in some antebellum colleges, of course, and the courses in moral philosophy that college presidents taught to seniors contained many issues and topics that later became the nucleus of the social science curriculum. But the institution of social science was desultory; the discussion of economic and political issues was something of an afterthought in the moral philosophy course, nearly always subordinate to religious concerns.[6] After the war social scientists, although not possessing quite the glamor of their colleagues in natural science or philology, aggressively sought complete independence from theological restrictions and the limitations of idealist and common-sense epistemology and developed a powerful esprit de corps and a passion for urging expanded teaching of social sciences in colleges and universities. Independent social science departments got underway with Cornell's founding in 1868 and Eliot's elevation at Harvard in 1869 and gained great momentum with Johns Hopkins' founding in 1876 and the establishment of the School of Political Science at Columbia in 1880.[7]

The academic social scientists' expansionist efforts formed part of the larger "mugwump" or "independent" movement in the United States in the last third of the 19th century. The mugwumps had been, or were descended from, members of the social elite before the war; they were largely of eastern birth and residence; they were committed to political independence, especially from the regular Republican machine of the era, and to civil service reform. All identified the years following the war as the scene of a crucial moral battle. They felt their values increasingly menaced by Greenbackers and labor unions who threatened, the independents thought, to expropriate the property of the rich; by what they viewed as the fanaticism or irrationality of Radical Republican reconstruction policy; and by the politicians, too incompetent in both a moral and technical sense to be called statesmen, who ruled the country.[8]

These men also felt threatened from within—by the backsliding from traditional ideals of service and social responsibility among men of their own class and even more frighteningly among the children of their class. Charles Eliot Norton—Boston Brahmin, Harvard's professor of art history, Dante scholar, and a founder of the *Nation*—urged in the midst of his disillusion with the crusade against slavery an improved education for the children of the elite. They needed education "in its nature moral,—an education in social duties, and in that enlightened self-interest which sees its advantage, not in a selfish accumulation of wealth regardless of the claims of those who assist in its production, but in such a division of profits as should raise the general standard of comfort. . . . Unless the ruling classes, upon whom rests the responsibility for remedial effort, are aroused from their selfish inactivity to a new sense of duty and to new exertions, no prophet is needed to foretell the approaching overthrow of social order."[9]

To ensure the maintenance of social order, the independents launched a large-scale educational campaign directed at the backsliders of their own generation and at all the children of the elite classes. Much of the effort was a journalistic one. It assumed that a mixture of exhortation and explication of how correct principles applied to current disputes would remind backsliders of the traditional values and of their duty to support them. Edwin L. Godkin's New York *Nation* was perhaps the premier effort. Founded in 1865 to support the extension of full citizenship rights to the freedmen, the *Nation* soon turned to defending liberal Republicanism, hard money, free trade, and property rights. Other journalistic efforts included the *North American Review* and *Harper's Weekly* and several daily papers in major eastern cities.[10] The independents, expanding on their Civil War experience in Loyal Publication Societies which distributed pro-Union pamphlets in the northern states and sought to place pro-Union news releases and editorial comment in small newspapers throughout the nation, formed several organizations—David Ames Wells's Society for Political Education was probably the most important—for circulating information about correct social and economic principles and for securing suitable comment in the media.[11] The Liberal Republican campaign in 1872 and the Independent movement of 1884 also should be included among the best men's efforts to educate the public in order to restore their social and political values to their rightful ascendency. The independents intended these campaigns, however futile they were as a means of gaining office, to teach politicians that they must abide by such principles if they were to keep the better classes' support.

Enlarging social science's place in the curriculum was another part of this educational effort. The vast majority of social scientists teaching at universities before 1880, at least, counted themselves among those who sought to reestablish classic principles of social and political organization as standards for Americans.[12] They proposed to teach the future elite—and university education then was pretty nearly restricted to the elite—correct principles of political and social organization, the laws governing social and political relations which had to be obeyed if the society were to function properly. Social science taught just those principles and laws through studying the development of English freedoms since Magna Carta (sometimes since village communities emerged in the German forests) and their extension and further safeguarding in the United States; how the constitution protected individual liberties, property, and the rights of minorities (in this case they meant the rights of the rich against the desires of the "mob") and how it limited the powers of democracy; and the laws and principles of classical laissez-faire political economy.[13]

The bond between the defenders of the traditional principles and the development of academic social science is vividly clear in Harvard's efforts to fill two places on the social science faculty in 1869–71—one in political economy and one in medieval history. Four of the five men seriously considered were intimately involved in the liberal journalism of the day. Charles Franklin Dunbar, chosen to profess political economy although he had never studied, taught, or written specifically on the subject, joined Harvard's faculty after an eight-year stint as editor of the Boston *Daily Advertiser*—the independents' newspaper in that city. Eliot's first choice for the position in medieval history was the Englishman Goldwin Smith, whose substantial historical qualifications included a period as Regius Professor of Modern History at Oxford, but even Smith was known primarily as a journalist, having once edited the *Saturday Review* and having established his American reputation as journalistic advocate of the British Liberal Party and the cause of Anglo-American understanding in the 1860s. Eliot also offered the post to Godkin, who had no experience or qualifications as an historian. Godkin finally refused it because Harvard would not let him remain the "responsible" editor of a weekly journal, although Eliot did expect him to continue writing for and taking a "lively" interest in the *Nation*. Henry Adams, who at the urging of his father, a prominent Liberal Republican, finally accepted the position, had made what reputation he possessed at the time not in scholarship but in his journalistic observations of Grant's Washington. The few historical pieces he had done covered only modern history.

Largely self-taught in the school of British Liberal political science and British and German evolutionary thought, Adams learned in Europe not the value of disinterested scholarship but the need to apply learning to the immediate improvement of political and social mores. Ironically, the fifth candidate—largely a self-proclaimed one—was the best qualified as a scholar and medieval historian. But John Fiske, although he shared the others' values and indulged in similar journalistic activities to some extent, took his scholarship a bit too seriously and followed his ideas to the point of proclaiming—so it seemed to the powers at Harvard—an anti-religious doctrine. Thus, he was never a serious candidate.[14]

All the serious candidates appeared to view teaching as another way of reaching the same goals that they had set for themselves as journalists. Godkin once described the Harvard offer as a chance to indulge his "burning longing to help to train up a generation of young men to hate Greeley and [Theodore] Tilton and their ways." Like Godkin, Adams did not see his move to Cambridge as the beginning of a new kind of career; rather, he planned to continue to urge reform of Grant's Washington upon his audience from his professorial chair in Cambridge. After coming to Harvard, Adams informed David A. Wells that "in order not to break entirely from old connections I have become editor of the North American Review, and propose to make it a regular organ of our opinions." Adams accepted the editorship at Harvard's request. It was only fitting that the duties of a professor of history at Harvard in 1870 should include those of the political journalist.[15]

These early university social scientists intended to make a direct difference in the world through their university teaching and their journalism and to make that impact sooner rather than later, immediately rather than gradually. The elite would be immediately reminded of the principles that it was their duty to uphold; their children, upon leaving school, would be prepared to assume responsibility, as public servants and citizens, for returning the country to the path of right policy.

In actuality, of course, the social scientists found that their efforts made little apparent difference. The political and social evils which first moved them to stress social science education burgeoned. Protectionist duties rose higher and higher; ill-informed but strangely popular schemes to undermine government commitments to honor the national debt multiplied; labor unions convinced more and more working men to submerge their precious individual liberties in collectives which would fight for higher wages they did not deserve and which the iron law of wages promised they could not receive. The independents most feared the violence—however caused—that accompanied labor's efforts, most notably in the great railroad strike of 1877. The most corrupt administration in the history of the United States won overwhelming reelection despite the strenuous efforts of the Liberal Republicans. Irresponsible and immoral plutocrats—whom Godkin was among the first to label "robber barons"—remained in the saddle, indifferent to and undeterred by the protests of the "best men" and their spokesmen in social science departments and liberal journals.[16] A decade and more of teaching aimed at reforming the society by recalling the elite to their responsibilities had accomplished little.

Worse yet, labor, soft money advocates, and self-interested protectionists were finding advocates for their causes in a new generation of social scientists, trained for the most part under the German historical school of economics.[17] By the early 1880s it was clear that academic economists did not speak with a single voice on the great issues of the day. The "new" economists began to write for and support the interests of an audience quite different from the elite one the earlier social scientists represented. For instance, Richard T. Ely, professor of political economy at Johns Hopkins, advocated Christian socialism, the rights of labor, the redistribution of resources in the United States. Such activities only increased popular resistance to the independents' laissez-faire ideas.

In response, social scientists in the older tradition intensified their commitment to popular education. They sought to increase their audience and the popular support for their views and to immunize the masses from the historical school's seductive doctrines. In these efforts they and their journalistic allies increasingly neglected their own previously announced values of moderation, rationality, caution, and calm. Instead their writings became increasingly shrill and emotional, their denunciations of evil increasingly bitter, their analysis and their conclusions increasingly oversimplified. Godkin's development as editor of the *Nation*, as John Sproat has amply demonstrated, followed this pattern.[18] The most appropriate case in point, however, is the career of James Laurence Laughlin, economist at Harvard, Cornell, and Chicago, advocate of banking reforms that finally culminated in the Federal Reserve Act, and militant defender of laissez faire before popular audiences.

Laughlin, who received his doctorate in history (1876) under Henry Adams, carried Adams' desire to use scholarship to reform and purify national life with him into the teaching of economics under Dunbar at Harvard from 1878 to 1888 and then into the departments he built first at Cornell

(1890–92) and at the University of Chicago (1892–1916). He left a secure and well-paying position as an insurance executive to teach at Cornell because, he explained to a friend, the "salary is good, the position independent, and the chance to influence opinion in favor of sound finance is considerable. As things now appear in the country, I cannot rest quietly without taking my part in the fight for honest money & sound taxation." But where these sentiments had led Adams to a concern with teaching the elite, Laughlin, coming at a later time when such elite-focused efforts appeared less effective, directed his teaching to a wider audience. In 1892 he complained that the "influence of scientific thinking in the United States has little or no authority with the masses of the people," especially in quelling public demand for radical reforms. A growing population swelled by immigration would, he felt, soon exhaust the country's natural resources, and as resources diminish, "labor and capital both get smaller rewards[.] [T]hen," he warned, "unless economically trained, even honest men, finding themselves cramped by barriers of their own creation, but brought into operation by natural laws, will not know what is really happening, and in entire ignorance of the truth may fly in the face of law and wreak signal damage on society as the supposed cause of their evil situation." To avoid this fate, "we must get ready to give economic instruction of a simple and elementary kind in every common school in the country, in such a way that it shall reach the ordinary voter, and influence the thinking of the humblest workman." Only the study of economic principles would train the volatile working class to bear the "iron law of wages" and the law of diminishing returns.[19] Laughlin thus substantially widened the audience and the responsibilities of the reforming social scientist.

Laughlin set out to follow his own advice. Between the publication of his doctoral dissertation in 1876 and the publication of his *Principles of Money* in 1903, he wrote almost exclusively to affect general public opinion. Laughlin's appointment at Chicago brought him to the headquarters city of William H. (Coin) Harvey's silver crusade, a proximity that convinced Laughlin of the desperate need for public education on economic questions. Accordingly, Laughlin composed newspaper columns in 1895, debated Harvey on the same platform, and in 1896 published a weighty volume arguing the hard money case which matched Harvey's popular *Coin's Financial School* cartoon for cartoon. Laughlin later claimed that his articles stopped the sale of Harvey's book,[20] an obvious case of wishful thinking. Wesley Clair Mitchell recalled that at the same time Laughlin was training his students at the University of Chicago to continue the fight against the free-silver agitation.[21] Laughlin remained committed to widespread public education as late as 1911 when he took a two-years' leave of absence in order to chair the executive committee of the National Citizens' League for the Promotion of a Sound Banking System. His purpose, he recalled, was to change "the thinking of a nation on an important public question." The league established offices in forty-five states, spent over $400,000 in two and one-half years of canvassing the nation, and published thousands of pages of propaganda, a large majority of which Laughlin personally edited. This propaganda consisted of "literature for the general reader and for speakers ... of a sort such that, even though complicated, ... could not only be easily understood by 'the man in the street,' but also be scientifically sound for editors and writers of important journals."[22] Laughlin clung to the assumption that the social scientist could effect social and political reform by building a large-scale political movement through education. In fact Laughlin's efforts at popular education failed to mobilize enough pressure to modify policy but they did make Laughlin's doctrines so suspect that policy makers excluded him from their deliberations.[23] As more and more economists came to discover after 1890, a more efficient strategy for relating economic ideas to policy was to adopt the role of the expert who advised policy makers without recourse to public education. This lesson Laughlin never learned.

The historical or "new" economists who rose to prominence in the 1880s agreed with Laughlin on the need for widening the economists' audience although they sought to teach that wider audience a message much different from Laughlin's. Like Godkin or Adams, they believed that changing public opinion was the most effective way of changing policy, but they aimed their messages considerably farther down the social scale than did the traditionalists—at the middle classes that filled Chautauqua tents and university extension classes and the skilled laborers who were organizing the crafts and trades. They understood that their support for labor and state regulation or control of monopolies would appeal to these classes more than to the elites whom Godkin and Adams sought to reach. But they did not hope to inspire a genuine "mass" movement; even at their most radical they appealed constantly to responsible public opinion and for piecemeal reform. They felt that reform required, however, the active support of the broad middle class of the country, both urban and rural, rather than just the support of the elite, and they sought to inspire such support. The historical economists' appeals differed somewhat in tone from those of men like Adams or Godkin. Where the traditionalists affected a certain cool aloofness and a moderate rationality, the historical economists appeared more passionate in their advocacy. Although the "new" economists were no more earnest than the traditionalists, their appeals had a more evangelical cast, reflecting in part the contrast between the younger economists' expectation that public opinion would effect positive changes in society and the traditionalists' desire to mobilize their audience to retard change or to restore a previous order.

The difference in tone also reflected a difference in background. Ely, Simon Nelson Patten, John Rogers Commons, Edmund Janes James, and Henry Carter Adams all came from rural or small-town America, the largest proportion from the middle west, and they all partook of the pious, preacherly cast of mind more characteristic of those regions. Indeed, for some a career of leadership as an economist took the place of a career of leadership as a minister, as A. W. Coats has ably demonstrated in the case of Henry Carter Adams. Urged by his pious Congregational parents, Adams entered Andover Theological Seminary in 1875 to prepare for the ministry. Finding the curriculum too rigid and his own faith unsure, he aimed instead for a career in reform journalism. He consulted Godkin about his choice of journalism as his way of improving the world. In 1876 Adams accepted a fellowship from the new Johns Hopkins University, intending to study constitutional law and history to prepare himself better for publishing a political quarterly. At Hopkins, however, he became enamored with political economy and decided to study it for journalistic preparation. Like theological training, the study of political economy, a subject which "comes into daily life— affecting the conditions and happiness of men" more than any other—would prepare him to better the social, political, and moral life of Americans.

While studying in Germany in 1878, he began to fear that political economy might indeed be too narrow, to suspect "that there is not enough chance to preach in" it. He vowed that in time he would move beyond political economy into political philosophy, a subject which touched all facets of social and moral problems and gave its students opportunity to be generalists in reform. Instead, Adams eventually expanded political economy to include political philosophy. He focused his work less on the technical points of economics (although he did significant work on taxation and railroad accounting methods) than on the larger problems of reconciling individual liberty and freedom with collective needs and the public interest. For him the economist's mission resembled the minister's. He committed himself as a teacher to getting his students to recognize "the necessity of thinking of these [social and economic] topics that are now coming to make up my life, indeed to take the place of religion." He also sought to arouse interest in the basic issues beyond the classroom. In the 1890s through his friendship with Felix Adler, head of the Ethical Culture Society, he addressed many ethical culture audiences and helped direct the Plymouth School of Ethics and the *International Journal of Ethics*.[24] Adams sought, then, to affect social, economic, and political policies by teaching correct facts and moral conclusions to a large audience, through preaching to all Americans.

Richard T. Ely is the prime example of an academic economist who combined economics and religious reform and who sought to influence policy through appeal to the "masses." Ely was born into a highly religious Presbyterian family in upstate New York. His father let crops rot in the fields rather than harvest them on Sunday and refused to grow barley—the crop best suited to the soil—because he knew it would be used to make beer. Although the younger Ely did not experience conversion, he shared his father's intense dedication to the eradication of sin and the betterment of mankind. Like Adams he felt that the academic economist fulfilled many of the same functions as the minister. Indeed, he even contemplated becoming a Universalist minister at one point, and his initial goals for graduate study—"to go to Germany to study philosophy and find the 'absolute truth'"—had a distinctly religious ring.[25] In Germany he shifted to the study of political economy and finally received a teaching position at Johns Hopkins in that subject.

He found the United States to which he returned in 1880 sharply divided on many economic and social issues and close to open conflict over the respective rights of capital and labor. He traced the causes of this impending conflict to the public's ignorance and lack of Christian toleration and brotherhood. Ignorance of labor's methods and aims and exaggerated views of its strength made people unnecessarily hostile to its organizing efforts, he recalled in his autobiography. The "ordinary man" had no "clear conception of the labor movement" and "was unaware even of the elementary differences between socialism and anarchism. There were a great many trees all around, but no one could see the forest for the trees." Ely wrote *The Labor Movement in America* (1886) to rectify this situation. "I thought I was doing something very remarkable and making a real contribution to human affairs." Although later he doubted whether he had done the right thing or written a very good book, "at the time I was full of enthusiasm and was fired with the thought that I was fulfilling a mission." "In the words of St. Paul, as I wrote to my mother at the time, 'Woe is me if I preach not this gospel!'"[26] Another book, *Social Aspects of Christianity* (1889), resulted from his belief that the impending conflict contained "an unprecedented, unparalleled opportunity for the church to direct the conflicting forces into such fruitful channels that they might have become powerful for the 'good of man and the glory of God.'" He appealed for "a great religious awakening which shall shake things, going down into the depths of men's lives and modifying their character. This religious reform must infuse a religious spirit into every department of political life."[27]

Ely wrote for the "ordinary man," not the elite. He regretted his inability as a lecturer to hold large crowds and give them the message. Instead, he had to depend on his writings. He wrote the first edition of his textbook for the Chautauqua Literary and Scientific Circle, to whose summer sessions in upstate New York both the educated and the "common people" flocked for information and enlightenment. He was very proud that this text "had a very wide circulation" and that "you could hardly find a hamlet anywhere of any size where somebody had not read this book and where it had not been discussed."[28] Between 1880 and 1900 most of his writing was popular. Besides the accounts of socialism, his text for Chautauqua, and his defense of the labor movement, he published *Problems of Today* (1888), *The Social Law of Service* (1896), and a host of popular magazine articles. At the same time he published only a handful of technical economic studies meant for professionals and policy makers. For seven years he actively participated at

Chautauqua meetings and he strongly promoted university extension. All these activities played a part in Ely's effort to use his economic training and knowledge to change American social life for the better by educating the masses to understand economic reality clearly.

Ely also sought to engage the emerging profession of academic economics in the same mass educational effort. Principal founder and publicist for the American Economic Association, he sought to make the academic economists' professional organization a popular platform from which economists who shared his goals could influence public opinion. "One aim of our association," Ely told the audience at the organizational meeting in 1885, "should be the education of public opinion in regard to economic questions and economic literature." Ely and his supporters modeled the association on the Verein für Sozialpolitik and committed it to the views of the "historical" or inductive school of economists who were seeking to overthrow the classical, laissez-faire ideas advocated by more traditional economists. The historical economists agreed generally that only an activist government—anathema to the classicists—could solve America's social and economic problems. Ely and other members of the historical school organized to press their views on public opinion and to loosen laissez faire's hold on the public and political mind.[29]

At the same time that the association's founders were intent on widening the academic economists' influence on practical affairs, they introduced a significantly new emphasis on research and science. The younger economists, with more than a little justice, denounced their predecessors' failure to do original research. All they did, the charge went, was to ransack the archive of long-codified and universally valid principles and subprinciples of classical theory to find those that best suited the specific situation at issue. The economist applied those principles whole in order to discover the best strategy for that situation—usually to do nothing but allow natural forces to run their course. Historical or inductive economists objected to this reliance on an arsenal of immutable principle. The historical school argued that the classicists' supposedly universally valid principles had been formulated in a specific historical and geographic context and were not necessarily applicable in other periods and places where conditions were different. This point of view naturally suggested a further fragmentation or relativism: because no two economic situations were alike, even within a single historical period, no general rules could apply. Instead of seeking to fit a situation to a general rule, the economist should conduct a thorough empirical investigation of the situation and induce from his findings the wisest policy to follow in that situation.[30]

For all its obvious failings as a doctrine upon which to build anything resembling a theoretical science, the historical school's point of view did stimulate vast quantities of empirical research. The historical economists identified themselves with the new university research effort, as accumulators of "new" knowledge. In investigating each specific economic situation, they discovered never-before-known facts and relations whereas their predecessors had mainly manipulated and reapplied already known knowledge. But in no way was the investigator or empiricist to be an ivory-tower scientist who discovered truth for its own sake. Each new fact also contributed to reform or social betterment. The historical economists required the economist to investigate contemporary economic problems to find the means of directing economic development in the public interest and to educate the popular audience to support the solutions to economic problems that he discovered. Science and reform in no way conflicted in their minds.

III

But Ely's vision of the American Economic Association as an organization of empirical economists bent on discovering solutions to immediate social problems and on generating widespread public support for those solutions did not materialize. Members of both the classical and historical schools came to reject the notion that the economist could serve as both investigator and popular educator. Ely's and Laughlin's commitments to popular education appeared to accentuate division and disagreement among economists. Many economists grew to believe that the public airing of disagreement would hinder their efforts to affect public policy. How could economists expect outsiders to listen to them if they could not agree among themselves as to the conclusions of economic science? In appealing for public support, advocates of various points of view often oversimplified the issues, partly to make their position more understandable and partly to make it more attractive to a large group. Their interest in public education led them to produce more controversy rather than less, to paint the opposite point of view as more evil and more irrational in order to place their own point of view in a better light. Such polarization obscured the wide range of agreement among economists of all schools and hindered rational discussion of the issues.[31]

Academic economists' efforts to gather public support for particular proposals also invited the public to participate in economic debate, on the same basis as academic economists. When Laughlin agreed to battle Coin Harvey on the latter's terms, he lost whatever authority he might have derived from his superior training and experience. Instead, he behaved as if he were no different from the amateur like Harvey. How could academic economists with their superior research ability and their superior knowledge claim special authority for guiding policy if they sought to affect reform in exactly the same manner as those economic thinkers without such training and knowledge? Academic economists did not clearly recognize this problem as they watched Ely engage in popular reform, for they had yet to develop a sophisticated and self-conscious notion of professionalization. A series of academic freedom cases involving economists—the first, ironically enough, a threat to Ely's promotion at Hopkins in 1886—brought the point home. When trustees, alumni, or administrators challenged the economists' right to hold and express heterodox views, academic economists argued that since they were scientists, they should not be subject to the judgment of those not trained as they had been. Economics was a matter of science, not opinion; of research and investigation, not belief. However, it was difficult to maintain this distinction and to claim immunity from the judgment of noneconomists when academic economists engaged in public debates with amateurs and appealed for popular support.[32] For these reasons a large number of academic economists coming to maturity after 1885 rejected the strategy of attempting to effect reform through popular education because they believed that it actually hindered the academic economist's efforts to relate his ideas to public policy.

In 1887 E.R.A. Seligman and Richmond Mayo-Smith of Columbia, Frank Taussig and Dunbar of Harvard, Henry W. Farnum and Arthur T. Hadley of Yale, Frank Fetter and Walter F. Willcox of Cornell, and Ely's erstwhile friends H. C. Adams of Michigan and E. J. James of Pennsylvania began carefully to plot Ely's ouster as the association's leader. In a formal written compact Dunbar, representing the traditional school, agreed to join the association and the others agreed to eliminate all the ideological statements Ely had included in the association's constitution in an effort to exclude traditional economists and to remove Ely from the crucial post of executive secretary. The association dropped the offending wording in 1888 and elected Dunbar president in 1892. In that year Ely stepped down—under some duress—as executive secretary and indeed allowed his membership to lapse for the remainder of the decade.[33]

The group that took control from Ely discarded the American Economic Association's emphasis on religiosity and popular education, but they did not intend to relieve the association or the academic economist of responsibility for using knowledge to affect policies in the real world. Indeed, a substantial portion of the extant association correspondence of the period from 1890 to 1910 is concerned with just how the academic economist was to make his views known and get them written into policy now that the strategy of popular education was discarded. The academic economists and their organization began to turn inward. Where once economists had deliberately sought the larger public's support for various policies, after 1885 they increasingly came to speak to each other. Ely and Laughlin wrote for the popular and semipopular press. Ely persuaded many ministers and supporters of the social gospel to join the American Economic Association; Laughlin included political figures and opinion makers of a more conservative and secular bent in the rival organization he had founded in 1883.[34] In the late 1880s, however, most academic economists sharply curtailed their semipopular publications and concentrated on the new professional journals that appeared in that decade—Columbia's *Political Science Quarterly*

(1886), Harvard's *Quarterly Journal of Economics* (1886), the American Economic Association's *Publications* (1886), and Pennsylvania's *Annals of the American Academy of Political and Social Science* (1890). In a process typical of academic professionalization, the economists quite deliberately developed specialized concerns and jargon and a number of exclusive forums in which they could use their new language to exchange ideas and information about these concerns. In this way they turned away from the emphasis on popular education and the extreme divisiveness, oversimplification, and bitterness which that emphasis seemed to entail.

However, the same leaders who engineered Ely's ouster and who founded exclusive professional journals were not at all happy with the limited audience that the association and its members reached. In 1899 the association invited a long list of officials, businessmen, and men of affairs to join. The association did so, the invitation stated, in the interest of "widening the constituency and increasing the usefulness of the Association." A financial crisis resulting from an absolute decrease in membership in the late 1890s precipitated this effort. But it also reflected a feeling that academic economists were speaking only to each other and not, therefore, exerting their rightful influence on public policy. In the first few years of the new century the association's leaders debated seriously the wisdom of including papers on practical affairs at the annual meetings and the association's responsibility for publishing a journal on practical economic questions. Having men like the President of the Sante Fe Railroad speak at the annual meeting, Taussig wrote in 1904, "adds to the interest and variety of the meetings." The leaders discussed the advisability of electing a businessman president in 1899. H. C. Adams advised Seligman in 1902 that he thought "our annual meetings ought to take up the particular questions of the year, and submit them to a discussion from the point of view of economics." As one example, he suggested that Seligman ask Carroll D. Wright, the Commissioner of the U.S. Bureau of Labor, "to show the meaning of his last bulletin on increasing prices—its meaning for men who live on salaries and for those who live on wages." In the same year Irving Fisher of Yale stated his desire "to see the meetings discuss topics of the day from a more practical point of view than is often taken, and with some regard for influence upon public opinion and legislation." He hoped that practical discussions would increase "the power of the Association as a factor in forming public opinion. . . . it seems to me that economists have altogether too little influence; they are too silent on public questions, and when they do speak their opinion commands less respect than it deserves." In 1909 and 1910 the association, again beset by financial difficulties due to lagging membership growth and still concerned with academic economics' influence on men of affairs, started another membership drive to enroll businessmen and government officials. As the various viewpoints quoted demonstrate, the academic economists found it very difficult to strike the proper balance between scholarly abstraction and practicality. They were never able to define clearly their organization in such a way that it retained both its professional exclusiveness and its influence on men of affairs who had not shared the economist's professional preparation.[35]

Just as the academic economists sought to use their professional organization both to distinguish them from society and to establish their contact with influential men in that society, the economists sought to use economic theory as a badge of professional exclusiveness and a source of authoritative conclusions about policy. In the 1890s academic economists displayed a growing concern with economic theory organized around Alfred Marshall's neoclassicism and the concept of marginal utility and a rapid waning of enthusiasm for the historical viewpoint and for simple empiricism.[36] Economists found theory newly attractive because it helped them distinguish themselves from politicians, men of affairs, and the general public. As part of their effort to professionalize, the academic economists sought to identify a body of knowledge which they could claim as their exclusive possession. The popular educational efforts of the 1870s and 1880s had submerged the distinction between the academically trained economist on the one hand and the average educated person on the other. Yet it was just this distinction that academic economists felt was increasingly necessary after 1890 both to protect their freedom to express opinions and findings without fear of reprisal from powerful amateurs and to support their claim that the public and policy makers should listen to their conclusions with special respect. Mastery of complex, jargonistic, and extended theory and the techniques associated with it came to distinguish the academic economist from the amateur and made his statements about economic affairs and his opinions about economic policy more accurate and authoritative than statements and opinions of those who had not mastered such theory. Any profession's claim to that combination of autonomy vis-à-vis the larger society and authority over certain issues which affect that larger society must rest on a belief that professionals, by dint of their special training, have skills, techniques, and knowledge that the rest of the society does not possess. After 1890 academic economists, only half consciously perhaps, came to believe that elaborate economic theory embodied their claim to professional skill and knowledge.

The economists could professionalize more readily around neoclassical theory than around the doctrines of the historical, inductive school. The historical school's view that economic generalizations were relative and that each economic problem must be approached *de novo* undermined the academic economists' claims that his superior training made his views more authoritative than those of men without that training. Although few members of the historical school advanced the extreme relativist position of which their doctrine was capable, many of that school's American critics identified just this tendency to eschew generalized and widely applicable principles as the inductive approach's great weakness.[37] Without the concept that the trained economist had mastered widely applicable principles and specialized techniques unknown to the general public, the economist could make little claim to authority.

The new theorists of the period after 1890 did not, as their classical predecessors had, conceive of theory as a scientific abstraction divorced from matters of policy and welfare. Since the 1830s classical economists, relying on the methodological formulations of J. S. Mill and Nassau Senior, had sought sharply to divide the scientific from the normative, the "is" from the "ought." In criticizing the historical school's reformist efforts in 1886 Dunbar voiced the traditional view that "economic laws, in strictness, deal with wealth; but the object of legislation is welfare." In 1891 he reminded his readers of

> the distinction often insisted upon by economists . . . between economic laws and the application of those laws in practical administration and legislation. The economic law, the deduction of pure science, is simply the statement of a causal relation, usually between a small number of forces and their joint effect, possibly between a single force and its effect. For the statement of that relation, the case has been freed from every disturbing element, and with the result . . . of giving a proposition which, however important, is only conditionally true. . . . But, when we come to the application of economics to legislation, we enter at once into a region of necessarily confused conditions, and also become conscious of objective ends often having little or no relation to any economic doctrine.[38]

This distinction between the science of wealth and the art of legislation or welfare has always been honored less in practice than in rhetoric, even by those most responsible for its development. It is significant that Dunbar's clear statement of the distinction came only when he was defending the classicists from the charge—advanced by the historical school—that they sought to impose their laissez-faire theory as a perfect and complete guide to policy in all situations. When free of the searching criticisms of the historical school, classical theorists were less prone to recognize the limitations of their work and to act accordingly. It is true, however, that the distinction between wealth and welfare did restrict economic theorists before 1890. They seldom called upon it to guide positive action; generally theory played a negative role. Science was capable of tracing the probable effects of a proposed policy and of warning against evils likely to ensue from its adoption. Thus classicists used Gresham's law to oppose silver coinage. It is also true that the distinction Dunbar cited made classicists largely content with theory as it stood. In studying the principles of political economy they aimed to elaborate details but not to change the theory substantially. They brought theory to bear on facts—for illustrative reasons if nothing else—but they did not study facts in order to modify theory. Theory, after all, was an abstraction and its failure to accord with facts resulted from the action of noneconomic complicating factors rather than from any weakness in the theory.

The new theorists opposed their predecessors on both counts. They sought to change theory from a negative brake on change to a positive guide to change and they sought constantly to test economic theory against facts and to amend theory when it failed to accord with the facts. Wesley Clair Mitchell, for example, gradually elaborated an empirical economic theory by constantly testing its reliability against the occurrences of the real world. Mitchell was very influential in convincing theorists to rely on quantitative analysis of real economic events rather than on logical deduction and speculation. For Mitchell's predecessors theory was an explanation that held only if certain ideal situations obtained—if the value of money or the demand for goods were held constant—and at best, therefore, had an attenuated relation to the real world where such ideal conditions never occurred. After Mitchell and others introduced mathematical analysis, index numbers, procedures for comparative analysis of large numbers of statistical time series of various economic indicators, and other sophisticated tools for handling empirical evidence, economists no longer had to rely on gross simplifications to generalize about the economic order. Mitchell believed that when economists could build their generalizations and principles on the basis of what really happened, economic theory would not simply be an exercise in mental gymnastics; it would be "useful" and practical, a positive guide for policy makers. After 1890 neoclassical theorists in general—whether armed with concepts of marginal utility and procedures for handling large stores of empirical information, or no—deemphasized theory's abstractness and stressed its applicability as a standard for guiding concrete economic policies. Dunbar's successor Taussig put it succinctly in arguing for the applicability of the principle of free trade, an aspect of economic thought not substantially affected by advances in methodology. Taussig began by echoing Dunbar's distinction between the science of wealth and the art of welfare but then drew a parallel between the principle of free trade and that holding "that the use of alcoholic liquors is overwhelmingly harmful." That principle alone would not allow the advocate to decide whether absolute prohibition or government regulation was most appropriate in a given situation, but "if he has the question of principle clearly settled in his mind, he will combat steadfastly popular errors about healthful effects of alcohol, and will welcome every promising device towards checking its use." Similarly, the principle that international trade is preponderantly beneficial because it is a form of the division of labor cannot in itself settle all trade policy problems. "But in considering any question of concrete commercial policy, it is necessary first to know whether a restriction on foreign trade is presumably a cause of gain or loss. Is a protective tariff something to be regretted, for which an offset is to be sought in . . . the way of advantage in other directions, or something which in itself brings an advantage?" The economic principle supplied the answer. "The essence of the doctrine of free trade is that *prima facie* international trade brings a gain, and that restrictions on it presumably bring a loss. Departure[s] from this principle, though by no means impossible of justification, need to prove their case; . . ."[39] The emphasis had shifted: theory was now presumed applicable until proved otherwise.

Developing all adequate economic theory solved only part of the economists' problem. No matter how accurate, theory could make little difference if economists found no way to apply it in the policy-making process. There remained, of course, the strategy of mobilizing public opinion behind the conclusions obtained when theory was applied to actual problems. However, this strategy threatened to embroil economists in the same discrediting divisiveness and oversimplification that had beset their predecessors. Academic economists did not totally reject popular teaching after 1890, for, like other social scientists, they continued to feel responsibility for public education and for molding public opinion. But few engaged in the kind of public campaigns that Laughlin launched in behalf of his national banking scheme.[40] Instead their appeals were general ones seeking public support for the idea of applying science to government and entrusting authority to scientifically trained administrators rather than party hacks.

Academic economists after 1890 sought to "make a difference" by directly influencing the policy makers. They became "experts" who transmitted the findings of economic investigation directly to policy makers without engaging in popular teaching or preaching. After 1890 large numbers of academic economists began to serve as informal and formal advisers to candidates for public office and to public office holders, as investigators for various branches of government, as drafters of legislation, as members of regulatory bodies, and as government administrators themselves. Academic economists did not invent the idea of the expert (natural scientists had preceded them in this role by some decades) and the process by which they received recognition as experts is far from clear.[41] A number of causes seem to have worked reciprocally to establish the "expert" as a necessary although sometimes unwelcome addition to the governing process. The United States was growing, it had assumed world-wide interests and responsibilities, its population was more heterogeneous than ever, its economy more complex. Increases in size, heterogeneity, and geographic mobility disrupted American society and brought increased conflict among a growing number of interest groups. Labor versus capital was the most obvious of the conflicts, perhaps, but there were hundreds of others—between large businessmen and small, between manufacturers and common carriers, between conservationists and speculators, and so on. The problems that beset the country as a whole influenced rapidly growing urban complexes even more strongly. It was no accident that the expert emerged as an important element in urban government earlier than he did at any other level. In the face of this complexity, reformers called on the government to adopt more efficient and businesslike procedures, including the specialization of function and the use of technical experts. Another cause lay in the change from "social Darwinism" to "reform Darwinism," from the theory of the small, noninterventionist state beloved of laissez-faire advocates to the doctrine of the interventionist, active state characteristic of progressive reform ideas. An active state needed knowledgeable men to direct its work. Academic economists both contributed to and benefited from this change in viewpoint; just how much their support for an active state was consciously or unconsciously tied to their professional self-interest requires further investigation.

The expert appeared also because many in the society came to believe that science—so successful in understanding and manipulating the physical world—ought to be applied to understanding and controlling the social world. The application of science to government was especially attractive to the upper and middle classes of American society because it promised to reduce conflict and restore order. Unaware or unwilling to admit that social conflict could reflect fundamental value disagreements or structural inequities in the society, the more comfortable social classes attributed the conflicts besetting their society to ignorance or emotionalism that blinded the parties involved to their true interests which, when identified, would surely turn out to be mutually harmonious. The social scientific expert, of course, would help discover that truth which would harmonize the competing interests and bring them into accord with those of the society at large.[42] Another reason for the expert's growing importance in the governing process was that economists successfully pressed their claim that they possessed a skill and knowledge that no one without economic training shared. The more successful they were, the more inevitable it became that society would call these specially equipped economists to public service. Monetary, trade, and resource policies were crucial problems for any government; economists claimed that they knew something about these matters that no one else knew; soon others became convinced that economists should help solve those problems.

Academic economists participated as experts in government in many different ways and at all levels. Most commonly in the early years they gave expert testimony before legislative and investigatory bodies. This form of participation was something of a transitional stage in that such testimony was aimed not only at lawmakers but at the general public. Yet the economist's testimony was not likely to be widely heard or regarded; indeed as the government grew, such testimony was buried so deeply in the outpourings of government documents that it reached only those intimately involved in the specific issue. Economists also informally advised candidates or public officials on specifically economic issues (as opposed to the general advice that academics had pressed on presidential candidates for some time). In the new century academic economists served more and more readily as publicly acknowledged expert advisers in the executive branch and on various legislative committees. Many economists advised or served on bodies charged with revamping municipal and state tax structures. Academic economists also played a large role after 1890 in organizing and strengthening the statistical and investigatory work of various government agencies. During World War I, of course, hundreds of academic economists advised or administered government agencies, especially the War Industries Board which was charged with supervising resource allocation within the war effort.[43]

The definition of the expert's function in the governmental process was not well established. Most often economists argued that their purpose was to carry out the wishes of the elected officials for whom they worked, to implement the goals of others. Publicly they claimed little independence or influence on substantive issues. This definition underlay the implementation of the famous Wisconsin Idea, a progressive experiment, according to its critics, in which "professors run the state." The Capitol and the University, at opposite ends of Madison's main thoroughfare, joined forces to serve the popular will. Social scientists from the university formed the Legislative Reference Service complete with a library for legislators' use and access to "experts" from all disciplines ready to use their knowledge to codify any legislator's goals—however agreeable or disagreeable the expert might find those goals—into legislation which would accomplish those aims and meet the test of constitutionality.[44]

Here the expert was defined as faceless and value free—in accord with the notion of social "science's" value neutrality. But the expert's influence on policy was greater than that. It is difficult enough to imagine that in determining what did or did not meet constitutional tests or accomplish a legislator's goal, the economist could keep his work value free. In Wisconsin and elsewhere, however, the interaction of expert and policy-maker went much further and the distinction between them became severely blurred. In 1904 Governor Robert M. LaFollette asked John Commons, a professor of economics at the university, to draft a state civil service law and then to serve as a commissioner. Commons refused the second invitation, but seven years later he drafted the state's Industrial Commission law—which regulated industrial safety and workmen's compensation, among other things—and then served a two-year term as one of three commissioners. Commons lost much of his advisory role and became instead an administrator and, at least in terms of day-to-day decisions, something of a policy-maker himself.[45] A similar enhancement of the economist's role occurred in the case of Henry Parker Willis, a Laughlin student from Chicago who simultaneously pursued three careers, as professor of finance (at George Washington University and then Columbia), as financial journalist (he finally became Editor-in-chief of the *Journal of Commerce*), and as an expert in banking for the government. Between 1911 and 1913 Willis helped the House Ways and

Means Committee draw up the Underwood Tariff Act. In 1912 and 1913 he advised the House Banking and Currency Committee on drawing up the Federal Reserve Act and thus exerted the influence on this legislation that Laughlin had sought to exert in a different manner. In 1914 Willis aided the Joint Committee on Rural Credits in preparing the Federal Farm Loan Act. In addition to helping draft the Federal Reserve Act, Willis joined the committee which organized the Federal Reserve System and also became the board's first secretary (1914–18), where he took an active part in drafting that agency's rules and regulations and in formulating its initial credit policies. From 1918 to 1922 he directed the board's division of analysis and research. In Willis's case the expert was far more than a neutral adviser; the expert played an important role in determining policy.[46]

Another instance of the expert determining policy occurred when President Wilson appointed Taussig as the first Chairman of the Permanent Tariff Commission—a commission for which Taussig had drawn up legislative specifications. An economist had directed the Tariff Board during the Taft Administration, but that body had been temporary and merely advisory. Wilson's commission was permanent and did have ongoing investigatory and administrative as well as advisory functions. Thus Taussig held a substantially independent position of some power where he could use his special training and his own theoretical conclusions to influence policy.[47]

Academic economists have been very reticent in discussing the power the expert could exert on policy. They have somewhat ritualistically deprecated their government service, arguing that independent scholarly and scientific work freed from the pressures of administration and politics gave them the most satisfaction. They imply that government service was thrust upon them and that they reluctantly accepted it. The historian should accept such rhetoric only in part. Economists did find government service frustrating because political considerations forced them to compromise the elegance of science and theory, and the pressures of time forced them to neglect important basic issues in order to guide day-to-day policies. Nor were economists very successful in effecting more enlightened economic policy since their hard work was often ignored or their findings subordinated to political expediency. The university, where the economist could follow his ideas to their logical end and discuss his results in an atmosphere in which truth rather than expediency governs, had many attractions.

Yet government service continued to attract economists because of their desire to make a difference, to make their knowledge felt beyond the university. Their reticence about acknowledging their motives sprang from the contradiction that lay at the heart of progressivism which simultaneously fostered the experts' elitist claim to authority and power while it sought to enhance the power of the electorate. The problem of justifying why specially trained expert advisers should have such an important role in the governing process without having to earn their right to influence policy by seeking electoral office genuinely disturbed and confused the economists. Like their academic predecessors, they believed in the right of the educated to lead, but the issue was less clear when the educated sought to lead by advising policy-makers privately and by manipulating highly complex technical procedures rather than by leading public opinion openly. In these circumstances academic economists found it very difficult openly to seek nonelective positions of influence or to acknowledge afterward that they had wanted or taken very seriously the positions that they had held.

Frank Taussig, in speculating on the form a tariff commission should take, reflected the combination of reluctance and eagerness, of fear of elitism and hope of accomplishment that characterized many of the academic economists who served the public as experts in the years after 1890. In the 1916 article for the general public, a draft of which the Wilson administration had used in drawing up the Tariff Commission legislation, Taussig immediately sketched the commission's limitations. "No administrative body of any kind can decide for the country whether it is to adopt protection or free trade, to apply more of protection or less, to enact 'a tariff for revenue with incidental protection' or a system of purely fiscal duties. Such questions of principle must be settled by Congress,—that is, by the voters." Nor was hope for "a 'scientific' settlement of the tariff" justified. "There are no scientific laws applicable to economic problems in the same way as the laws of physics are applicable to engineering problems." Some conclusions of economics are "well established"; others "very tentative and provisional." "I believe some things are established concerning the working of protective duties; but I would not for a moment pretend that there is such a consensus of opinion on the subject as to give us a body of principles applicable at once in legislation, or such as to enable us to decide at once a method of procedure."[48]

Despite these disclaimers, Taussig felt that a tariff commission "could be helpful" in many ways. It could substitute "more careful preparation" for the "haphazard" and "rough and ready" means of framing tariff legislation. "It could aid in the accurate, honest, and consistent carrying out of whatever policy Congress,—that is, the party to which the voters had given control of legislation,—might wish to carry out."[49] A permanent commission could, moreover, explain objectively to legislators just what effects suggestions and amendments pressed by special interests would have. Taussig favored a commission whose main duties were administrative and judicial —like those of the Interstate Commerce Commission and the Federal Trade Commission. A commission established solely to advise on legislation would urge unnecessary changes simply to justify its existence. The Tariff Commission should primarily adjudicate conflicts arising from detailed questions of classification and the determination of ad valorem rates and supply Congress and the Executive with statistical information on foreign trade and American production.

Taussig believed that, ideally, highly competent, permanent officials in the executive branch should perform these functions.[50] But he realized that permanent positions paid too poorly to attract competent persons. The incompetents that did occupy them, simply because they were permanent and thus often the only "experienced and well-informed" officials in their section of the executive branch, exercised "great influence in shaping current administrative practice and the details of legislation. It has been said with much truth that the Government of the United States is run by $1,500 clerks. We have sore need in our public service of a body of able, well-paid, permanent officials, whose positions shall not be affected by party changes, who shall not simply follow in mechanical fashion the precedents of their offices as they have found them, who shall be able to give intelligent advice as well as useful information." Since Taussig realized that such a core of permanent, impartial officials was unlikely to develop in the executive branch, he accepted the independent commission as the best alternative for introducing impartial expertise in government.[51]

Taussig again repeated his distinction between advice and policy making, but held wide the door for an independent commission to effect long-run policy improvement.

> It does not follow that a tariff board can be of no service whatever in guiding Congress and the country on the larger and more difficult questions of industrial policy. It could undertake investigations on the character and the development of American industries, on the conditions of competition between foreign and domestic industries, on the prospects of growth and development for American industries, which would throw light on disputed questions of industrial policy. Investigations of this sort, however, take time, and are more likely to be carried out with sole regard to the ascertainment of the facts if they are not undertaken with direct reference to any pending legislation or proposals for legislation. They should be conducted slowly, quietly, without any flourish of trumpets. They are more likely to command the respect of Congress and of the public if carried on by a board which had already established its usefulness and its impartial spirit by routine work more nearly of all administrative sort. The more ambitious and high sounding its regular duties, the less likely is it to be really successful. Let it be given mainly the duty of assisting Congress in the intelligent elaboration of whatever policy the country has decided to follow, and make no pretense of removing the determination of policy from the quarter where in the end it necessarily belongs: Congress and the voters.[52]

The voters were to set policy, Taussig said, but a commission could influence policy making profoundly so long as it kept itself and its findings out of the public spotlight. Taussig could not have been completely unaware of this contradiction. A man who could speculate that low echelon bureaucrats "run" the government must have realized how much power over policy those who administered laws and those who controlled the flow of information to policy makers and administrators exercised. He claimed that powerful role for the economic expert like himself but did so only gingerly since it contradicted so many public beliefs about power in a democracy. "Making a difference" through the exercise of expertise could never be publicly acknowledged in the way that "making a difference" through educating public opinion had been.

The National Bureau of Economic Research was another example of the new strategy with which academic economists sought to relate thought to action. The National Bureau, financed by private and foundation grants, was chartered in 1920 "to encourage, in the broadest and most liberal manner, investigation, research and discovery, and the application of knowledge to the well-being of mankind; and in particular to conduct, or assist in the making of exact and impartial investigations in the field of economic, social and industrial science, and to this end to cooperate with Governments, universities, learned societies, and individuals."[53] That the phrases about "the application of knowledge to the well-being of mankind" and cooperation with other agencies more concerned with policy were more than routine statements of the scholar's faith that his work has some meaning beyond the academy is clear in the careers and interests of two of the bureau's leaders, Edwin F. Gay, its first president, and Wesley Clair Mitchell, its longtime director of research.

Gay, professor of economic history at Harvard, briefly Editor of the New York *Evening Post*, and first Dean of the Harvard Business School in the years when that school was dedicated to training for public service as well as business, devoted his whole life to mobilizing social science in the service of society. Extensive study in Germany had imbued Gay with Gustav Schmoller's belief that history, economics, political science, sociology, ethics, and psychology must cooperate in finding scientific solutions to the world's problems. To this end he helped found the National Bureau, the Social Science Research Council, and the Council on Foreign Relations. As his editorship of the *Evening Post* suggests, Gay had not completely repudiated the older strategy of educating public opinion as a means of using economic and social scientific knowledge to alter social policy. Between 1910 and 1912 he drafted a new factory inspection bill for a Massachusetts Citizens' Committee and built popular support for it through his work with the American Association for Labor Legislation, the Women's Educational and Industrial Union, and the Boston Chamber of Commerce. At the same time he conducted an educational campaign in behalf of profit-sharing plans. In Washington during the war Gay emerged as more the expert economic administrator than the educator of public opinion. As Director of the Shipping Board's Division of Planning and Statistics, Gay had to devise trade policies that would free the maximum shipping capacity for the war effort. Soon he was heading several different government planning and statistical groups and had become something of a czar in Washington. After the war he sought to influence policy through the private scholarly research agencies. He planned and organized large-scale statistical research projects that served policy makers' immediate needs for information on immigration, philanthropy, recent economic trends, trends in corporate organization, or comparative international wage statistics. The National Bureau was but one agency in which Gay meant to use his training to influence public policy.[54]

Gay's colleague Mitchell had a more theoretical orientation to economics but was always concerned with developing economic theory that was "useful." In 1911 he outlined his "case for economic theory." Theoretical knowledge of causal interconnections had a great practical value in human affairs. "We putter with philanthropy and coquette with reform when we would fain find a definite method of realizing the demand for social justice which is so strong an element in human nature. And tho we are so often discouraged by the futility of our efforts, we stick manfully to our tasks and try to do what little we may to alleviate at retail the suffering and deprivation which our social organization creates at wholesale. What we need as a guide for all this expenditure of energy is sure knowledge of the causal interconnections between social phenomena."[55] Mitchell himself held several government positions which enabled him to apply economists' findings directly.[56]

But Mitchell tempered Gay's enthusiasm for direct involvement by contending that the thinker must stand back somewhat from the day-to-day efforts to patch up and administer the system in order to work out comprehensive explanations of interconnection. The laboratory biologist, not the practicing physician, had made the fundamental discoveries which eased the burden of sickness; so it would be with social issues. The bureau was the laboratory in which economists could elaborate social theory for eventual application to solving social problems. Mitchell thought that eventuality was relatively immediate. Although the early bureau is best known for its long-running projects on business cycles and on the measurement of national income, it also performed (largely at Gay's insistence) much work of a more immediately practical sort—work done for or in cooperation with other agencies concerned with immediate policy issues.[57] The National Bureau's Board of Directors always included men of affairs, in part to ensure that its work spoke to real problems. In 1935 Mitchell, noting that the need for scientific investigation of economic and social problems had not lessened since 1920, reaffirmed his desire to have the bureau's work influence the nation's policies.

The country's economic record for the last decade is botched by colossal errors of judgment during the boom years, by ineffective efforts to check the depression, and by inspirational attempts to stimulate recovery. That economics has not saved us from these blunders is due partly to the disregard of it by both individuals and officials, but this very disregard is chargeable largely to the uncertainties of economic knowledge. No sensible man supposes that fact finding will put economics upon a strictly scientific basis in short order, or stop wishful thinking. But neither does any sensible man deny that more exact knowledge of economic processes and their interrelations will contribute toward wiser economic behavior in proportion as it is applied to the problems that face us as individuals and as a nation. The need for more exact knowledge grows greater as our economic organization becomes more complex and as proposals for drastic changes multiply.

Proof that the bureau had already had some effect lay in the wide use of its reports in practical affairs and in scientific publications.[58]

The National Bureau did not explicitly define itself as an organization mainly interested in influencing policy makers instead of public opinion, but that is the way it functioned. Its findings reached other researchers, government officials, and men of affairs. It made its findings available to the public, of course, but did nothing to simplify or popularize them. Indeed, Mitchell's introduction of sophisticated quantitative measures effectively prevented all but the most expert laymen—i.e., those businessmen and officials who held key managerial roles in the economy—from understanding the progress of economic research. Quantitative techniques made empirical research in economics as esoteric and exclusive as the most complex and logically rigorous deductive theory. Thus, Mitchell could stress the empirical and the need for minute investigation of specific events without abandoning any of the professional's claim to authority and expertise and therefore avoid the problems that had plagued the inductive economists of an earlier generation.

The National Bureau offered academic economists a chance to make a difference in the society according to a new strategy that required them to focus their teachings on a narrow elite of policy makers rather than on the wide audience of "informed" public opinion. The new strategy did not require a total rejection of the older one. Most academic economists, indeed, continued to spend most of their working hours endeavoring to teach the children of the upper strata to become responsible citizens well-informed on economic issues. Even within university teaching, however, the economist's focus shifted increasingly to graduate training, to the creation of more expert economists. Moreover, institutions like the Tariff Commission and the National Bureau succeeded in shifting, psychologically at least, the locus of making a difference from the university to other institutions.[59] Although academic economists continued to try to teach the public to respect the scientific method applied to social problems and to trust experts, they spent little time trying to convince the public of the wisdom of particular policies. As Commons put it in describing his own experience in developing a means of influencing the "real" world around the turn of the century, "I learned . . . that the place of the economist was that of advisor to the leaders, if they wanted him, and not that of propagandist to the masses."[60]

The new definition of the economist's role—as an adviser and teacher who sought to influence policy makers directly—had not lessened his concern with making a difference in the real world. Professionalization and the stress on scientific and quantitative methods had not lessened this overriding concern with using an understanding of economic developments to better the world and soon. Rather, the new definition of the economist's role was but a new strategy for achieving the same basic purpose that underlay the formation of economics as a university discipline. Economists had originally sought to make themselves significant and to make a strong impact on the society by teaching proper economic principles to large segments of the society who would in turn force policy makers to abide by those principles. After 1890 academic economists, discouraged at the slight progress their group had made, sought to achieve a significant impact on the society by working ever more closely with those in power and by influencing their actions directly. In the process they inevitably deemphasized the importance of teaching, in the classroom and in the popular press. This new strategy promised much, both for the economists' professional image and for the harnessing of economic processes to the quest for social justice. But, as the economists themselves recognized, the introduction of the expert and the short-circuiting of popular influence on public policy held grave dangers for a democracy.

Notes

1 Two studies which do not subscribe to the progressive view and which are consequently more insightful than most histories of social science disciplines are Bernard Crick, *The American Science of Politics: Its Origins and Conditions* (Berkeley and Los Angeles 1959), and Albert Somit and Joseph Tanenhaus, *The Development of American Political Science: From Burgess to Behavioralism* (Boston 1967). John Madge, *The Origins of Scientific Sociology* (Glencoe, Ill. 1962), ch. 1, views the science toward which sociology has progressed as one "concerned not merely to formulate knowledge but also to do something with it" (p. 3). It is just this view of science that most histories of social science fail to incorporate, a failure that has led them to misconstrue the nature of change in those disciplines.
2 On the social and class values of professionalizing social scientists, see the suggestive discussions that bear obliquely on the point in Richard Hofstadter, *Anti-Intellectualism in American Life* (New York 1963), pt. III, and Robert H. Wiebe, *The Search for Order, 1877–1920* (New York 1967), chs. 5–7.

3 On American anti-intellectualism and its relation to the university, see Hofstadter, *Anti-Intellectualism*, pt. IV; on the academics' ambiguous relation to the "real world," see Laurence R. Veysey, *The Emergence of the American University* (Chicago 1965), ch. 2, esp. 61–63, and pt. II, passim.

4 For a survey of opinions on the relation of economic thought to action and of the cycles of controversy among economists, see T. W. Hutchison, *"Positive" Economics and Policy Objectives* (London 1964), esp. ch. 1.

5 I have chosen to concentrate on economics because the process under discussion occurred more rapidly and clearly in economics than in other social sciences. However, extensive research and reading in the history of political science and sociology does not suggest that the process of development in those fields differed in anything but detail except that the latter disciplines took somewhat longer to professionalize. I have not attempted to apply the viewpoint argued here to psychology and anthropology since neither of these disciplines took the form of a social science—i.e., a focus on the behavior of men in society—in the 19th-century United States.

6 Michael J. L. O'Connor, *Origins of Academic Economics in the United States* (New York 1944); Edwin R. A. Seligman, "The Early Teaching of Economics in the United States," in *Economic Essays: Contributed in Honor of John Bates Clark*, ed. J. H. Hollander (New York 1927), 283–320; Joseph Dorfman, *The Economic Mind in American Civilization, 1606–1865, Volume Two* (New York 1946), chs. xxv and ff; Anna Haddow, *Political Science in American Colleges and Universities, 1636–1900* (New York 1939); Gladys Bryson, "The Emergence of the Social Sciences from Moral Philosophy," *International J. of Ethics* 42 (April 1932), 304–23, and "The Comparable Interests of the Old Moral Philosophy and the Modern Social Science," *Social Forces* 11 (October 1932), 19–27; Wilson Smith, *Professors & Public Ethics: Studies of Northern Moral Philosophers before the Civil War* (Ithaca, N.Y. 1956).

7 Robert L. Church, "The Development of the Social Sciences as Academic Disciplines at Harvard University, 1869–1900," Ph.D. diss., Harvard Univ. (1965), chs. 1–4; Walter P. Rogers, *Andrew D. White and the Modern University* (Ithaca, N.Y. 1942); R. Gordon Hoxie *et al.*, *The History of the Faculty of Political Science, Columbia University* (New York 1955); Hugh Hawkins, *Pioneer: A History of the Johns Hopkins University, 1874–1889* (Ithaca, N.Y. 1960), ch. x (at Hopkins the difference in the rate of development between the social sciences and the hard sciences and the humanistic "sciences" is most clear); John B. Parrish, "Rise of Economics as an Academic Discipline: The Formative Years to 1900," *The Southern Economic J.* 34 (July 1967), 1–15. The disciplines subsumed under the term "social science" in the late 19th century were history, political science, and political economy. Sociology had yet to be formally introduced; psychology remained a part of philosophy, and anthropology essentially a part of archaeology.

8 Hofstadter, *Anti-Intellectualism*, ch. VII; Geoffrey Blodgett, *The Gentle Reformers: Massachusetts Democrats in the Cleveland Era* (Cambridge, Mass. 1966), and John G. Sproat, *"The Best Men": Liberal Reformers in the Gilded Age* (New York 1968), portray this group of men most insightfully. The general matter in the paragraphs that follow relies on these general works, on my reading of numerous biographies and autobiographies of these men, and on my reading of several collections of their correspondence—especially the Edwin Lawrence Godkin Papers and the Charles Eliot Norton Papers, Houghton Library, Harvard University.

9 Charles Eliot Norton, "The Poverty of England," *North Am. Rev.*, 109 (July 1869), 153–54. On Norton see Kermit Vanderbilt, *Charles Eliot Norton: Apostle of Culture in a Democracy* (Cambridge, Mass. 1959), esp. 75–100.

10 On the founding of the *Nation*, see William M. Armstrong, "The Freedmen's Movement and the Founding of the *Nation*," *JAH* 53 (March 1967), 708–26, and the works cited therein.

11 George Winston Smith, "Broadsides for Freedom: Civil War Propaganda in New England," *NEQ* 21 (September 1948), 291–312; Frank Freidel, "The [New York] Loyal Publication Society: A Pro-Union Propaganda Agency," *Mississippi Valley Hist. Rev.* 26 (December 1939), 359–76; Fred Bunyan Joyner, *David Ames Wells: Champion of Free Trade* (Cedar Rapids, Ia. 1939), ch. IX, esp. 147–50; Irwin Unger, *The Greenback Era: A Social and Political History of American Finance, 1865–1879* (Princeton, N.J. 1964), 136–42.

12 Political independence was not, of course, confined to social scientists on college campuses—leading academics in all fields, many students, and a large number of college and university presidents also joined the movement.

13 On history and political science, see John Higham, *History* (Englewood Cliffs, N.J. 1965), pt. II, ch. 1, and pt. III, chs. 1–2; Edward N. Saveth, *American Historians and European Immigrants, 1875–1925* (New York 1948); on political economy, see Sidney Fine, *Laissez Faire and the General-Welfare State: A Study of Conflict in American Thought, 1865–1901* (Ann Arbor, Mich. 1956), chs. II–III; Joseph Dorfman, *The Economic Mind in American Civilization, Volume Three, 1865–1918* (New York 1949), ch. III.

14 For a detailed discussion of these appointments, see Church, "Development of the Social Sciences," ch. I. President White of Cornell offered social science positions at the same period to Smith, Godkin, and Fiske (Smith accepted). Biographical information on the five candidates is found in Frank William Taussig, "Introduction" to Charles Franklin Dunbar, *Economic Essays*, ed. O.M.W. Sprague (New York 1904), vii–xvii; Elizabeth Wallace, *Goldwin Smith: Victorian Liberal* (Toronto 1957); Sidney Lee in *DNB*, Suppl. 1901–11, s.v. Smith, Goldwin; Rollo Ogden, *Life and Letters of Edwin Lawrence Godkin* (New York 1907); Charles William Eliot to Godkin, 18 July, 23 July, and 27 August 1870, Godkin Papers; Godkin to Eliot, 6 August, 25 August, and 29 August 1870, Charles William Eliot Papers, Harvard Univ. Archives, Harvard Univ.; Ernest Samuels, *The Young Henry Adams* (Cambridge, Mass. 1948); Milton Berman, *John Fiske: The Evolution of a Popularizer* (Cambridge, Mass. 1961); and John Edward Higgins, "The Young John Fiske: 1842–1874," Ph.D. diss., Harvard Univ. (1960). Many have assumed that because Adams set out for Germany in 1858 "to become a scholar," he was prepared to assume a scholarly post in the United States upon his return from Europe. But his German training amounted to but a few, poorly understood lectures. George McKee Elsey, "The First Education of Henry Adams," *NEQ* 14 (December 1941), 684; Samuels, *The Young Henry Adams*, 56.

15 Godkin to Charles Eliot Norton, 28 July 1870 in Ogden, *Godkin*, II, 62 [I have been unable to locate the original letter]; Adams to Wells, 25 October 1870 in John Eliot Alden, "Henry Adams as Editor: A Group of Unpublished Letters Written to David A. Wells," *NEQ* II (March 1938), 148.

16 The independents' increasing disillusion and mounting fear is evident in reading through the editions of the *Nation* in the 1870s. See also the sources listed in n. 8 for their thought in these years.

17 On the German historical school and its influence in the United States, see Jurgen Herbst, *The German Historical School in American Scholarship: A Study in the Transfer of Culture* (Ithaca, N.Y. 1965), chs. 6–8; Dorfman, *Economic Mind*, III, 87–98, 160–74; Dorfman, "The Role of the German Historical School in American Economic Thought," *Am. Economic Rev.: Papers & Proc.* 45 (May

1955), 17–28; Daniel M. Fox, *The Discovery of Abundance: Simon N. Patten and the Transformation of Social Theory* (Ithaca, N.Y. 1967), 22–24; Jack C. Myles, "German Historicism and American Economics," Ph.D. diss., Princeton Univ. (1956); Joseph A. Schumpeter, *History of Economic Analysis* (New York 1954), pt. IV, ch. 4. On the best men's reaction to the new school, see Sproat, "*The Best Men*," 155–57.

18 Sproat, 19.

19 Laughlin to Henry Villard 17 May 1890, Henry Villard Papers, Houghton Lib., Harvard Univ.; Laughlin, "The Study of Political Economy in the United States," *J. of Political Economy* 1 (December 1892), 1–6; Laughlin, *The Study of Political Economy: Hints to Students and Teachers* (New York 1885), 44–49. All biographical information on Laughlin in this essay comes from Alfred Bornemann, *J. Laurence Laughlin: Chapters in the Career of an Economist* (Washington, D.C. 1940), unless otherwise noted. Dorfman, *Economic Mind*, III, 274, quotes Laughlin to the effect that he believed his devotion to practical questions had prevented him from making theoretical contributions of "sufficient value to recall." Laughlin was not the only conservative economist of the late 19th and early 20th century interested in mass education. C. J. Bullock of Harvard (1869–1941) and Irving Fisher of Yale (1867–1947) fit the same mold. Dorfman, *Economic Mind*, III, 239, 371.

20 Laughlin, *The Federal Reserve Act: Its Origins and Problems* (New York 1933), 3. The book, made up of Laughlin's newspaper articles of 1895, was *Facts About Money: Including the Debate with W. H. Harvey* ("*Coin*") (Chicago 1895). Laughlin appears in Harvey's *Coin's Financial School* (1894) as the interests' financial apologist whose arguments Coin demolishes. See *Coin's Financial School*, ed. Richard Hofstadter (Cambridge, Mass. 1963), 160–61, 174–75, 185, 190.

21 W. C. Mitchell, "J. Laurence Laughlin" [rev. of Alfred Bornemann, *J. Laurence Laughlin: Chapters in the Career of an Economist* (Washington 1940)], *J. of Political Economy*, 49 (December 1941), 879–80.

22 Bornemann, *Laughlin*, 49–53; Laughlin, *Federal Reserve Act*, chs. I–IV [quotations from 70, 90].

23 Laughlin, *Federal Reserve Act*, 43–49, 53–61, 63–64, 82–84, 99, 104–37, 184–85, claimed that he greatly influenced the shape of the Act but that his role could not be publicly acknowledged because of political pressures. Carter Glass, *An Adventure in Constructive Finance* (Garden City, N.Y. 1927), and H. Parker Willis, in his review of Laughlin's *Federal Reserve Act, Columbia Law Rev.* 23 (1933), 1281–85, and in a letter to Mitchell, 8 March 1934, W. C. Mitchell Papers, Special Collections, Columbia University Library, emphatically disagree with Laughlin's assessment. Willis advised the committee which drafted the Federal Reserve Act.

24 Biographical information in this paragraph comes from A. W. Coats's persuasive account, "Henry Carter Adams: A Case Study in the Emergence of the Social Sciences in the United States, 1850–1900," *J. of Am. Studies* 2 (October 1968), 177–97. The three quotations come from documents quoted in that article— H. C. Adams to his parents, 22 October 1877, 184; Adams to his parents, 29 October 1878, 186; Adams to Herbert Baxter Adams, 13 and 23 April 1883, 188. For a discussion of Adams' concerns as an economist, see ibid., 195; Dorfman, *Economic Mind*, III, 164–74. Another discussion of religious themes in late 19th century American economics is John Rutherford Everett, *Religion in Economics: A Study of John Bates Clark, Richard T. Ely, Simon N. Patten* (New York 1946).

25 Richard T. Ely, *Ground Under Our Feet: An Autobiography* (New York 1938), 34. Biographical information in this and the following paragraphs comes from ibid.

and Benjamin Rader, *The Academic Mind and Reform: The Influence of Richard T. Ely in American Life* (Lexington, Ky. 1966).

26 Ely, *Ground*, 71–72.

27 Ibid., 72–73; Ely is summarizing *Social Aspects of Christianity and Other Essays*, new and enl. ed. (New York 1889), 147–48, but although he indicates that he is quoting directly from it, he is not.

28 Ely, *Ground*, 81.

29 On the formation of the American Economic Association, see Ely, "Report of the Organization of the American Economic Association," *Publications of the Am. Economic Ass.* 1 (March 1886), 5–32 [the quotation comes from p. 15]; Ely, "The American Economic Association: With Special Reference to Its Origin and Early Development: An Historical Sketch," ibid., 3d ser., II (April 1910), 47–92; Ely, *Ground*, ch. IV; A. W. Coats, "The First Two Decades of the American Economic Association," *Am. Economic Rev.* 50 (September 1960), 555–74; Dorfman, *Economic Mind*, III, ch. IX; Fine, *Laissez Faire and the General-Welfare State*, ch. VII; Fox, *Discovery of Abundance*, 33–43; Rader, *Academic Mind and Reform*, 33–40.

30 On the historical economists, see, besides the sources listed in n. 17, the discussion of W. J. Ashley in Robert L. Church, "The Economists Study Society: Sociology at Harvard, 1891–1902," in Church *et al.*, *Social Sciences at Harvard, 1860–1920: From Inculcation to the Open Mind* (Cambridge, Mass. 1965), 61–78.

31 Mary O. Furner, "Advocacy and Objectivity: The Professionalization of Social Science, 1865–1905," Ph.D. diss., Northwestern Univ. (1972), ch. V, esp. 120–21, makes this point for a somewhat different purpose in her illuminating discussion of methodological and ideological controversies among academic economists in the 1880s. I learned a great deal on this point, and on all others relating to the professionalization of academic economics, from a draft of her dissertation which I had the good fortune to read while working on this paper. This valuable study won the Frederick Jackson Turner Prize of the Organization of American Historians in 1973 and is scheduled for publication by the University Press of Kentucky early in 1974. See also, e.g., Taussig to Charles W. Eliot, 17 May 1901, Eliot Papers, and Taussig's sentiments described in Furner, "Advocacy and Objectivity," 257.

32 Furner, "Advocacy and Objectivity," points out the relation between professionalization and a desire to protect academic freedom throughout—indeed, I believe she emphasizes too much the defensive motives behind professionalization. On the academic freedom cases, see, besides Furner, Richard Hofstadter and Walter P. Metzger, *The Development of Academic Freedom in the United States* (New York 1955), ch. IX; Veysey, *Emergence of the American University*, ch. 7; Elizabeth Donnan, "A Nineteenth-Century Academic Cause Célèbre," *NEQ* 25 (March 1952), 23–46. While economists of almost all shades of opinion flocked to Ely's defense in 1886 and 1887, several wrote privately that Ely brought much of the trouble on himself by concentrating on popular education rather than on scholarly work. See Coats, "First Two Decades," 560, n. 9.

33 The most accurate account of the changes in the leadership of the American Economic Association is found in Furner, "Advocacy and Objectivity," ch. VI; see esp. 135–36 for revealing quotations from Mayo-Smith and Dunbar in letters to H. C. Adams, dated 10 June and 1 July 1887. For additional insight into the shift in power and the motives behind it, see Rader, *Academic Mind and Reform*, 117–22; Joseph Dorfman, ed., "The Seligman Correspondence, I and II," *Political Science Quart.*, 56 (March and June 1941), 107–24, 270–86. In one of his last acts as secretary of the association, Ely scheduled the annual meeting

at Chautauqua, much to the consternation of many other economists who wanted to sever their relation with popular education and reform. The resulting furor attested to the changing self-concept among economists, see Furner, "Advocacy and Objectivity," 140–42, and Coats, "First Two Decades," 565, ns. 18–20.

34 Coats, "First Two Decades," 562 and n. 12; A. W. Coats, "The Political Economy Club: A Neglected Episode in American Economic Thought," *Am. Economic Rev.* 51 (September 1961), 624–37.

35 Taussig to Walter F. Willcox, c. 13 May 1899, Taussig to Frank A. Fetter, 3 December 1904, H. C. Adams to Seligman, 14 May 1902, Fisher to Seligman, 20 February 1902, all in the Am. Economic Ass. Papers, Special Collections, Northwestern Univ.; Coats, "First Two Decades," 571–72; A. W. Coats, "The American Economic Association: 1904–1929," *Am. Economic Rev.* 54 (June 1964), 263–38.

36 Dorfman, *Economic Mind*, III, 237–41.

37 For a typical critical view of the historical school, see Frank William Taussig, "The Present Position of the Doctrine of Free Trade" [Presidential Address to the Am. Economic Ass. 1904], *Publications of the Am. Economic Ass.*, 3d ser., 6 (February 1905), 56–58.

38 Dunbar, "The Reaction in Political Economy," *Quart. J. of Economics* 1 (October 1886), 7; Dunbar, "The Academic Study of Political Economy," ibid., 5 (July 1891), 409; Hutchison, *"Positive" Economics and Policy Objectives*, 27–41.

39 See Mitchell to John Maurice Clark, 9 August 1928, an autobiographical letter reprinted in Lucy Sprague Mitchell, "A Personal Sketch," in Arthur F. Burns, ed. *Wesley Clair Mitchell: The Economic Scientist* (New York 1952), 96–98; Mitchell to Lucy Sprague, 18 October 1911, another autobiographical letter reprinted in ibid., 66–67; Arthur Burns, "Introductory Sketch," ibid., 27 and passim; Frederick C. Mills, "Professional Sketch," ibid., 121–23; Dorfman, "Professional Sketch," ibid., 126–34; Taussig, "Present Position of the Doctrine of Free Trade," 63–65 [which contains the quotation]; Taussig, "Minimum Wages for Women," *Quart. J. of Economics*, 30 (May 1916), 411–12; Dorfman, *Economics Mind in American Civilization, 1918–1933, Volume Four* (New York 1959), 236–47, esp. 238 [Taussig], 360–77, esp. 360–64 [Mitchell].

40 One exception was the National Tax Association, a group of businessmen, academics, and government officials who sought tax reform. Seligman was its president from 1912 to 1915; C. J. Bullock was one of its most ardent supporters and members in the late teens and the 1920s. See the many letters in the Bullock Papers, Harvard Univ. Archives, Harvard Univ.

41 A. Hunter Dupree, *Science in the Federal Government: A History of Policies and Activities to 1940* (Cambridge, Mass. 1957), chs. VIII–XV. Some economists had served as experts before 1890, but they had done so largely on an informal basis and in a manner indistinguishable from that of noneconomists. Nonacademics like Wells and Edward Atkinson had played a larger role as economic "experts" than did the academics of the pre-1890 era (Fine, *Laissez Faire and the General-Welfare State*, 49–51); Carroll D. Wright was the 19th century's most prominent expert and he was not an academic economist at all (except in his last years after he had established his reputation as an expert); his preparation was in Law and politics. See James Leiby, *Carroll Wright and Labor Reform: The Origin of Labor Statistics* (Cambridge, Mass. 1960).

On the expert in general see Hofstadter, *Anti-Intellectualism*, ch. 8; Wiebe, *Search for Order*, chs. 5–7; Sidney Kaplan, "Social Engineers as Saviors: Effects of World War I on Some American Liberals," *JHI*, 17 (June 1956), 347–69; Charles Forcey, *The Crossroads of Liberalism: Croly, Weyl, Lippmann, and the*

Progressive Era, 1908–1925 (New York 1961); Morton White, *Social Thought in America: The Revolt against Formalism*, new ed. (Boston 1957); Samuel Haber, *Efficiency and Uplift: Scientific Management in the Progressive Era, 1890–1920* (Chicago 1964); Jay M. Gould, *The Technical Elite* (New York 1966), ch. III; Barry D. Karl, "Presidential Planning and Social Science Research: Mr. Hoover's Experts," *Perspectives in American History*, III (1969), 345–409; Leonard White, *Trends in Public Administration* (New York 1933), ch. XIX; James Weinstein, *The Corporate Ideal in the Liberal State, 1900–1918* (Boston 1968), esp. 189–213.

42 By the same token it might be argued further that the reliance on science served the interests of the middle and upper classes. Science was supposed to represent disinterest, neutrality, what was best for all, but the middle and upper classes were the ones that found rationalism and neutrality most congenial to their values and style of thinking. Moreover, the fact that social scientists came overwhelmingly from the middle and upper strata of the society assured those strata of representation and a powerful voice were science to be applied in the process of government. The upper and middling strata of America supported science in government to some degree, I believe, to counter the growing threats to their power coming from organized labor and ethnic bloc voting on the one hand and from the "malefactors of great wealth" on the other.

43 There is no study of the economic "expert" in government. White, *Recent Trends in Public Administration*, 271–72, states that the federal government employed 25 "economic and political science" experts in 1896 (all statisticians) and 848 in the period 1928–31. The trend—and the wide variety of kinds of employment—is clear in reading obituaries and biographies of economists prominent in the early part of the 20th century.

44 On the Wisconsin Idea, see Charles McCarthy, *The Wisconsin Idea* (New York 1912); Rader, *The Academic Mind and Reform*, 172–81; John R. Commons, *Myself: The Autobiography of John R. Commons* (New York 1934), ch. v.

45 Commons, *Myself*, 100–107, 153–65.

46 B. H. Beckhart in *DAB*, suppl. 2, s.v. "Willis, Henry Parker"; Dorfman, *Economic Mind*, IV, 314–22.

47 Joseph Frederick Kenkel, "The Tariff Commission Movement: The Search for a Nonpartisan Solution of the Tariff Question," Ph.D. diss., Univ. of Maryland (1962); Taussig to David F. Houston (Secretary of Agriculture in Wilson's cabinet), 17 December 1915, Woodrow Wilson Papers, Libr., of Congress, enclosing draft to Taussig's "The Proposal for a Tariff Commission," *North Am. Rev.*, 203 (February 1916), 194–204. Portions of Taussig's draft were incorporated into the Tariff Commission Bill. Taussig also advised the American Commission to Negotiate Peace on matters of international trade and played a part in drafting the third of the Fourteen Points. He served on the Price Fixing Committee of the War Industries Board and took part in Wilson's Second Industrial Conference. Before the World War he had served the Commonwealth of Massachusetts as an expert on taxation.

48 Taussig, "Proposal for a Tariff Commission," 194–95. We may note that in this context Taussig is more reticent than usual about the applicability of theory in judging among policy alternatives although we must also note carefully his use of "at once" twice in the above passage.

49 Ibid., 197.

50 Ibid., 201–2, and see material on 12, 18 of the draft in the Library of Congress which does not appear in the published article.

51 Ibid., 202–3.

52 Ibid., 204.
53 "Charter" quoted in [Wesley Clair Mitchell], *Retrospect and Prospect, 1920–1936*, National Bureau of Economic Research (New York 1936), 6. On the founding of the bureau, see Herbert Heaton, *A Scholar in Action—Edwin F. Gay* (Cambridge, Mass. 1952), 196–203; Burns, "Introductory Sketch," 30–35; L. S. Mitchell, "Personal Sketch," 101–3.
54 Heaton, *Gay*, passim. On the early intentions of the Harvard Business School, see the draft report, "School of Business and Public Service," in Taussig's hand in Business School Archives, Baker Library, Harvard University, undated (probably December 1906); Wallace B. Donham and Esty Foster, "The Graduate School of Business Administration, 1908–1929," in *The Development of Harvard University Since the Inauguration of President Eliot, 1869–1929*, ed. Samuel Eliot Morison (Cambridge, Mass. 1930), 533–48.
55 Mitchell to Lucy Sprague, 18 October 1911, loc. cit., 66–67. See also Mitchell, "Statistics and Government," *Publications of the Am. Statistical Ass.*, 16 (March 1919), 223–35; Dorfman, *Economic Mind*, iv, 360–66, 375–76.
56 Dorfman, "Professional Sketch," 134–36. Mitchell served as chief of the Price Section of the First World War's War Industries Board, he chaired President Hoover's Research Committee on Social Trends, he served on the National Planning Board of the Federal Emergency Administration of Public Works during the thirties, and later as chairman of the Technical Committee which was attached to the President's Committee on the Cost of Living to settle some problems involving index numbers so that war production would not be hampered. On the Committee on Recent Social Trends, see Karl, "Presidential Planning and Social Science Research."
57 Mitchell to Lucy Sprague, 8 October 1911, loc. cit., 66–67; Heaton, *Gay*, 201. The Bureau researched *Business Cycles and Unemployment* (1923) for President Harding's Conference on Unemployment; for the Committee on Recent Economic Changes it published *Recent Economic Changes*, 2 vols. (1929), *The Planning and Control of Public Works* (1930), *Economic Tendencies in the United States* (1932), *Industrial Profits in the United States* (1934), and *Strategic Factors in Business Cycles* (1934). It published *International Migrations* (1929, 1931) for the Social Science Research Council and International Labour Office; the Carnegie Corporation requested *Trends in Philanthropy* (1928), the Association of Community Chests and Councils, *Corporate Contributions to Organized Community Welfare Services* (1930), and the National Planning Board, *Public Works in Prosperity and Depression* (1935). See [Mitchell], *Retrospect and Prospect*, 11–12.
58 Ibid., 22.
59 Barry D. Karl, "The Power of Intellect and the Politics of Ideas," *Daedalus* 97 (Summer 1968), 1006–7, makes a somewhat similar point about the shift in the academics' focus as the control of research money and professional recognition shifted from the individual university and its president to the national research bodies.
60 Commons, *Myself*, 88; Weinstein, *Corporate Ideal in the Liberal State*, 189–90.

113

DONNISHNESS

Sheldon Rothblatt

Source: S. Rothblatt, *The Revolution of the Dons: Cambridge and Society in Victorian England*, London: Faber and Faber, 1968, reprinted Cambridge: Cambridge University Press, 1981, pp. 181–208.

1

'Cambridge,' complained Seeley in 1867, 'is like a country invaded by the Sphinx. To answer the monster's conundrums has become the one absorbing occupation.'[1] The questions of the sphinx dealt with life, those of the tripos with easily-tested knowledge, but it is perverse to reproach Seeley for a poor simile. The tripos certainly kept honours students extremely busy, for success was generously rewarded. Well before mid-century a high finish in the tripos guaranteed a college fellowship; and until late in the nineteenth century a first class honours degree was still the road to post graduate academic distinction in all the colleges except Trinity. Fellowships were a reward for undergraduate industry rather than a recognition of teaching ability or future scholarship.

The tripos was a written comprehensive examination which originated in the eighteenth century. Originally an examination in mathematics (arithmetic, geometry, algebra, trigonometry, mechanics, optics, astronomy and Newton's *Principia*), it was considered to be the oldest and most famous written competitive examination in England. In 1824 a tripos was established in classics, but mathematics enjoyed a unique prestige for another thirty-three years. Until 1857 no honours candidates except noblemen were permitted to sit the classical tripos without having first taken the mathematical honours examination. But while mathematics dominated university examinations, classics were important in college competitions, especially at King's. Until 1851 scholars of King's proceeded directly to a degree without taking university examinations. As a result – and because Eton resisted the introduction of mathematics until 1840 – mathematics was virtually unknown in King's.

The tripos examinations stressed method – technique, precision, logic and rigour – and method was transferable: the man who understood the principles of argument and knew how to derive generalizations from a body of factual material could subsequently teach himself any subject. If necessary, the tripos could also be defended as preparation for professional life. Mathematics and classics were of obvious value to the schoolmaster; logic and argument were the tools of the lawyer and politician; generalization enabled the clergyman to read God's will; scientific method was essential to the physician.

The tripos was held to be scientific in ideals, content, and in its method of determining ability. Unlike Oxford, Cambridge ranked its honours men on a strict order of merit, from the senior wrangler or senior classic down. This intensified the competition for honours and made many believe that the tripos system of marking was a scrupulously objective method of selection. As Francis Galton wrote in 1869, 'The fairness and thoroughness of Cambridge examinations have never had a breath of suspicion cast upon them.'[2] The order of merit had faults, however, that did not go unrecognized. Ranking could only be accurate within each year's grouping, making it difficult to compare men of different years who might be competing for the same college fellowship. It also reinforced the character of the tripos as an examination on set knowledge; textbooks were especially compiled to offer the student unimaginative lessons to be gotten up quickly by rote. Nowhere was there a suggestion of original synthesis, analysis or a developing frontier of knowledge.

The nature of the tripos made it a useful device for controlling students. Success in the examinations required considerable advance preparation and cramming, as well as speed and stamina during the long hours of the examination week. The competition was strenuous, and bets were laid in advance as to the probable winners. 'True to their sporting instincts the English had contrived to turn even the university examinations into an athletic contest.'[3] If a student were conscientious, if he needed the academic recognition and financial reward that the tripos could bestow, if he crammed to the point of injuring his health – particularly in his last year – he would have little time for mischief.

The university of course did not rely solely on the tripos to 'guard the inexperienced against the temptations of youth and the dangers of wasteful extravagance.'[4] The colleges and university had established a number of purely disciplinary measures and institutions: walls, gates and ditches surrounding the colleges were meant to restrict student mobility and prevent townsmen from disturbing the college peace. Compulsory chapel and college lectures, dinners in hall and college examinations were given a disciplinary purpose; and a variety of punishments – admonitions, rustication, expulsion, prohibitions and literary impositions – were customarily meted out for violations. College deans and chaplains, retaining their religious functions, were also made responsible for student conduct, as was the tutor, who ceased to be primarily a teacher.

Responsibility for overseeing the activities of students away from the colleges belonged to the university. Proctors flanked by subordinates called 'bulldogs' policed the streets in order to prevent town and gown conflicts and to enforce regulations regarding academic dress – the latter especially useful in detecting violators. The university also established curfews, licensed boarding and lodging houses, and required prior notification of all dinner and supper parties given in lodgings or in the town. Shopkeepers – particularly wine merchants – were licensed to trade with students; and tutors were given the authority to review student accounts. All bills in fact – college, university and tradesmen's – were first received by college tutors.

Regulations governing student conduct had been framed in a period when undergraduates were of secondary school age; but by 1850 or 1860 entering freshmen were eighteen or nineteen – a year or two older than earlier in the century. Customary restraints no longer applied; but many of the older dons continued to act as if the majority of undergraduates were schoolboys and bravely tried to implement the existing regulations. Discipline was undermined, however, by jurisdictional disputes between the university and its constituent colleges; college loyalty frequently conflicted with university authority. By mid-century it was still customary for the proctors to report undergraduates suspected of sexual offences to the colleges rather than, as an ancient statute directed, to the Vice-Chancellor's Court; and college justice tended to be more lenient. A statute of 1858 attempted to restore serious offences to the Vice-Chancellor's Court. But even the Vice-Chancellor – himself the head of a college – was reluctant to act against college interests.

University authority was further hampered by disputes with the town corporation. The university's far-reaching regulation of local tradesmen, its assumption of police power within the town, its high-handed treatment of prostitutes and the inquisitorial nature of its examination of prisoners in the university prison – so much at variance with common law – aroused the suspicion and hostility of borough officials. Undergraduates on a spree benefited from the resentment.

Poll or pass men, who comprised the majority of undergraduates in the university, were the principal beneficiaries of relaxed university discipline. They were usually addressed as idle and dissolute, but some of the recrimination was unjust. There were good reasons for avoiding the honours examination, especially before 1851. There were only two honours subjects and both were highly specialized and technical, requiring schoolboy cramming which could impair health. Many of the poll men were secure of the future and saw no reason to abandon three years of leisure and recreation for the rigours of a highly competitive examination. Sons of noblemen and gentry, as well as sons from other wealthy families, frequently adopted this attitude – even those of considerable intellectual ability. The largest proportion of poll men intended to take holy orders and aspired to nothing more than a country rectory. Ambitious students preparing for ecclesiastical careers invariably read for honours. The great bishops and public school headmasters of the nineteenth century took honours degrees.

When the poll degree first came under serious scrutiny in the early 1860's, exhausting argument and discussion resulted in two major reforms. A third or 'special' examination in either theology, philosophy, history, political economy, natural science and engineering (mechanical science) was added as a final degree requirement. In addition, the examination schedule itself was tightened to enable poll men to graduate about six months before honours men, since 'it had long been objected that the Cambridge course for this degree consumed more time than could be spared by young men who were designed for professions, and who would have to spend some further time on education elsewhere to prepare them for their special duties.'[5] This explanation was partly euphemistic, for throughout the century many medical students at Cambridge took the special examination in natural science mainly because they wished to enjoy a period of leisure before commencing a clinical routine in the London hospitals. Scientists and teachers like Michael Foster and Clifford Allbutt, anxious to raise the standards of the Cambridge Medical School, vainly tried to turn all the medical students to the natural sciences tripos. By 1885 students reading for pass degrees deserved much of the criticism directed at them. The establishment of new triposes in philosophy, biological science, theology, law, history and Semitic and Indian languages, the reform of classics and mathematics and the introduction of two-part triposes, enabling a student to read more than one subject, removed many of the traditional objections to the honours degree, a fact generally recognized when for the first time in the history of Cambridge, honours degrees outnumbered pass degrees.[6]

Dons and royal commissioners, despite their occasional discomfort about poll men, were reluctant to abolish the pass degree because they feared that inevitably the standard of the honours degree would be lowered. They did not believe that the quality and intellectual distinction of the tripos could be maintained if the poorest students were required to take honours degrees. There were also more positive reasons for retaining the pass degree. Some students did not benefit from early specialization. Their interests and abilities developed late, and the pass degree at least gave them a chance to explore more subjects, to read widely and generally. If they failed to make use of this comparative leisure and latitude, they had only themselves to blame.

In several ways the poll man was an asset and could be used to further some of the important educational reforms of the nineteenth century. Since he often had a family or other guaranteed position awaiting him upon graduation, the colleges were not obliged to assist him in finding employment, and tutors could concentrate on the honours students whom they were anxious to help. Furthermore, since the poll men were invariably pensioners, their tuition fees and miscellaneous college expenditures could be used to subsidize the more expensive education of honours students, especially those who had entered as sizars or possessed limited means. In general the colleges were reluctant to make poor students pay the increased lecture and tuition fees necessitated by the mid-Victorian teaching reforms. The poll man may have been especially useful during the agrarian depression when most college incomes declined and dons were doubly anxious to meet scholarship and exhibition payments. How important a subsidy of scholars and sizars the fees of poll men were is difficult to determine from college accounts, but there are indications the subsidy was valuable. When the cost of educating students rose sharply during the inflationary period following the first world war, a nearly desperate Trinity Hall threatened to revert to a policy of admitting the 'idle rich'.[7]

Despite, however, objections to the tripos as narrow and cramped and despite the fact that the poll men could be used to further some of the reforms begun in the late 1850's, the existence of the poll degree was a continuous embarrassment to the Victorian dons, a standing refutation of their claim that Cambridge was a highly competitive society open to talent from all social classes and groups.

Conspicuous among the idle poll men of the first half of the nineteenth century were the young aristocratic bravos who gambled on horses in nearby Newmarket, frequented disorderly houses, gladly returned or provoked the insults of town bargees and turned athletic contests into wild brawls.[8] Their pranks came close to imperilling the lives of dons and other students. An American at Trinity in the 1840's did not believe that young English aristocrats deserved to be called gentlemen. Relating a disgraceful episode in the Union Debating Society in which two undergraduates assaulted one another, he wrote unctuously that 'English young gentlemen at a public meeting are more ungentlemanly than any *class* of our people (for a meeting of Irish or other foreigners in New York is not to be considered an American meeting), they never look upon the occasion in a serious light, but seem to consider it the most natural one for a lark.'[9] Albert Pell was one of the wealthy aristocratic students of the 1840's who soon saw that he 'might be as idle and unstudious as [he] chose.' He left an instructive account of how he and other privileged and raffish undergraduates passed their time:

'In the year that I entered Trinity one of the proctors . . . rendered himself very unpopular from his diligence and severity. He was feared and disliked. He was attended in his patrols by a wonderfully active little "bulldog", nimble and long-winded as a hare. He chased a little friend of mine twice or three times round Rose Crescent, Market Place, and Trinity Street, when, on the very point of making his capture, he slipped and broke his leg, poor fellow! His master had become so very unpopular and disagreeable that it was decided he must be punished by a dip in the river. Mr. Smith, however, was on his guard, and frustrated the attempt by retreating to his college stronghold, the outer gate of which was promptly closed by the porter. The Trinity men by this time had got together in the street, and using a builder's plank as a battering-ram, smashed the door, only to find a strong chain stretched across the doorway inside, under which the assaulters would have to stoop in entering. As on the threshold we saw a Caius man with poker uplifted on guard, we all hesitated. Meanwhile the Trinity dons had been sent for – Peacock, Sedgwick, and Whewell. On their coming up, a townsman ventured the attempt of thrusting Whewell aside, whereupon that wondrous example of stature and wisdom took the rapscallion by the coat-collar into an angle of the church opposite and pummelled him unmercifully – a warning to us undergraduates that we had better take ourselves off, which we did. Mr. Smith had so impressed me by the exercise of his University authority, that long afterwards, on meeting him unexpectedly in Regent Street in the evening, I bolted for a moment down a convenient passage.'[10]

In truth the majority of dons had no heart for such disagreeable and dangerous disciplinary assignments and vacillated between permissiveness and a stern paternalism. When wearied by the attempt to enforce a uniform standard of conduct, they turned their attention away to the amusements of a bachelor society. The authority of the university, they said, had not been compromised. Nowhere among the students were there signs of determined insubordination, nowhere indications that students would rise *en masse*, challenge the authorities and force the closing of the university as happened in Russia in the early 1850's. Cambridge undergraduates were not renegade gentry or alienated continental intellectuals. They were pillars of the establishment; two-thirds of them came from clerical and landed families, and the misconduct of a few exuberant poll men could not be regarded as anything more serious than the customary irregularities expected from the youth of the governing classes.

In the late 1850's and early 1860's, however, some tutors took a different view of the polloi. Regarding idleness and wanton behaviour as inappropriate to a university environment, no matter what the social background of students, they made a positive effort to gain the respect and affection of undergraduates who were usually ignored, except when they were deliberately provocative. Leslie Stephen, a tutor of Trinity Hall, and, it has been said, the first of the muscular Christians, led the way by making sports, particularly rowing, activities recognized and supported by the college: 'The undergraduates saw that their tutor's heart was in the College and, what was more, in their personal pursuits. It was Stephen who presided at Bump Suppers and wrote the College Boating Song, and they noticed that his enthusiasm was as frenzied as their own when the boat went head of the river. "I shall never forget the joy with which he caught hold of my hand and shook it," said the stroke of the boat on that occasion. "He very nearly upset us all into the river, and, if I had not used some strong language, I believe he would have done so." Undergraduates could forget that he was a parson, for Stephen was ready to take the lead in every new enthusiasm.'[11]

The active participation of college fellows in student sports begins before the return of Maurice and Seeley to Cambridge but is part of the same change of attitude which led those thinkers to stress the importance of teaching. Ultimately the renewed interest in students may be traced to Dr. Arnold; but in Cambridge it may be said to begin with the appointment of the first Graham Commission in 1850. Dons began to respond to the external pressures on the university, to demands that Cambridge broaden its curriculum, remove its civil disabilities and lower its expenses in order to attract more students. Dons were beginning to see the implications of the liberal reforms of the second quarter of the nineteenth century and the rationalist attack on religious orthodoxy. If society was in confusion and values changing, then Cambridge could no longer rely on compulsory chapel, obsolete regulations or the tripos – the sphinx that always asked the same menacing questions – to provide the essential teaching of the university. A more positive and dynamic effort had to be made to reach the mind of the nation through its youth and potential leaders. Students had to be taught to understand themselves, and Cambridge had to give them standards by which to measure the aims of their time.

Leslie Stephen resigned his tutorship in 1862 and left for London two years later, well on his way to agnosticism and convinced that Cambridge did not care whether a good man came or went. Signs of a transformation in the university, however, were apparent at the time of his departure. Within the next decade a revolution occurred. Donnishness was in retreat.

2

In the middle of the nineteenth century there were two undergraduate conceptions of a don which passed under the heading of donnishness. Both emphasized the separation of dons from students. The first conception recalled the amiable neglect and indifference which were the characteristics of an isolated, ageing and idle bachelor community still allied in tastes and values to a hard-drinking and an athletic, county society. Gourmandizing, convivial wine parties and gambling were the typical activities of the amiable don. At best this don possessed a certain gracious demeanour and a talent for witty and pleasant conversation; at worst he was an irresponsible and abandoned man, such as Macaulay described in 1854 when he reminded Whewell of 'two reverend gentlemen who were high in college office when I was an undergraduate. One of them never opened his mouth without an oath, and the other had killed his man.'[12]

The agreeable don remained part of the literature of university stereotypes until at least the First World War. He could be found at undergraduate festivities, sharing their food and their card games; he was noted for his devotion to antiquarian history or eccentric hobbies; he was frequently an expert on college plate and the portraits in Hall; and he kept a close watch on the condition of the lawns and cobbles. Such dons were J. M. Image, a Trinity tutor in the 1880's remembered as 'an agreeable fellow of the old school'; John Cooper, a Trinity tutor in the 1850's – 'an amiable right-handed man, of no particular force' – and William Collings Mathison, another mid-century Trinity tutor, an accomplished musician and 'to those whom he liked, generous and kind; but . . . I do not gather that the junior members of Trinity suffered much when he married and retired to a college living in Norfolk.'[13] Such too was the Master of Trinity Hall in the 1850's, 'an ancient megatherium, who liked his bottle in the evening and asked only to be left in peace.'[14] Undergraduates soon learned there was little to be gained from the genial topers, accepted the situation and went their own way.

Throughout the nineteenth century donnishness mainly designated the distant and uncompromising don, known to all undergraduates as a vain pedant, a morose scholar, or an arrogant and humourless college authoritarian, old before his time. 'A drawback to the society of the place,' wrote Leslie Stephen, 'was the extraordinary rapidity with which the more permanent residents became superannuated in the eyes of their colleagues. A don of thirty was ten years older than a rising young barrister of forty.'[15] The crabbed and ageing don was expected to show neither friendliness nor sympathy. When instructing small classes his manner was generally formal, antiseptic and unenthusiastic. In his stiff and solemn posture of dignity he attempted to convey a suggestion of moral excellence; his function was not to excite the mind but to correct youthful irregularities and make productive human beings of rebelliously-inclined undergraduates, in which endeavour he was bound to be misunderstood. 'Talk not of an Old Don as an old dry stick who delights in Greek particles and mazy problems and long series,' protested 'Sapere Aude' of St. John's. 'You comprehend us not, our mission, our high and holy purposes,' to make young men 'perform the daily routine of their profession quietly in harness.'[16]

The stereotypes of the genial don and the pompous, priggish don are undergraduate conceptions of their teachers and as such not altogether reliable estimates of the motives and personalities of the collegiate fellows. There are in the complaints of the 1850's, '60's and '70's recognizable generational elements; and even in the late nineteenth century the epithet 'donnish' was being applied in the sense of the earlier period to dons who were neither stuffy nor wastrels. Certainly appreciations of the intelligence and kindness of many of the older fellows can be found in reminiscences to offset some of the more disparaging remarks about their learning and teaching. Because their scholarship was narrow, in the language of the time 'masculine', does not mean they eschewed intellectual problems or failed to take learning seriously.

Although some of the charges of donnishness were student misconceptions, erroneous interpretations of manner and behaviour, they are not totally unfounded. There were always pockets of serious scholars in Cambridge, but the number varied radically from college to college, and the majority of able and ambitious fellows did not stay long enough to provide any continuity in collegiate teaching or inspire needed reforms. College teaching was not considered a career or a profession, except for tutors; and as there were relatively few official teaching positions within the colleges, there was no reason for successful young fellows to remain. Those who did stay took holy orders, settled into a routine and waited for vacancies to occur in college livings. For every don respected by students, there were many more who rarely saw undergraduates – except perhaps in hall, chapel and in the courts – and gave no attention to their academic or personal problems.

Student complaints about donnishness are in part attributable to unrealized expectations. Earlier generations of undergraduates were certainly aware that Cambridge was not noted for the uniform excellence of its teaching or the inspired learning of the collegiate fellows; but, with some exceptions, undergraduates were content, like Macaulay, to wander at liberty over the college grounds, to rejoice in their freedom from close supervision, to study, or not to study, as they chose. This was clearly no longer the case by mid-century. The serious student of 1850 or 1860 needed dons more than his predecessors. One reason was that the pressure for success in the tripos had increased. Macaulay had 'gulfed' the mathematical tripos, failed to place, and yet he had been elected to a fellowship. This was not likely to occur in the 1860's.

But there was another reason why the undergraduate of the 1850's and 1860's needed the dons, and why therefore he expected more of them. The reading man of the mid-Victorian period might have been taught by the Arnoldians in some of the public or older grammar schools; and one effect of Dr. Arnold's influence was to increase the dependence of the serious student on the teacher by enhancing the role of teacher, by investing it with an awesome moral authority, at times even a mystique. For the force and brutality which governed the relations between masters and pupils in the older public schools, making them equals on the battlefield until might prevailed, Dr. Arnold substituted a relationship between teacher and student which depended on admiration and occasional hero-worship. This was why when a great Victorian master was found to have feet of clay, as happened at Harrow with Vaughan, the disclosure could be acutely distressing to the student.[17]

The young man, like Sidgwick, who drank deeply of Rugbeian ideals and values, came to Cambridge fully expecting the same kind of close and dedicated teaching, the same sense of communion between teacher and elect, the same kind of prophetic leadership he had experienced in the sixth form. His earnestness and seriousness sometimes rubbed off on bright undergraduates whose own schooling had not been so principled and who were more inclined to join the fashionable or sporting sets. The reading man of the mid-Victorian period needed a teacher who would take an interest in his studies, in his career and in his personal problems. No longer a schoolboy, and indeed one or two years older than his counterparts earlier in the century, he did not expect to find himself subject to petty and minute regulations or virtually ignored by his teachers. His expectations disappointed, his emotional and psychological needs unsatisfied, he had no alternative but to dismiss his seniors, sometimes indiscriminately, with the invidious epithet 'donnish', to fall back on his own resources, or, as happened, to seek inspiration and companionship elsewhere.

The students of the 1850's who accused the fellows of donnishness became the new dons of the 1860's. They criticized their predecessors for confusing manner and knowledge, form and content. They found absurd the argument that Cambridge was a place of moral education because each college had a chapel, less absurd but equally unsatisfying the assertion that it was a place of intellectual education because it had a famous honours examination. They deplored the donnish practice of treating undergraduates as schoolboys, of stressing formal rules and regulations instead of seeking the loyalty of students and trying to capture their minds. In place of the 'old college system' with its antiquated routine and curious combination of formality and leniency, they proposed another idea or ideal of what a collegiate university should be, an ideal which was historical and new at one and the same time. The clearest statement of that ideal was made in 1850 by an Oxford don, Mark Pattison, the Subrector and Tutor of Lincoln College; but it exactly captures the discontents within Cambridge and expresses the mind of the new generation. Just before he became sour and cynical, engrossed with thoughts of his possible insanity, embittered by the improbable circumstances that deprived him of the headship of Lincoln and consequently no longer favourably disposed to the college idea – probably because he despaired of its realization – Pattison had a romantic moment in which he told the Royal Commission on Oxford that, 'The perfect idea of the Collegiate system proposed to take up the student from quite tender years, and conduct him through his life till death. A College was not divided into tutors and pupils, but like a Lacaedaemonian regiment . . . all were students alike, only differing in being at different stages of their progress. Hence their life was truly a life in common, with a common direction and occupation, and subject to one law. The seniors were at once the instructors and example of the juniors, who shared the same plain food, simple life, narrow economy, looking forward themselves to no other life. And in that mode then was obtained that which, then as now, constituted the truly invaluable element of the College system – the close action of the teacher on the pupil, of the matured character on the unformed, of the instructed on the learning mind, not indeed without a very beneficial reaction of the young on the aging man, an influence not unknown to the great and experienced men who originated and promoted Colleges. This insensible action of the teacher's character on the pupils' is the most valuable part of any education. . . . But it is contended that this influence is not now exerted by the body of Fellows on the Undergraduates. College life has ceased to be the life in common, even for the Fellows. . . . The relation between the student and the College official is, in general, as distant and technical as that between the officer and the private in our army. The young men associate with, and form one another's character mainly. There remains, however, a very powerful means of influence of the kind above described in the relation of the College tutor to his pupils, felt in some degree at present, and capable of still greater extension. But this is incident to his function as tutor, and is in no way dependent on the circumstance of the Undergraduate being accommodated within the walls. It might be favoured, certainly, by the pupil doing what he does not do now, living with the tutor. But it would exist exactly as it does now, let the pupil be lodged where he would. Indeed little as are the restraints and obligations which College discipline professes to impose on the student, the body of resident Fellows are too often an obstacle in the way of their enforcement. If there be any action of the character of the Corporation of the College on the student, its value must be entirely dependent on the *personnel* of that Corporation. It is to be feared that the moral and religious standard with which a well-disposed youth comes up from a pious home, would not be elevated by close and habitual intercourse with the Senior Common Room.'[18]

Pattison's sentimental, monastic reconstruction of the college idea contrasts markedly with the donnish notion of a college as a building of stone and mortar inhabited by starched clerics playing stock roles and instructing students with the aid of a uniform religious creed. For Pattison, the college was of little use if it survived in form only. The real college was more than walls and gates. It was a life in common, a set of common values, a human relationship, a Porch or Lyceum – exactly what the new generation of dons was saying.

As Pattison suggested, the tutor was especially culpable for the neglect of undergraduates, for as the main adviser to students and principal teaching officer, more was expected of him than of the average fellow. This is precisely what Leslie Stephen realized when taking off his clerical collar and gown – the symbols of established authority – he put on patched flannels to chase the boats along the towpath. In effect he was inviting every college tutor to remember his duties. At the same time, he was trying to determine what those duties were, for by 1860 the exact responsibilities were strangely unclear. Although the office of tutor was of considerable antiquity, originating in the sixteenth century,[19] it had developed informally and the exercise of tutorial functions had become very much an individual matter.

The tutor was appointed by the college head and in smaller colleges generally succeeded the master. The number of tutors varied according to the size of the college. In a small college there might be only one tutor, but in a large college like Trinity there were usually three tutors of equal status – although more was not inconceivable – each with a staff of assistant tutors. The tutor was usually responsible for admissions, for the assignment of rooms and lodgings, for advice on general expenses. He was also in charge of the college teaching programme and was authorized, but not obligated, to use the tuition fund to hire lecturers. Since the tuition fund, composed of student fees, was not part of college revenue or subject to review, and since student caution money was also deposited with the tutors, there was opportunity for peculation. Although caution money was returned when the student graduated, the tutor could invest the money and collect interest in the interim.[20] Instances could be recalled where tutors put off paying tradesmen's bills for which they had received money from their students in order to accrue the interest.[21] Some tutors may have made a personal use of the tuition fund, either investing the money or lending sums at interest to students for periods of several years. In 1874 the Cleveland Commission briskly reproved tutors who regarded the disposition of tutorial funds as a private matter.[22]

Where tutorial responsibility was least clear was in the exercise of those functions which related to the moral and physical welfare of students. The tutor was supposed to be a father to the student, and some tutors performed this function remarkably well. Gunson of Christ's was a famous tutor, George Peacock and James Lemprière Hammond of Trinity – a vivacious Channel Islander – were others. J. W. Clark claimed that Hammond 'made me';[23] and both Sidgwick and Henry Jackson, another famous reformer, relied heavily on Hammond's advice in the beginning of the reform period.[24] But although there were conscientious tutors in the first half of the nineteenth century, few undergraduates found the tutorial arrangements satisfactory. 'The Tutor is supposed to stand *in loco parentis*,' wrote Bristed, 'but having sometimes more than a hundred young men under him, he cannot discharge his duties in this respect very thoroughly, nor is it generally expected that he should.'[25] Bristed was referring to Trinity tutors, but there is no reason to believe that tutors in smaller colleges were generally more successful. Leslie Stephen's contention that Cambridge did not care whether a good man came or went was still valid. Sooner or later the best tutors left.

3

'I am convinced that the Tutor frequently has not sufficient knowledge of the pupil's intellectual habits and progress to guide him on points which might be referred to the Tutor's judgment, or to give to that judgment the influence which it ought to possess. This want of acquaintance with the student's progress is due to the fact of that progress being dependent almost entirely on Private Tuition, while the unrecognized existence of that mode of teaching prevents any necessary communication between the College and Private Tutor.'[26]

The tutor performed a teaching function, but at some point in the eighteenth century – it is difficult to know when – this aspect of his office began to decline in importance, becoming virtually a formality by the early Victorian period. Increasingly, and to a much greater extent than at Oxford, the essential teaching at Cambridge passed out of the colleges and into the hands of private teachers or tutors called coaches.

The private tutor or coach had been an integral part of English education for over a century. Locke approved of home tutors, and tutors were to be found outside the great public schools coaching boys in subjects not provided in the foundation. In addition private tuition was provided in many grammar schools.

In Cambridge private tuition survived mainly because the tripos was used to award fellowships; and fellowships were essential to any intelligent and ambitious graduate of moderate means anxious to launch himself into the Church, the public schools, politics or a learned profession. In 1781, 1807, 1815 and 1824 the university attempted to limit the amount of time students might spend in preparation with coaches; but since the colleges did not provide adequate substitutes, coaching naturally continued and even accelerated after the creation of a classical tripos in the 1820's. In 1854 William Hopkins, the most famous of the early Victorian mathematical coaches, declared that the teaching of mathematics had never before been so completely and systematically in the hands of private tutors.[27] It was certainly apparent that coaches were not simply providing supplementary or remedial instruction. They were the most important teachers in the university: and all undergraduates were forced to use them.

Private tutors were mainly college fellows, college lecturers or B.A.'s kept from a fellowship by marriage. Nearly all resident fellows were coaches for at least one period in their career. Because coaching was a full-time activity, the college lecturer who coached was not inclined to stimulate his classes at the expense of his pocket;[28] and college lectures were therefore neglected. No reading man regarded them with sufficient confidence to forego private tuition. College lectures did not even cover the full examination syllabus; honours students in classics received instruction only in composition and not translation. Moreover, few undergraduates found the repetitious, dull and routine classes they were frequently compelled to attend little more than formal, schoolboy lessons.

Little teaching assistance could be expected from the professors, whose lectures were expected to embody the results of original work. A few lectures, such as those given by the Regius Professor of Greek in the 1840's, were valuable to the classical reading man; but most bore no direct relation to the triposes. Even when professorial lectures were related to the ordinary degree most pass students preferred the coaches. And whenever a new pass examination was introduced or alterations made in an existing one, attendance at professorial lectures decreased even more.[29]

The reputation of a coach was measured by his ability to cram an undergraduate, to drill him intensively for a high place in the examination lists. He was hired to do a job, and his performance could be strictly measured by the number of first class honours or poll men he coached. His labours were given a market price and evaluated in commercial terms. A well-paid coach had to be competitive, sure of his technique, well-organized and willing to work at least six hard tutorial hours every day, as well as grade written exercises and problem sets. The best private tutors in fact developed a system of drill and exercises that was later used as a model for examination papers set by lecturers in history, philosophy and some branches of mathematics.[30]

Coaching was an intercollegiate activity. The coach drew his pupils from all colleges by virtue of reputation. The student was not a captive bound over to the lecturer as he was in the college, but a voluntary attendant, willing to work, open to suggestion. And since the student came willingly, he was under no obligation to remain; if he felt at any time that the coaching sessions had become unprofitable, no statute could detain him. The coach was a hired teacher, a sophist in search of clients. He had to take the initiative in all relations with the student, win his confidence, convince him that no better coach existed. This entailed a knowledge of the student equal to a knowledge of the subject taught; and the student soon realized that he could expect from the coach the warm and personal interest which college officers failed to provide. Whewell himself, a sworn enemy of coaching, frankly admitted in 1852 that 'the pupil values more what he has to himself, what he pays for himself, or what is given to him in a familiar and companionable tone.'[31] And thirty years later, when classics but not mathematics coaching had almost ceased, a writer to *The Cambridge Review* asserted that an undergraduate went to a private tutor not because his college lecturer was incompetent, but because he was recognized as an individual.[32]

Virtually every graduate living in Cambridge, whether a fellow or not, tried coaching because the remuneration was exceptionally good. If not occupied with other duties an ordinary private tutor could teach perhaps a dozen students every term, seeing each student several times a week for approximately one hour per visit. At £7 a student for a term's coaching an ordinary private tutor could make £252 per academic year, or about £50 less than the customary value of a fellowship in the mid-nineteenth century. If the services of an ordinary coach were required daily, 'whole tuition' as it was called and very common in the second quarter of the nineteenth century, he could double his fees and add appreciably to his basic income. Ordinary coaches not greatly in demand of course earned less. The best classics coach who handled on the average more students than an ordinary coach and worked a longer, fatiguing schedule, or the crack mathematics coach who taught even more students, naturally received higher annual incomes. Frequently too their fees were greater. As Hopkins remarked, it was possible for an outstanding coach to make £700–800 per academic year,[33] and even more if he coached in the Long Vacation when he could expect to make 10 guineas per student. This was an extraordinary amount, almost within the definition of an upper middle class income.[34] If coaching were combined with a fellowship or college lectureship, the total emoluments available to the successful private tutor might equal the income of the Lady Margaret's Professor of Divinity, the most highly endowed chair in Cambridge.[35] Few coaches earned the maximum amount, but the range of possible remuneration was nevertheless tempting.

Money alone, however, did not make a resident fellow take private pupils. Many fellows became coaches in lieu of any other satisfactory alternative. There were simply not enough official teaching positions within either the university or the colleges; and research was not an attractive choice because only professors were expected to write. Reformers like Seeley and Sidgwick, who proposed that all teachers unite German scholarship and English teaching, encountered formidable opposition. There was not much sympathy for a class of *gelehrten*, regarded as isolated and politically unimportant. It was feared they would 'distract the energies of the nation from the broad highways of civic life and lead them into the by-paths of abstract study, so that, while thought and speculation might be busy and free, political action might be inert and shackled.'[36] As Seeley noted, Cambridge was considered a place of moral edification from which obedient and observing men returned to society; and this view of university education discouraged scholarship, denounced in some quarters as a continental apology for anarchic free-thinking.

Dons who did not hold a college office had to make a difficult choice. If they remained in Cambridge, they had either to coach or fill their time with some kind of routine. Time was on their hands – hence the lengthy meals, parties and hard drinking – and coaching was therefore important not only because it paid well, but because it was so time-consuming. But it was also an endless and wearisome routine, competitive yet arid. It required repeating the simple rules of Euclid and grammar term after term and in the Long Vacation. Tripos teaching was a feverish activity in which a man stood absolutely still; and sensitive men inevitably became profoundly dissatisfied with themselves.

William Hopkins was one of the few coaches to have surmounted the deficiencies of the tripos syllabus. By refusing to be donnish and by encouraging his students to take a speculative and philosophical view of mathematics, he conveyed a genuine love of learning. Marriage had kept him from a college career, and he turned to coaching as the only satisfactory alternative. Among the undergraduates whom he coached were George Gabriel Stokes, William

Thomson (Lord Kelvin), James Clerk Maxwell and Isaac Todhunter, some of the most important names in English science and mathematics. Next to his pupil, Edward John Routh, he produced more senior wranglers than any other coach. He is reported to have said in 1849 that he had nearly two hundred wranglers to his credit, of whom seventeen were senior and forty-four were in one of the first three places.[37]

Routh succeeded Hopkins as a 'wrangler maker', coaching more than six hundred students in the period 1855–88, and producing from this group no less than twenty-seven senior wranglers, twenty-four of whom were consecutive. He himself had been senior wrangler in 1854, the year that Clerk Maxwell was second, and like Hopkins he managed to make original contributions to mathematics. There is no doubt, however, that his work as a coach detracted from his reputation as a mathematics scholar, for he was by-passed for the Sadlerian Professorship of Mathematics in 1863 after announcing his intention to stand.[38] Like Hopkins, Routh had married and was forced to vacate his fellowship in 1864. Not until 1883 was he made an honorary fellow of Peterhouse, a distinction which provided neither the privileges nor satisfaction of a regular fellowship.

Although he was employed as a lecturer by Peterhouse and Pembroke, Routh's college teaching suffered for the sake of his coaching. He was firmly committed to the challenge of the tripos and accepted its limitations. His methods were both a reflection of the demands of the tripos and his sober, taciturn, efficient manner. His organization and clarity were considered exemplary. He taught in classes of six to ten, set weekly problem papers, gave moot tripos exams and rated his students according to merit. He devoted himself single-mindedly to the formula which produced success: set problems, set books, set solutions: 'Independence on the part of a student was not encouraged; for independence would rarely, if ever, be justified by the event. Foreign books were seldom mentioned: Routh himself had summarized from them all that could be deemed useful for the examination. . . . Regularity and steady diligence were two demands which he always made from his pupils.'[39] Routh knew how to raise the level of individual performance, but not the level of individuality. As a manufacturer he was unsurpassed: he used the best materials and turned out finished, machined products. It may perhaps be suggested that had William Hopkins not been so prone to the distractions of meta-mathematics, he might have produced a coaching record more equal to that of his famous successor.

Although hired teachers, Hopkins and Routh retained their self-respect. It is difficult, however, not to concur with Heitland that Richard Shilleto, the most famous Victorian classics coach, was a pathetic figure. A Salopian trained under Butler, he was widely known as a Thucydides scholar and occasionally lectured in King's and Trinity; but he spent most of his time coaching students in Shrewsbury alcaics and elegaics. Early marriage ruled out a Trinity fellowship; and heavy drinking, according to Heitland, kept him from the Regius Professorship of Greek, to which an Ely canonry was attached. Shilleto had taken holy orders but could not live down his reputation as an alcoholic and eccentric acquired after years on the fringes of university and college life. The bitterness of his situation, the exclusion and dependence which characterized his life, is obvious from the alternately sarcastic and suppliant letters to undergraduates in which he alluded to his position as an outsider. 'Will you come on Thursday evening, and, if you have such strange tastes, take a cup of tea?' he once wrote an undergraduate. 'It will undoubtedly be followed by a Tankard if not of Audit at least of Guinness.'[40] His teaching technique was derived from the schools: it was narrow, exact and formal. He exhausted himself by applying it in his prime to about a dozen students every day, six days a week. This gruelling life of disappointment was only partially redeemed by an amended Peterhouse statute of 1867 which allowed him to become the first married scholar to assume a fellowship in the college.[41]

By the end of the 1850's, Macaulay's ideal of the independent scholar, he who 'read Plato with his feet on the fender,' was almost out of fashion among even the best reading men. Ironically, his own nephew rushed into the arms of Shilleto the moment the uncle's influence was removed.[42] Progressively coaching had become *de rigeur* in Cambridge.

4

In the second quarter of the nineteenth century lecturers and fellows left the colleges to serve as coaches, and college teaching declined. In the 1850's and 1860's members of royal commissions and select committees suggested that the colleges adopt coaching methods and compete with private tutors, but many dons resisted this solution. Whewell, especially depressed by the increase in private teaching, considered coaching exclusively a university matter. He idealized the college, regarding it as an inviolate society, and refused to commit Trinity to any course which might corrupt its purpose. If lecturers took over the functions of coaches, he argued, the worst abuses of coaching would be transferred to the colleges. Lectures would be tied directly to the examinations, and lecturers would give students only such technicalities as they could master with little effort.[43]

Whewell's reluctance to commit Trinity to an attack on private tuition convinced many critics that the colleges could not easily be persuaded to take the initiative in the reform of Cambridge teaching. Their doubts increased when they reflected that the small colleges relied on private tuition to provide teaching they were unable to afford and that few lecturers and fellows cared to deprive themselves of an excellent source of revenue. By mid-century there was considerable support for the opinion that only university teaching or an intercollegiate arrangement could solve the problems arising from coaching.

Hopkins and the Graham Commission advocated a programme of teaching that was actually a prototype of the university lecture system established by statute in 1882. Sub-professors or public lecturers drawn from outstanding coaches or college lecturers were to be added to the university teaching staff. Most professors were to continue to devote themselves to scholarship and research, although some could participate in the new scheme. In the 1860's Seeley suggested a compromise measure that would inspire life into college teaching but at the same time would make the colleges more competitive and university-minded. He proposed an intercollegiate scheme of teaching with lecturers occupying a position midway between the professoriate and the teachers of the old college system. The colleges would retain their teaching staffs; all college lectures would be open to students from other colleges; small colleges would specialize instead of attempting to offer a full programme of studies. Seeley also advocated abolition of the order of merit; and he agreed with other reformers that coaching could not be superseded unless the new university lecturers were given every advantage enjoyed by coaches. Celibacy and the requirement of ordination would have to be eliminated.

The problem of remuneration still remained. Unless lecturers were adequately paid, no coach would consent to lecture. Hopkins and the Graham Commission decided that salary guarantees would have to be made if a university teaching staff was to be recruited; but both also agreed that the standard of teaching improved when lecturers were forced to compete for students, as coaching was successful precisely because students voluntarily sought out the better teachers. They therefore suggested that lecturers be paid partly by fees and partly by salary. Hopkins set the minimum salary for lecturers at £300, the customary value of a fellowship, and suggested that lecturers could earn an additional £150 more in fees. He proposed to raise the lectureship endowment by diverting bequests no longer providing educational benefits or by the remission of university taxes imposed on degrees, and by adding to the sums thus released annual contributions from the colleges that could consist of fees collected from undergraduates for obsolete services.[44] The Graham Commission also suggested that the colleges contribute to the support of the university lecturers; and in order to forestall collegiate hostility added that lecturers might be induced to exchange a high salary for a guarantee of permanent employment.[45] This was still another attempt to tempt teachers away from private tuition, for coaching was a precarious occupation, particularly for the non-fellow who had no other source of income or the inept teacher who failed to attract students. It was the economic insecurity of coaching as well as demand that inflated its fees.

The Graham Commission found little enthusiasm in the colleges for its proposals to strengthen university teaching in order to diminish the importance of coaching. Only Trinity, Peterhouse and Christ's were willing to accept a 5 per cent tax on distributable income for university purposes; and only Christ's was willing to open its fellowship competition to the entire university – an essential step if the small colleges were to acquire sufficient teaching talent to forgo their dependence on private tuition.[46] Furthermore, another alternative to coaching, intercollegiate lectures supported exclusively by the colleges, had not been started. As Seeley remarked in 1867, 'Trinity refuses to let the men of other colleges attend its good lectures, and the small college refuses to excuse its own students from attending its own inferior lectures.'[47] In addition, new honours courses raised problems of staffing even more serious than for classics and mathematics. The colleges were reluctant to detach endowments in order to establish fellowships and provide scholarships in new, untried tripos subjects like philosophy, introduced in 1851 but even a decade later cautiously advertized and unsatisfactorily rewarded.[48] All in all, coaching was still the rough remedy.

5

The significance of the system of private tuition that developed in Cambridge at the end of the eighteenth century and expanded in the second quarter of the nineteenth century has been completely overlooked by historians of university education. Coaching was not simply a substitute for the teaching which the colleges neglected and which the university was unable to perform. It was the only practical school of education in Cambridge, the only place where a prospective university teacher could prove his worth in a competitive situation. Coaching provided jobs for married men and supplementary income for the young resident don with no college duties; it supported the B.A. who had failed to receive a fellowship and was awaiting another chance; it enabled young dons like Sidgwick, unsure of their religious belief, to divorce themselves from college life while deciding whether to assume holy orders. Coaching was also the means by which many impecunious sizars and sons of poor parsons earned enough money to repay tutors and creditors for an expensive university education;[49] it enabled Henry Knights to become bishops. Despite its obvious educational limitations, coaching was a major contribution to the reform of teaching in the second half of the nineteenth century; for in the coaching relationship mutual respect developed between teacher and student, donnishness could not survive. Nevertheless, no reform was possible in Cambridge as long as coaching remained unchallenged.

Notes

1 John Robert Seeley, 'Liberal Education', in *Lectures and Essays* (London, 1870), p. 163, first published in F. W. Farrar's *Essays on a Liberal Education* (London, 1867).

2 Francis Galton, *Hereditary Genius* (London, 1962), p. 59.

3 Noel Annan, *Leslie Stephen* (London, 1951), p. 24.

4 Graham Commission (1852), Report, p. 16.

5 *Student's Guide* (1866), p. 277.

6 After 1885, however, the percentage of honours degrees increased slowly. In 1902 approximately 53 per cent of the degrees given in Cambridge went to honours men, and in 1913–14 about 62 per cent. The number of honours students and degrees varied radically from college to college. From 1851–1906 one-third of all Cambridge students took pass degrees and over one quarter went down without taking any degrees. See *Student's Guide* (1866); Return Relating to the Universities of Oxford and Cambridge, 1866, li, p. 69; Royal Commission on Oxford and Cambridge (1922), Appendices, 154 and 185; and Alfred Isaac Tillyard, *A History of University Reform from 1800 to the Present Time* (Cambridge, 1913), pp. 299–301.

7 Evidence submitted to Royal Commission of 1919, Cambridge University Library Box VI, folder 5, p. 18.

8 Perhaps the last example of how violent an undergraduate mob could be was the notorious assault on the Newnham gates in 1921, prompted by the vote taken on degrees for women. A photograph of the mob leaving the Senate House is in the Whibley Papers, Pembroke College.

9 Charles Astor Bristed *Five Years in an English University*, 2 vols (New York, 1852), I, pp. 180–1.

10 Albert Pell, *Reminiscences* (London, 1908), p. 77. For other episodes see D. A. Winstanley, *Early Victorian Cambridge* (Cambridge, 1940) (hereafter EVC), pp. 374, 417–18.

11 Annan, *Leslie Stephen*, pp. 32, 30–6. Another don who was successful in subduing young bloods was Henry Latham, Senior Tutor of Trinity Hall. 'He was a remarkable figure, unrivalled in the power of controlling full-blooded Undergraduates. No man understood better the need of enforcing order and obedience; no man saw more clearly that petty regulations and frequent interference only serve to make dignity ridiculous and corrupt the moral bonds of discipline. . . . To bring young men together and keep them out of mischief . . . was a function not always performed by College Tutors with success.' William Emerton Heitland, *After Many Years* (Cambridge, 1926), p. 143.

12 EVC, pp. 396–7. Macaulay's letter is in the Whewell Papers, Trinity College Library.

13 John D'Ewes Evelyn Firth, *Rendall of Winchester* (London, 1954), p. 20; A. E. Shipley, '*J.*' *A Memoir of John Willis Clark* (London, 1913), pp. 85–6.

14 Annan, *Leslie Stephen*, pp. 41 and 41 n.

15 Leslie Stephen, *Life of Henry Fawcett* (London, 1885), p. 76.

16 'The Confessions of an Old Don', *The Eagle*, V (1867), pp. 106–11. References to donnishness may be found in Iris L. Osborne Morgan, *Memoirs of Henry Arthur Morgan* (London, 1927), p. 21; Terrot Reaveley Glover, *Cambridge Retrospect* (Cambridge, 1943), pp. 58–62; Walter Leaf, *Some Chapters of Autobiography* (London, 1932), p. 79; J. P. Whitney, 'Sir George Prothero as a Historian', p. 1, King's College Library Q.32.33; Headlam Papers, letter dated August 28, 1908, King's College Library N.21.52; A. W. Verrall, *Collected Literary Essays* (Cambridge, 1913), pp. xxxii et seq. See especially Galton's description of Hopkins in Karl Pearson, *The Life, Letters and Labours of Francis Galton*, 4 vols (Cambridge, 1914–1930), I, p. 163: 'Hopkins to use a Cantab expression is a regular brick; tells funny stories connected with different problems and is no way Donnish; he rattles us on at a splendid pace and makes mathematics anything

but a dry subject by entering thoroughly into its metaphysics. I never enjoyed anything so much before.' Galton was at Cambridge in the 1840's.

17 Phyllis Grosskurth, *The Woeful Victorian* (New York, 1965), pp. 33, 20–41.
18 Report of the Commissioners appointed to inquire into the State, Discipline, Studies and Revenues of the University and Colleges of Oxford, together with the evidence and Appendix. 1852 (1482), xxii, *Evidence*, pp. 43, 48–9.
19 D. A. Winstanley, *Unreformed Cambridge* (Cambridge, 1935), p. 267.
20 Ewart Committee, Evidence, p. 56.
21 Ibid. Bristed, I, p. 115, did not think tutors took undue advantage of tradesmen. The fault, he said, lay with students who paid bills late.
22 Report of the Commissioners appointed to inquire into the property and income of the Universities of Oxford and Cambridge (Cleveland Commission), 1873 (*c.* 856) xxxvii, pp. 31–2.
23 Shipley, p. 86.
24 Jackson to Maitland, November 13, 1905, Cambridge University Library Add. 4251 (13) 713, published in John Roach, 'The Victoria County History of Cambridge', *Proceedings of the Cambridge Antiquarian Society*, LIV (1960), p. 123. Hammond was a Trinity tutor from 1854–64.
25 Bristed, I, p. 15.
26 William Hopkins, *Remarks on the Mathematical Teaching of the University of Cambridge* (1854), p. 23.
27 Ibid., p. 7.
28 Isaac Todhunter is a good example of a college teacher who neglected lecturing because of coaching. See Edward Miller, *Portrait of a College* (Cambridge, 1961), pp. 87–8.
29 EVC, pp. 177–81.
30 *Student's Guide* (1893), pp. 71–2.
31 Graham Commission (1852), Evidence, p. 417.
32 *Cambridge Review* (May 12, 1880), p. 66. Heitland also complained that college lecturers 'did not study their pupils personally so as to diagnose individual cases. Even the set lectures to full classrooms were apt to be a blend of what men either knew or did not want to know at all'. *After Many Years*, p. 128.
33 For coaching fees see Chapter 2.
34 J. A. Banks, *Prosperity and Parenthood* (London, 1954), considers £900 to be an upper class income about 1851. Other historians use £1,000 as the lower limit of an upper middle class income. See F. Musgrove, 'Middle-Class Education and Employment in the Nineteenth Century', *Economic History Review*, 2nd series, XII (August, 1959), pp. 99–111.
35 The Lady Margaret's Professorship of Divinity was worth £1,085 per annum in 1885 and possibly more earlier. See the returns compiled by Thorold Rogers and published in the *Pall Mall Gazette* (November 5, 1886), p. 2, and Graham Commission (1861), p. 6.
36 Lord Houghton, 'On the Present Social Results of Classical Education', in *Essays on a Liberal Education*, p. 368.
37 Dictionary of National Biography.
38 Cambridge University Library Add. 6580 (55). Arthur Cayley was elected instead.
39 A. R. Forsyth, 'Edward John Routh', *Proceedings of the London Mathematical Society*, ser. 2, V (July 5, 1907), xvi. Also J. J. Thomson, *Recollections and Reflections* (London, 1936), pp. 35–42.
40 G. M. Trevelyan, *Sir George Otto Trevelyan, A Memoir* (London, 1932), pp. 40–1. 'Audit' is a reference to the ale served in colleges.

41 For Shilleto see Heitland, p. 131, EVC, p. 412, and Reginald St. John Parry, *Henry Jackson* (Cambridge, 1926), p. 15. Jackson wrote to his sister in 1860 that 'Shilleto nearly poisoned himself on Monday: just before going to bed he drank a glass of furniture varnish by mistake for his ale, and was so frightened that he telegraphed to his sister that he should not be surprised if he were dead tomorrow. He seems all right again today.'

42 Trevelyan, *G. O. Trevelyan*, pp. 42, 38–9. Macaulay died in December 1859.

43 Graham Commission (1852), Evidence, p. 417.

44 Hopkins, pp. 36–7.

45 Graham Commission (1852), Report, pp. 81–3.

46 Ibid., (1861), pp. 7–8, 16.

47 Seeley, 'Liberal Education', p. 167.

48 *Student's Guide* (1863), pp. 150 and 152.

49 'When the student takes his degree, he obtains by pupilizing enough to render further assistance unnecessary, and soon begins to pay off his debt, and when he gets his Fellowship, he clears himself very speedily. It is in fact pledging his labour and time two or three years ahead, and though such a mortgage may in some cases prove an awkward incumbrance, the general result is good: it enables many first-rate men to get a first-rate education, which they could not otherwise have obtained.' Bristed, I, pp. 114, 214.

114

THE ACADEMIC ROLE

Sheldon Rothblatt

Source: S. Rothblatt, *Tradition and Change in English Liberal Education*, London: Faber and Faber, 1976, pp. 174–94.

Ideals of scholarship arriving from the Continent were instrumental in restoring pride to the average Oxbridge don, long demoralized by having an insufficient amount of work to do and depressed by such restrictions as the celibacy clauses attached to fellowships. Fellowships were only technically college appointments. The conditions of tenure actually had nothing to do with teaching or scholarship. The award was a prize, and since the role model for a fellow was not academic, few objected to its being enjoyed away from the university. The fellow rarely aspired to be a scholar or a scientist or a professor. The highest achievements for a person of university education were outside the institutions. It was certainly more prestigious to be the headmaster of a great public school than to be a don, or to become a bishop or a judge. The ultimate honour was cabinet office.

Between 1850 and 1870 a profound role crisis developed within Oxford and Cambridge, bringing into the open questions of career choice, self-esteem, and social status. The crisis was started by the realization that English society was no longer dominated by the values of a landed aristocracy, and that the unofficial yet solid connection between Oxford and Cambridge and the aristocratic-governed State and Church was about to be broken. Pressure for reform was applied in two forms: from Parliament, which threatened to produce greater changes than it actually accomplished, and from undergraduate admissions into the universities on a scale never before experienced. Clearly, a reorientation was required and a complete rethinking of academic roles and university purposes. In this setting the revival of learning—to use one of the slogans of the period—opened up the possibilities of a calling.[1]

The fellowship system had to be the target, for most of the endowments that could be used for education were tied up in special trusts. Demands that the fellowship system be overhauled had been made periodically—in the late eighteenth century, for example, and in the 1830s; but what was consistently

354

absent, besides pressure from Parliament, were a sense of urgency and an ideological element. It was one thing to request the end to celibacy restrictions or geographical quotas, or to insist that holy orders be eliminated as a condition for the life tenure of fellowships, and quite another to require that fellowships released in this way be used for teaching and learning. That is why the ideals associated with the knowledge revolution made a difference. They provided an emotional dynamic in the service of reform, the conviction of a mission or a religious conversion; advocates came close to proclaiming the advent of a millennium. With education reunited to its true purposes, after so many years of wasted efforts and trivial ends, national resolve was bound to be strengthened and national achievement was certain to follow. We now recognize these claims as overdone, and perhaps overstatement could not be avoided as sides were being drawn, but the grand objectives do adequately express the faith of the nineteenth century in the power of education to provide culture, recover moral integrity, and produce, in the long run, a better life for society. By 1880 the necessary changes had been effected. The career academician emerged at Oxford and Cambridge, as he had emerged elsewhere in England, as the dominant type of university person. The fear of melancholy which had so worried the Georgians was removed once and for all by a new work ethic, and since it was now legitimate for dons to apply themselves to specialized reading or laboratory research, there was no need to worry about the charge of pedantry. Aided by the liberation of fellowships from historic restrictions and also by the establishment of new university teaching positions, the numbers of teachers active in the universities increased rapidly. In the decade following 1876, the Oxbridge university staff alone doubled, and throughout the colleges more fellows were engaged in the task of tuition than had been the case in centuries.

Initially, the most conspicuous influence of the revival of learning was on teaching. The renewed interest in character formation theory at the college level stimulated young dons, leading them to seek out promising undergraduates whose values they might influence. The ideal of universal knowledge also carried with it a heavy teaching commitment, since it was, at one level, an answer to the problem of premature subject concentration. Classical teaching was too often dull and repetitive, 'pedantic and meagre', and the ideal of universal knowledge held out the promise of a new, elevated view of the interconnectedness of learning. Insofar as all scholars were agreed that disciplining the faculties must remain the proximate end of education, universal knowledge at least made clear why this was so, giving the student an ultimate goal to aim for. Universal knowledge was also supposed to be instrumental. It was addressed to what its exponents considered the broadest problems of their generation.

The royal commissioners of the 1850s had definitely been interested in improving the teaching at Oxford and Cambridge. This was, in fact, their primary purpose. Parents whose sons pushed enrolment figures to unprecedented levels in the 1860s were certainly interested in the quality of Oxbridge teaching, especially in view of its extraordinary expense. The costs of university residence were much too high, partly because of the social pressures undergraduates exerted upon one another—a pattern of spending for conspicuous consumption started in the preceding centuries by extravagant scions of noble families—and partly because of the prevalence of private teaching. Everyone knew that the assistance of coaches in passing examinations was indispensable, but the solution was a simple one. The colleges could easily absorb coaching if more fellows were employed in teaching. The need to pay large extra amounts for collegiate instruction when basic tuition costs were already exorbitant seemed an anomaly, an old regime abuse surviving into an age of progress. A generation of parents in a society which had undergone historic reforms in its systems of economic production and political representation and had made changes in the structure of local government and in the character of public administration did not wish to see its standard of living eroded by needless educational expense.

The central objective of the first movements to reform the universities was certainly teaching. It was what that famous academic Tory, Cardinal Newman, wanted, a teaching university, a place for teaching universal knowledge, as he defined it in his famous lectures. This was nearly as true for the professoriate in general, for that part of the university faculty supposedly committed to the task of advancing knowledge in the several fields of scholarship and science, as it was for the collegial fellowship. Halford Vaughan was an exception. He saw no reason why a professor should have to teach or even reside in a university when his object was original learning, but this was assuredly a minority viewpoint. The great Oxbridge professors of the mid-Victorian period are as famous, perhaps more famous, for their teaching as for their contributions to the advance of knowledge. Seeley and Sidgwick at Cambridge, Jowett and T. H. Green at Oxford, were as intensely interested in teaching as in original scholarship. Seeley was, in fact, more interested in teaching, although of a special kind. Jowett saw no fundamental difference in the functions performed by professors and tutors; both were essentially teachers.[2]

In mid-Victorian Oxbridge the professorial system and the collegiate or tutorial system were mutually supporting. Even more, the reinvigoration and expansion of professorial teaching were vital to the success of the awakened collegiate system. For a professorship now became the capstone of an academic career and thus an incentive. The professoriate was necessary to the fellowship, allowing the fellow to become a career teacher, something he had not been for centuries, thus stopping the drain of so many excellent minds into occupations outside the university.

The teaching solution adopted at Oxford and Cambridge, while historically significant, was not in all respects novel. The professor as teacher was the British tradition. It was true of the Scottish professors, who throughout the eighteenth and well into the nineteenth centuries wrote distinguished books on philosophy and the social sciences and gave lectures to undergraduates of secondary school age. As the new English universities of the nineteenth century were founded, beginning with University College, London, in the late 1820s, it was the professorial rather than the tutorial system that was adopted, Durham being an exception. The professorial system was far cheaper for students and parents, as no special provision for residence and individual tutoring had to be made and no expensive buildings and gardens had to be maintained in order to create an appropriate atmosphere. Character, if it was to be shaped at all, was shaped intellectually in the classroom. All that was required for the professorial system were lecture halls where large numbers of students could crowd. Furthermore, professorial income could be pegged to attendance, as it often was in Germany, a decision that could, however, and frequently did cause financial hardship, dampening educational innovation and driving some professors out of the universities in search of new patrons, new clientele, and sources of supplementary income. Nevertheless, professorial teaching was the answer for institutions of limited endowments.

The renewed interest in teaching produced some interesting discussions in the mid-Victorian period and later on the relationship of the teacher to his subject of study and the relationship of both to the student. Two positions or models developed. In the first, the teacher was regarded as more important than the subject he taught. This was called the Christian or saintly model, of which charisma in the explicit Weberian meaning was a prime characteristic. The Christian teacher inspired students by his example, by the right conduct visible in his own life. He was in touch with values beyond the banality of everyday life, or he lived those values universally recognized but not universally observed. Knowledge was important insofar as it awakened an interest in values, but never as important as the values themselves. Learning for its own sake was secondary. This model and its variations had obvious uses in those theories of liberal education concerned with character formation.

In the second model the teacher was looked upon as subordinate to his subject; ego gave way to the discipline, personality to knowledge. This was the Socratic model, based upon a characteristic nineteenth-century tendency to identify Socrates with the man described in Plato's dialogues and to read into the characterization an interpretation not supported by the facts. The Socratic model of the teacher soon became identified with the German conception of a professor as someone who imparted scientific method or the scientific spirit. The great Manchester chemist Henry Roscoe, who had studied under Bunsen at Heidelberg, cited him as an example of the true teacher and scientist humbled by a sense of the limits of his knowledge, his allegiance always to the subject and never to himself. 'His modesty was natural and in no degree assumed. In his lectures, when giving an account of some discovery he had made, or some new apparatus or method of work which he had instigated, I never heard him mention himself. It was always "man hat dies gesunden," or "es hat sich so herausgestellt." In his old age, and looking back on his lifework, he writes me that he "feels as keenly as ever how modest and contemptibly small is the amount which I have added to the building of Science." [3] One is reminded of Droysen's famous statement about history. When the facts speak for themselves, the teacher has merely to present them.

The Socratic model was reinforced in the nineteenth century by social science determinism, by the belief in impersonal forces and inevitable cycles or laws of historical movement. The individual was powerless to effect change: he could only understand it, and, at most, clarify its inevitable direction. In the Socratic model personality characteristics were secondary, competence and training foremost. As Sir Walter Raleigh said in 1911, using the Socratic model in connection with his own subject, literary criticism, 'The vanity of teaching ... often tempteth a man to forget that he is a blockhead. ... In our time we make fuller and more settled provision for teaching. But learning is still the real business, and the most that a teacher can do is to help with sympathy and advice those who are travelling the same way with him.' [4]

It is clear from the remarks of Bunsen in science and Raleigh in literature that in the course of the nineteenth century one part of the renewed interest in the teaching of undergraduates began to separate and attach itself to the research ideal. The Socratic model was the link between the teaching revolution and the knowledge revolution, and the person who regarded himself as the scholar or scientist had to be prepared to recognize the autonomy of his subject. 'The spirit of learning,' said Raleigh, 'is a good and humble thing, much better than the spirit of teaching.' [5] Increasingly, the whole question of the personal inspiration of the teacher, as well as his moral conduct, the example he as an individual was supposed to set, raised by the notion of the teacher as saint, diminished in importance as the ideal of advancing knowledge spread throughout the international university world. It remained an important consideration for undergraduates, for whom the years after the age of eighteen were still important for self-exploration. But for the scholars and scientists who were at work altering the fundamental precepts of liberal education, the teacher as saint was the wrong model. It drew attention away from learning to self, increasing personal arrogance and simplifying the problem of the place of knowledge in an industrial and scientific world. Theologians were as unattracted to the saintly model as other scholars. As the Dean of the Faculty of Theology in the University of London said in 1911 when he advocated the creation of an 'ideal' or research university in London, 'You must make provision for chairs ... , not merely for the sake of the students of the University, but for the good name of the University itself. It is not merely the business of a professor to be lecturing and teaching, perhaps elementary work to students, it is also his business to carry on the work of research.'[6]

At the very centre of the knowledge revolution was *Lehrnfreiheit*, the unrestricted pursuit of truth, which meant that some teachers were free to innovate and others devoted themselves to preserving the traditional learning; but for either group intellectual freedom was the most precious ornament of academic life. This had not been the situation earlier, when dons were dismissed from their fellowships or tutorships for advocating unorthodox views on the religion of the Church of England. Academic freedom bore some relationship to the Georgian independence ideal that had emerged in London towards the end of the eighteenth century, but it was really closer to what the Victorians considered the essence of professional behaviour. Georgian independence was basically independence from some person or group; it was much closer to being a 'liberty'. It did not imply duties or responsibilities to be given in return for independence. It was primarily a status to be enjoyed. The Victorian conception of professional independence incorporated a service ideal. Education was the foundation of the service, although exactly what service to provide and how to provide it caused academicians as much difficulty as did the definition and meaning of a liberal education.

We must not exaggerate the degree of discipline specialization or expertise implied by the phrase 'professionalism'. Certainly in the first instance, the knowledge revolution did not automatically mean the emergence of the expert, whether in government, industry, or the universities. There are degrees of professionalism as there are degrees of amateurism. A simple contrast does not really give us the historical condition we may seek. In the early Victorian period Edwin Chadwick considered himself an authority in the area of public health, yet he had nothing but contempt for medical men. In the field of epidemiology he was mainly influenced by the theories of civil engineers. Before the physician could be respected as an expert in questions of community sanitation, it was necessary for him to upgrade his professional qualifications, a situation that did not occur in England until after the 1860s. Even then it was possible to find leading government bureaucrats who may have been trained physicians, but who otherwise showed very little competence, or perhaps even basic interest, in public medicine or in the control of contagious diseases. In the second half of the nineteenth century, the school inspectors employed in the Department of Education were likely to be highly intelligent, efficient, and conscientious, but also without any special competence or experience in the administration of mass education. Their qualification was limited to a first-class degree from Oxford or Cambridge and a friend or acquaintance in the Department. Unquestionably, the cream of the Oxford honours schools or the Cambridge tripos were an improvement over the aristocrats and their cousins

359

who controlled the civil service departments before 1850, but we must not overstate the degree of specialized education or special qualification required for one group to gradually replace another. In fact, the first phase of the knowledge revolution as represented by university persons such as the Mark Pattison of 1850 was an attempt to get away from specialism, which was seen to be the principal barrier to the creation of a vital liberal arts syllabus.

In the last decades of the nineteenth century the specialist ideal, which had already established itself in the newer universities, began to influence Oxbridge as well. Of course, some Oxbridge dons of 1900 still congratulated themselves on resisting the fragmentation of learning and praised one another for upholding the principles of general education. But the issues in which the question of a liberal education was sometimes raised indicate that the protagonists no longer possessed an unmistakable idea of the suitable forms of liberal instruction. In 1905, for example, a large number of tutors and lecturers protested against the plan of the Regius Professor to introduce a thesis essay based on original sources into the syllabus of the Oxford History School. A thesis existed as part of the history curriculum at Manchester, where the Regius Professor had been trained; but the dons argued that it would introduce an undesirable professional element into what was 'a liberal education through history'. Examinations, however, they regarded as well within the spirit of liberal arts teaching.[7]

The trend, nevertheless, was towards specializing and contributing to original research. A teaching knowledge of a subject was becoming insufficient as a test of professional competence. More was required. Even the long-standing belief that a practising—an acclaimed—London barrister was qualified to be a professor of law or a legal historian without also being a seriously-trained legal scholar was challenged in university circles. In 1886, when he was elected to the Downing Professorship of the Laws of England at Cambridge, Maitland raised the question with customary wit: 'My own belief to the last moment was that some Q.C. who was losing health or practice would ask for the place and get it.[8] If not every university subject had become professionally academic as we now understand the phrase, requiring an advanced degree in the subject or other proof of research competence, and if there was still room in English academic life for the man of general education who had achieved some eminence outside the university, there can be no doubt that this form of amateurism was becoming deeply resented. In the same year that Maitland received his appointment to the Downing chair, the famous Victorian churchman and sometime Headmaster of Harrow, Henry Montagu Butler, was named Master of Trinity College, Cambridge, a position in the gift of the crown. One of the greatest Cambridge men of his generation, Henry Sidgwick, confessed himself depressed and dissatisfied 'at the snub given to academic work' by Butler's appointment. Sidgwick liked him personally. They had been together at the university, and Butler was a serious and important man. But he was not a scholar, had made no contributions to the advance of learning, and, consequently, in Sidgwick's eyes was not a professional academic person.[9]

As long as universal knowledge was the goal of many prominent and serious members of the academic community, it was still possible to have learned amateurs in the university world, but by the end of the nineteenth century, as the great comprehensive *summas* and positivist theories of social development became less interesting and valuable to scholars, as the newer universities registered real advances in the solution of scientific and technological problems, the model of the man of general education was being superseded. While a grand philosophical overview was still important in the minds of some scholars and likely to appear as the stated objective of specialties still in the process of definition, most academics associated intellectual achievement with narrower areas of concentration.[10] The growth in the number of fields, subjects, and specialties that are the rule of the university today can be followed throughout the second half of the nineteenth century and into the twentieth century. It is easy to appreciate the excitement so often expressed in biographies, testimonies, and addresses and lectures of the period. It is no wonder that the life of the mind was so highly praised when learning appeared fresh and endless, when the terrifying applications of science to weaponry had not yet stunned the imaginations of men and women, when ideas of racial or national superiority had not yet been legitimized in Europe by academic decree, and when theories of the absurd had not penetrated the culture and education of western civilization.

Specialism fragmented the university world as it had never been fragmented before. The official scholastic curriculum of the seventeenth century, although it was supplemented by a revolution in scientific thinking, had imposed a unity on the educational life of the university and defined an overall purpose to study. The recovering university of the early nineteenth century had concentrated on a select number of subjects and carefully ordered the priority given to other subjects. The expansion in the number of fields after 1850, the establishment of new chairs, and the revival of the professional schools ended whatever educational unity had hitherto existed. Seen in this perspective, the universal knowledge ideal was both the last attempt to unify the educational purpose of the university and the first phase of the process that destroyed the unity.

Specialism became essential to academic professionalism and to professionalism generally as it had not been in the eighteenth century. To be sure, there was a professional movement of substantial proportions in the Georgian period, but its primary objective was not competence itself but competence as validated by status. Georgian writers, architects, painters, and physicians were more interested in their social standing than in their reputations as professional men. Status professionalism developed in a society where style and manners were co-determinants of prestige, and prestige was more important than career. As this was the case, career preparation through university education was essentially unnecessary. A university education would have been important only if it had been solidly based on the ideal of the gentleman so closely associated with rank and position. As we have seen, it failed to fulfil this requirement.

Unlike status professionalism, occupational professionalism, Victorian in origin, depends upon competence as validated by the diploma; but this is only one guarantee that the professional man has been adequately trained. In addition, the association of professional men, highly organized and self-regulating, determines both the educational criteria and the working ethics of the profession. Merit as defined by the association and guaranteed by the university is more important than social standing, which, if it is achieved at all, is achieved through distinction in the profession. Career is foremost, and general education by itself is insufficient to guarantee success.

Occupational professionalism and specialism, although they did not necessarily originate together, soon joined. At the core of the union was the professionalization of academic life. Since it was the specialty that provided the academic person with his self-assurance and his success, it was in his interest both to advance his subject and to enlarge its general importance. The accomplishment of this took various forms, depending upon the nature of the subject. New constituencies and new audiences were created, as they were created in Georgian times, and new alignments between academic persons and non-academic communities appeared.

The civic universities are an excellent example of this process of professional growth. From the start, the newer universities were closely identified with the manufacturing industries of the Midlands and the North. 'The thrust bearing lubrication, colliery pumps, vanadium steels, chrome leather, gas fires, sparking plugs, and radio tuning all owed much to the work of the professors while products like cheese, soap, beer and the quadruple expansion engine were all considerably improved by their work.'[11] This pattern of involvement, while to continue past 1914, underwent various alterations. As some industries developed their own research facilities, the civic universities gave more attention to projects that can be called pure research.

Initially, Oxbridge regarded the connections between the newer universities and the industrial regions of England with distrust and disdain. Although Cambridge professors in the early Victorian period had worked in several government-sponsored research projects, they had refrained from offering their services to the new manufacturing districts. Of course, it must be added that in the earlier period industry had not developed to the point where university research of any kind was useful in production. Industry returned the disdain, and it continued into the later Victorian period and well into the twentieth century. By and large, the great scientific achievements of Cambridge—the discoveries in atomic physics that took place at the Cavendish Laboratory, for example—had no connection whatsoever with industrial enterprise. As long as dons were able to develop their specialties without substantial monetary assistance from outside, they could mock the new universities and freely indulge their wit.

> He gets degrees in making jam
> At Liverpool and Birmingham.[12]

But already in the Victorian period there were important signs of malaise. It was sensed, particularly, but not exclusively, by representatives of newer subjects, that the historical conditions allowing Oxbridge complete supremacy in higher education were passing, and that a new effort at accommodation between the ancient universities and important interests outside was necessary. During the first world war the sharp donnish distinction between applied and pure research disappeared in the interests of patriotism and national survival.

Specialization was both a cause and a consequence of the diversification of academic life in the second half of the nineteenth century. Or to explain it another way, it is not absolutely clear that interest in an academic specialty in every case preceded its professional development. Other variables were important—the availability of academic employment, for example. The German case, whereby chairs in new disciplines were sometimes established because the professorial system closed off academic mobility, is well known. The acceptance of a new subject into the university world, whether in Germany or in England, was not automatic. Despite the belief that knowledge must advance and that innovation was essential to the continued vitality of a university, academics zealously guarded their areas of influence. Recognition had to be fought for, sometimes in bitter competition with established fields. Specific goals had to be elaborated, financial support obtained, positions acquired, a place in the curriculum, in the library, or in the laboratory to be found. Efforts had to be made to enlist the interests of students and obtain other forms of public support. Publicity and advertizing became necessary, and large claims were sometimes made on behalf of young subjects in order to assure their support and survival. The history of the university in the past hundred years is certainly a wonderful account of new ideas and discoveries, but it is also an account of academic manoeuvring on a new scale. It is to a considerable extent the history of precisely those professional or pedagogical associations that arose to defend and promote developing academic or occupational interests. The internal histories of all universities have been profoundly affected by the growth of professional associations. The collegiate structure, because it is mainly, if not solely, used for teaching, has been the most successful in resisting the implications of specialism, although it, too, ultimately derives its academic direction from the faculty boards and from the examination system.

The growth of professional associations generally between 1850 and 1900 was an extraordinary development. In 1850 they were comparatively rare.

There were naturally philosophical and literary societies within the universities and journal publications. But the number of such groups was limited, and their place in both university life and in the development of academic specialism was not significant. When in the 1850s dons testified before the royal commissions investigating the teaching, discipline, and finance of the ancient universities, they usually did so as individuals. The one single important group to appear in the 1850s was the Oxford Tutors' Association, which lobbied successfully for college teaching, but the Oxford Tutors' Association was not, strictly speaking, a professional organization. Its task was not to certify skills, but to defend an interest within one single academic institution. The same was true of another pressure group composed of professors which formed in opposition to the tutors. By the end of the century the number of groups, academic interests, associations, and specialties that could be expected to testify before a government commission or committee of inquiry was staggering. When the reorganization of the University of London was considered at the end of the nineteenth century and the beginning of the twentieth, representatives of medical and legal associations, of hospitals, colleges, and schools all came forward to present their views on liberal and professional education, as did ad hoc groups formed to represent teachers of different income and status categories, field workers in social science subjects, and representatives from architectural firms. Throughout England, business, industry, and even local government began to take an interest in the work of university-trained professionals.

Specialism and professionalism account for changes in the development of the modern university which appear as contradictions. Specialism produced differentiation within the university, complicated its structure of governance, and changed academic roles. The development of the academic career gave university scholars and scientists a greater interest in the internal affairs of their institutions than they were allowed to have in the days of the Oxbridge prize fellowship system and the nonresident professor. Interests were turned inward to the institution, as they had once been forced outwards away from it. But at the same time, the organization of specialists into professional associations, arranging national and international meetings, sponsoring special projects, publishing journals and newsletters, created an extended university community such as had not existed in principle since the Middle Ages. Specialism also enabled academic persons to look outwards from their institutions by involving them in the many activities of an enormously complex industrial society, voracious in its demands for new skills and proficiencies.

It is a paradox of the modern university that while the number and level of its contacts to outside communities have vastly increased through the activity of its members, its overall size, internal differentiation, and international character, its involvement in administration, teaching, and research has given it a complete self-absorption. University faculties feel little need for the kind of social contacts yearned for by isolated Georgian dons. Unless there are some compelling institutional reasons to do so—usually fund-raising in some form or public relations—the average university teacher is content to remain with his peers. Whatever the necessity for outside contacts, they rarely have anything to do with career or personal advancement except in the most remote and indirect sense. The modern university faculty member has his professional identification, his standing in the community of scholarship and science, and his special institutional affiliation; but he has no social model in the narrow sense on which to form himself. He knows of no single outside reference group as important to him as the gentlemen of Georgian England were indispensable to the monks and pedants of Oxford and Cambridge. The importance of this change for the history of a liberal education is that 'getting-along' has ceased to be a social problem for dons, even if 'getting-on' remains.

Yet another paradox of the modern English university (or, for that matter, Scottish and American ones) is the degree to which it has been able to balance its internal values against outside interests. A high degree of intellectual autonomy co-exists with numerous obligations to groups outside—to government, to industry, to the professions, to broadcasting, and to journalism. The contemporary university has been able to assume a primary place in modern social and economic life which the Georgian university could not, and it has been able to do this without developing or trying to develop shared intellectual or social values with the rest of society. This is a point certainly worth remembering when the university is denounced for being completely the servant of the State or subservient to the dominant economic interests within it.

Yet despite the great degree of intellectual freedom existing within universities, it is unduly optimistic to conclude that conflicts affecting the intellectual autonomy and self-governing status of universities do not exist and will not exist. By no means is the modern university absolute master in its own kingdom. Not even the University Grants Committee of the Treasury, representing as it mainly does the academic community, is a perfect guarantor of university independence. Any time an educational institution assumes or is forced to assume relationships with influential bodies outside itself, questions affecting the priority of studies within the university and the values professed by it inevitably arise. Decision-making is then to some extent shared, especially if money is involved. But to speak for a moment only of yesterday, it is certain that one great historical achievement of the past century has been the extent to which scholars and scientists have been able to choose their subjects and develop them largely through professional control of the content. If research problems did not always originate within the universities, certainly methods for solving the problems were developed there and new projects and lines of inquiry started.

Academic professionalism, original research, the new involvement with outside institutions inevitably created a basic change not only in the concept of liberal education, but also in the whole function or purpose of a university, in what Newman, adapting Coleridge, had called its 'idea'. Of course, that 'idea' was closely related to the type of education provided within the university, and so it had been customary to view the university as a liberal arts institution. It was common in the early nineteenth century to regard the university as always having been a liberal arts institution and to deny that it had ever had any other rival purpose. 'The most ancient part of the University of Paris was the faculty of arts or philosophy,' wrote a don in 1835. In his view the *trivium* and *quadrivium* were no less than the twin pillars of a liberal education, conveniently corresponding to the philology and mathematics taught at Oxford and Cambridge. 'The original functions of a University were those of a "school of arts", out of which the three professional faculties were subsequently developed. It was a *studium generale*, and could send forth *sophistae generales*, and *magistri artium*, with reference only to the acknowledged elements of a liberal education, and without any regard to the professional destination of its students.'[13]

It was precisely at the turn of the century that the historian and theologian Hastings Rashdall challenged and overturned this long-standing conclusion regarding the origins of the university. He argued—and his viewpoint has prevailed—that professional education had always been the distinguishing characteristic of the university. In his monumental study of the European university and in the lectures he gave around the kingdom, he publicized his findings in an obvious effort to promote support for a university ideal with which he was completely in accord. No longer was it improper for universities to relate their education directly to careers or to train their students for specific professional occupations, as in fact they had long been doing. There had always been some attempt by someone to twist the strands of a liberal education round some honourable career. A correct understanding of the origins of the European university showed that this was the only proper course. The Rashdall view legitimated the developing situation—the new idea for a university—by giving an historical explanation for it. He used historical method, as others of his generation were using it, to trace the origins of institutions in order to clarify the meaning of their development, and the message was clear: polite education and character formation were later and undesirable accretions.

Once career preparation was seen to be the true purpose of a university education, one of the oldest hurdles in the history of liberal education could be surmounted. General education was unnecessary if there were so many occupations in society for which a university education could prepare undergraduates. Why should university faculties trouble themselves over a definition of education that put them in the awkward position of having to identify those occupations appropriate for a university-educated person and those not? Why be jesuitical? A veil was lifted, as Professor Dale of University College, London, had tried to lift it in the early nineteenth century when he said there were no differences between liberal and professional forms of education.[14] He was roundly criticized. And yet the problem was not so easily resolved, for perhaps there had been a point to the defence of liberal education through the centuries and possibly there remained a lesson worth considering even in a mature, industrial society. A disquieting sense of a lost and valued principle continued to trouble the minds of academicians, even as they struggled to eliminate traditional categories and ideas from their understanding of the purposes of a liberal education. Some of the difficulties involved in accepting Rashdall's discovery are beautifully illustrated in a report issued by the University Grants Committee on 3 February 1921:

'There is indeed no inherent antagonism between a liberal and vocational training,' the report began, continuing with the Rashdall conclusion: 'Universities began in mediaeval times as groups of teachers and students devoted to the study of some profession, and since a large number of students in the departments of the Arts and Pure Science Faculties of a modern University enter the teaching profession, their University training is in a sense as vocational as that of students taking courses with more directly utilitarian applications.' Here the committee was guilty of adopting a common fallacy. Because students will use their education for entry into a particular occupation does not mean the education they received is designed with that job in mind. As if to recognize the fallacy, the committee then contrasted the arts and pure sciences courses with subjects 'more directly utilitarian', although another qualifying sentence immediately followed: 'It is clearly impossible to draw a hard and fast line between pure theory and practical application.' Not wishing to abandon the attempt completely, however, the committee then resorted to a traditional definition: 'The difference between a liberal and vocational training lies not so much in the subject studied as in the spirit in which it is pursued. What is essential is to maintain that breadth and proportion of view which are implied by a University standpoint.' Yet further on in the same report, the requirement of breadth was gently nudged aside, still struggling, as specialization, the antithesis of breadth, was eased into its place. 'The bases on which all Applied Science is founded are ever broadening as the boundaries of knowledge are extended,' the committee observed. 'It follows that University courses must tend to become increasingly exacting if they are to be continuously informed with fundamental scientific principles.' No fundamental literary principles, but fundamental scientific principles. It is true that the phrase 'increasingly exacting' need not be, strictly speaking, tied to specialization, but that is certainly the overall drift and context of the report. The entire discussion is far away in 'spirit' from what the Georgians believed the nature of a liberal education to be, and not at all what they would have understood as 'that breadth and proportion of view which are implied by a University standpoint.'[15]

The report is a characteristic document of the twentieth century, an unsuccessful attempt to combine principles of education which were once certainly antithetical and still do not reconcile easily. A reluctance to abandon the past forces the ideas of yesterday to dress in uncomfortable and unsuitable clothes. Over and over again we can notice the same attempt by scholars and scientists and men and women of ideas to define liberal education by joining principles and values that at bottom have different historical origins and acutely different cultural meanings and purposes.[16]

Surveying the course of university history from 1914, a twentieth-century Georgian would have noticed an enormous change in the influence exerted over education in general, over the professions, and over government by English universities. Never since the mid seventeenth century had they been so important, and never had their relationships with so many other institutions been so involved and far-reaching. The examination system, which had been one of the great changes of the early nineteenth century, gave the universities *de facto* control over the curriculum of the secondary schools through school-leaving and scholarship examinations, and over higher education in general through the university extra-mural teaching movements and the local examinations. The schools periodically rebelled against this power, demanding showdown conferences to resolve outstanding differences, but once established, the benevolent tyranny remained. Through examinations the future elite was drawn out of the secondary schools into the universities, and the standard of high school education generally was maintained nationally. What existed in 1900 or 1914 had not existed in 1650 or in 1750, 1800 or in 1850: educational systems organized on a national scale providing instruction for hundreds of thousands of children and young persons at least through elementary school and for many of them through secondary school, all orchestrated from above by a number of government departments whose members were recruited from the universities, particularly from Oxbridge. And the lever which moved this mass was the belief in the supremacy of the discipline and in the autonomy of the subject. It was quite out of the question to rank subjects according to either their intrinsic worth or their utility. What was important was scientific method. No matter what the subject, it could be treated scientifically. Scientific modes of comprehension were the essence of any kind of education, whether liberal or professional, whether in medicine, metallurgy, business administration, classics, genetics, or in the deciphering of cuneiform tablets.

Notes

1 See Sheldon Rothblatt, *The Revolution of the Dons* (London and New York, 1968), Part II.

2 Report of the Royal Commission on Durham University, Parliamentary Papers 1863, XLVI. Evidence, 95.

3 Sir Henry Enfield Roscoe, *Life and Experiences* (London and New York, 1906), 47.

4 Walter Raleigh, *The Meaning of a University* (Oxford, 1911), 17–18.

5 Ibid.

6 Report of the Royal Commission on University Education in London, Parliamentary Papers 1911 (Cd. 5911), XX, 500.

7 A. T. Milne, 'History at the Universities: Then and Now', in *History*, LIX (February, 1974), 40.

8 C. H. S. Fifoot, *Frederic William Maitland, A Life* (Cambridge, Mass., 1971), 92.

9 Arthur Sidgwick and Eleanor M. Sidgwick, *Henry Sidgwick, A Memoir* (London, 1906), 460–1.

10 For a summary of the two positions, plus an excellent review of the issues involved in the creation of modern academic associations, see the materials collected by the Sociological Society entitled *Sociological Papers* (London, 1905), British Museum Ac 2263.

11 Michael Sanderson, *The Universities and British Industry 1850–1970* (London, 1972), 93.

12 Ibid., 93–5. Lord Ashby has commented on the important change in the relations of the new Victorian universities and their lay governing councils. The latter were supposed to guarantee some kind of interplay between industry, commerce, local public life, and the universities; but in time initiative came solely from inside the universities, and the influence from outside dissipated. See A. C. Crombie, ed., *Scientific Change* (London, 1963), 727.

13 Quoted in John William Donaldson, *Classical Scholarship and Classical Learning* (Cambridge, 1856), 20, 25.

14 Thomas Dale, *An Introductory Lecture* (London, 1828), 8.

15 Report of the University Grants Committee, 3 February 1921, 10.

16 But to be fair, it must be reiterated that the muddle is as much Victorian as twentieth-century. See the address by the Professor of Greek at St. Andrews entitled *The End of Liberal Education* (Edinburgh, 1868). His argument bounces back and forth from character formation to 'an increased perception of the inward power and freedom of the human spirit', to cultivating intellect, to the 'simple love of truth', and to finding 'the highest form under which we ourselves and this universe, and the Great First Cause, and the relation of each to all, may be most perfectly conceived'.

The recent symposium on higher education in the United States arranged by *Daedalus* (Fall, 1974) certainly proves that American efforts to define liberal education are vexed and uncertain. It also illustrates how universal is the tendency to extract specific educational ideals and values from confining historical contexts. For example, in the course of one essay, Martin Meyerson, President of the University of Pennsylvania, moves through almost all the customary attributes and purposes of liberal instruction as if ambiguities do not exist. Liberal education is equated with breadth, with being 'flexible, civilized, and responsible', with learning for its own sake, with the 'analytic method that has been the ideal of the arts and sciences', with humane objectives and with a life of service united to a calling. Meyerson goes on to repeat the common opinion that 'Humanistic and scientific learning have been divorced. In the eighteenth and nineteenth centuries science was seen as part of the humanistic achievements of man, a liberating force. Now science is confused with technology and is sometimes viewed by humanists as a threat to the values of our culture.' If my own argument is correct, this view has to be substantially qualified, at least for England. I have also been suggesting that the omnibus ideals commonly associated with liberal education are contradictory in historical terms and are more than the tradition can bear, whether in England or elsewhere. This is not to say that they are unworthy but to question the possibility of their realization in our own time.

115

EMERGING CONCEPTS OF THE ACADEMIC PROFESSION AT OXFORD 1800–1854

Arthur Engel

Source: L. Stone, *The University in Society*, vol. I: *Oxford and Cambridge from the 14th to the Early 19th Century*, Princeton: Princeton University Press, 1974, pp. 305–51.

I. Introduction

Throughout the 18th and early 19th centuries, the University of Oxford was the object of bitter public denunciations. It was argued that the colleges were "close corporations," eccentric, uncompetitive, and often corrupt in their elections to fellowships; operating simply to distribute their income and other benefits among the members of their foundations. The examinations for degrees were denounced as meaningless rituals, emptied of all educational content.

Despite these criticisms, until 1854 the university continued to be governed by the statutes given by Archbishop Laud in the early 17th century. The examination system was reformed beginning in 1800, but the structure of university and college institutions remained unchanged. The government of the university was in the hands of the Hebdomadal Board, consisting of all heads of colleges and halls together with the two proctors, the chief disciplinary officers of the university. All students were required to be members of a college or hall in order to matriculate and be eligible for degrees in the university.

The university also provided a number of professorships (nineteen in 1800, twenty-five by 1854). The professors were appointed in various ways. The six Regius Professors were appointed by the crown. A few were elected by large assemblies (the Lady Margaret Chair in Divinity by all who had taken divinity degrees in the university, the Poetry Professorship by all M.A.'s who kept their names on the books of their colleges). Most professors,

371

however, were selected by smaller boards consisting generally of the heads of certain colleges together with certain important public officials. According to the statutes, the professors were to provide instruction through public lectures. The problem was that most of the professorships were in areas outside of the curriculum (geology, astronomy, modern history, medicine, etc.). Therefore, the professors could expect few students to attend their lectures. Also, the endowments for many of these chairs were so small (in some cases as little as £50 per annum) that the professors were often either nonresident or involved in other tasks within the university. The result was that most of the professors ceased to lecture in the 18th century and fulfilled no real function within the university.

Thus, by the Laudian Statutes, the colleges became the center of the life of the university. The colleges were autonomous corporations, governed in most cases by their fellows and the heads, elected by the fellows. The headships were generally given to one of the fellows or former fellows of the college. Virtually all of the fellowships were restricted to men born in particular localities, or to those who had attended particular schools. Most colleges were also required by their statutes to prefer candidates who could prove descent from the founder of the college. A fellowship entitled its holder to a share in the income derived from the property held by the college as a charitable foundation. In general, the fellowship was tenable for life on the conditions of taking holy orders within a specified period, remaining unmarried, and not holding a church living or other income over a certain value. The colleges also owned advowsons; i.e., the right to appoint clergymen to church livings. These livings, when they fell vacant, were offered to the fellows of the college in order of seniority. Teaching and administrative duties within the college were performed by several of the fellows, selected either by the head, or by co-optation, or on a system of rotation, while the remainder of the fellows were free to use their fellowships simply as incomes to enable them to begin their careers, generally within the church.

The fellows of colleges made up the vast majority of the dons; i.e., the senior academic community of the university. There were about 500 fellowships divided among the nineteen colleges. The college officers—the tutors, lecturers, deans, bursars, etc.—were all selected from among the fellows of each college. Aside from these fellowships, there were only about fifty other official positions in the university; the twenty-four headships of colleges and halls, the professorships, the eight Canonries of Christ Church and a few other university offices. These fifty positions were the only ones in the university in the early 19th century which could be held by married men. Some of these positions, notably the headships of colleges, the Canonries at Christ Church, and a few of the professorial chairs were rich prizes providing fine houses and large incomes. Many of the others, however, provided little more than an honorarium.

In the early 19th century, one more class was added to the senior academic community: the coaches. The coaches were called into being by the reform of the examination system. Beginning in 1800, the examination system was gradually transformed from a formal ritual into a genuine competitive test. The examination statutes of 1800 and 1807 set up honors examinations in *Literae Humaniores* (classical studies; including history, literature and philosophy, as well as languages) and in science and mathematics. The ordinary "pass" school was also made into at least something of a genuine test of knowledge. All through the 18th century, the examination for the B.A. had been a purely formal ritual of answering standard questions known in advance, and reading a "wall lecture," so called because the examiners would generally leave during the reading of the lecture. It was purely a formal requirement that the lecture be read and the examiners were not required to judge its quality.

One unintended result of the reform of the examination system was that a demand was created for teaching beyond that which was provided by the colleges. The quality of collegiate instruction depended in large part on the ability and energy of the individual tutor or lecturer. In general, however, collegiate instruction was by "catechetical lectures"; i.e., classes composed of all students in the college, regardless of attainments, who wished to present a particular classical text for the examination. In class, the text would be read and translated, the lecturer making remarks on both the language and the substance of the work. This method was ill-adapted to the needs of both those students whose classical preparation was weak and those students who wished to take the honors examinations. The system of coaching grew up to meet the needs of these students for more personal and intensive teaching. The coaches were outside of the official body of collegiate and university instructors. For a fee of about £10 per term, a coach would undertake to give private instruction to a student generally in the last year before his examinations. The coaches in Oxford in most cases were young men who had taken these examinations recently and who wished to remain in Oxford in the hope of obtaining a fellowship. It was of course possible for a man to marry and remain in Oxford as a coach; however, the uncertainty of the income and the lack of any official status made the position undesirable as a career.

In the early 19th century, the Oxford don was by profession a clergyman, not a university teacher. In most cases, holy orders were a condition for holding his fellowship, and he was destined to resign his fellowship after about ten years in order to fulfill the duties of a country parson. The church was the only profession smoothly connected to the holding of a fellowship. It was, of course, possible for a man to use his fellowship income to support himself while attempting to make a career in law or medicine. However, the colleges could not provide clients or patients, while they could provide church livings. The result was that even in those colleges such as Merton, in which fellows were not required to be in holy orders, the great majority did, in fact, choose this path. Typically, a man would take a fellowship soon after receiving his B.A., and for the next ten to fifteen years he would draw an income from the college. During this period, he would take deacon's and then priest's orders and he would probably spend some part of this time as a curate or holding a poor living. If the living was in or near Oxford, he would live in his rooms in college. It was also probable that at some point during his tenure of the fellowship, this hypothetical don would be called upon to take a college office—dean, tutor, bursar, etc.—which would alike require residence. At the end of this period of ten to fifteen years, the don would probably have acquired enough seniority among the fellows to be offered one of the college livings. He would then take the living, resign his fellowship, and leave Oxford for a career in the church. Clearly, for this man, the fellowship and teaching duties in Oxford were not a career for life; they were a prize and a rung on a ladder leading to a career in the church.

By the end of the 19th century, this career link had become the exception rather than the rule. The outward structure of a fellowship had changed little, but its function had been altered drastically. Most fellows, and virtually all of the younger ones, were engaged in teaching within the colleges. Further, their teaching was no longer an interlude before commencing their true career, it was their career itself. Many would remain in Oxford all their lives as teachers and scholars and even those who left often went to positions at other universities. The outlines of the academic life as a profession had already been drawn.

This transformation has not gone unnoticed by the historians of the university. The earliest historians of this period regarded this change as part of the general process of the elimination of corruption.[1] Depending on the individual historian's temperament, the 18th century university might be viewed with either indignation or amusement; but all were agreed in accepting the 18th century denunciations at face value. Since these first historians were the heirs to this transformation, their works inevitably partook of the nature of self-congratulation. The more recent historians have modified this portrait by removing the overt value-judgment while maintaining the same essential view. The 18th century attacks have been seen as emanating from political and ecclesiastical party conflict rather than simply from righteous indignation.[2] In its adherence to High Church, Tory, even Jacobite orientations, the university was truly, in Mathew Arnold's phrase, the home of "lost causes and impossible loyalties."

For W. R. Ward, the most recent historian of the university, the great revolution of the 19th century was the removal of Oxford from the arena of politics in order to allow it to concentrate on its prime tasks of education and research. One problem in his account is that since these latter functions are taken for granted as the proper tasks of the university, their antecedents have gone unanalyzed. The relationship of this transformation to the events and movements of the early 19th century has not been explained. No attempt has been made to relate the development of an academic profession to the attacks on Oxford by the *Edinburgh Review*, the reform of the examination system, or the Tractarian Movement. Ward concludes with a guarded compromise: "The shape of Oxford in the [eighteen-] 'eighties . . . bore the marks of Manchester as well as Westminster, of Berlin as well as Christ Church."[3] Perhaps this is a useful antidote to the view based on Mathew Arnold's Oxford, "so unravaged by the fierce intellectual life of this century," and Max Beerbohm's "city where nothing is ever born and nothing ever quite dies." Essentially, Ward argues that the institutional and intellectual peculiarities of Oxford had only the effect of hopelessly confusing the ideological conflicts of this period: "The development of the professorial and tutorial ideals described here gave rise to sharply differing notions of the organization, instruction and social function of a university, but so complex was the university constitution, and so complicated was English parliamentary life for much of the period, that a headlong clash of ideals could hardly ever take place."[4]

The present essay is an attempt to trace the complex and oblique way in which these ideals did clash. It also tries to show that crucial to the intellectual conflicts and institutional changes at Oxford in the first half of the 19th century was the question of whether the university was to provide careers for academic men; and, if so, what sorts of careers these were to be in terms of functions, status, and income.

II. Early reform proposals

The idea of university teaching as a profession played little or no part in the reform debates of the late 18th and early 19th centuries. Complaints about the fellowship system were concentrated on the venality of elections and the lack of a proper life of discipline and poverty for the fellows. The reformers generally confined themselves to simple denunciations, but when they did venture to suggest reforms, the suggestions can be seen as directly counter to the encouragement of an academic profession. One writer suggested that fellowships ought to be limited to twenty years' tenure rather than to be held on condition of celibacy. He argued that the existing system "occasions many persons spending their whole life in a College, without doing any the least service to their country, but to their own hurt, being generally, as they advance in years, over-run with spleen or taking to sottishness."[5] The author admitted that the twenty-year limit might be relaxed for two fellows, at the most, in each college if they had served as tutors for fifteen years: these men should be allowed their fellowships for life on the ground that since they are "pretty much obliged to keep to academical learning they cannot so well pursue the study of some profession."[6] The author did not indicate that any educational advantage would accrue to the student or university from this extended tenure in the tutorial office. He merely recognized that since the tutor would not have been able to prepare himself for any profession, it would be unfair to take away his fellowship after twenty years.

Even in regard to the venality of fellowship elections, the reformers did not complain that fellowships were not given to the men of the highest intellectual merit; rather, they complained that fellowships were given to rich men who did not use them as their sole means of support.

> Fellowships are rarely given to Scholars of *low condition*, whatever be their Merit. Men of *Family* and *Fortune* are, now, not only ready to *accept* of them, but make great Interest to procure them. . . . *Possessed* of the Endowments, they live not in the simple, frugal Manner, so necessary to Health, and Study and Virtue, which their Founders designed they should. . . . A Founder's Endowment is no longer considered as a charitable Provision for *intire* Maintenance, or as laying any obligation upon those who accept of it to observe his Rules, but as a Branch of their Revenue in general to be spent in the manner they like best.[7]

Clearly, these men had no conception of university teaching as a lifetime career or of a fellowship as providing a satisfactory stipend for a teacher.

The first criticisms of Oxford which questioned this idea of academic life in the university were in the famous articles of the *Edinburgh Review* of 1808–10.[8] Although the main thrust of the attack was directed against the system of classical education at Oxford, the reviewer also criticized the lack of scholarly activity within the university. In discussing the classical texts published by the Clarendon Press at Oxford, the reviewer observed that "though this learned Body have occasionally availed themselves of the sagacity and erudition of Runken, Wyttenback, Heyné and other *foreign* professors, they have, of late, added nothing of their own, except what they derived from the superior skill of British manufacturers, and the superior wealth of their establishment; namely, whiter paper, blacker ink, and neater types."[9] There was no overt call in the *Review* for the university to take the advancement of learning as one of its goals, but this was the clear implication of this taunt. It was certainly taken as such by Edward Copleston, then a Fellow and Tutor of Oriel College, who took upon himself the task of defending the university against these attacks:

> If we send out into the world an annual supply of men, whose minds are imbued with literature according to their several measures of capacity, impressed with what we hold to be the soundest principles of policy and religion, grounded in the elements of science and taught how they may best direct their efforts to further attainments in that line . . . I think we do a greater and more solid

good to the nation, than if we sought to extend over Europe the fame of a few exalted individuals or to acquire renown by exploring untrodden regions, and by holding up to the world ever ready to admire what is new, the fruits of our discovery.[10]

It is interesting that Copleston identified the advancement of knowledge with a system of teaching through public, professorial lectures to large classes even though no mention was made of the professorial system in the *Review* articles. Copleston noted that the system of instruction at Oxford was "not by solemn public lectures, delivered to a numerous class from a Professor's Chair, but by private study in their respective colleges."[11] The system of collegiate lectures, he argued, was more effective as a means of instruction since the student was given more individual attention and the instructor could gear his teaching to the capacities and previous knowledge of each of his students.[12] He added:

> I would not undervalue these higher doings [public lectures]; but we must be cautious how they lead us our of the track of plain and sober industry. A thirst for distinction may interfere with homely duties more really important to mankind. Our husbandry is truly on a large scale; but let us beware how we sacrifice, after the example of vain, ostentatious breeders, the food of some twenty or thirty, for the sake of making a proud shew of one.[13]

The advancement of knowledge and public lectures were linked together by Copleston by the fact that he considered them both "more exalted" and "higher doings" which benefited the few at the expense of the many. Likewise, teaching and the system of collegiate lectures were thought to be bound together since both were "homely duties" conducive of "greater and more solid good" than the advancement of knowledge or professorial lectures. This connection between the professorial system and the advancement of learning was to have a long history in the ideological debate over the nature of an academic profession in 19th century Oxford. The conception of professorial lectures as the "higher" form of teaching was also to have a long life, although it would eventually be overthrown by the idealization of the tutorial system which was to replace the collegiate, catechetical lecture as the prime mode of Oxford teaching.

Although this controversy of 1808–10 may be seen as the first glimmering of the debate from which there eventually developed the idea of an academic profession at Oxford, it was not until the 1830s that direct attacks were made on the existing structure of academic life. It is significant that it was also in this period from 1800 to 1830 that the working of the new system of examinations established in 1800 began to have its effect. These new examinations put a great strain on the teaching resources of the colleges. It was discovered that richly endowed colleges with from ten to upward of forty M.A.'s on their foundations were unable to provide adequate instruction to enable their students to pass the new examinations. The inadequacy of collegiate tuition was made up by the development of a class of private coaches who prepared students individually for the examinations. These coaches were never officially recognized by the college authorities, in fact, they were often condemned as mere crammers. Nonetheless, by the 1830s, they had become an important, though embarrassing, element in the academic system.[14] This situation inevitably stimulated both a greater emphasis on the teaching function of the colleges and a serious questioning of the institutions and mechanisms by which these inadequate collegiate teachers were selected and supported.

As usual, the *Edinburgh Review* was the first to attack. In 1831, Sir William Hamilton wrote two articles[15] in which he argued that university education ought to be conducted by professors who taught one subject which they knew well, rather than by college tutors each of whom had to teach all subjects, though generally not qualified to teach any particular subject in depth. He argued that the fellows, from among whom the tutors were always selected, were not elected for their intellectual merit, but rather, were usually chosen according to the capricious will of the founder of the college and through fortuitous circumstances. Most importantly, he argued that the institution of the fellowship was not calculated to induce men to view teaching as a serious occupation.

> The fellow who in general undertakes the office [of tutor] and continues the longest to discharge it, is a clerical expectant whose hopes are bounded by a college living and who, until the wheel of promotion has moved round, is content to relieve the tedium of a leisure life by the interest of an occupation, and to improve his income by its emoluments. Thus, it is that tuition is not engaged in as an important, arduous, responsible, and permanent occupation; but lightly viewed and undertaken as a matter of convenience, a business by the by, a state of transition, a stepping-stone to something else.[16]

The old criticism of the venality and corruption of fellowship elections took on a new specificity in the situation of the 1830s. Instead of criticizing these practices as misappropriations of charitable endowments, one reformer argued that "the manner of the appointment of . . . tutors, and the body out of which they are chosen, do not in general afford the least security for their being fit repositories of the trust committed to them."[17] One step toward the solution of the problem was that fellowships should be awarded on the basis of intellectual merit. Thus the reformer was forced to sanction the altering of founders' wills or even parliamentary intervention in order to achieve his end.[18] Other reformers believed that the root of the problem was the system by which fellowships had to be resigned on marriage.

> If a person who has neglected all means of improvement, be once selected Fellow anywhere, he is far less likely to give up his advantages by marriage, than a man of cultivated and powerful mind. The former has looked to his fellowship as a maintenance, and thinks that if he lose it, he shall never get so good a thing again. Thus the natural inclination to marry, thwarted by the Oxford law of restriction, cannot but operate to draw off from the Colleges just those men whom the University should wish to keep; and if those who remain clinging to her through life are but the refuse intellect of the place, it is not to be wondered at; We believe that the Colleges which have the cleverest body of Fellows, generally find them pass off most quickly, either by marriage or by other appointments. This appears more desirable than stagnation; yet a quick succession of very young tutors is by no means desirable. On the present plan the two evils co-exist to a great degree.[19]

These critics of the 1830s did not all go so far as Hamilton in implying that the colleges should be reduced to boardinghouses for those rich enough to afford them and that all instruction be given over to university professors. Some proposed both a reform of the fellowship system and a revival of the professoriate,[20] in order to obtain more effective teaching. Others timidly asserted that "professorships should be made the means of as much good as the altered system of education will permit."[21]

In his articles, Hamilton did not emphasize the deficiency of Oxford from the viewpoint of the advancement of knowledge. Only at one point did he mention this weakness while alluding to the ideal of the German professorial system.[22] Another critic, however, concentrated more on this point, although he also dealt at great length with the deficiencies of Oxford teaching. Significantly, the ideal of the advancement of knowledge as a function of the university was again tied closely to the ideal of the professorial system as it existed on the Continent and particularly in Germany. In Oxford,

> philology itself, in which one would expect Oxford to excell, is not known as the science which it has become in the hands of the inquisitive Germans. . . . That Oxford has exceedingly fallen back in comparison with her ancient fame, cannot be denied. Once she stood on a par with the most celebrated foreign universities. Even more recently her Professors were of leading rank in oriental studies. Now we hear of Paris, Copenhagen and Petersburg as the center of numberless publications in the languages of the East and North; but of Oxford, nothing of the kind. She seems to have long been living

on German classics and on French and Cambridge mathematics. The Germans have so outstripped her in Greek, Latin, Arabic, and Hebrew criticism, in Philology at large, in Biblical antiquities, in Ecclesiastical and other ancient history, that for a length of time she will have nothing to do but translate from German authors.[23]

The defenders of Oxford against these criticisms, especially those of Hamilton, did not really come to grips with the proposal to reorganize Oxford so that teaching would be recognized as a career for life. James Ingram, the President of Trinity College, Oxford, simply enumerated a list of eminent men who had been Oxford tutors, as a defense of the university against Hamilton's criticisms. Further, he blandly asserted that the existing system of education combined satisfactorily the professorial and the tutorial modes of instruction.[24] Another defender of the university, the Reverend Vaughan Thomas, repeated Copleston's argument that the personal supervision provided by the collegiate lecture was a far more effective method of education than large professorial lectures.[25] No mention was made of the substantive accusations leveled against the existing collegiate system. The reason for this neglect of specific accusations seems to have been that the defenders basically rested their support of the existing system at Oxford on its efficiency in preserving the university from the religious heresy rampant in the continental universities. Thomas accused the *Edinburgh* reviewer of being "just fresh from the classroom of a Dr. Birchschneider or a Dr. Wagschneider, or some other Teutonic Gamaliel, with a name as unutterable as his blasphemies."[26]

> Be the imperfections of our seminaries what they may, I am acquainted with no other situations where young men can be so largely stored with principles that may enable them to detect the fallacy, and to escape the contamination of those metaphysical novelties, which are said to have gained a wide and dangerous ascendancy on the continent. After the recent downfall, and amidst the rapid decay of similar institutions in foreign countries, OUR UNIVERSITIES are the main pillars, not only of the learning, and perhaps the science, but of the virtue and piety (whether seen or unseen) which yet remain among us.[27]

III. The Tractarian movement

It is ironic that this last quotation from a pamphlet by the Reverend Vaughan Thomas was to be cited approvingly in 1837 by the *British Critic*, the organ of the Tractarian party in Oxford, since it was this movement which, in the 1840s, was to do most toward undermining the credibility of this defense. As one journal remarked after Newman had been received into the Roman Catholic Church,

> Within a recent period the hereditary instinctive confidence of England in its Universities has been broken by painful revelations. The nation has been compelled to believe, what once it would fain have rejected, as a monstrous libel. The nation has been compelled to accept as a fact, that for years the Universities have been the seat of a dangerous, and too successful conspiracy against the faith of which they were supposed to be the bulwarks.[28]

High Churchmen might complain that "Tractarian" was simply being used by the enemies of the autonomy of the universities as an effective brush to tar the supporters of that autonomy,[29] but there can be no doubt that, in fact, after the flight of Newman and other Tractarians to Rome, Thomas's type of argument was largely discredited. Oxford could no longer be regarded as a reliable defender of the Church of England.

But the effect of Tractarianism on the development of the idea of an academic profession was not merely to discredit Oxford as a support for the Established Church. In the late 1830s and 1840s, the Tractarians were one of the few articulate groups within Oxford with a coherent program for reform. Their program was visionary and seemingly calculated to annoy the traditional Tory supporters of the university. Indeed, its main effect seems to have been to divide the defenders of Oxford. The Tractarians argued that the university must overtly embrace a monastic ideal, rather than compromise with the utilitarian values of the day. Only in this way could the university preserve its autonomy and its essential character. Their indictment of the *status quo* emphasized the futile and suicidal attempt to compromise with the spirit of the times.

> If persons like ourselves might presume to offer its [the University's] members any counsel, it would be never to forget that their present life is but a continuation of the life of past ages, that they are, after all, only in a new form and with new names, the Benedictines and Augustinians of a former day. The monastic element, a most important ingredient in the social character of the Church, lingers among them, when the nation at large has absorbed it in the frivolous or evil tempers and opinions of an advanced period of civilization. . . . Institutions come to nothing when they abandon the principle which they embody; Oxford has ever failed in self-respect, and has injured its inward health and stability, as often as it has forgotten that it was a creation of the middle ages, and has affected new fashions or yielded to external pressure.[30]

In a review of G. R. M. Ward's translation of the Statutes of Magdalen College, Oxford, the monastic ideal was made more specific. The college ought to return to its original function as a home for forty "poor scholars," the fellows of the college, and a president, all united in a common life of frugality, prayer, piety, and theological study. The model was not to be a theological college for the training of parish clergy, like the Dissenter's Homerton or the Roman Catholic's Maymooth[31] nor should it be modeled on "some Prussian or French academy."[32] Rather, the ideal was to be St. Maur, the monastery devoted to the collection of theological documents by monk-scholars of the Order.[33]

These ideals in themselves would have been enough to alienate many of the defenders of the *status quo*; however, this effect was intensified by the language of these articles. One Tractarian reviewer casually remarked that "it is really losing time and toil to deny what is as plain as day, that Oxford has, and ever has had, what men of the world will call a popish character."[34] This was clearly waving a red flag before the Anglican bull. In discussing the proper social background for a clergyman, another Tractarian reviewer took the opportunity to strike out at the Anglican ideal of merging the character of squire and parson: ". . . if it is thought that gentlemanlike habits are well-nigh indispensible for the clergy (as who will deny their advantage) it must be remembered also that the Catholic Church embodies all that is most ennobling in the universe, and that it can only be where her institutions are crippled and imperfect that she can take at secondhand from the world qualities which in their true sense, none can bestow more amply than herself. Gentlemen, therefore, the Church must have; but they must be priest-gentlemen, not samples of the squirearchy."[35]

The significance of the Tractarian movement in the development of the idea of an academic profession was not merely in its role as one of the defenders of the university from "external pressure." Through both the manner and the content of the movement's promulgation of an internal idea for the reform of the university, it helped to divide and weaken the forces of established power within the university. To the Tractarians, the university was not as monolithic as it might seem to the external critic. They saw that power was in the hands of a tight oligarchy of heads of houses, most of whom were hostile to their ideas. The Tractarians therefore wished to undermine the power of the present rulers of the university, while still preserving its autonomy.[36]

This type of internal criticism became much more prevalent in the 1840s and its effect was to polarize opinion, and to bring into the open hitherto unrecognized ideological differences among the reformers. Previously, the attacks on the university had been diffuse, varied, and contradictory; attacks on the structure of academic life had been combined with general denunciations of idleness, luxury, corruption, and immorality. In this situation of incoherence and lack of theory, the defenders of the university had been free to view all attacks as motivated simply by ignorance and foreign ideas. The increasing national prominence of the Tractarian Party in Oxford, however, undermined the old plea for the university as the defender of the purity of the Anglican Church. Moreover, the new examination statutes of the period 1800–1807 had stimulated a need for teaching within the university. By the 1840s, this situation had affected enough of the resident fellows of the colleges to create new and articulate reform groups within the university.

In general, these groups started with the major premise that the university ought to provide lifetime careers for academic men. In itself this was a great step from the earlier denunciations of idleness and luxury. One can argue that these earlier attacks were external both in the sense that they originated with men outside the university and in the more important sense that they viewed the university as a monolithic and homogeneous enemy because of its Tory politics and its exclusion of all Dissenters. Not unnaturally, the question of academic careers was rather a side issue for these external critics. As we have seen, the opinion that teaching at Oxford ought to be a serious and lifetime occupation had been mentioned by the critics of the 1830s, but for these men it was not the main thrust of their argument. Similarly, the advancement of learning, which had been assumed also by the Edinburgh critics as early as 1808–10 to be a major role of the university, was also a function capable of justifying a lifetime career. But this also was merely one more point in the attack on Oxford, rather than the major thrust of their argument: the university might be denounced for falling behind the Germans or the French in the production of scholarship, but this charge was not pursued.

The new critics who first began to appear in print in the 1840s took this earlier side issue as their point of departure. Some of them may be characterized as internal critics, in that they were often Oxford residents: either fellows and tutors of colleges or professors in the university. For them, the question of the provision of the possibility for an academic career was of primary importance. These men saw their task as the development of an ideology which would justify the fulfillment of the need for more specialized teaching through the creation of careers for life within the university.

For these men the university was not the monolithic structure it seemed to the external critics. Like the Tractarians, they saw different internal groups struggling to gain or to retain power within the university. Furthermore, as the ideology of these internal critics became more explicit in the 1840s, it became apparent that there were important, even irreconcilable, differences among them. If one took the idea of developing an academic profession seriously, rather than merely using it as one of several methods of attacking the existing institution, the question soon arose as to the type of academic profession it ought to be. Was it to be organized to fulfill the role of teaching, or the role of the advancement of learning? Even if one accepted both of these roles as legitimate, conflict still remained over which group was to have power within the university or which function was to predominate. Thirdly, what institutions were to be used to create these careers? Were the college fellowships to be transformed to meet the requirements of these new roles, or were the professorial chairs to be remodeled for this purpose? Lastly, there remained the crucial question of status. Were the members of this new profession to match in status and income the older "higher" professions of physician and barrister? In the 1840s, the issue of the development of academic careers came to the surface in the reform debates and as this issue became more explicit, these questions and the resulting splits within the "reform group" became more important.

The issue of Tractarianism was, of course, a *leitmotif* running through all reform positions during this period. The very presence of the movement in Oxford was taken as a symptom of intellectual malaise. One reviewer wrote of "Oxford theology," that "it never could have been produced in a place where scientific thought or historical criticism had flourished. Had Oxford minds understood the laws of evidence, or had they been imbued with the principles of mathematical proof, Newman and his disciples would have laboured in the fire. Had even logic flourished as a science, Puseyism must have been strangled at birth."[37] The reviewer could argue that his proposed reforms of the educational system at Oxford would eliminate Tractarianism and, implicitly, would have prevented it had they been instituted sooner. In this example, the author, who wished to alter the curriculum toward more practical subjects, used the need to combat Tractarianism in order to advance his argument. However, this issue was flexible enough to lend itself to other uses as well. Another critic, desirous of establishing a system of professorial instruction with emphasis on the function of learned research, could argue that Tractarianism grew because of the lack of scholarly research at Oxford. "If we have no original philosophy of our own we must import it from abroad," remarked Bonamy Price.[38] This argument was doubly effective in that it could be used not only to explain the malaise of Tractarianism but also to criticize the other great enemy of Anglican orthodoxy, German historical criticism of the Bible.[39] Price concluded, "Surely it is not necessary to say more in order to make evident the urgent need there is of English learning, and, above all, at the Universities."[40]

IV. Practical subjects vs. scholarly research

These reformers of the late 1840s all used the issue of Tractarianism in order to demonstrate the need for reform, phrasing their specific explanation of the growth of this movement in Oxford in such a way as to justify their own remedies. However, their ideas of reform conflicted in basic ways. This period saw the development of the idea that the revival of "the professorial system" would be the cure of Oxford's deficiencies. This theme had been touched first by the critics of the *Edinburgh Review*, but at this period the suggestions became specific enough to reveal that the reformers were in fact fundamentally split into two groups. Both wished to see the professoriat expanded, given greater scope in the educational work of the university and provided with the opportunity for a professional career within the university. However, divergences in fundamental orientation between the two groups meant that their definitions of this academic career were quite different.

One group was essentially interested in changing the curriculum of the university in order to provide training in more practical subjects. One reviewer wrote that "we cannot think that universities will be at all more successful in cultivating either truth or taste in the abstract, if everything that can be called practical, we may add, professional, be removed to a distance from them."[41] These reformers had a dangerously narrow path to tread. On the one hand, their major critique was of the Coplestonian idea of liberal education: i.e., that the purpose of the curriculum was simply to provide abstract training or mental discipline. According to this theory, at the university one derived from the study of classical languages and literature the habits of thought and intellectual skills which could later be applied to the study of any particular profession. The reviewer criticized this conception of education with the comment that its effect was "to rear clergymen, schoolmasters, and gentlemen, by imparting to all indifferently the knowledge which is professional to the schoolmaster."[42] However, in attacking this concept of education, the reformer had to be careful to avoid the danger of advocating the transformation of Oxford into a place of vocational education. This would render his argument liable to dismissal by the Coplestonian rejection of utilitarian motives in education. (This criticism was soon to be given its classic statement in Newman's *On the Scope and Nature of University Education*, delivered in Ireland in 1851.[43]) The reformer had, therefore, to walk a tightrope between "liberal education" and "practical, professional education." "Deprecating, as we do, low utilitarian notions, which would undervalue all mental culture that does not yield immediate and palpable fruit, we yet cannot but think that abstract science and what is vaguely called liberal knowledge, will wander into absurd or unprofitable vagaries if they are not at intervals checked by demanding some fruit of them."[44]

It was at this point that the ideal of an academic profession became crucial. Clearly, the main goal of these reformers was to reorganize the studies of the university to provide more direct training for the professions. At the same time, they had to avoid "low, utilitarian" notions. The solution was to argue that physiology, jurisprudence, history, etc., were all appropriate subjects of university education: i.e., appropriate sources of abstract "mental culture," and that the teachers of these subjects must be "*students of truth* not practitioners for gain."[45] Thus, by constructing a scholarly ideal for the teacher, the taint of vocational education was removed.

For these particular reformers, the establishment of some provision for an academic profession at Oxford grew out of their ideas for changing the curriculum. They argued that so long as teaching in the university was in the hands of young men who would have to seek a life career elsewhere, it would be hopeless to expect the successful teaching of the "progressive sciences." For these new subjects, it was necessary that the teachers be "men of mature age and whose lives are given to their peculiar branch."[46]

The emphasis among these reformers was clearly on the role of teaching for this academic profession. The idea that the teacher should also be a "student of truth" was only called on to attempt to absolve the reformers of "low, utilitarian" motives. One reviewer stated his attitude toward the function of the existing fellowship system in the bluntest possible terms. He argued that fellowships had no function and ought to be transformed into salaries for teachers.

> The possession of a fellowship implies the right to receive so much money for doing nothing. As, however, the founders did impose duties on the fellows, let the duty of affording public instruction be imposed on them, in place of the duties required by the founders, which are either become illegal or obsolete; and if needful, let two or more fellowships be consolidated to provide an adequate stipend for an efficient public teacher; and above all, let the fellow be allowed to marry. This permission will deprive the efficient instructor of his inducement to leave the university.[47]

The reviewer argued that in this way the 557 fellowships in the colleges could be transformed into about 200 professorships of £450 per annum. Thus, an adequate staff of teachers would be provided for instruction in the new progressive sciences.

Not all of these reformers wished to see the fellowship system destroyed, but all, at the least, wished the professorships and fellowships to be transformed into career positions for teachers. One reviewer wrote, "The body of fellows employed in tuition, in strict subordination to the professors, would be an invaluable assistance. The number of fellows in each college might be easily so arranged that they should all be employed, and all render tuition gratis; for surely common sense suggests that they should do something for their fellowships. . . ."[48] These reformers also believed that teachers should be free to marry and that if the fellows were to continue in existence, they should serve in strict subordination to the professors.[49]

At this time, these reformers were called advocates of the professorial system. There was, however, another position which also involved advocacy of the professorial system, yet which differed markedly from this ideal. The first group of reformers was interested primarily in reforming the curriculum; they advocated the development of academic careers only as a necessary corollary to their major goal. The second group saw their main goal as the development of the university as a center of learned research. The creation of an academic career was, therefore, a major objective in its own right. This second ideal of the professorial system reached its full expression in the evidence and report of the Oxford University Commission of 1852. However, in its general outlines, one can see it also in the years immediately before the calling of the commission, for example, in the views expressed by Bonamy Price in 1850.[50] At this time, Price was a Master at Rugby but he was later to become Professor of Political Economy at Oxford.[51] If one examines Price's argument carefully, one can see the fundamental difference between it and the ideals of the first group of reformers. Where they placed their emphasis on the deficiencies of the university as a place of education, Price explicitly placed his emphasis on the deficiencies of the university as a seat of learning. "One of the primary functions of the University—the pursuit of really profound knowledge for the benefit of the nation and the University—is almost entirely abandoned. Study and self-improvement and original investigation are sacrificed to the educational office. . . ."[52]

Price argued that the root of the problem was that the university did not offer a man the possibility of a career. Beyond the college fellowship, which had to be vacated at marriage, the university provided only a small number of professorial chairs, most of which were insufficiently endowed, and the college headships, for which literary excellence was not generally considered to be an important qualification.[53] In any case, the positions were too few and too unrelated to original research to serve as a stimulus to the scholarly labors of tutors. Of the college fellows and tutors, Price wrote:

> They cannot look upon their office as their home, or their profession. It cannot be anything else than a temporary post . . . the evil here is that the Tutorship is a preparation for no other post; it leads to no further station for which it trains and qualifies the tutor. A tutor must ever be on the lookout for some call which shall terminate his teaching; and this fact alone is sufficient to show that he cannot connect the cultivation of knowledge with his office.[54]

Superficially, this argument seems similar to that of the first group of reformers, who were also calling for the establishment of careers within the university. The purpose of the reform, however, was exactly the opposite. For the first group, a career had to be provided for teachers because this was the only way in which subjects of practical or professional value could be introduced into the curriculum. For Price, the curriculum had to be broadened because this was the only way in which the university could provide a proper scope of activity for learned men.[55]

Price argued that the solution was to create within Oxford attractive positions awarded on the basis of literary merit toward which the fellows and tutors might aspire. He suggested that the professorships could serve as such positions if there were more of them, if they were better endowed, and if they were better integrated into the studies of the university. To achieve this he proposed that the curriculum should be altered so that the existing examination in classical languages and literature could be taken after two years of study. During this period, the student would be instructed by college tutors, to whom their tuition fees would be paid. After this, the final year could be devoted to preparation for a second set of examinations in history, divinity, and philosophy. During this period instruction would be largely through professorial lectures with some tutors also specializing in these subjects. There would be three professors for each of these three subjects and tuition would be divided among them (to some degree on the basis of student attendance). Each professor would give two courses of lectures, one for undergraduates preparing themselves for the examinations and one for advanced students; i.e., fellows, tutors, and coaches specializing in the subject. The tuition fees together with the endowment of the chair would provide an income for each professor of about £1500 per annum.[56]

In this way, Price argued that an orderly professional hierarchy for academic men would be created within the university. The fellow and tutor would have some stimulus to advance his own learning. If he were successful in producing original research, he could look forward to one of those well-paid professorial chairs as the reward for his ambition and industry. The fellowship would become a step on the ladder of a genuine profession rather than, at best, a mere prize for past performance. Price explicitly compared the prospects for a man remaining at Oxford with those of men entering the learned professions as barristers, physicians, and clergymen. He found that the existing institutions were ill-adapted to providing professional careers within the university. With these reforms, however, Price argued that it would be possible to provide careers analogous to those possible in these other professions.[57]

> Were the educational system of Oxford placed on this footing, the prospect opened to the young Batchelor, if he decided to become a resident would be altogether different from what it is now. He would have a real profession, and that a noble one. As a Fellow, he would enjoy maintenance from his College; and by continuing his studies under the direction of a professor, he would, in the fullest sense, be carrying out the purpose for which the founders of his College bequeathed to him that maintenance. As a private tutor [i.e., a coach], he would be keeping up his course of improvement. In due time he would become professor; and that with a mass of knowledge which had been constantly accumulating from the day of his entrance into the University. Here too progress would be sustained. The responsibilities of his office, and the immediate value of knowledge in the Academical system, would be effectual guarantees that the efforts to advance would be unbroken; the University would gain a great name in science, recognized and honoured as such

throughout England; and beyond all estimation would the influence of Oxford be increased in the country, when her professorships—not from accident, but from the necessary actions of the institutions—were known to contain the highest literary authorities which the nation could boast; and it would not then be easy to tempt men away from the University. For a post which implied a sphere of action worthy of it—which conferred station, wealth, authority, influence and, not least, increasing self-improvement—such a post would indeed be one of the noblest things which this land contained.[58]

It is obvious that this high ideal of a scholarship-oriented academic profession which could compete in status and wealth with the rewards of the other higher professions was far removed from that of the first group of reformers who desired to create careers for teachers of practical subjects at salaries of £450 per annum. It is also obvious that Price's ideal would be much more attractive to those within Oxford. It was this position which, in the debates over the Royal Commission of 1852, came to be recognized as the ideal of the professorial system. The specific reform suggestions were modified under the pressure of debate, but the ideal remained.

This ideal did not appeal, however, to all portions of the university. In particular, the heads of houses and those fellows who viewed themselves primarily as clergymen were bound to be hostile to reform of this sort. The tutors of colleges also tended to regard this plan as an attempt to degrade them into mere students and subordinates of the professors and to allow the latter to encroach on their monopoly of official teaching in the university. The tutors had reform-ideals of their own, for the existing institutions were just as unsuited to their aspirations as they were to the ideals of the professorial reformers. The third group of opponents were those who really took practical or professional education seriously. They came to see that they could not cooperate fully with men whose basic goal was to use the university to support learned research, and who supported broadening of the curriculum only to the extent that it would contribute to the task of integrating these learned men into the studies and educational work of the university.

V. The Royal Commission 1850–52

The Royal Commission of 1852 was the arena within which these three ideas of academic life crystallized and attained the form they were to retain. The task of framing specific reforms or defending existing institutions led to the conscious articulation of rival concepts of academic life.

The calling of the commission by Lord John Russell in 1850 was the result of long-term, cumulative, and diverse grievances combined with a situation in which the strongest argument for the *status quo*—the position of the university as the bulwark of Anglican orthodoxy—had been destroyed by the Tractarian Movement and the defections to Rome. The very existence of this movement in Oxford could be used effectively to discredit opposition to the commission. One satire written at this time contained a mock legal opinion for some "Stable-keepers"; i.e., the Hebdomadal Board, protesting against a "Subcommission"; i.e., the Royal Commission, appointed by the government to inquire into their affairs. The "barrister" for the "Stable-keepers" concluded,

> Having read your case submitted for my opinion, I have no hesitation whatever in declaring that the Subcommission of March 1851 is . . . neither constitutional nor legal. . . . The true source of power being his Holiness the Pope and under him the Cardinal Wiseacre, and the only Bull now in force in Oxford being decidedly opposed to its proceedings, it follows that Aniseed [the "Secretary of the Subcommission"] and his associates are acting on no better authority than the recommendation of one John Russell, a discharged servant of the temporal power.[59]

The revocation within recent memory by the Hebdomadal Board of Dr. Pusey's license to preach in Oxford for two years was also considered by some residents, not only by Tractarians and their sympathizers, to have been unduly harsh, vindictive, and dictatorial. This intemperate action had demonstrated to some the structural flaws in the existing system of university government and the need for reform.

Nonetheless, the Royal Commission was not able to attain recognition for its legitimacy among large segments of the university. To most residents of Oxford, the prospect called up nightmare visions of the "bad old times" of the 17th century, when first the Puritan Commonwealth and then James II had attempted to crush the autonomy of the university.[59a] This feeling was, naturally, strongest on the part of the heads of houses, who, as the Hebdomadal Board, were the dominant power in the existing structure of university government. However, such sentiment was also profound among the majority of the college residents. Although they often harbored resentment against the Hebdomadal Board, yet they also knew well that the critics of the university who had called for a government commission were united in hostility to the collegiate system which was the basis of the position of the college residents within the university.

The result was that, with the single exception of Pembroke College and its Master, Dr. Jeune, the heads of houses and many of the college officials refused to recognize the legitimacy of the Royal Commission. They refused to sit on it, nor would they supply it with evidence of their opinions or the factual information which the commissioners desired. The result was that the commission fell by default, in large part, to those critics of the university who were advocates of a scholarly professorial system. The Royal Commission's report was the perfect forum for their position since this reform group could expect no sympathy front the existing collegiate or university institutions.

Since the Hebdomadal Board refused to recognize the legitimacy of the Royal Commission, they were forced to articulate their own views through a commission of their own. They collected and printed evidence and wrote a report in which the traditional view of the university could be presented. In this view, a conception of academic life as essentially a rung in the hierarchy of the Established Church could be consciously stated and defended.

It was at this point that the majority of the working residents of the university, the college tutors, were placed in a dilemma. They could not lend their aid and voice their opinions before a Royal Commission essentially hostile to the collegiate system. On the other hand, they could not silently acquiesce to the views on university government and academic life promulgated by the report of the Hebdomadal Board. The experience of fifty years of increasing importance for the system of examinations in the work of the university had engendered a consciousness of group identity as college teachers among many of the tutors, and a desire to see this role established as a full professional career. In this situation, an association of college tutors was formed and a series of pamphlets published as a forum for their ideas of university reform. This view was opposed to both the suggestions of the Royal Commissioners and the views of the Hebdomadal Board.

With this political background, it will now be possible to examine each of the conceptions of academic life as they emerged from the debates surrounding the Royal Commission of 1852. The report of the Royal Commission expressed the view of those who wished to see the establishment of academic careers in Oxford on a scholarly professorial model. One could argue that this was the central point of the commissioners' plan for reform. In all of their suggestions, the raising of the status, powers, and importance of the professoriate was stressed at the expense of the existing collegiate organization. In remodeling the government of the university, the commissioners' suggestions would have destroyed the dominance of the heads of houses, giving power instead to the professors, who would form a majority in a "revived Congregation" which was to have taken the place of the Hebdomadal Board.[60] In their plans for university extension, the commissioners were also most enthusiastic about a proposal which would have destroyed the monopoly of the colleges over admission to the university. They advocated the creation of a class of noncollegiate students who could matriculate in the university and stand as candidates for degrees without being members of any college.

The commissioners' intention was to make the Oxford professoriate into a class of dignified professional men whose primary task would be the advancement of learning. In relation to the educational work of the university, the professors were to be formed into faculty boards which would have exclusive control over studies and the examination system.

> It is generally acknowledged that both Oxford and the country at large suffer greatly from the absence of a body of learned men, devoting their lives to the cultivation of Science, and to the direction of Academical Education; it is felt that the opening of such a career within the University would serve to call forth the knowledge and ability which is often buried or wasted, for want of proper encouragement.[61]

The commissioners proposed to establish a hierarchically organized profession of academic men. At the bottom would be the fellows and tutors of the colleges, who would essentially take over the role previously fulfilled by the unofficial coach, i.e., the close personal supervision of the studies of the college student: ". . . if the multiplicity of labours now required from College Tutors is diminished, they will be able to do much that is at present expected from private tutors [coaches]."[62] The "multiplicity of labours" to be removed from the college tutors were essentially the tasks of teaching subjects (as opposed to drilling students), forming the examinations, and judging the student's performance. The tutor would simply drill the student in the texts necessary for the subjects of examination.

The institution of the fellowship would be little altered except that restrictions of family or locality would be removed, so that fellowships might be awarded on the basis of intellectual merit. Essentially, the fellowship would remain as a prize to enable a young man who had distinguished himself in his studies at Oxford to support himself while beginning his professional career. The only difference would be that a new career option would be opened to the young fellow; instead of having to choose between the church, the law, and medicine, he would have one more choice: a professional career as an academic.

> If the Professoriate could be placed in a proper condition, those Fellows of Colleges whose services the University would wish to retain, would be less tempted and would never be compelled to leave it for positions and duties, for which their academical labours had in no way prepared them, but would look forward to some sphere of usefulness within the University for which they would have been fitted by their previous occupations.[63]

From the tone of this statement it is clear that this new career open to fellows would not merely be one of several choices but would be the most appropriate one for the winners of academic distinction. The commissioners pointedly attacked the use of the fellowship as a rung in the professional hierarchy of the church: ". . . it is evident that, for literary men, Academical rather than Ecclesiastical offices are the fittest rewards and the most useful positions."[64] In regard to the use of advowsons by colleges to provide church livings for fellows, the commissioners argued that "it is very doubtful whether either literature or the Church derive any benefit from the ecclesiastical patronage of Colleges. That a College should be deserted by any of its abler men in their full strength, for a country living, in which they are for the most part lost to learning, is a great evil even when they are succeeded by young men of promise."[65] However, the commissioners did not suggest that the fellowships themselves be made into professional career positions but, rather, that they would continue to serve as preparations for the professions. Consequently, the commissioners advocated no change in the requirement that fellows resign their positions when they marry.

This profession to which the fellows might aspire within the university would be organized into a two-tier hierarchy. The basic teaching of the university would be in the hands of a class of university lecturers or subprofessors, who would be appointed by faculty boards composed of the professors. Although the commissioners were somewhat vague on the exact position of these lecturers, it seems clear that they would rank above the tutors and that the position would serve as an entrée into the academic profession for the tutors: ". . . it is evident that such an intermediate grade of Lecturers would at once serve the purpose of opening prospects of advancement to the Tutors, Collegiate and Private. . . ."[66] These university lecturers would specialize in particular subjects and would be free from all clerical and celibacy restrictions. The commissioners also tentatively suggested that perhaps in the case of a college fellow appointed to a university lectureship, the man might be permitted to marry and yet retain his fellowship.

At the summit of the academic profession would be the university professors. It would be to these positions that the lecturer might look for professional advancement. The professors and the faculty boards, composed exclusively of professors, would have full control of the examination system and the appointment of lecturers. Their own tasks would be the cultivation of their subject and the administration of the examination system, while the actual teaching would be largely in the hands of the lecturers and the college tutors. The position of a professor would also be attractive enough to serve as an object of ambition to the lower ranks. Aside from being removed from most teaching and having controlling power in the university, the professor would also have a handsome income. The commissioners suggested that the annual income of a university professor ought to be at least £800 from endowment in addition to fees which would make a total minimum income of £1000 to £1500. The commissioners further suggested that this income be obtained through making the professors *ex officio* fellows of colleges and suppressing and combining several fellowships to make the necessary income.

This Royal Commission plan for the creation of a hierarchical academic profession within the university was important as a fully explicit expression of the idea of a scholarly professorial system. However, in terms of practical results, it was virtually a dead letter. When the government came to formulate the Oxford University Bill of 1854, these recommendations were almost completely ignored. Instead, the major provision of the Act was to give each college leave to alter its statutes under the eyes of a Board of Executive Commissioners. This meant the death of the Royal Commission's plan, which was seen as a threat to all collegiate interests. To the heads of houses, it threatened the loss of their dominance in the government of the university; to the fellows, it threatened to make them underlings of the university professors.

The commissioners might well have predicted this reaction, if they had paid attention to the evidence which was submitted to them. The majority of those who submitted evidence to the commission were in favor of the establishment of some sort of profession within the university, but only a few, most notably H. H. Vaughan, Regius Professor of Modern History, submitted schemes similar to the one adopted by the commissioners, which place the professoriate in a dominating position within the university. This was an ominous sign for the commission's plan since most of the strongest opponents of reform refused to submit evidence at all. The positions taken by those who did submit evidence reveals quite clearly the paucity of support for the commissioners' plan, even among those who supported some measure of reform in the university.

The fundamental issue was power. Many witnesses advocated the integration of the professors into the teaching work of the university, particularly in teaching the "higher aspects" of the subjects.[67] According to their proposals, the professors would be responsible for teaching the students in their third year. This third year was often conceived of as a concession to the demands for "professional education,"[68] since at the least, it could be viewed as distinctly pre-professional. Those intended for careers in law would study modern history, law, and political economy with the professors in those fields while those intended for careers in medicine would study with the professors of the natural sciences. The commissioners rejected this proposal, citing with approval Professor Vaughan's view that such a plan would degrade the professor into merely "a Tutor of the third year." Although they did not reject the desirability of "catechetical instruction" by professors, the commissioners implied that this task would be more suitable to the role of the subordinate university lecturers.[68a]

Many witnesses also called for the recognition of the claims of advanced study.[69] Some saw this role as the task of the professors, though Professor Vaughan was one of the few who advocated combining this role with control over the examination system.[70] Others preferred to allow the fellow to use his position for this purpose with the prospect of being allowed to hold his fellowship for life without the celibacy restriction after a ten-year probationary period (during which time the fellow would be required to live in Oxford and devote his time to study and research).[71] Other witnesses wished to see the fellowships used for the provision of a teaching career.[72] Ten years of service as a tutor would entitle a fellow to hold his fellowship for life without celibacy or clerical restrictions. But the commissioners explicitly rejected both these views of the fellowship. For them, it could never be a provision for life but only a stipend to be used by a young man preparing for a professional career.

The plan for the expansion of the professoriate was attractive to those witnesses who could not countenance any tampering with college foundations but who nevertheless wished to see life careers for teachers within Oxford. One witness argued that the creation of a class of university teachers would make "provision in the University itself, unclogged with the heavy restriction of celibacy, for men of high academic honours. Justice to the able men, who now, amidst many difficulties, discharge most conscientiously the duties of college tuition, requires that Oxford should not be wanting to herself in holding out to her best sons adequate encouragement to continue in her service."[73] These positions would be desirable in providing higher positions within the university toward which the college fellow might aspire. Of course, the commissioners also saw this as an advantage of their plan. The problem was that their scheme actually reduced the current position of the college fellow, subordinating him to the professor, while holding out to him the possibility of a professorship in the future. But this future possibility was not likely to be considered by the tutors an adequate recompense for their present loss, and the commissioners might well have understood this from a study of their own evidence. This evidence revealed a variety of discontents with the existing state of the university, but few for which the commissioners' plan could be considered an acceptable solution.

VI. The Tutors' Association

The publication of the Royal Commissioners' Report in 1852 galvanized into action the college tutors, who were the most coherent of these discontented groups. In the Royal Commission's Report, there was a basic consistency in the evidence submitted by college tutors. They complained of the temporary nature of their occupation as tutors. As Mark Pattison, then tutor of Lincoln College, expressed it, "The transitory nature of the occupation, which in most cases being adopted 'in transitu' to a totally different pursuit, has none of the aids which in the regular professions are derived from regard to professional credit, and the sustained interest which a life-pursuit possesses."[74] This complaint about the temporary nature of the occupation of tutor was generally combined with another about the lack of the possibility of specialization in subjects. Arthur Hugh Clough, formerly a Tutor of Oriel College, complained of the task of the tutor "with his three hours a day of subjects not always his choice, very often his unpleasant necessity, and belonging to the most various and heterogeneous departments. I can conceive nothing more deadening to the appetite for learning than this three-hour-a-day tuition, leading as it does in general, and always must be expected to do, to no ultimate learned position—a mere parenthetical occupation uncontemplated in the past and wholly alien to the future."[75] The plan of the Royal Commissioners did little to answer these complaints of the tutors. It confirmed their position as fellows as temporary and merely preparatory to a professional career, and it degraded their teaching into that of mere drill instructors under the supervision of the professors.

Essentially it was the threat presented by the recommendations of the Royal Commissioners which forced the tutors into unified action and a definite expression of their ideas. About sixty tutors came together to form the Tutors' Association. They decided to publish a series of pamphlets expressing their views on various aspects of university reform and on the commissioners' recommendations.[76] In these reports of the Tutors' Association were contained an ideal of an academic career which was designed to rival that of the Royal Commissioners.

In their diagnosis of the defects in the system of instruction in the university, the Tutors' Association came strikingly close to the Royal Commissioners. They identified two main problems: "The first is the want of a body of instructors who, confining their attention to a single branch of study, shall be capable of prosecuting it to its utmost limits. . . . The second deficiency is the want of all adequate means of producing and retaining within the University men of eminence in particular departments of knowledge."[77] For the Royal Commissioners, the first of these problems was to be dealt with by the creation of the group of university lecturers who would each specialize in a particular subject. The second problem would be solved by the selection of professors for literary merit and providing for them positions within the university which could attract and retain such men. For the Tutors' Association, the commissioners' plan to create new classes of teachers within the university was completely unnecessary in order to meet these admitted deficiencies. It argued that the existing teachers of the university— i.e., the college tutors—could supply both of these needs if they were offered a professional career: "Hardly any of the present teachers of Oxford can look upon their occupation either as the business of their whole life, or as affording any preparation for a subsequent employment . . . his tutorial position is not, under the existing restrictions of College Fellowships, such as most men will regard with satisfaction as a permanent occupation."[78]

For the Tutors' Association, this situation contrasted unfavorably with that of the university teacher in Germany, where "the German teacher is a scholar or a philosopher by profession, instead of being compelled, as is too often the case at Oxford, to take up scholarship or philosophy as a mere temporary occupation."[79] Clearly, the implication was that if these "restrictions" were removed and if each fellow were permitted to confine his teaching to one subject or set of texts, the college tutor might then be able to view his occupation as a professional life-career and could be expected to be as much a scholar as his German counterpart.

The Tutors' Association based its case for the superiority of its reform proposals to those of the Royal Commissioners' upon (1) the superiority of the system of tutorial instruction to professorial lectures as a mode of education, and (2) the disadvantages and unfairness of granting dominating powers in the university to the professoriate.

In criticizing professorial lectures as a mode of education,[80] the Tutors' Association relied heavily on the traditional Coplestonian defense of liberal education. They argued that the professorial system had three major defects in relation to the system of collegiate instruction: in lectures to large classes, there was an inherent tendency to attach "too much importance to the person teaching and too little to the things taught"; the lecturing situation tended to place a premium on innovation for its own sake rather than for the sake of "Truth"; and lectures provided an easy and superficial education, memory being the major mental faculty cultivated, while the faculties for thinking were not developed.

In regard to the increased powers of the professoriate envisioned by the commissioners, the Tutors' Association argued that "it would not be doing justice to many of the Tutors of Oxford, to degrade them to mere mouthpieces or subordinates of superior teachers."[81] They argued that many tutors in Oxford were equally qualified to hold a professorial chair, yet under the commissioners' plan, if one were appointed, he would suddenly be raised to a position of dominance over all the others. This situation would certainly induce many able tutors to leave the university. In general, the Tutors' Association concluded that the Royal Commissioners' plan to give the professors a dominating voice in the university "would destroy the independence of thought among the equal members of an intellectual republic, to make way for the energetic rule of all official despotism."[82]

The Tutors' Association was not, however, opposed to the expansion of the professoriate. Rather, so long as they could be certain that the professoriate would not infringe upon the independence of the college tutors, they were willing actively to support the expansion of the number of university professors. They suggested several areas among the traditional classical studies of the university in which more professorial chairs would be useful, although they were less certain of the need for them in the new subjects of natural science and modern history.[83] Clearly, new professorships in classical studies would be attractive in that they would provide possibilities for advancement to the college tutors, whereas this would not have been true of these new subjects, which were not taught on the college level. The Tutors' Association did suggest a somewhat lower annual salary for professors than the Commissioners' plan would have allowed: £600 plus fees rather than £800 plus fees. Even so, the proposed salary would make the professorial chairs in almost all cases considerably more attractive than they had been. This salary, with duties of three lectures per week rather than three classes per day, would make these professorial positions into definite objects of ambition to the college tutor even without the broad powers in university government which the Royal Commissioners wished to give to the professoriate. Under the Tutors' Association plan the professor would not have a voice in the government of the college either, since the funds for endowing the chairs would be derived from a general tax on collegiate revenues. Fellowships would not be directly utilized for this purpose.

In regard to the fellowship system, the general principle of Tutors' Association was that fellows ought to be resident and involved for the most part in tutorial work. The theme of providing more opportunities for teaching was a constant motif in their reform suggestions. In discussing plans for university extension, the Tutors' Association suggested that one of the benefits of expanded enrollment of students would be that "it is important to provide work for that large number of Fellows who may be expected at any one time to be resident in Oxford."[84] They argued that the present situation "excludes from Oxford many teachers who would add fresh life and energy to her instruction."[85] It is obvious that the Tutors' Association felt that there was a substantial number of fellows who wished to make Oxford teaching a career, but who could not be employed in the limited number of college tutorships then available. Taken together, their advocacy of university extension, subject specialization by college tutors and cautious expansion of the professoriate may be seen as a unified plan to overcome this problem.

One interesting point was that although the Tutors' Association placed their case for expansion almost wholly on the needs for teaching in the university, they tended to define their role as "learned men" rather than exclusively as teachers. They argued that the university ought to function as an antidote to that utilitarian spirit of efficiency and productivity which dominated a commercial country. For them, the university ought to be the "centre and source for the exercise and encouragement of that unproductive thinking which to be successfully prosecuted must be adequately endowed. . . ."[86] This emphasis on learning may be viewed as an expression of the superior status of scholarship in relation to teaching. In relation to the traditional gentlemanly ideal, teaching was often related to trade, the metaphors of business and retailing being used in regard to this activity. Even the more old-fashioned defenders of the teaching role of the university, such as Copleston, tended to view teaching itself as a "homely duty."[87]

This status situation was, of course, translated into concrete material terms. One witness before the Royal Commission stated the prevailing view with great bluntness. In regard to whether professors were to be defined as teachers or learned men, he wrote that "if it be required only to have a body of tolerably competent teachers, moderate endowments are sufficient. But if it be desired that the University Professors should generally be amongst the most distinguished cultivators of their respective sciences to be found in the country, then much more liberal endowments are necessary."[88] This argument would clearly hold for the fellows as well. Material and status advantages dictated at least a perfunctory bow in the direction of scholarship by the Tutors' Association. In advocating that the fellow might entitle himself to a professional career in Oxford either on the basis of teaching or on the basis of residence for the purposes of advanced study, the tutors avoided the unpleasing status connotations of reducing the fellowship from an independent income to a mere salary for a teacher.

In regard to the crucial question of celibacy restrictions on fellowships, the Tutors' Association was caught in a dilemma. The logic of their argument for the provision of an academic career pointed clearly in the direction of allowing tutors to marry while retaining their fellowships. However, in defending the collegiate system and their own position within the colleges against the onslaught of the Royal Commissioners' scheme, the tutors had to rely on the argument stressing the "sacredness" of founders' statutes and the "illegality" of tampering with them. Since married fellows were explicitly forbidden in the statutes of every college, the Tutors' Association could not advocate the marriage of fellows without destroying their own best argument against the Royal Commissioners' plan for interfering with the autonomy of the colleges. The result was that the Tutors' Association had to content itself with weakly suggesting that perhaps fifteen years of residence in Oxford as a fellow for the purposes of either teaching or private study might entitle the fellow to marry and yet retain his fellowship.

The basic dilemma for the Tutors' Association was the problem of reconciling their strong loyalty to the college system with their desires for reform in the direction of providing life careers for teachers within the university. In the face of the threat to the collegiate system represented by the report of the Royal Commission and the impending Parliamentary Bill, the tutors were forced into the defense of the *status quo*. In a letter to Gladstone in 1853, Charles Marriott, one of the leaders of the Tutors' Association, declared that the founders' will "is *everything* as a *typical germ*, giving the principles and organization of the Foundation. And I look upon a diminution of a Founder's numbers as almost sure, in one way or another, to truncate the living body which he intended to exist."[89] Unfortunately, this type of argument could cut both ways. It was meant to attack the plans of the Royal Commissioners, but it could be used to frustrate all desires for reform, including those of the Tutors' Association itself.

VII. The report of the Hebdomadal Board

While the Tutors' Association was formulating its conception of an academic career in opposition to that of the Royal Commissioners, the Hebdomadal Board was busy collecting evidence and preparing its report. The original idea of the Hebdomadal Board was that the university residents might present a united front against the commissioners. However, they were not able to reach agreement with the representatives of the Tutors' Association on the important question of representation on the committee which would prepare the Hebdomadal Board's report. The heads of houses were quite unwilling to admit the propriety of accepting college tutors as a separate class within the university. Dr. Hawkins, the Provost of Oriel, in discussing the government of the university, expressed well the attitude of the heads on this question of representation. He wrote that "if any change should be recommended in the Hebdomadal Board, it should not be such as should destroy its *representative* character; as representing, that is to say, all the several Societies of which the University is actually composed. . . . Nor do I perceive any good reason for a special representation of the Professors, or the Tutors, or any other Functionaries, with reference to Academical Legislation generally. . . ."[90] This attitude was, of course, as unsatisfactory to the Tutors' Association as the attitude of the Royal Commissioners themselves. This cleavage was regretted. Dr. Cotton, the Vice-Chancellor, wrote of the need for "*singleness of action*" and stigmatized the Tutors' Association as "a self-constituted" body.[91] Yet the existence of an articulate idea of an academic career among the tutors made it quite impossible that they could join forces with the Hebdomadal Board.

The report of the Hebdomadal Board took as its task the defense of existing institutions against both the plans of the Royal Commissioners and those of the Tutors' Association. Essentially, the report ignored the issue of the provision for an academic career. For the heads, there was no need to make such careers possible. The particular plan of the Royal Commissioners was denounced on the traditional grounds that it would destroy the liberal character of Oxford education and would be inimical as well to the interests of Anglican orthodoxy:

> . . . the system of the Commissioners, with its ample staff of well-endowed Professors, its array of Lecturers, and its multitude of Unattached Students, is one which this University has never known and, we may be permitted to hope, will never know. For, remote as are such results from the contemplation of the Commissioners, it would tend, we fear, to substitute Information for Education, and Sciolism for Religion.[92]

In discussing possible alterations in the fellowship system, the report also recommended no changes in regard to encouraging either increased specialization in subjects or increased residence of fellows for the purposes of either teaching or study, both of which were recommended by the Tutors' Association.[93] In discussing university extension, the report concerned itself only with the maintenance of the collegiate system, giving no mention of the desire of the Tutors' Association to expand the possibilities for employment of fellows within Oxford.[94] Similarly, in regard to the government of the university, the report attacked both the Royal Commissioners' plan for professorial dominance, and the Tutors' Association's plan to represent the "resident M.A.'s" as a separate class in the government of the university.[95] Their own plan was to leave the government of the university unchanged, compromising only to the extent of suggesting the appointment of "Delegacies" of members of Convocation to make suggestions on given subjects. Essentially, the report defended the existing system and institutions of the colleges and university in virtually every detail. They concluded that the only changes required were for Parliament to give the university an enabling act which would permit the university and the colleges to alter or abrogate statutes which the course of time and altered conditions had rendered obsolete. Their hope was not that this would be used for any substantive changes but merely that it would be used to bring the statutes into consonance with the actually existing system of the university.

This report of the Hebdomadal Board, though diametrically opposed to the Royal Commissioners' report in virtually all substantive areas, was nonetheless similar to it in one formal respect: in ignoring the evidence which was placed before it. The report of the Hebdomadal Board bore as little relation to its evidence as the report of the Royal Commissioners bore to its evidence. These two sets of evidence present many similarities which link them more to the suggestions of the Tutors' Association than they do to either of the "official" reports.

The witnesses before the Hebdomadal Board's commission were as opposed as the Board's report itself to the Royal Commissioners' plans for the dominance of the professoriate. But for many of these witnesses, a definite desire for the development of an academic career in Oxford was evident. Even Dr. Pusey, the commission's most important witness and most vociferous opponent of German ideas of professorial dominance, developed in his testimony basic criticisms of the existing fellowship system from the viewpoint of lack of specialization and lack of residence on the part of fellows. He denounced the system whereby "the incomes of colleges have practically been employed in eking out poor curacies."[96] He argued that the fellowships ought to be used for resident teachers and scholars, and not as prizes to help young men begin their professional careers outside the university. Specialization of subject was also demanded: "The greatest disadvantage of the Tutorial system, at least in smaller colleges, is that the same Tutor is required to teach upon too varied subjects."[97] Pusey argued that one attractive aspect of university extension would be that it would necessitate "an addition in the number of Tutors employed, and this increase of Tutors would facilitate the division of subjects."[98] Pusey concluded that if these reforms were instituted "more Fellows might readily be induced, or might be glad, to stay, if there were definite occupation for them."[99] Finally, Pusey went even beyond the Tutors' Association in advocating the removal of the celibacy requirement in order to facilitate the development of a genuine profession: ". . . since the Heads and Canons are allowed to marry, in order to retain older men for important offices, there is nothing which can be objected to, on any principle, in allowing certain Tutors and Lecturers to marry, and yet retain their fellowships."[100]

Although Dr. Pusey developed these ideas for an academic career based on the college fellowship more fully than other witnesses, the call for increased residence and specialization appeared in several of the witnesses' evidence.[101] William Sewell, Fellow and Tutor of Exeter, one of the strongest opponents of the Royal Commission among the college tutors, even suggested that the desire of the fellows for teaching work was so great that no expansion of teaching opportunities in Oxford alone would satisfy it. In a public letter addressed to the Vice-Chancellor, Sewell proposed a plan for affiliating new colleges to be built in other cities in England with Oxford colleges. The method of "affiliation" which he recommended was to utilize the Fellows of the Oxford college as the tutors and lecturers of these new colleges. One important advantage of this plan, for Sewell, was that it "would immediately open a wide field of occupation for Fellows of Colleges, who, being at present not engaged in tuition, are often obliged to quit the University, to seek a maintenance. . . ."[101a] The implication was clearly that many Fellows left the university, not to seek the richer prizes available in the world, but simply because the university did not provide them with sufficient opportunities for teaching work.

In regard to the professorships, the witnesses revealed the same ambiguity on this question as the witnesses before the Royal Commission and the Tutors' Association. They were unanimous in their dismissal of any plan which would make the professors as a class into the rulers of the university. However, the idea of expanding the number and value of professorial chairs in order to provide higher positions for college tutors proved attractive. One witness asserted:

> I hold firmly that, among other wants, the University needs a great extension of the Professorial body . . . there is at present hardly any means of keeping in the University men of ability, who wish to marry. There is no sort of promotion in their own calling offered to able and successful College Tutors. We want some means of

permanently fixing in Oxford men of eminence in their several pursuits, which can only be done by offering them situations of emolument equal to at least the more moderate "prizes" in other professions. And surely it would be better for a situation of this sort, rather than a College Living, to be the goal set before the College Tutor. The diligent and able Tutor should have, as in other professions, the prospect of rising to a higher place in his own line, that is, to a University Professorship.[102]

As in the evidence before the Royal Commissioners and the Tutors' Association, the logic of this conception of the function of the professorship necessitated the defining of the professorial role primarily in terms of research. One witness recommended that the professor not be permitted to give more than two courses of lectures per year "in order that sufficient time may be secured to every Professor for carrying on his private studies, and for advancing the progress of the science which he professes." In this way, "provision [could be] made for securing the services of men who have attained the greatest eminence in their several departments of Literature, Science, and Art. . . ."[103] One could argue that it was necessary to define the professor primarily as a scholar in order to justify the high position which he would have to hold if his position were to function as an object for the ambitions of the college tutors. A scholarly conception of the professoriate was, of course, also useful in justifying the exclusion of the professors from the educational work of the university which was the preserve of the college tutors.

VIII. The act of 1854 and beyond

If one views the two sets of evidence given to the Royal Commissioners and the Hebdomadal Board, together with the reports of the Tutors' Association, a remarkably consistent ideal of an academic career emerges. This ideal was a distinctive Oxford product, produced to suit its conditions and to fit the aspirations of Oxford dons. Whereas the ideals of academic life which had been expressed in the period prior to the Royal Commission and in the commission's report itself had grown from basic criticisms of the colleges and of the ideal of liberal education, this new ideal grew out of basic acceptance of the Oxford system. Essentially, the idea was to expand the possibilities for careers within the university while altering the system of collegiate autonomy and the traditional concept of education as little as possible. This ideal was particularly important because, in its broad outlines, it was this conception of an academic career which was to prevail.

This conclusion was really inevitable in the Oxford University Bill of 1854. The task of framing a bill was left to Gladstone, M.P. for the university, who had been in close contact with the leaders of the Tutors'

Association.[104] Essentially, it was their plan which was instituted in the bill, and the Royal Commissioners' plan for professorial dominance in the university and for basic instruction by a staff of sub-professors was completely ignored. The main positive act of the bill was to constitute a new governing body for the university along the lines suggested by the Tutors' Association. The powers of the heads of houses were decreased and that of the "resident M.A.'s" was considerably enhanced. Some attempt was made in Parliament to frame new statutes for the individual colleges but this plan was abandoned when the loyal sons of the university in Parliament offered so many amendments that the entire bill would have been destroyed if these provisions had been pressed. The result was that colleges were simply left to remodel their own statutes under the scrutiny of a set of Executive Commissioners notably sympathetic to the collegiate system.[105] Given the balance of Oxford opinion which was revealed in the evidence before the two commissions and in the Tutors' Association reports, it was inevitable that this "tutorial profession" would eventually prevail.[106]

The actual implementation of this ideal was the slow but steady task of the next half-century. The task could not be accomplished at one stroke by the writing of new statutes in each college under the surveillance of the Executive Commissioners. In most colleges, the governing body still contained a majority of men committed to the older nonprofessional and clerical ideal of a fellowship. In Christ Church, the only college for which a detailed study has been done of this period, the governing body consisted of the Canons of the Cathedral only. The "students" were similar to the scholars and fellows of other colleges except that they had no power in the governance of the college. Ideas of a "tutorial profession" were strong among the students, but they were ignored by the canons and the commissioners in the writing of statutes. The result was that the discontent of the students led to a revision of the statutes in 1867. The avowed purpose was to raise the students to the level of the fellows of the other colleges. The most important result of these revised statutes was that the senior students, especially those involved in college work, were given the dominant voice in the government of Christ Church.[107]

In most colleges, the major result of these new statutes written under the auspices of the Executive Commission was to destroy the restrictions of place of birth, schools (to some extent), and families on elections to fellowships. Clear distinctions were also made between scholars and fellows and there was some movement toward equalizing the position of fellows, both in governing powers and in income.

This period also saw efforts to provide the "more specialized teaching," about whose absence many dons had complained in their evidence before both the Royal Commission and the commission appointed by the Hebdomadal Board, as well as in the pamphlets of the Tutors' Association. Prior to the Royal Commission, in 1849 and 1850, the Hebdomadal Board had approved the establishment of two new examination schools, one in natural science and the other combining law and modern history. These were clearly responses to the calls for more practical and professional training within the university, since they could be viewed as appropriate preprofessional studies for physicians and barristers, respectively. The existence of these new examination schools had been effective in preventing the Royal Commissioners from dealing with the reform of the curriculum since it was argued that this new statute had not yet had time enough to prove its effectiveness in satisfying critics of the university.

The effect of these new examination schools was to create a demand for teaching which the colleges were not well able to satisfy. Only a small number of students in each college, at least at first, were interested in reading for these new schools (in large part because virtually all of the prizes, exhibitions, scholarships, and fellowships were still to be given for classical studies). The result was that colleges were unwilling to elect fellows for the specific purpose of teaching the few students in these subjects.

The solution to the problem of providing collegiate instruction in these new examination schools was for one lecturer to be paid by several colleges to supervise all of their students in one of the new subjects. This system eventually evolved into the "combined lectures" which were to point the direction toward the solution to the problem of providing more specialized teaching work for college tutors. The "combination" system began in about 1865 among the collegiate teachers of modern history. It was a private and informal arrangement among the individual teachers and was not officially sanctioned by the colleges or by the university. Since a very small number of fellows and lecturers did all of the collegiate teaching in modern history, it was not surprising that they were the first to decide to act together. Each teacher would open his collegiate lectures to any student of the other teachers in the "combination" who wished to study the particular subject on which he was lecturing. This arrangement was more efficient than for each to attempt to cover all of modern history by himself. It also had the added advantage of allowing each collegiate teacher of modern history to specialize in a particular period or aspect of his subject. This system had to face strong opposition on the ground that it tended to turn the fellow or lecturer into a professor and, therefore, destroyed the distinctive, personal advantages for the student of the collegiate system of instruction. However, the practical advantages of the "combination" system, the fact that the new subjects could not be taught effectively on a purely collegiate basis, insured the success of the system in modern history and its expansion to the other new subjects as well.

When the "combination" system eventually was adopted by the teachers of classical studies, these practical advantages were clearly less important. Each college had enough students reading *Literae Humaniores* to justify three or four classical tutors. There was no pressing, practical need for "combination" in order to fulfill a minimum standard of providing collegiate instruction for an examination school. Nonetheless, the system was attractive to many of the teachers of classical studies since it held out the promise of providing them with greater opportunities for specialization than were possible while each college remained an autonomous educational unit. It proved difficult in practice, however, for either of the two classical "combinations" which began in the late 1860s to operate effectively. There were among the colleges only ten fellows and lecturers specializing in modern history while there were more than sixty collegiate teachers of classical studies; the informal modes of decision-making which were appropriate to the modern history "combination" proved ineffective for co-ordinating the teaching of classical studies. It was not until the establishment of official "Boards of Faculties" in the 1880s after the work of the Oxford Commission of 1877 that the problem of providing increased opportunities for specialization was finally solved. The "combined lectures" were important because they provided the model for this successful solution. The college fellow and tutor would maintain his primary loyalty to his college while he would also have a secondary commitment to the faculty board on which he was represented. One function of these boards was to allow the collegiate teachers opportunities for more specialized teaching work by co-ordinating effectively the lectures to be given in each subject.

In 1877, the Oxford Commission was called largely as a result of dissatisfaction within the university with the settlement of the 1850s. Teaching fellows resented the drain on college resources of the "prize fellows." Mark Pattison, the Rector of Lincoln College, and others, resented the lack of endowments for learned research. In 1871, there had been a financial commission for the university which had revealed the great wealth of Oxford and its eccentric distribution among the colleges and between colleges and the university. There seemed to be little relation between the size of the endowments and the educational and research work of the institution. The avowed purpose of the Commission of 1877 was to reallocate these resources and to remodel the fellowship system to provide more encouragement for academic careers.

Along with the establishment of faculty boards, the most important result of this commission was that it finally solved the problem of how collegiate institutions could be altered to allow fellows engaged in college work to marry. Beginning in the late 1860s, there had been a few colleges who had been able to obtain alterations in their statutes which allowed college tutors to marry while retaining their fellowships. However, there had been no general and comprehensive solution to this problem. As a result of the recommendations of the Commission of 1877, a new category of "official fellow" was established especially to fit the needs of collegiate teachers who wished to marry and devote themselves to academic work as a life-career. The college system, however, retained a strong prejudice against the married fellow. The communitarian and personalistic ideals of the college were ill-adapted to the married man living in North Oxford, coming into college to teach and occasionally to dine. It was said that J. L. Strachan-Davidson, Master of Balliol in the 1920s, would not attempt to prevent a fellow from marrying but would signal his disapproval by refusing to speak to him for several years.[108] Even today, the unoccupied bedroom in the married don's college rooms seems to stand as a constant reproach to his refusal to reside in college.

Largely unsuccessful efforts also were made during this period to enhance the power, income, and status of the professoriate. Attempts were made to increase the professors' power by making them the *ex-officio* chairmen of the new "Boards of Faculties." The college tutors, however, were successful in foiling this plan as a threat to their autonomy. As a compromise, all professors were given *ex-officio* positions as members of the boards while the college tutors only elected representatives. The Commission of 1877 also tried to improve both the income and the status of the professoriate by reallocating collegiate funds to the payment of professors who would automatically become fellows of the colleges which provided their income. This reform was also only partially successful, however, since the colleges were often able to curtail the amount of collegiate funds to be used for this purpose. The very serious and long-term decline in college income derived from property after the mid-1870s due to the "agricultural depression," finally destroyed these hopes of largely augmenting and strengthening the professoriate. The collegiate income to be used for this purpose simply did not exist anymore.

IX. Conclusion

The academic profession which emerged from these events was firmly based on the collegiate system and on the ideal of liberal education. Recruitment was by the individual colleges through their fellowships. The primary role of the academic man was as a teacher of subjects whose value was conceived of in terms of "mental discipline" rather than as "useful information." The status-value of the fellowship, which remained the basic institution of the profession, was carefully preserved. A fellowship provided an independent income rather than a salary, which could be considered analogous to the honorarium received by the barrister rather than a fee. In this way, the traditionally degrading status-connotations of receiving payment for services rendered were avoided. The secondary conception of the don as a learned man, a "center of unproductive thinking," also served to satisfy similar status needs.

In regard to the educational work of the doll, the idea of liberal education was flexible enough to be remodeled to fit his desires for increasing specialization. The argument in favor of the introduction of new subjects was simply altered from the older one that they would make the system of university education more practical to a new one that they would be as beneficial as the traditional classical studies for inculcating mental discipline.[109]

This model of an academic profession, however, was not without its difficulties. One was that so much emphasis had been placed on the personal nature of the tutorial relation in order to set out its distinctive advantages over impersonal professorial lectures that it was difficult to justify the position of the tutor as a married man living outside the college. By the 1880s, however, the principle was at least grudgingly admitted that "official fellows" engaged in tutorial work might be allowed to marry and yet retain their fellowships.

The other great difficulty in this model for an academic profession was the absence of a true professional hierarchy to provide higher positions toward which the college tutor might strive. Fear of professorial dominance made it impossible to grant the professors any genuine role in the educational work of the university and without this task it proved difficult to justify the creation of a large enough number of professorial chairs. The idea of "the endowment of research" provided a justification for some expansion of the professoriate, but the decline of college and university endowment income due to the "agricultural depression" made the provision of more professorships impossible without infringing on the position of the college tutors. In 1892, there were forty-seven professorships in the university, as opposed to the twenty-five there had been in 1850. This was a considerable expansion, yet the total number of chairs was still not great enough for the professorship to be viewed as a normal promotion for the college fellow.

Thus, the first half of the 19th century in Oxford saw the articulation of a viable, though imperfect, ideal of academic life as a professional career. The idea of an academic profession itself certainly owed much to comparison with foreign university systems, particularly those of Germany. However, the particular ideal which was effected at Oxford was, in its specific outlines, a distinctive product of Oxford conditions, developed from a traditional and enduring conception of Oxford education and suited to the material and status-aspirations of Oxford dons.

Notes

1 See A. D. Godley, *Oxford in the 18th Century* (London 1908); A. Hamilton Gibbs, *Rowlandson's Oxford* (London 1911); C. E. Mallet, *A History of the University of Oxford*, vol. III (New York 1928).

2 See W. R. Ward, *Georgian Oxford* (Oxford 1958); also the excellent brief background chapter in V. H. H. Green, *The Young Mr. Wesley* (London 1961) 13–40.

3 W. R. Ward, *Victorian Oxford* (London 1965), xv.

4 Ibid., xi.
5 Anon. [attributed by Cordeaux and Merry, *Bibliography of Writings Relating to the University of Oxford* (hereafter C&M)] to the 3d Earl of Macclesfield, "A Memorial Relating to the Universities," in *Collectanea Curiosa*, ed. J. Gutch (Oxford 1781), iii, 56.
6 Ibid., 58.
7 "Supplement: Well-Wishers to the University of Oxford," *The General Evening Post*, no. 2546 (London 11–13 January 1750). (Attributed by C&M to R. Newton, Principal of Hart Hall, Oxford.)
8 See review of "Traité de Mechanique Céleste, par P. S. LaPlace," in *Edin. Rev.* no. 22 (January 1808), 249–84; review of "The Oxford Edition of Strabo," *Edin. Rev.* no. 28 (July 1809), 429–41; review of "Essays on Professional Education by R. L. Edgeworth," *Edin. Rev.* no. 29 (October 1809), 40–53; review of "Woodhouse's Trigonometry," *Edin. Rev.* no. 33 (November 1810), 122–35.
9 Review of "The Oxford Edition of Strabo," *Edin. Rev.* 28 (July 1809), 431.
10 Anon. [E. Copleston], "A Reply to the Calumnies of the *Edinburgh Review* against Oxford containing an account of the studies pursued in that University" (Oxford 1810), 150. The other defenses of Oxford against the criticisms of the *Edin. Rev.* do not go beyond simply agreeing with Copleston on every point. See "Replies to the Calumnies against Oxford," *Quart. Rev.* 7 (August 1810), 177–206; also "Three Replies to the Calumnies against Oxford," *Brit. Critic* 37 (1811), 346–56.
11 Ibid., 145.
12 Ibid., 145–47 and passim.
13 Ibid., 149.
14 An Oxford student guidebook of 1837 complains of the growing prominence of private coaches in the university. The author does not approve of this development but his discussion of the subject indicates its *de facto* importance at this time. See *The Student's Guide to a Course of Reading Necessary for Obtaining University Honours by a Graduate of Oxford* (Oxford 1837), 97. The growth in the importance of private coaching can be gauged by the fact that another student guidebook of 1860, though still hostile to private coaching, is forced to admit that "as to the Formal Examination, there are but few, if any, colleges, where the help supplied is of itself sufficient to insure a man a high place in the Class List. It is pretty nearly a universal rule with class-men to read two terms at least with a Tutor [coach] before the day of trial." *Pass and Class: An Oxford Guide-Book*, by Montagu Burrows M.A. (Oxford 1860), 60.
15 "Universities of England—Oxford," *Edin. Rev.* 53 (June 1831), 384–427, and a review of "The Legality of the Present Academical System of the University of Oxford, Asserted against the New Calumnies of the *Edinburgh Review* by a Member of Convocation," ibid. 54 (December 1831), 478–504.
16 [Sir W. Hamilton], "Universities of England—Oxford," 396–97.
17 A Graduate of Cambridge, "Letters to the English Public on the Condition, Abuses and Capabilities of the National Universities," no. 1 (London 1836). See also "Thoughts on Reform at Oxford," by A Graduate (Oxford 1833), esp. 15–16.
18 "Thoughts on Reform at Oxford," 10–12.
19 Review of "The Oxford University Calendar (1837)," *Eclectic Rev.*, N.S. 2 (July 1837), 15.
20 Ibid., see 21–23 esp. See also "State of the Universities," *Quart. Rev.* 36. 71 (1827) 216–68. This critic is primarily interested in the development of professional education at Oxford as a method of raising the social status of some

of the lower professions (principally surgeons and solicitors). He argues that this goal could be attained only if each of the teachers in the university were able to concentrate on one subject and view teaching as a permanent career. Under his system, the professor would give public lectures while the college tutor would work with the student in a more personal way. The author conceives of his reforms as modeled on the German professorial system and contrasts this system with the Scottish universities in which personal contact with the *privat docent* or college tutor is lacking.

21 *Eclectic Rev.*, 19 (above, n. 19).
22 Review of "Legality of the Present Academical System . . . Asserted," 486.
23 "Reform of the University of Oxford," *Eclectic Rev.*, 4th ser., 2 (August 1837), 125.
24 Anon. (J. Ingram, D. D. [C&M]), "Apologia Academica or Remarks on a Recent Article in the *Edinburgh Review*" (Oxford 1831), esp. vi–x, 12–33.
25 A Member of Convocation [Rev. Vaughan Thomas B. D. (C&M)], "The Legality of the Present Academical System of the University of Oxford asserted against the New Calumnies of the *Edinburgh Review*" (Oxford 1831), esp. 116–19.
26 A Member of Convocation [Rev. V. Thomas], "The Legality of the Present Academical System of the University of Oxford re-asserted against the new Calumnies of the *Edinburgh Review*" (Oxford 1832), 22–23.
27 Quoted from the Rev. V. Thomas's second pamphlet (above, n. 26), in "Attack on the Universities—Oxford," *Brit. Critic* 22 (October 1837), 399–400. See also the first part of this article in *Brit. Critic* 22 (July 1837), 168–215.
28 "University Reform," *Oxford Protestant Mag.* 1 (March 1847), 5–6. Another critic launches his attack on the system of education pursued at Oxford with the argument that the Tractarian Movement was a symptom of the failures of Oxford education and that these ideas could not have taken hold in a more wholesome intellectual atmosphere. See "The Present State of the University of Oxford—Its Defects and Remedies," *Tait's Edin. Mag.* N.S. 16 (August 1849), 525–39, esp. 530.
29 See the four pamphlets attributed by C&M to the Rev. W. Sewell, "The University Commission or Lord John Russell's Post-Bag" (Oxford 1850), esp. no. 4, p. 9, and no. 3, p. 31.
30 "Memorials of Oxford," *Brit. Critic* no. 47 (July 1838), 144.
31 "The Statutes of Magdalen College, Oxford," *Brit. Critic* no. 54 (1840), 387. This unsigned article was written by James Hope (late Hope-Scott), a young follower of J. H. Newman. Newman suggested to Hope that he write this review. Newman also saw the review in draft and judged it "very good and interesting." A. Dwight Culler, the historian of Newman's educational ideals, has written that this review "gives the most extensive account we have of the sort of reform that Newman would have espoused" (92–93); see A. Dwight Culler, *Imperial Intellect: A Study of Cardinal Newman's Educational Ideal* (New Haven 1955), 92–95.
32 Ibid., 365.
33 Ibid., 394.
34 "Memorials of Oxford," 146.
35 "Statutes of Magdalen College," 390.
36 In 1851, Newman had the opportunity to make a constitution for the Catholic University of Ireland, of which he was rector. In his plan, the major legislative power in the university was placed in the hands of the "senate"—of which three-quarters were the resident teachers of the university. The other one-

quarter would be fellows of the university who would be eminent men from outside the university who would take doctoral degrees in the various faculties. The heads of houses in Newman's university were to have only domestic powers. This plan indicated strikingly the hostility of the Tractarians to the power of heads of houses. It was also significant that these legislative plans were strikingly similar to those developed by the Tutors' Association in Oxford. To this degree, they showed the Tractarians as proponents of the "tutorial ideology" which was developing during this period. See Culler, *Imperial Intellect*, ch. VIII, esp. 158–59.

37 "Present State of the University of Oxford," 530. The issue of Tractarianism is used similarly in "Oxford and Cambridge: University Reform," *Brit. Quart. Rev.* 3 (1 May 1846), 358–76, esp. 376.

38 Bonamy Price, *Suggestions for the Extension of Professorial Teaching in the University of Oxford* (London 1850), 20. See also 19–20 for critique of Tractarianism.

39 Ibid., 21.

40 Ibid., 22.

41 Oxford and Cambridge: University Reform" *Brit. Quart. Rev.* 3 (1 May 1846), 365–66. See also "Reform of Oxford University," *Tait's Edin. Mag.* 16 (October 1849), esp. 709 for another example of the same argument.

42 Ibid., 368.

43 See J. H. Newman, *On the Scope and Nature of University Education* (1852), ed. W. Ward (London 1965), esp. Discourse IV, "Liberal Knowledge its Own End," 80–102.

44 *Brit. Quart. Rev.*, p. 365 (above, n. 41).

45 Ibid., 366.

46 Ibid., p. 368. See also "The Present State of the University of Oxford," esp. 536 for another example of the same argument.

47 "Reform of Oxford University," 708. For a similar argument see, "Oxford and Cambridge: University Reform," 371.

48 "Present State of the University of Oxford," 533.

49 See n. 44, and "Oxford and Cambridge," 375, ". . . the professors ought to have a chief voice in deciding the course of academic instruction."

50 Price, *Suggestions for the Extension of Professorial Teaching*.

51 Price was elected Drummond Professor in 1868 after a heated struggle with J. E. Thorold Rogers, who had previously held the chair. The great irony was that Price, the great exponent of the use of professorial chairs as rewards for profound learning, was elected a professor himself because of the orthodoxy of his religious views. It was asserted that Rogers was sympathetic to Nonconformity and this decided the electors to choose Price.

52 Price, 8.

53 Ibid., 14–17.

54 Ibid., 12–13.

55 Ibid., 6–8.

56 For Price's specific suggestions for reform, see ibid., 25–31.

57 Ibid., 11–12.

58 Ibid., 32–33.

59 *Eureka, No. II. A Sequel to a Sequel to Lord John Russell's Post-Bag* (Oxford 1853), 13. This anonymous pamphlet was a specific parody of the four pamphlets published by the Rev. W. Sewell in 1850 (above, n. 29).

59a See the reprints of a 17th century account of the trials of the university published by the Rev. Vaughan Thomas in 1834 and again in 1850. "A Ballad in

Macraronic Latin entitled *Rustica Descriptio Visitationis Fanaticae*, being a country clergyman's tragi-comical lament upon revisiting Oxford after the root-and-branch reform of 1648 (1649), by John Allibond, with preface and notes, the verses being done into doggerel 1834 in *Usum Parliamenti Indoctorum, Ejusdem Nominis Secundi*," 3d ed. (Oxford 1850).

60 This "revised Congregation" would consist of all professors (at least fifty under the commissioners' plan) together with all heads of houses and the senior tutors of each college totaling forty-one including the halls).

61 *Oxford University Commission* (1852), Report, 94 (hereafter *OUC* Report).

62 Ibid., 90.

63 Ibid., 94.

64 Ibid., 94.

65 Ibid., 171.

66 Ibid., 100.

67 See "Answers from the Rev. Richard Congreve, M.A., Fellow and Tutor of Wadham College, Oxford," 151–54, esp. 153; "Answers from the Rt. Rev. Thomas Vowler Short, D. D., Bishop of St. Asaph," 164; "Answers from N. S. Maskelyne, Esq., M.A., Deputy Reader in Mineralogy in the University of Oxford," 185–91, esp. 188. All in *OUC* Evidence.

68 For the use of law professors for pre-professional training for barristers, see "Answers from Stephen Charles Denison, Esq., M.A., late Stowell Fellow of University College, Deputy Judge Advocate General," 197–200. For a similar argument for medicine, see "Evidence of H. W. Acland, Esq. M.D., Lee's Reader in Anatomy, Late Fellow of All Souls," 235–39. Only Charles Lyell advocated the establishment of full professional training in medicine in Oxford; see 119–23. All in ibid.

68a "Many of the Lecturers, at least might have classes not larger than those which attend College Tutors, and would naturally adopt the same mode of teaching." *OUC* Report, 101. For the commissioner's entire argument, see 99–101.

69 See "Answers from the Rev. H. L. Mansel, M.A., Fellow, Tutor, and Dean of Arts, of St. John's College, Oxford," 19–21, esp. 20; "Answers of the Rev. Robert Scott, M.A., Rector of South Luffenham and Prebendary of Exeter; Late Fellow and Tutor of Balliol College, Oxford," 110–14, esp. 112. All in *OUC* Evidence.

70 See "Answers of Henry Halford Vaughan, Late Fellow of Oriel College, and Regius Professor of Modern History," 82–92; "Answers from Sir Edmund Head, M.A., K.C.B., Governor of New Brunswick, and Late Fellow and Tutor of Merton College, Oxford," 157–61, esp. 160–61 for an argument for professorial control over the examination system, but with less emphasis on the role of the professor in learned research. In ibid.

71 See "Answers from John Conington, M.A., Fellow of University College, Oxford," 115–19, in ibid.

72 See "Answers from the Rev. Bartholomew Price, M.A., Fellow, Tutor, and Mathematical Lecturer of Pembroke College, Oxford," 59–67; "Answers from the Rev. W. Hayward Cox, B.D., Late Fellow of Queen's College and Formerly Vice-Principal of St. Mary's Hall, Oxford," 92–99, esp. 97. All in ibid.

73 "Answers from the Rev. John Wilkinson, M.A., of Merton College, and Rector of Broughton Gifford, Wilts," 75, ibid.

74 Ibid., 48.

75 Ibid., 213.

76 See Ward, *Victorian Oxford*, 180–84 for formation of the Tutors' Association; also "No. 1. Recommendations Respecting the Extension of the University of

Oxford, Adopted by the Tutors' Association, January 1853" (Oxford 1853), 4 (hereafter *Tutors' Association*, No. 1).

77 "No. 3. Recommendations Respecting the Relation of the Professorial and Tutorial Systems as Adopted by the Tutors' Association, November 1853" (Oxford 1853), 62 (hereafter *Tutors' Association* No. 3).

78 Ibid., 62.

79 Ibid., 63.

80 Ibid., 74.

81 Ibid., 75.

82 Ibid., 76. For the Tutors' Association's attack on professorial dominance in the government of the university, see "No. 2. Recommendations Respecting the Constitution of the University of Oxford, as adopted by the Tutors' Association, April 1853" (Oxford 1853).

83 *Tutors' Association, No. 3*, 78–79.

84 *Tutors' Association, No. 1*, 29.

85 *Tutors' Association, No. 1*, 8.

86 *Tutors' Association No. 3*, 64.

87 See "Answers of Herman Merivale, Esq., M.A., Late Fellow of Balliol College and Professor of Political Economy, Oxford," in *OUC* Evidence, 200–202.

88 "Answers from W. F. Donkin, M.A., Savilian Professor of Astronomy, Mathematical Lecturer and late Fellow of University College, Oxford," in ibid., 108; also see 106–10.

89 BM Add. MSS. 44251 pt. I fols. 74–6 (Gladstone Papers), quoted in Ward, *Victorian Oxford* 184, n. 26.

90 "Evidence of the Rev. E. Hawkins, D.D., Provost of Oriel College, pp. 349–379," in *Report and Evidence Upon the Recommendations of Her Majesty's Commissioners for Inquiring into the State of the University of Oxford, Presented to the Board of Heads of Houses and Proctors, December 1, 1853* (Oxford 1853), Evidence, 370 (hereafter *HBC*, Evidence).

91 "Evidence of the Rev. R. L. Cotton, D.D., Provost of Worcester College, Vice Chancellor," 381–95, in ibid., 381.

92 Ibid., Report, 59–60.

93 Ibid., 94–98.

94 Ibid., 42–45.

95 Ibid., 65–86.

96 "Evidence of Rev. E. B. Pusey, Regius Professor of Hebrew and Canon of Christ Church," pp. 1–175, in ibid., Evidence, 79. Also see 112–13 for his objection to the use of law fellowships in "eking out the income of Junior, and other, Barristers until they marry."

97 Ibid., 78.

98 Ibid., 78.

99 Ibid., 79.

100 Ibid., 112.

101 See "Evidence of the Rev. Edward Arthur Litton, M.A., Vice-Principal of St. Edmund Hall, Late Fellow of Oriel College," 405–13; "Evidence of Edward A. Freeman, Esq., M.A., Late Fellow and Rhetorical Lecturer of Trinity College," 415–40; "Evidence of the Rev. James T. Round, B.D., Formerly Fellow and Tutor of Balliol College," 463–95, all in ibid., Evidence.

101a William Sewell, B.D., *Suggestions for the Extension of the University; submitted to the Rev. the Vice-Chancellor* (n.p. [Oxford] n.d. [1850]), 10. Sewell printed this pamphlet because he considered the Royal Commission to be "illegal" and, therefore, he had refused to answer the set of questions which the commissioners had submitted to him. He felt, however, that some statement ought to be made in order to guard against a charge of indifference which might be placed on his refusal were he to remain silent. Since Sewell's motivation was identical to that which compelled the Hebdomadal Board to establish a committee of their own and to collect evidence after the Royal Commission's Report had been published, this pamphlet may be considered as part of the evidence submitted to the Hebdomadal Board.

102 "Evidence of Edward A. Freeman, Esq., M.A., Late Fellow and Rhetorical Lecturer of Trinity College," in *HBC*, Evidence, 433.

103 "Evidence of the Rev. James T. Round, B.D., Formerly Fellow and Tutor of Balliol College," in ibid., 471.

104 See Ward, *Victorian Oxford* 180–200.

105 Ibid., ch. ix, 180–209.

106 See Appendix, below, for expansion of academic careers in 19th century Oxford.

107 See E. G. W. Bill and J. F. A. Mason, *Christ Church and Reform 1850–1867* (Oxford 1970).

108 See J. W. Mackail, *James Legh Strachan-Davidson, Master of Balliol: A Memoir* (Oxford 1925), 56–59.

109 Professor Donkin, in his evidence before the Royal Commissioners of 1850, advocated the use of his subject, astronomy, in the undergraduate curriculum on the basis of the traditional ideals of liberal education rather than by stressing the need for professional, or even "pre-professional," studies: "I think it is to be considered that practical astronomy is not merely a means of obtaining astronomical results, but is also capable of being made highly useful as an instrument of intellectual discipline and cultivation . . . [it] requires very clear conceptions and exact reasoning, without involving (so far as it needs to be taught for educational purposes) the more abstruse parts of Mathematics." *OUC* Evidence, 110.

116

WOMEN AND MEN

A. H. Halsey

Source: A. H. Halsey, *Decline of Donnish Dominion: The British Academic Professions in the Twentieth Century*, Oxford: Clarendon Press, 1995, pp. 216–34.

The participation of women in higher education is patchy, passionate, and peculiar because we are living through a period in which vigorous reforms are taking place with a view to establishing fair or equal chances in what remains, despite many slights and denials, one of the most attractive careers for women in paid employment in modern society. In one sense the establishment of an equal position for women in teaching is relatively easy in that such posts are culturally assimilable to the traditional 'caring' role of women in the domestic economy. Leonora Davidoff and Catherine Hall have written a beautifully detailed portrait of the role of the bourgeois wife in keeping her husband 'on stage' in a business career from behind the screen in the family home (Davidoff and Hall 1987). Historically, an educational career was one of the obvious paths out of domesticity into professional life for Victorian women. Marriage was, of course, the culturally favoured career. The nurse and the governess were relatively respectable alternative positions in society, while actresses, courtesans, and prostitutes were ancient but more or less scandalous, 'deviant' cultural figures.

This is not the place to detail either the history or the sociology of women's penetration into the educational world.[1] In her study of ten Victorian pioneers of the path out of domesticity into public professional life, Julia Parker has been at pains to emphasize the special qualities of both Victorian middle-class culture and the high resolve of those like Annie Besant, Octavia Hill, Florence Nightingale, or Beatrice Webb, who overcame a multiplicity of familial and social obstacles to their ambition. If we compare the circumstances of women moving out of domestic and family life in the last quarter of the twentieth century with those of the Victorian women discussed by Mrs Parker, 'what is immediately striking is the vulnerability of the women of the present day. The Victorian ladies had three important strengths: adequate material resources, strong family networks and, whether or not religiously inspired, a commitment to work which they could see as crucially important in bringing about a more just and merciful society' (Parker 1988: 194). Today both social circumstance and definitions of femininity are transformed: religious belief has declined, fertility has fallen, family networks have weakened, and the vocation of social service is less compelling. Modern women are subject less to the motives of the heroine and more to the mundane necessities of earning a living, even in the higher professions.

The modern female professional is also almost as different in her social position from her earlier twentieth-century forebears as described by Talcott Parsons (Parsons 1949). By the 1930s and 1940s, to be sure, a career in the professions had been made more acceptable as an alternative to marriage: but the cultural dominance of feminine domesticity was still overwhelmingly great. As Parsons put it:

> The majority of married women, of course, are not employed, but even of those that are a very large proportion do not have jobs which are in basic competition for status with those of their husbands. The majority of 'career' women whose occupational status is comparable with that of men in their own class, at least in the upper-middle and upper classes, are unmarried, and in the small proportion of cases where they are married the result is a profound alteration in family structure.
>
> (Parsons 1949: 223)

For Parsons at mid-century the analysis of sex roles turned fundamentally on 'the interrelations of the occupational system and the conjugal family' (Parsons 1949: 223). For Julia Parker, writing of women in the 1980s, 'the step from domestic into outside work remains a difficult one when family responsibilities are also retained' (Parker 1988: 195).

Academic women provide an illuminating case in the study of the history and sociology of professional employment among women. The teaching role has been historically compatible with perceptions of femininity, by contrast, for example, with business: and therefore the educational career was relatively attractive to middle-class girls in Victorian times. Moreover, the motives of these girls were both material and cultural. As Josephine Butler remarked in 1868:

> The desire for education which is widely felt by English women, and which has begun to find its expression in many practical ways, is a desire which springs from no conceit of cleverness, from no ambition for the prizes of intellectual success, as is sometimes falsely imagined, but from the conviction that for many women to get

knowledge is the only way to get bread, and still more from that instinctive craving for light which in many is stronger than the craving for bread.

(Butler 1868)

Higher education and the Victorian woman

Attempts to change regulations governing the admission of women to university degrees, though dependent on improving the secondary education of girls, began to acquire momentum simultaneously with school reform. The key figure in many of these battles was the fanatically motivated Emily Davies. She had reacted to the failed attempt of Elizabeth Garrett to sit the London University matriculation examinations by petitioning various university boards to allow girls to sit their pre-university local examinations and, in 1863, Cambridge University allowed a trial examination to be held (Kamm 1966: 52). The trial became a permanency four years later and Oxford followed suit in 1870. But Emily Davies wanted to achieve a higher goal—that of the entry of women into the universities generally and, therefore, female access to formal degree qualifications. There was opposition from many sides, not only against the entry of women as such, but also in the guise of proposals that they should sit 'modified' examinations. It was on this latter basis that London University became the first to admit women in 1869. In the same year Emily Davies started a college in Hitchin within which women, though taking the same examinations as men in Cambridge, had no official status. In 1874 this college moved to Girton, Cambridge, and by 1881 its students were admitted to degrees.[2] By the end of the 1890s women were placed on an equal footing with men with respect to the granting of degrees in all the major universities and Girton, as a womens' college, had been joined in Cambridge by Newnham College. Like Somerville and Lady Margaret Hall in Oxford, the differences between these two women's colleges reflected the unease which continued to exist about the admission of women to sit examinations alongside men. Girton scholars, like those in Somerville, sat the same examinations as their male fellow students. Those at Newnham and Lady Margaret Hall were allowed to take a more 'relaxed' approach and sit modified versions of the male examinations. Thus attitudes towards the higher education of women remained markedly ambiguous. The pioneers of the movement were anxious to allay the suspicions of the college authorities as well as to overcome the prejudices of male undergraduates against the supposed 'blue stocking' invasion. There was in other words a struggle to demonstrate both that 'college girls' were upright and respectable citizens and at the same time that they were not contaminated by pursuing high educational qualifications, disqualifying themselves from marriage (Delamont 1978).

The early female graduates and employment

Resistance to the new and unfamiliar female graduate was based on a cultural distinction between the public and the private sphere defining distinctive male and female roles. This distinction proved to be one which education alone could not overcome. And the struggle of many middle-class women to enter the previously restricted public world of employment was, correspondingly, a long and bitter one. Teaching was one of the few professional careers open to the new graduates. It was mainly available in primary and secondary schools, and even here there were warnings that supply would exceed demand. Such warnings were thinly disguised antifeminism. A late Victorian protest was apposite.

> There are not yet 800 women graduates at London and Cambridge. Of these the majority are assistant mistresses in public or private schools, visiting teachers, lecturers, or head mistresses. There were in 1881, according to the census of that year, 123,000 women teachers and over 4 million girls between the ages of 5 and 20; and yet already this little handful of graduates is told that it is in excess of the demand and that it must take lower salaries in consequence.
>
> (Collet 1890)

So does monopsony reinforce cultural prejudice. Though women were becoming more acceptable as recruits to middle-class employment, the established conceptions of appropriate sex roles was stubbornly persistent.

It was no doubt plausible to argue, as did the International Federation of University Teachers in 1966, that 'women have always been admitted into the teaching profession, unhampered by any traditional prejudice against them; on the contrary, it is generally accepted that women have special gifts for educating the young, teaching them and forming their character' (International Federation of University Women 1966: 20). Nevertheless, the entry of female graduates into the higher levels of teaching was contested and limited. The leap from the lower to the higher professions was never an easy one, and the following comment made at the beginning of the twentieth century is still often echoed today:

> In most of the new co-educational universities, teaching positions were nominally open equally to women with men, but in practice a woman had to be exceptionally well qualified and much more distinguished than a man in order to gain an appointment.
>
> (Holcombe 1973: 66)

Some, like the early Somerville graduate Lillian Faithfull, who became Vice-Principal of the 'Women's Department' at King's College London in 1894, went on to have successful academic careers (Spender (ed.) 1987: 351). But many found themselves confined in their academic employment to women's colleges. Change was slow and limited. A woman could take a medical degree by 1885 in Edinburgh but not in many of the London colleges and was refused membership of the BMA until 1893. Careers in law remained firmly closed until the passing of the 1919 Sex Disqualification (Removal) Act, and it was not until 1925 that the Civil Service opened its administrative grade examinations to women (Kamm 1966: 203). Moreover, all these professions, including school-teaching, operated marriage bars which disqualified women from working once they were married.

Women students and the expansion of higher education

We have already described the expansion of student numbers in the British universities and, more recently, the polytechnics (Table 4.6). The number of male full-time undergraduates in 1988/9 was an increase of 11,400 on the 1970 figure, while the number of female undergraduates went up by 52,700 in the same period. The emergence of the polytechnics in the 1970s pushed the proportion of women students in higher education further still. The polytechnics specifically targeted groups unlikely otherwise to enter higher education and, at least in their initial stages, were particularly attractive to women. The Secretary of State for Education in the mid-1960s, Anthony Crosland, declared:

> There are two categories of students whose importance to the nation can hardly be overestimated. First, there are the tens of thousands of students who want to do a full-time course which, although not of degree standard, leads to one or other of the many professional qualifications marked by a certificate or an associateship. Secondly, there is the huge and growing army of part-time students at all levels, almost all of them already in employment. Now the universities cannot cater for these without a complete transformation of the university system of a kind which would not be practicable for many years ...
>
> (Robinson 1968: 252)

Here was a vast, unsatisfied demand and, in the first years of the new polytechnics, female full-time students outnumbered males by some 11,000. Over the next decade, however, men drew level, and the 1988/9 figures show the numbers of men to be slightly greater at 147,900 compared to 146,700 women. The continued rise in the student population in the 1980s was largely confined to the polytechnic sector, with the numbers entering the universities rising much more slowly. The Open University, as we have seen, also provided more opportunities, especially for part-time women students.

Between them the polytechnics and the Open University gave spectacular increases in part-time opportunities for women. By 1990 women made up 43 per cent of all students in higher education—an increase of about 10 percentage points in less than twenty years.

These advances are impressive, but it should also be noticed that women are distinguished from men in their academic interest and their qualifications. There is still a high propensity for women to enter areas linked to traditional sex roles or stereotypes such as nursing, teaching, and the arts. They are accordingly heavily outweighed by men in the sciences and applied sciences including engineering. In this respect there has been little change since the 1960s, when women formed 42 per cent of arts students, 22 per cent of medical students, and 3 per cent of those studying technology (International Federation of University Women 1966: 6).

Women in the senior common rooms

Despite the large increase in female students in higher education, barriers against an academic career remained, with the consequence that the numbers of women in the higher ranks of teaching are disproportionately low (Table 1), just as they are in law and medicine. The gap between the sexes is narrowing, but its persistence deserves explanation.

Are the differences caused by prejudice? Sex discrimination is widely complained of. It is denounced in the AUT publication *AUT Women*. The 1990 Hansard Report was heavily critical of the universities, describing them as 'bastions of male power and privilege', arguing that, in certain cases, the under-representation of women in top positions represented a situation worthy of examination by the Equal Opportunities Commission (Hansard Society 1990: 68). It can reasonably be replied that universities and polytechnics try to be good employers and are willing practitioners of the statutory policy of equal opportunity between the sexes. But women

Table 1 Men and women in British universities (1989/90), distribution by rank, full-time academic staff (%).

	Men	*Women*
Professors	11.4	1.7
Readers/Senior lecturers	22.3	8.9
Lecturers	57.5	65.5
Others (research, teaching, etc.)	8.6	23.9
TOTAL	100.0	100.0
(No.)	(38,098)	(9,488)

Note: These figures include 10,836 men and 4,995 women employed in research only.
Source: USR, *University Statistics*, 1989–90, table 29.

420

are well known to be a minority in the senior common rooms. They constituted 10 per cent of the university staff in 1964. By 1976 that percentage was marginally increased to 11.6 and in polytechnics it was 13.6. In 1989 our sample numbers indicated a further rise to 14 per cent among those with full-time posts carrying both teaching and research duties (that is, excluding research-only staff) in the universities and 21 per cent in the polytechnics. The USR census for 1989, however, with its wider definition of full-time and part-time staff, and including those with research duties only, indicates that the proportion of women employed in university academic staffs was 20 per cent. Thus significantly more women have entered the senior common rooms in recent decades. But, as we shall see below, inequalities of rank persist in that men have tended to retain the more secure and more senior positions.

In pursuit of explanation we can begin with an empirical map of the similarities and differences between the women and men we find in the senior common rooms of polytechnics and universities. Their origins, their domestic position, their distribution between university groups, subject areas, and academic ranks are set out in Table 2 for the higher education system as a whole, and the further differences between the universities and polytechnics appear in Table 7.

To put the statistics into context, we should note that if social background, marital status, household income, faculty membership, rank, and university group were unrelated to sex, the percentages would be equal in each row of Table 2. If the whole system were equally and equally competently staffed by men and women, all the odds ratios would be equal to 1. They are not.

The academic professions remain predominantly male. There is strong social selection in the passage from junior to senior common room. The juniors are now over 40 per cent women, the seniors 20 per cent. But what kind of selection? Genetic capacities may presumably be ruled out. The relatively high female proportions in education, literature, language, and social studies suggest continued differential socialization. The proportions run in the universities and the polytechnics from approaching half in language and literature departments of polytechnics to as low as 2 per cent in the engineering and technology departments of universities. Explanations for such uneven distribution presumably lie in the experiences of girls in their families and schools. Sex differences in recruitment among university groups are not wide, though the relatively low figures for Scotland and the older redbricks invite explanation. The rank and tenure distributions in both universities and polytechnics suggest further selective processes. In both sectors women are scarce in the upper ranks and the secure appointments and concentrated in the lower teaching ranks and in the army of research workers on fixed-term contracts (see Tables 2 and 7). Again, the explanations are not obvious.

421

Table 2 Women and men in higher education in Great Britain, 1989: origins and distribution.

	Men	Women	Odds ratio or significance of difference
Age (mean years)	46.4	43.5	$p<0.00$
Social background (%)			
Origin in service or intermediate classes	83.1	89.6	1.75[a]
Origin in manual classes	16.9	10.4	0.57[a]
Private secondary schooling	30.2	28.9	0.94
State secondary schooling	69.8	71.1	1.05
Marital status (%)			
Married	80.9	58.3	0.32[a,b]
Living as married	5.8	9.9	1.87[a]
Separated/Divorced	5.8	9.9	1.87[a]
Widowed	0.7	1.6	2.57
Never married	7.2	18.2	2.85[a,b]
Household income (mean %)			
Salary	72.7	61.8	$p<0.001$
Other earnings	7.0	3.8	$p<0.001$
Spouse's income	16.8	31.0	$p<0.001$
Subject area (%)			
Arts	15.3	24.7	1.85[a]
Social Sciences	27.5	41.3	1.83[a]
Natural Sciences	28.2	13.5	0.39[a]
Engineering/Technology	15.6	3.7	0.20[a]
Medicine/Health	11.6	16.0	1.41[a,b]
Agriculture/Forestry/Veterinary Science	1.8	0.9	0.51
Rank (%)			
Professoriate	15.3	3.9	0.22[a]
Reader/Sen. lecturer/Principal lecturer	42.2	38.1	0.83
Lecturer	42.5	58.0	1.89[a,b]
University group (%)			
Oxbridge	4.0	3.4	0.89
London	10.3	12.4	1.13
Old redbrick	16.0	11.5	0.69[a]
New redbrick	7.1	5.5	0.77
New Robbins	8.0	8.5	1.04
Technological	5.9	4.6	0.77
Scotland	9.9	5.7	0.56[a]
Wales	3.7	2.1	0.55
Polytechnics	34.6	46.3	1.62[a]
Terms of employment (%)			
Full-time	96.0	92.7	0.51[a]
Part-time	4.0	7.3	1.95[a,b]
Contract terms (%)			
Till retirement	79.0	67.4	0.54[a]
No specific term	11.7	16.4	1.53[a]
Fixed term	5.4	12.7	2.48[a]
Probationary	2.4	3.2	1.40
Other	1.5	0.2	0.16[a]

[a] Statistically significant at the 0.05 level or less.
[b] Distribution differs between universities and polytechnics.
Note: Odds ratios and probabilities (*p*) are not controlled for the effects of other variables. N varies slightly on different variables due to missing values and is approx. 1861 for men and 298 for women.
Source: A. H. Halsey, 1989 survey.

There are differences too in the career patterns and connections to family life. Women academics are on average three years younger than men. They are more likely to come from middle-class origins, though there is little difference in their schooling.

Academic women and family

More men than women are married. A higher proportion of women are cohabiting or are separated or divorced or widowed or never married. These differences hold even when age (women being somewhat younger than men) is taken into account. Although the numbers of 'unpartnered' people are low they include separated or divorced women (who may have responsibility for child care) as well as those who have never married.

Those women who are in a partnership appear to function as secondary bread-winners. If we examine the percentage of household income that comes from the salary of the respondent it turns out that less than half of the household income enjoyed by partnered women comes from their own salaries compared with over two-thirds (69.6 per cent) of the income accruing to partnered men. Women also tend to earn less from other sources, though this form of income is minor for both sexes according to our data.

More women work part-time in their academic appointments than do men (Table 2). And this is true for the partnered more than the unpartnered women. The differences are however fairly small. Well over nine out of every ten of men and women in both the universities and the polytechnics are full-time. It is simply that our samples included 6.8 women against 5.2 per cent men part-timers in the universities and 8.3 women against 1.7 per cent men in the polytechnics. It is also clear that women are much more likely to have less secure contracts than men. Over three-quarters of the men compared with two-thirds of the women among the full-time employees of universities or polytechnics have tenure until retirement. None of this description is new or surprising. We already know that women in paid employment in general are likely to have lower rank, to be paid less, to be more likely to be part-time or temporary, and to be secondary bread-winners to their partners (Purcell 1988).

Academic women and careers

This outline of the structural position of women in the academic professions reflects their late and uncertain entry as well as the continuing struggle to adapt to the conflicting pressures of the formal as distinct from the domestic economy. We must now ask how this struggle impinges on the performance of women in their professional role (Table 3). Purcell suggests that because women see themselves as secondary bread-winners they are inhibited from seeking career advancement in the way to which men are habituated. The

423

Table 3 Women and men in higher education, 1989: teaching and research.

	Men	Women	Odds ratio or significance of difference
Allocation of time (mean % adjusted for age)			
Teaching undergraduates	33.1	35.2	$p<0.05$
Doing research	23.22	20.8	$p<0.01$
Would like to teach undergraduates (%)	28.3	30	n.s.
Would like to do research (%)	37.4	35.4	$p<0.05$
Supervision of research students (%)	59.7	47.1	0.61[a]
Insufficient time for research because of teaching commitments (%)	64.3	81.8	2.49[a,b]
Index of career-related activities (mean adjusted for age)			
All	5.69	4.82	$p<0.001$[b]
Non-professors	5.16	4.72	$p<0.01$

Notes: As for Table 2.
Source: A. H. Halsey, 1989 survey.

general view is that women in work are more concerned about working conditions and the social relations of employment than with advancement in their career.

In addition it has been found (Rose and Fielder 1988) that if a promotion involves change in geographical location, married women are expected to follow their husbands, even if this involves demotion or job loss for the wife. The converse does not hold true to the same extent.

There is some evidence of such predispositions among academic women at the present time. We have already noted the general pattern of attitudes towards mobility between institutions and posts. If we look at sex differences from this point of view we find from responses to questions about preferred posts which were asked of the university sample that social or family considerations are more important to women than to men in making decisions about moving from one job to another (Table 4 and Appendix 2).

There are congruent patterns of response to related questions. As Park has pointed out (Park 1991: 26), women express more discontent with working conditions than do men, who are more inclined to grumble about salaries. University women are also more dissatisfied with academic life than either university or polytechnic men. University women more frequently give lack of job security as a reason for wanting to leave academic life and this presumably is partly a reflection of their less secure contracts. In general it may be that women are less satisfied because their conditions are typically worse, not because they are women.

Purcell also suggests that women tend to be marginalized into 'caring' rather than decision-making roles in their profession. Talcott Parsons noticed much earlier in the century (Parsons 1949) that a sexual division of labour was characteristic of professional employment such that, for example, women doctors were disproportionately engaged in paediatric as against surgical specialisms. There is a general tendency for professional and domestic roles to be assimilated to each other. This is borne out by our finding that women in 1989 spent a greater proportion of their time than men teaching undergraduates (Table 3) and correspondingly they spent rather less of their working time in research activity. This pattern holds in the polytechnics as well as the universities, even though polytechnic teachers generally give proportionally more time to teaching than to research whatever their sex. In this connection it is significant that there is little difference between the sexes in the percentage of time *ideally* allocated between the teaching and research functions. It should, however, be emphasized that these differences are small and in any case they are subjective estimates which may themselves be the outcome of differences in male and female consciousness.

On the other hand it is objectively true that men do more supervising of research students than do women. In the universities 70 per cent of the men compared with 56 per cent of the women were currently (in 1989) supervising research students. The comparable figures in the polytechnics were 34 and 23. Such a difference of activity may well be reflected in greater opportunities for men to publish, and this is particularly likely in that men are more concentrated in the sciences where research students are more likely to be cast in the role of apprentice researchers than they are in the humanities where the women tend to gather. At all events women more than men see the teaching burden as an obstacle to research. In the universities three-quarters and in the polytechnics still more of the women thought that teaching commitments left insufficient time for research (Table 3).

Other career-related activity was pursued more vigorously by men according to an index constructed from our questions (Appendix 2 contains the details). This may, however, be not so much a sex difference as a consequence of the fact that women, carrying greater domestic responsibilities, are less visible and high ranking in their profession. Hence their lower participation in such activities as refereeing applications for grants, speaking at other institutions, and so on. However, there are also other causative factors at work: when this analysis is refined to exclude professors and to control for age, differences between men and women are seen to be slighter. So a general picture emerges of academic women as somewhat but not enormously more involved in the teaching side of the work of the polytechnic or university rather than in research or in the associated activities of the academic professional life.

From studies of the labour market generally, Purcell also suggests that women are less likely to be involved in trade union activity, although she states that this is not the case for the academic professions. In our survey

Table 4 Women and men in higher education, 1989: careers and attitudes.

	Men	Women	Odds ratio or significance of difference
Academic attitudes (mean)			
Binary equality (factor score)	−0.18	1.10	*p*<0.001
Élitist teacher orientation[a]	−0.11	0.67	*p*<0.05
Élitist research orientation[a]	−0.14	0.93	*p*<0.01
Career			
Promotions over past decade (mean)			
Age below 35	0.75	0.61	*p*<0.10
Age 35–49	0.53	0.45	*p*<0.05
Age 50+	0.20	0.29	*p*<0.10
Give non-career reason for moving to another institution[b]	−1.28	−0.86	*p*<0.001
See themselves as likely to obtain a chair[b] (%)			
More likely	26.3	15.4	0.49[c]
Less likely	25.3	38.3	1.87[c]
Have seriously considered leaving academic life (%)	35.8	41.4	1.27[c]

Notes:
[a] Controlled for subject and age.
[b] Universities only.
[c] Statistically significant at the 0.05 level or less.
Source: A. H. Halsey, 1989 survey.

women's union membership is slightly greater than that of men, and women record holding union office as frequently as men. Thus 74.2 per cent of the women and 69.8 per cent of the men were members of a union and 24 per cent of women compared with 23 per cent of men had held some kind of office. Perhaps women's interest in union activity results, as Purcell suggests, from a political perspective which is at once both consensus-seeking and more radical. There is some evidence in our survey to support this generalization in the case of the academic professions (Table 5).

Table 5 Women and men in higher education, 1989: trade union activity.

	Men (%)	Women (%)	Odds ratio or significance of difference
Trade union member	70.1	74.0	1.23 n.s.
Trade union office-holder	22.9	24.6	1.13 n.s.

Source: A. H. Halsey, 1989 survey.

A factor analysis of sex differences

At this point, we can look at another major theme of our general analysis of academic attitudes—the question of the binary division between polytechnics and universities. Factor analysis can illuminate the issue in terms of sex differences. Using this method Muriel Egerton shows six factors which together explained more than half the variance (reported in more detail in Appendix 2).

Analysis of the factors in terms of sex differences shows that men and women differ most conspicuously in their attitudes to the binary divide. Women are relatively much keener on its dissolution. Out of the six factors this factor, relating to the equalities and inequalities between universities and polytechnics, accounted for most variance (18 per cent). The difference between university women and men was much greater on this factor than that between polytechnic men and women, with university women being relatively more favourable to dissolving the binary divide (Table 7).

No sex differences were found on a second factor, relating to the importance of teaching as against research. However, men and women did differ with respect to a third factor, related to the autonomy of universities and polytechnics against industry and government. This suggests that women are more inclined to adopt an élitist teaching orientation than men. Sex differences were also found in a fourth factor, suggesting that women are more inclined to favour an élitist researcher orientation than men. The latter two factors, which indicate support for the autonomy of higher education, and separate teaching from research, while valuing both, can be interpreted as reflecting traditional academic values. Women are concentrated in the humanities and social sciences, and these subjects may be more 'traditionalist' than the pure or applied sciences, where research is more frequently carried out in collaboration with industry. However, even when discipline was taken into account, women were somewhat more inclined to adhere to the more traditional positions. No differences between men and women were found on the final two factors, related to the expansion of higher education, and to the status and conditions of academic employment.

Finally, we may examine directly the effects of sex on the probability of promotion into the professoriate and so complete our discussion of career success from Chapter 9, where we ignored the distinction between the sexes. The correlates of career success are set out for men and women in Table 6. The corresponding table without sexual distinction is Table 9.1. As before, it must be remembered that the odds ratios (or probabilities) do not take into account any linkages or 'interactions' between the variables we include in the analysis and, also as before, the analysis of *net* effects appears at Appendix 2. We should also again remember that staff with only research duties are not included in this analysis. The differences between

Table 6 Correlates of career success: differences between men and women, 1989.

	Men (no. = 1,861)	Women (no. = 298)	Odds ratio or significance of difference
Qualifications			
1. Degree class			
(*a*) First class (%)	33.9	29.5	0.83 n.s.
2. Graduation			
(*a*) Oxbridge (%)	24.3	20.1	0.77 n.s.
(*b*) London (%)	17.9	17.6	0.99 n.s.
3. Doctorate (%)	61.1	46.3	0.54[a]
(*a*) Oxbridge (%)	11.7	8.4	0.68[a]
(*b*) London (%)	12.4	10.6	0.82 n.s.
Research orientation			
1. Research mainly (%)	27.8	20.5	0.65[a]
2. Both teaching and research (%)	28.7	27.5	0.96 n.s.
3. Teaching mainly (%)	43.3	52.1	1.42[a]
Publications			
1. Articles			
(*a*) 20+ (%)	43.3	21.0	0.36[a]
(*b*) Controlled for age of subject and binary type			0.51[a]
2. Books			
(*a*) Number (mean)	2.26	2.28	*p*=0.914 n.s.
(*b*) controlled for age and binary type	2.24	2.37	*p*=0.783 n.s.
Index of career-related activities (mean adjusted for age)			
All	5.69	4.82	*p*<0.001[a,b]
Non-professors	5.16	4.72	*p*<0.01[a,b]

Notes: As for Table 2.
Source: A. H. Halsey, 1989 survey.

Table 7 Sex differences between universities and polytechnics, academic staff, 1989.

	Universities			Polytechnics		
	Men (*n = 1618*)	*Women* (*n = 234*)	*Odds ratio*	*Men* (*n = 854*)	*Women* (*n = 202*)	*Odds ratio or significance of difference*
Marital status						
Married	82.3	54.7	0.25[a]	78.4	62.0	0.45[a]
Never married	7.2	22.0	3.67[a]	7.4	14.0	1.99[a]
Subject area (%)						
Health/Medicine	11.4	12.9	1.35	1.5	5.3	5.52[a]
Rank (%)						
Lecturer	49.0	77.3	2.88[a]	31.6	43.6	1.49[a]
Part-time	5.2	6.8	1.34 n.s.	1.4	8.0	5.36[a]
Full-time	94.8	93.3	0.74 n.s.	98.3	92.0	0.19[a]
Teaching and research (%)						
Insufficient time for research because of teaching commitments	56.3	81.4	2.82[a]	79.5	86.9	1.57[a]
Index of career-related activities (mean)	6.47	5.49	$p < 0.000$	4.28	4.11	$p < 0.02$
Binary equality (factor score)	−3.32	−0.98	$p < 0.001$	4.29	4.54 n.s.	

Notes: As for Table 2.
Source: A. H. Halsey, 1989 survey.

men and women in promotion chances are related significantly to doctoral qualifications, research orientation, and research performance. Men more frequently hold doctorates and have more frequently taken them in Oxbridge, though first degree Firsts and place of graduation do not differentiate between the sexes. The research discriminations, both attitudes and performance, are real but not large. Men are on average more research-minded and more productive with consequently better chances of promotion. The pattern of predictive associations will look different when net effects rather than gross correlations are considered: for example, qualifications are better predictors in the context of all the factors identified for women than for men, as also high productivity in research. Both of these effects, it may be surmised, stem from the fact that women academics generally are relatively less involved in research and lean more towards teaching. The outstanding woman researcher is therefore more visible to selection committees appointing candidates to chairs.

With respect to research productivity it appears that women do have a higher proportion of non-producers and lower proportions of very high producers, and this difference obtains also for the record of publications in the last two years—a measure which offsets the tendency for women to be relatively recent recruits. In sum the male performance is superior but not spectacularly so. And the university/polytechnic difference certainly dwarfs sex differences in higher education as a whole.

Summing up we may in general say that our portrait of academic women is very similar to the picture which has emerged from studies of women in employment generally. There is only partial assimilation, there is some tendency towards a sexual division of labour, the direction is one which assimilates professional to domestic roles in that teaching in some aspects is, so to say, *in loco parentis*. The outcome is that women in this privileged profession put themselves, or are put, at a disadvantage in the competititon to produce research. They are partially subordinated to men. Yet, to repeat, we cannot offer a comprehensive explanation of the markedly poorer prospects of professorial promotion which have so far been women's lot. All that we can do is to point to a continuing problem. A female professor of arts wrote to us: 'I am not a feminist of any school, but it is a fact that the percentage of women in academic posts decreases as you go up the ladder. I am frequently the only woman . . . on committees of the university, though (it) has a respectable number of women professors.'

Notes

1 More detail may be had from Park 1991: ch. 1.
2 Ironically Cambridge was, in fact, the last university to grant women full status; it was not until 1921 that women could receive even titular degrees and not until 1948 did they become co-equal with men.

References

BUTLER, J. (1868), 'The Education and Employment of Women', in D. Spender, (ed.), *The Education Papers: Women's Quest for Equality in Britain* (London, 1987).

COLLET, C. (1890), *The Economic Position of Educated Working Women: A Discourse* (London).

DAVIDOFF, L., and HALL, C. (1987), *Family Fortunes* (London).

DELAMONT, S. (1978), 'The Domestic Ideology and Women's Education', in S. Delamont and L. Duffin, *The Nineteenth Century Woman: Her Cultural and Physical World* (London).

Hansard Society (1990), Report of the Hansard Society Commission on Women at the Top (London).

HOLCOLME, L. (1973), *Victorian Ladies at Work: Middle-Class Working Women in England and Wales 1850–1914* (Newton Abbot).

International Federation of University Women (1966), *The Position of the Woman Graduate Today: A Survey* (London).

KAMM, J. (1966), *Rapiers and Battleaxes* (London).

PARK, A. M. (1991), 'Women Working in Higher Education' (M.Phil. thesis, University of Oxford), ch. 1.

PARKER, J. (1988), *Women and Welfare: Ten Victorian Women in Public Social Service* (London, 1988).

PARSONS, T. (1949), 'Age and Sex in the Social Structure', in *Essays in Sociological Theory Pure and Applied* (Chicago), 218–32.

PURCELL, K. (1988), 'Gender and the Experience of Employment,' in D. Gallie (ed.), *Employment in Britain* (Oxford).

ROBINSON, E. (1968), *The New Polytechnics* (London).

ROSE, M., and FIELDER, S. (1988), 'The Principle of Equity and the Labour Market Behaviour of Dual Market Earners', Working Paper 3, *The Social Change and Economic Life Initiative* (Oxford).

SPENDER, D. (ed.) (1987), *The Education Papers: Women's Quest for Equality in Britain* (London).

117

PATTERNS OF PROVISION
Access and accommodation

Carol Dyhouse

Source: C. Dyhouse, *No Distinction of Sex? Women in British Universities, 1870–1939*, London: University College London Press, 1995, pp. 11–55.

Admitting women

Josephine Kamm, an early historian of women's education, observed that in the long struggle to obtain university degrees for women "Britain blazed no trail".[1] In this respect British universities lagged behind their American counterparts, as well as the universities of the Commonwealth.[2] Access came later, and accommodation was often rather more meagre. Phoebe Sheavyn, who was Senior Tutor to Women Students at Manchester University in the early 1920s, compiled a brief survey for the International Federation of University Women around 1924, in which she contrasted the poverty of provision for women in British universities with the dignified and spacious arrangements that she had seen in the United States.[3]

Dr Sheavyn was well placed to comment on educational provision and social opportunity; she came from a relatively poor social background, and as a young woman she had taught in a Board School in the Midlands, allegedly "after her hemming had passed the scrutiny of a male inspector with a magnifying glass".[4] Following some depressing teaching experiences she became a governess in the family of an architect who had encouraged her to sit for the Oxford Local Examinations. This had led to a scholarship at the new College of Aberystwyth. She was awarded a first-class honours degree in English by the University of London in 1889, her master's degree in 1894, and a D.Litt. in 1906. Between 1894 and 1896 she held posts as Reader and then Fellow of Bryn Mawr in Pennsylvania, where she was able to acquire first-hand knowledge of American provision for the higher education of women, before returning to England as Tutor and Lecturer at Somerville. In 1907 she left Oxford to take up an appointment as Senior

Tutor to Women Students and Warden of Ashburne Hall in Manchester.[5] Sheavyn's life history was extraordinary in terms of her social mobility, variety of experience, and sheer longevity (she lived to be 102), but these were some of the qualities that rendered her a sharp social observer.

In Britain, the University of London was, in 1878, the first university to admit women to its degrees (with the exception of medicine), and University College London (UCL), which opened most of its classes to women in the same year, has laid claim to being the first coeducational university institution.[6] But the pattern is complex, and much depends on definitions. Neat chronological lists of dates of entry are not easy to draw up and call often be misleading. Women were frequently allowed access to classes before, or in some cases after, being allowed to sit degree examinations. There were sometimes special qualifications for women: St Andrews University in Scotland had offered a higher certificate (the LA, later LLA or "Lady Literate in Arts") to women students from 1876.[7] Students in the newer university colleges prepared for the degrees of the University of London before these colleges obtained their separate charters. Women were cautiously admitted to classes in Owens College, Manchester, in 1883, for what was originally designated as a trial or probationary period of five years. Access to degrees in Manchester (then part of the "Victoria University" federation of Manchester, Liverpool and Leeds) came slowly and in instalments.[8] At first, only the pass degree and four honours schools in the Faculty of Arts were open to women, although by 1897 they were admitted to all degree examinations except those in engineering and medicine.[9] Apart from Oxford and Cambridge, Durham was the last university in England to admit women to its degrees. In Durham a supplementary charter licensing their admission to all courses and degrees (with the exception of divinity) was obtained in 1895, although women were excluded from membership of Convocation until 1914.[10] None of the charters granted to the new civic universities in England excluded women. In Scotland, legislative changes of 1889 and 1892 empowered the four Scottish universities to admit women to classes and degrees.[11] The charter of the University of Wales, granted in 1893, stipulated women's eligibility for degrees and also offices, stating specifically that they should be treated as full members of the university.[12]

However, as stated above, much depends on definitions. Women students were often admitted to classes in colleges that later became part of chartered institutions of full university status. The College of Science in Newcastle, originally part of the University of Durham, accepted women students before Durham did.[13] Mason College in Birmingham, Firth College in Sheffield, the Yorkshire College in Leeds, and the university colleges in Nottingham, Reading and Bristol all admitted women students to some or all of their classes before they received their charters. The pattern is blurred further by arrangements for instruction in medicine: almost everywhere it was opposition from faculty in the medical schools, and their links with senior staff and managers of local hospitals and infirmaries, that delayed the universities' formal provision for the full acceptance of women students to classes and examinations. In Edinburgh, the bitter struggles between, on the one hand, Sophia Jex-Blake and the group of women who battled to obtain a medical education in the 1870s, and, on the other, the medical faculty, led by Professor Robert Christison, arguably produced a backlash, which left the university authorities confused and wary about the rights of women to full access to university facilities, particularly the women students of medicine.[14] In Glasgow, the existence of a separate medical school for women in Queen Margaret College delayed the university's sense of any need to open its own medical classes to women, even after the incorporation of Queen Margaret College into the university in 1893.[15] Even in University College London, with its proud tradition of pioneering coeducational provision, women were not admitted into the Faculty of Medicine until 1917.[16]

The Ladies' Educational Associations

If medical schools served to delay the full admission of women, female students were often admitted to classes taught at least partly under the aegis of university authorities before their admission to degrees. This was not only in connection with the separate qualifications or certificates offered to women students such as the St Andrews' LA mentioned above. Here we have to consider the work of the Ladies' Educational Associations founded, for the most part, in the 1860s and 1870s. There were a large number of these associations, and they were originally founded for a number of purposes.[17] Following the opening of the Oxford and Cambridge and other university Local Examinations to women in the second half of the nineteenth century, these associations frequently supervised the arrangements whereby girls and women sat for these examinations, also acting as support groups for women teachers. Others were more specifically concerned to promote the higher education of women, to which end they organized classes and lecture series, sponsored scholarships and bursaries, and lobbied their local institutions of higher education for access and facilities. There were Ladies' Educational Associations in almost all the larger towns and many of the smaller ones too: some of these were relatively informal and have left little documentation, others were highly organized, long lived and powerful. The best known was the North of England Council for Promoting the Higher Education of Women, founded in 1867 to unite the local educational associations in Manchester, Liverpool, Leeds, Sheffield and Newcastle.[18] The activities of Anne Jemima Clough and Josephine Butler in connection with the council, together with its role in pioneering the University Extension Movement and its influence on the foundation of Newnham College, have received a good deal of attention from historians. Twelve towns were represented on the council between 1867 and 1874.[19]

Negley Harte has illuminated the role played by the London Ladies' Educational Association in facilitating the process whereby University College came to admit women in 1878. The London Association, founded in 1868–9, was modelled to some extent on the North of England Council. With the key support of Henry Morley, Professor of English, and other sympathetic professors from University College, the London Ladies' Educational Association began to organize "lectures for ladies" originally outside college premises. Gradually these lectures were introduced into the college, although for propriety's sake the classes were kept strictly separate from the men's classes. Gradually a number of mixed classes were introduced: after 1878 these came to predominate and as the college came formally to accept women students the London Ladies' Educational Association disbanded.[20]

This pattern was echoed, with local variations, elsewhere in Britain. In Yorkshire the Yorkshire Ladies' Educational Association arranged for Cambridge Extension lectures, which effectively developed into the arts departments of the Yorkshire College, later the University of Leeds. Indeed, in 1882 the Yorkshire Ladies presented Edward Baines, as representative of the college, with a cheque for a thousand guineas, in recognition of the college's role in facilitating women's access to higher education in the area.[21]

Ladies' Educational Associations were also important in Scotland, particularly in Edinburgh and Glasgow. Sheila Hamilton has looked in detail at the work of the Edinburgh Ladies' Educational Association (ELEA), founded in 1869.[22] Like the London Association, this was a highly respectable body which worked closely with university professors who were sympathetic to the need for higher education for women, and in particular with David Masson, Professor of English Literature and Rhetoric. Lecture series organized by the association were well attended and of a wholly reputable standard: they were all given by professors wearing gowns. This made it comparatively easy for the university authorities to agree, in 1872, to offer a special certificate for women who had qualified to a certain standard in literature, philosophy and science.[23] In 1874 the first three ladies, Flora Masson, Margaret Mitchell and Charlotte Carmichael, later to be the mother of Marie Stopes, received their certificates.[24]

The institution of a special certificate for women fell short of the aspirations of many feminists, and it is hardly surprising to learn that Emily Davies wrote to the Edinburgh Ladies' Education Association in 1872 expressing her alarm over the injurious effects of setting up a separate standard for women.[25] However, as Sheila Hamilton has argued, the comparatively cautious, accommodating strategies of the ELEA helped to soothe some of the tension and controversy generated in Edinburgh by the campaigns of the women bent on studying medicine. As Professor Masson observed, the ELEA effectively developed into a kind of female Faculty of Arts, the students of which were taught by university professors, but not yet entitled to sit examinations for degrees.[26] In 1879, the ELEA renamed itself the Edinburgh Association for the Higher Education of Women, the role of professors on its Council and executive committee was strengthened, and the new association began to issue an annual calendar similar in format to the university's own.[27] The association continued to petition for full access to degrees.

In Glasgow, similarly, there was co-operation between the Glasgow Association for the Higher Education of Women and the university. John Caird, the Principal of Glasgow University, presided over the large public meeting at which the association was formally constituted in 1877.[28] Again, a pattern developed whereby sympathetic professors lectured and provided accommodation for classes organized by the women's association. In 1883 a gift from Mrs Isabella Elder, a wealthy local widow, allowed the Glasgow Association to open its own college close to the university. Queen Margaret College was incorporated in 1884. The college was not at the outset formally affiliated to the university, although the Senatus elected two members of its governing body, and there were teaching links.[29] The college developed on the periphery of the university, opening its own medical school in 1890, and the Glasgow Association continued to campaign for the admission of women to degrees. Following the ordinance of 1892, the college became formally a part of the university; in effect, the "women's department", although women students continued to be known as "Queen Margaret students".[30]

The Ladies' Educational Associations, then, played an important part in facilitating women's access to the universities. They had powerful patrons and supporters of both sexes. The president of the Glasgow Association was Princess Louise, Marchioness of Lorne, and the executive committee of the Edinburgh Association in 1878 was headed by the Duchess of Argyll. Some of the office holders and many of the subscribers to these associations were the wives and daughters of wealthy local citizens, or widows and unmarried daughters with considerable wealth at their disposal, who were in a position to make significant educational endowments. This is an important theme that will be returned to later in the chapter. Supporters and subscribers also included a large number of professors' wives and daughters. (We have seen that Flora Masson was one of the first to receive a certificate in Edinburgh in 1874.) The support of university professors and teachers sympathetic to the cause of women's education was crucial in fostering academic links, and in ensuring that the educational work of the associations was of an appropriate standard. This meant that when the universities opened their degree examinations to women, there were women whose previous attendance at classes enabled them to qualify almost immediately, without much further study. In Edinburgh, for instance, the "first eight ladies" who graduated in arts in 1893 had all been students of the Edinburgh Association for the Higher Education of Women,[31] and in Glasgow, the medical classes at Queen Margaret College had been carefully arranged so that in 1892 attendance at these classes qualified students to proceed immediately to university examinations. Marion Gilchrist, a student at Queen Margaret College, became the first woman to obtain a Scottish medical degree in 1894.[32]

Women students: numbers and social composition

Compared with the number of women who had attended lectures organized by the local Educational Associations in university towns, the number of women graduates was at first small. In Glasgow, three more Queen Margaret College students received their medical degrees in 1894, and arts degrees were awarded to two women in the following year.[33] In Aberdeen, the first four women graduates were capped in 1898.[34] In England, four women students obtained their BA degrees from the University of London in 1880;[35] degrees were conferred on four women students in Manchester in 1887.[36] The sight of these early women students graduating was still unusual enough to provoke public interest and merriment at the turn of the century. When Birmingham University mounted its first degree day procession in July 1901, and the first female student was presented to Joseph Chamberlain, it is recorded that the male undergraduates shouted out "Go on, Sir, kiss her", although Chamberlain did not oblige.[37]

From around 1900, however, the number of women students rose steadily, especially in arts departments, all over Britain. In London in 1927, over 500 women students graduated.[38] Figures from the University Grants Committee (UGC) show that women represented 16 per cent of the student population of Great Britain in 1900: this proportion rose to 24 per cent in 1920 and 27 per cent in 1930, falling again to 23 per cent on the eve of the Second World War.[39] The proportion of women was higher in the Scottish universities and in the University of Wales. By 1899 one quarter of the students in Aberdeen's Faculty of Arts were women, and by 1913 nearly half.[40] In St Andrews, women students represented 40 per cent of the total student population as early as 1907–8. The proportions were 31 per cent in Aberdeen, 24 per cent in Glasgow, and 18 per cent in Edinburgh for the same year.[41] By 1937–8 the UGC figures show a total of 11,299 full-time women students enrolled in British universities (including Oxford and Cambridge but excluding Ireland). There were 37,890 men, so women represented nearly one quarter of the total.[42]

Writing about what he saw as the revolutionary changes that higher education had effected in the status and aspirations of women, Charles Grant Robertson observed that by 1939 women graduates were "as plentiful as tabby-cats, in point of fact, too many".[43] There were indeed a number of educationalists and social observers who argued that the network of provision for women students had been spread widely enough by that date. This was not least because the increase in career opportunities for educated women had not kept pace with their supply. Teaching remained the major occupational outlet for women graduates.[44] Margaret Tuke, Principal of

Bedford College, complained that the universities "were apt to be regarded, as far as women were concerned, as institutions for the training of teachers", noting that the figures at her disposal indicated that between half and three quarters of all women graduates were destined to enter the profession.[45] As early as 1914, Edith Morley lamented the fact that too many girls committed themselves to teaching because it appeared to be the only route to obtaining a grant for higher education, and there were few other professions to which they might aspire.[46] R. D. Anderson has argued that women's access to higher education was intimately related to the fluctuating market for teachers.[47] The decrease in the proportion of women students over Britain as a whole in the 1930s, although accounted for to a considerable extent by a decrease in their numbers in Scotland, can be related to the Depression and a falling off in the demand for schoolteachers during that decade.[48]

Those who petitioned for women's access to the universities in the 1870s almost invariably emphasized the need for improving the education of women teachers. We have already noted the close connections between the Schoolmistresses' Associations of the 1860s and 1870s, and the Societies for the Higher Education of Women. The Edinburgh Ladies' Educational Association, in pressing the Universities Commission in Scotland to consider women's entitlement to degrees in the 1870s, pointed to the fact that both Edinburgh and St Andrews universities had instituted Chairs in Education, and argued that since the majority of teachers were women, they could be seen as having an obligation to attend to their needs.[49] Similar arguments were made elsewhere. In 1885 the Edinburgh Association established its own college, St George's, for the training of women teachers in connection with the Teachers' Training Syndicate of the University of Cambridge.[50] The Cambridge Syndicate had been set up in 1879: it made provision for lectures in the theory, history and practice of education, conducted examinations that could be prepared for in Cambridge or elsewhere, and issued certificates to candidates who were successful in these examinations.[51] The Cambridge Day Training College for Women, with Miss E. P. Hughes as Principal, was founded a few years later in 1885. The Cambridge certificate was keenly supported by Miss Clough, and by Frances Buss of the North London Collegiate School, and it became widely respected among headmistresses across the country. In 1883 the University of London established a postgraduate diploma in education, and the Victoria University followed with a similar qualification in 1895.[52] By 1900 there were secondary training departments in 21 universities and university colleges in Britain.[53] As has often been observed, training for teaching at the secondary level was more popular among, and taken much more seriously by, women than men at this time.[54]

The universities' involvement in teacher education generally grew rapidly after the 1890s, and followed the foundation of the "day training colleges", which were the ancestors of the modern university departments of education.[55]

In 1890 the government drew up regulations for the administration of grant aid to day training colleges in connection with the universities and university colleges. Students were to receive their general education in the ordinary classes of the university, while their professional training was to be the responsibility of the day training college. Academic and professional work could be fitted into a two year course of training, although students might also remain for three years if they wished, and were able to take a degree. A number of universities responded immediately to the invitation to establish day training departments, seeing this as an opportunity to expand student numbers. Day training colleges were established in 1890 in Manchester, Newcastle, Nottingham, Birmingham, Cardiff and King's College London. Similar institutions were set up in Sheffield, Cambridge, Liverpool and Leeds in the following year. Oxford, Bristol and Aberystwyth followed in 1892, Bangor in 1894 and Reading and Southampton in 1899. Exeter's day training college was established in 1901; University College London instituted a day training college in 1892, but this was shortly afterwards disbanded.[56] Experience eventually showed the combination of academic and professional study in a concurrent course to be an arduous undertaking, particularly for the weaker students, and after 1911 a three year academic course, followed by one year of training, became the preferred pattern.[57]

After 1910 the Board of Education's scheme for training secondary teachers allowed students who pledged their intention to teach to be eligible for grant support over four years, which covered tuition fees for three years of degree work and a last year in the education department.[58] The grant also included a maintenance allowance. The intake of students bent on a career in either elementary or secondary schoolteaching was of crucial importance to the new universities. W. H. G. Armytage argued in 1955 that

> it is not too much to say that the civic universities in their struggling years, and the university colleges all along, owed the very existence of their arts faculties and in many cases their pure science faculties to the presence of a larger body of intending teachers whose attendance at degree courses was almost guaranteed by the State.[59]

In the University of Wales around the turn of the century, we find that in Bangor in 1897, 98 out of a total of 258 students were in the day training college; in Cardiff and Aberystwyth teachers in training constituted about a quarter of the student body.[60] P. H. Gosden notes that in the University of Leeds the number of students holding teacher training grants represented about a quarter of the entire student body through the inter-war years.[61]

Large numbers of these intending teachers were women. Gosden notes that it was as "King's Scholars", as grant-aided trainee teachers were called, that women students first became a visible presence in the University of Leeds.[62] The day training colleges in Bristol and in Nottingham were originally set up for women only. J. B. Thomas has calculated that in Bristol in 1895–6, 42 per cent of all students in the Faculties of Arts and Science were day training college girls, and they even represented 35 per cent of those reading mathematics.[63] Mabel Tylecote observed that the advent of the day training college in Manchester in 1892 greatly strengthened the "women's department" in the university, effectively doubling the number of women degree students between 1891–2 and 1892–3.[64] From 1899–1914 one third, or in some years approaching a half, of all Manchester's women students were members of the day training college, and as a result women were beginning to outnumber men in the Faculty of Arts as early as 1904–5.[65]

The term "day training college" is somewhat misleading because, as J. B. Thomas has pointed out, from very early in their history these departments or colleges attracted students from beyond their immediate localities and the question of residence had to be considered.[66] This was seen to be a particularly important matter where women students were concerned. University authorities were not easy about allowing their female charges to live in unsupervised lodgings: parents might not approve. More importantly, the Board of Education did not approve, and allocated grants for maintenance, education and training only to students living in recognized colleges and hostels. The Board of Education regulations were crucial in spurring the provision of supervised hostels and halls of residence for women, the development of which will be discussed in a later chapter. These early halls and hostels involved careful chaperonage, limiting the extent to which female student teachers interacted with the rest of the student body. The potential for such interaction was further limited by the tendency of other students and some academic departments to look down on the teacher-training contingent, who were often from somewhat more humble social origins. In Durham Miss Roberts, who was appointed as first Principal of the University Women's Hostel in Claypath in 1899, remembered that "the Training College Girls had a few acquaintances among the townsfolk, but none of the students under my care ever had undergraduate friends".[67] This informal social apartheid seems to have continued for some time. Even though Durham was such a small city and considerable numbers of the students at the training colleges sat for university degrees and certificates, by the 1920s, C. W. Gibby, who was appointed to a lectureship in chemistry at the university in 1926, recalled a pattern of segregation:

> Social life in Durham was very pleasant, and I received great kindness from people, many of whom were more than a generation older than myself. People connected with the Castle, Hatfield, St Mary's and the Cathedral mixed with one another, but in an orbit which hardly touched St Chad's and St John's, and entirely ignored the training colleges. . . . I don't think there was any animosity; it

was probably a kind of snobbery, a feeling that the members of the new colleges were "not quite, don't you know".[68]

The women university students at St Hild's College in the 1920s formed their own society separate from the central Women's Union Society in Durham.[69] Similarly in Bristol, Marian Pease, who was appointed Mistress of Method to the new day training college in 1892, remembered that she had been "anxious not to swamp" the small body of about 20–30 women students who were preparing for London degrees in Bristol at that time with her group of 60 teacher trainees.[70] It was no doubt partly her social tact that disinclined her to encourage social intercourse between these two groups of students. In Bristol women trainee teachers lived in separate, and often substandard hostels, a situation that the Board of Education viewed with "grave concern" and found objectionable by 1918.[71]

In other universities, such as Birmingham or Manchester, there appears to have been much less segregation between intending teachers and the rest of the student body, and in some women's hostels the perceived advantages (both social and educational) of mixing the two groups were emphasized from the outset. In any case, the institution of the four-year, consecutive pattern of training after 1911 served to reduce the differences and to facilitate the integration of teacher trainees with the rest of the student body. Phoebe Sheavyn commented in 1924:

> In some Universities, and particularly in those which still offer a two-year training course for teachers in Elementary Schools, the "training students" form a class somewhat apart from the other, regarded as to some extent socially, and perhaps also intellectually, inferior. In others no distinction whatever exists, except that the "training" student has to satisfy the fairly stringent regulations of the Board of Education, in regard to making satisfactory progress year by year.[72]

In 1928 Margaret Tuke asserted that a university education was by then an option for "the average woman", or even a necessity, "sometimes an unwelcome necessity", for those who needed to earn their own living and could not rely on their parents for support. In her opinion standards had declined somewhat from the "pioneer" years at the end of the nineteenth century. "The number of women students in the universities in England has increased during the last fifty years from seventy-one to more than 9,000", she wrote, "and if the keenness for learning today cannot be compared with that of the seventy students of 1877, we cannot be surprised".[73] It is clear from her article that Tuke was more sympathetic towards women who sought knowledge as "an end in itself" and were in pursuit of "a tradition of taste and culture which cannot be gained in one generation", than she was towards those who looked upon their university education as "mere training for a career".[74]

In the last quarter of the nineteenth century attendance at university lectures had indeed been characterized by the presence of large numbers of ladies of leisure, many of them married, who were in pursuit of general culture: some of them seeking perhaps to make good the deficiencies of their earlier education, others looking for entertainment or some kind of social purpose. Many women enrolled for classes without any intention of sitting examinations or working towards degrees. Focusing on evidence mainly from the Oxford women's colleges, Janet Howarth and Mark Curthoys have suggested that there was a "dual market" for women's higher education in the late nineteenth and early twentieth centuries.[75] Women students in Oxford came overwhelmingly from the professional, commercial and industrial middle class, but within this category there were wide variations in status and income. The majority of women went on to engage in paid work at some time in their lives, but a significant minority – around one in eight – did not. The majority of the early cohorts of women students at Oxford – around 70 per cent – did not marry, although this pattern changed after the war, and particularly by the 1930s marriage became more common. Howarth and Curthoys argue that although most women who went up to Oxford in the early days probably envisaged teaching as a career, a sizeable number had no specific vocational objectives, nor did they have any real need to contemplate such objectives. This was because either they were possessed of sufficient independent means, or their chances of making "good" marriages were high.

Did this "dual market" persist elsewhere? Most university towns had their affluent suburbs, and the daughters of the civic bourgeoisie from Clifton in Bristol, from Edgbaston in Birmingham, from Alderley Edge in Manchester and from the elegant squares and terraces of Edinburgh's New Town, may have continued to attend their local universities in pursuit of general culture rather than through vocational aspiration. Tylecote estimates that about half of the students in the Women's Department in Manchester between 1886 and 1891 were "ladies" who attended a single course, in English literature perhaps, or in German. Others worked at several subjects, but only a small proportion aimed at a degree:

> The "ladies" were not registered students, but possessed cards admitting them to certain lectures. The registered students were termed "women".[76]

However, the number of students attending classes without any intention of sitting for degrees undoubtedly declined fairly sharply before 1914. In Glasgow the proportion of women graduating represented 24 per cent of the total of women entrants in 1895–6: by 1910–11 this proportion had risen to 71.8 per cent.[77] Sheila Hamilton has pointed out that the numbers of what were often referred to, rather deprecatingly, as "debutante attenders" fell off steeply before 1911, and this pattern seems to have been common in most institutions. Phoebe Sheavyn observed in the 1920s that "English girls of aristocratic or wealthy parentage do not as yet go to the University in large numbers; most of the students come from homes of limited means".[78] It seems likely that the great majority of the women who attended universities, particularly outside Oxbridge, by around 1914, did so in the hope that it would improve their opportunities of earning a living, either before marriage, or in the event of their not marrying at all.

Of course, many women may have hoped that the wider social networks of university life would extend their choice of marriage partner. From the 1890s onwards, satirical features in *Punch* magazine regularly mocked the courtship aspirations of women students. A cartoon in the *Morning Leader* in July 1905 was headed "Don't crush", and depicted a queue of women purchasing railway tickets to Bangor in response to announcements "that at least six professors at Bangor University" had "married lady students" in that year.[79] Winifred Peck, a student at Lady Margaret Hall in Oxford just before the First World War, recorded that no girl who became engaged while in the college was allowed to stay, since a student who needed a degree for her livelihood was felt to be more deserving of the room.[80] There are endless examples of women tutors' hostility to the idea of girls' getting engaged while at university: Marjorie Schofield (née Woodward), a student at St Mary's, Durham from 1921 to 1924, recalled that Miss Donaldson, the Principal, disapproved strongly when she became engaged to a fellow student at the Castle, insisting that she must have "broken the rules" in order to do so.[81] But chaperon regulations and restrictions on social intercourse between the sexes had relaxed considerably by the 1930s. Barbara Lees (née Brockman) who studied at Reading University in that decade records that

> Reading in my time was known as the matrimonial university because so many students found their marriage partners there – in fact there was a joke in those days about naming a new Hall Wedmore (one of King Alfred's famous battles), and I remember well an Economic History lecture given by Dr Peyton when a student asked "What *is* husbandry?" When the lecturer had recovered from his astonishment he replied "What most young ladies come up to this university for". I met my husband at Reading – as my daughter also met hers.[82]

Judith Hubback, whose study *Wives who went to college* was published in 1957, noted a popular belief that university was "the best possible marriage market for an intelligent girl", because there she would "meet such a high concentration of her mental equals".[83] Hubback's study was based on completed questionnaires from over one thousand women who had graduated in English universities between 1930 and 1952: 36 per cent of these women reported having met their husbands while at university.

The evidence we have on the social class origins of students in Britain's universities after 1914 is often fragmentary and much depends, of course, on categorization. Most authorities agree, however, that women students came from the same social background as the majority of male students: broadly speaking from the middle and lower-middle classes. There were regional variations however, and in universities where costs were lower there was a larger representation of what might be regarded as working-class students. Lindy Moore has argued that this was, for instance, the case in Aberdeen.[84] Glasgow, Birmingham, the Welsh university colleges, Nottingham, Liverpool and Leeds may also have had larger proportions of working class students than elsewhere.[85] However, as R. D. Anderson has cautioned from his study of Scottish university students in the early twentieth century, "the non-middle-class element in universities was not primarily working class, but a stratum that brought together children of skilled workers, shopkeepers and small farmers".[86] There were, in any case, fewer women from the working class than there were men, because here "both the scholarship machinery and the psychology of motivation traditionally favoured boys".[87]

Women medical students came from significantly more affluent social backgrounds than did university women as a whole, not least because medicine involved a longer and more expensive course of study. Wendy Alexander has looked closely at the backgrounds of early women medical students in Glasgow and she calculated that the number of these students who came from professional backgrounds was approximately double the university average for all women students, while those from intermediate or working-class backgrounds were about half.[88] She cites an article from "the ladies' newspaper" *The Queen* in 1894, which estimated the total cost of a medical education for a woman living away from home at around £600. The cost of studying medicine in Glasgow was relatively cheap by contemporary standards but, even so, Alexander estimates that it cannot have been less than around £400 (including class and examination fees, lodging, equipment and textbooks) by around the turn of the century.[89] She suggests that if we follow F. Musgrove's analysis of middle-class incomes at this time, professional men, well-to-do clergy, superior tradesmen, lesser gentry and industrial managers might have expected (as the middle-middle class) to earn £200–£1,000 p.a.; whereas upper-middle class men would have commanded above £1,000 p.a.[90] The fathers of Alexander's sample group of women were divided fairly evenly between upper-middle and middle class groups, but with some from the lower-middle class. Clearly the strain of supporting a daughter's medical education at around £100 p.a. would have been difficult or nigh impossible for these groups without some form of external support.

Elizabeth Bryson's autobiography, *Look back in wonder* (1966), is the story of an exceptional woman and can hardly be considered representative, but it nevertheless illustrates some of the strategies adopted by someone from a background of material deprivation but firm educational purpose.[91] Dr Bryson (née Macdonald) was born in Dundee in 1880, the fourth child of a family of nine, of whom seven managed to acquire a full university education. From an early age, inspired by stories of Sophia Jex-Blake in Edinburgh, Elizabeth dreamed of studying medicine. With the support of a determined mother (who pieced together an income by giving music lessons) and the help of bursaries, Elizabeth enrolled as a student at St Andrews University in 1896. She learned that the authorities would not permit her to begin studying medicine until she was 19 years old (she was only 16 in 1896), and so she read for an arts degree first, graduating MA with first-class honours in English a few months before her nineteenth birthday. She had been spurred in her motivation to do well in these examinations by the hope that she might win a scholarship of £100 p.a. for two years, and indeed,

> When the results were posted up there was only one name in the list for First Class Honours and, believe it or not, that name was mine. My first thought – I had won the Scholarship! Joy unbelievable![92]

The following day however Elizabeth was summoned to a meeting of the university Senate, and congratulated on her success in the examination, but the Principal

> went on in a somewhat subdued tone – to say how sorry they all were that they could not award me the Scholarship that I had undoubtedly earned. Why? Because I was a woman! It would require an Act of Parliament to alter the terms before the award could be made to a woman. I was completely silent, dumb with disappointment.[93]

The coveted scholarship went to a man with second-class honours in the examination: Elizabeth was given a bursary of £30 p.a. Undeterred, she went on to five years more study at the Bute Medical School in St Andrews and the new University College in Dundee. She continued to live at home and to support herself with the bursary and by working as assistant dispenser in a local chemist's shop for £1 a week during vacations. Matters for her family were greatly eased by the Carnegie bequest in 1901–2, which guaranteed the fees for students of Scottish birth or extraction in the universities of Scotland. Elizabeth Macdonald completed her medical training in 1905, her distinction in the degree examinations helped to secure her one of the first Carnegie research scholarships, and she proceeded to advanced work in gynaecology. Her work was considered quite outstanding, but as a woman she was barred from hospital appointments in the area, so in 1908 she emigrated to New Zealand.

Scholarships, grants and costs

In 1914 Edith Morley collected details of the costs of tuition and residence for women students in British universities, which showed that tuition fees for an arts degree ranged from around 10 guineas p.a. (Aberdeen, St Andrews) to around £20 p.a.[94] Fees for courses in science were slightly higher. The cost of residence in university halls or hostels for women students at this time ranged rather widely from £32 to £60 p.a. The fees for students in the Oxford and Cambridge women's colleges were then around £105 p.a. (including tuition, examination fees and residence). By the 1920s Phoebe Sheavyn estimated the cost for Oxbridge women students at £135–£150 p.a., again including tuition, board and lodging, but not including the cost of books or personal expenditure. Next in order of expense came London, where the fees for residence in college were higher than elsewhere, at around £90–£100 p.a. In the larger towns and cities in England, Sheavyn estimated the cost of university residence for women at around £70 p.a., whereas in the smaller civic institutions and in Wales and Scotland it was between £40 and £50 p.a. Tuition fees, according to Sheavyn's estimates, ranged from around £15 to £45 p.a. in arts subjects, with the cost of science subjects again rather higher.[95]

The question of women's eligibility for university scholarships and bursaries arose almost as soon as they enrolled as students in the civic universities. Most accounts of the stormy years when women fought to enter medicine in Edinburgh give prominence to the affair of the Hope Scholarship in 1870.[96] Edith Pechey's outstanding performance in the chemistry class in Edinburgh in that year theoretically entitled her to this scholarship, which gave the holder free admission to laboratories for research purposes. Pechey's moral claim to the scholarship was strengthened by the fact that its endowment fund derived from the profits that Charles Hope, Professor of Chemistry 50 years earlier, had made from a series of lectures be had delivered to the ladies of the community. Pechey was given a bronze medal, but the scholarship on this occasion was awarded to the male student who had come second in the examination on the grounds that the women students, who had been taught separately, could not be considered to have been full members of the class. The decision was not a popular one, and the whole affair helped to exacerbate sexual politics in Edinburgh.[97]

In Manchester the question of women's eligibility for Owens College Scholarships arose in the 1880s, provoking much discussion about what the wishes of the founders of these scholarships would have been, could they have foreseen the admission of women. A test case arose when a woman applied for the Victoria Scholarship in classics, but evidently she was not allowed to compete for it as the legal position was doubtful.[98] However, Mr Thomas Ashton responded by endowing a special Victoria Scholarship for Women, and after 1885 some of the older scholarships and prizes were in fact opened to women. The institution of scholarships for women in Manchester owed much to local benevolence, particularly to the strong network of supporters for the Women's Department, who had close links with Manchester High School for Girls. Several annual scholarships of £20 p.a. were offered by this group between 1883 and 1892.[99] In Durham, similarly, the 1890s brought considerable debate over women's eligibility for entrance scholarships. It was generally agreed that "it would not be convenient that the scholarships now open to men should be taken away from them or thrown open equally to women students", and this resulted in the foundation of a new scholarship for women, available from 1897.[100] In many towns the local Ladies' Educational Associations and their supporters were active in setting up special scholarships for women. In Edinburgh Miss Houldsworth and Sarah Mair of the ELEA both provided funds for bursaries in each of their names in the 1870s and 1880s.[101] In Bristol the Catherine Winkworth Scholarship Fund was set up in 1879 to provide scholarships for women as a memorial to Catherine Winkworth; the subscriptions included a significant donation by the committee of the Clifton Association for the Higher Education of Woman.[102] Several of the scholarships established by the local educational associations were attached to the women's halls of residence that were built in the last years of the nineteenth century.

Many of the new scholarship schemes in universities were open to men and women equally. In St Andrews, the Taylour Thomson Bequest of £30,000 in 1883 stipulated the donor's desire that bursaries should be made available to students of both sexes, in equal numbers, and in the case of women, used to assist them in qualifying for the medical profession.[103] (It was a Taylour Thomson bursary that enabled Elizabeth Macdonald to begin her studies in St Andrews in the 1890s.) Scholarships in the newer universities were less likely to be exclusively for men. Marjory Fry noted in 1909 that all Birmingham's scholarships were open to women.[104] However, informally awards to women might still provoke comment: Birmingham's Professor of German, H. G. Fiedler, wrote to Charles Harding, who had founded a scholarship in modern languages (and incidentally was Fiedler's father-in-law), informing him that in 1903 the scholarship had gone to a woman student from the local high school, and commenting that "she seems decidedly a bright girl ... though I would rather have commenced work with a man".[105]

Another noteworthy source of funding for women students in the late nineteenth and early twentieth centuries was the Gilchrist Educational Trust founded in 1865, and originating from the bequest of the eccentric but liberally inclined Dr John Borthwick Gilchrist (who had died in 1841).[106] A considerable proportion of the income from this bequest of £70,000 went into scholarships and fellowships for women in Oxford, Cambridge,

London and at several of the newer universities. Recipients of Gilchrist awards included Sara Burstall (later headmistress of Manchester High School), Clara Collet, Alice Zimmern, Enid Starkie, Helen Wodehouse and E. M. Butler (both of these last two women were destined to become professors) and a number of women who rose to prominence in the educational world.[107] The trustees of this bequest included men of liberal views in education and also, before 1939, three women: Dr Sophie Bryant (headmistress of the North London Collegiate School), Margaret Tuke of Bedford College, and Lynda Grier of Lady Margaret Hall. They prided themselves, with some justification, on being one of the first public bodies to make significant provision for women in higher education.[108]

Apart from Board of Education grants to teachers in training, and the scholarships and bursaries attached to particular universities, the main source of support available to women students before the First World War came from local authority grants. Local authority scholarships were the biggest single source of support to university students generally: in the two years 1911 and 1912 their total cost amounted to £56,893, the average value of an award being around £43–4 p.a.[109] However, the system of awards was extremely patchy: local education authorities (LEAs) differed widely in their practices, some (around one third in 1911–12) making no awards to university scholars at all. Girls were almost everywhere at a disadvantage.[110] In 1911–12, of the 464 university scholarships made by LEAs in England, 373 went to boys and only 91 to girls.[111] In 1916 the Board of Education's Consultative Committee Report on scholarships for higher education pointed out that since there were fewer endowed schools for girls, the proportion of girls who received their full secondary education in grant-aided schools was conspicuously greater than that of boys, "yet the provision of scholarships to take such girls to the universities is even more conspicuously less".[112] Few authorities reserved special awards for women, and some of them gave their few successful girl scholars around £20 less p.a. than the boys.[113]

The 1916 committee strongly recommended that more scholarships should be made available to girls. According to G. S. M. Ellis, whose report on the scholarship system, *The poor student and the university*, was published in 1925, by 1914 "the supply of public scholarships for women was lagging behind the demand for higher education in a most alarming manner".[114] By 1922–3, Lord Haldane noted that local authority expenditure on grants had increased to £220,000,[115] but many believed the amount continued to be inadequate, and girls were still failing to secure anything like their equal share of awards. There were energetic appeals to private benefaction in the localities. In Manchester, for instance, a public meeting in the town hall was held in 1918 "with the object of raising a fund to provide a more adequate supply of University Scholarships for Women", and through the efforts of Mrs Hope Hogg, Warden of Ashburne Hall of Residence for Women, C. P. Scott and other sympathizers, nearly £7,000 was raised within a few months.

By 1936, when administration of this fund passed to the university, about 57 entrance scholarships had been made available by the Manchester committee.[116]

In 1920 state scholarships (originally 200 in number) were introduced by the Board of Education, partly as a result of the recommendations of the Consultative Committee report of 1916. These covered fees and offered up to £80 maintenance p.a. in case of need. They were suspended as a result of economy measures in 1922 but reintroduced in 1924.[117] It is interesting that the Board of Education was immediately embroiled in a controversy about the proportion of scholarships that should go to girls. Originally they were divided equally, with half going to boys and half to girls. However, many more boys reached the required standard in School Certificate examination than did girls, and there was pressure from headmasters to allocate more scholarships to boys. When the number of state scholarships was increased from 200 to 300 in 1930, it was decided to allocate 188 scholarships to boys, leaving 112 for girls. There were bitter complaints from headmistresses and from teachers in girls' high schools who pointed out that boys had many more sources of funding available to them than girls. Board of Education officials were uncertain as to how to handle the situation. They observed that:

> The Regulations as they stand would not prevent us from making a larger allocation to girls at the expense of boys, if the argument is considered a determining one. Apart, however, from the question of policy which the argument involves, it is probable that anything short of a substantial addition to the number allocated to girls would not satisfy the Headmistresses, and that anything which satisfied them would raise a protest from the Headmasters.[118]

Officials also argued that as future teachers, girls had other sources of funding open to them, and observed that, in any case, were the girls to be judged in open competition with the boys (a notion that the 1916 Consultative Committee had clearly argued *against*, on the grounds that adolescent girls were subject to particular strains during their school years[119]), girls would gain many fewer awards than boys. The matter remained contentious throughout the 1930s.

The amount of controversy generated by this debate indicates just how coveted state scholarships were. In 1928 Margaret Tuke estimated that "a considerable proportion of women students (certainly not less than 50 per cent of the whole number) hold scholarships drawn from public funds".[120] Nevertheless, any ladder of opportunity from elementary school to university was harder to find, and offered fewer footholds, for girls than for boys. In Birmingham, societies offering loans to women students were said to be swamped by applications, and the archives of women's halls of residence everywhere contain evidence of wardens making heroic efforts to piece together small loans and bursaries for students who found themselves in acute financial difficulty.[121] The annual report of the Central Employment Bureau for Women in 1924 drew attention to the extraordinary number of requests for loans towards the cost of university fees and training received from individuals in that year, noting that:

> Many parents belonging to the professional and middle classes are passing through a time of exceptional hardship and strain. Out of their small incomes it is impossible for them to meet the expense of training their daughters and yet it is essential that these girls should be prepared for work in which they may be self-supporting.[122]

The loan fund that had been established by the bureau in 1910 was considered quite inadequate, and attempts were made to seek co-operation and support from benevolent and trust funds elsewhere. Between 1910 and 1925 loans were found for 225 needy female students in universities and teacher training. Cases of individual difficulty rose steeply in the 1930s, when the evidence suggests that expense increasingly debarred many women from embarking upon a university education in the first place.

Making space for women

What sort of accommodation did the universities make for their first women students? Provision was usually rather meagre, and given the social mores of the late nineteenth century, women were carefully secluded from the men. There are many stories of broom cupboards, of poky rooms in dingy basements and of side doors and separate entrances at this time.

Negley Harte, celebrating University College London's early admission of women students, nonetheless observes that women were treated as "second-class citizens in all manner of ways".[123] Mary Adamson, studying science at UCL in the 1880s, recalled a distinctly "chilly" rather than a "cheery segregation" between men and women students.[124] Adamson was enrolled as a student at Bedford College but sought access to teaching at UCL when she found that Bedford was unable to provide advanced teaching in science. She was allowed to join the physics and botany classes at UCL, but allegedly was told that admission to the chemistry class was unthinkable, as the women students would be "scarred for life and have their clothes burnt off them as the men threw chemicals around". Adamson was not allowed to enter the physics lecture theatre through the main door. She remembers being obliged to use a little door at the back. She had to sit high up and well back from the men. In the botany class, she was also made to arrive well beforehand and to sit quite separately from the men. The only other room that the women might frequent in college was a vast, semi-dark cloak room stretching under the portico and entered from the open air. It had hat pegs all round and some big, bare tables and a nondescript female was seated permanently by the fireplace. Quite a number of women students frequented it, largely Slade students who were all very lively and friendly with one another and the fireside woman. I think this must have been the only room available to women and that they had not then access to the dining room, for they had to take snacks of food in it, and occasionally a seedy waiter would hasten in with a covered plate of food, dab it on a table, and beat a hasty retreat.[125]

Similar conditions prevailed elsewhere. The Women's Department in Brunswick Street, Manchester, was in "a depressingly small and dark" house, "gloomy and dingy, full of draughts and smoking chimneys". This afforded few social opportunities, although there was a reading room, "redeemed from utter dreariness only by photographs of Michael Angelo's Sistine prophetesses placed there by Miss Wilson" (the first Tutor to Women Students).[126] Tylecote records that women's admission to classes in Owens College was marked by the acquisition of an umbrella stand:

So it came about that the first property the women held in Owens was the famous umbrella stand acquired in 1886. Next year came the cession of "a little room under the roof, approached by a small staircase behind an iron gate" with loopholes in the staircase walls. Mummies occupied the neighbouring museum, and stuffed lions, tigers and gorillas lurked in the corridor outside. The room was "transformed into a common room and each student" (writes one of them) "did her part in contributing something towards its furniture and decoration".

The women were again required to use separate entrances, and a maid-of-all-work was obliged to fetch any books they might need from the library. Another small common room was provided in 1888, but when the students asked if they might make tea in it the Principal forbade this on account of the risk of fire. "The fact that the teacups were washed in the fire buckets no doubt emphasized the apparent irresponsibility".[127] Women medical students did not fare much better. They were originally allocated one small room

which had to serve them as a dissecting room and cloak room, and the exigencies of the timetable frequently compelled them to take their lunch there.[128]

One of the conditions of admitting women to medical classes had stipulated a separate women's dissecting room. According to Catherine Chisholme, one of the first women medical students, Miss Wilson was "much relieved that it was not necessary to smoke in the dissecting room".[129]

Conditions had improved slightly in Manchester, but by no means everywhere, by the time of the First World War. In Edinburgh, the women students in the Old Buildings occupied a "dungeon" in the basement with no natural light and "with toilet facilities of a very spartan, dingy kind".[130] In Aberdeen, at Marischal, the women students again rejoiced in the occupancy of a windowless room popularly known as "the dungeon", or "coffin".[131] At King's a room comfortable for 10 or 12 students was being used by 60 or 70 women by 1897. Alternative accommodation was provided in 1899 and again in 1904, but the situation remained unsatisfactory and during the war the women complained bitterly about the stultifying effect of inadequate, cramped facilities on social life: "the hideous crimson divan (of the broken springs) and the appalling array of hard, straight-backed chairs. . . . No power on earth could make the Ladies' Room an attractive or an inviting place".[132] Edna Rideout, who enrolled as a student in Liverpool University in 1912, remembered the tiny common room used by women students in the Victoria Building during her first term: the women's coats and hats being piled up on the balcony where they caused considerable obstruction, frequently falling down into the Victoria Hall, then "the inviolate stamping-ground of men students", below.[133] The novelist Storm Jameson, a student at Leeds University from 1909 to 1912, recalled the "sordidly shabby" common room used by the women students. As Secretary of the Women's Representative Council she decided to try to improve things through the acquisition of a new carpet, incurring the wrath of the Professor of Classics who was Treasurer of the Students' Union, and who inveighed that "in his very long experience no undergraduate, male or female, had ever behaved in so unprincipled a way".[134]

Benefactions and the shape of provision

The quality of accommodation offered to women students in these years depended a great deal on local benefaction. In Manchester the cost of running the Women's Department was estimated at £1,150 p.a. in the 1880s. The committee responsible for the department had agreed to make a grant of £500 p.a. to Owens College during the five year trial period of women's admission to the university, but income from fees was not sufficient to cover these expenses. A bequest of £10,000 from the will of Mrs Abel Heywood, received in 1887, greatly eased the situation.[135] When it came to providing accommodation for the women's union, which was founded in Manchester in 1899, Mrs James Worthington of Sale stepped in with a grant of £5,000 "to provide a comfortable club house and refectory for the women students", the capital to be used towards the erection of a permanent building and the interest for the maintenance of a house that the Council had leased in Oxford Road. She and Mrs Tout worked indefatigably to furnish the house, Mrs Worthington

> completing her work by a gift of some Tanagra figures and a number of water-colour drawings from her own collection which were placed in the "exceedingly cheerful and pretty" drawing room.[136]

The local Ladies' Educational Associations played an important role in providing accommodation for women students. The Edinburgh Association for the Higher Education of Women moved from Shandwick Place to a flat in 8 Hope Park Square in 1893, and these comparatively spacious rooms accommodated the first women's union and societies, supplying the deficiencies of the drab premises offered by the university in the Old Quadrangle.[137] In Glasgow, the women students had their administrative and social headquarters in Queen Margaret College, originally donated by Mrs Elder and made over to the University Court by deed of gift after the admission of women in 1892. Mrs Carnegie, the wife of the Scottish benefactor, provided union facilities for the women at St Andrews and Dundee in 1904.[138] In Liverpool, Emma Holt, the unmarried daughter of a wealthy local ship-owner and merchant, provided a house as a first hall of residence for women students, and gave liberally towards the cost of the women's wing of a new student union building, erected in 1913.[139] Almost everywhere the furnishing and decoration of women's common rooms depended on the generosity of local benefactors and well-wishers, some male, but mainly female, or the efforts of the women students themselves. In Southampton University College, the women expressed their gratitude to their fellow men students for the donation of a collection of photographs of the men's cricket and football teams, which graced the previously bare walls of the women's common room.[140] The women in Bristol were perhaps luckier – their reading room was brightened by "a delightful collection of photographs of eminent women", "including the 'advanced women' of medieval times who were not afraid to run the gauntlet of public opinion, and study both science and classics", and "the Pioneers in the Education of Women"; the collection having been donated by Miss Helen Blackburn in 1894.[141]

In *A room of one's own*, Virginia Woolf lamented at length on women's inability to endow the education of their daughters, and the long history of painful and difficult fund-raising that had characterized the foundation of the early women's colleges.[142] Writing in 1890, J. G. Fitch observed that any and all of the provision for the higher education of women in Cambridge by that time was attributable to private benefaction: women students had "neither asked nor received material aid in any form" from the university's resources, "the admission of women has not yet cost the university a shilling".[143] Feminist writing on education at this time was frequently spiked by a bitterness derived from the conviction that women had been historically swindled out of resources: the nunneries had been plundered for endowment of men's colleges; endowments for the education of children had been appropriated by boys' schools; the founders of the ancient universities had included wealthy women.[144] But the newer universities and university colleges rested on a very different financial footing. The state contributed practically nothing to the cost of these foundations, which depended almost entirely on voluntary contributions. Fees contributed only a small proportion of their income, let alone their operating costs, hence the observation of one recent historian who has described the civic universities as being "built on charity".[145] The stories of the male benefactors from wealthy industrial and commercial families who played such a key role in financing the new institutions, the Frys, Wills, Palmers and so forth, has often been told, but the part played by women benefactors has been less singled out for comment.

Women's benefactions were not on the same scale of course, since as W. D. Rubinstein has commented, "women in Britain were not often very wealthy in their own right".[146] But whether individually, as wealthy widows and unmarried daughters, or collectively, as subscribers to Ladies' Educational Associations or new foundations, women's contributions were still important in the developing network of provision for higher education. We have already observed the Yorkshire Ladies' Association presenting Edward Baines and the Yorkshire College with a thousand guineas in recognition of the college's contribution to women's higher education in 1882. Collective efforts from women continued to be very important well into the present century. The historian of Leicester University records that the foundation of a university college in Leicester owed much to the women of the city and country whose bazaar, organized in aid of the college funds in May 1922, raised an impressive £15,000.[147]

Some of the highly significant ways in which the outlook and intentions of individual benefactors could serve to shape the character of provision are apparent in the early history of the single-sex colleges for women. Bedford College, founded by the wealthy widow and feminist Elizabeth Reid, was possessed of a constitution and trust fund, the conditions of which had been carefully drawn up to ensure female governance.[148] Royal Holloway College, founded and endowed by Thomas Holloway in 1883 in memory of his wife, was bound by the terms of the founder's will, which stipulated that future trustees and governors of the college should all be male. The exclusion of women (and staff) from the governing body was a highly unsatisfactory arrangement, deplored by the Haldane Commissioners in 1909, but could not be changed until 1912.[149]

The wills drawn up by early benefactors of universities elsewhere in Britain similarly influenced the extent of women's access and provision. The will of John Owens, the founder of the college in Manchester that bore his name, had stated specifically the donor's desire to provide the means "of instructing and improving young persons of the male sex" in university subjects. This necessitated legal change in 1871 to circumvent the restriction.[150] The principal benefactor of University College Dundee was Miss Mary Ann Baxter of Balgavies, who originally donated £120,000 for the foundation of the new college (she later added another £10,000). Her co-benefactor and distant relative, John Boyd Baxter, also contributed sums of £5,000 on two separate occasions. These two benefactors did not always see eye-to-eye, but as a historian of Dundee has remarked, since Miss Baxter was giving nearly all the money, "she would dictate terms".[151] Dundee College, established on her conditions, was governed by a deed drawn up in 1881 stipulating that the college should promote the education of both sexes. There was to be no religious test, nor was any religious subject to be taught. Women students enrolled in Dundee well before they gained full access to the associated University of St Andrews. Seventy-five of the first students to be enrolled in Dundee were women, stimulating the local poet, William McGonagall, into an unforgettable eulogy of Miss Baxter – "Give honour to whom honour is due/Because Ladies like her are very few" – and her efforts – "For the ladies of Dundee can now learn useful knowledge/By going to their own beautiful college".[152]

Sometimes the generosity of local benefactors keen to promote the cause of women's education ran well ahead of the enthusiasm of university authorities. This appears to have been the case in Durham. Since Durham was a collegiate university with regulations requiring residence, the question of providing a college or hall for women students was an important issue. In 1881 the Senate in Durham agreed that women might be admitted to all the courses and degrees in the university (except in theology), but stipulated that they must reside in a college or hall licensed by the Warden and Senate, and under the control of the university. There the matter appears to have stood for some time: with the university expecting the Durham Ladies' Educational Association and other supporters to build and endow a college, and these supporters waiting for the university to provide one.[153] In 1886 the Senate rejected an offer made by Canon Brereton to convert Hatfield Lodge into a women's college: this may have been because it was having second thoughts about whether the university's charter did indeed empower it to grant degrees to women. In 1895 however, Senate petitioned the Crown for a supplementary charter giving the requisite powers, and this was granted in the same year.[154]

The university's "rather lukewarm attitude" towards women students continued to be apparent in its reluctance to settle the question of a women's college.[155] Senate had appointed a committee to investigate possibilities and this committee had recommended that the university make £5,000 available for a new building, provided that the same amount could be raised by the supporters of women's education. It was subsequently decided to reduce this contribution to £2,000, with £3,000 being made available on loan. By

1898 more than £6,000 had been promised to the "hostel fund", the enthusiasm of the women's supporters was high, and plans and builders' estimates for the construction of a new college were being invited in the hope that the foundations could be laid before the end of the year. Nothing came of these plans. Instead, the university agreed to rent a rather depressingly damp and dingy house at 33 Claypath, to accommodate the women students in 1899. By that time, many of those who had promised or actually donated money for a new college were becoming anxious and concerned about the lack of progress. Senate responded with some indifference, merely noting that the funds raised so far were not considered sufficient, and should they wish it, subscribers could have their subscriptions reimbursed.[156]

Laura Roberts, who had been appointed Principal to the women students in the far from salubrious accommodation in Claypath, has left us a full account of her experience of the university in these years. She recorded that from the very beginning she

> sensed the positive hostility or total indifference with which the residence of women students was regarded by most of the dwellers in the College, and by many of the University authorities; while the bachelor Bursar to whom the choice of a house, its decorations and its furnishings, had been committed, was said to dislike not only the movement, but the entire female sex.[157]

In her study of women scientists in America before 1940, Margaret Rossiter has remarked on the role of what she has called "coercive (or creative) philanthropy" – "the offering of large gifts with key strings attached" – in furthering opportunities for women in higher education.[158] Sometimes the strategy was successful, but in other cases the tactic could misfire: university authorities might accept a gift, but neglect its conditions or deflect it to other use. In other cases there might be endless controversy over the precise retentions of the benefactor, which could well end up by absorbing resources and frustrating the benefactor's general purpose. It is instructive to look at the difficulties raised in Glasgow by the Muirhead bequest of 1889 in this context.

In a will drawn up in 1889, Dr Henry Muirhead expressed strong feelings of indebtedness to the women in his life and his concern at how little "real, good solid and scientific education" had fallen to women's share. In view of these considerations he proposed to bequeath the greater portion of his savings for the purpose of erecting and endowing an institution or college for "the education of women by women, as far as that can practically and judiciously be carried out". The women students were "to receive education to fit them to become medical practitioners, dentists, electricians or chemists etc."[159] In a memorandum attached to the will Muirhead stipulated that he did not wish clergymen to have anything to do with the management of his proposed college, "for creeds are the firmest fetters to intellectual progress", nor did he want medical men as trustees, because "their trade unionism" was opposed to women entering the medical profession.[160] In 1892 agents of the Muirhead trustees wrote to the Secretary of the University Court in Glasgow enclosing excerpts from the will and offering to confer with the court in devising a joint scheme for the medical education of women. Interestingly, an earlier attempt at co-operation with Queen Margaret College seems to have come to grief because the two parties could not agree on terms. However, negotiations with the university foundered over a number of issues. The trustees' plan to establish a "Muirhead College" near Glasgow's Victoria Infirmary was not favourably regarded by the committee of the University Court, which argued that the university was not a mere examining body to test work done in affiliated colleges and empha-sized its unwillingness to enter into any system of joint control.[161] Further, as the historians of the Victoria Infirmary have pointed out, the infirmary's constitution made it unable to provide exclusively for the clinical instruction of female students. The politics involved in these protracted and controver-sial negotiations were undoubtedly complex. In 1908, the trustees decided to use the money for scholarships, and more substantially for the endowment of two new university chairs at the Royal Infirmary.[162] Muirhead's vision of a college of science and medicine for women, governed by women, had failed to materialize.

The higher education of women in Glasgow suffered from another pro-tracted controversy over the precise terms of a benefaction in the 1890s. In this case the benefactor in question, Mrs Isabella Elder, was still alive, and prepared to put up a spirited fight with the university authorities who, she maintained, had insulted her generosity and ignored her purposes. The con-troversy is interesting because it illuminates the complexities that surrounded the issue of "separate but equal" educational provision for women in these years. Mrs Elder was the wealthy widow of John Elder, a marine engineer and shipbuilder. It was her generosity that had largely brought about the establishment of the separate college for women in Glasgow, Queen Margaret College, with its own premises in North Park House (more recently the headquarters of BBC Scotland). From 1890–2 Mrs Elder had additionally met the costs of the associated medical school for women. Between 1892 and 1893 the university assumed responsibility for the college with its associated medical school, following a deed of gift from Mrs Elder. Corres-pondence between the latter and Principal Caird in 1892–3 makes it clear that Mrs Elder's understanding was that her gift of the college was made on certain conditions, the most important of which was that the college should continue in name and that its students should receive separate but equal teaching from the professors of the university.[163] Mrs Elder expressed her unease about newspaper reports that had unfavourably compared provision for women students in Glasgow with arrangements in Edinburgh. These reports had intimated that women in Edinburgh were to be taught by recognized teachers of the university, while in Glasgow the women would receive separate tuition from Queen Margaret tutors, who did not have the same standing. It seems that at this point Mrs Elder considered revoking her offer of Queen Margaret College, in favour of setting up an endowment fund for women students at the university. She decided against this on receiving an assurance from Principal Caird, who emphasized that women in Glasgow would be immeasurably better off than those in other universities in Scotland on account of their possession of a separate college. He pointed out that the university would not otherwise be able to afford any additional accommodation for women, that the university classrooms and laboratories were already full to overflowing with male students, and that since local opinion was so unfavourable to the idea of mixed classes in medicine, *without* the gift of the college, the medical education of women in Glasgow could not go any further. Correspondence from Mrs Elder makes it clear that at this stage she felt reassured about the situation.[164]

However, further difficulties soon arose in connection with the teaching offered to arts students in Queen Margaret College. As women came to be offered access to classes in Gilmorehill, university teachers became reluctant to organize what they saw as duplicate classes for the women in Queen Margaret College. When in 1894–5, it became apparent that there were to be no history classes organized in the college, and that any women students wanting to study the subject would have to join the men, Mrs Elder instructed her solicitors to write to Principal Caird indicating her view that this amounted to a breach of their agreement.[165] Matters were exacerbated when Richard Lodge, newly appointed to the Chair in History, wrote rather aggressively to the Secretary of the University Court expressing his strong disinclination to teach any extra classes in order for the women to be taught separately. He protested that he had been given no indication of any need for this at the time of his appointment and that he would regard any duplication as "an extraordinarily irksome and intolerable burden". In fact, if he had known that two sets of classes were to be part of his duties, he would not have applied for the post in the first place.[166]

Discontent rumbled on through solicitors' letters; the university authorities trying to placate Mrs Elder with various attempts at compromise, such as the teaching of some subjects in Queen Margaret College in alternate years. Eventually the University Court sought the opinion of Counsel, circulating this advice (in the form of a memorandum marked "Strictly private and confidential") to its members in 1896.[167] The legal advice received from John Rankine and J. B. Balfour was that Queen Margaret College no longer existed as a separate college, it was simply part of the university. More importantly, a deed of gift was not a contract, in that negotiations prior to its execution could not be "admitted to aid in its construction or to control its terms".

There the matter seems to have rested, at least as far as the University Court was concerned. Feelings in Queen Margaret College appear to have been divided. Undoubtedly many of the students were content to attend mixed classes, in spite of the inconvenient distances involved. However, another enduring problem stemming from the deed of gift of 1892–3 was that no provision had been made for the representation of the women of Queen Margaret College on the University Court. As Frances Melville, Mistress of the college from 1909 observed, this was "perhaps unfortunate, certainly significant" for the after conduct of college affairs.[168] Mrs Elder nursed her grievances over what she continued to consider an "unpardonable breach of faith". In 1899, frail with ill-health, she found an opportunity for revenge. The university wanted money for a chapel, a project with which (as she wrote to Principal Storey) she *might* have had every sympathy: but in view of the way in which they had treated her gift to the women students of the university, she felt wholly unable to contemplate any further benefaction.[169]

The advocates of university education for women in Glasgow in the 1880s and 1890s were, then, divided. Mrs Elder and Janet Galloway, the first Mistress of Queen Margaret College, were clearly in favour of "separate but equal" provision. However Frances Melville, who followed Janet Galloway as Mistress of Queen Margaret College, was more reclined to see the benefits of integration. Marion Gilchrist, the pioneer medical student at the college, reflecting in 1948 on the controversies of her youth considered that

> in Glasgow and Edinburgh, where special medical schools for women were started and paved the way for the entrance of women to the medical profession, these held back their progress and for a time prevented the women from getting equal teaching. St Andrews, including Dundee, and Aberdeen Universities opened all doors and had mixed classes. Now St Andrews has the first woman professor, Margaret Fairlie – distinguished in obstetrics and gynaecology.[170]

The most forceful objection to arguments for separate provision stemmed always from the conviction that separate would mean inferior, or be judged so. This conviction lay at the root of Emily Davies' thinking, and fuelled the arguments of what Sara Delamont has referred to as the "non-compromising" feminist advocates of women's higher education.[171] The belief that women's education should not be judged by a separate standard ensured the collapse of Thomas Holloway's plans for Royal Holloway College to develop into a fully-fledged university for women, with power to confer degrees on its own students. In a conference held at Royal Holloway in 1897, there was very little support for the idea of seeking a separate charter for the college.[172] This cleared the way for the scheme for its future development much preferred by Emily Davies and its recently appointed

Principal, Emily Penrose, which was that Royal Holloway should aim at becoming a constituent college of any new teaching university of London. At the conference, Dr Sophie Bryant of the North London Collegiate School argued not only that there was no demand for a separate university for women, but that increasing numbers of girls were demanding "a university education of the established type". It was too late in her view, to say "that this type is, or was, established for men only".[173]

But Bryant's words were somewhat premature. The early years of the new century saw a number of influential educationists arguing precisely that the existing forms of higher education had been devised for men, and that women needed something different. This was an argument that could undoubtedly be made from a feminist as well as a non-feminist perspective. However, between 1900 and the outbreak of war, there was a significant strand of public opinion that favoured a more feminine, home-based curriculum for women.[174] This generated immense controversy, but profoundly affected the development of higher educational provision for women students in King's College London.

It is appropriate to conclude the foregoing discussion of patterns of endowment in women's education with reference to the history of King's College, because if elsewhere in the country provision for women was hampered by scarce resources, the history of King's College for Women was shaped by what was almost an embarrassment of riches in the years before the war.[175] This had certainly not been the case in the early years of what was originally the "Ladies' Department" of King's College in Kensington Square, which had come into existence in the 1880s, and developed into a vigorous academic community under the guidance of Lilian Faithfull, as Vice-Principal in the 1890s. Student numbers rose steadily in these years (to over 500 in 1906), and the department showed every sign of maturing into a fully-fledged college for women on the pattern of Bedford or Royal Holloway. Accommodation was cramped however, and the committee of management had begun to seek space for expansion.

In 1907 Lilian Faithfull was appointed headmistress of Cheltenham Ladies' College, her successor in what was now called the "Women's Department" in Kensington was Hilda Oakeley. Hilda Oakeley's appointment coincided with a period of curriculum innovation in the department that was ultimately to determine its whole future: this was the introduction, in 1908, of a new course in "home science". Enthusiasm for the new course brought together a group of women who sought to raise the status of domestic subjects, and who were genuinely convinced of the need for a more scientific and economically based study of the household with its associated concerns of nutrition, sanitation and hygiene. Proponents of this view included Mabel Atkinson, May McKillop, and several members of the Women's Industrial Council, as well as the growing numbers of women teachers of cookery and domestic subjects in the schools. The scheme drew further support from influential men in the universities such as Professor Arthur Smithells of Leeds, and Herbert Jackson, Professor of Chemistry at King's, who firmly believed in the need to foster a more feminine variant of science. The scheme was, of course, highly controversial, and for those women who adhered strongly to the belief that there was "no sex in intellect" it could appear as a highly retrograde development.[176] Hilda Oakeley's position was undoubtedly one of some ambivalence; she understood "the doubt, suspicion and dismay" with which many feminists greeted the proposal to educate women in home science, while on the whole publicly defending the scheme as an important educational innovation.[177]

Any lingering doubts about the intellectual validity of the home science course were soon to be swamped by a tide of public support and benefaction. While *Punch* was busy mocking the idea of girls matriculating on the basis of their culinary proficiency with apple dumplings and beef stew, enthusiasts for the scheme, firm in their belief that a university standard in home science would improve the efficiency of the nation's mothers, were actively canvassing the support of wealthy aristocratic patrons.[178] Lord Anglesey donated £20,000, the Dukes of Westminster and Devonshire, the Earl of Plymouth and Lady Wantage each gave £500. Mrs Wharrie added another £20,000, Sir Richard Garton the same amount. Thomas Dewey, Chairman of the Prudential Assurance Company, volunteered an astonishing £30,000. By 1912 over £100,000 had been raised. In conjunction with other developments, this munificence was to have a "cataclysmic" effect on "the Cinderella department" in Kensington.[179] In 1910, the London County Council asked Senate to consider "whether it would not be in the interests of the higher education of women generally that the College should aim at the development of the Home Science Department and should gradually abandon the other part of its work". The report of the Haldane Commission on the University of London in 1913 was of similar mind. In the teeth of opposition from Hilda Oakeley and the supporters of the Women's Department in Kensington Square, who "implored the Committee's permission to live and to retain the College's integrity", the recommendations were adopted, and King's College for Women disintegrated in all but name. The new department of Household and Social Science moved to spacious premises in Campden Hill in 1915 (a site originally intended for the women's college as a whole) while the rump of the staff and students from the arts and science departments in Kensington went to the Strand, inaugurating co-education in King's.

Oakeley records that there the women were welcomed by the student body "with striking openness of mind", a fine common room being allocated for their use.[180] She was clearly trying to make the best of things; as a woman with a self-confessed fear and dislike of controversy, she had found the last few years deeply traumatic. Reflecting on the events of 1908–15 twenty years later, she insisted that she had had no idea at the time of her

461

appointment of the place that home science was to occupy: no-one at that time could have predicted its "sensational" growth. She confessed that, as public representative of the college, she felt bound to give the idea of home science a fair hearing, whereas had she *not* been in this position, she might well have aligned herself with the scheme's opponents:

> In part the contest was painful, because it brought me into opposition to women with whose general standpoint I was in essentials in agreement, and in whose camp I should have wished if possible to be.[181]

As things developed, she felt King's College for Women had been forced into playing the part of "Iphigenia for the University Agamemnon, a necessary sacrifice to the Olympian powers", and a victim of "forces too powerful for us to withstand".[182] It is important to remember that Oakeley had been attracted to King's precisely because it had begun to establish a tradition of high academic standards and seemed likely to develop into a fully independent women's college. She had found her previous post as Tutor to Women Students in the co-educational environment of Manchester University uncongenial.[183] But by 1915 she found herself in a similar position in the Strand, her title now being "Warden" rather than "Vice-Principal". In 1915, feeling that her work was "no longer essential", she resigned.[184]

Oakeley was replaced by Miss Eleanor Plumer, who took charge of the women students for the next two years. The Delegacy advertised the post as "that of the Head of the Women's side of a Co-educational College", believing that:

> While a strong corporate life for the College as a whole is desirable, opportunities must be provided for both men and women students to have certain activities in their separate common rooms, apart.[185]

The post was later designated that of "Tutor to Women Students". The experience of women in positions of this kind will be the subject of the next chapter.

The development in King's, like those in Glasgow, serves to illustrate the complexity of issues and motives surrounding decisions about whether the interests of female students were best secured by incorporating them in educational arrangements alongside men, or whether women's education should aim at separate or distinct forms of provision. The political implications of decisions of this kind could be decidedly ambiguous. Arguments over difference, which could depend either on the notion of women having special educational needs as women, or stem from the awareness of their vulnerable position as newcomers to higher education, less secure in their entitlement to resources, could be made equally from a feminist or from a conservative position. Mrs Elder's advocacy of separatism was based on her belief that this was the best way to earmark resources for women. The controversy in London was more concerned with divided perceptions about women's interests and the curriculum, although questions of resource allocation were by no means absent. Events in both London and Glasgow reveal a complex interplay between projects espoused by benefactors and the strategies of recipient institutions. The route towards securing women's best interests was rarely clear.

Notes

1 J. Kamm, *Hope deferred, girls' education in English history* (London, 1965), p. 268.
2 *Ibid.*, pp. 268–70.
3 P. Sheavyn, *Higher education for women in Great Britain* (London, n.d. (*c.* 1924)), p. 19.
4 E. Huws Jones, *Margery Fry, the essential amateur* (London, 1966), p. 57.
5 *Ibid.*, see also "A greeting to Phoebe Sheavyn", *Yggdrasill* (the magazine of the Ashburne Hall Association, December 1966), and "A salute to Dr Phoebe Sheavyn", *Bryn Mawr Alumnae Bulletin* (1), 1966–7. (I am grateful to Dr Dulcie Groves for this reference.)
6 N. B. Harte, *The admission of women to University College London: a centenary lecture* (London, 1979), p. 3.
7 R. N. Smart, "Literate ladies: a fifty year experiment", *Alumnus Chronicle* (59) (University of St Andrews, June 1968), pp. 21–31.
8 M. Tylecote, *The education of women at Manchester University, 1883–1933* (Manchester, 1941), pp. 13, 26.
9 *Ibid.*, pp. 42–51.
10 C. E. Whiting, *The University of Durham 1832–1932* (London, 1932), pp. 147–54.
11 S. Hamilton, *Women and the Scottish universities c. 1869–1939: a social history*, PhD thesis (University of Edinburgh, 1987), p. 140.
12 W. G. Evans, *Education and female emancipation, the Welsh experience, 1847–1914* (Cardiff, 1990), p. 210.
13 M. Hird (ed.), *Doves and dons: a history of St Mary's College, Durham* (Durham, 1982), n.p., *c.* p. 2.
14 Hamilton, *Women and the Scottish universities*, p. 162.
15 "Petition from Women medical students concerning the opening of classes to women, 20 April 1904", *Minutes of Senate* 103 (University of Glasgow), p. 336.
16 Harte, *Admission of women*, p. 17.
17 R. D. Pope & M. G. Verbeke, "Ladies' educational organisations in England, 1865–1885", *Paedagogica Historica* **16**(2), 1976, pp. 336–61: and N. Jepson, *The beginnings of English university adult education: policy and problems* (London, 1973), pp. 31–45.
18 S. Lemoine, *The North of England Council for Promoting the Higher Education of Women*, MA thesis (University of Manchester, 1968).
19 *Ibid.*, see also Kamm, *Hope deferred* p. 252ff; Pope & Verbeke, "Ladies' educational organisations", p. 346ff; S. R. Wills, *The social and economic aspects of higher education for women between 1844 and 1870, with special reference to the North of England Council*, MA thesis (University of London, 1951).

20 Harte, *Admission of women*, pp. 8–9.
21 D. R. Jones, *The origins of civic universities: Manchester, Leeds and Liverpool* (London, 1988), pp. 100–101. On the role of the Yorkshire Ladies' Association see also I. Jenkins, "The Yorkshire Ladies' Council of Education, 1871–91", *Publications of the Thoresby Society Miscellany*, **16**(134), 1978.
22 Hamilton, *Women and the Scottish universities*, Chapters 1 & 2; E. Boog Watson, *The Edinburgh Association for the University Education of Women, 1867–1967* (Privately printed, n.d.); K. Burton, *A memoir of Mrs Crudelius* (Edinburgh, 1879).
23 Hamilton, p. 76ff.
24 *Ibid.*, p. 86.
25 *Ibid.*, p. 85.
26 *Ibid.*, p. 79.
27 *Ibid.*, pp. 102–3.
28 *Ibid.*, p. 110ff.
29 F. Melville, "Queen Margaret College", *The College Courant* (Journal of the Glasgow University Graduates Association, Whitsun, 1949).
30 *Ibid.*, see also O. Checkland, *Queen Margaret Union, 1890–1980: women in the University of Glasgow* (Glasgow, 1980), and Hamilton, pp. 110–18.
31 W. N. Boog Watson, "The first eight ladies", *University of Edinburgh Journal* 23, 1967–8; Hamilton, p. 163.
32 Hamilton, p. 179.
33 *Ibid.*, p. 180.
34 *Ibid.*, p. 146.
35 M. Tuke, "Women students in the universities", *Contemporary Review* **133**, p. 72, 1928.
36 Tylecote, *The education of women*, p. 43.
37 M. Cheesewright, *Mirror to a mermaid: pictorial reminiscences of Mason College and the University of Birmingham, 1875–1975* (Birmingham, 1975), p. 33.
38 Tuke, p. 72.
39 R. D. Anderson, *Universities and elites in Britain since 1800* (London, 1992), pp. 22–3. More detailed figures can be found in the *University Grants Committee report for the period 1929–30 to 1934–5* (London, 1936). (See Appendix ii)
40 L. Moore, *Bajanellas and semilinas: Aberdeen University and the education of women 1860–1920* (Aberdeen, 1991), pp. 43–4.
41 *Ibid.*, p. 44.
42 University Grants Committee, *Returns from universities and university colleges in receipt of Treasury grant, academic year 1937–8* (London, 1939), p. 6.
43 C. G. Robertson, "The provincial universities", *Sociological Review* **31**, p. 253, 1939.
44 A. Gordon, "The after careers of university educated women", *The Nineteenth Century* **37**, pp. 955–60, 1895; M. Sanderson, *The universities and British industry 1850–1970* (London, 1972), p. 315; J. W. Berman, *A sense of achievement: the significance of higher education for British women, 1890–1930*, PhD thesis (State University of New York at Buffalo, 1982), Chapter 5; K. Scobie, *Women at Glasgow University in the 1920s and 1930s*, MA dissertation (University of Glasgow, 1986); C. Logan, *Women at Glasgow University: determination or pre-determination?* MA dissertation (University of Glasgow, 1986); T. Watt (ed.), *Roll of graduates of the University of Aberdeen, 1901–25* (Aberdeen, 1935).
45 Tuke, "Women students" p. 76.
46 E. Morley (ed.), *Women workers in seven professions* (London, 1914), p. 12.
47 Anderson, *Universities and elites*, p. 57.

48 *Ibid.*, p. 23; University Grants Committee Report, 1929–30, 1934–5, p. 4.
49 Hamilton, *Women and the Scottish universities*, pp. 98–9; Moore, *Bajanellas*, pp. 21–2.
50 Hamilton, pp. 108–9.
51 J. B. Thomas (ed.), *British universities and teacher education: a century of change* (Lewes: Falmer Press, 1990), p. 3.
52 R. W. Rich, *The training of teachers in England and Wales during the nineteenth century* (Cambridge, 1933, this edn Bath: Cedric Chivers, 1972), p. 274.
53 *Ibid.*, p. 274.
54 *Ibid.*, p. 263.
55 J. B. Thomas, "The day training college: a Victorian innovation in teacher training", *British Journal of Teacher Education* 4(3), 1978, pp. 249–61.
56 Rich, p. 227; J. B. Thomas, "Victorian beginnings", in *British universities and teacher education*, p. 14.
57 W. H. G. Armytage, *Civic universities, aspects of a British tradition* (London, 1955), p. 255; Thomas, "Day training college to Department of Education", in *British universities and teacher education*, p. 26.
58 P. Gosden & A. Taylor, *Studies in the history of a university 1874–1974* (Leeds, 1975), p. 50.
59 Armytage, p. 256.
60 Thomas, "Day training college to Department of Education", p. 28.
61 Gosden, in Gosden & Taylor, p. 50.
62 *Ibid.*, p. 57.
63 Thomas, "Victorian beginnings", p. 28.
64 Tylecote, *The education of women*, p. 47.
65 *Ibid.*, pp. 53–4.
66 Thomas, "Day training college to Department of Education", p. 26.
67 Hird, *Doves and dons*, c. p. 10.
68 C. W. Gibby, "Academic Durham in 1926" *Durham University Journal* LXXIX(2), p. 5, December 1986.
69 Minute books, St Hild's College University Students' Society, 1920 and 1929, MS 378.42811–15 F 20 (archives, Durham University).
70 M. Pease, "Some reminiscences of University College, Bristol", unpublished MS (archives, University of Bristol, 1942), p. 12.
71 D. W. Humphreys, "The education and training of teachers: the first fifty years", in *University and community: essays to mark the centenary of the founding of University College Bristol*, J. Macqueen & S. Taylor (eds) (Bristol, 1976), p. 47.
72 Sheavyn, *Higher education for women*, p. 6.
73 Tuke, "Women students", pp. 76–7.
74 *Ibid.*, p. 76.
75 J. Howarth & M. Curthoys, "The political economy of women's higher education in late nineteenth and early twentieth century Britain", *Historical Research* 60(142), pp. 208–231, 1987.
76 Tylecote, *The education of women*, p. 27.
77 Hamilton, *Women and the Scottish universities*, p. 390.
78 Sheavyn, *Higher education for women*, p. 19.
79 J. Gwynn Williams, *The University College of North Wales: foundations, 1884–1927* (Cardiff, 1985), plate 50.
80 W. Peck, *A little learning, or a Victorian childhood* (London, 1952), p. 166.
81 Hird, *Doves and dons*, c. p. 36.
82 B. Lees, "A family at Reading", unpublished MS in possession of author.
83 J. Hubback, *Wives who went to college* (London, 1957), p. 25.

84 Moore, *Bajanellas*, p. 122.
85 Anderson, *Universities and elites*, p. 54, pp. 56–7. An early historian of Nottingham claimed that according to Treasury inspectors in 1901–2, "Nottingham University College stood at the head of all English university colleges in the number of students who entered from elementary schools and that the opportunities offered to young working men of promise were very considerable" E. Beckett, *The University College of Nottingham* (Nottingham, 1928), p. 54.
86 R. D. Anderson, *Education and opportunity in Victorian Scotland: schools and universities* (Oxford, 1983), p. 318.
87 Anderson, *Universities and elites*, p. 57.
88 W. Alexander, *First ladies of medicine* (Glasgow, 1987), p. 14.
89 *Ibid.*, p. 18.
90 F. Musgrove, "Middle-class education and employment in the nineteenth century", *Economic History Review* **23**, pp. 99–111, 1959–60, cited by and discussed in Alexander, p. 19.
91 E. Bryson, *Look back in wonder* (1st edition 1966; Dundee, 1980).
92 *Ibid.*, p. 130.
93 *Ibid.*, p. 131.
94 Morley, *Women workers*, pp. 82–136.
95 Sheavyn, *Higher education for women*, p. 20.
96 C. Blake, *The charge of the parasols: women's entry to the medical profession* (London, 1990), p. 114ff.
97 Hamilton, *Women and the Scottish universities*, p. 35.
98 E. Fiddes, "Introduction" in Tylecote, *The education of women*, pp. 13–14.
99 Tylecote, p. 45.
100 Hird, *Doves and dons*, c. p. 3.
101 E. Boog Watson, *Edinburgh Association for the University Education of Women, 1867–1967* (Edinburgh, n.d.), pp. 14–15.
102 M. J. Shaen, *Memorials of two sisters: Susanna and Catherine Winkworth* (London, 1908), pp. 260–1, 330. See also minute book relating to Catherine Winkworth Scholarships Fund (archives, Bristol University).
103 Note on Taylour Thomson Bequest (November 1883), University of St Andrews, *Minutes of Senate* **20**, p. 426.
104 Brochure advertising University House, 1909 (University House archives, special collections, Birmingham University).
105 Professor H. G. Fiedler to Charles Harding, 5 October 1903 (special collections, FH 79, Birmingham University).
106 Lord Shuttleworth, "The Gilchrist Educational Trust: pioneering work in education", an address delivered before the Bolton Education Society, Cambridge, 1930; "A sketch of the life of Doctor Gilchrist, with particulars of the educational trust founded by him", (archives of the Gilchrist Educational Trust, London, 1881).
107 See minutes of the Gilchrist Educational Trust, 1874 to present.
108 Lord Shuttleworth, p. 9, and list of trustees in appendix.
109 Lord Haldane, "Foreword" in G. S. M. Ellis, *The poor student and the university* (London, 1925), p. vi.
110 Ellis, p. 11.
111 *Ibid.*, p. 10.
112 Board of Education, *Interim report of the Consultative Committee on scholarships for higher education*, (London, 1916), Cd. 8291, vol. VIII, p. 65 para. 119.
113 Ellis, *The poor student*, p. 32.
114 *Ibid.*, p. 9.

115 Lord Haldane, Foreword to Ellis, p. vi.
116 Tylecote, *The education of women*, pp. 115–16.
117 Board of Education files on state scholarships, ED 54, nos 34, 35 and 37 (Public Record Office).
118 PRO, ED 54, No. 37: letter from Assistant Mistresses Association dated 20 May 1930 and comments, memorandum relating to interview with headmistresses, 18 January 1932, and headmasters, 9 May 1933.
119 Board of Education, *Interim report of the Consultative Committee on scholarships*, 1916, p. 65, para 120.
120 Tuke, "Women students" p. 76.
121 Report from the Senior Tutor to Women Students in Birmingham (n.d., *c.* 1935? University collection, Heslop Room, Birmingham University Library), 3 vii 1–2, 3 vi 7–8, 1926–47; Marjorie Rackstraw's typescript notes on Barbara M. Paterson, a first year arts student in Masson Hall, Edinburgh, in the 1930s, in (uncatalogued) box of papers relating to Masson Hall (archives, Edinburgh University); J. Lee, *This great journey* (New York, 1942), p. 56ff.
122 Central Employment Bureau for Women and Student Careers Association, *Report*, April 1924, p. 5.
123 Harte, *Admission of women*, p. 18.
124 M. Adamson, "University College and women science students, 1884–1885", unpublished manuscript (archives, University College London, UCL MEM 1B/18).
125 *Ibid.*
126 Tylecote, *The education of women*, pp. 24, 32.
127 *Ibid.*, p. 35.
128 *Ibid.*, p. 51.
129 Dr C. Chishohne to Mabel Tylecote, June 1934, cited in Tylecote, *The education of women*, p. 51.
130 H. Wilkie, "Steps which led to the appointment of a Woman Superintendent of Studies" *University of Edinburgh Journal*, 1971–2, pp. 136–8.
131 Moore, *Bajanellas*, p. 71.
132 *Ibid.*, p. 73.
133 E. Rideout, unpublished MSS reminiscences (archives, Liverpool University, D 255/3/3).
134 S. Jameson, "The University of Leeds in 1909–12", unpublished MS (archives, Leeds University), p. 15.
135 Tylecote, *The education of women*, p. 43.
136 *Ibid.*, p. 60.
137 Hamilton, *Women and the Scottish universities*, p. 165.
138 *Ibid.*, p. 158.
139 T. Kelly, *For advancement of learning: the University of Liverpool 1881–1981* (Liverpool, 1981), pp. 116–17.
140 *University of Southampton students handbook 1904–5* (special collection, Southampton University), p. 61.
141 "The women's reading room", *The Magnet* (21 June 1900), pp. 161–2 (archives, Bristol University).
142 V. Woolf, *A room of one's own* (Penguin, 1973), pp. 21–5.
143 J. G. Fitch, "Women and the universities", *Contemporary Review* **58**, pp. 250–1, 1890.
144 C. S. Bremner, *Education of girls and women in Great Britain* (London, 1897), pp. 122–5.
145 Jones, *The origins of civic universities*, p. 95.

146 W. D. Rubinstein, *Men of property: the very wealthy in Britain since the Industrial Revolution* (London, 1981), p. 250.
147 J. Simmons, *Leicester and its university* (Leicester, 1963), p. 33.
148 M. Tuke, *A history of Bedford College for Women, 1849–1937* (Oxford, 1939), Chapters 1, 2 and Appendix I.
149 C. Bingham, *The history of Royal Holloway College, 1886–1986* (London, 1987), pp. 120–2.
150 E. Fiddes, "Introduction" in Tylecote, *The education of women*, pp. 1–2.
151 M. Shafe, *University education in Dundee, 1881–1981: a pictorial history* (Dundee, 1982), pp. 11–12.
152 *Ibid.*, p. 15.
153 Whiting, *The University of Durham*, p. 148.
154 *Ibid.*, p. 153.
155 Hird, *Doves and dons*, c. p. 5.
156 *Ibid.*, c. p. 7.
157 *Ibid.*, c. p. 9.
158 M. Rossiter, *Women scientists in America: struggles and strategies to 1940* (Baltmore, 1982), pp. 46–7.
159 S. D. Slater & D. A. Dow, *The Victoria Infirmary of Glasgow 1890–1990: a centenary history* (Glasgow, 1990), pp. 179–80.
160 Report of committee on negotiations with Muirhead trustees, March 1895, Appendix, Glasgow University Court minute book, no. 4 (archives, Glasgow University, GUA 50569).
161 *Ibid.*, p. 3.
162 Slater & Dow, p. 180; M. Gilchrist, "Some early recollections of the Queen Margaret Medical School", *Surgo* (March 1948).
163 Correspondence between Mrs Elder and Principal Caird, 11–17 October 1892 (GUA 62398).
164 *Ibid.*; Mrs Elder to Principal Storey; 15 April 1899, (DC 21/290–2).
165 A. J. and A. Graham to Principal Caird, 9 November 1895 (GUA 62401).
166 Correspondence between R. Lodge and Alan Clapperton, Secretary to the University Court, Glasgow, 27 January 1896, (GUA 62415).
167 "Memorial for the Queen Margaret College Committee of the University Court of Glasgow" Court minute book, no. 5, 1896 (GUA 50570).
168 F. Melville, "Queen Margaret College", *Pass It On* (special edition, 1935), p. 5.
169 Mrs Elder to Principal Storey, 2 April and 5 April 1899 (archives, Glasgow University, DC 21/290–2).
170 M. Gilchrist, *Surgo* (March 1948).
171 S. Delamont, "The contradictions in ladies' education", in *The nineteenth-century woman: her cultural and physical world*, S. Delamont & L. Duffin (eds) (London, 1978), p. 154.
172 Bingham, *History of Royal Holloway College*, pp. 91–2.
173 *Ibid.*, p. 90.
174 C. Dyhouse, *Girls growing up in late Victorian and Edwardian England* (London, 1981), p. 162ff.
175 N. Marsh, *The history of Queen Elizabeth College* (London, 1986), Chapters 1–3. Much of the following information is taken from this source.
176 Dyhouse, pp. 168–9.
177 H. D. Oakeley, "King's College for Women", in F. J. C. Hearnshaw, *The centenary history of King's College London, 1828–1928* (London, 1929) pp. 489–509; Oakeley, "Education in home science" in *History and progress* (London, 1923), pp. 220–29; and Oakeley, *My adventures in education* (London,

1939), p. 138ff, and her outcorrespondence file relating to the establishment of the home science course (archives, King's College London, KWA/GPF 11).

178 Marsh, *History of Queen Elizabeth College*, pp. 39–40.

179 *Ibid.*, pp. 43–6.

180 Hearnshaw, *The centenary history of King's College*, p. 508.

181 Oakeley, *My adventures in education*, pp. 146, 149.

182 *Ibid.*, pp. 149, 152.

183 *Ibid.*, p. 135.

184 *Ibid.*, p. 156.

185 Draft advertisement for administrative officer of King's College for Women, 3 July 1917 (archives, King's College London, KWA/GPF 20).

118

RECONSIDERING A CLASSIC

Assessing the history of women's higher education a dozen years after Barbara Solomon

Linda Eisenmann

Source: *Harvard Educational Review* 67(4) (1997): 689–717.

In this article, Linda Eisenmann examines the role and impact of Barbara Solomon's now classic text in women's educational history, *In the Company of Educated Women: A History of Women and Higher Education in America*. Eisenmann analyzes how Solomon's book influenced, defined, and in some ways limited the field of women's educational history. She shows how current historical research — such as the study of normal schools and academies — grew out of Solomon's work. She points out where the book is innovative and indispensable and where it disappoints us as teachers and scholars in the 1990s. Eisenmann criticizes Solomon for placing too much emphasis on women's access to higher education, thereby ignoring the importance of wider historical and educational influences such as economics, women's occupational choices, and the treatment of women in society at large. Finally, Eisenmann examines the state of subsequent research in women's higher educational history. She urges researchers to investigate beyond the areas defined by Solomon's work and to assess the impact of these neglected subjects on women's experiences in education.

In 1985, Harvard University scholar Barbara Miller Solomon published a comprehensive historical study of women's higher education in the United States that became an instant classic. *In the Company of Educated Women: A History of Women and Higher Education in America* offered the first book-length synthesis of women's academic progress since Mabel Newcomer's 1959 effort, *A Century of Higher Education for American Women,* and was the first in its field to employ the new data, methods, and insights made available by the contemporary surge in women's history.[1]

Benefiting from the expanded work of specialists in the new field of women's studies, Solomon synthesized secondary sources and reexamined primary materials, proclaiming women's higher education "an unfinished revolution" that continues to pose complexities for women.[2] Access constituted Solomon's major analytical theme, as she told the stories of successive generations of women pushing first for initial entry, and then struggling to make higher education meaningful to their sense of their own life opportunities. Cognizant of biases and omissions in earlier histories, Solomon's book included — more than any other single history of women's higher education — the stories of nontraditional institutions and students, adding sections on historically Black colleges, Catholic schools, and two-year institutions. She also included the stories of poor women and immigrants to those of middle-class and privileged students. Overall, she stressed that her book was not a history of institutions, but rather of generations of women. Thus, Solomon discussed successive eras in layers, detailing the institutions, curricula, clientele, job opportunities, and public debates surrounding women's education from the colonial era to the 1980s.

As the single most comprehensive and available historical study of women's higher education, Solomon's book appears widely in courses on women's history, higher education, and the history of education. It also constitutes the major source for nonhistorians seeking a solid and accessible discussion of women's higher education, and is consulted frequently by a wide range of readers. Now that *In the Company of Educated Women* has reigned as the strongest resource in the field for a dozen years, the time is right for assessing the book's role and impact as the classic source. The time is also propitious for examining the state of subsequent research in women's higher educational history that might supplement, or supersede, Solomon's ideas and for offering recommendations about future work. This article treats each of these issues in turn.

First, I outline briefly Solomon's approach and her analysis, suggesting where the book is innovative and indispensable, but also noting where it disappoints us as teachers and scholars in the 1990s. I argue, in terms of the book's legacy, that Solomon's framing of women's educational history as a story of access to traditional institutions, while vital, may actually have limited later historians' approach to questions and debates, encouraging them to focus their questions on these traditional settings. In the second part of this article I discuss new research that extends Solomon's work on the history of women's advanced education. Solomon urged her colleagues to consider the nineteenth-century normal schools and academies as appropriate components of higher education, to investigate the experience of a more diverse group of women, and to reevaluate the use women made of their education throughout successive eras.[3] Each of these areas has produced substantial work in the last dozen years, some building on Solomon and some going in entirely new directions. Finally, in the third section I explore some research areas that remain underdeveloped, suggesting that the field of women's higher education may not yet be ready for a new Solomonesque resynthesis.

The Solomon legacy

In 1995, a panel of seven historians of higher education, convened to assess the legacy of Barbara Solomon's work, concluded unanimously that they "could not imagine teaching a history of education course without *In the Company of Educated Women*."[4] With its thorough presentation of American women's push for higher learning from colonial times through the post–World War II era, the book provides a basis for understanding women's education before colleges had opened for women and carries us through women's fight for equal access over subsequent generations. However, those same historians who lauded Solomon's work also admitted that the book cannot stand alone as the story of women's education; it requires heavy supplementing in the areas of racial, ethnic, geographic, economic, and intellectual history.

Until Solomon, no historian had tried to analyze the entire sweep of women's higher educational history since Mabel Newcomer's *A Century of Higher Education for American Women* in 1959. Newcomer, much as she tried to cover a wide variety of women's institutions, had fallen back on the environment she knew best as a Vassar professor: the eastern women's colleges. Even as she reminded her readers that three-quarters of all colleges were coeducational, Newcomer found women's experiences too diffuse in those larger institutions and turned instead to the separate women's colleges, where she could observe the particular arrangements that had been crafted for women in curriculum, residential life, and vocational guidance. Surprisingly few individuals appear in Newcomer's story: institutions rule the day and leaders control the institutions. Writing in a particularly dismal era for women's intellectual participation, Newcomer recognized the limiting effect that societal norms have on women's choices; focusing on women's actual efforts was the extent of her challenge to those limits.

Historian Patricia Palmieri has suggested that, just as Newcomer was as positive as the 1950s climate allowed, Solomon offered a type of scholarly challenge to the more pessimistic 1970s and 1980s view that colleges had failed women, at least in terms of their equal participation and performance. Solomon, Palmieri asserts, "restored a balance in the scholarly domain" by showing that women, over time, had asserted their place in higher education and had, in fact, repeatedly pushed colleges to accommodate their needs.[5] That is, a calculus that women remained far behind men in the 1980s should not overshadow the achievement women made in this educational arena.

Between Newcomer and Solomon came the resurgent women's movement and the first two decades of women's studies scholarship. Whereas
Newcomer and her contemporaries had no language with which to analyze
discrimination against women, Solomon could rely on scholarly explications
of ways that economic and educational structures had inhibited women's
advancement.[6] Solomon drew on older, factual material to document
women's early efforts, including such works as Emilie J. Hutchinson's 1929
study, *Women and the Ph.D.*, and Jeanne Noble's 1956 work, *The Negro
Woman's College Education,* both of which outlined the early history
of women's opportunities on a large scale.[8] Solomon also relied on dozens of
institutional histories, biographies, novels, diaries, editorials, and newspaper
articles to capture both the spirit and realities of earlier generations of women.
By 1985, however, Solomon was also able to reinterpret this material with
a feminist consciousness constructed by a new generation of historians and
sociologists. Karen Blair's *The Clubwoman as Feminist,* for example, helped
Solomon understand that women's clubs were more than safe opportunities
for privileged women to share knowledge; rather, according to Blair, these
clubs allowed women to claim power and influence in activities that men
ceded to their authority, at the same time providing educational opportunities for many women unable to attend formal college.[8] Solomon could
also use Nancy Cott's explanation of *The Bonds of Womanhood: "Woman's
Sphere" in New England, 1780–1835* to understand that the limits of a
designated female sphere of activity and influence could also develop as
a center of power for women where religion, domesticity, and education
were tailored to women's particular needs.[9] And, although access sustained
a primary role as the organizing principle of Solomon's book, she did
heed Jill Ker Conway's 1974 reminder that access alone never guaranteed
women's full participation, using that caveat to look at issues for women
once they had entered collegiate doors.[10]

In twelve chapters plus an "Afterthought," Solomon addressed three
main eras of women's participation in higher education: the antebellum era
(from the colonial period, with its few institutions, up to 1860), the growth
period (1860 to 1920, the era of greatest proliferation of institutional types
from women's colleges to land grant universities), and the modern period
(1920 to the Second World War, which actually produced a decline in
women's percentages of participation in higher education). One last chapter,
entitled "The Promises of Liberal Education — Forgotten and Fulfilled,"
brought the story to the present, with a firm focus on the contemporary
women's movement.

Solomon's approach is recursive. She describes the general conditions for
women in a particular era, both in education and in society. In subsequent
chapters, she swings back through that same time period to explain which
women participated in higher education, what they studied, and how female
students eventually used their education. Throughout her discussion, she

tends to offer bits of women's lives to illustrate small points, but then does not develop those pieces into fuller stories. Instead she moves into other points, frustrating those readers who are seeking a more linear narrative. Because of her insistence on inclusivity, Solomon jumps among institutional types as well, sometimes leaving a dutiful but "tacked on" feeling to her discussion of Catholic colleges, historically Black institutions, and normal schools. In the chapters on women's use of their education, Solomon moves systematically through topics, treating teaching, the professions, marriage rates, and women's reflections on their college lives era by era.

Although offering a thorough discussion of women's collegiate participation, Solomon does not offer much additional context — another concern of those who would rely on the book for a thorough story. Economic history is woefully lacking in her explanation of women's occupational choices; intellectual history is limited to precise arguments about the usefulness of higher education; and except for the occasional connection to movements like suffrage and temperance, general U.S. history is altogether too absent from the discussion. This seeming neglect, however, results front Solomon's careful reliance on the extant secondary sources available to her to explain women's progress in collegiate life; she achieves a synthesis in her self-described "narrative," but never promises a new theoretical paradigm — particularly for a field where little theory existed.

Yet even with what appear now as limitations, the book advanced several categories of analysis — which Sally Schwager describes as Solomon's "sensibilities" — that were relatively new to the study of women's higher education in 1985 and that still ground our understanding. Extending work by David Allmendinger on poor students who attended college, Solomon looked at the economic standing of students, freshly examining the issues of financial aid and student self-support.[11] In turning the lens on women who needed help to attend college, she also promoted studying the role families played as sponsors for female students. Perhaps because of Solomon's earlier strong study of New England's immigrants, Schwager notes that Solomon was one of few historians to recognize the important role of immigrant parents who pushed their daughters into school.[12] Although the attention to historically Black and Catholic colleges seems forced and limited to a 1990s reader, Solomon's commitment to including those institutions and their students goes beyond the lip service of earlier studies. Even with little secondary work at her disposal, Solomon recognized the need to look at racial and ethnic diversity on predominantly White college campuses, perhaps laying groundwork for later comparative analyses.

Another advance by Solomon — a place where her focus on access is beneficial — was her resuscitation of the history of academies, and her claim that these pre-collegiate antebellum institutions were appropriate forerunners of higher education. By the turn of the twentieth century, high schools and colleges had developed into recognizable institutions, superseding the academies and female seminaries in influence and prominence. Relying on older work and a smattering of new sources, Solomon acknowledged the role that academies — many of them with all-female student bodies and headed by women — had played in offering both liberal and vocational opportunities to a range of nineteenth-century women. Finally, although her look at women's experiences after college, posed by many as the "after college what?" question, often ignores some of the influences women exerted outside traditional jobs and professions — such as their role in reform movements — Solomon tried to relate the purposes of women's education to actual results, going beyond scholars who had argued that women sought schooling primarily to expand their intellects.[13]

Overall, Solomon stressed that for women, "education evoked opposition" — thus the resistance to access.[14] Opposition sometimes occurred in students' own families, as daughters struggled for identity outside the family unit; it also developed from society, with educated women challenging expectations for female roles. On coeducational campuses, women were tolerated but rarely welcomed, finding barriers to their full participation and development. Across institutional settings, Solomon found that women learned as much from their female and male peers as they did in their classrooms, and her book attends to what Frederick Rudolph labeled "the extracurriculum" for its importance to students' lives.[15] With her themes of access, opposition, curriculum, and career development as guides, Solomon's story of female participation in higher education inevitably contains as many examples of frustrations and impediments as of successes and accomplishments.

Subsequent historical research

When a single book dominates and synthesizes a field of study, it also may shape the way subsequent scholars ask questions and frame debates in that field. Having waited twenty-five years for a synthesis like Solomon's, have historians of higher education been overly influenced by her approach, her data, and her paradigm? In what areas have Solomon's ideas held sway, and where have they sparked new approaches?[16]

Three of Solomon's constructs seem to have maintained primacy in the way that historians of women's education ask their questions, perhaps limiting the vitality of their investigations: first, her implicit hierarchy of women's colleges on top and others, especially the normal schools, arraying themselves toward the bottom; second, the dominance of access as an organizing principle; and third, the lack of attention to other agencies' influence on higher education, especially foundations, the government, and accrediting groups. In this section I discuss Solomon's impact on each of these areas and highlight recent work that is beginning to stretch her construction.

The implicit hierarchy

Solomon certainly succeeded better than Newcomer and others at attending to a range of institutional types in her story of women in higher education. Historian Patricia Albjerg Graham, in her 1975 call for future research, "So Much to Do: Guides for Historical Research on Women in Higher Education," lamented the continuing focus on women's colleges, highlighting a fact Newcomer herself had raised: by 1890, 70 percent of women attended coeducational institutions, a figure that continued to rise throughout the twentieth century.[17] Further, as Susan B. Carter asserted in her economic study of hiring patterns for female faculty, the land grant institutions were significant employers of women professors, even though far too many were shunted into teacher training departments and home economics.[18] Solomon unquestionably heeded Graham's challenge, noting that "the debate over the advantages of the separate college environment is largely anachronistic."[19] She included significant data on women in state universities, clarifying that, especially in the Midwest and West, coeducational state colleges and universities provided the primary collegiate experience for women students. Their access into these institutions hailed a major advance for women's education. Generally, the push to segregate women into separate settings was an eastern and southern phenomenon, one far outweighed by the number of women attending land grant and other public institutions. Solomon described fears about the "feminization" of the collegiate environment that appeared in the early part of the twentieth century, as women's presence at coeducational campuses and in the curriculum was growing. In fact, she expressed concern that an inherent class bias against these large, coeducational settings prompted both contemporary and modern preferences for the separate, all-female environments.

Nonetheless Solomon, somewhat like Newcomer, often fell back on the Seven Sisters and other women's colleges with their prominence and superior archives for filling out women's stories. This reliance is understandable since, in terms of traditional leadership, women's institutions provide the most data: many (but not all) of the female colleges hired women presidents and faculty, for example.[20] In addition, in the early years of these schools' existence, women students and professors proved the most self-conscious about their roles as pioneers. Thus, the women's colleges built stronger archives for both faculty and student experiences, and their women leaders recorded more of their own backgrounds and accomplishments. The ready availability of data for certain populations parallels the issue in writing any social history: how does the scholar uncover and honor the experience of less literate people or those whose traditions and opportunities do not favor recording their experience?

However, as both Patricia Palmieri and Margaret Rossiter have shown, women's institutions faltered in their commitment to female professors by the 1930s, when a male faculty was assumed to signal quality.[21] As women's overall participation slackened from its high in the 1920s, women's colleges may have maintained their commitment to female students, but not concomitantly to women faculty.[22] Solomon herself notes that "the assumption that women's colleges consistently offered female role models is an oversimplification."[23] Combined with the fact that women's colleges made up only 5–15 percent of institutions open to women from the 1940s to the 1980s, their seeming status as the most important setting for studying women should be challenged.

Only in the last decade or so, however, have historians of women's education begun serious efforts to rejuvenate the normal schools, the public institutions, and the female academies as worthy and important sites for studying women's participation. Perhaps the influence of social history needed time to affect the field, or perhaps women had too often fallen into the trap of trying to prove their equality with the elite men's institutions. Recent research provides correctives that were unavailable to Solomon in two important areas. First, historians of these more "marginal" institutions remind us that higher education — especially in the nineteenth century — was far more permeable as a system than a sense of hierarchy would suggest. Second, the normal schools and the female academies were frequently sources of both real access and power for women students and faculty.

In the last ten years, normal schools have attracted renewed attention, although not initially because of their role in educating a largely female population. Two book-length studies inaugurated a fresh look at the normal schools as providers of training for several generations of nineteenth- and early twentieth-century teachers. Jürgen Herbst, in *And Sadly Teach,* devoted keen attention to these institutions, tracing their theoretical lineage from German forebears who brought aspects of the normal model and of Pestalozzian pedagogy to the United States.[24] Although Herbst began with the birth of U.S. normal schools in Massachusetts, the intriguing part of his book was his demonstration that the normal school model, when transported to the public institutions of the Midwest and West, transmogrified into a new sort of "people's college" that served as basic higher education for men and women, whether or not their main goal was to prepare as teachers. Since most college graduates of the nineteenth century (and almost all of the women) became teachers, the normal schools played a vital role as they dotted the central part of the country with their new opportunities.[25]

A team of educational historians working with John Goodlad in his large study of teacher training in the United States also studied the normal schools, but as only one setting where teachers were taught. Whereas Herbst traced the legacy of the normal schools themselves, the Goodlad group studied the range of places where teachers received training, examining the effects of training in normal schools, academies, land grant universities, and liberal arts colleges.[26] The Herbst and Goodlad books, along with Donald

Warren's edited volume, *American Teachers: Histories of a Profession at Work,* focused a new lens on normal schools as both separate institutions and as elements within a system.[27]

The attention to normal schools in these works was seized upon by a new generation of scholars, who examined them specifically for the role they played for women. Christine A. Ogren, Laura Docter Thornburg, and Mary Alpern examined normal schools throughout the country, highlighting the degree to which women served as educational leaders. Thornburg studied the career of Julia Ann King, first "preceptress" of the Michigan normal school, examining King's influence as a practicing teacher and head of one of the primary teacher-training centers in that part of the Midwest. Ogren studied seven normal schools throughout the nation, finding similarities to women's colleges in students' involvement in academic and extracurricular activities, and those institutions' commitment to vocational preparation. She clarified ways that women used normal training as both teacher preparation and general education.[28] Mary Alpern's findings supported Ogren's suggestion of the normal schools' academic and career strengths. Alpern questioned earlier assumptions that female "normalites" (a rejuvenation of an old term) were not serious students, citing others who had claimed that women students neither intended nor pursued lengthy careers as teachers and that they viewed teaching only as either a way station until marriage or a fallback in case of widowhood. Studying the Albany, New York, normal schools, Alpern traced 428 students, finding that women taught, on average, for 10.3 years and men 11.7. Of women who never married, the average tenure was twenty-two years. By examining social-class origins as well as subsequent careers, Alpern confirmed new findings that normal schools indeed strengthened women's educational and career options.

Ogren, Thornburg, and Alpern also highlighted the degree to which normal school graduates diffused their technical training beyond their local areas. The women's colleges, and the more famous female academies, such as Emma Willard's Troy Female Seminary, had long been recognized for their ability to "seed" like institutions. In her important 1979 article on "The Diffusion of Feminist Values" through Troy Seminary, Anne Firor Scott traced dozens of schools founded by graduates of Troy.[29] The women's colleges, too, were known to create "daughter schools" in the western part of the country. Margaret Nash recently studied the ecology of institutions for women in one part of Ohio, beginning with the Western Female Seminary in Oxford, a daughter school of Mount Holyoke College.[30] Looking, as Nash has, at the range of institutions serving women in a given area confirms the notion that "higher education" was in fact a flexible nineteenth-century concept depending on availability of institutions, funding, and stability.

Other new work on academies has begun to clarify the issues of student choice and its relationship to curriculum, markets, and vocational preparation.

Nancy Beadie applied an economic analysis to student decisions on academy attendance, discovering that women's attendance, not men's, often directed the curricular emphases of these schools. Women paid for not only basic education, but also for science and music courses, encouraging academy founders to tailor curricula to female needs and expenditures.[31] Kimberley Tolley has traced women's curricular choice as well, focusing especially on their higher demand than men for science courses in both the nineteenth and early twentieth centuries. Her work, along with Beadie's, suggests that academies provided significant and advanced curricular opportunities for women who did not attend the now better known eastern women's colleges.[32]

None of this work on the variety of institutions that prepared women for their most populous profession was available to Solomon when writing *In the Company of Educated Women*. Her call for other sites of female leadership and academic success has been more fully realized with such subsequent illumination of these little-studied female institutions.

Access as the organizing principle

Women's history as a field came of age in an era when women were pushing for equal rights and equal access to men's institutions, careers, and opportunities. The "difference debate" of the 1980s and 1990s, in which some women claimed the right to differential treatment while others fought for the right to equal treatment, did not hold sway in the early years of the post-1960 women's movement. Instead, women focused on winning equal treatment and access to the same opportunities open to men.[33] Writing in 1985 from an institution that had long resisted granting women an equal place, Solomon focused steadily on the issue of women's hard-fought battle for access to collegiate life. She was not unaware of the complications that women faced once they arrived on college campuses; in fact, her focus on student life and the curriculum was dedicated to clarifying women's complicated maneuvering in a setting that rarely welcomed them. Because of her focus on access, however, she may have downplayed some other aspects of women's participation that indeed affected the development of higher education, such as their parallel involvement in non-educational settings, their treatment once they had achieved access, and the possible costs of women's educational entry points.

Work like Nancy Cott's and Karen Blair's, mentioned above, allowed historians to look for instances where women established authority without access to mainstream institutions. Cott looked at both religion and education as sites for women's power; Blair proclaimed the women's clubs as sources of education and influence for their all-female membership. Separatism as a conscious strategy by women was highlighted by Estelle Freedman, spurring historians to look for ways that women injected vitality into those areas ceded to them.[34] Linda Kerber furthered the construct of "separate spheres" as a potent organizing principle for historical investigations of women.[35]

In educational history, as in other areas of women's history, this notion of separate spheres of influence inspired scholars who were aware of barriers that had been erected to keep women in their separate institutions or in tributaries of the mainstream. Polly Kaufman, for example, offered a study of the Women's College at Brown University, showing how a parallel women's institution flourished alongside a reluctant male partner.[36] Lynn Gordon examined the women who coeducated the Universities of Chicago and California at Berkeley, exploring the different ways these schools welcomed women.[37] Carolyn Terry Bashaw and Jana Nidiffer explored the creation of the profession of dean of women as a formal recognition by university heads that women needed both tending and containing on coeducational campuses.[38] These fine educational studies build on Solomon's construction of women's educational history as a story of access sought or access denied, and fill out her presentation of women's participation in the mainstream.

Denial of women's full and equal participation prompted a different development, however, which Solomon addressed only occasionally. Lacking the opportunity to connect education with wider public life, women developed what Sally Schwager addresses as "counter-institutions" to the colleges where they could exert their influence, especially in the nineteenth century and in the Progressive Era.[39] Blair's recognition of the significance of women's clubs at the turn of the century signals one way women created offshoots from colleges and universities. Reform movements grabbed women's attention and their energies: temperance, suffrage, prison and moral reform, and any number of activist causes allowed women these opportunities for self-education and leadership. In the nineteenth century, these movements often took the place of absent collegiate education. Women like Elizabeth Cady Stanton, Frances Willard, Harriet Beecher Stowe, and Margaret Fuller preceded the era of widespread collegiate education, yet they established vital careers as informal educators through their writing and activism. In the Progressive Era, when women generally had experienced more formal education, the counter-institutions led to new careers and new agencies, such as the development of social work through women's efforts, the influence and reach of settlement houses, and the establishment of national government agencies like the Women's Bureau and the Children's Bureau.[40] In describing the pre-academy era, Solomon attends to some of these efforts. However, a full story of women's education might find these vibrant informal settings just as significant as the formal educational institutions where women were so long resisted.[41]

Geraldine Jonçich Clifford, who has studied both the history of teachers and of women in coeducational institutions, worried that writing women's history through the lens of access focuses historians too heavily on a story of victimization. She lamented a dedication to writing the history of the "education of women" and urged instead claiming the mainstream for women by writing the history of "women in education." Thus Clifford would ask, "How did the presence of women make a difference in colleges and universities? What did their presence pay for? speed up? permit?" She explained, for example, that the dominant historical paradigm of colleges developing into universities coincided with the growth of coeducation, yet the two phenomena are usually treated separately.[42] Lawrence Veysey and Roger Geiger, for example, wrote histories of the growth of research universities in which women seldom were mentioned; gender held little significance in their stories.[43] Coeducation, when attended to at all, usually appears in histories of women's education either as their push for access or their challenge to prevailing academic cultures.[44]

Clifford wondered how the story might change if the two were intertwined. She noted early challenges, especially in the Midwest and West, to using state funds for higher education when the elementary and grammar schools were still needy. The study of women's entry into teaching shows that women's consistent use of colleges to prepare as teachers ameliorated public sentiment about the use of tax money for collegiate training. Because of women's clear use of higher education as a road to teaching, that sector was able to assert its claim as a useful public benefit.[45]

Clifford also suggested that women influenced institutions they did not attend. Citing the sector of prestigious men's colleges that resisted the inclusion of women the longest, she explained that the Ivy League and other men's colleges were allowed to craft their own specialized education for men, "capturing a constituency" and becoming renowned as the most elite of educational sites until the final push for coeducation in the late 1960s brought women into their midst. Further, looking at the absence of women in southern colleges and universities might explain how those institutions lagged behind many of the larger public institutions when growth occurred in the decades after the Civil War. As both Clifford and historian of southern education Bashaw explained, southern institutions were among the only ones not to coeducate after the Civil War, clinging to their antebellum single-sex focus. Had they proceeded with coeducation, like the premier institutions in the Midwest, southern colleges might have grown more rapidly into the mainstream of higher education.[46]

This notion of women's influence even where they were physically absent challenges Solomon's focus on access, as does the development of counter-institutions outside the educational panoply. Generally, however, historians of women's higher education have tended to follow Solomon's lead, looking first to issues of access and only more rarely at a different way of reconceptualizing the history.

Influence of outside agencies

The lack of wider historical context in *In the Company of Educated Women* appears most strikingly in the absence of a discussion of how outside agencies — especially the federal government, foundations, and accrediting agencies — influenced the development of higher education. Perhaps focusing so tightly on the specific issues of women and their access to collegiate institutions steered Solomon away from examining some important other factors that affected the way institutions grew and oriented their missions, programs, and clientele. Although these agencies seldom targeted women's issues directly, they nonetheless affected women as a share of higher education participants. Solomon might have argued that her book never promised a full history of higher education, but her overlooking of governmental and nongovernmental influences has not encouraged historians of women to investigate these potent sources of influence.

The federal government played a fairly quiet role in higher education until after World War II, when the G.I. Bill of Rights, the expansion of federal financial aid, and the explosion of research dollars poured money into colleges and universities. Yet before 1945, both the Morrill Land Grant Acts (1862 and 1890) and the Smith-Hughes Act for vocational education (1917) provided new funds and new missions that shaped the development of many collegiate institutions. Solomon did note the importance of the land grant acts for creating large public institutions, and she mentions the struggles women had with opportunities for vocational education. But the real significance of the land grant institutions in the lives of women students and faculty members has been underestimated in traditional stories of higher education. As Clifford noted, the use of public money after the Civil War for widening the purview of higher education caused initial skepticism. Although Justin Morrill and his congressional colleagues had deemed colleges and universities an appropriate site for federal largesse to improve "the industrial, military, and mechanical arts," those institutions lagged well behind the federal funding in actually producing new scientific and agricultural research. Once the pump was primed, however, universities eventually expanded and began attending to the service needs of the nation. Although women took less advantage of some land grant university curricula (whether by choice or by force), they certainly flocked to both the home economics and teacher-training departments of these public institutions.

Likewise, the Smith-Hughes Act pumped money into vocational education, primarily at the secondary school level. Although generally an initiative that affected the schools, two facts about the use of federal vocational education funds bear on women's role in higher education. First, women pursued high school training more frequently than men, pushing especially into commercial education programs (and virtually ignoring attempts to "vocationalize" housework in the curriculum), increasing their overall access and participation in education. Second, the success of vocational education in the secondary schools prompted their growth into comprehensive high school institutions, which in turn allowed higher education to differentiate itself more clearly from high schooling and to offer more "tracks" of its own to increasing numbers of high school graduates. Since these developments affected the growth of colleges and universities (for instance, allowing them to eliminate their longstanding preparatory programs for ill-prepared entering students), it would appear that early federal influence in fact helped direct both the course of higher education and women's participation.[47]

Certainly, the more obvious governmental influences of the post–World War II era — the G.I. Bill, financial aid legislation, and research support — affected women both directly and indirectly, despite Solomon's relative inattention to these effects. The G.I. Bill was never intended as an educational effort; its primary concern was to ease the return of veterans into the job market and, secondarily, to reward them for wartime service. Women vets were equally eligible for provisions, and in fact used the bill in proportions equal to their military participation — about 3 percent.[48] However, the G.I. Bill produced an interesting unexpected consequence that reduced women's role on campuses. During the war, women's participation in higher education had soared, with so many college-age men in the service. The steady presence of women as students sustained many colleges that would otherwise have closed for lack of paying customers. Wartime women students also proved themselves capable of running campus organizations and providing academic leadership, both on the student and faculty levels. In fact, many restrictions against women that were relaxed during the pressures of wartime permanently opened doors after the crisis ended. At Harvard University, for example, wartime women students integrated classes with men for the first time; without these female students, numbers would have been too small to continue. After the war, Radcliffe women retained the right of shared classes, echoing a development on other campuses around the country. Hunter College, the largest women's college in the world in the 1930s, permanently adopted coeducation after experimenting with G.I. Bill male students. Yet, generally, women's high participation as students and their enhanced leadership roles diminished with the influx of male veterans, leading to a decade-long decline in women's participation as both students and faculty. In a nation eager to return to perceived normalcy, women's continued press for an enhanced presence in academe fell by the wayside.

The availability of financial aid and research dollars offers divergent stories of impact on women. Financial aid — especially in its consolidated form in the 1965 Higher Education Act — served women well, allowing their increased attendance at traditional colleges as well as in continuing education and community colleges. However, the increase in federal research dollars failed to enhance women's opportunities for advanced training, a story seldom told in the discussions of the growth of research universities. Research schools stand atop the academic hierarchy, but represent the very institutions where women have been least visible. Only with Rossiter's work on academic scientists in the United States have historians begun to look at how women were excluded or limited in the distribution of funds and fellowships that would have produced research scientists and scholars.[49]

Since the turn of the twentieth century, both private foundations and regional accrediting boards have affected the direction of higher education, yet the effect of their policies on women has hardly been studied. Here is a prominent area where, as Clifford suggested, the integrated involvement of women in higher education should be examined, rather than requiring a separate study of women's educational history. The Carnegie Foundation for the Advancement of Teaching, for example, affected higher education at several points. In the 1910s, their inducement of a large pension fund for penurious faculty members affected the way that various institutions planned and organized their curricula, their faculties, and their degree programs. Several institutions chose to abandon denominational affiliations in order to qualify for Carnegie funds; others enhanced library and curricular offerings in designated areas. Accrediting boards had the same effect later in the century, often pushing institutions seeking their imprimatur to develop research-oriented Ph.D. programs and to send more of their own faculty on for advanced training. With no governmental or system-wide force pushing on higher education, the foundations and accreditation agencies stepped in to exert a heavy hand on institutions, pushing and prodding them to upgrade facilities, curricula, and personnel.[50]

Women were seldom valued in these enhancements, and female institutions and programs either fell behind or were more clearly placed outside the increasingly obvious mainstream. One female organization, the American Association of University Women (AAUW), followed the accrediting boards' approach, using its own public list of approved colleges to exert the same push for upgraded facilities and training on some women's campuses. Later, the AAUW also tried to embarrass certain coeducational institutions by calling public attention to their low numbers of women faculty and trustees, although the effort produced only mild results.[51] Women, of course, were not the only population to suffer in the push for bigger and better resources. Black colleges and Catholic institutions faced the same pressures, with their leaders sometimes having to decide how to shunt money into developing only certain schools, knowing that others would fill a different, more generalist role.[52] The story of how foundations and agencies affected higher education's development has most often been told as a shining tale of producing a worthy elite; less frequently has it been examined for its overall effect on the system and its various populations.

New areas for research

Any discussion of the most promising or underdeveloped areas of historical research in women's higher education risks the same critique that we are applying to Solomon's work. That is, we ask here whether Solomon's conceptual framework may have directed research into certain paths and whether her lack of attention to other areas may have limited subsequent historians' inquiry. By singling out the following areas, I may be guilty of the same judgments for which I challenge her. Nonetheless, I would like to suggest three areas of historical research in women's higher education that seem particularly promising at this moment, especially for asking new questions of old issues and for focusing attention on women whose collegiate stories have been too long quiet. The three include: 1) as discussed above, a wider focus on institutions significant in women's educational development, especially the academies and normal schools; 2) attention to women's development as educated professionals, especially as academics; and 3) increased attention to marginalized populations of women and their participation in higher education, including African American, Latina, Asian American, and Native American women. Although this third area of racial and ethnic concerns should not be separated out from the wider study of women's higher education, doing so here provides an opportunity to focus appropriately on new work. Work in all these areas remains surprising small; in some the literature is growing; in others, the field remains relatively open.

Range of institutions

In this article, I have already examined historians' recently expanded attention to normal schools and academies within the panoply of women's institutions. After a long period of neglect where historians assumed easy explanations for the role and clientele of these schools, scholars are now claiming them as significant players, rather than as aberrant non-colleges with little impact on higher education's long-term development. Perhaps because both institutions were frequently female dominated, normal schools and academies have been treated as stepsisters in most traditional educational histories. And, because these schools generally did not connect to the most prestigious women's colleges, educational histories of women have often ignored their influence as well.[53] Yet, if historians heed Clifford's call to integrate women's educational participation into the historical mainstream, these institutions will assume a more prominent role in the overall story. Ogren, Thornburg, Alpern, Beadie, Tolley, and Nash are beginning this work by regenerating interest in these institutions and also by examining the marginalized populations of women who turned to these less prestigious institutions for their advanced education.

By adding fuller discussions of both normal schools and academies, higher education can be studied more accurately as a flexible system or a set of options rather than a hierarchy. As Herbst showed, the midwestern version of normal schools assumed a very different form than the earliest versions in the Northeast. Likewise, from curricular and career standpoints, early academies and seminaries sometimes functioned more like colleges than many colleges did. By not integrating all these institutions into our studies, we stratify the system more than is necessary.[54]

Women as academic professionals

Barbara Solomon's book enriched the usual story of higher education by trying to connect women's post-collegiate lives to their collegiate preparation. The work draws criticism, however, for her lack of connecting women's professional pursuits to wider concerns of U.S. society. Although research on women as professionals is still young, some efforts are extending Solomon's ideas and providing a rich new base.[55] The strongest and most comprehensive — in many ways the model for such investigations — is Rossiter's two-volume study of women scientists in America. Exhaustively researched and carefully presented, Rossiter explores the history of science as an endeavor, as a curriculum, and as a career. While using women's experience as the organizing principle, she also investigates the fuller practice of science and compares men's and women's opportunities, preparation, and progress. Although it covers more than higher education, Rossiter's work belongs in higher education history for two reasons. First, she examines women's preparation for science careers within colleges, universities, and graduate schools, noting, for example, the difficulties experienced by women's colleges in supporting expensive laboratories. And, even when she traces women scientists in a host of non-academic job settings, Rossiter cites their collegiate preparation and experiences. Second, she devotes considerable and careful attention to women academic scientists, exploring the experience of women professors at small women's colleges as well as at large public institutions. She fulfills some of the promise that Solomon, Patricia Graham, and Susan Carter had hoped for by explicating the career issues for faculty women at coeducational universities. Overall, Rossiter concludes that women scientists were unable to capitalize on or sustain research and career opportunities over time; their advances in wartime, for example, were withdrawn or evaporated when men reasserted control of funding and research agendas.[56]

A new project that follows Rossiter's lead by studying the universe of women in one profession is Mary Ann Dzuback's focus on women academic social scientists from 1890 to 1940. Like Rossiter, Dzuback's self-created data base of faculty women allows her to study patterns of training, employment, career persistence, and accomplishment over time. Similar to Rossiter, who found enclaves of academic women who perpetuated their work by hiring their own students, Dzuback has observed how certain collegiate departments proved receptive and supportive to women social scientists, while many more continued to ostracize or ignore women academics. Dzuback's research in the economics department at Berkeley, for example, finds that the presence of one or two women faculty members, joined by the support of a few influential male colleagues, could sustain women's participation in the face of wider university ambivalence. Her research stresses ways in which women's activities "transgressed" the boundaries that had been assigned to them in academe, claiming "space" and access for their work.[57]

Palmieri, although drawing a tighter circle around the group she studies, has also presented an in-depth examination of a group of academic women, revealing strong connections between the work lives of one campus group and the wider society that affected women's opportunities. Palmieri's study of the female faculty community at Wellesley College between the 1880s and 1920 is noteworthy for its expansive coverage of these women's home lives, career preparation, and subsequent faculty work. Because Wellesley, more than some of the other women's colleges, challenged tradition by sustaining an all-female faculty, Palmieri is able to examine a women's setting that was both consciously separate from the mainstream and desirous of partaking in its scholarly opportunities. Palmieri succeeds especially well in demonstrating links between the faculty members' own training, their personal commitments to progressive causes, and their use of these commitments in their own classrooms.[58]

Rossiter, Dzuback, and Palmieri lead the present study of women academics' lives. Except for Rossiter, whose time period extends to 1972, little historical work has yet been produced on more recent faculty women (or, more generally, on women's higher education in the post–World War II era). My own ongoing study of various institutional efforts at gender equity in the 1950s and 1960s should fill a gap by looking at how advocates for women used philanthropy and special programs to build an array of structures to support women. The fellowship programs, research centers, and women's studies departments that these advocates created after 1960 sparked and later sustained women faculty's stronger movement into the academic mainstream.[59]

Much of the recent work that advances understanding of women as professionals appears via biography, both on women as faculty and as educational leaders. Biography, of course, has long been a staple of discussions on educated Americans' lives. However, feminist research and new approaches to writing women's biographies have generated thoughtful new work that expands our understanding of the role of education in women's lives.[60]

For example, in addition to work on women as faculty members and school leaders, scholars are beginning to examine women teachers' lives, finding a more complex picture of their career and leadership opportunities than previously assumed. Since the teaching profession long absorbed the bulk of women's college and normal school graduates, it deserves attention in studies of women's higher education. Yet teaching — numerically dominated by women but headed by influential men — was often judged a feminized "semi-profession" and suffered in attention when scholars turned to the more egregious fights for access to the traditional male fields of law, medicine, and business.

Recent work emphasizes teachers as actors in their own career decisions, rather than as functionaries subject to male leadership. Kathleen Weiler has investigated the range of career opportunities pursued by female teachers in California, reinvigorating the leadership role of county superintendent that allowed women considerable flexibility and autonomy in wide geographic and functional settings.[61] Kate Rousmaniere, whose interests include teachers' roles in union work, studies New York City teachers' preparation, activity, and progress.[62] Ruth Markowitz also focuses on New York teachers, with particular attention to how ethnicity influenced the lives of women teachers.[63] Turning to a particular type of teacher, Barbara Beatty explores how preschool teachers developed their profession from a vantage point outside the traditional school and college mainstream. In her examination of the development of preschool education, Beatty argues that over the course of the twentieth century, leaders of the kindergarten and preschool movements pushed colleges and normal schools to include child development and kindergarten training among the options available to women teachers.[64]

Jo Ann Preston's work on the feminization of the teaching profession connects the first two areas of new research: challenging the notion of an academic hierarchy and studying women as educated professionals. She examines the sites of women's preparation for teaching, comparing the preparation available at normal schools vs. academies. Preston suggests that academies and seminaries provided more liberal arts oriented training than did the normal schools, provoking her belief that subsequent teacher education (including its current organization) suffered from the direction sparked by the normal approach. Preston doubts that normals very often provided the kind of real advanced preparation that Ogren discovered, although she continues to find both settings dedicated to the needs of female students.[65]

These studies exemplify the connections of women's collegiate training to the wider sweep of social issues surrounding and sometimes limiting them. Whereas Solomon, and Newcomer before her, kept their lenses focused on women's lives within collegiate settings, recent authors are drawing parallels between what women students and leaders sought for female academic training, the actual career opportunities that faced women as graduates, and the structural issues that affected women's development.

Diverse populations

Recent scholarship has begun to disaggregate the groups of women who participated in higher education, examining the specific experiences of racial, ethnic, and religious groups who sometimes formed separate institutions and sometimes pushed for a place within the mainstream. Historians have not yet, however, integrated this work into the overall story of women's higher education, causing it to remain a patchwork of secondary material awaiting a synthesis or broader framework, or appearing as appendages to wider histories in the way that Solomon wrote. Like the populations it discusses, this scholarship has too frequently been allowed by historians to sit at the periphery of traditional history.

Linda Perkins, whose work appears in this Symposium, stands as one of the most thorough scholars of African American women's role in higher education. Perkins's particular contribution lies in explicating the situation both for women at historically Black colleges, where they often competed with men, and at predominantly White institutions, where they were tolerated, but rarely welcomed. In earlier work, Perkins highlighted the dilemma faced by many African American women in the nineteenth century as they confronted the "cult of true womanhood" and its prescriptions for femininity. In the early to middle part of that century, "true womanhood" idealized women's purity and domesticity, generating a constellation of expectations that did not especially encourage women's pursuit of a useful education. Perkins explained how believers in such notions virtually omitted Black women because of strong racial prejudices that defied ever seeing these women as pure. Yet when African American women nonetheless persisted in their own Black colleges, their contributions were eventually downplayed by African American men, who needed to bolster their sense of men's contribution to "race uplift." Black women were doubly disadvantaged then: they were excluded from White opportunities and devalued in Black settings where they had made initial progress.[66] As Perkins shows in her new study African American women continued to navigate these difficult waters, slowly making inroads in the predominantly White settings and asserting their place in Black colleges.

Scholars are beginning to reassess Black women's role in the famous debate between Booker T. Washington and W.E.B. DuBois that frequently characterizes — and sometimes limits — the presentation of early twentieth-century African American educational history. Generally, historians assume that Black educational philosophy veered between the economic self-help focus of Washington (with its careful dependence on White philanthropy and its attendant demands) and the seemingly more virile declaration of DuBois's professional and classical training. Women were presumed to follow one or the other of these approaches, depending on predilection, opportunity, or connection to one of the major figures. Scholars have recently begun to look more deeply at the separate institutions created and sustained by female African American school founders, discovering that these women borrowed from both educational camps, depending on need and opportunity. Kathleen C. Berkeley and Ann S. Chirhart focus on Black southern school leaders, noting that when finances, curriculum, or other needs dictated, they could bend their missions to meet the needs of their clientele, sometimes professing vocational and classical training for women at the same time. These studies complicate the view not only of Black educational history, but also of women's role within it. As such, they serve as models of how adding women more purposefully into overall educational history clarifies the story.[67]

Women of other racial and ethnic groups have, as yet, received less concerted attention from historians of higher education. Developing work on Hispanic American, Asian American, and Native American women generally limits its focus to the schools where, arguably, the basics of the story need first to be investigated.[68]

Victoria-María MacDonald has surveyed educational historians' work on Hispanic Americans, noting three successive stages of analysis: pre-1960, characterized by use of anthropological perspectives on conditions of schooling; the 1960s and 1970s, featuring politically charged work responding to the Chicano movement, but which also benefited from a more sophisticated understanding of ethnic differences in uses of schooling; and the present, examining the political goals and activities of Hispanic American communities in their pursuit of self-efficacy.[69] Specific attention to women in these general histories is sporadic, however. As MacDonald explains: "The educational history of Hispanic American women occupies a nebulous position between the few works which examine the history of schooling for Hispanic Americans and the post-1970s flowering of scholarship on the history of women. Consequently, researchers . . . must seek information from widely scattered articles."[70] Looking specifically at higher education produces little from a historical perspective. Raymond Padilla and Rudolfo Chavez's *The Leaning Ivory Tower* and Felix Padilla's *The Struggle of Latino/a University Students* address Latinas in the higher education setting, but their work has a more contemporary than historical focus.[71]

Similar issues arise in the historical study of Asian American women. Work is beginning on Asian Americans in separate schools and "mixed" schools, but the majority of this work neither specifically extricates women's experience nor examines higher education. Historian Eileen Tamura has written on the experience of the Nisei generation of Japanese Americans in Hawaii, but once again the focus is on schooling rather than higher education. The same is true for Thomas James's *Exile Within: The Schooling of Japanese Americans 1942–1945*, a study of the educational experience in the World War II relocation camps.[72] As with Latinas, much prominent work on Asian American experiences in higher education considers current concerns, such as those gathered in the strong anthology by Don T. Nakanishi and Tina Yamano Nishida.[73] As Sucheng Chan reminds us, the Chinese Exclusion Laws of the 1880s and other restrictive immigration quotas until 1943 eliminated most Asian women's early opportunities in the United States.[74] Asian women's participation in higher education was severely hampered by the long-term effects of these restrictions, perhaps explaining the focus on recent collegiate experience in much of the historical scholarship.

Native American women have received attention in recent years, both for their part in general educational histories of Native Americans and in a few separate studies on women. Scholars Ardy Bowker, David DeJong, Devon Mihesuah, David Wallace Adams, and Tsianina Lomawaima have examined the education of Indians, the last two from the perspective of the boarding school experience.[75] Adams, in his prize-winning study of how Indians were "educated for extinction," includes some attention to how cross-cultural gender expectations figured in the White leaders' plans for providing assimilative education to Native American girls and boys. Mihesuah's work offers the deepest focus on women in one actual institution. These works, however, treat pre-collegiate schooling, which was often the highest level available to most Native Americans; the tribal colleges that grew after the 1960s have yet to be the focus of much historical work.[76]

Catholic women reveal a long and influential history in higher education, with religious teaching orders responsible for founding scores of colleges for women beginning in 1895. Beyond institutional histories, the overall experience of Catholic collegiate women or religious teachers remains relatively unexamined by educational historians. A few works, including those by Eileen Mary Brewer, Barbara Misner, and Nikola Baumgarten, focus on religious women, emphasizing the opportunities for education, community-building, and leadership offered to Catholic women who chose convent life.[77] Generally, however, scholars are just beginning to examine the historical experience of Catholic collegians either in separate institutions or as contenders within mainstream higher education. Philip Gleason, for example, traces the ongoing Catholic effort to respond to changing collegiate missions, curricula, and values; Kathleen Mahoney studies Catholics who entered the collegiate mainstream. This tendency of Catholic youth to "drift" into nondenominational colleges caused great concern among Catholic leaders, who disagreed over the virtues of separatism or engagement for Catholics in American life, a theme explored by both Mahoney and Gleason.[78] Mary Oates's anthology of primary and secondary historical sources remains the single best work on Catholic collegiate women, but it does not assume an analytical focus, leaving this population awaiting fuller explication.[79]

Conclusion

In the twenty-five years that elapsed between Newcomer's and her own synthesis of women's higher education history, Barbara Solomon benefited from an explosion of educational studies. Lawrence Cremin led the way for seeing education as a whole array of learning opportunities beyond but including formal schooling where men, women, and children learned about life, scholarship, and culture.[80] Such an approach clearly created more room for women than in earlier, school-based histories. At the same time, historians of women's lives began to look at how women used their "separate sphere" of influence in areas like religion, reform work, teaching, and domestic life.

Solomon infused her work with new scholarship from these areas, but it was the story of women's push for access into collegiate institutions that most captured her attention, perhaps because it best demonstrated women's concerted work in claiming a place in one important part of mainstream U.S. culture. The story of access is clearly vital; we need a record of women's initial entry and subsequent participation in various fields and institutions. We also need, as Solomon recognized and provided as far as possible, a disaggregated record that shows how women of different racial, ethnic, religious, and social-class backgrounds experienced and instigated the push for equal treatment.

In taking a long view, Solomon proposed a generational breakdown to understand how and where women pushed for educational equity. She divided her study among the antebellum era, the late-nineteenth and turn-of-the-twentieth centuries, and the post–World War II period, describing institutions, clientele, curriculum, and purposes as they developed for the women of each era. Through this framework, Solomon could differentiate, for example, the experience of middle-class White women from that of Black women, finding a clear difference between available opportunities and ease of access. The discussion by era also enabled her to focus on institutions like the normal schools, academies, and women's colleges that established precedents and prospered in certain eras, only to be superseded by subsequent developments.

Some of Solomon's approaches and conclusions may, however, have nudged later historians into following her lead rather than asking different questions sooner about women's role and contributions in a wider array of settings. Although she likely did not intend such a focus, Solomon produced a book that gives prominence to women's colleges, even as she calls for more attention to normal schools and public institutions. She also underestimates the influence of outside agencies such as the government and accrediting bodies on the development of higher education. Most of these emphases, however, resulted from the lack of secondary material available to Solomon when she wrote a history designed to synthesize and organize the scholarship on women in higher education.

Current scholars can hope that, with unceasing attention to women's history and to the histories of previously "marginal" groups, there will not be such a long wait for another re-crafting of the story of women's participation. However, higher education as a whole has been awaiting an equivalent synthesis for three decades. Most scholars continue to start with the 1960s histories created by Frederick Rudolph and Laurence Veysey for the fullest explications of how higher education developed from the colonial period to the present. Some recent and excellent work has studied particular segments of the collegiate enterprise, offering the new raw material for an updated historical synthesis. Roger Geiger has revised Veysey's story of the development of the research university, attending more to outside influences and research activities than to Veysey's more philosophical study. And, in a scheme reminiscent of Solomon's discussion of women, he has presented the history of higher education through "generational" characteristics produced in knowledge, constituents, and purposes.[81] David Levine has examined changes in higher education between the two World Wars, finding that interwar period to be a significant time for the growth of the business-college connection.[82] Ellen Schrecker has studied the effect of McCarthyism and its era on the collegiate enterprise.[83] Bruce Leslie has focused on changes in faculty life, including the impact of professionalization on prestige and pay.[84]

These studies, plus scores of smaller-scale monographs, have not yet produced a reworking of the American story of higher education, let alone one that includes the considerable strong work on women and diverse populations. Yet if ambitious historians heed Geraldine Clifford's call, the next synthesis will no longer find separate chapters on "the education of women" (à la Rudolph) or scattered index references to African American women or Hispanic Americans as students and faculty. These individual contributions seem not yet ready to cohere into a fuller story that blends the variety of populations, institutions, and purposes of U.S. higher education. One key to such a blending, however, may be to diminish the focus on separatism and access while still honoring the efforts of women and others to assert their place in traditional academe. Solomon's invitation to travel "in the company of educated women" may offer a guide for incorporating both new and familiar territories into a reconfigured map.

Notes

1 Barbara Miller Solomon, *In the Company of Educated Women: A History of Women and Higher Education in America* (New Haven: Yale University Press, 1985); Mabel Newcomer, *A Century of Higher Education for American Women*

(New York: Harper, 1959). Barbara Miller Solomon, who died in 1992, was a senior lecturer in American history and literature at Harvard University for much of her career. Through her advocacy of women's history, which included directing the Radcliffe library now known as the Schlesinger Library on the History of Women in America, Solomon influenced the establishment of women's studies at Harvard. She also held posts as associate dean at Radcliffe and assistant dean at Harvard.

2 Solomon, *In the Company of Educated Women*, p. xvii.

3 Normal schools were institutions dedicated to teacher training that began in the United States in the late 1830s. Because they frequently offered students a review of elementary material before they extended a second or a third year of pedagogical training, these institutions have not always been considered "higher education." Similarly, academies and seminaries predated collegiate education in the eighteenth and nineteenth centuries. Many of these latter institutions arguably offered curricula equal to some of the early colleges.

4 The panel was convened by the author at the annual meeting of the American Educational Research Association in San Francisco in April 1995, as "Ten Years after a Classic: Historical Research and Teaching on Women's Higher Education a Decade after Barbara Solomon." Panelists included Carolyn Terry Bashaw, Geraldine Jonçich Clifford, Patricia Palmieri, Linda Perkins, Sally Schwager, Linda Eisenmann, and Mary Ann Dzuback (chair). Although the present article had its genesis in the panel, it extends the discussion and, except where noted, represents my own thinking on Barbara Solomon's book and its impact on the writing of women's higher educational history.

5 Patricia Palmieri, comments made at "Ten Years after a Classic."

6 For a discussion of how women scholars of higher education in the 1950s failed to connect women's status with wider societal issues, see Margaret Rossiter, "Outmaneuvered Again — The Collapse of Academic Women's Strategy of Celibate Overachievement," Paper presented at the Berkshire Conference of Women's Historians, Vassar College, June 1993; and Linda Eisenmann, "Befuddling the 'Feminine Mystique': Academic Women and the Creation of the Radcliffe Institute, 1950–1965," *Educational Foundations, 10* (1996), 5–26.

7 Emilie J. Hutchinson, *Women and the Ph.D.: Facts from the Experiences of 1,025 Women Who Have Taken the Degree of Doctor of Philosophy Since 1877*, Institute of Women's Professional Relations, Bulletin No. 2 (Greensboro: North Carolina College for Women, 1929), and Jeanne L. Noble, *The Negro Woman's College Education* (New York: Teachers College Press, 1956).

8 Karen Blair, *The Clubwoman as Feminist: True Womanhood Redefined, 1868–1914* (New York: Holmes and Meier, 1980).

9 Nancy F. Cott, *The Bonds of Womanhood: "Woman's Sphere" in New England, 1780–1835* (New Haven: Yale University Press, 1977).

10 Jill Ker Conway, "Perspectives on the History of Women's Education in the United States," *History of Education Quarterly, 14*, No. 1 (1974), 1–12.

11 Allmendinger produced provocative work in the 1970s on poor students — both male and female — who used scholarships or other support to attend college. Interestingly, Solomon cites only Allmendinger's piece on women, ignoring his wider study of collegiate students. See David F. Allmendinger, *Paupers and Scholars: The Transformation of Student Life in Nineteenth-Century America* (New York: St. Martin's Press, 1975), and David F. Allmendinger, "Mount Holyoke Students Encounter the Need for Life-Planning, 1837–1850, *History of Education Quarterly, 19* (1979), 27–47.

12 Barbara Miller Solomon, *Ancestors and Immigrants: A Changing New England Tradition* (Cambridge, MA: Harvard University Press, 1956); Sally Schwager, "Ten Years after a Classic."

13 "After college what?" was a question asked by many individuals and authors as women and men considered their post-collegiate career and family opportunities, especially in the late nineteenth century. Helen Starrett encapsulated the concerns in her pamphlet "After College What? For Girls" in 1896. Joyce Antler used the notion to explore the competing senses of duty faced by college women graduates around the turn of the century; see "'After College What?' New Graduates and the Family Claim," *American Quarterly*, 32 (1980), 409–435.

For a discussion of the importance of studying differences between college students' "origins" and their "destinations," see Roger L. Geiger, "The Historical Matrix of American Higher Education," *History of Higher Education Annual*, 12 (1992), 7–28.

14 Solomon, *In the Company of Educated Women*, p. xviii.

15 Frederick Rudolph, *The American College and University: A History* (New York: Vintage, 1962). Rudolph was the first educational historian to integrate residential life, athletics, and extracurricular activities into his discussion of collegiate effectiveness.

16 I am grateful to historian Harold Wechsler for raising this question of how to consider the legacy of Solomon's book.

17 Patricia Albjerg Graham, "So Much to Do: Guides for Historical Research on Women in Higher Education," *Teachers College Record*, 76 (1975), 421–440. The figure for coeducation is cited in Newcomer, *A Century of Higher Education*, p. 49.

18 Susan B. Carter, "Academic Women Revisited: An Empirical Study of Changing Patterns in Women's Employment as College and University Faculty, 1890–1963," *Journal of Social History*, 14 (1981), 675–699.

19 Solomon, *In the Company of Educated Women*, p. 208.

20 Several of the Seven Sister colleges supported women either as faculty or presidents. Among them, only Wellesley College sustained an all-female faculty and presidency for a substantial period of time. Vassar and Smith colleges, for example, both opened with male presidents.

21 Patricia A. Palmieri, *In Adamless Eden: The Community of Women Faculty at Wellesley* (New Haven, CT: Yale University Press, 1995); Margaret Rossiter, *Women Scientists in America: Struggles and Strategies to 1940* (Baltimore: Johns Hopkins University Press, 1982), and Margaret Rossiter, *Women Scientists in America: Before Affirmative Action, 1940–1972* (Baltimore: Johns Hopkins University Press, 1995).

22 Patricia Graham first called attention to the fact that women's participation in higher education had, in fact, peaked in the 1920s, only to fall over subsequent decades. Women's percentage of all undergraduates was 47 percent in 1920, 43 percent in 1930, 40 percent in 1940, and 31 percent in 1950. From there, the percentage began a slow climb. Women now constitute the majority in higher education. Patricia Albjerg Graham, "Expansion and Exclusion: A History of Women in American Higher Education," *Signs: Journal of Women in Culture and Society*, 3 (1978), 759–773.

23 Solomon, *In the Company of Educated Women*, p. 208.

24 Johann Pestalozzi (1746–1827) was a Swiss-born educator whose ideas greatly influenced the early American normal schools. Pestalozzi believed in the power of love and nurturance as a way to influence children's behavior (thus eliminating the reliance on corporal punishment), and he advocated women as "natural"

teachers of children. Much of his pedagogy replicated maternal instruction, suggesting the use of common household objects in his practical modes of teaching. Only after education of the senses could reason be exercised, he argued. See Jürgen Herbst, *And Sadly Teach: Teacher Education and Professionalization in American Culture* (Madison: University of Wisconsin Press, 1989) for a full discussion.

25 Herbst, *And Sadly Teach.*

26 John I. Goodlad, Roger Soder, and Kenneth A. Sirotnik, *Places Where Teachers Are Taught* (San Francisco: Jossey-Bass, 1990).

27 Donald R. Warren, *American Teachers: Histories of a Profession at Work* (New York: Macmillan, 1989).

28 Christine A. Ogren, "Where Coeds Were Coeducated: Normal Schools in Wisconsin, 1870–1920," *History of Education Quarterly, 35* (1995), 1–26; Christine A. Ogren, "Education for Women in the United States: The State Normal School Experience, 1870–1920," Diss., University of Wisconsin, 1996; Laura Docter Thornburg, "Rewriting the History of Teacher Education through the Life of the Woman Teacher: A Case of Julia Anne King and the Michigan State Normal School," Paper presented at the annual meeting of the History of Education Society, Toronto, Canada, October 1996; Mary Alpern, "A Successful Experiment in Teacher Education: The Founding and the Early Years of the Albany Normal School," Diss., Cornell University, 1996.

29 Anne Firor Scott, "The Ever-Widening Circle: The Diffusion of Feminist Values from the Troy Female Seminary, 1822–1872," *History of Education Quarterly, 19* (1979), 3–25.

30 Margaret A. Nash, "'A Salutary Rivalry': The Growth of Higher Education for Women in Oxford, Ohio, 1855–1867," *History of Higher Education Annual, 16* (1996), 21–37.

31 Nancy Beadie, "Defining the Public: Congregation, Commerce, and Social Economy in the Formation of the Educational System, 1790–1840," Diss., Syracuse University, 1989; Nancy Beadie, "Emma Willard's Idea Put to the Test: The Consequences of State Support of Female Education in New York, 1819–67," *History of Education Quarterly, 33,* No. 4 (1993), 543–562.

32 Kimberley Tolley, "The Science Education of American Girls, 1784–1932," Diss., University of California, Berkeley, 1996; Kimberley Tolley, "Science for Ladies, Classics for Gentlemen: A Comparative Analysis of Scientific Subjects in the Curricula of Boys' and Girls' Secondary Schools in the United States, 1794–1850," *History of Education Quarterly, 36* (1996), 129–154.

33 The issue of "difference" divided feminists early in the century and raises concerns among them now, as well. In the 1910s, in the struggles over the Equal Rights Amendment and protective labor legislation, some feminists believed that women's differences should allow them differential treatment and protection, for example, for limits on the number of hours they could be forced to work or prohibitions against certain dangerous work settings. ERA advocates, on the other hand, pushed for equal treatment. The debate plays out among modern scholars, too, with some suggesting that women are different in their approach to morality or to learning, and other feminists concerned about the implications of such findings.

34 Estelle B. Freedman, "Separatism as Strategy: Female Institution Building and American Feminism, 1870–1930," *Feminist Studies, 5* (1979), 512–529.

35 Linda K. Kerber, "Separate Spheres, Female World, Woman's Place: The Rhetoric of Women's History," *Journal of American History, 75,* No. 1 (1988), 9–37.

36 Polly Welts Kaufman, ed., *The Search for Equity: Women at Brown University, 1891–1991* (Hanover, NH: Brown University Press, 1991).

37 Lynn D. Gordon, "Coeducation on Two Campuses: Berkeley and Chicago, 1890–1912," in *Woman's Being, Woman's Place: Female Identity and Vocation in American History*, ed. Mary Kelly (Boston: G. K. Hall, 1979), pp. 294–317; Lynn D. Gordon, *Gender and Higher Education in the Progressive Era* (New Haven: Yale, 1990).

38 Carolyn Terry Bashaw, "We Who Live 'Off the Edges': Deans of Women at Southern Coeducational Institutions and Access to the Community of Higher Education," Diss., University of Georgia, 1992; Jana Nidiffer, " 'More than a Wise and Pious Matron': The Professionalization of the Position of Dean of Women," Diss., Harvard University, 1994; Jana Nidiffer, "From Matron to Maven: A New Role and New Professional Identity for Deans of Women, 1892 to 1916," *Mid-Western Educational Researcher: Special Issue on Midwestern History* (1995), 17–24.

39 Sally Schwager, comments made at "Ten Years after a Classic."

40 For good general discussions of women's roles in these reform movements, see, for example, Gordon, *Gender and Higher Education in the Progressive Era*; Ellen F. Fitzpatrick, *Endless Crusade: Women Social Scientists and Progressive Reform* (New York: Oxford University Press, 1990); Kathryn Kish Sklar, *Florence Kelley and the Nation's Work* (New Haven, CT: Yale University Press, 1995).

41 In creating the *Historical Dictionary of Women's Education in the United States*, I included both formal and informal educational opportunities and organizations, arguing that "women's history has demonstrated that telling the full story of women's participation in American life involves traditional institutions as well as alternate routes" (p. 4). In preparing the dictionary's index, I observed that the informal educational connection appearing most often in all the entries was women's ties to the suffrage movement. Linda Eisenmann, ed., *Historical Dictionary of Women's Education in the United States* (Westport, CT: Greenwood Press, forthcoming).

42 Geraldine Jonçich Clifford, comments made at "Ten Years after a Classic." See also Geraldine Jonçich Clifford, *Equally in View: The University of California, Its Women, and the Schools* (Berkeley, CA: Center for Studies in Higher Education and Institute of Governmental Studies, 1995); and Geraldine Jonçich Clifford, " 'Shaking Dangerous Questions from the Crease': Gender and American Higher Education," *Feminist Issues*, 2 (1983), 3–62.

43 Laurence Veysey, *The Emergence of the American University* (Chicago: University of Chicago Press, 1965); Roger Geiger, *To Advance Knowledge: The Growth of American Research Universities, 1900–1940* (New York: Oxford University Press, 1986); Roger Geiger, *Research and Relevant Knowledge: American Research Universities since World War II* (New York: Oxford University Press, 1993).

44 See, for example, Gordon, *Gender and Higher Education in the Progressive Era*.

45 Clifford, comments made at "Ten Years after a Classic."

46 Clifford and Carolyn Terry Bashaw, comments made at "Ten Years after a Classic."

47 For good discussions on the impact of vocational education on women (although they focus primarily on schools, not colleges), see John L. Rury, *Education and Women's Work: Female Schooling and the Division of Labor in Urban America, 1870–1930* (Albany: State University of New York Press, 1991) and Jane Bernard Powers, *The "Girl Question" in Education: Vocational Education for Young Women in the Progressive Era* (London: Falmer Press, 1992).

48 Keith W. Olson, *The G.I Bill, the Veterans, and the College* (Lexington: University Press of Kentucky, 1974) remains the best source on the origins and impact of the bill.

49 Rossiter, *Women Scientists in America.*

50 On the Carnegie Foundation, see Ellen Condliffe Lagemann, *Private Power for the Public Good: A History of the Carnegie Foundation for the Advancement of Teaching* (Middletown, CT: Wesleyan University Press, 1983). For a good discussion of the effects of one accrediting organization, see Lester F. Goodchild, "The Turning Point in American Jesuit Higher Education: The Standardization Controversy between the Jesuits and the North Central Association, 1915–1940," *History of Higher Education Annual, 6* (1986), 81–116.

51 On the AAUW's role as accreditor, see Marion Talbot and Lois K. Mathews Rosenberry, *The History of the American Association of University Women* (Boston: Houghton Mifflin, 1931); and Susan Levine, *Degrees of Equality: The American Association of University Women and the Challenge of Twentieth-Century Feminism* (Philadelphia: Temple University Press, 1995).

52 For a thorough discussion of the effect of philanthropy on Black institutions, see James D. Anderson, *The Education of Blacks in the South, 1860–1935* (Chapel Hill: University of North Carolina Press, 1988).

53 In fact, some female academies did pave the way for elite women's colleges, although others phased out after decades of academy status. Mount Holyoke College, for example, began as Mount Holyoke Female Seminary in 1837. Interestingly, Mount Holyoke's push for collegiate status — although ultimately quite successful — made it among the last of the Seven Sisters to emerge as a college (1887). The others began as separate collegiate institutions or as "coordinate colleges" attached to older male institutions (e.g., Radcliffe as coordinate with Harvard, Barnard as coordinate with Columbia).

54 As early as Thomas Woody's classic, *A History of Women's Education in the United States,* (New York: Science Press, 1929), scholars recognized that the name of an institution did not always match our assumptions about its curriculum, clientele, or purpose.

55 Although this section primarily describes women as academic professionals, considerable new work is appearing on women in the professions. See, for example, Ellen Fitzpatrick, *Endless Crusade: Women Social Scientist's and Progressive Reform* (New York: Oxford University Press, 1990); Robyn Muncy, *Creating a Female Dominion in American Reform, 1890–1935* (New York: Oxford University Press, 1991); Virginia Drachman, *Women Lawyers and the Origins of Professional Identity in America: The Letters of the Equity Club, 1887 to 1890* (Ann Arbor: University of Michigan Press, 1993); Darlene Clark Hine, *Speak Truth to Power: Black Professional Class in United States History* (Brooklyn, NY: Carlson, 1996); Darlene Clark Hine, *Black Women in White: Racial Conflict and Cooperation in the Nursing Profession, 1890–1950* (Bloomington: Indiana University Press, 1989). For a general overview, see Linda Eisenmann, "Women, Higher Education, and Professionalism: Clarifying the View," *Harvard Educational Review, 66* (1996), 858–873.

56 Rossiter, *Struggles and Strategies* and *Women Scientists in America.*

57 Mary Ann Dzuback, "Women and Social Research at Bryn Mawr College, 1915–1940," *History of Education Quarterly, 33* (1993), 579–608; and Mary Ann Dzuback, "Joining the Ancient and Universal Company of Scholars: Women in Social Science Graduate Study, 1890–1940," Vice-Presidential Address at the annual meeting of the American Educational Research Association, Chicago, March 1997.

58 Palmieri, *In Adamless Eden.*

59 Linda Eisenmann, "Weathering 'A Climate of Unexpectation': Gender Equity and the Radcliffe Institute, 1960–1995," *Academe, 81,* No. 4 (1995), 21–25; and Eisenmann, "Befuddling the Feminine Mystique."

60 Ellen Condliffe Lagermann encouraged a wider approach to recognizing and assessing educational influences, especially in women's lives, with her *A Generation of Women: Education in the Lives of Progressive Reformers* (Cambridge, MA: Harvard University Press, 1979).

61 Kathleen Weiler, "Women and Rural School Reform: California, 1900–1940," *History of Education Quarterly, 34* (1994), 25–47.

62 Kate Rousmaniere, *City Teachers: Teaching and School Reform in Historical Perspective* (New York: Teachers College Press, 1997).

63 Ruth Jacknow Markowitz, *My Daughter, the Teacher: Jewish Teachers in the New York City Schools* (New Brunswick, NJ: Rutgers University Press, 1993).

64 Barbara Beatty, *Preschool Education in America: The Culture of Young Children from the Colonial Era to the Present* (New Haven, CT: Yale University Press, 1995).

65 Jo Anne Preston, "Gender and the Formation of a Women's Profession: The Case of Public School Teaching," in *Gender Inequality at Work*, ed. Jerry A. Jacobs (Thousand Oaks, CA: Sage, 1995); and Jo Anne Preston, "Gender and the Professionalization of School Teaching: An Investigation of Changes in Teacher Education in 19th Century New England," Paper presented at the annual meeting of the American Educational Research Association, Chicago, March 1997.

66 Linda Perkins, "The Impact of the 'Cult of True Womanhood' on the Education of Black Women," *Journal of Social Issues, 39* (1983), 17–28. See also Linda Perkins, "African-American Women and Hunter College, 1873–1945," *The Echo: Journal of the Hunter College Archives* (125th anniversary edition, 1995), 17–25.

67 Kathleen C. Berkeley, "The Sage of Sedalia: Education and Racial Uplift as Reflected in the Career of Charlotte Hawkins Brown, 1883–1961," and Ann S. Chirhart, "'The Rugged Pathway': Beulah Rucker, African American Education, and Modern Culture, 1920–1950," Papers presented at the annual meeting of the History of Education Society, Toronto, October 1996.

68 The terms "Hispanic American," "Asian American," and "American Indian" used here all are general terms for a wide array of people with varied cultural, linguistic, and educational histories. I use them here to represent the widest scope of historical studies.

69 Victoria-María MacDonald, "'Immigrants' or 'Minorities': Exploring the Complex Historiography of Hispanic American Education," Paper presented at the annual meeting of the History of Education Society, Toronto, October 1996.

70 Victoria María MacDonald, "Hispanic American Women's Education," in Eisenmann, *Historical Dictionary of Women's Education in the United States.*

71 Raymond Padilla and Rudolfo Chavez, *The Leaning Ivory Tower: Latino Professors in American Universities* (Albany: State University of New York Press, 1995); Felix M. Padilla, *The Straggle of Latino/a University Students: In Search of a Liberating Education* (New York: Routledge, 1997).

72 Eileen Tamura, "Gender, Schooling, and Teaching, and the Nisei in Hawaii: An Episode in American Immigration History, 1900–1940," *Journal of American Ethnic History, 14*, No. 4 (1995), 3–36; Eileen Tamura, *Americanization, Acculturation, and Ethnic Identity: The Nisei Generation in Hawaii* (Urbana: University of Illinois Press, 1994); Thomas James, *Exile Within: The Schooling of Japanese Americans, 1942–1945* (Cambridge, MA: Harvard University Press, 1987).

73 Don T. Nakanishi and Tina Yamano Nishida, eds., *The Asian American Educational Experience: A Source Book for Teachers and Students* (New York: Routledge, 1995). See, especially, the section "Higher Educational Issues and Experiences:

Access, Representation, and Equity." The book offers a good historical section, but none of the four articles focuses on higher education or on women. See also, for current concerns, Joanne Faung and Gean Lee, *Asian American Experiences in the United States: Oral Histories of First to Fourth Generation Americans from China, the Philippines, Japan, Asian India, the Pacific Islands, Vietnam, and Cambodia* (Jefferson, NC: McFarland, 1991).

74 Sucheng Chan, "The Exclusion of Chinese Women," in *Entry Denied: Exclusion and the Chinese Community in America, 1882–1943*, ed. Sucheng Chan (Philadelphia: Temple University Press, 1991), pp. 94–146.

75 Ardy Bowker, *Sisters in the Blood: The Education of Women in Native America* (Bozeman: Montana State University, Center for Bilingual/Multicultural Education, 1993); David DeJong, *Promises of the Past: A History of Indian Education in the United States* (Golden, CO: North American Press, 1993); Devon Mihesuah, *Cultivating the Rosebuds: the Education of Women at the Cherokee Female Seminary, 1851–1909* (Urbana: University of Illinois, 1993); David Wallace Adams, *Education for Extinction: American Indians and the Boarding School Experience, 1875–1928* (Lawrence: University Press of Kansas, 1995); Tsianina Lomawaima, *They Called It Prairie Light: The Story of Chilocco Indian School* (Lincoln: University of Nebraska Press, 1994).

76 See, for example, the brief discussion by Michael A. Olivas, "Indian, Chicano, and Puerto Rican Colleges: Status and Issues," in *The History of Higher Education: ASHE Reader Series*, ed. Lester F. Goodchild and Harold S. Wechsler, 2nd ed. (Needham Heights, MA: Simon & Schuster, 1997), pp. 677–698.

77 Eileen Mary Brewer, *Nuns and the Education of American Catholic Women, 1860–1920* (Chicago: Loyola University Press, 1987); Barbara Misner, *Highly Respectable and Accomplished Ladies: Catholic Women Religious in America, 1790–1850* (New York: Garland, 1988); Nikola Baumgarten, "Beyond the Walls: Women Religious in American Life," *U.S. Catholic Historian*, *14*, No. 1 (special issue, Winter 1996).

78 Philip Gleason, *Contending with Modernity: Catholic Higher Education in the Twentieth Century* (New York: Oxford University Press, 1995); Kathleen Mahoney, "Adrift: Catholics and American Higher Education," Paper presented at the Spencer Foundation Winter Forum, Cambridge, MA, February 1995. See also William Leahy, *Adapting to America: Catholics, Jesuits, and Higher Education in the Twentieth Century* (Washington, DC: Georgetown University Press, 1991).

79 Mary Oates, *Higher Education for Catholic Women: An Historical Anthology* (New York: Garland, 1987).

80 Lawrence Cremin reoriented the study of educational history through his monumental three-volume study of education in the United States. His now-familiar view of education expanded our previous school-based understanding to include those "agencies, formal and informal, [that] have shaped American thought, character, and sensibility over the years" (*American Education: The Colonial Experience*, p. xi). See his *American Education: The Colonial Experience, 1607–1783* (New York: Harper and Row, 1970), *American Education: The National Experience, 1783–1876* (New York: Harper and Row, 1980), and *American Education: The Metropolitan Experience, 1876–1980* (New York: Harper and Row, 1988).

81 Veysey, *The Emergence of the American University*; Geiger, *To Advance Knowledge* and *Research and Relevant Knowledge*. Roger Geiger, "The Historical Matrix of American Higher Education," *History of Higher Education Annual*, *12* (1992), 7–28.

82 David Levine, *The American College and the Culture of Aspiration* (Ithaca, NY: Cornell University Press, 1986).

83 Ellen Schrecker, *No Ivory Tower: McCarthyism and the Universities* (New York: Oxford University Press, 1986).

84 Bruce Leslie, *Gentlemen and Scholars: College and Community in "The Age of the University," 1865–1917* (University Park: Pennsylvania State University Press, 1992).

INDEX